The Book of
BUILDINGS

The Book of
BUILDINGS

*A Panorama of Ancient, Medieval,
Renaissance, and Modern Structures*

Richard Reid

Rand McNally & Company
Chicago • New York • San Francisco

Contents

INTRODUCTION 6

Ancient Classical World

Published in the United States
of America, 1980
by Rand McNally & Company

First published in Great Britain
by MICHAEL JOSEPH LIMITED

Copyright © 1980 by Dorling Kindersley
Limited, London.
Text copyright © 1980 by Richard Reid

ISBN 0-528-81103-7
Library of Congress Catalog
Card Number 80-51521

Printed in the United States of America
by Rand McNally & Company

Byzantine & Medieval World

Modern Classical World

Modern World

Introduction

"Coming into Canterbury," Charles Dickens wrote in *David Copperfield,* "I loitered through the old streets with a sober pleasure that calmed my spirits and eased my heart. There were the old signs, the old names over the shops . . . the venerable Cathedral towers . . . the battered gateways . . . the ancient houses . . . ." For Dickens, as for many writers, the creation of a powerful sense of place is often achieved by a description closely associated with architectural forms. In addition to providing a reassuring frame of reference, this awareness of the quality and character of the environment is a reflection of a continuous concern with our surroundings.

Building and architecture play a major part in that concern, and it is to a better understanding and appreciation of their elements that this book is addressed. The intention here is to try to unravel the mystery a little and to show that architecture is neither quite as sophisticated as some would have us believe, nor as basic as many pretend, but is in reach of everyman, regardless of background knowledge.

To many the word Architecture is a generic term for any kind of building, good or bad, a misunderstanding probably arising from the fact that the term, first used in the mid 16th century, is derived from the Latin word *architectura* which means literally chief craftsman or master builder. In the 19th century Ruskin wrote that architecture is nothing but ornament applied to building. Others have made a distinction between architecture and building, seeing the two as different yet related. Sir Nikolaus Pevsner in his *An Outline of European Architecture* sees the cathedral as architecture, the bicycle shed as building—building being any enclosure of sufficient scale for a person to move about in, the term architecture being reserved for those buildings designed with a view to aesthetic appeal.

The distinction between building and architecture is easier to understand if we accept the notion that building came first, then the decorated building and finally architecture. The earliest human habitations were shelters excavated either by enlarging caves or burrowing into cliffs. The development of elemental structural forms such as the post and lintel and the building of the first weather-proof structures on open ground coincided with our first primitive cultural endeavours as we attempted to embellish these structures with ornamentation. The next step was to question the idea of erecting a building and then decorating it afterwards. Why not make a building sufficiently delightful in its own right so that there would no longer be a need to decorate it? To make architecture, in fact.

The most quoted definition of Architecture is that by Sir Henry Wotton who, in his *The Elements of Architecture* (1624), wrote that architecture must fulfill three conditions, firmness, commodity and delight. Firmness meant that it had to be soundly built of good materials; commodity that it had to be conveniently planned for its purpose; delight that it had to give pleasure to the eye of a discriminating beholder. Mere building was transformed into architecture by a synthesis of all three ingredients.

Architecture is, therefore, not a generic term for all building; it is a qualitative term for buildings of a particular excellence. All architecture has to be well built and well planned. But if we accept the existence of both building and architecture, we have to accept the existence of two parallel traditions, one a regionalist tradition seen, for example, in the simple, utilitarian structures of the Mediterranean, the other a more grand design tradition epitomized by, say, Versailles. The former reflects the life and activities of people directly whereas the latter, influenced and concerned with theories of architecture, fashions, impressiveness and the like, reflects the pomp and ceremony of public occasions.

Any example of building or architecture fits somewhere between these two extremes. The constant in both is that form is dictated by purpose. Form is not plucked out of thin air, it is shaped by the particular use of the building, the technology available, the materials at hand, the constraints of site and cultural context as well as the history of the building type. Such considerations are as important for our understanding of modern building and architecture as they are for our appreciation of the historic. Too often we separate the two, so that we have Historic Architecture and Modern Architecture instead of simply Architecture. By separating the two we fail to see the necessity for a sense of continuity between our historic past and present and to recognize that somewhere in that continuity may lie the future.

There is a fine balance between building and architecture. The first is more concerned with nature, the second with art. But this balance can too easily be lost. As Thoreau wrote " . . . the lover of art is one and the lover of nature another, though fine art is but one expression of our love of nature. It is monstrous when one cares but little about trees and much about Corinthian columns, and yet this is exceedingly common."

This book is not a history but a topographical guide to building and architecture in Europe and North America. It ranges from the simple utilitarian beginnings in the domestic life of Minoan Greece to the 20th century cities that are sprouting in Texas and California. While I have concentrated primarily on the forms of building and architecture I have also attempted to discuss some of the factors affecting architecture, such as social history. For example, the demand for wool in the Netherlands in the 15th century encouraged sheep-farming in England, and the consequent prosperity led to the erection of large parish churches in the sheep-rearing counties. In the 12th century the Cistercian movement was able to accommodate variations of the Romanesque in Northern Italy and Germany which were austere enough to meet with their approval, but in England, where the established style was too weak, they insisted on purely Burgundian features. As the book is about building and not just architecture, I have, in addition to some of the high points of architectural genius in any particular country, also included examples of the ordinary and everyday buildings to be found in rural environments, such as the simple cottage or the agricultural barn.

To make this information more readily accessible—while attempting to indicate a sense of continuity between historic past, present and, hopefully, future—I have divided the book into four main sections: the Ancient Classical World, the Byzantine and Medieval World, the Modern Classical World and the Modern World.

The Ancient Classical World, covering Minoan and Greek, Etruscan and Roman, ranges from 3000 BC to the 5th century AD. Although the time span is great and the difference in both proportions and quality of detail between the buildings of the Greek World and Roman World is marked, the average traveler will surely have an overwhelming impression of consistency and convergence in thinking.

The Byzantine and Medieval World, on the other hand, while covering a frontier as big as that of the Roman, and spanning a time scale a third of that of the Ancient Classical World, is all disparity and divergence, with each and every building marked by its particular, and often different, cultural, historical, geographical, geological or climatic context as seen in the examples included of Early Christian, Byzantine, Carolingian, Romanesque and Gothic work.

The Modern Classical World, which covers a period from the mid-15th century in Italy to early 19th-century Europe, includes the Renaissance, mannerism, Baroque, rococo and Neoclassicism. Most other books refer to this period either as the Renaissance or as the Classical period. But the Renaissance clearly only refers to a part of it, and the Classical on its own seems more to do with the ancient world than this more recent period. It therefore seemed more appropriate to distinguish it from the Ancient Classical World by referring to it simply as the Modern Classical World.

The end of the Modern Classical World, however, and the beginning of the Modern World vary between Europe and North America. The Modern Classical, which was almost burnt out in Europe by the late 18th century, was only just beginning in North America at that time; in fact, architecture in North America was still concerned with white columned mansions until the Civil War. The turning point for the Modern World in Europe was the French Revolution and the European wars which followed it, although in terms of technology European architecture was not significantly affected until the 1830s.

In addition to covering the principles of the building periods, I hope that the four sections also convey a notion of the effect of time and distance, and not just place, in architectural development; for example, the slowness of the Renaissance to catch on in Northern Europe or, in contrast, the rapidity with which the ideas of the Modern World were transmitted back and forth across the Atlantic, often gaining enrichment in the crossing.

The gazetteer has further been subdivided under building types—religious buildings, castles and palaces, domestic buildings, civic and public buildings, industrial and commercial buildings. The interest here is in observing the relative importance or lack of importance attached to a building type at any one particular period. In the 17th century, at the height of Amsterdam's commercial prosperity, the city built its fine Town Hall; in the 20th century power and prosperity is reflected in such vast projects as the Rockefeller Center, New York City, or Place Bonaventure, Montreal. The Greek architectural fame rests mainly on magnificent temples, the Roman on large civic and public works, the medieval on great cathedrals, the Renaissance on palazzos, the modern on the skyscraper and the domestic house. For hundreds of years architecture could be discussed simply by referring to religious buildings. In the 20th century the only country producing any new churches of note is Finland.

Since this is principally a guide book, the major countries included have been divided into reasonably manageable areas. The divisions in many instances are ones of convenience rather than reflecting specific regional boundaries. Having taken the same amount of time to visit many of these areas that most holiday makers have at their disposal, I have attempted to give the reader examples of buildings that might lie within reasonable reach of a holiday trip. But many buildings are included not because they themselves have to be seen, but because they give an indication of buildings of similar characteristics in the particular locality, region or country. This book is not only about the buildings in it, but also about those not in it, of how to recognize them and what kind of interpretation to put on them.

The exciting thing about building and architecture is that it can tell us so much about the character and quality of our historic past and present. Everybody is affected in one way or another by buildings—we are born in them, live in them, work in them, and more often than not die in them, yet the layman probably knows less about them than almost anything else that affects his life. While he can usually accept historic architecture, popular opinion is of the belief that modern architecture is bad architecture. But, surely, isn't that so called bad architecture merely bad building? Architecture, after all, is still very much alive and well; we don't always have the eyes to see it. I hope this book may contribute a little in showing that the modern world has as much to offer in quality as the historic, if you accept that our particular period has not been around for quite as long. If the historic style is dead, the principles are still very much alive.

Form

In the design of all buildings, from the simplest rural structure, reflecting the needs of an everyday way of life, to the most grandiose monument, built to commemorate the glorious aspirations of its age, there is one constant and common factor – their form is governed by the purpose for which they were designed.

1 Ely Cathedral (*c.* 1080)
2 Moot Hall, Elstow (16thC) Bedfordshire
3 Dutch gabling
4 Pont du Gard, Nîmes (*c.* AD 14)
5 Castle, Manzarenes el Real (15thC)
Right Town Hall, Middelburg (1412-1599)
Previous page Parthenon, Athens (447-432 BC)

6 Golden Gate Bridge, San Francisco (1937)   **Right** Capitol, Washington DC (1793-1867)
7 Fallingwater, Mill Run (1935), Pennsylvania

Facades

A façade is a key element in architecture because outwardly it proclaims the purpose of a building. It can also be a reflection of a building's interior life; the arrangements of the plan are often expressed in it. And the façade can give us the first clue to a building's age and style. Some façades, like the soaring mass of a cathedral, are seen in isolation; others, such as a simple timber-frame house, are often seen in the context of a village street, its buildings seemingly glued together.

1 Hôtel Carnavalet, Paris (*c.* 1545)
2 Tithe barn, Oxfordshire (13thC)
3 Main façade, Cremona Cathedral (13th-16thC)
4 Monastery of Sainte-Marie-de-la-Tourette, Lyons (1955)
5 Main façade, Monastery of the Escorial, Madrid (1562-84)
Right West front, Amiens Cathedral (1220-88)

Previous page San Xavier del Bac, Tuscon (1783-97)
6 City Hall, Toronto (1958-65)

Right Spanish Mission, Santa Ines (*c.* 1804),
California

6

Entrances

Entrances are not just gates or doors but can also include the passage by which a place may be entered as well as the area beyond the threshold. Entrances link together different spaces. In both their form and decoration they give us some indication of the type of space we are about to enter – witness, the white columns of a Palladian villa, the unadorned timber door of a cottage, the carved portal in the grim walls of Mycenae....

1 Petite Palais, Paris (1900)
2 Rotunda, Vincenza (*c.*1550)
3 Lion Gate, Mycenae (*c.*1400 BC)
4 Royal Naval Hospital (1698-1702)
Right Prior's Door, Ely Cathedral (*c.*1080)

5 Elevator door, Chrysler Building,   **Right** Pierce-Nichols House, Salem (1782),
   New York City (1928-30)   Massachusetts

Structure

The structure of a building is usually dictated by the technical, economical and social considerations prevailing at the time of construction. Ultimately, however, whether you are in the presence of an agricultural barn or a Gothic cathedral, the quality of the architecture is really that of the structure. The structure is the bones of the building. In some cases, the skeleton acts as the framework for the flesh of architecture; in others, the skeleton itself is exaggerated to create a more vivid image.

1 Tithe barn, Oxfordshire (13thC)
2 Cast-iron greenhouse, Lyons (19thC)
3 Cathedral, Cordoba (AD 785)
4 Flying buttresses, York Minster (13th-15thC)
5 Cloisters, Gloucester Cathedral (14thC)
Right Angel roof, St Wenthreda, March
  (*c.* 1550) Cambridgeshire

6 Sainte-Chapelle, Paris (13thC)
Right World Trade Center, New York City (1962-77)

Enclosure

To enclose means to surround, to envelop. A building is any enclosure of sufficient space for a person to move about in. Buildings act as enclosures against weather, noise and intrusion. But to be enveloped in the stillness of a great mosque, to stand in the arcaded shadows of an Italian piazza, or to shelter under the umbrella of Gothic vaulting is to experience an exhilaration that goes far beyond the utilitarian nature of enclosure and creates a particular sense of place which is memorable in its own right.

1 St Mark's Square, Venice
2 Gallery, Herrenchiemsee Castle (1878-85)
3 King's Gallery, Brussels (19thC)
4 Vaulting of nave, Bourges Cathedral (1195-1515)
Right St Sophia, Istanbul (532-37)

5 Interior, Philip Johnson's House, Canaan
(1948), Connecticut

Right King's College Chapel, Cambridge
(1446-1515)

5

Elements

Separate elements, like windows, walls, doors, corridors, stairs and chimneys, represent the component parts of a building. When we look at a Georgian terrace or a row of Victorian houses we register the difference through the various parts; the proportions of the windows, the details around a door, the manner in which the materials have been used. These elements represent an architectural language, a vocabulary through which buildings express their period and their purpose.

1 Interior, Pembroke Castle (13thC)
2 Spiral staircase, The Monument, London (1671-77)
3 Timber-frame house, Lavenham (16thC)
4 Baptistery, Pisa (1153-1265)
5 Georgian doorway, Dublin (18thC)
6 Chimneys, Hampton Court (1514)
Right Spiral staircase, Château Blois (1498-1638)
Overleaf Cloisters, Collegiate Church, Santillana (12thC)

Decoration

Delicate stucco work on a façade, a window frame
enlivened by Baroque molding, an intricate pattern
of polychrome work across a roof – such decoration
has usually been added to enrich a structure.
In certain instances, however – and perhaps most
notably in some of the Baroque church interiors – the
decoration is of such exuberance that the division
between structure and decorative work is dissolved.

1 Choir stalls, Chester Cathedral (12thC)
2 Hotel de Jacques Coeur, Bourges (1443)
3 La Sagrada Familia, Barcelona (1881)
4 Public House window, London (19thC)
5 Cupola, Duomo, Florence (1296-1492)
6 Stained glass window, Canterbury Cathedral
  (early 13thC)
7 Angel, Canterbury Cathedral (*c*. 1448)
8 Hôtel Dieu, Beaune (1443-51)
Right Alhambra, Granada (1338-90)

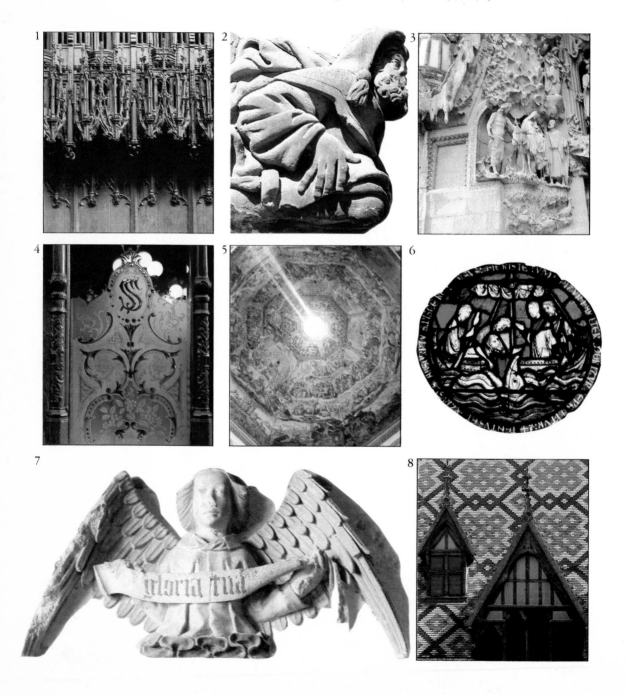

9 Frieze, St Mark's, Venice (1063-73)
10 Middle tower, Château, Chambord (1519-17thC)

11 Façade, Carson Pirie Store, Chicago (1899-1904)
Right Chrysler Building, New York City (1928-30)
Overleaf Church of die Wies (1745-54)

9

10

11

Such an ambitious work is impossible to tackle without becoming indebted to the work of many brilliant academics.

The classic introductory book on architecture is Banister Fletcher's *A History of Architecture.* The range is global. A shorter, sharper book is Nikolaus Pevsner's *An Outline of European Architecture.* But the one most concerned with presenting architecture as a visual subject is Doreen Yarwood's *The Architecture of Europe.* Clearly such concise and informative works were in my mind in writing this book.

Of the many historians in the field I am indebted in particular to the following for their work on Greek and Roman architecture: A. W. Lawrence, John Ward-Perkins, J. J. Coulton, Barry Cunliffe, Jean Charbonneaux, Roland Martin, Francois Villard and A. J. McKay; for the Byzantine and Medieval World: Joan Evans, Geoffrey Webb, Wolfgang Braunfels, William Anderson and Wim Swaan, Kenneth John Conant and Richard Krautheimer; for the Modern Classical World: Leonardo Benevolo, Peter Murray, Ludwig H. Heydenreich and Wolfgang Lotz, Wend Graf Kalnein and Michael Levey, Anthony Blunt, John Summerson and Kerry Downes; for the Modern World: Henry-Russell Hitchcock, Leonardo Benevelo, S. Giedion and Charles Jencks, with particular reference in America to the works of Vincent Scully, William Jordy, William H. Pierson and David Gebhard; in Canada to Alan Gowan; in Scandinavia to Thomas Paulsson's *Scandinavian Architecture* and to J. M. Richards' *800 years of Finnish Architecture,* in particular several of his photographs which he allowed me to use as reference for drawings; in eastern Europe to Brian Knox, Dezsö Dercsény, Hubert Faensen and Vladimir Ivanov, Jan Bialostocki and Kathleen Berton.

For vernacular building I am indebted, among others, to the writings of Alec Clifton-Taylor, R. M. Brunskill, Hans Jüngen Hansen, editor of *Architecture in Wood,* Gillian Darley, Peter Smith, Eric Mercer and Makoto Suzaki.

There are colleagues to whom I owe a debt for their advice and criticism, in particular Professor Piero Sartogo, Professor Jean-Francois Mabardi, Professor Gerhard Freising, Francine Haber and Dr Roger Dixon. I am also particularly grateful to Dorling Kindersley, who have been the real architects of the book; to the various artists for their beautiful drawings; to Mary Ellen McEuen who, despite her own busy family life, typed the manuscript. And last, but not least, my own family who, with remarkable equanimity, have accepted the sudden squealing of brakes as I pulled up, often on the most hazardous of highways, to take yet another photograph.

Finally I would like to dedicate this book to Margery Smith who shared our home and several journeys in search of buildings but died before the book was complete.

How to use this book

The Book of Buildings is divided in three ways: by period (Ancient Classical World, Byzantine & Medieval World, Modern Classical World and Modern World); geographically (by region, country or group of countries), and by building type (Religious buildings, Castles & Palaces, Domestic buildings, Civic & Public buildings and Commercial & Industrial buildings).

For the convenience of travelers, some countries have been sub-divided into manageable areas. Maps showing these geographical divisions, which remain constant for all four sections of the book, are found on pp. 422-432.

To find the pages covering a specific age in a particular region, consult the contents list at the front of the book. Once a period and place have been isolated, individual buildings can be referred to in the text and the captions.

The main entry for a building is followed by its address and dates. A single date indicates the year in which a building was begun. When dates cannot accurately be established, the *circa* symbol (*c.*) is used. No dates are given when they are speculative and might be misleading. In captions, dates and full addresses are given only to those buildings which have not been mentioned in the text.

A glossary of technical terms appears on pp. 434-438. Glossary terms are identified at their first appearance on each double-page spread by italic type in the text and Roman type in captions.

Ancient Classical World

GREEK ARCHITECTURE

The Minoan Period (c. 3000–1200 BC)

Greek architecture began in the primitive Bronze Age world of the Aegean civilization (*c.* 3000-1000 BC) whose major centers were along the coast of Asia Minor, in southern Greece and Crete. From about 2500 BC, Crete grew slowly in wealth and power. It took some five centuries, however, before the Minoan civilization began to flourish.

Minoan power and wealth were based on substantial trading throughout the eastern Mediterranean, under the protection of a powerful navy. At home, affluence and self-confidence were expressed above all in elaborate palaces, such as those at Knossos, Phaistos and Mallia, built between about 2000 and 1800 BC, and often reconstructed in the following centuries to repair earthquake damage. The palaces, whose large

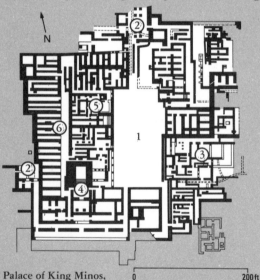

Palace of King Minos, Knossos, plan *The largest and most famous of the palaces on Crete, it was added to and its sections amalgamated over 500 years until it was finally destroyed around 1400 BC.*

1 Central courtyard
2 Entrances
3 Royal apartments
4 Great stairs to state-rooms
5 Throne-room
6 Long gallery and magazines

number of rooms inspired the legend of the Labyrinth for the later Greeks, were constructed around a central court, their plans conveying the sense of freedom and openness that resulted from the mercantile supremacy of Crete. Indeed, external defenses were practically nonexistent, as the powerful navy was expected to

repulse any attack long before it reached the island's shores. Many of the palace apartments were two or more stories high and connected by elaborate staircases. Walls were of rubble and stone, faced with stucco.

The Minoan palaces reached their most advanced forms during the 16th century BC. After this zenith, Minoan power began to dwindle and a huge volcanic eruption on Thera, the island due north of Crete, sometime between 1500 and 1450 BC, probably combined with internal revolt and a raid from the mainland, brought about its collapse.

The Mycenean Period (1500–1000 BC)

By the time of the Minoan collapse, power had already shifted to the mainland, to a society very different from that of Crete. Mycenean life was militaristic and defensive, individual communities often warring with one another.

Mycenean cities were dominated by grim citadels, as at Mycenae and Tiryns, strategically placed on high ground and protected by massive walls of enormous limestone boulders and fortified gates. Mycenae itself became the capital of the society to which it gives its name during the 14th and 13th centuries BC. Here Greek kings, including Agamemnon, were protected within the fortification with his immediate subjects living in the dwellings outside the citadel walls. As in Minoan Crete, the rooms of the palace were grouped around a central courtyard but were smaller and more compact. The distinctive feature of the courtyard was the megaron, a large oblong hall used for both domestic and ceremonial purposes. It occupied one side of the courtyard and had an entrance portico and vestibule.

Mycenean rulers celebrated elaborate funeral rituals either in chamber tombs cut out of the hillside and reached by a roofless passage, or in magnificent subterranean tholos tombs, such as the Treasury of Atreus, Mycenae (*c.* 1325 BC). These were circular chambers cut out of the hillside in which the funerary monument was covered by a conical stone vault.

The Greek "Dark Ages" (1200–800 BC)

From about 1200 BC onward waves of invaders brought an end to Mycenean civilization, and little is known of what happened in Greece at this time — the assumption is of a succession of small, poor, warring states, each enjoying a much lower material standard of life than had prevailed in Mycenean Greece.

By about 800 BC, a recognizably Greek culture began to emerge. Most of the Aegean world spoke the same language; trade revived; a written language and similar pottery styles developed.

The Hellenic Period (c. 800–323 BC)

The prevailing political structure of Hellenic Greece was the city-state, a relatively small and cohesive area, ruled over at first by a hereditary aristocracy. The aristocrats were later replaced by tyrants, dictators who were themselves supplanted during the sixth century BC by some method of collective government, a form of government that reached its apogee in the democracy of fifth-century Athens. A constant feature of Greek society was a fervent religious belief. Each city's gods were consulted frequently, even on day-to-day affairs.

The architecture of Hellenic Greece naturally reflects these preoccupations. Although domestic dwellings must have been more numerous, the most important monumental building type was the temple. The major buildings, whether secular or sacred, were all public, as befitted a society in which civic wealth and power could, to some extent, be measured by the size and majesty of buildings.

The Hellenistic Period (323–146 BC)

Classical Greece may conveniently be said to have come to an end on the death of Alexander the Great in 323 BC. But although his huge empire collapsed almost immediately, the political and cultural influence of Greece remained strong for several centuries. Indeed, the whole Hellenistic period became a key point of reference as Rome developed its own styles.

In contrast with Hellenic Greece, many of the best buildings of the Hellenistic period are civic, not religious, as in the restored Stoa of Attalus, Athens, *c.* 150 BC. For the first time, Greek architects began to design groups of buildings as a harmonious whole, linked by colonnaded porticos and stoas. Alexandria, the greatest Greek city of this time, was laid out on a regular grid plan, with streets intersecting at right angles and forming equal perimeter blocks, the epilogue of Greek urbanism.

Construction & Design

The earliest buildings of Hellenic Greece were of sun-dried bricks, timber and decorative terracotta. Later, stone and marble became the chief materials. Mortar was rarely used, the finely cut blocks being held by metal dowels and cramps.

Although Greek architects were aware of the arch and vault, their approach was relatively conservative. The megaron, with its portico entrance and low-pitched roof, was the model for the Greek temple. The earliest temples were timber, their forms later

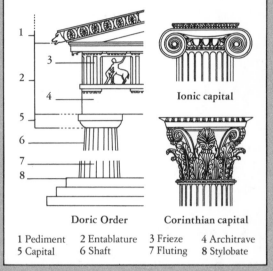

Greek Orders

Generally, every component of a Greek temple complies with the Order of the whole so that recognising just one component, such as a capital, gives a key to the whole. However, the total effect of a Doric temple with its simpler lines, squatter columns and sense of weightiness, contrasts with the taller elegance, or power, of Ionic and Corinthian temples.

Ionic capital

Doric Order

Corinthian capital

1 Pediment	2 Entablature	3 Frieze	4 Architrave
5 Capital	6 Shaft	7 Fluting	8 Stylobate

translated into mud-brick, and finally stone. The two basic elements of timber structures — vertical supports (columns) and horizontal members (entablatures) — were transformed into the three carefully proportioned Orders, or styles, of Greek architecture, the Doric, Ionic and Corinthian. Each Order consisted of a column, which generally stood on a base, and a capital supporting a horizontal lintel, the entablature. The entablature itself was divided into architrave, frieze and cornice, one above the other. The gable of the roof above the entablature was closed by a triangular pediment.

From about 600 BC the Doric Order was employed in stone primarily on the Greek mainland and in southern Italy and Sicily. The Ionic was developed simultaneously in Asia Minor, while the Corinthian did not appear until later, in the Hellenistic period.

Greek architecture was essentially of the exterior. Limited structural progress was more than offset by a very sophisticated concern for proportion. From early Doric temples, a swelling, or entasis, was built into column shafts to correct the optical illusion of straight lines curving in. By the time of the Parthenon, Athens, this preoccupation with correct appearance

Stoa of Attalus, Athens, plan
Covered colonnades, sometimes two-story, providing sheltered walks were built as part of building groups and as retreats near temples and theatres. The plan of the Stoa of Attalus, right, shows how a row of shop units was included.

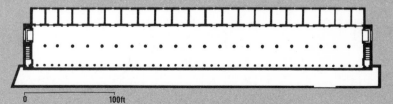

0   100ft

had spread to every exterior line of the building, mostly to prevent any sense of sagging horizontal or bending vertical lines. Even the spacing of columns was subtly altered.

Decoration

Concern for the outward appearance of their buildings led Greek architects to devote much attention to decoration. Stone, marble or bronze sculpture was used for decorative friezes, relief work on pediments and for statues. Subjects varied from scenes of daily life to episodes from legend. Decorative ornamentation included natural motifs such as the acanthus leaf, honeysuckle and palm, as well as griffins' and lions' heads. Stone ornamentation was painted in bright colors and gilded, and walls decorated with murals.

Religious buildings

Temples were the chief monumental buildings of Greece and within the limits of their technical knowledge Greek architects, builders and artists sought always for beauty and harmony. The temple, the house of the gods, was to be as aesthetically pleasing as possible,

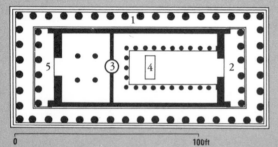

| Parthenon, | 1 Peristyle | 2 Pronaos | 3 Naos |
| Athens, plan | 4 Cult statue | 5 Opisthodomos | |

The earliest temples were based on the Mycenean megaron, though Hellenic architects soon began to expand on this original model. The most important part was the naos, the central room where the statue of the god was housed. The naos received little light, as it was usually roofed and was divided by folding doors from the pronaos, a portico or entrance room. The pronaos emphasized the space in front of the temple where the altar was placed. It was here, outside the temple, that worshippers congregated. At the far end of the naos there was usually the opisthodomos, a room in which the treasure of the temple might be kept.

The front of the pronaos and, in many Greek temples, all four sides, was flanked by a single or double row of columns forming the portico and peristyle. The position and number of these columns has been classified and named. With a columned portico the temple is said to be prostyle, with a portico front and rear, amphiprostyle, and with a complete encircling colonnade, peripteral. A temple is also said to be distyle (two), tetrastyle (three), hexastyle (six),

octastyle (eight), decastyle (10), or dodecastyle (12), according to the number of columns included in its portico. The entire building stood on a raised platform, or stylobate, although strictly speaking the stylobate refers to the top step of the platform only. Most temples were grouped in sacred enclosures or sanctuaries on high ground, an acropolis or citadel, away from and above the city, and entered through elaborate gateways (propylaea), as in Athens. Protected by walls, the acropolis was originally a place of refuge.

Civic & Public buildings

The main civic building was the agora. There political assemblies were held, civic, social and commercial affairs conducted. Around it were grouped other administrative and public buildings, shops and temples.

Other major public buildings included the bouleuterion, a large covered rectangular meeting-place with raised seating on three sides; the palaestra, or wrestling school, used for all sorts of physical training; the prytaneum, for civic receptions, and the gymnasium, the Greek version of today's sports' halls, with facilities for running, jumping, wrestling and so on.

Early Greek drama was performed in the open air in a natural hollow of ground with the audience sitting on the surrounding hillsides. Later theatres were modeled on these beginnings and consisted of three main elements, the stage, orchestra and auditorium. The stage, or skene, was a simple structure with a false front which served as a backcloth to the orchestra and provided changing facilities. The orchestra was a circular paved space used by the chorus. The auditorium, or cavea, was semicircular in form with seating cut out of the hillside. All the major Greek cities had a theatre, one of the best examples being that at Epidauros (c. 350 BC). The

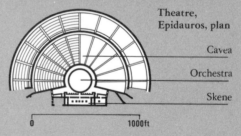

Theatre, Epidauros, plan

Cavea

Orchestra

Skene

Greek odeion was a similar type of building to the dished theatre, but used for musical contests. One of the most impressive is the Odeion of Herodes Atticus, Athens (c. AD 161).

The Greek stadium was a running track. They were planned parallel to a ridge of land so that the slopes of the ridges could be used for spectators' seating. The course was some 600 ft long with a straight and semicircular finish, as at the Stadium, Athens, which was rebuilt in 1896. The hippodrome was a similar structure, but larger so that it could be used for horse racing.

ROMAN ARCHITECTURE

The Etruscan Period (750–100 BC)

The beginnings of Roman architecture are to be found in the work of the Etruscans. Thought to be from Asia Minor, they settled in central Italy, between Florence and Rome, at the end of the seventh century BC. Theirs was a primitive culture, in part of Hellenic descent. They were remarkably skilful builders and fortified their cities with massive stone walls and towers built of polygonal blocks or large, partly-burnt bricks. They developed vaulting with dressed stone and their city walls were pierced by arched gateways, such as the Arch of Augustus, Perugia (2ndC BC).

Etruscan temples were first wooden-framed with mud-brick walls, but from the fourth century BC walls and columns were of stone. The Etruscan, or Tuscan Order (see p. 30) was a simpler and cruder version of the Greek Doric Order, with a plain, rounded capital and unfluted column shaft.

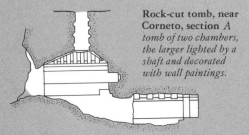

Rock-cut tomb, near Corneto, section *A tomb of two chambers, the larger lighted by a shaft and decorated with wall paintings.*

The Etruscans also built magnificent tombs, located outside their city walls. There were two types, a circular burial mound with a stone base and earth cover and a rectangular tomb cut in the rock. Good examples of both exist at Cerveteri, (*c.* 500 BC). The design of many of these tombs was like that of contemporaneous houses. Some even had an open outer chamber, similar to the atrium, or inner courtyard, characteristic of Roman domestic buildings.

The Roman Period (300 BC–AD 365)

The Roman Republic had been founded by a small Latin tribe in 509 BC. Its beginnings were unremarkable and, like that of the Etruscans, its architecture was humble and unpretentious.

Gradually, however, the Republic began to expand, defeating first the Etruscans, then Sicily and Carthage. Greece came under Roman control in 146 BC and by the third century AD Rome controlled an empire that covered most of the known world, from the Persian Gulf in the east to Hadrian's Wall on the English frontier with Scotland. This expansion accompanied dramatic developments in all aspects of living, from religion to road making, from written record to law and administration, developments which have had a profound effect on the history of mankind ever since. Despite their antipathy toward the Greeks, the Romans were awed by their intellectual, philosophical and artistic achievements, and during the third century BC Roman architects rapidly fell under the spell of the Greek world. It was only two centuries later, as the Republic transformed itself into an empire, that Rome began to acquire the buildings and monuments appropriate to its status as a world capital. It is in the difference between the new Roman architecture and Greek architecture that the driving force and principles of Roman architecture are found. Both architectures made use of columns and decorated elements like capitals and entablatures, but the Greeks had seen architecture as a means of serving the gods. The Romans, by contrast, believed that it should reflect the might and power of the builder or patron. The basis of their architecture was engineering. Pragmatic by nature, they concerned themselves with problems such as enclosing vast spaces with vaults or domes, building bridges and huge aqueducts. Decorative enrichment was provided by the application of Greek-style ornament.

The Romans were skilled town planners. However, their townscapes, unlike those of Hellenistic cities, did not adhere rigidly to a controlling grid. They saw planning as a spatial art where selfcontained building complexes are joined by interconnecting axial lines which are picked out and reinforced by triumphal arches, colonnades, fountains and monuments.

Construction & Design

The quality of Roman architecture depended entirely on its ability to build across huge spaces. The keys to this were the development of the Etruscan stone arch and the use of concrete, a material which revolutionized the architecture of the classical world as much as steel did in the modern world.

The most important element was the round arch which could form a barrel vault on parallel walls. A further development was the groin or cross-vault, formed by the intersection of two barrel vaults over a

Roman structural elements
Based on the strength of the round arch, Roman engineers developed the barrel or tunnel vault — really an elongated round arch between parallel walls — and from this the groin or cross vault.

Round arch

Barrel vault

Groin vault on a square bay

square bay. Buttresses were also introduced, especially the "spur" buttress and the flying buttress which became a characteristic feature of Gothic structure. The Romans tended not to emphasize such supports.

Many buildings were of brick rendered with concrete. Some were of brick-faced concrete with a stucco finish. Travetine, a hard limestone, was also used. There were two types of brick, sun-burnt and kiln-burnt. They were usually 1½ inches thick and 1 foot square. When bricks were used as a facing, cut stone was employed on the corners of the building to protect them.

Whereas Greek architects employed the Orders as structural elements of their buildings, the use of the arch in Roman architecture meant that the Orders became primarily a means of articulation, or dividing the design. The Romans used all three Greek Orders, though the Corinthian, with its highly decorative quality, was the favorite. They frequently employed different Orders on each story, something the Greeks would very rarely have done. The Tuscan Order was not popular with the Romans, perhaps because it was comparatively plain. Roman architecture did invent one new Order, however, the Composite, an amalgam of Ionic and Corinthian.

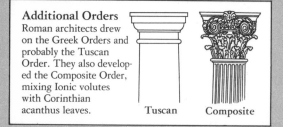

Additional Orders
Roman architects drew on the Greek Orders and probably the Tuscan Order. They also developed the Composite Order, mixing Ionic volutes with Corinthian acanthus leaves.

Tuscan　　Composite

Decoration

Much decorative work was based on Greek prototypes, and large quantities of sculpture were imported from Greece. In addition, a native style of realist figurative sculpture was developed, exemplified in numerous equestrian statues, such as that of Marcus Aurelius, the Campidoglio, Rome. Floors were usually in decorative marble panels or marble mosaics laid in elaborate patterns.

Religious buildings

Roman temples are an amalgam of Greek and Etruscan models. They were usually an integral part of the townscape with the raised portico adding grandeur to the urban ensemble of buildings. The cella (the Roman naos) was generally wider than in Greek temples. Outside, the front portico was the major feature and the whole building was raised on a high podium, instead of the Greek stylobate. Where Greek temples had a stepped base with the steps running all around the temple, the higher Roman podium was mounted by a flight of steps at the front only. The larger

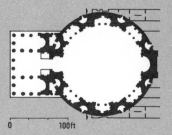

Pantheon, Rome, plan *Walls some 20 ft thick were the Roman solution to supporting the dome of the rotunda. A plan shows how niches cut into this thickness below the line of thrust.*

0　　100ft

temples, such as Mars Ultor, Rome (14–2 BC), stood in colonnaded courtyards, sometimes entered via triumphal arches.

Numerous circular and polygonal temples were built, such as the Temples of Vesta, Rome (AD 205), and Tivoli (*c.* 80 BC). The most extraordinary, the Pantheon, Rome (AD 120-24), is the best preserved of all Rome's ancient buildings and became the prototype for the centralized churches of the Renaissance. Unlike most temples, its architects did not emphasize its exterior but instead the cella inside, with its huge hemispherical dome and elaborate coffering. The cella is lighted by an unglazed circular opening in the crown of the dome.

Palaces & Domestic buildings

The major palace remains in Rome are those that crown the Palatine Hill, where successive Emperors added their own complexes. The most interesting are those of Domitian (r. AD 81-96). In Nero's Golden House, Rome (AD 64), came the first attempt to break away from the strict right-angled geometry, a movement that culminated in the magnificent collage of parts at Hadrian's Villa, Tivoli (AD 118), which spreads over the undulating countryside.

Domestic buildings were of three main types. The domus, or private house, consisted of rooms planned around an atrium, or inner court, with a colonnade beyond. Good examples are found at Pompeii and Herculaneum. The second type is the villa, or country house. A typical example is the Villa of Maximian, Piazza Armerina, Sicily (4thC AD), with its characteristic asymmetrical layout. Finally, the insula, a multistory apartment block, consisted of a central courtyard with shops on the street frontage. Good examples are found in Ostia, among them the House of Diana (2ndC AD). The insula was a prototype of the Renaissance Palazzo.

Civic & Public buildings

At the center of every Roman town or city was the Forum, both a meeting- and a marketplace. The earliest fora were generally irregularly shaped, but during the Empire most were rebuilt about strong axial lines. Many of the major public buildings, the basilicas, market halls and administrative offices, were planned around them. The earliest Imperial forum in Rome is the Forum Romanum, which was replanned on grandiose lines by Julius Caesar.

A whole series of artifacts, such as triumphal arches erected to commemorate victorious military campaigns, enhanced the civic quality of Rome. The first of these arches was built in about 200 BC. Decorated ornately with scenes from the campaigns, they had either one or three openings. Of particular interest are the Arches of Titus (AD 82); of Septimius Severus (AD 203), and of Constantine (AD 312). Numerous town gateways and archways were also built. These were either intended as defensive strong points, complete with vantage courts, or as ornamental portals to fora or at main street intersections.

Basilicas were the law and business centers of the Roman world. They usually consisted of three or five aisles with galleries and the body of the basilica rising to twice the height of the side aisles. Entrance was from the side or, more often, from the end, opposite the tribunal, which was usually on a raised dais in a semicircular apse. Good examples are the Basilicas of Trajan, (AD 98-113) and Constantine (AD 310-13), both of which are in Rome.

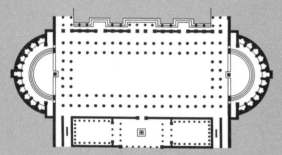

Basilica of Trajan, Rome, plan *The classic Roman basilica plan with large open "nave", and surrounding colonnades forming double side aisles. This example has a tribunal in an apse at each end and entrance at the side.*

Roman basilica, section
The arrangement of high nave and lower side aisles in a Roman basilica shows how the building was a prototype for Christian church building for centuries to come.

Thermae played a major part in Roman daily life. These palatial public baths were both community and recreation centers. One of the best examples is Thermae of Caracalla (AD 211-17). This consisted of a complex of baths with accommodation for 1600 built on a high platform above the furnace and service rooms and surrounded by a park enriched with fountains and statuary. There was also a stadium, and the whole center was enclosed by a great structure of apartments, shops and lecture rooms. The Thermae of Diocletian (AD 302) was similar, although on a vaster scale with accommodation for 3000 bathers.

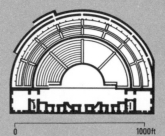

Theatre, Orange, plan *(c. AD 50). An advanced example, this theatre in France shows how Roman engineering produced an enclosed theatre building which did not depend on a natural site.*

Greek plays were presented in Rome as early as the third century BC. Roman theatres were freestanding, an elaborate stage building backing the stage itself and engaging at either side the walls forming the exterior façade of the building. Both the stage building and the façades of the Roman theatre were usually arcaded in tiers and articulated externally. by Orders. The seats were supported on a semicircle of tiered and galleried corridors made structurally possible by the development of the arch. Although several theatres were built in Rome, the Theatre of Marcellus (23-5 BC) is the only one that survives. Theatrical performances were superseded in popularity by gladiatorial combats, held in amphitheatres such as the Colosseum (AD 72-80). Amphitheatres, adapted from the freestanding theatres, were built in every major city. Circuses, developed from the Greek stadium, were used for chariot and horse racing. The best surviving example is the Circus of Maxentius (AD 309), built in Rome itself.

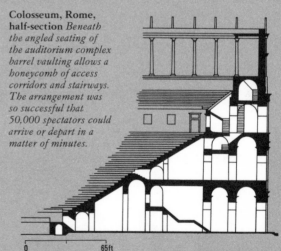

Colosseum, Rome, half-section *Beneath the angled seating of the auditorium complex barrel vaulting allows a honeycomb of access corridors and stairways. The arrangement was so successful that 50,000 spectators could arrive or depart in a matter of minutes.*

Roman engineering skills came into their own in the construction of bridges (some of which had enormous spans) and aqueducts, all based on the round arch on brick and concrete piers. Aqueducts are particularly typical of Roman pragmatism, supplying major cities and providing the immense quantities of water required for public fountains and baths, Rome itself being served by 11 large aqueducts. In time, a reliable water supply was provided throughout the empire.

31

Southern Greece

Religious buildings

The **Temple of Hera, Olympia** (7thC BC), one of the earliest Greek temples to be built in stone, is the oldest and best preserved building at Olympia. Remains include some of the columns, the *stylobate,* and parts of the *naos* walls. Typical of the *Hellenic* period, external massing dominated internal planning. The **Temple of Apollo, Corinth** (6thC BC), with its heavy *Doric peristyle,* was equally monumental, as was the **Temple of Athena Polias, Athens** (6thC BC), of which only the foundations remain. The latter was the first of the great structures to be built on the Acropolis and was later replaced by the Parthenon. Other examples of early Hellenic temples include the **Old Temple, Sanctuary of Hera** (7thC BC), Argive Heraion, possibly the earliest *peripteral* building in the Peloponnese, and the **Temple of Zeus, Olympia** (470-456 BC), the most important temple within the Altis, or inner sanctuary, and one of the largest in Greece.

With the **Parthenon, Athens** (447-432 BC), the Greek temple achieved a level of sophistication unparalleled in the building world. Designed by Ictinos and Callicrates, the building has a highly classical exterior, including the legendary optical corrections necessary to prevent the illusion of sagging horizontal lines and concavity of the vertical lines. Internally the layout was equally radical. In order to accommodate the monumental gold and ivory statue of Athena by Phidias, a relatively spacious naos was provided for the first time in temple architecture.

Two other buildings by Ictinos were equally innovatory. The **Telesterion, Eleusis** (5thC BC), was the first great hall of Greek architecture. Its construction was made possible by new technology that allowed its vast roof to be carried on only seven rows of seven columns. It was a monumental cube with room for 3000 worshippers. At the **Temple of Apollo, Bassae** (5thC BC), the innovation concerned decoration. Here the *Ionic colonnade* within the naos was a purely decorative feature, not structural.

Both the concern for internal spatial rearrangement and this preference for decorative rather than structural effect profoundly changed temple designs. The external proportions and structure of the **Hephaisteion, Athens** (449-444 BC), were dictated by the temple's decorative internal design. Other examples are the tiny Doric **Metroon, Olympia** (4thC BC), and the **Temple of Athena Alea, Tripolis** (*c.* 395 BC).

Later, more exuberant sculptural and decorative themes predominated. The graceful, miniature **Temple of Athena Nike**, or **Nike Apteros, Athens** (427 BC), designed by Callicrates, shows that the use of slender columns and a combination of styles was increasing. Bare side walls contrast with decorative porches, while the whole is linked by an encircling *frieze* and a continuation of the column bases along the foot of the naos.

Reconstructions of the **Tholos, Epidauros** (360 BC), in the local museum show the qualities of this Doric temple by Polycleitus. It was considered the finest of all *tholoi.*

Parthenon, Athens *The mathematical precision of the Parthenon made it more an awesome machine than a building. It was the genius of Phidias, the master sculptor, that brought it alive. Of his work only the western* frieze *(details left) along the top of the* naos *wall remains virtually intact on the building.*

Temple of Apollo, Bassae *The reconstruction of the interior, above, shows the once beautiful crafting of this temple. The remains are shown, right. It was built high in the Arcadian mountains as a thanksgiving for deliverance from an outbreak of plague in the state of Phigalia.*

Temple of Apollo, Corinth *One of the great Doric temples in Greece, the remains include ponderous columns with marked entasis to compensate for their shortness, and flat, splayed Doric capitals.*

Hephaisteion, Athens *Originally known as the Thesion, it is the best preserved of the Greek temples because it was later converted into a church. Standing elegantly aloof on its low, stepped podium, it has a small naos and is traditional in plan except for the east end which is more spacious.*

Temple of Poseidon, Sounion *(c. 444 BC). A stately temple with confident Doric peristyle. It was designed by the architect of the Hephaisteion, Athens. Perched near the edge of a cliff, it forms a conspicuous silhouette when viewed from the sea.*

Temple of Athena Nike, Athens, *above. This tiny marble temple stands gingerly on a rocky spur of the Acropolis, Athens, in front of the line of the Propylaea. The demure scale and Ionic style were clearly designed to balance the monumental gateways rising behind it.*

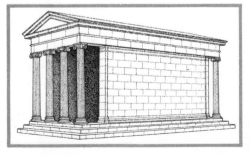

Temple on the Ilissus, Athens *(449 BC). The remains are partially preserved, but this reconstruction shows how fragile was Callicrates's design. A four-columned Ionic portico is duplicated front and rear, while the whole stands on a stepped terrace.*

33

Southern Greece

The building of the **Erechtheion, Athens** (421-405 BC), on the Acropolis, marked the beginning of a concern for the spatial relationships within a group of buildings. It was designed as an unobtrusive counterweight to the Parthenon, its position balancing the plan of the Acropolis. The central block, with the additions of the north porch and the porch of the *caryatids* on the south side, give the building a delightful asymmetry. The sculptured *frieze* crowning the central block and extending around the north porch lends coherence.

Many idyllic locations became the sites of sacred precincts in classical Greece. Within them little regard was given to the relationship of one building to another. In the **Sanctuary of Zeus, Olympia** (6th-5thC BC), the principal temples were enclosed in a central area called the *Altis*. This sanctuary was associated with the Olympic Games and is set in a lush, green valley shaded by evergreen oaks, poplars and pines. At the **Sanctuary of Asclepius, Epidauros** (c. 380 BC), are the remains of a religious center and spa devoted to the cult of Asclepius. It is set in a broad, pineclad valley. The **Sanctuary of Poseidon, Isthmia** (c. 582-146 BC), also famous for its games, was one of the four Panhellenic sanctuaries celebrated in the Odes of Pindar. There are other sites of sanctuaries at the ancient towns of **Sounion** (5thC BC) and **Bassae** (5thC BC).

Primitive in comparison with Classical Greece, *tholos* tombs were characteristic structures of Bronze Age Mycenae. The **Treasury of Atreus,** **Mycenae** (c. 1300-1250 BC), is the finest of all remaining tholos tombs and is thought to be the tomb of Agamemnon. A monumental approach cut into the *tufa* led to the circular chamber which was *corbelled* and had a conical roof. The **Treasury of Clytemnestra, Mycenae** (13thC BC), another tholos tomb, had an ornamental façade carved in colored stones. Above the door *lintel* is the triangular element, common to tholos tombs, which dispersed the load.

Castles & Palaces

Citadel palaces were also typical of the Mycenaean period. A product of the ever violent times of the *Helladic* period, they exploited Cretan mercantile supremacy and became the centers of small, powerful empires. The **Citadel, Tiryns** (13thC BC), has primitive megalithic fortifications, but in contrast the palace was built of sun-dried bricks and wooden columns. Rooms were planned around an outer court and an inner *colonnaded* court with its sacrificial altar. The principal room was the megaron, or great hall. At the **Citadel, Mycenae** (c. 1400 BC), are remains of grim fortifications, the palace and the magnificent Lion Gate in the massive citadel walls.

The **Palace of Nestor, Pylos** (1300-1200 BC), was planned around a large interior court which was entered by a *propylon*. It was from such primitive beginnings of megaron and entrance gate that the temple and propylaea of Classical Greece were ultimately to develop.

Temple of Athena Polias, Athens *(6thC BC). A section of the limestone pediment (in the Acropolis Museum) shows how this temple's monumental character was once enhanced by rich sculptural and painted decorations. It was modeled on the design of the Temple of Apollo, Corinth.*

Temple of Zeus, Nemea *(340-320 BC). The remains of this elegant Doric temple show us its unusually slender columns. To the south of the temple is a palaestra with attendant baths.*

Erechtheion, Athens *Its irregular plan was designed for an awkward, sloping site, to accommodate hallowed ground and for the worship of three gods, Erechtheus, Poseidon and Athene, which called for separate chambers. There are windows, three Ionic porches of different scales, and a* caryatid *porch.*

Decorative details

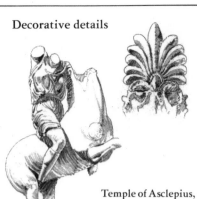

Temple of Asclepius, Epidauros *Detail of an* antefix, *above (Epidauros Museum); detail of a mounted Amazon from the west pediment, above left, and "Victory with Cock" from the west front, left, (National Museum).*

Temple of Zeus, Olympia *(470-456 BC). One of the carved groups decorating a* metope, *above, and a detail of a kneeling girl, right, (Olympia Museum). Statues from the pediments of this temple are among the finest of ancient Greek sculpture.*

Temple of Olympian Zeus, Athens *(c. 170 BC). This was the largest temple in Greece, with a giant* peristyle *of* Corinthian *columns which are unusually thickly proportioned.*

Treasury of Atreus, Mycenae *The tomb, a vaulted chamber 47 ft in diameter, was approached by a long narrow passageway (the burial chamber itself was a chamber off the tomb cut into rock). The magnificent entry façade was originally dressed in white, red and green stones in geometric patterns.*

Citadel, Mycenae *(c. 1400 BC). The Lion Gate, right, was the principal entrance to the citadel and is the most ancient sculpture remaining in Europe. The reconstruction of the citadel, below, shows the fortress was magnificently austere.*

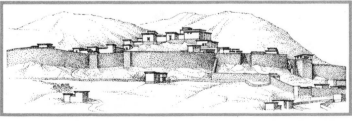

Southern Greece

Civic & Public buildings

Continual warfare in ancient Greece required an upper town, or acropolis ("city on the height"), that was the last refuge in a siege. Here the principal temples and treasuries were built. Not until the 5th century BC was the **Acropolis, Athens,** transformed into a sacred precinct. The **Larissa, Argos** (6thC BC), is built on an equally impregnable height. At **Messene** (*c.* 369 BC) the site required a series of walls and towers for defense. The skilful siting of towers and passageways and the use of handsome masonry show an awareness for military and aesthetic concerns.

Propylaea were the entrance gateways to sanctuaries, palaces and *agoras.* The most monumental and imposing, the **Propylaea, Athens** (437-432 BC), marks the western entrance to the Acropolis. It was designed by Mnesikles and consists of a main gateway with a dominating façade flanked by asymmetrical porches. The **Great Propylaea, Eleusis** (*c.* AD 120), was a close copy, but the **Lesser Propylaea, Eleusis** (54 BC), consisted of a tall, narrow *portico* placed at the rear of a recess in the sanctuary walls.

Buildings for the meetings of Ancient Greek Councils took various forms. The **Bouleuterion, Olympia** (6th-3rdC BC), was awkwardly planned with two separate, round-ended, oblong halls, side by side, and a square room between. The **Bouleuterion, Athens** (*c.* 5thC BC), was almost square with room for about 700 people. Larger public meetings were originally held in the open air but, with technological advances, high, covered assembly halls like the **Thersilion, Megalopolis** (4thC BC), were built. This was a huge oblong building accommodating 6000.

The beauty of the Greek theatre lay in its relationship to the landscape. The **Theatre, Megalopolis** (4thC BC), was the largest in Greece. It is beautifully sited with magnificent views and seating for 20,000. The **Theatre, Epidauros** (3rdC BC), with seating for 14,000, is one of the best preserved classical buildings in Greece. Other examples include the **Theatre, Argos** (4thC BC), the **Theatre, Sikyon** (3rdC BC), and the **Theatre of Dionysus, Athens** (342-326 BC).

The odeion was the concert hall of the ancient classical world. The **Odeion of Herodes Atticus, Athens** (AD 161), was one of the largest buildings erected in ancient Athens, with seating for 6000. Also of interest: the **Odeion of Agrippa, Athens** (*c.* 15 BC), which was roofed by a single span and seated 1000; the **Odeion, Corinth** (1stC AD); and the **Odeion, Patras** (2ndC BC, restored 1960).

Used first for foot races and later for other athletic events, stadia were usually planned parallel to a hillside so that seats could be easily cut out of the slope. The **Stadium, Nemea** (4thC BC), lying in a natural hollow, was the site of the Nemean games, one of the four great Panhellenic festivals, which were held biennially. The **Stadium, Olympia** (4thC BC), the oldest in Greece, could seat 40,000 spectators. Stadia are also found at **Epidauros** (3rdC BC) and **Athens** (*c.* AD 160).

Arcadian Gate, Messene (*c. 369 BC*). *The fortifications at Messene were constructed for defense as well as display. This particularly well-preserved gate consisted of an inner and an outer entrance, separated by a circular court.*

Citadel, Tiryns *The earliest walls of this fortified palace are so thick (17-56 ft) and crudely hewn that the classical Greeks attributed them to the mythical Cyclops. The walls themselves contained large galleries and chambers.*

Theatre, Epidauros *Designed by Polycleitos, the theatre has astonishingly good acoustics. This elegant doorway is one of the two entries to the orchestra, one at each end of the scene building.*

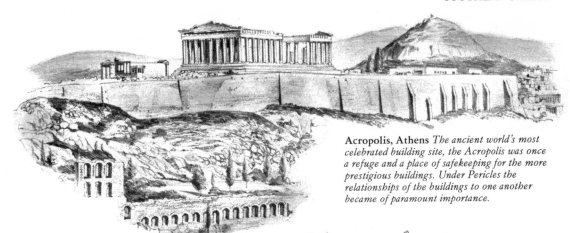

Acropolis, Athens *The ancient world's most celebrated building site, the Acropolis was once a refuge and a place of safekeeping for the more prestigious buildings. Under Pericles the relationships of the buildings to one another became of paramount importance.*

Propylaea, Athens *This detail of a* capital *is from one of the six* Ionic *columns that lined the central passageway and supported the marble ceiling between the front and rear* Doric *porticos.*

Great Propylaea, Eleusis *Remains of the sanctuary entrance built under the auspices of the Roman Emperor, Antonious Pius. His portrait bust on the medallion ornamented the main* gate *pediment. The gate was approached by six marble steps.*

Lesser Propylaea, Eleusis *Reconstruction of the entrance to the innermost court of the sanctuary. Centered in a recess, the* portico *was supported on orthodox* Corinthian *columns on the outer façade. The inner façade had* caryatids *instead of columns. The* entablature *had an elaborate* frieze, *of which portions remain.*

Theatre of Dionysus, Athens *The theatre was reconstructed in stone in the 4th century BC to seat 17,000 spectators. The marble seats of honor, above, were added later in the 1st C BC.*

Stadium, Athens *Reconstructed by Herodes Atticus on an established site, and then faithfully restored in 1896, it occupies a natural valley with seating for 60,000.*

Southern Greece

The **Library of Hadrian, Athens** (AD 117-138), was designed symmetrically around a large rectangular garden with a long central pool. It was enclosed by a huge wall, *buttressed* externally by *Corinthian* columns. The more spacious rooms opposite the main entrance, and entered through a porch, housed the library, whereas the rooms arranged around the cloister were probably used for workrooms or for archives. The library has all the monumentality of Imperial Rome rather than the regional characteristics of earlier public buildings in Southern Greece.

Wherever they settled, the Romans built public baths that were not only designed for luxurious bathing but were also the centers of social life. They were as characteristic of Roman civilization as the amphitheatres. The **Roman Baths, Athens** (AD 124-131), had four main halls with the characteristic three-bath chamber to the side. The **Roman Baths, Argos** (2ndC AD), were lavish, with a *frigidarium* equipped with three plunge-baths together with three *caldaria* fitted with marble lined baths.

Gymnasia consisted of courts for athletics, bathing pools, dressing rooms, rest rooms and lecture rooms. The **Gymnasium, Epidauros** (4thC BC), consisted of a huge *colonnaded* court with surrounding rooms. The entrance is at the northwest corner through an elaborate *propylaeum*. Also of interest is the **Great Gymnasium,**

Olympia (3rdC BC). Next to it is the **Palaestra, Olympia** (3rdC BC), a wrestling school not dissimilar in plan to a gymnasium, consisting of an open colonnaded court, 148 ft square, with rooms built behind three sides. *Palaestra* and gymnasia were essentially Greek meeting places. It was the Romans who later combined them with lavish baths, which were to develop into the large scale imperial *thermae*.

The **Choragic Monument of Lysicrates, Athens** (334 BC), is an example of the many monuments erected to display a tripod — a prize for athletic or artistic prowess. Lysicrates had directed the best chorus at a drama festival and this monument celebrates the event. The dome that caps the structure was cut from a single block of marble. The ornament on the dome would have once carried the bronze tripod itself. The monument is the earliest example of an *entablature* with both a *frieze* and a *cornice* with dentils, or small square blocks of masonry.

Commercial & Industrial buildings

Stoas, usually long, colonnaded buildings and mostly used for business, were built around public places or as shelters at sanctuaries. Only the foundations of the **Stoa of Zeus, Athens** (5thC BC), remain but it was once an elegant building with a central *Doric portico* and projecting wings. The **Stoa of Attalus, Athens** (150-138 BC,

Library of Hadrian, Athens *Part of the east wall with its elegant screen of* Corinthian *columns. Of particular interest is the way in which the columns were raised on bases to give greater height, the bases being free-standing* pedestals *rather than* engaged plinths.

Gateway, Agora of Caesar, Athens *This Roman gate in Greek style marked the entrance to the market at the foot of the north slope of the Acropolis. It appears flat and two-dimensional compared to the layered effect in the façades of Hadrian's Library and Hadrian's Arch.*

Arch of Hadrian, Athens *(c. AD 138). Erected by Hadrian, the arch divided the new city from the old. The upper openings framed statues, while vertical columns, bracketed out from the* entablature, *edged the archway.*

rebuilt 1953-56), was originally erected by the King of Pergamon and used as an arcade along the east side of the Agora, or town square. Other examples include the **South Stoa, Corinth** (146 BC), one of the largest secular buildings in Classical Greece, the **Stoa of Eumenes, Athens** (197-159 BC), used as a shelter and promenade near the Theatre of Dionysus, and the **Stoa of Basileios, Athens** (5thC BC), which was a surprisingly small building which could accommodate only a hundred people.

The social and commercial center of Greek cities was the agora. The **Agora, Athens,** consisted of a large central space with buildings arranged in an irregular fashion along three sides, the Stoa of Attalus dominating the fourth side. The Panathenaic Way, the processional road that climbed the slope of the Acropolis, crossed diagonally in front of the Stoa of Attalus. The **Agora, Corinth,** was far more organized. It was a vast marketplace on two levels. A row of shops and a monumental rostrum marked the transition between the two levels. The main entrance was near the northeast corner, with a flight of steps and grand propylaeum. During Roman replanning, the latter was replaced by a characteristic triumphal arch. The **Agora of Caesar, Athens** (c. 12-2 BC), was a large square with a smaller colonnaded courtyard, the whole paved with marble. Its building was financed by Caesar and Augustus.

Choragic Monument of Lysicrates, Athens, *right. A diminutive* tholos *with acanthus leaf decoration placed on top of a tall, square, limestone base makes this monument a delightful* Baroque *folly. This is the first known external use of Corinthian columns.*

Tower of the Winds, Athens *(1stC BC). A monument of Roman Athens, it is an elegant marble octogon with a pyramidal roof built to house a waterclock, sundial and weathervane. The sides of the tower correspond to the eight winds.*

Stoa of Attalus, Athens *View showing the first floor interior. The outward facing side is fronted with shops, while the remainder provided promenades and a viewing platform overlooking the Agora.*

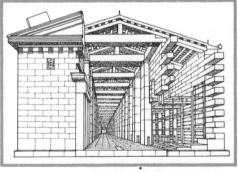

Arsenal, Piraeus *(c. 330 BC). Reconstruction of the Arsenal showing an enormous hall under a single roof. It was one of several giant, shed-like structures built to house the Athenian navy and for the storage of sailing tackle on the peninsula of Eëtioneia. Only fragments remain.*

Stoa of Zeus, Athens *Distinctly different from the simpler, oblong structures, the façade of this stoa was broken with a recessed center, emphasized by two projecting wings.*

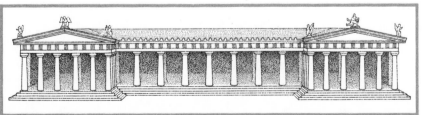

Central & Northern Greece

Religious buildings

The late *Helladic tholos* tomb, the **Treasury of Minyas, Orchemenos** (*c.* 1300 BC), is unsophisticated in comparison to work found at Delphi, but has a magnificently carved ceiling in the rectangular side chamber leading off the tholos. At **Marmara**, near Delphi, the center of the rectangular **Sanctuary of Athena** is occupied by three buildings: the **Treasury of Massalia** (*c.* 530 BC), a *Doric* **Treasury** (490-460 BC) and the marble **Tholos** (*c.* 390 BC), remarkable for its circular design. Architectural expertise in the 4th century BC led to a series of magnificent circular buildings, of which this tholos is the earliest example. Classical in spirit and style, it has an external Doric *peristyle* contrasting with a paved interior of *Corinthian* halfcolumns. To the west of the tholos stood the *prostyle* **Temple of Athena Pronoia** (*c.* 360 BC).

Greek sanctuaries, designed to accommodate a procession, were linear in layout, as for example the **Pythian Sanctuary**, or **Tremenos of Apollo, Delphi**. Buildings and monuments faced the processional way that led to the temple façade, the dominating point of the plan. The **Temple of Apollo** (366-329 BC) was an exact reproduction of an earlier temple, which it replaced. The earlier temple had set a precedent in that it was an architecture of façades, the front façade being entirely covered in marble while the rest remained in limestone. The columns of both temples were also thinner than usual, since marble is a particularly hard rock. The architects, now technically more confident, were in effect working more as artists than as engineers. Access to the temple was via the Sacred Way, beside which stood a series of votive monuments, including the massive **Monument of the Admirals**, the **Bull of Corcyra** and the **Kings of Argos**. Beyond are a series of treasuries, notably the **Treasury of the Athenians** (490 BC), the first known example of a Doric building constructed entirely of marble. It resembles a miniature temple and consists of a porch, facing the Sacred Way, with two columns between the end walls of the *naos*. A sculptured *frieze* adds relief to the three blank walls. The **Treasury of the Siphnians** (526-525 BC), an *Ionic* temple which had two *caryatids* between the side walls at the end of the naos, and the **Treasury of Sikyonians** (5thC BC) are also of interest.

In northern Greece, the **Mausoleum of Galerius, Salonika**, a magnificent *rotunda* built in AD 311 and now the church of St George, was originally designed to be the founder's tomb. Thessalonike was the capital of Galerius's quarter of the empire and a processional way joined the rotunda to his **Palace**. The triumphal **Arch of Galerius** (AD 297) marked the point where the processional way crossed the Via Egnatia. Parts of it have survived.

Domestic buildings

Remains of private houses at **Dystos** (5thC BC) are among the few surviving examples of the period. Standardized in plan, each house originally consisted of an entrance passageway, an inner

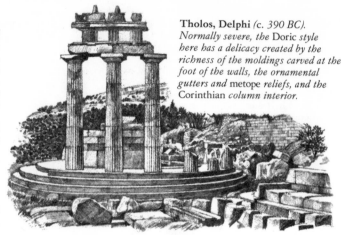

Tholos, Delphi *(c. 390 BC). Normally severe, the* Doric *style here has a delicacy created by the richness of the moldings carved at the foot of the walls, the ornamental gutters and* metope *reliefs, and the Corinthian* column interior.

Temple of Apollo, Delphi *A product of reactionary architecture, it was a reproduction of an earlier temple, destroyed in 373 BC. The architrave above these columns was decorated with shields captured from the Persians and Gauls.*

Theatre, Delphi *(4thC BC). Set in a rough, mountainous landscape, the theatre has a superb view westward across the Temple of Apollo and the winding Sacred Way leading up to it. Delphi was thought to be the gods' favorite abode on earth.*

court, a living room, two bedrooms and, in some cases, an upper story. Ceilings were low. Houses at **Olynthus** (5th-4thC BC) had varied interiors but the court, usually cobbled, was normally the largest unit and was entered directly from the street or through a passage. Olynthus was the most important of the Greek cities on the Macedonian coast and was laid out in a grid of perimeter blocks, 330 ft by 130 ft, and divided into rectangular house units 80 ft square. Of special interest is the **Villa of Good Fortune**, from which prototype more spacious plans were evolved, a notable example being the **House of the Lion Hunt, Pella** (*c.* 300 BC), which consisted of three open courts off which led a dozen rooms, three of which were decorated with mosaics.

Civic & Public buildings

The **Theatre, Delphi** (4thC BC), one of the best preserved in Greece, is reached from the Sacred Way by a Roman staircase. The **Stadium** (5thC BC), built in the highest part of the city, was hewn out of rock on its north side and supported on blocks of masonry on its south. Parts of the Roman **Triumphal Arch**, which decorated the southeast entrance, remain. The **Theatre, Dodona** (297-272 BC), restored between 1960 and 1963, had a *scene building* with a *stoa* as an outer façade, together with a central arch opening onto the stage. At the top, behind the auditorium, a well-preserved gate leads into the *acropolis*.

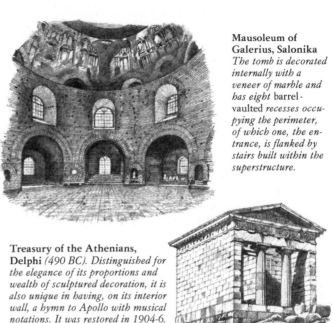

Mausoleum of Galerius, Salonika *The tomb is decorated internally with a veneer of marble and has eight* barrel- *vaulted recesses occupying the perimeter, of which one, the entrance, is flanked by stairs built within the superstructure.*

Treasury of the Athenians, Delphi *(490 BC). Distinguished for the elegance of its proportions and wealth of sculptured decoration, it is also unique in having, on its interior wall, a hymn to Apollo with musical notations. It was restored in 1904-6.*

Military fortifications

In Aristotle's view fortifications had to satisfy two needs: defense and architectural excellence. The first was achieved by stout towers, the second by handsome masonry and the aesthetic effect of monumental gateways.

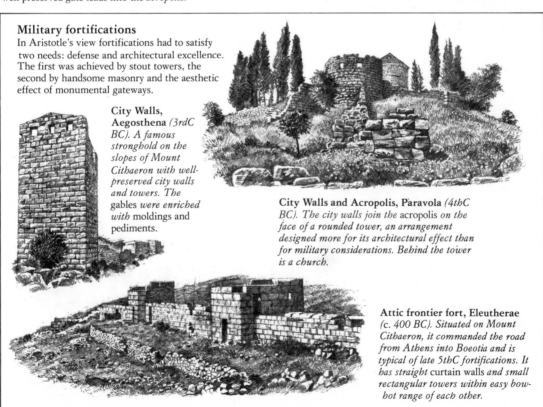

City Walls, Aegosthena *(3rdC BC). A famous stronghold on the slopes of Mount Cithaeron with well-preserved city walls and towers. The* gables *were enriched with* moldings and pediments.

City Walls and Acropolis, Paravola *(4thC BC). The city walls join the* acropolis *on the face of a rounded tower, an arrangement designed more for its architectural effect than for military considerations. Behind the tower is a church.*

Attic frontier fort, Eleutherae *(c. 400 BC). Situated on Mount Cithaeron, it commanded the road from Athens into Boeotia and is typical of late 5thC fortifications. It has straight* curtain walls *and small rectangular towers within easy bow-shot range of each other.*

41

Greek Islands

Religious buildings

The **Temple of Aphaia, Aegina** (6thC BC), stands on a pine-clad hill on the tiny triangular island. Considered the most perfectly developed of the late archaic temples, it was built on an artificial terrace and enclosed by a wall. Remarkable sculptures adorned the *pediments*, and the *entablature* was once richly painted.

The **Sanctuary of Athena, Rhodes** (4thC BC), fills most of the southern section of the *acropolis* at Lindos. It was approached through a monumental *stoa* and a gigantic stairway leading to the L-shaped *propylaea*. Beyond the propylaea was the small **Temple of Lindia, Rhodes** (*c.* 348 BC), which stood serenely on a cliff edge.

The **Sanctuary of Asclepios, Kos** (2ndC BC), was more elaborate and ambitious in planning. Within it the great *Doric* **Temple of Asclepios** stands on the highest of three terraces. Stairways connected it to the lower terraces. Also of interest is the *Ionic* **Temple of Antis, Kos** (3rdC BC).

The **Sanctuary of Hera,** or **Heraion, Samos** (6thC BC-2ndC AD), was more disorderly in plan, but the siting of the first **Great Temple** (6thC BC) there made it more coherent. This temple was enlarged in 525 BC, and numerous temples were added later by the Romans.

The **Sanctuary of Apollo, Delos** (6thC BC), contained such an extraordinary number of buildings within a confined area that attempts were made to relate the later buildings in the sanctuary (stoas, treasuries and dining halls) to the major temples that stand to the east of the

Sanctuary of Athena Lindia, Rhodes *A view from the stairway that leads from the lower terrace of the sanctuary to the* propylaea *and temple of the upper terrace. The* Doric *columns in the foreground form the* portico *to the* stoa *in front of the sanctuary proper.*

Temple of Artemis, Corfu *(c. 580 BC), right. Now in the local museum, this detail of* pediment *decoration from the monumental temple was a prototype. Previously the* typanum *area would have been painted with a simple decorative motif rather than carved.*

Fountain, Ialyses, Rhodes, *left. This limestone building is an elegant fountain shelter, consisting of a six-columned Doric* colonnade *fronting a long rectangular recess carved out of the rock face. The water trough is beyond the colonnade against the back wall.*

Terrace of Lions, Delos *Five of the original nine lions remain, guarding the avenue that led from the sanctuary on the island to the Sacred Lake. Such avenues were traditional in the Near East and Egypt.*

Temple of Aphaia, Aegina *Sculpture of a fallen warrior from the east pediment of the temple that shows episodes from the Trojan War. Now in the Glyptothek, Munich.*

Sacred Way: the **Temple of Apollo** (477 BC), the **Temple of Athena** (425-417 BC) and the **Porinos Naos** (6thC BC). Also of interest on Delos are the Ionic **Temple of Artemis** (*c.* 179 BC) and the **Temple of Isis** (2ndC BC).

Castles & Palaces

Cretan towns were politically unified and protected by a powerful Cretan navy. Such stability allowed remarkable palaces to grow slowly outwards, almost organically, from great central paved courts. The archetype is the **Palace of King Minos, Knossos** (1700-1400 BC). Characteristic is the asymmetrical placing of doors. Also of interest: the **Palace, Phaestus** (*c.* 1700 BC), and the **Palace, Mallia** (*c.* 1500 BC).

Domestic buildings

In the houses at **Delos** (mostly 2ndC BC), rooms were grouped around an open court, which in less congested areas was *colonnaded* on all sides. The **House of Hermes** has a reconstructed two-story courtyard: the **House of Comedians**, an unusual two-story *peristyle*, and the **House of Masks** have beautiful mosaic pavements.

Civic & Public buildings

To the north of the sanctuary at Delos stands a huge open court, the **Agora of the Italians** (*c.* 110 BC), with its Doric peristyle and Ionic colonnaded gallery above. Northwest of this, west of the Sacred Lake, is an avenue called the **Terrace of Lions** (7thC BC).

Agora of the Italians, Delos
Remains of the Doric peristyle which surrounded what was once a huge, open court. It was built and used by Roman merchants as a social and business center. The peristyle provided a basic structure at the back of which shops and offices were built.

Palace of King Minos, Knossos, Crete

In 500 years of building the plan of the palace grew around a large central court to cover over 3 acres. The spacious state rooms were on the first floor of the western wing and were approached by an elaborate ceremonial route and grand staircase.

West Magazines *The victuals magazines consisted of 18 long apartments on the ground floor. Liquids were stored in jars, many of which have been preserved.*

Bull's Head, Rhyton
The bull was once considered sacred on ancient Crete. This masterpiece of Minoan art (now in the local museum) is a serpentine vessel that was used to pour wine in honor of the bull deity.

Frescoes *The "Ladies in Blue," right above, were found in the eastern wing of the Palace. The "Fresco of the Dolphins," right below, once crowned the door of the Queen's megaron. Both examples are now to be found in the local museum.*

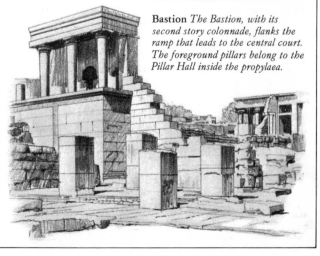

Bastion *The Bastion, with its second story colonnade, flanks the ramp that leads to the central court. The foreground pillars belong to the Pillar Hall inside the propylaea.*

Rome

Religious buildings

Numerous temples were built during Rome's struggle for supremacy over Italy. Of the group of temples at **Largo Agentina** (300-100 BC), the circular **Temple B,** and **Temple C** standing on its high *podium,* are both *Etruscan* in origin. The **Temple of Fortuna Virilis** (*c.* 40 BC), Forum Boarium, is more typically Roman, an amalgam of Greek sensibility and Etruscan *portico* and podium. The **Temple of Divus Julius** (*c.* 29 BC) was built on a tall podium to accentuate height. A flight of steps links the temple to a platform and altar which marks the spot where Julius Caesar was cremated. Also of interest is the **Temple of Venus Genetrix** (*c.* 46 BC).

The **Temple of Mars Ultor** (14-2 BC), built in the Forum of Augustus, is a fine example of length being sacrificed for height in temple design, with eight columns across the façade and only nine down each side. The **Temple of Castor and Pollux** was equally lofty. While there was a striving for height and, later, monumentality and lush carving, there was little uniformity of plan. The **Temple of Concord** (7 BC-AD 10) had its *cella* running lengthways across the temple so the temple façade only coincided with the cella front at one end. The **Temple of Antoninus and Faustina** (AD 141), built on the north side of the Forum Romanum, has a deep portico reached by steps. The awesome **Temple of Venus and Rome** (AD 123-141) has an unusual plan, consisting of two cellas with *apses* back to back. The **Temple of Divus Hadrianus** (AD 145) is equally expressive of the Roman ceremonial and religious fervor of the period. Cella wall and columns of the long north side still stand in the Piazza di Pietra.

The **Pantheon** (AD 120-124) is perhaps the most remarkable of Roman temple buildings. An impressive monument of the Emperor Hadrian, it was dedicated to all the gods of the celestial pantheon. The *cupola,* the largest ever built before the development of reinforced concrete, symbolizes the vault of the heavens. The central opening, providing the only source of light, represents the sun and is sufficient to light all parts of the building when the massive doors are closed.

Roman funerary architecture was as diverse and idiosyncratic as its domestic architecture. The **Mausoleum of Hadrian** (AD 135) was the most important of the monumental tombs. Now the Castle of S. Angelo, it originally consisted of a high, square podium faced in white marble with equestrian groups at the corners. On this was an enormous drum with a *peristyle* enriched with statuary. Above this was a huge circular tower surrounded by funerary trees and crowned by a *quadriga.* The main feature of the **Mausoleum of Constantia** or S. Costanza (4thC AD), is its use of wall mosaics. Such decoration was later developed as a leading art form in the *Byzantine* Age. The **Mausoleum of the Villa of the Cordiana** (4thC AD) consisted of an upper hall for the celebration of the funeral rites, and the burial chamber below. Also of interest is the **Mausoleum of Augustus** (28 BC), an imposing cylindrical tomb some 290 ft in diameter.

Round Temple, or Temple of Portunus *(1stC BC). Sited in the Forum Boarium, this well-preserved round temple is the work of a Greek architect and is strongly* Hellenistic. *It is built of marble and stands on a high, eight-stepped* podium. *Twenty* Corinthian *columns form the* peristyle.

Tomb of Caecilia Metella *(c. 20 BC). A massive tomb built on the Appian Way in imitation of the monumental Mausoleum of Augustus.*

Temple of Castor and Pollux *Standing in the Forum Romanum, it was originally dedicated in c. 484 BC. The remaining Corinthian columns with their uniquely carved* capitals *belong to a restoration of the Augustan Age.*

Temple of Antoninus and Faustina *The steps leading to the deep portico of this temple lie between extensions of the podium walls. The cella walls are plain, without engaged columns. In 1602 it became the Church of S. Lorenzo in Miranda, when the pediment and roof structure were altered.*

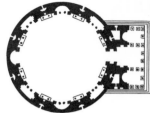

Pantheon, *left, with plan above. The most perfectly preserved of all Rome's ancient buildings, it consists of a circular* rotunda *(142 ft in diameter) molded to a giant portico. Around the interior of the temple are seven great recesses where statues of the gods were positioned.*

Temple of Fortuna Virilis *in the Forum Boarium. This rather small but beautiful* Ionic *building shows Greek influence throughout, although the deep portico is typically Roman. The temple has engaged columns down the sides and along the back of the cella.*

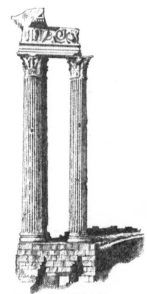

Temple of Vespasian *(AD 94). These columns are the remains of a six-columned, Corinthian portico which had an ornate entablature. The temple was begun by Titus and completed by Domitian.*

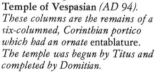

Temple of Saturn *(AD 284). Built in a commanding position close to the Capitol, it is raised on a high podium reached by a flight of steps. From Republican times it was the repository of the state treasury. Moldings in the* architrave *were omitted to accommodate an inscription.*

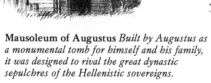

Mausoleum of Augustus *Built by Augustus as a monumental tomb for himself and his family, it was designed to rival the great dynastic sepulchres of the Hellenistic sovereigns.*

45

Rome

The **Pyramid of Caestius** (12 BC) was an exotic tomb, Egyptian in influence. It was built of brick and cased in marble, while figure paintings decorated the interior. The **Tomb of the Baker Eurysaces** (40-30 BC), Porte Maggiore, consists of a rectangular marble block relieved by cylindrical decorative shapes.

As interment became more common than cremation, mausoleums were rejected in favor of more spacious tombs in the form of temples. A typical example is the **Tomb of the Pancrati** (2ndC AD), in the Via Latina, its simple brick exterior contrasting with elaborate internal decoration. Some interiors, of which the most splendid is the **Tomb of the Caetennii** (2ndC AD), were exuberantly *baroque* in decoration.

The **Catacombs of Domitia** were used as places of worship and common burial by the early Christians. Rectangular niches were cut for the bodies in the network of subterranean tunnels. There were also large chambers that were frequently decorated and *stuccoed*. Of particular interest are the **Basilica of SS. Nereo e Achilleo** and the **Greek Chapel**, Catacomb of Priscilla.

Castles & Palaces

The **Flavian Palace** (AD 92), the Palatine, is the most spectacular of the group of palaces on the Palatine Hill. It consisted of three parts: the Flavian Palace, the reception area containing the Throne Room; the Imperial Palace, the private residence of the emperor and his family, and the Palatine Stadium or Racecourse. But the most lavish of royal palaces was **Nero's Golden House** (AD 65). Irregular in plan, its most astonishing feature was the octagonal fountain hall, which is still intact. A forerunner of later Roman building, it was an architecture of the interior, an envelope enclosing light and space.

Domestic buildings

Of domestic buildings the most interesting are the remains of the **House of Livia,** an *atrium* style house of several stories built on the Palatine Hill, and the **Villa of Sette Basse** (AD 140-160) in the Via Latina, a luxurious suburban villa built around three sides of a large garden *peristyle*.

Civic & Public buildings

Roman theatres were freestanding, the seats supported on a semicircle of tiered and galleried corridors. Several were built in Rome, but the **Theatre of Marcellus** (23-15 BC) is the only one to survive.

Amphitheatres were an adaptation of the freestanding theatre building and are to be found in every major Roman town. But the sheer size of the **Colosseum** (AD 72-80) is unique. Its construction resembles two Theatres of Marcellus placed back to back, the four stories of the outer wall climbing to nearly 165 ft.

The **Circus Maximus** (AD 320) similarly catered to popular taste. Developed from the Greek stadium, Roman circuses were used for chariot and horse racing. The best preserved is the **Circus of Maxentius** (AD 309).

Temple of Divus Romulus *(c. AD 300). This temple consists of a starkly simple* rotunda *with a classically austere but well-preserved doorway. The building was later used as the vestibule to the Church of SS. Cosma e Damiano.*

Temple of Vesta *(AD 205), Forum Romanum. Circular in form, the design was probably derived from* Etruscan *temples. Here the Vestal Virgins kept alight the sacred fire, symbolic of the hearth, center of Roman life.*

Tomb of Annia Regilla *(2ndC AD), Via Appia. An unpretentious family tomb with elaborate molded* entablature. *Such structures were usually* vaulted *or gabled with a gaily painted or* stuccoed *interior.*

Temple of Minerva Medica *(4thC AD). Thought to be a* nymphaeum *from the Villa of Licinii. The circular* cupola, *one of the largest in Rome, is set on brick* ribbing, *a technique more advanced than that used for the Pantheon.*

Imperial Palaces *(begun AD 3), Palatine Hill. Impressive even as ruins, the palaces had a commanding view of civic life in the valley below. First begun by Augustus, succeeding emperors added their own extensions, decorated on a lavish scale.*

Colosseum, *below. Begun by Vespasian and completed by Domitian, it was the most lavish of all amphitheatres. The structure was more a feat of engineering, made possible by the use of concrete, than architecture. A canopy sheltered the 50,000 spectators from the sun.*

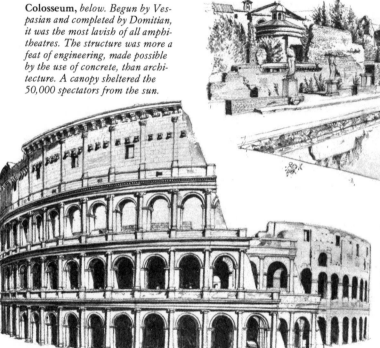

House of the Vestals *(AD 66). Built next to the Temple of Vesta, it was here the Vestal Virgins lived in two galleried stories built around a long rectangular courtyard, enriched with statuary and a series of ornamental pools.*

Circus Maximus, *below. Reconstruction of the largest, oldest and most famous of all Roman circuses. It was adorned with costly marbles, mosaics, columns and statuary and could accommodate 250,000 spectators.*

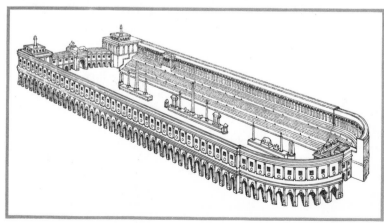

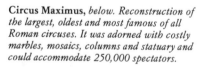

Theatre of Marcellus *The only surviving ancient theatre in Rome, it owes its preservation to its conversion in the Middle Ages to a fortress, and then during the 16thC to a palace.*

Rome

Civic & Public buildings

Around the *forum* were grouped the major civic, public and religious buildings. The oldest was the **Forum Romanum** (5thC BC), a shapeless affair laid out between the seven hills of ancient Rome. Imperial Rome required grander and more spacious civic places and so, gradually, the disorderly nature of the *Italic* marketplace gave way to the splendor of the **Forum of Caesar** (*c*. 51 BC), the first of Rome's great imperial forums. Successive emperors added their own, first the **Forum of Augustus** (42-2 BC), then the **Forum of Vespasian** and the **Forum of Nerva** (AD 97). The largest, the **Forum of Trajan** (AD 98-113), consisted of the forum proper, the Basilica of Trajan, the Temple of Trajan and a market hall complex built on the slopes of the Quirinal Hill.

Basilicas, the law and business centers of the ancient Roman world, were developed from the Greek temple. They usually comprised three or five *aisles* with galleries or columns above supporting the wooden roof. The **Basilica of Aemelia** (14 BC) consisted of a long narrow hall lit by a *clerestory* and surrounded by an internal *colonnade* with gallery above. The east side was open, but the long south side was enclosed by a row of shops. The **Basilica of Julia** (AD 12) housed the law courts. It was open on three sides with the west side enclosed by two stories of shops and offices. Only part of the monumental entrance, the *nave* and the southeast aisle, remain of the **Basilica of Trajan** (AD 98-112). It was felt to epitomize the grandeur of Roman imperial might at its peak. The central nave is 384 ft long and 87 ft wide, with double aisles either side and *apsed* ends. The model for the **Basilica of Maxentius** (AD 310-313) was the architecture of the great Roman bath buildings. Its magnificent *vaulting* makes a complete break from the earlier basilicas.

Palatial public baths *(thermae)* were as expressive of the hedonistic fervor of Imperial Rome as the amphitheatres. The **Thermae of Agrippa** (*c*. 20 BC) were the earliest but only fragments remain. The **Thermae of Titus** (AD 80) were built on part of the ground that belonged to Nero's Golden House but little remains except a *portico.* The **Thermae of Trajan** (AD 109) were considerably larger. An elaborate precinct was built surrounding the baths, complete with libraries, meeting halls, recreation and other social areas.

Size was the major characteristic of the baths that followed. The **Thermae of Caracalla** (AD 211-217) had accommodation for 1600 bathers. A complex of baths was built on a high platform above the furnace and service rooms. Surrounding this was a park enriched with fountains and statuary. There was also a stadium and associated facilities. The whole was enclosed by a great structure of apartments, shops and lecture rooms. The **Thermae of Diocletian** (AD 302) was not dissimilar in plan, although on a vaster scale still, with accommodation for 3000 bathers.

Forum of Nerva
This detail is from the frieze above the remaining columns of the temple of Minerva, built in the center of the forum. Flamboyant decoration is typical of the late Flavian Age.

Forum Romanum, *left. Reconstruction of the forum as seen from the Campidoglio. Note the profusion of victory columns. In the background to the right is the Palace of Caligula on the Palatine Hill.*

Basilica of Maxentius
Completed by Constantine, it consisted of a central nave, crowned by an enormous groined vault, with the south and north aisles divided into three parts, each with a great semicircular vault.

Basilica of Julia *Originally built in the Forum Romanum by Julius Caesar, it was destroyed by fire and remodeled by Augustus.*

Forum of Augustus, *right. Built at the edge of the Quirinal Hill, this forum once had a two-story* colonnade *on three sides with the Italic styled Temple of Mars Ultor, that dominated the whole complex, on the fourth. On either side of the temple were* porticos, *which were carried on caryatids.*

Tabularium *(78 BC). Built to house the public archives of the Roman State, the Tabularium was sited against the Capitoline Hill and formed a monumental backdrop to the western end of the Forum Romanum.*

Thermae of Trajan, *right. Nero's Golden House was burned down in AD 104 and Trajan built these baths on the site of the ruins. This was the main apse of the compound that surrounded the whole baths complex.*

Curia *(AD 303), above. Façade of the Curia, the seat of the Roman Senate. It was reconstructed by Diocletian after a fire in AD 283 and now stands austere, with its neighboring buildings in ruins. The original bronze doors are today found in S. Giovanni in Laterano, Rome.*

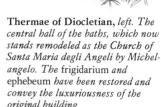

Thermae of Diocletian, *left. The central hall of the baths, which now stands remodeled as the Church of Santa Maria degli Angeli by Michelangelo. The frigidarium and ephebeum have been restored and convey the luxuriousness of the original building.*

Thermae of Constantine *(AD 315). This personification of the River Tigris is one of the many statues that once adorned the baths.. Today it stands with the statue of the Nile by the steps to the Palazzo Senatorio.*

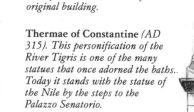

Rome

The civic quality of Rome was enhanced by a whole series of artifacts. Triumphal arches, erected to commemorate victorious campaigns, were first built about 200 BC. They were ornately decorated with scenes from the campaigns concerned, and victorious generals would ceremonially pass through them. The first triumphal arches in Rome, on the Field of Mars, had a single opening. Three openings are characteristic of the more flamboyant *Imperial* period. The **Arch of Titus** (AD 82) is one of the single opening type. It was built by Domitian and stands on the upper part of the Via Sacra. The arch is decorated with reliefs commemorating Rome's capture of Jerusalem, showing a triumphal procession with captive Jews, Titus triumphant and the spoils taken from the Temple at Jerusalem. The **Arch of Septimus Severus** (AD 203) has three openings. Eight *Composite* columns stand detatched from the legs of the archways on *pedestals,* ascending to the extensions of the *entablature*. It was built to commemorate victories over the Parthians and it was crowned by a *quadriga* showing the Emperor and his two sons. The **Arch of Constantine** (AD 312) also has three openings. The verticality of the arch is emphasized in the *attic* story by statues, which continue the lines of the *Corinthian* columns below.

There were also numerous town gateways and archways that were built for defense, complete with flanking towers and *vantage courts,* like the **Porta Appia,** or Porta San Sebastiano (AD 275-280), the **Porta Ostiensis,** or Porta San Paolo (4thC AD), and the **Porta Latina** (3rdC AD). Others were ornamental entrances to *forums* or they marked primary street intersections, such as the **Arch of Janus** (4thC AD). Originally dominating a crossroads, this gateway has a square plan with an arch in each face. Later it was used as a shelter for the dealers in the Forum Boarium, the cattle market that became an important commercial center with a port on the Tiber. Nearby is the **Arch of Argentari** (AD 204), built by the merchants and bankers of the forum.

The city was also dotted with Pillars of Victory that were erected to commemorate the exploits of victorious generals. **Trajan's Column** (AD 113) was built by the senate and people of Rome to commemorate Trajan's victories over the Dacians. It is a giant, 115 ft hollow *Doric* column with an internal staircase and was originally surmounted by a bronze eagle. An inscription dated AD 114 says that the column marks the height of the hill that had to be removed to make the site level. The **Column of Marcus Aurelius** (AD 174) commemorated the Emperor's victory on the Danube and stands in the Piazza Colonna. The original statue of Marcus Aurelius was replaced in 1589. Another monument of interest is the **Column of Antoninus Pius** (AD 161).

Obelisks, such as the **Egyptian Obelisk** (6thC BC), were much in evidence during Rome's Imperial times, when Egyptian fashion was cultivated. Originally shipped from the Nile to the Tiber, they were later salvaged from the ruins of Imperial Rome to embellish Christian Rome.

Porta Appia *A major entrance, this gateway in the Aurelian Wall defended the Via Appia. It originally had two archways. The clean, functional lines of towers and gateway are typical features of the fortified arch.*

Trajan's Column *Built behind the Basilica of Trajan, it stood in an open,* colonnaded *court flanked by two libraries. From the library galleries details of the column decoration could be seen. The 787-ft* spiral frieze *illustrates events from the Emperor's two campaigns. In the ornamented* pedestal *there is an entrance to Trajan's tomb chamber.*

Arch of Titus Composite Order *columns mark the corners of the structure and the sides of the arch itself. The underside of the arch is deeply* coffered, *with a relief carving at its center showing the deification of Titus.*

Porta Ostiensis, *or Porta San Paolo. Flanked by two semicircular towers, the original gateway had two arches until a later reconstruction. Behind, on the city side, is a vantage court and this makes use of the two original archway gates.*

Arch of Janus *Erected in the reign of Constantine. No doubt there was an attic story, probably capped by a circular pavilion with a conical roof as this would emphasize the symmetrical quality of the huge, fourfold arch.*

Porta Flaminia, *or Porta del Popolo (220 BC), below. The gateway was originally flanked by two semicircular towers. These were replaced by rectangular bastions, which were themselves demolished in 1877. The city side of the gateway remodeled by Giovanni Bernini in 1655.*

Porta Latina, *above. An interesting combination of the more austere, early gateway complete with semicircular towers, which belongs to the first period of the Aurelian Wall, with the later addition of a clear, classical arch façade with a row of windows above the gateway, dating from the time of Honorius.*

Egyptian Obelisk *(6thC BC). One of the smallest obelisks in Rome. It was found in 1666 in the Dominican monastery garden and returned to its original site in the Temple of Isis. The elephant base was designed by Giovanni Bernini in 1667.*

Arch of Constantine *Erected in honor of Constantine to commemorate his victory over Maxentius in AD 312. Ornamented with sculptures and reliefs salvaged from other monuments, it is characteristic of the populist works built in Rome prior to the founding of Constantinople in AD 330.*

Rome

Civic & Public buildings

The **Aurelian Wall** (AD 270-280) was built as a matter of urgency under the increasing threat of Barbarian attacks. It was a vast undertaking, over 10 ft thick, 25 ft high and 12 miles in length. The gateways are stone; elsewhere the material is concrete. It took ten years to complete, by which time Aurelius, the instigator of the scheme, had been assassinated. This military architecture of the frontier, with its boldness of structure and simplicity of line, left so indelible an impression on Roman taste that it was little wonder later civic works appeared to assimilate much of the wall's scale and character.

Commercial & Industrial buildings

In addition to the Imperial forums there were some built for more specific purposes. The **Forum Boarium**, a cattle market, was laid out between the Tiber and the Palatine. The remains of the **Forum Holitorium** and its riverside wharves, originally Rome's vegetable market, have been partially covered by the church of S. Nicola in Carcere. Several buildings in Rome combined meat and fish markets. The **Macellum Magnum** (AD 59) was an elaborate version of that in Pompeii. It consisted of a rectangular two-story enclosure of offices with a central *pavilion*. Nothing, however, remains. The most magnificent of all are the **Markets of Trajan** (AD 100-112). They were built in a monumental crescent on the northern edge of Trajan's forum, forming a grand, curving street between the forum and its northeastern *apse*. The complex was hollowed out of the Quirinal Hill and served as a general market for trading as well as for the distribution of corn. It was constructed of brick-faced concrete and, with the exception of the main market hall, consisted of repetitive units of the standard Roman taberna, that is a single-roomed, *barrel-vaulted* shop with a wide door.

The **Horrea Aggripiana** (1stC BC) was one of many warehouses within ancient Rome. It was built under Agrippa and comprised a main court surrounded by tabernae. There are also remains of the **Horrea Galbae** and the **Horrea Piperataria**, among others.

Water was of great importance to the Romans, as is testified by the great many ruined aqueducts found in the areas they once ruled. It has been estimated that some 350 million gallons of water were needed daily in Rome alone, for domestic use, the *thermae* and numerous fountains. The early city was adequately supplied from local springs and wells but, as the population increased and consumption rose, a more abundant and reliable supply was needed. By the 1st century BC the dynamics of transporting water were well understood and the building of structures perfected. Several undergound channels were built but the **Aqua Marcia** (144 BC) was the first to be built above ground. Of particular interest are the **Aqua Julia** (33 BC), the **Aqua Claudia** (AD 38), the most impressive Roman aqueduct which carried water some 45 miles from Subiaco to Rome, and the **Aqua Traiana** (AD 109).

Rampart Walk, Aurelian Wall, Porta Latina and Porta Appia *The first wall encircling Rome was built in the 6thC BC but, as the population spread beyond it and Barbarian attacks became imminent, Aurelius was prompted to build the massive wall which survives to the present day.*

Tiered rampart walks, Aurelian Wall, Viale Castrense *The wall has 38 projecting towers, one every 100 Roman feet. There were 19 main gateways and a number of smaller openings strategically sited between them.*

Aurelian Wall *It was enlarged and reinforced by Honorius in AD 403. The wall enclosed an area of some 3400 acres and was so soundly built that it remained the main defense of Rome until the second half of the 19thC.*

Pons Fabricius *(62 BC). A simple but elegant bridge of twin arches, each measuring nearly 82 ft, connecting the left bank of the Tiber to the Tiber island. It is one of the best preserved of all the Roman bridges.*

Pons Mulvius, *or Ponte Molle (109 BC). For more than 2000 years this stone bridge of semicircular arches carried on massive piers was the principal entrance to the city of Rome. The additional arches cut higher in the piers were to allow flood water to pass freely.*

Trajan's Market *This is utilitarian architecture on a vast scale, comprising 150 shops, offices and a two-story hall, constructed on five levels. Above right, part of the complex of administrative offices which, together with a court, is located on the third floor of the building.*

Pons Aelius, *or Ponte San Angelo (AD 134), below. A monumental bridge built under Hadrian's command, spanning the Tiber to his mausoleum on the right bank. Statues, which were replaced by those of angels in the 17thC, decorated each pier.*

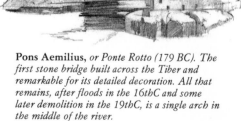

Pons Aemilius, *or Ponte Rotto (179 BC). The first stone bridge built across the Tiber and remarkable for its detailed decoration. All that remains, after floods in the 16thC and some later demolition in the 19thC, is a single arch in the middle of the river.*

Central Italy

Religious buildings

The **Capitolium, Ostia Antica** (*c.* AD 120), stood on an unusually high *podium.* Brick built and richly marbled, it was clearly designed to dominate the surrounding apartments. In Latium, the **Temple of Jupiter, Terracina** (1stC BC), was built on a platform carried by colossal supporting arches, still standing, on the summit of a mountain dominating Terracina and the sea. The remains of the **Temple of Hercules Victor, Tivoli** (80-50 BC), show that it was a grandiose theatre-temple built on a majestic terrace. The **Temple of Fortuna Primigenia, Palestrina** (130-110 BC), consists of a monumental temple complex in which seven terraces climbed the hillside to a round temple. The central stairs of the temple building itself were reached at right angles by two enormous ramps, which are still standing. Another early round temple is the **Temple of Vesta, Tivoli** (*c.* 80 BC). Also of interest is the **Temple of Hercules, Cori** (*c.* 100 BC) with its elegant 30-ft columns.

In Umbria, the **Temple of Minerva, Assisi** (1stC AD), is a majestic building with a *Corinthian portico.* Placed centrally along one side of the forum, now the Piazza del Commune, it was later converted into a church.

The religious tolerance of the Romans resulted in diverse types of religious building. The **Synagogue, Ostia Antica** (2ndC BC), is typical. Such buildings were spaciously planned and usually consisted of a tall central structure carried on columns and surrounded by an *aisle.*

Typical of Etruscan wealth are the elaborate tombs in the **Banditaccia Cemetery, Cerveteri:** the **Tomb of the Thatched Roof** (7thC BC), with its starkly vaulted roof; the **Tomb of the Cornice** (*c.* 500 BC), and the **Tomb of the Alcove** (3rdC BC). Later tombs, like the **Tomb of the Volumnii, Perugia** (2ndC BC), had very large halls, often with side chambers.

Castles & Palaces

Hadrian's Villa, Tivoli (AD 118-133), the most fascinating of the imperial villas, is an extravagant collage of buildings based on models seen during the Emperor's travels. The plan is twisted to accommodate the gently undulating site.

Domestic buildings

The best collection of ancient classical domestic buildings in the area is at **Ostia Antica.** The **House of Fortuna Annonaria** (2ndC BC) is a typical single family house built around a *colonnaded* courtyard. The centrally heated room is one of the earliest yet found in Ostia. The **House of Cupid and Psyche** (*c.* AD 300) had a luxuriously marbled, centrally heated *triclinium* and spacious central corridor. The **House of Diana** (2ndC AD) combined shops and multi-story dwellings, a result of increased population and rising land values in the city. The **House of Lararium** (2ndC AD) consisted of apartments built around a central courtyard. Also of interest in Ostia Antica: the **House of the Triple Windows** and the **House of the Charioteers.**

Temple of Hercules, Cori *The tall, elegant* atrium *of this temple makes use of* Doric *columns — unusual for a Roman temple. A small* Romanesque *church has been built into the remains of the temple.*

Synagogue, Ostia Antica *Based on the plan of a small provincial* basilica. *Centered in the wall behind the bema, or raised platform, would have been a small* apse *where sacred scrolls were kept.*

Temple of Vesta, Tivoli *The idyllic ruins of this temple are perched on a rocky prominence. Hellenistic in influence, the* peristyle *columns have unusually florid, late* Republican *capitals, as shown in the detail above.*

The Canopus, Hadrian's Villa, Tivoli *(c. AD 130). This ornamental waterway was a nostalgic recreation of the original Canopus, a canal leading to a shrine in ancient Egypt. At the southern end was a loggia, carried on caryatids modeled on those at the Erechtheion, Athens.*

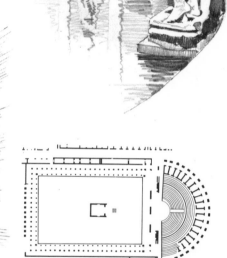

Island Villa, Hadrian's Villa, Tivoli *(AD 118-125). This was the Emperor's private retreat within the villa complex, surrounded by three concentric circles of wall, portico and moat. A medley of concave and convex-shaped rooms surround a miniature courtyard.*

House of Diana, Ostia Antica *Really a block of apartments, the rooms have windows facing the street in contrast to the inward looking Pompeian houses. Like later Renaissance palaces, the apartments were planned around a central arcaded courtyard.*

Theatre and Forum of the Corporations, Ostia Antica *(c.12 BC), below and in the plan above. A combination of theatre with a colonnaded forum built behind the stage. The forum was used as a sheltered retreat for the audience and has the Temple of Ceres at its center. Later, shops and offices were added.*

55

Central Italy

Commercial & Industrial buildings

As early as the 5th century BC, before Mediterranean trade had much developed, granaries were needed for the storage of corn and other foods shipped from Sicily and the *Etruscan* coastal towns to Rome and the Latium cities. The models for these commercial buildings were the warehouses of the Middle East, but it was the development of concrete and vaulting that turned such simple structures into the grandiose buildings of Rome.

It was in such everyday architecture that Rome had most effect on the architecture of Ostia Antica, Rome's port. Outstanding among such buildings was the insula, or apartment block, the design of which was to be used until the 20thC. The plan could be adapted to a number of uses. The **House of Lararium** (2ndC AD) is an example. A block of apartments around a central courtyard, it had shops and a market on the ground floor. Indeed, this palazzo type of apartment house, which was to play such an important role in the Renaissance, was so accommodating that it was with little effort that one was transformed into the **Barracks of the Vigiles** (AD 117-138), the headquarters of the local fire-brigade. The **Horrea Epagathiana** (*c.* AD 145-150) also shows that little modification was needed to turn the typical apartment house into a multi-story, privately owned warehouse. The major modification necessary for warehouses and granaries of this type was the adoption of ramps instead of stairs to the upper stories.

The **Granary of Hortensius** (*c.* AD 30-40) was one of the most important commercial buildings of the time. It consisted of three large warehouses for storing corn and commercial commodities prior to their shipment along the Tiber to Rome. But by the beginning of the 3rd century AD the rise in land values and the increase in population demanded more economical planning. Classical *Orders* associated with civic and public buildings were abandoned, plain brick arches and *piers* becoming the rule.

Civic & Public buildings

The **Baths of Neptune, Ostia Antica** (AD 117-138), differed from the Pompeian baths in that the bathing block was to one side of a *colonnaded palaestra* and had a line of shops along the main street frontage.

Arch of Trajan, Ancona *(AD 115). An elegant marble arch, simply ornamented with framed decorative panels and originally with applied bronze wreaths. It was built over a raised footway to honor the emperor Trajan, who had ordered the harbor to be built.*

Horrea Epagathiana, Ostia Antica *View showing the main entrance with shops. A passageway led through this entrance to the internal* colonnaded *courtyard. It was built by two wealthy freedmen, an example of the private enterprise which flourished at the time.*

Insula, Ostia Antica, *above. Reconstruction of the façade of the Insula, with a cookhouse on the ground floor. This type of building can be seen in many Italian towns to this day.*

Main Decuman Road, Ostia Antica *The road passes along the eastern edge of the theatre, of which the ground floor remains. Behind is the Piazzale of the Corporations, used by the audience during intervals.*

Northern Italy

Civic & Public buildings

The most numerous and varied of the Roman structures in northern Italy are the arches and city gates. The **Arch of Augustus, Susa** (*c.* 5 BC), a simple commemorative arch, has three-quarter columns on a *plinth* at the four outer corners and a plain *attic*. The façade of the **Arch, Aosta** (24 BC), is divided into three equal parts, with the arch, rather awkward in scale, squeezed in centrally. The **Arch of Augustus, Rimini** (27 BC), was one of a pair of arches built to mark the completion of the Via Flaminia. Its twin stood beside the Pons Mulvius in Rome.

At Turin there are the remains of the somewhat elaborate **Porta Palatina** (1stC AD). It had a double central carriageway with a gallery above between two 16-sided towers. The **Porta dei Borsari, Verona** (1stC AD), has a flamboyant façade, which has a double carriageway with two *arcaded* galleries above. The **City Gate, Volterra** (300 BC), is a graceful *Etruscan* arched gate with *Hellenistic* style heads on the *key* and *springer stones*. The **Porta Praetoria, Aosta** (1stC BC), is a double gateway of three arches. On the left are the remaining arcades of the **Theatre** (1stC BC) and remains of the stage. There are also considerable remains of the Roman **Town Walls** (1stC BC), forming a rectangle 875 yd by 685 yd. The center of the town still retains a Roman plan almost intact.

Perhaps the most interesting Roman building in the area is the **Amphitheatre, Verona** (1stC AD), which is exceptionally well preserved, with most of the stone seats still complete. Unlike contemporaneous Roman theatres in France, which were more architecturally decorative, this is simple and utilitarian, an expression of the new medium of concrete. It is the third largest Roman amphitheatre still in existence.

Arch of Augustus, Susa *An early example of an arch as an independent building. It has four engaged three-quarter columns and a straight entablature with a plain attic. The arch is sparsely adorned, save for carving on the frieze, and is believed to be the work of a local craftsman.*

Porta dei Borsari, Verona *A pleasant architectural oddity, it has contrasting curved and triangular pediments. It was originally flanked by projecting towers and was probably inspired by contemporary work in the eastern provinces of the empire.*

Bridge of Tiberius, Rimini *(*c.*AD 21). Particularly well preserved, with its parapets still standing, it is a handsome bridge of five equal arches constructed of dressed stone. Each pier is embellished on its outward face with two columns supporting an entablature complete with pediment.*

Amphitheatre, Verona *Constructionally, this building is similar to the Colosseum, especially in the use of dressed stone for its more important architectural elements. It could accommodate as many as 28,000 spectators.*

Southern Italy

Religious buildings

The innovatory spirit of mainland Greece was largely alien to the Greek world of Sicily and southern Italy. The colonists, clinging nostalgically to *Hellenic* traditions, froze the Classical rules so that it is here (with the exception of the Temple of Zeus, Olympia) that the purest temples of the Classical period are found.

Of interest in Sicily are the temples at **Selinunte: Temple E** (480-460 BC), not dissimilar in proportion and volume to the Temple of Zeus, Olympia; **Temple G**, one of the largest temples in antiquity, reflecting the wealth of 6th-century BC Selinunte, and **Temple C** (550-530 BC). At **Agrigento**, the **Temple of Olympian Zeus** (*c.* 470 BC), the second largest of Greek temples, consists of two *porticos* with *engaged columns* along the sides. Also of note are **Temple D** (460 BC) and **Temple F** (430 BC). At **Syracuse** is the **Temple of Apollo** (*c.* 565 BC), a pioneer building characterized by an extraordinary heaviness. It is the earliest Greek temple to have a continuous outer ring of columns. The **Temple of Athena, Syracuse** (480 BC), was later incorporated into the Cathedral there. Its original design was concerned with solid mass and perfect form rather than grandeur of detail. At **Segesta** is the unfinished **Doric Temple** (5thC BC).

The classical concepts of mainland Greece were also employed at **Paestum**, an ancient Greek colony on the southern side of the Bay of Naples. It enjoyed a long period of prosperity, resulting in fine temples and tombs. The **Basilica**, or **Temple of Hera** (565 BC), has archaic columns with exaggerated *entasis*. The **Temple of Neptune** (5thC BC) is the best preserved of all Greek temples. It is a building of great severity since it had no decorative sculpture. Another building of interest at Paestum is the **Temple of Athena**, or **Ceres** (6thC BC).

The pre-Roman civilization of Southern Italy was permeated with Greek culture. The **Temple of Apollo, Pompeii** (2ndC BC), is a hybrid with *Italic orientation* and Greek *peristyle*. This, like the **Doric Temple** in the Triangular Forum, was a product of Pompeii's increasing prosperity following the final Roman victories over the Etruscans. Apart from minor wayside and domestic shrines, the religious life of Pompeii was catered for by seven other temples. Among these are the **Temple of Jupiter Meilichius** (1stC BC), a tiny temple dedicated to a Greek cult and heavily influenced by Greek culture; the **Temple of Venus** (1stC BC), commanding views over both shore and port; the **Temple of Isis** (1stC BC), which is Egyptian in influence, and the **Temple** of **Fortuna Augusta** (*c.* 3 BC).

Hellenistic mainland Greece was the inspiration for much of the ancient tomb architecture of Southern Italy. In Pompeii, both monumental sepulchres and grandiose mausoleums can be seen in the **Tombs, Via de Sepolcri**, and the **Necropolis, Via Nocera**. Of interest in **Santa Maria Cápua Vetere** are the **Mausoleum, La Carceri Vecchia** (2ndC AD), and the **Mausoleum, La Connochia** (2ndC AD).

Temple of Neptune, *or* Hera II, Paestum
The design of this temple gives an impression of force and power with its ponderous columns and over-strong entablature. Metopes and pediments were left bare of carved decoration.

Doric Temple, Segesta, *above. Detail of the simple capitals and entablature of this mighty temple. Never completed, the shell remains, stark and unadorned.*

Temple of Fortuna Augusta, Pompeii *This reconstruction shows the small temple dedicated to the deified emperor as it once was north of the forum. The tall* podium *faced with limestone slabs still stands. The temple was damaged during the earthquake of AD 62 and was being rebuilt at the time of the eruption of 79.*

Sanctuary of Chthonic Divinities, Agrigento *(5thC BC). The sanctuary enclosed the most sacred ground in Agrigento. In the foreground is a large altar. Beyond is part of the Temple of the Dioscuri.*

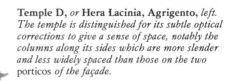

Temple D, *or* **Hera Lacinia, Agrigento,** *left.*
*The temple is distinguished for its subtle optical
corrections to give a sense of space, notably the
columns along its sides which are more slender
and less widely spaced than those on the two
porticos of the façade.*

Temple E, Selinunte
*View of the northeast
corner. In Sicily and
other colonies, tem-
ples still employed
forms which had long
disappeared in main-
land Greece. A major
difference was the col-
umns, which re-
mained thicker than
those in Greece.*

Temple F, *or* **Temple of Concord,
Agrigento** *The temple remains in
an exceptionally good state of preservation complete with outer entablatures and pediments. The design is
light and elegant compared with the
massive grandeur of the other temples at Agrigento.*

Capitolium, Pompeii *(1stC BC). Standing
between two triumphal arches (one of which
can be seen below), the temple (to the left)
closes the northern end of the forum. The high,
molded* podium *had a deep* Corinthian *portico.*

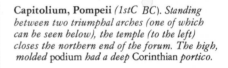

Temple of Athena, *or* **Ceres, Paestum**
*Although this temple has a conventional plan,
its colonial builders modified the details of the
Orders used. The* Doric *capitals spread wide and
the* trachelion *decoration shows* Ionic *influence.*

Necropolis, Via Nocera, Pompeii *This group
of tombs is among a succession of sepulchres
and grandiose mausoleums, complete with
statues and burial inscriptions, which line some
820 ft of the road to Nocera outside the city of
Pompeii. Burial outside a city's walls was
mandatory under Roman law.*

Southern Italy

Domestic buildings

A former palace of the Emperor Tiberius, the **Villa Jovis, Isle of Capri** (AD 14-17), is perched magnificently on a cliff with a drop of 1000 ft to the sea. Because the only source of water supply was rain, which had to be stored, the courtyard was built over a network of vaulted cisterns, around which the villa is informally arranged. The age old disciplines of symmetry were also disregarded in the **Villa of Maximian, Piazza Amerina** (AD 286-305), Sicily. It is an elaborate hunting lodge set in the well-forested and watered interior of the island and has all the charm of the antique Italian villa.

It is in Pompeii, however, that the development from *Italic* to later Roman houses is most clearly seen. The **House of the Surgeon** (4thC BC) has the austerity typical of early Italic houses. It is rectangular in plan, cavernous and with little natural light. The **House of the Sallust** (3rdC BC) is similar but with the addition of four shops on either side of the front entrance. The first *Hellenistic* influences are seen in the **House of the Faun** (2ndC BC), with its series of courtyards and gardens. The **House of the Pansa** is a synthesis of Hellenistic and Italic domestic forms. It is a large mansion occupying an entire city block. The *peristyle* behind the Tuscan *atrium* contains a great pool.

Architectural forms remained unchanged after Sulla's colonists established themselves in the city in 80 BC. Greater emphasis, however, was placed on pictorial art, as in the **House of the Labyrinth** (1stC BC) and the **House of Venus** (1stC BC). The lack of large building plots led some of the richer merchants to join several smaller residences into one, notably with the **House of the Dioscuri**. Most of the other houses, however, such as the **House of the Silver Wedding**, were merely modified. The **House of the Vettii** is perhaps the most luxuriously decorated, having a graceful *frieze* of cupids in the *triclinium* and a gallery of mythological pictures in the remaining rooms. The elegant **House of the Tragic Poet** is named after a mosaic found in the *tablinum*. The **Villa of Julia Felix** and the **House of Marcus Loreius Tiburtinus** (AD 62-79) are memorable for their spectacular gardens.

The most notable of the suburban villas is the **Villa of Mysteries**. It is spacious and airy, with terraces and hanging gardens surrounding it on three sides and a semicircular windowed verandah on the fourth. Of particular note is the painting of the "Mysteries" in the triclinium.

In Herculaneum the houses were more modest in scale but a number, including the **House of the Stags** (1stC AD) and the **House of the Telephus Relief,** had panoramic views to the sea. The **House of the Bicentenary** is perhaps the most beautiful of all in Herculaneum, while the **House of the Carbonized Furniture** is an excellent example of a middle-class dwelling. The **House of the Wooden Partition** and the **House of the Beautiful Courtyard** clearly marked the transition from atrium home to courtyard house, so characteristic of Renaissance Rome.

House of Venus, Pompeii *The rapid mercantile expansion of the city restricted available building space and thus architectural expression. Here, as in many contemporaneous villas, artistic endeavor took the form of elaborate decorative work.*

House of Marcus Loreius Tiburtinus, Pompeii *One of the largest and noblest of Pompeian buildings, with spacious living quarters and a large garden with a terrace, trees and statuary. The grandiose entrance had two seats for clients outside and shops on either side.*

House of the Large Portal, Herculaneum *A small dwelling, it has a* portal *comprising a double door with brick* half-columns, *surmounted by* capitals *adorned with figures of winged victories.*

House of the Faun, Pompeii *The main entrance, with its powerful* tufa *pillars mounted on elegant capitals and walls richly ornamented with* stuccoes, *leads to an imposing Tuscan atrium.*

House of the Gilt Cupids, Pompeii *The peristyle is rich in statuettes, relief carvings and
small columns with carved heads. The far end
of the garden enclosure is raised and approached
by a short flight of stairs.*

House of the Labyrinth, Pompeii
*View of the atrium and peristyle.
One room has an Ionic colonnade,
finely decorated with views of
Hellenistic buildings which are
rendered in perspective.*

**House of the Beau-
tiful Courtyard,
Herculaneum,** *left.
Among the most
unusual houses in the
city, it has a central
courtyard with a stone
staircase along one
side instead of the tra-
ditional atrium. This
was an innovation
which was later to be
much copied.*

House of the Stags, Herculaneum
*A shelter supported by pillars on the
terrace, it was designed as a vantage
point for viewing the bay and sea.*

Samnite House, Herculaneum *(120 BC),
below. The* loggia-*gallery, a feature imported
from Asia Minor, has columns or half-columns,
the spaces between them being sometimes
enclosed and sometimes windowed.*

**Villa of Maximian, Piazza
Amerina,** *Sicily. View of the peristyle court and adjoining living
quarters. The villa had a monumental triple entrance and a forecourt in
the shape of a horseshoe.*

Southern Italy

Civic & Public buildings

The **Forum, Pompeii** (*c.* 150-120 BC), was the center of the city's religious, political and economic life. Within its *porticos* stood the major public buildings of the city, of which the **Basilica** (2ndC BC) was the most grandiose. Seat of the court and business meeting place, it consisted of a central *nave* and surrounding *aisles* with a two-story *tribunal,* the width of the nave, at its western end. Entry to the *forum* from the north was via a **Triumphal Arch** (2ndC BC) flanking the **Temple of Jupiter** (1stC BC).This, like the **Arch of Caligula,** the **Porta Nocera** and the **Porta Stabiae,** was delightfully simple and utilitarian. The **Porta Marina,** the main sea gate, consists of two arches, the smaller for pedestrians, the other for chariots and beasts of burden. In complete contrast is the **Arch of Trajan, Benevento** (114 AD), a sober, slightly stocky arch of Greek marble, richly embellished with symbolic and allegorical relief sculpture.

The public baths at Pompeii are unique for their remarkable state of preservation. The oldest public baths of the Roman age were the **Stabian Baths** (2ndC BC). The principal entrance on the Via dell' Abbondanza led through a small, square vestibule into the *palaestra,* which was surrounded by porticos on three sides. The **Central Baths** (AD 63-79) were reminiscent of the traditional *Hellenistic* gymnasium, while the **Forum Baths** (1stC AD) were a smaller scale, but extraordinarily elegant, version of the Stabian Baths. In Herculaneum, the **Forum Baths** (1stC BC) were the town's principal bathing establishment. The *barrel vaulted* changing rooms are particularly well preserved, complete with seats, shelves for clothes and mosaic floors. Also of interest is the **Suburban Baths, Herculaneum** (1stC AD).

Modeled on Hellenistic lines, the **Large Theatre, Pompeii** (1stC AD), was built around a natural inlet in a hillside and had accommodation for 5000. The magnificent auditorium of the **Theatre, Syracuse** (*c.* 335-230 BC), Sicily, was hewn almost entirely from the local rock. It is one of the largest ancient Greek theatres in existence. Also of note are the **Theatre, Segesta** (3rdC BC) Sicily, and the **Theatre, Benevento** (2ndC BC).

Built as permanent premises for gladiatorial performances, the **Amphitheatre, Pompeii** (*c.* 70 BC), is the oldest of Roman *amphitheatres.* It was built in a convenient hollow and so lacked the substructures of later examples. The **Amphitheatre, Santa Maria Capua Vetere** (1stC AD), was the largest after the Colosseum, Rome, and was the scene of the slave rebellion led by Sparticus. The **Amphitheatre, Pozzuoli** (1stC AD), was the third largest in Italy and remarkable for its complex of service corridors and sub-structure planning.

Commercial & Industrial buildings

The **Eumachia Building, Pompeii** (1stC AD), occupies a large, central site and was the headquarters of the guild of fullers. The **Macellum, Pompeii,** a rectangular, porticoed enclosure, was the fish and meat market.

Central Baths, Pompeii *These baths consisted of a quadrangular exercise yard surrounded on three sides by shops and offices and on the fourth by the baths complex.*

Palaestra, Herculaneum *(1stC AD).* Part of the Forum Baths *complex, the* Palaestra *was an essential element of the men's section, complete with fountain and swimming pool. On the street frontage there were shops and offices.*

Porta Nocera, Pompeii *Eight gateways were cut into the ramparts of Pompeii. The Porta Nocera is one of the south facing gates. It was used by both pedestrians and wheeled vehicles.*

Forum, Pompeii, *left. The most complete and best preserved of its type, this was the first of the* Italic *marketplaces to be redeveloped to match the imperial* forums *of Rome. It was the center of civic life and the site for religious sacrifices.*

Suburban Baths, Herculaneum, *above. A high* portal *entrance with columns led down via a flight of steps to this elegant vestibule. It was lit and ventilated from above, as was the rest of the complex.*

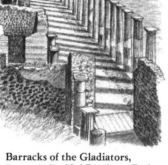

Barracks of the Gladiators, Pompeii *(2ndC AD), above. Built at the rear of the Great Theatre, the space was originally used by the theatre audience during intervals. It was transformed into a barracks in the Imperial Age.*

Cardo IV, Herculaneum, *left. A narrow, residential street, its variety of façades, doorways, porches, projecting upper stories and plain* arcades *must have presented a delightfully picturesque scene.*

Theatre, Segesta *One of the finest of Greek theatres, the beauty of the building lay in its particular relationship to the landscape. The view over the distant countryside is magnificent, while the adaption of auditorium to site is such that structure and setting are fused.*

Odeion, Pompeii *(c. 80-75 BC). A small, permanently roofed theatre, it was designed for recitations and musical performances and could accommodate 1000 people. There were two zones of seats, the upper separated from the lower by a balustrade.*

63

Britain

Religious buildings

The **Temple of Mithras, London** (c. AD 200), is one of the best preserved temples of Roman Britain. It originally lay under the foundations of Bucklersbury House but was unearthed in 1954 and the remains — walls and two rows of pillars — reassembled in the forecourt of Temple House. Smaller finds from the site are now housed in the British Museum.

Castles & Palaces

The Romans conquered Britain in AD 43 and for three centuries built military complexes, fortresses, towns, palaces and villas. **Hadrian's Wall** (c. AD 122) was their major defensive work in Britain. It ran the width of Britain from Bowness-on-Solway, Cumbria, to Wallsend-on-Tyne, Northumberland, 81 miles distant. There was a ditch on both sides of the wall, a network of forts, a service road and supply depots.

Most Roman forts, normally housing 500 to 1000 men, were built on standard patterns with headquarters, barracks, granaries, workshops, a hospital and quarters for officers. The **Roman Fort, Cripplegate** (2ndC AD), in London, was typical, although there the soldiers were primarily engaged on ceremonial duties related to the city rather than on military tasks.

Domestic buildings

The noblest of the early country mansions of Roman Britain is the splendid Flavian **Villa, Fishbourne** (c. AD 71-80), near Chichester. It covered 6.5 acres, and remains include one

wing of the building, with mosaic floors, and much of the extensive garden. **Lullingstone Villa, Eynsford** (c. AD 180-380), in Kent, built on an embankment of the River Darenth, began as a simple residence but in the 4th century was developed into a luxurious manor house with dining and reception halls at the center. In Sussex, **Bignor Villa, Petworth** (4thC AD), is notable for an unusually fine series of mosaics.

Civic & Public buildings

Much of the Roman work at York and Chester is buried under medieval buildings, but interesting remains of the **City Wall, London** (c. AD 200), can be seen behind the ruined Wardrobe Tower, Tower of London, as well as in **Wakefield Gardens** and the **Barbican.** Surviving *bastions* are probably medieval. At **Lincoln**, one of the major towns of Roman Britain, two of the stone gateways survive in remarkable condition: the **Newport Arch**, North Wall and the **Gate**, (4thC AD), in Orchard Street. At **Verulamium**, **St Albans**, Hertfordshire, there are remains of the *colonnaded* stage and auditorium of the **Theatre**.

One of the best preserved Roman buildings in western Europe is the **Roman Baths, Bath** (3rdC AD), parts of which are still in use. Other examples include the magnificent **Bath Building, Wroxeter** in Shropshire, complete with exercise halls and a large swimming pool, and remains of the **City Baths** in Leicester. The finest example of a paved Roman road in Britain is found at **Blackstone Edge**, near **Littleborough** in Lancashire, once linking Manchester and Ilkley.

Lighthouse, Dover *(1stC AD), Kent. The earliest Roman lighthouse in Britain, it stands on a hill by Dover Castle. When required, a bonfire was lit at the top to guide mariners. Another lighthouse stood across the Channel at the port of Boulogne.*

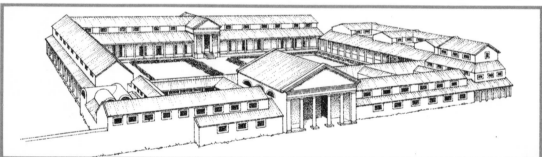

Fishbourne Villa, Chichester *Reconstruction. The villa originally consisted of a large* colonnaded *courtyard with additional courtyards designed as formal gardens. The principal room, dominating the whole complex, was the audience chamber.*

Multiangular Tower, York *(AD 71). The tower is all that remains of a fortress and was originally situated in what was the southwest corner of the building. It is, however, one of the most impressive Roman structures still standing in Great Britain today.*

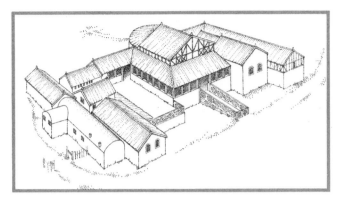

Lullingstone Villa, Eynsford *Reconstruction. The villa was the center of a small estate and has fine mosaics and other decorative features. It is notable for having one of the earliest private Christian chapels in England, identified as such by numerous finds made possible by new techniques of excavation.*

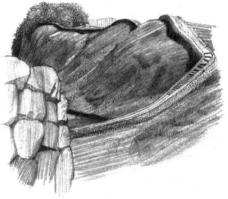

Hadrian's Wall *At every Roman mile along its length there was a small fort (a milecastle) and between each pair were two turrets. The wall, 14.5 ft in height, was topped by a battlement of almost 7 ft and was for its greater part between 8 ft and 10 ft in width.*

Military Baths, Chesters Fort, Hadrian's Wall *A major feature, as of all Roman settlements, was the baths, which were outside the fort. This was a large building, set in a river bank, comprising rooms with baths of different temperature.*

Great Bath, Bath *This Roman town developed around its curative hot springs. The Great Bath had a surrounding colonnade and was probably open to the sky. Fragments of the plumbing and the mosaic flooring remain. Two other, smaller baths were built nearby in rectangular halls.*

Roman Forts of the Saxon Shore (3rdC AD)
There were at least 10 forts, built at strategic points by the sea, guarding the natural gateways of southeast Britain. Each held a garrison and adjoined a harbor from which a fleet operated.

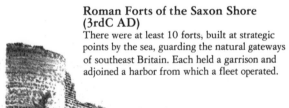

Portchester Castle, Portchester, *Hampshire. The most westerly of the forts. Its entire wall-circuit, complete with semicircular bastions and gateways, remains.*

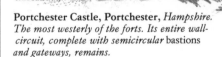

Pevensey Castle, Pevensey Bay, *Sussex. More than 10 acres in extent, it was among the largest of the forts. The walls, generally 11.5 ft thick, have round-fronted bastions.*

France, Germany & Iberian Peninsula

Religious buildings

In France, the **Maison Carrée, Nîmes** (*c.* 19 BC), standing on a tall *podium,* is the best preserved Roman temple in existence. Nothing remains of the **Temple of Janus, Autun** (2ndC AD), however, save the square *cella,* a monumental tower 43 ft high. A *portico* with a low roof ran around the outside of the building. Other religious buildings include the **Basilica, Trier** (AD 300), Germany — all that is left of Constantine's imperial palace — and the **Temple of Diana, Evora** (AD 200), Portugal, which was built on a 50-ft-high podium.

Civic & Public buildings

The **Theatre** and **Odeion, Lyon** (AD 117-138), France, is interesting as an example of a Hadrianic complex, but the **Amphitheatre, Arles** (1stC AD) is in a far better state of preservation. Of the arches, the **Triumphal Arch of Tiberius, Orange** (*c.* 30 BC), is one of the earliest surviving triple arches. A contemporary is the **Arch of the Julii, Saint Remy** (*c.* 25 BC). The **Triumphal Arch of Germanicus, Saintes,** was not built until AD 19. It consists of a double archway and has rectangular *piers* with *engaged columns* on the corners. Other notable buildings include **Porte Saint-André, Autun** (*c.* 16 BC), a double arched gateway with arcade above, which was flanked by semicircular projecting towers, the **Tower of August, La Turbie** (5 BC), and the **Monument of the Julii, Saint Remy** (1stC BC).

In Germany, the **Porta Nigra, Trier** (4thC AD), a monumental gateway, is possibly the most impressive monument. It has a double archway, each equipped with a *portcullis,* and flanking semicircular towers, while behind was a *vantage court.* Trier, one of the oldest and most prosperous towns of northern Gaul, became an imperial residence and the capital of Gaul following the reorganization of the Roman Empire under Diocletian. It reached the height of its prosperity under Constantine (r. 306-337). Other remains there include the **Imperial Baths** (4thC AD), the third largest in the Roman Empire, and the **Amphitheatre** (*c.* AD 100).

Commercial & Industrial buildings

The outstanding Classical structures in Spain are aqueducts and bridges. Because of the immense quantities of water required for public fountains and baths, funds were allocated for the construction of a series of aqueducts supplying major towns. Of these, the aqueduct bridge is the most impressive construction. Examples include the **Aqueduct, Segovia** (2ndC AD), the **Aqueduct, Mérida** and the **Aqueduct, Tarragona.** Also of interest is the **Bridge over the Tagus, Alcantara** (AD 106). The most intriguing remains of all, however, are those of the **Roman Arch, Medinaceli** (2ndC AD), which stands weather-beaten and alone. It consists of a large main arch with flanking doorways, while above are *pediments* and *pilasters* and a plain *attic.*

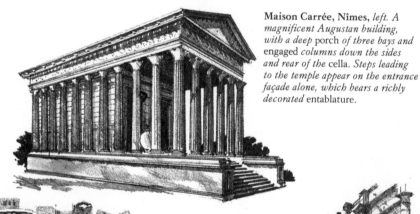

Maison Carrée, Nîmes, *left. A magnificent Augustan building, with a deep* porch *of three bays and* engaged *columns down the sides and rear of the cella. Steps leading to the temple appear on the entrance façade alone, which bears a richly decorated* entablature.

Amphitheatre, Arles, *below. Technical advances in the new building materials of concrete, by then well advanced in Rome, are conspicuously lacking here. This amphitheatre is contemporary with and stylistically similar to the one at Nîmes.*

Amphitheatre, Nîmes *(AD 1stC), right. While Italian models emphasized the horizontal continuity of the encircling* cornices, *this stressed the vertical throughout the façade by the projection of* pilasters *and half-columns.*

Arch and Monument of the Julii, Saint Remy
The monument's pedestal is decorated in low relief, while above are engaged Corinthian columns supporting a circular story with entablature and roof. The arch is typical of Roman arches in Provence.

Arch of Tiberius, Orange *Tiberius inscribed his name on this arch, which is notable for its fine relief carving and its accentuated central arch with projecting pediment and cornice.*

Temple of Janus, Autun *(AD 2ndC). Remains of the cella. Typical of Gallo-Roman temple architecture was a basic form comprising a square, circular or octagonal cella with a single door.*

Bridges and aqueducts
Roman engineering was at its most impressive in this field. Many were of enormous spans and a number of the aqueducts still supply towns with water.

Pont du Gard, Nimes *(c. AD 14). The bridge is part of an aqueduct, comprises 3 tiers of arches and measures nearly 885 ft.*

Bridge over the Tagus, Alcantara
An impressive structure, built under Trajan. Simple proportions disguise the fact that the six arches have different spans.

Aqueduct, Segovia
Stonework blocks were left rough to give visual strength to the unusually slender piers. The structure still carries the city's water supply.

Porta Nigra, Trier *The masonry is crude since the gate was never finished. It was designed to be both a defensive post and a symbol of Roman might. As with much late Roman work, it was built in imitation of earlier Imperial models.*

Turkey & Yugoslavia

Religious buildings

The **Archaic Temple of Artemis, Ephesus** (c. 560 BC), was one of the largest classical Greek temples and was the first to have any distinctive *Ionic* features. To emphasize the entrance, two rows of eight columns, an unprecedented number, were employed. It was destroyed by fire in 356 BC but another temple, the "Later" temple, was built on the same site. It was identical in plan but even more lavish in decoration. In complete contrast is the Roman **Temple of Hadrian** (2ndC AD). It was an ornate but modestly scaled building, remarkable for a façade carried on the outer corners on rectangular *piers* rather than columns, and for the central *portico,* which is arched up on to a *pediment,* a plan derived from Syria.

The **Temple of Athena Polias, Priene** (c. 334 BC), the religious center of the city, was of the Ionic Order at its most classic. The *entablature* was in two parts, omitting a *frieze.* The **Temple of Apollo, Didyma** (3rdC BC), built on a high, stepped platform, was an Ionic shrine. It stood in an open court, originally planted with bay trees. The 120 columns, 6 ft in diameter and 64 ft high, were the tallest and thinnest of all Greek temples. Much of the decorative work belongs to the *Hellenistic* age.

The outstanding achievements of 4thC BC architecture were the perfecting of the *tholos,* the *Corinthian capital* and Ionic temple and the

adaptation of the temple form to tombs. The best known example of the last in Turkey was the **Neried Monument, Xanthus** (410-380 BC), which took the form of an Ionic temple on a base of approximately equal height. Only the base remains. Other fragments are in the British Museum. Further examples include the **Mausoleum, Halicarnassus** (4thC BC), of which the remains are again in the British Museum, and the **Lion Tomb, Coridus** (4thC BC), so named from the enormous sculpture of a lion on a platform at the top of the tomb.

Castles & Palaces

In Yugoslavia the most impressive Roman work is the vast **Imperial Palace of Diocletian, Split** (3rd-4thC AD). With one side facing the Adriatic and covering an area of 8 acres, it was a combination of Roman fortress and residential villa. Within the palace stood Diocletian's elaborate mausoleum.

Civic & Public buildings

At **Priene,** the supreme example of Hellenistic urbanism, there was an absence of the empty spaces associated with earlier Greek planning; the buildings were no longer designed as isolated units but as an ordered, harmonious sequence. The **Ekklesiasterion** or Council Hall (c. 200 BC) was a large hall remarkably free of internal

Temple of Apollo, Didyma *(3rdC BC), right. View of the staircase leading from the court to the high platform on which the shrine stood. It had doors on either side of the staircase which led, through tunnels, to the* pronaos.

Sanctuary of Asklepius, Pergamon *(AD 140-175). Part of the* rotunda *engaging the southeast corner of a large complex. It is an early example of the use of brick in Asia Minor and was modeled on the Pantheon.*

Temple of Athena Polias, Priene, *left. The building is situated on a high terrace rising above the northwest corner of the agora and is nearly twice as long as it is broad. Above: detail of the* pilaster *strip of the* naos *walls, now housed in the British Museum.*

structure and capable of accommodating 700 people. The **Theatre** (*c.* 300 BC) provided the first Hellenistic example of a raised stage along the façade of the *scene-building,* bringing the actors more into view. The **Agora** (2ndC BC) was entered via a Gateway, added in 156 BC and is considered to be the earliest Greek example of an ornamental arch.

At **Pergamon,** where the site was more difficult to develop, terraces were cut into the hillside. The **Library** (2ndC BC), which included a lecture hall, was built at the back of the *stoa,* with the stoa portico acting as its front façade.

Public buildings of the **Civic Center, Miletus** (*c.* 150 BC), were a model for centuries to come. The center's chief feature was the ornate **Council House** (175-164 BC), which reproduced the curve of a theatre's auditorium. The *propylaeum* had intricately detailed capitals and its frieze was embellished with a relief depicting weapons and shields. The *axial* planning of the **Agora, Assos** (2ndC BC), was a departure from the usual grid planning and became a characteristic feature of the Hellenistic Age. Two long stoas splayed outward toward the west end, which was closed by a temple on axis with the marketplace.

Roman civic architecture is seen at its best preserved in the **Theatre, Aspendus** (2ndC AD), the **Library of Celsus, Ephesus** (*c.* AD 135) and the **Serapaeum, Pergamon** (3rdC AD).

Theatre, Priene *The most characteristic creation of* Hellenic *architecture was the theatre. This is an outstanding example of the fully developed classical form, with raised stage bringing the actors into better view.*

Ekklesiasterion, Priene *One of the best preserved of Greek council halls. Around the top of the seats there originally ran a passageway, which was lined with 14 columns.*

Palace of Diocletian, Split *The ceremonial courtyard, which led to the residential wing. The entire palace was protected by massive walls, fortified with towers. The south side, facing the sea, had a series of open arcades on the first floor overlooking the Adriatic. This was the area of the Emperor's private apartments.*

Stoa, Priene *(2ndC BC), above. Reconstruction of the interior. Most* stoas *contained an inner* colonnade *to increase the amount of covered space. Behind the stoa were shops and offices.*

Aqueduct of Pollio, Ephesus *(AD 4-14). One of the earliest examples where the main structure was built of coursed rubble laid in mortar and with the surface dressed in stone.*

Byzantine & Medieval World

The Emperor Constantine (ruled AD 306-37) made Christianity a state religion of the Roman Empire in 324 and six years later inaugurated his new imperial capital in the Hellenic town of Byzantium, which was rebuilt and renamed Constantinople ("city of Constantine"). This momentous event had an enormous impact, not only politically in shifting the whole balance of the Roman Empire from the east to the west, but also socially and culturally.

Two distinct types of building had been handed down from the ancient classical world shaped first by the Greeks, then by the Romans: the rectangular hall, or basilica, and the round temple, expitomized by the Pantheon. With the gradual division of the Roman Empire into two halves — the Eastern Roman Empire (Byzantium) and the Western Roman Empire — architecture developed in two distinct ways. The east followed the circular temple plan with a domed roof, or at least combined the dome with the basilican plan, while the west adopted the basilica with a simple pitched roof. In Byzantium, the Greek cross plan (four arms of equal length) focused attention on a central point under the dome. In the west, the Latin cross plan (three short arms and one long one) encourages attention to be drawn up to a focal point, with a long perspective accentuated by colonnading.

There is an unbroken sequence from Roman architecture to Early Christian architecture, then via Carolingian and Romanesque architecture, to Gothic. Byzantine architecture, in comparison, is an offshoot of architectural history which reached its climax with the zenith of the Byzantine Empire. The continuity of the western architectural line depended on the strength of the western church for, although defensive building played an important role, all the periods of the medieval world are dominated by ecclesiastical building. This strength was gained at the expense of the Eastern Orthodox Church which was overcome politically as the Turks gradually reduced the Byzantine Empire, Constantinople falling in 1453. The Orthodox Church only survived in areas of European Russia and its very orthodoxy ultimately restricted the development of its architecture away from traditional forms.

Early Christian Architecture

The Christians of third- and early fourth-century Rome met in churches converted from private homes, partly to avoid being harassed and persecuted by the authorities, and partly because the pagan associations of the official religious architecture were incompatible with their beliefs. Once Christianity had been recognized by Constantine, however, the number of converts increased, and larger, more spacious meeting houses became needed. For these the traditional basilica was the most suitable model, and its long high nave and lower flanking aisles became the prototype of the first Christian churches.

Byzantine Architecture

After the Imperial Roman capital was established at Constantinople in AD 330, it took about two centuries before architects began to break away from traditional Roman classicism. Gradually classical concepts, especially the use of Orders, were discarded. By the fifth century a domed religious building with a Greek cross plan had become established in the form of "martyria" — martyrs' shrines. These could only be built after the problems of supporting a dome over a square bay had been suitably resolved.

Throughout the sixth century Byzantine architecture made real progress as Roman engineering genius overcame the inflexibility of the circular plan. Domed, centralized churches were combined with elements of the basilica form allowing magnificent new interiors

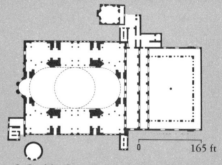

St Sophia, Constantinople, plan *The great central dome is supported by the four central piers, half-domes on two sides and four great external buttresses.*

culminated by St Sophia, Constantinople (532-37). Such an interior is wholly unclassical, the molding of spaces, so that one subtly gives way to another, and the play of light being all important.

Romanesque Architecture

In the years around AD 800, Charlemagne's empire, which stretched from northern Spain to eastern Germany, brought short-lived unity to western Europe for the first time since the collapse of the Roman Empire. With it came a renaissance of art and learning. Though its architecture took much from Roman examples, it was essentially provincial in nature, and no uniform style developed.

The first truly international Romanesque style did not develop until the second half of the 10th century, at the same time as the monastic movement began to expand and prosper and new orders were founded.

In Romanesque churches the dominance of the altar was accentuated by the long perspective of the basilican nave. It is plain to see how architects adapted the semicircular arch and the groin or cross-vault from ancient Roman prototypes to suit the basilican form. The massing of the various elements of construction was bold and dignified using the simple geometry of basilican section with its high nave and low side aisles. Transepts and towers were articulated internally and externally by decorative blind arcading. The tympana over the main entry portals were magnificently sculpted.

Despite the obvious internationalism of the Romanesque style, however, its real quality was derived from the interpretations put upon it by local craftsmen, so that we speak not so much of countries but more of schools, not of France or Italy but of Aquitaine and Apulia, Poitou and Pisa.

Gothic Architecture

The aim of Gothic builders was to bring light and spaciousness into dark interiors. They achieved this by dispensing with weight and mass in external walls, increasing window space and so letting light flood in. The beginning was in the Abbey of St Denis (1085-1151), in Paris, where the heavy Romanesque walls of the choir are pierced by magnificent windows, made possible by structural elements such as ribs, pointed arches and flying buttresses.

Mullioned window *The increased window space in Gothic, as compared with Romanesque and earlier churches, provided large areas of glass that had to be supported and strengthened by mullions. These supports themselves became integral parts of the Gothic design.*

Solid Romanesque walls gave way to skeletal Gothic window-walls, their dramatic effects inside heightened by the composition of light and shade. The internal walls, which often contained three stories of arcades and galleries (the first to the height of the aisles, the second and third, the triforium and clerestory, above this) were carried on loadbearing piers and ribs, while the external walls were supported by flying buttresses. The Gothic period was, to an extent, an age of machines. Agriculture was being revolutionized by the use of machines used to harness wind and water power, the mechanical clock was developed and the suction pump driven by a rod and crank invented. Cast iron was similarly a product of the Middle Ages and vital both for the strengthening of construction and for strong, effective building tools and machinery. The soaring

Gothic cathedrals in many ways epitomized the spirit of the times. Increasing prosperity, and a fuller and more complex intellectual life were paralleled by the skillful innovations of the architect-engineers who worked on the great medieval cathedrals, abbeys and parish churches built by the church and the monastic orders. There was a considerable sense of public rivalry that could be fulfilled through religious architecture, and citizens encouraged the building of a higher spire or a higher vault. Records were set and broken, a fact that is underlined by the height of the spire of Strasbourg Cathedral (1230-1365), which at more than 138 ft remained the tallest building in the world until Robert Mills's Washington Monument (1836-54), and the iron and steel construction of the Eiffel Tower (1887-89). This spirit of rivalry was largely crushed when the choir of Beauvais Cathedral (1247-1568), which was nearly 165 ft high, crashed to earth in 1284.

Religious buildings were not the sole result of the architects' skills. The monarchy and nobility had elaborate castles built for them and fortified manor houses for defensive purposes, and in the towns burghers and merchants, enjoying unprecedented independence and wealth, constructed impressive town halls, guild halls and cloth halls.

Although the Gothic period was dominated first by France, then by England, each country — Germany, Spain, the Netherlands and so on — interpreted the style in its own particular manner. In Italy, however, where the classical tradition was still strong, comparatively little was built in the Gothic style, and then only in buildings such as Milan Cathedral, where the influence of northern Europe was significant.

Construction

The builders of the early Christian basilicas used the same structural techniques as their predecessors. A simple trussed roof covered a central nave and flanking aisles and supported columns, placed either close together if an entablature was carried or further apart if there were arches.

In Byzantium the structural problems were more complex. The thrust exerted by the structure of larger domes had previously been met by massively thick walls or by clumsy abutments. To incorporate such domes in a flexible design made up of square and oblong bays, the problem of making a strong but unobtrusive transition from dome to bay was solved by

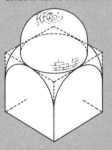

Supporting a dome *The strongest base for a round dome is circular, so fitting a round dome over a square bay requires extra support in the upper corners of the bay. These curved triangular inserts are called* pendentives.

71

the insertion of stone brackets, or pendentives, in the corners of the bay to provide a circular base for the dome. Once this smooth transition was achieved Byzantine architecture became increasingly exotic, some churches being roofed with an amazing combination of domes. A characteristic feature of Byzantine buildings is the way in which these complex internal structural forms of vaults and domes can be seen in the external form of the church. Among the building materials employed, marble columns from older buildings were often reused. The domes themselves were usually built of brick, but sometimes of light stone or interlocking clay pots.

Romanesque architects inherited the long nave and simple trussed roof from Early Christian basilicas, but their churches, cathedrals and abbey churches were narrower and often vaulted. The apse terminating the nave was roofed with a half-dome. Roman groin, or cross-vaults were used throughout Europe until the early 12th century, when they were superseded by ribbed and panel vaulting, in which a rib cage supports thin stone panels. The major limitation of the style was that bays were square to comply with the round Roman

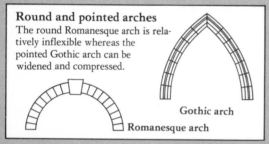

Round and pointed arches
The round Romanesque arch is relatively inflexible whereas the pointed Gothic arch can be widened and compressed.

Gothic arch

Romanesque arch

arches that supported them. Walls were generally of rubble and concrete faced with brick or stone and were occasionally stuccoed. Columns were built of ashlar masonry with a rubble core and were carved with decorative patterns.

The search for lightness, both spatial and structural, was the hallmark of the Gothic period. A key element was an elaborate system of external buttresses that avoided the need for thick walls. Gradually these buttresses, particularly flying buttresses, began to play

Flying buttress *This elegant form of buttress is a particularly characteristic feature of Gothic architecture. The immense thrust from a cathedral roof was partially carried down through the arm of the buttress to the upright and to the ground. The more or less weighty the pinnacle and upright, the more or less thrust the buttress takes.*

a major role in carrying the thrust from the stone roofs. The walls between were replaced by large windows mullioned to withstand the wind. The major innovation,

however, was the development of the pointed arch, which directed the thrust to the abutment more precisely. As the pointed arch is of infinitely variable width between certain limits, the bays that it supported could be rectangular as well as square. Vaulting therefore became far more flexible and so plans could better fulfill functional requirements. By the late Middle Ages, masons had mastered the art of the vault so superbly that they could turn its form to intricate decorative purpose as well.

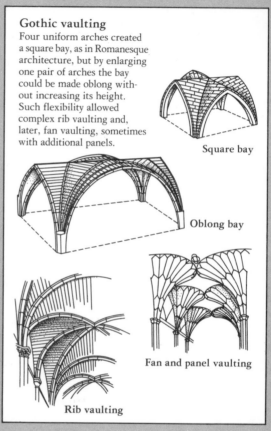

Gothic vaulting
Four uniform arches created a square bay, as in Romanesque architecture, but by enlarging one pair of arches the bay could be made oblong without increasing its height. Such flexibility allowed complex rib vaulting and, later, fan vaulting, sometimes with additional panels.

Square bay

Oblong bay

Fan and panel vaulting

Rib vaulting

Design

Early Christian basilicas were comparatively low, with a long central nave and flanking aisles. The focal point was the altar which was placed in the center of the sanctuary and separated from the nave by a triumphal arch. The columns were usually Corinthian, sometimes Ionic, and were often quarried from existing buildings. Light came from windows in the clerestory above the nave. At one end, terminating the vista, was a semicircular apse. At the other was a narthex, or porch, sometimes approached through an open courtyard. One or two round churches were also built, such as S. Constanza, Rome (*c.* 350).

The centralized plan in Byzantine churches combined the domical prototype from the East with a basilica designed in a series of square bays. The central dome was often raised on a high drum pierced by windows. In larger buildings this weakened the walls, which then had to be buttressed. Smaller drums were frequently built around the central drum. There was usually a narthex (a vestibule or portico) at the west end.

In comparison with the long, low early Christian basilicas, Romanesque churches were lofty and boldly massed. Unlike the early Christian basilica, in which you advanced toward God, here you were surrounded by Him. Arcades consisted of huge circular arches. The thickness of the walls was expressed by the deep reveals of windows, doors and arches. A wheel window was often placed over the west door in Romanesque churches whereas in Gothic churches this was usually a rose window. Many churches had twin-towered west façades. Major innovations included adding chapels to the choir, as at S. Philibert, Tournus (*c.* 950-1120), the use of double transepts, first seen at the Abbey of Cluny (*c.* 1088), and adding a second apse and choir, as at St Michael's, Hildesheim (*c.* 1001). These additions increased the area behind and to the sides of the altar, giving more of the feel of a centralized church.

Decoration

Although early Christian basilicas followed the form of their Roman prototypes, they were stripped of extraneous decorative detail. Inside, colorful glass mosaics decorating the apse, the triumphal arch and walls above the nave arcading added richness. Themes were generally dedicatory or ceremonial with large, boldly drawn figures shown frontally. Floors were of marble, which was usually laid in elaborate geometric patterns.

The Byzantine Empire had plentiful supplies of marble and the walls of Byzantine churches were usually faced in colorful marbles. Domes and vaults were decorated with either glass or marble mosaics. In later buildings frescoes were often preferred. Elaborately carved screens were also constructed. The Roman brick used for the superstructure was also employed externally in elaborate decorative patterns.

In Romanesque buildings, the very structure itself was carved, in contrast with Byzantine and early Christian churches, in which a decorative veneer of marble or mosaic was applied. At first, capitals were based on Corinthian and Ionic prototypes, but during the eleventh century these were gradually replaced by decoratively carved cushion-type capitals. By the late Romanesque periods, however, variations on the

Corinthian capital had once again begun to appear. Gradually, too, the decorative spirit of the interior was extended to enrich the more austere exterior, and arcades and capitals in abbey cloisters, for instance, became elaborate works of art. In the 12th century, portals were adorned with elaborate figures, decorative molding and sculpted tympana depicting winged dragons, centaurs, lions, monkeys and other fabulous creatures. Some churches, such as some in Lower Saxony, have Byzantine inspired frescoes and mosaics.

Portals took on new significance in the Gothic period, when the triple portals common in the French Romanesque were drawn closer together, the central one becoming dominant. Door jambs, tympana and side walls were richly decorated with statuary. The creatures favored by masons of the Romanesque period were replaced by figures, often of the church's patrons, that articulated the portal-like pillars, becoming a kind of Gothic caryatid.

Gothic is a carved architecture, its high point best represented by Chartres Cathedral (1194-1260). Moldings were often elaborately carved, often with animal and vegetable forms. The window-wall created new opportunities for creative work, as in the stained glass of the cathedrals at Bourges (1192-1275) and Strasbourg (1230-1365), where biblical stories were boldly illustrated. The Romanesque wheel window was replaced by the rose window. Set high above the entrance portal between twin towers, it welded the often complex façades into a taut harmony.

Italy

In Italy the major developments during the Romanesque period took place in Lombardy. Churches generally had a basilican plan, and the nave and flanking aisles were usually covered by a stone barrel vault. The gabled entrance façade was articulated by a corbel table frieze, and the semicircular apse often had an eaves gallery, an influence from northern Europe. A wheel window most often crowned the central porch. Projecting porches were preferred to recessed portals. The porch itself was carried on free-standing columns supported on the back of crouching beasts. The elegant round or square campanile, or belltower, was separate from the main church. Many baptisteries were built; these were generally octagonal or circular in plan. Tuscany was more deeply rooted in the classical tradition than Lombardy, as S. Miniato al Monte, Florence (1018-62), with its elegantly paneled marble façade, shows.

Italian Romanesque architecture set great store by the enrichment of external surfaces, as demonstrated by the work of the Pisan School, with its characteristic open arcaded galleries covering the western façades. In southern Italy and Sicily, many churches display a mixture of Byzantine, Muslim and Norman influences and have domes instead of vaults. In many cases their interiors are decorated with beautiful mosaics applied to ceiling vaults and nave and aisle walls.

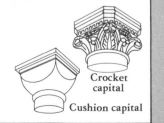

Capitals
Romanesque capitals tended to be simplified into the cushion type with little carved decoration. The crocket capital was used as Gothic architecture began to be developed.

Crocket capital

Cushion capital

73

The largely horizontal classical tradition was so strong in Italy that the verticality of Gothic Europe made little impression, except in the Cathedral, Milan (1387-1483), and even here there is not so much Gothic form but rather an amalgam of Gothic decorative features. The Gothic style was largely bypassed, and the classical tradition led through the Romanesque directly to the Renaissance.

France

Little remains of the numerous churches built in France before the Roman legions departed in the fifth century. A few Carolingian churches are still standing, among them St Martin, Angers (11thC). The first major Romanesque works are the Cathedral, Périgueux (c. 1120-50) and Ste Etienne, Périgueux (11thC), the Abbaye aux Dames (1062-1110) and the Abbaye aux Hommes, Caen (1068-1115), and St Sernin, Toulouse (c. 1077). Norman architects developed major new features, the twin-towered west façade with tall galleries. The main regional schools of the Romanesque period were Auvergne, Burgundy, Normandy and Poitou.

Gothic architecture predominated in France from about 1150 to the mid-16th century. French cathedrals are wider and loftier than the cathedrals built at the same time in England. Side projections are comparatively small. The east end usually has an apse which contains a processional aisle and ring of chapels known as a chevet. Like Greek temples, French cathedrals developed through the refinement of proportions within clearly defined constraints. The walls between the buttresses, now no longer so important as supports, were transformed into magnificent traceried windows, their stained glass depicting biblical stories. Important examples of French Gothic cathedrals are Amiens (1220-88), Bourges (1195-1515), Chartres (1194-1260), Laon (1160-1225), Notre Dame (1163-1260), Rheims (1211-90) and Rouen (1202-30).

United Kingdom

In Anglo-Saxon Britain (410-1066) buildings were constructed including fragments from the remains of Roman buildings or with details roughly based on Roman models. There were two main schools of architecture centered on Kent in the southeast and in Northumberland in the north. Characteristic features were a central or western tower on the main axis, semicircular arches and windows with round or triangular heads. Decorative details were probably based on timber prototypes and consisted of long and short work, particularly at the angles of the tower, and pilaster strips. Good examples are churches at Earls Barton (c. 935), Bradford-on-Avon (c. 700) and Sompting (11thC).

After the conquest of 1066, the Norman settlers instituted an enormous building program, in which virtually every cathedral and abbey was reconstructed and numerous new cathedrals and castles were started. It was this surge of new construction work that introduced the Romanesque style to England. Bold and massive forms, semicircular arches, ponderous cylindrical or polygonal piers and flat buttresses are characteristic features. The windows were small and deeply splayed. Ribbed and panel vaulting was introduced. Molding, which included zigzag chevron and beakhead ornament, was precise and geometrically simple, and carved foliage was generally bold. Major examples are the Chapel of St John, Tower of London (1078), and the Cathedral, Durham (1093-15thC).

English Gothic was heralded by the new choir designed by William of Sens, the French master-mason, for Canterbury Cathedral (1071-1503), after the disastrous fire of 1174. An interesting innovation was the introduction of double transepts, an idea taken from the Cluniac monasteries of France that now became a characteristic English feature. In the Early English Gothic period (1189-1307) tall, narrow lancet windows are a typical feature. Projecting buttresses and pinnacles were developed, the pointed arch slowly came into use,

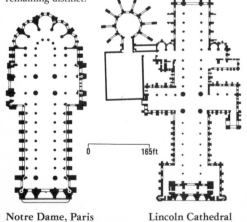

French and English Gothic cathedral plans
The two plans below of Notre Dame, Paris, and Lincoln Cathedral, show the differing Gothic styles developed in France and England. Notre Dame has a wider nave but an altogether more compact plan with the short transept arms joining the chevet on both sides. In the English cathedral there is no merging of elements, the nave, transept arms, choir and chapter-house remaining distinct.

0   165ft

Notre Dame, Paris   Lincoln Cathedral

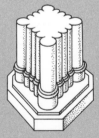

Compound piers *Massive piers are a feature of Romanesque (particularly Norman) architecture. In the transition from Romanesque to Gothic, the visual massiness of these piers was gradually eroded and became articulated by various multishafted designs. This articulation was usually continued above the capital across the spans of the arches themselves.*

and compound columns replaced the massive Norman columns. Walls remained massive, the decoration of their surfaces limited. Good examples of the Early English style are the cathedrals of Wells (12th-14thC) and Salisbury (1220-1260).

In the Decorated Gothic period (1307-77) walls became less thick, the size of the windows increased, and angle buttresses were introduced. At first window tracery consisted of geometrical forms, but later curvilinear or flowing lines were introduced. Richly decorated or pierced battlement parapets became frequent, and more and more intermediate ribs were used in vaulting. Surface texture was richer. Richly decorated or pierced battlement parapets became frequent, and more and more intermediate ribs were used in vaulting. Surface texture was richer and carving more naturalistic than before, a good example is the Angel Choir, Lincoln Cathedral (1185-1280).

In the Perpendicular Gothic period (1377-1485) the emphasis in both window tracery and wall paneling was on the vertical. Windows were enlarged, piers became more slender and fan vaults with numerous ribs and panels became characteristic. More hammer-beam roofs were built. The Tudor rose, the portcullis

Hammer-beam roof
The hammer beam itself projects from the top of the wall and supports an arched brace in the pitch of the roof. Various multiples of this design were also used.

and the fleur-de-lys were typical ornaments and decoration was generally lavish. Good examples are Westminster Hall, London (1394-1402), with its magnificent carved roof, King's College, Cambridge (1446-1515), and Henry VII's Chapel, Westminster Abbey (1503-19), London.

Under the Tudor monarchs (1485-1603) secular buildings predominated. Houses were usually timber-framed, with lathe and plaster panels, and brick became a fashionable material. Moats and elaborate gatehouses were retained as architectural features, though they had long since lost their original defensive purpose.

Spain

Medieval Spain was exposed to complex cultural influences. The Muslin invasion and subsequent occupation from the eighth century onward (which was not finally concluded until 1492 and covered most of the Iberian peninsula except a small area in the north) had profound cultural consequences. In architecture the horseshoe-shaped arch, decorative brickwork, polylobed arches and blind arcading crowning portals, as in the Cathedral, Córdoba (785), all became characteristic. At the same time, the Visigoths, who

had fled to the mountains of Asturia in northern Spain, built a number of fine churches, such as Santa Maria de Naranco (848). During the 10th century many Christians came north from the Moslem occupied territories, bringing with them features such as the horseshoe arch and ribbed cupolas. These were merged with the Visigothic tradition to form the Mozarabic style. Elsewhere the reverse happened. Moslems in areas reconquered by the Christians adapted their own techniques and styles to Christian ideas, and so the Mudejar style developed which included decorative features such as artesonado ceilings, azulejos and decorative strapwork on belfries.

The first Romanesque works in Spain were built in Catalonia, as in San Clemente, Tahull (12thC), a region cut off by mountains from Mozarabic influences and closely linked with France and Italy. The corbel table frieze, blind arcading and pilaster strips have characteristic Lombardic features. The buildings constructed along the pilgrimage routes in northern Spain were greatly influenced by current architectural fashions and the great pilgrimage church of Santiago de Compostela (1077-1128), at the end of one of the most famous routes in the Christian World, is the major Romanesque building in Spain.

Cistercian monks from Burgundy introduced the Gothic style to Spain in the early 12th century. Most of the early cathedrals, such as those at Burgos (1221-1457), Toledo (1227-1493) and Leon (1255-1303), were modeled on French prototypes; Notre Dame, Paris, and Rheims, for instance. Structurally these cathedrals are more cumbersome and less vertical than their French models. They are generally short and wide and have small projections, and many have chevets.

The turbulent history of Spain in these centuries is reflected in the numerous castles, fortifications and city walls still visible. The strategic, rocky sites chosen resulted in considerable irregularities in plan. The great period of castle building was the 14th and 15th centuries, most notably in Castile. The late 15th century brought the development of the Isabeline style, in which key architectural elements such as portals were enriched with exotic carvings and sculptures. This gradually gave way to the plateresque style of the Renaissance.

Germany

The Romanesque style in Germany began when Roman basilicas were taken over for Christian worship. The first new buildings came in the Carolingian period (9th century), such as the Palatine Chapel, Aachen Cathedral (792-805). Under the Ottonian dynasty of the 10th and 11th centuries enormous churches were built in Saxony, such as St Michael's, Hildesheim and in the Rhineland, as in the cathedrals of Cologne (1248), Speyer (1031-61) and Maria Laarch (1093-1152). Characteristic features were the aisled basilican nave, a ground plan based on a square module (first developed at Hildesheim), numerous round, square or polygonal towers, some with helm roofs, a double chancel, often double transepts, decorative blind arcading and eaves galleries. As in Italy, the Romanesque in Germany was so dominant that the Gothic style was introduced late. Even when it was taken up, it retained the solid, static character of the Romanesque. The major influence was the classic French style of building such as Amiens Cathedral, as is seen in the Choir of Cologne Cathedral. Some magnificent brick churches were built in the 13th century, such as the Marienkirche, Lübeck (1251-1351), and in Westphalia and Southern Germany there are magnificent hall churches as at Munster (1745-54) and St George's, Dinkelsbühl (1448-92).

Belgium and the Netherlands

The major Romanesque church buildings in Belgium are at Invelles (10thC), Liège (12th and 13thC), and Tournai (13thC), and in the Netherlands at Maastricht, in Holland. Bold and very simple, they all have a ponderous west façade and a huge tower. The Gothic period not only produced interesting cathedrals and churches but also magnificent civic buildings, as in the 13th and 14th century cloth halls at Ypres and Bruges, both of which have monumental belfries, and the 15th and 16th century town halls at Brussels and Ghent. German Gothic was the major influence in eastern Belgium and northern Holland, whereas the low-lying areas of Brabant took more from the French Gothic of Sens, Noyon and Laon Cathedrals. In Holland, barn-like churches were built of brick, giving a generally austere appearance.

Religious buildings

The classic French cathedrals such as Chartres, Rheims and Amiens epitomize the Gothic style. They were all built to a broad cruciform plan, with transepts projecting only slightly. Their naves are three storeys high, consisting of a nave arcade, triforium and clerestory. Their west façades, conceived as the Gate of Heaven, have twin towers and magnificent sculptured portals. At the east end is a semicircular chevet, or ring of chapels. (In England the east end of the Gothic cathedral was generally square.)

In Germany, hall churches are characteristic of the Late Gothic period. These consist of a single large space composed of three aisles of equal height, unlike contemporary cathedrals, which had a high nave and low side aisles with galleries above. Other characteristics are a single, wide-pitched roof carried on lofty columns and the nave lighted by the windows of the flanking aisles. Good examples are St George's, Dinkelsbühl and the choir of the Cathedral, Vienna (1404-1491).

Although there were many religious relics and venerated burial places throughout western Europe, Jerusalem, Rome and Santiago de Compostela drew the greatest number of pilgrims. The routes the pilgrims took were already major highways, complete with monasteries and hospices. During the 11th century many of these were extended, and new priories, each a comfortable day's journey apart, were founded. One of the more important routes went through France via Chartres, Orleans, Tours and Poitiers. A good example of a pilgrimage church is St Sernin, Toulouse.

Towers

Towers built for various purposes, detached or as features of buildings are in themselves an element of Medieval architecture worthy of individual attention.

A characteristic of Romanesque churches in Italy is the elegant campanile, or belltower, built detached from the body of the church and often articulated by blind arcading on pilasters and pierced by roundarched openings. In northern and central Italy many blank-faced, square-planned towers were built with just a few openings high up. Initially they were the solution to local problems of personal defense and refuge in case of fire in cities crammed with wooden buildings. Later they became symbols of wealth, and families rivaled one another in the height of their towers. Florence once had 150 such towers.

Churches and cathedrals with mighty twin-towered west façades are characteristic of Norman Europe. The towers themselves usually have round or polygonal plans and are variously decorated with arcades, statuary and openwork sections. Although few French cathedrals have spires, Gothic towers are usually crowned with elegant spires that draw the eye upward. In Germany in particular, late Gothic spires are on a monumental scale with elaborate openwork designs.

Castles & Palaces

The earliest castle designs took the form of a motte and bailey. The motte was a steep-sided, flat-topped mound of earth surrounded by a ditch and surmounted by a square, two-story wooden tower surrounded by a wooden fence. Earth from the ditch was used to build the mound. The bailey (there were sometimes more than one) was an open area linked to the motte by a wooden bridge across the ditch, which was filled with water (a moat) or sharpened stakes.

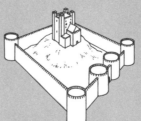

Motte and bailey
The motte and bailey defense arrangement was translated into stone with the keep surrounded by a bailey, which was itself defended by a curtain wall.

This kind of primitive castle was known in western Europe from the early years of the 11th century and in simpler forms even earlier. They were all of wood, were frequently burnt down and as frequently re-erected. They were essentially private fortresses, places of refuge in times of danger, and were owned, not only by kings but by their favored vassals to whom grants of land had been made. In time these wooden structures gave way to more defensible fortresses of stone, of which the foremost example in England is the Tower of London (11thC) with its White Tower or great keep. During the feudal period, however, many of these stone castles were fortified by powerful barons and princes and civil war became endemic.

A strong king, however, built castles not only to defend his domains but to extend them. In this respect, Edward I of England is the outstanding instance, for he built a chain of forbidding fortresses from 1277 onward to control the sea and valley routes of Wales during his campaigns to subjugate the Welsh. Magnificent examples include those at Caernarvon (c. 1285) and at Chepstow (1067-79), which with other castles formed a strategic chain. A later development was the concentric castle, seen at its best at Beaumaris (1295).

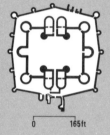

Beaumaris Castle, plan
The curtain wall defenses of Beaumaris Castle display a perfectly concentric design, which presented a similarly threatening face to attack from any angle.

0   165ft

On the continent of Europe, and more especially in France, whole towns were given defensive walls and were in fact castles on a vast scale to provide shelter for citizens in times of war. An outstanding example is the walled town of Carcassone (13thC). In other cases, such as the great medieval castle of Fougères in Brittany, the castle was so powerful that it afforded adequate protection to the villages without its walls.

The massive castles of the 12th and 13th century were not impregnable, however. Refinements, such as machicolations — parapets projecting on brackets on the castle walls, with openings in the floors to enable defenders to drop molten lead and missiles on assailants — prolonged the life of the great castles, but they became progressively more vulnerable to mines and, after the invention of gunpowder, to cannon fire. Redesigning the square keep and square towers in circular form, which better deflected missiles, could prolong their usefulness but little. In time the great castles were abandoned and fell into decay, replaced first by smaller fortified homes, and then, as civil wars became less common, by more comfortable houses where, as in Elizabethan England, the moat gave way to the formal garden. These ruins were largely disregarded until the Gothic Revival in the 19th century, when they were remodeled or built anew as romantic but undefendable versions of their grim originals. Similar reproductions are found in many parts of southern Germany and Austria, where they are perched on awkward mountain sites and embellished with picturesque turrets, towers and battlements.

The English red-brick Tudor palaces seem set midway in refinement between the heavily fortified castles of the 12th to 14th centuries and the Renaissance palaces of Europe. The original sumptuous building of Hampton Court (1514-19) for Cardinal Thomas Wolsey epitomizes the style with quadrangles, turrets, cupolas and octagonal-towered gateways. That such palaces expressed the insular confidence of Tudor England is evident in the building of Nonsuch, Surrey (1538), when the Renaissance was well underway in Europe, This extravagant palace, built by Henry VIII and demolished in the reign of Charles II, did indeed include many Renaissance motifs but these were restricted to the extravagant decoration executed by foreign craftsmen. The structure itself, although imitating Chambord, in France, was a traditional half-timbered one.

Domestic buildings

Timber and mud were the materials available to peasants throughout the Middle Ages, and only the nobility used stone for their fortified houses and castles. The simplest peasants' huts were cruck-framed buildings

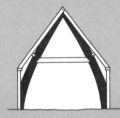

Cruck-frame, section
The cruck-frame cottage was based on two or more "A"-shaped supports comprising two heavy blades of timber joined at the top.

consisting of two curved blades of timber joined at the top, erected in 16 ft bays and thatched, rather like a tent. Larger houses were built with a box frame of timber members. These were originally built as great halls; the main room, which was open to the roof, was used for both eating and sleeping, and there were few private rooms. Gradually a distinction between sleeping and living areas grew up and the number of bedrooms increased. By the 16th century many manor houses, spacious and elegant, were built around a central court.

Civic & Public buildings

One way the bourgeoisie of medieval Europe found to express its increasing prosperity was in constructing magnificent public buildings. Medieval Italy produced a wealth of town halls, each standing at the edge of the main public square. Good examples are the Palazzo Pubblico, Siena (1289-1309) and the Palazzo Vecchio, Florence (1298-1314). A characteristic feature is the slender tall tower and castellated roof line. In England charitable foundations built hospitals and almshouses as well as guildhalls such as that at Lavenham, Suffolk (c. 1629). In the Netherlands the wealthy merchants of the 15th and 16th centuries built magnificent trade halls and town halls.

Northern Italy

Religious buildings

The grandiose church architecture of 4th-century Italy is well exemplified by **S. Lorenzo, Milan** (*c.* 370). Although rebuilt in the 12th and 16th centuries, the original octagonal plan and monumental proportions of the *double-shell* design remain. *Baptisteries* were usually square, as at **Aquileia** (*c.* 450), or rectangular.

The simple plan and structure of **S. Simpliciano, Milan** (4thC), a domed cross, shows the Italian model that inspired small church architecture all over the Christian world. **SS. Felice e Fortunato, Vicenza** (5thC), is another example of this model.

A standard *basilica* plan did not develop in Ravenna until the late 5th century. The classic example of **S. Apollinare Nuova, Ravenna** (490), is a blend of *capitals* in the Constantinople style, polygonal *apse* of Aegean origin, exterior *pilasters* and brick banding of Syrian influence and the finest mosaics in Europe.

The chief characteristic of *Byzantine* churches is their centralized plan, with a dominating, central dome over the body of the church. **S. Vitale, Ravenna** (546-48), is particularly interesting as the body consists of an inner and an outer octagon, covered by a dome constructed of interlocking earthen pots and covered by a timber roof.

The *Romanesque* architecture of 9th-century Lombardy was of major international importance, characterized by dramatic *vaults* enriched by moldings, galleries and elaborate scupltured motifs. To this were added two distinctive features: the *rib vault* and the square-planned belltower decorated with pilaster strips and *corbel tables.* Examples of the style are the **Abbey Pomposa,** (1063); **Basilica of S. Abondio, Como** (1063-*c.* 1095), and **S. Fidele, Como** (12thC).

St Mark's, Venice (1063-85), the most westerly stronghold of the Eastern Empire, has a Greek cross plan covered by five domes rising on high *drums,* the central dome being the largest. The *crocketed* pinnacles, *ogee* arches and canopied niches of the façade are later *Gothic* enrichments. Column capitals and other internal details are modeled on Justinian originals.

S. Michele, Pavia (1100-60), is a fine example of the mature *Lombardic* Romanesque style, but the *nave* roof has oblong single bays of rib vaulting, characteristic of the French Romanesque. Other examples are the **Cathedral, Piacenza** (*c.* 1122), with its wide, *apsed transepts,* and **S. Savius, Piacenza** (1107). The **Cathedral, Parma** (12th C), another example, has a dramatic stone façade with flanking towers. The *gable* is capped by a continuous, stepped gallery-arcade and rich cornice. Entry is via an elegant *barrel-vaulted* porch with covered balcony above. Nearby stands the monumental baptistry. There is a similar cathedral group at **Cremona** (1129-48).

S. Ambrogio, Milan (*c.* 940), is a Lombardic basilica with fine *atrium* and *narthex.* The martyr's chapel, in the form of a tomb *cella,* is characteristic of northern Italy. **S. Zeno Maggiore, Verona** (*c.* 1123), is one of the finest wooden roofed basilicas to be found in Lombardy.

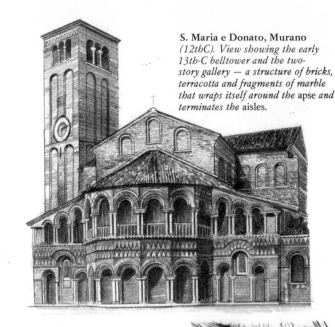

S. Maria e Donato, Murano *(12thC). View showing the early 13th-C belltower and the two-story gallery — a structure of bricks, terracotta and fragments of marble that wraps itself around the* apse *and terminates the* aisles.

S. Vitale, Ravenna. *Elaborate* capitals *in the* chancel, *part of the rich interior of one of the great* Byzantine *buildings of 6th-C Europe. It is a simpler variation of the original octagonal,* double-shell *plan developed in Constantinople with SS. Sergius e Bacchus.*

S. Abondio, Como *This Benedictine abbey church, cathedral in scale, has double aisles with a deep sanctuary of two rib-vaulted bays, and a ribbed apse. The latter, flanked by classic, paired bell-towers, is decorated internally with Lombardic arches and bands.*

S. Michele, Pavia
The magnificent, stone-built west façade of the church. The cliff-like gable, fronting both nave and aisles, is articulated *vertically by* shafting *decorated by lines of beast sculpture and capped by an* arcaded gallery.

S. Apollinare Nuova, Ravenna
South wall of the nave *with its beautiful mosaic* frieze *depicting a procession of 26 martyrs leaving the palace of Theodoric toward Christ. Opposite, on the north side of the* basilica, *the frieze shows 22 virgins.*

S. Zeno Maggiore, Verona *The stern simplicity of the façade of this fine* Romanesque *basilica is brought alive by this elegant, projecting marble porch. The porch ceiling is a semicircular vault, and this is covered by a gabled roof. The flanking reliefs illustrate stories from the Book of Genesis.*

St Mark's, Venice, *below. The façade of the basilica, with its five entrance portals, is largely 12thC. It is a marvelous multicolored collage of materials brought from many lands. The marble facing came from the East, and the* porphyry *and alabaster columns from Constantinople and Alexandria.*

The Baptistery, Parma *(1196-13thC), above. A monumental, octagonal-shaped* baptistery *built of brick and faced in stone. It has sculptured* portals, *tiers of arcaded galleries and* buttresses *capped by* crocketed pinnacles.

Northern Italy

A church of major architectural significance was built in Ravenna under the rule of Galla Placidia. It had a cross plan, with *aislcless* arms, but as at **S. Croce** (*c.* 425), only the *nave* survives. To one side stands the **Mausoleum of Galla Placidia** (*c.* 425), with its distinctive *blind arcading* and classical *cornices.* The interior contains beautiful mosaics. Placidia also built the *basilica* of **S. Giovanni Evangelista** (424-34), which was largely rebuilt in 1944 to repair war damage. The influence of Greece dominates this church, as is seen in the rooms projecting out from the *narthex* and the *impost blocks* above the *capitals.*

Toward the end of the 5th century, octagonal *baptisteries,* like the **Battistero Neoniano,** or **degli Ortodossi, Ravenna** (*c.* 400-450), became common in northern Italy, as opposed to the earlier, square-planned version. The Battistero Neoniano is Milanese in influence and was converted from a Roman bathhouse.

The **Mausoleum of Theodoric, Ravenna** (*c.* 526), built of huge blocks of *ashlar,* is an amalgam of Imperial Rome and the Near East. Many galleried basilicas in northern Italy were similarly influenced by the architecture of both Constantinople and the Balkan provinces. Such borrowing of styles was usually fragmentary. The basilica of **S. Apollinare in Classe, Ravenna** (539-49), has, for example, Eastern-type *apses,* while the interior decoration, column shafts and capitals were designed in a Constantinople style. **S. Foscara, Torcello** (*c.* 1000), has a Greek cross, octagonal plan. The **Cathedral, Torcello** (rebuilt 1008), has a beautiful mosaic floor and column capitals of *Byzantine* influence which contrast with the strong *Lombardic* flavor of the building seen particularly in the tall, *arcaded* belltower and the overall simplicity of the interior.

An important characteristic of the religious architecture of northern Italy is the tall, detached, Lombardic belltower, decorated with *pilaster strips* and *corbel tables.* The belltower of S. Apollinare in Classe is the most impressive and tallest tower in Ravenna. Other fine examples are at the Benedictine **Abbey, Pomposa** (1063), and **S. Satiro, Milan** (*c.* 1043).

In a number of churches apse walls are enriched by *eaves galleries* contained within giant arches. Characteristic of northern European architecture as a whole, good examples can be seen at the **Collegiate Church, Castell'Arquato** (1122), and **Modena Cathedral** (*c.* 1099).

The six-domed basilica of **S. Antonio, Padua** (1232-1307), recalls St Mark's, Venice, but without the decorative extravaganza. Although the basilica is a Byzantine structure, the spiky bell-towers, the cone rising above the central dome, the internal plan and the decorative details are all *Gothic.* Also of interest are **SS. Giovanni e Paolo, Venice** (1260-1385), with its beautiful brick façade with pointed windows, its molded cornices and lofty *clerestory;* **S. Maria Gloriosa dei Frari, Venice** (1250-1338); **S. Anastasia, Verona** (13thC); **Capella degli Scrovegni, Padua** (*c.* 1300-5); and **Fidenza Cathedral** (1207), with its elaborate west door.

S. Antonio, Padua *Six domes on* pendentives *cover* nave, transepts *and* choir. *The* chevet, *with nine radiating chapels, is like contemporaneous French examples. The wide spreading,* gabled *screen front, with* arcaded gallery *above pointed arches is* Lombardic Romanesque.

S. Tomaso in Lemine, Alemno San Bartolomeo *(11thC), Bergamo. This pilgrimage church is an impressive two-story, circular structure topped by a* cupola *and* lantern. *Within, the gallery has an arcade with particularly fine* capitals.

Battistero Neoniano, Ravenna *The octagonal plan and marble retaining wall date from* c. 400. *The top of the outer walls is* articulated *by* pilaster strips *and finished by a* corbel-table frieze. *The interior has arched bays with mosaic decoration.*

S. Ambrogio, Milan *(940). The* narthex, *or long arcaded forecourt, was built* c. 1140 *to replace a* Carolingian *forecourt. The arcades are joined to the façade of the abbey church by a wide sweeping gable. The entrance to the narthex is via a handsome* atrium.

Collegiate Church, Castell'Arquato *This beautiful Romanesque church has four* apses, *the largest of which, in the view above, displays an* eaves gallery. *The interior is plain but there are fine capitals.*

S. Giovanni Evangelista, Ravenna *The columns dividing the* aisles *from the nave of this* basilica *have* impost blocks *above the capitals, like truncated, inverted pyramids. The walls of the aisles are articulated by pilaster strips and have unusually generous windows.*

S. Giulio, Lago d'Orta *(rebuilt 9th-12thC). Detail of a lectern, carved in black marble, from the 11th-C pulpit of this island basilica. The pulpit is supported on elegant pillars, two wreathed in decorated strips, with classical capitals.*

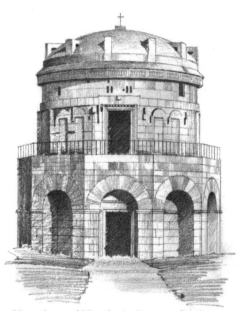

Mausoleum of Theodoric, Ravenna *Similar to the imperial mausoleums of Rome, this is an impressive domed structure which once had a galleried upper story of short, transverse* barrel vaults *carried on a ring of* colonnettes *and* arches. *The dome was made from one block.*

81

Northern Italy

S. Petronia, Bologna (1390-1437) is wholly *Gothic* with a northern European flavor and, unlike many contemporaneous buildings, it made no attempt to move toward the *Renaissance*. The interior is reminiscent of Milan Cathedral with its profusion of decorative details, spiky miniature spires and sculptured *arcading,* but here the similarity ceases as Milan, the largest medieval cathedral next to Seville, was to become part of the new classicism (see p. 192).

Castles & Palaces

There are some fine medieval castles in northern Italy such as **Castello d'Estense, Ferrara** (*c.* 1385), which consists of a rectangular block with corner towers enclosing a courtyard. **Castello di Giorgio, Mantua** (1395), is similar. **Sirmione Castle** (1290-1310), which included a fortified port, was built to control traffic on Lake Garda. **Castello Visconteo, Pavia** (*c.* 1360-1365), exemplifies the transformation from castle to palace. It has spacious private apartments surrounding the *cloisters,* with corner towers and a deep moat as sole defense.

Venetian palaces were clearly designed for comfort. The best examples are **Palazzo Loredan** (13thC), **Palazzo da Mosto** (13thC) and **Palazzo Falier** (13thC). Many of the Gothic palaces are characterized by elaborate *traceried* openings as at the palazzi **Foscari** (15thC), **Pisani** (15thC), **Cavalli** (15thC) and **Contarini-Fasan** (14thC), which has alternating Istrian stone *quoins* and richly carved cable-molding on its façade.

Civic & Public buildings

Civic architecture was on a particularly grand scale in Venice. The **Doge's Palace** (12thC), the seat of government, was part of a monumental town planning scheme carried out over several centuries. The palace, with its arcades of pointed arches, carved *capitals* and horizontal lines of open tracery, is the epitome of Venetian Gothic. Civic buildings of note outside Venice are the **Broletto, Como** (1215); the **Broletto, Monza** (13thC); **Palazzo Pubblico, Cremona** (1206-45), and the **Palazzo Pubblico, Piacenza** (1280).

A product of medieval life in Italy was the communal tower which served both as belltower and watchtower. A good example is the **Torre del Commune, Verona** (1172). It is a square-planned tower of striped stone and brickwork with a belfry crowned by an octagonal *lantern.* Other towers of interest are the **Campanile of St Mark's, Venice** (10thC), which was rebuilt after it collapsed in 1902, and the **Torrazzo, Cremona** (1261-84), the tallest in Italy at 400 ft.

Commercial & Industrial buildings

Many of the palaces in Venice were merchants' places of business. In addition the **Fondaco dei Turchi** (*c.* 1225) — the emporium of the Turkish merchants — has a *Byzantine* arcade and *loggia* flanked by towers. It was rebuilt in the 19th century. The **Loggia dei Mercanti** (1382-84) has projecting *tribune* and forked battlements which are characteristic of northern Italy.

S. Foscara, Torcello *(c. 1000). Planned as a Greek cross-octagon, the building originally had a dome, but this collapsed. The classical Byzantine church structure was modified to accommodate Western Liturgical traditions by the introduction of short open aisles in place of the more usual closed forechoirs.*

S. Petronia, Bologna *Perhaps the greatest of the few Italian churches that are wholly* Gothic *in spirit. Designed to eclipse the cathedral at Florence, it would have been one of the largest churches in Italy but the eastern section was never built. The main façade was left unfinished.*

S. Apollinare in Classe, Ravenna *(532-49). This single-aisled basilica has a 9th-C crypt below the raised eastern apse, an impressive nave with Byzantine column shafts, marble veneers and capitals, and one of the earliest circular belltowers in Ravenna.*

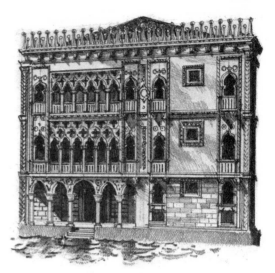

Doge's Palace, Venice *Begun in the 9thC and extensively enlarged in the 13th and 14thC, the building was completed in the* Renaissance. *The façades, built 1309-1424, have open* arcades *on the first and second stories. The third story was rebuilt in the 16thC.*

Palazzo Ca d'Oro, Venice *(1422-40). Gothic at its best in Venice designed by the architects of the Doge's Palace. The arcaded entrance has two further arcaded stories above, decorated with characterisitc* tracery *and elegant projecting balconies. The façade was once gilded.*

Broletto, Como *The town hall is one of the very few Romanesque civic buildings in Italy. The elegant façade, raised above an open, arcaded ground floor, is built in alternate courses of black and white marble.*

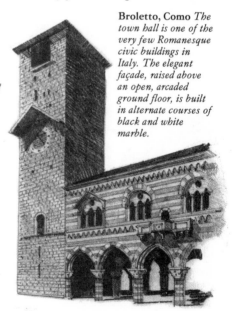

Palazzo del Commune, *or* **della Ragione, Verona** *(c. 1193). The* Romanesque *courtyard was given a monumental Gothic external staircase in 1446-50, but with the exception of a tower, the Torre delle Carceri, the main façade was rebuilt in the 19thC.*

Ponte di Castel Vecchio, *or* **Scaligero, Verona** *(1335). A beautiful fortified bridge, with ornate forked battlements along its length and defensive towers on either bank. The bridge, first built on Roman remains, was destroyed during World War II and has since been rebuilt.*

Central Italy

Religious buildings

Religious architecture of the period in central Italy is either of the *Romanesque* or a continuation of the classical tradition of Ancient Rome. **Siena Cathedral** (*c.* 1225), with its semicircular *arcades* and arches that traverse the *nave,* is a good example. The building is cruciform in plan with an irregular hexagon at the crossing of nave and *transepts* covered by a dome and *lantern.* The whole stands on a stepped platform and has a magnificent west façade in white, red and green marble. The clean simplicity of outline is classical, the detail Romanesque. A characteristic of Italian Romanesque as a whole is the concentration of ornamental detail on the façades. The *portal* of **S. Maria Maggiore, Tuscania** (12thC), is beautifully sculptured, while the façade of **S. Pietro, Tuscania** (11th-12thC), teems with grotesque monsters, reptiles and birds. The latter has a *rose window* which has been restored.

Italian *Gothic* was more of a transition between Romanesque and *Renaissance* classicism than a developed branch of the style. The Italian concern for balance and harmony shunned the dynamic verticals of northern European Gothic and restricted itself to a show of Gothic motifs. **Orvieto Cathedral** (1290-1330) has a façade which is as strictly geometrical as that at Siena, but the *gables,* rose windows and *finials* are unmistakably Gothic. The miniature church of **S. Maria della Spina, Pisa** (1323), built on the banks of the Arno, is equally contradictory. Its shrine-like façade has a full compliment of Gothic decoration including *crocketed* gables and pinnacled canopies, and yet in spirit it is still not quite Gothic. **S. Croce, Florence** (1294-1442), has a Gothic interior, with widely spaced columns and timber roof, but a classically proportioned western façade. But one of the best examples of Gothic as a transitional style is seen in the contrast between the Romanesque and Gothic interior and the Renaissance façade of **S. Maria Novella, Florence** (1278-1350 and 1456-70, see p.203). The church was designed as a huge Latin cross. The *clerestory* of the nave is pierced with circular windows.

In the year following the overwhelming victory of the Pisan navy over the Saracens of Sicily, the Pisan Republic began its grandest building venture by laying the foundations of **Pisa Cathedral** (1063-1118 and 1261-72). This, together with the **Baptistery** (1153-1265) and the **Campanile** or **Leaning Tower** (1174-1271), formed one of the finest examples of grouped cathedral buildings in the world. The Romanesque Cathedral is the major example of the Pisan style. Its façade is made up of tiered arcades with a row of seven large arches at ground level. The plan is cruciform with far-spreading transepts, making the arms of the church only about 65 ft shorter than the body. The Campanile has a circular plan and has seven stories crowned by a bell chamber. Conspicuous and original features of these buildings are their marble paneling, arcading and *colonnades.* The use of such marble paneling and arcading, freestanding or applied, became a characteristic of the Pisan school in the 12th and 13th centuries.

Siena Cathedral
View of one of the aisles *showing the dividing* colonnade *of banded black and white marble columns, and pointed* vaulting. *The spatial quality of Italian churches is remarkable, and is usually determined by a central* cupola *over the crossing.*

Orvieto Cathedral *The Cathedral has a basilican plan of nave, aisles and projecting semicircular chapels. To this was added the striking façade of triple porch and triple gable and, rather like Siena Cathedral, it was finished in striped marble and alabaster.*

S. Maria Maggiore, Tuscania *The façade of this standard basilica was built of local stone, but marble was used for the ornamental features such as the pilasters and carvings on the doorway and the arcading above.*

S. Maria Novella, Florence *Part of a great Dominican monastery, the church was planned as a huge Latin cross with chapels. The Romanesque cloisters are called the "Chiostro Verde" because of the green of their frescoes.*

S. Michele, Lucca *(1143-14thC). The glory of this church is its magnificent façade. The four arcaded galleries above the entrance are decorated with geometric patterns of colored marble inlay, and fantastic animals.*

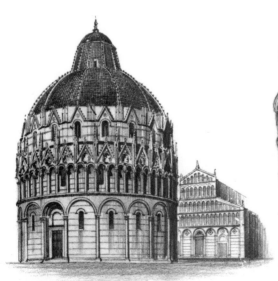

Baptistery, Pisa *This building, circular in plan, has a vaulted interior while the exterior is articulated by engaged columns on the ground story which includes four portals. The Gothic dome was added in the 14thC.*

Cathedral *and* **Campanile, Pisa** *The Cathedral, above, is a basilica in plan. The exterior, with its shallow wall arcading, is finished in bands of red and white marble. The Campanile, left, has a celebrated lean due to soil subsidence. Six stories of decorative marble arcading rise above a tall ground story of half-columns.*

Central Italy

A classical tradition was always very strong in Tuscany. One of the most remarkable examples of this tradition is the *basilica* of **S. Miniato al Monte, Florence** (1018-62), with its façade of colored marble set in geometric patterns in the central *gable* end and above a decorative *arcade*. The proportions and geometry of this façade greatly influenced the façade of the **Badia Fiesolana, Fiésole** (*c.* 1090), with its fine inlaid marble work. Both churches clearly anticipate the new classicism of the *Renaissance*.

Lucca has a beautiful series of churches. The earliest is **S. Frediano** (1112-47), a basilica with double *aisles* and a tower with arcaded openings. The **Cathedral** (1196-1204) is also basilican in plan but the interior was rebuilt in the 14th and 15th centuries in a *Gothic* style. The façade of **S. Michele** (1143-14thC) has oriental designs.

S. Maria di Portonova, Ancona (1034), is the church of a once rich Benedictine abbey. Its structure is a variation of the typical *Byzantine* cruciform domed church, having single aisles in the *nave* and double aisles at the *crossing*. The crossing itself is lighted from above, through the central *cupola*. **S. Maria di Collemaggio, L'Aquila** (1287), has a beautiful red and white patterned façade with classical *cornices* and a *rose window* above the sculptured, central *portal*. Other interesting churches in the north of central Italy are **S. Eugenia, Spoleto** (10thC), which has a high *vaulted* nave with a spacious gallery above the aisles, and the **Church of the Pieve, Pienza** (12thc), a Romanesque church.

The dramatic cathedral building group at **Florence**, consisting of the **Cathedral** (1296-1462) itself, the **Campanile** (1334-59) and the **Baptistery** (11thC), is very different in spirit from the group at Pisa. The Cathedral does have the vertical massing of northern European Gothic but the colored marble paneling, the small, *traceried* windows, the absence of *buttresses* and pinnacles and the horizontality of the applied geometry are distinctly Italian. The dome, which heralds the Renaissance, was added by Filippo Brunelleschi between 1420 and 1434.

Churches of the mendicant orders were often built as an expression of saintly poverty. A characteristic is a long nave without *transepts*. In Umbria, a famous example is the basilica of **S. Francesco, Assisi** (1228-53). It has two stories consisting of an upper and lower church. The basilica is part of a complex that includes the monastic building that partially overhangs the valley to the north on arched supports.

Castles & Palaces

Most typical of the medieval strongholds in central Italy is the **Castle, Volterra** (1343), with its round corner towers and *machicolations*. The huge circular *keep* at the heart of the fortress, added in 1472, has a *scarped* base. Also of interest is the **Castle, Prato** (1237).

Of palaces, the **Palazzo Papale, Viterbo** (1257-66), is notable with an external stairway leading to the main hall. The fine Gothic *loggia* was added in 1267.

S. Miniato al Monte, Florence *Breaking from the* basilican *tradition the church is divided into three main sections, of which the raised eastern portion has a* crypt *which is open to the* nave.

Lucca Cathedral *While the interior of the Cathedral is* Gothic, *the façade is Pisan Roman-esque with a spacious narthex built in 1204. The Cathedral became a place of pilgrimage from the 11thC through its possession of the "Volto Santo" crucifix.*

Pieve di S. Maria Assunta e S. Donata, Arezzo *(c. 1210). The effect of the superimposition of graded arcades on this church façade is surprisingly classical, a distinct departure from the articulation by way of gable and polychromy as seen in the façades of Pisa and Lucca.*

S. Pietro, Tuscania *(11th-12thC).* *The* rose window, *left, and flanking paired windows of this church show Spanish influence. It is a three-aisled, wooden-roofed basilica with a marvelous façade which is an amalgam of styles from Burgundy, Tuscany and Lombardy.*

Baptistery, Florence *A face of the octagonal Baptistery. Originally a 5th-C church, it was converted to a* baptistery *in the 11thC. The faces are in three stages of dark green and white marble, the whole crowned by a low roof and lantern. The famous bronze doors were added in the 14th and 15thC.*

Campanile, Florence *The belltower has four principal stages with a belfry, crowned by an arched corbel-table at the top. The structure is embellished with panels of colored marble, sculptured friezes and inlay. It was begun by Giotto di Bondone and finished by Nicola Pisano.*

S. Francesco, Assisi (1228-53)
The church of this great pilgrimage center has a two-story *nave* making an upper and lower church, both *vaulted,* without *aisles* and each terminated by the polygonal *apse.* The apse, in turn, marks the west end of the Great Cloister (1470).

The south front

The Great Cloister

Cathedral of S. Ruffino, Assisi *(1144). The fine* gable *façade has round-headed doors and windows,* pilaster strips, *molded panels and carvings of grotesque animals. It is the three splendid rose windows that make the façade so distinctive. The central one is supported by three carved angels.*

Central Italy

Civic & Public buildings

Lofty watchtowers and fortified façades which were often crowned with *machicolations* and battlements are typical features of the civic architecture of medieval central Italian towns. The civic buildings they adorn are *Romanesque* in their solidity but *Renaissance* in proportion and in complete contrast to the civic buildings of northern Europe which were, to a greater or lesser extent, adapted from ecclesiastical architecture. The **Palazzo Pubblico, Montepulciano** (14thC), is a fine example. It is symmetrical in design, resembling a Renaissance palazzo but has a tall central tower. The **Palazzo dei Priori, Volterra** (1208-57), is four stories in height with heavy-looking battlements and a further square tower rising up from the front wall, capped with a belfry. The **Palazzo Pubblico, Siena** (1289-1309), has an asymmetrically positioned tower, the **Torre del Mangia** (1338-48). At its base is the **Capella di Pianza** (1352-76), an open *loggia* with round arches, beautifully decorated with arabesques. Other notable civic buildings are the **Palazzo del Podestà**, or **Bargello, Florence** (1255), the **Palazzo Vecchio, Florence** (1298-1314), and the **Palazzo del Municipu, Perugia** (1293-97).

In many towns to the north of central Italy, a notable architectural feature is the covered *portico* that forms a loggia, usually dominating one side of a square. The **Loggia dei Lanzi**, or **della Signoria, Florence** (1376-81), is a graceful structure with lofty semicircular arches on *compound piers*. It formed part of a scheme intended to embrace the whole Piazza della Signoria. Other examples are the **Bigallo, Florence** (1352-58), a tiny arcaded loggia designed for the display of foundlings in need of the charity of wealthy citizens, and the **Loggia della Mercanzia, Siena** (1471), designed by Sano di Matteo.

Tall, bleak, square-planned towers were built in great numbers for private defense in the cities of central and northern Italy. Florence originally had 150 and the towers of Lucca rose like a forest. Families rivaled one another in the height of their tower. At **San Gimignano** the **Palazzo Communale** (1228-1323) has a tower nearly 174 ft high which carries a mark beyond which no private tower was allowed to rise.

Ponte Vecchio, Florence *(1345). The building bridge, or pont-maison, often with houses five stories high on it, was a feature of medieval cities. The Ponte Vecchio is of Roman origin but was given its present form by Taddeo Gaddi. Today it is lined with shops.*

Palazzo Pubblico, Siena *The lower floors of this austere but graceful building are of stone and the upper ones of brick. The central section alone rises to four stories. The elegant arcade along the street frontage is characteristic of the city.*

Palazzo Vecchio, Florence *A handsome, rectangular fortress-like palace, the stone façade is* rusticated *and has elegant windows. The 13th-C tower rises up, off center from the battlements and machicolations of the front wall.*

San Gimignano *12th- and 13th-C towers such as these, usually square in plan, undecorated and with few openings, were built both for private defense and as places of refuge in case of fire among the predominantly wooden buildings of cities.*

Rome

Religious buildings

Fourth-century Rome saw a classical revival in churches. The major buildings of early Christian Rome are **S. Paolo fuori le Mura** (386-9thC, rebuilt 19thC), which has column shafts built from Roman spoils with classical *capitals,* and **S. Maria Maggiore** (432-40) with its wide *nave* flanked by two *aisles* in classical proportion. **S. Costanza** (*c.* 350) was originally the mausoleum of Constantine's daughter and only later converted into a church. Sixteen huge *clerestory* windows flood the central, domed nave with light. **S. Stefano Rotondo** (*c.* 468), one of the oldest and largest of the circular churches in Rome, recalls much of its classical spirit.

Less luxurious but equally important are parish churches such as **S. Clemente** (*c.* 380). St. Clement's House was originally used by the early Christians of the city as a meeting place and a sanctuary. The simple oratory was later replaced by a *basilica* which was enlarged in the 8th and 9th centuries. A new church was erected in 1108 using fragments of the old building which had been destroyed by the Normans. Another fine example is **S. Sabina** (422-32) which served as the prototype for the developing standard Roman basilica. It is elegant and lavishly decorated inside.

In Rome the *Romanesque* period was one of decline. The most original work consisted of additions to existing buildings such as the brick *campanile* (12thC) added to **S. Georgio in Velabro** (6thC). Rome has 36 of these fine 12th- and 13th-century towers. Good examples are found at **S. Maria, Trastevere** (1148), and **SS. Giovanni e Paolo** (1206). The campanile of **S. Maria in Cosmedin** (*c.* 1200) has seven stories of *arcading,* the *impost* line carried as a *string course* around the tower.

The few examples of large scale Romanesque architecture in Rome are the *cloisters* (*c.* 1200) of S. Paolo fuori le Mura, and the cloisters (*c.* 1227) of **S. Giovanni in Laterano,** but despite the originality of the work the enduring classical tradition of the city gave churches of the period a basilican character. Indeed, classicism was so pervasive that **S. Maria sopra Minerva** (13thC) is the only *Gothic* church in Rome, and this has a *Renaissance* façade.

S. Paolo fuori le Mura *View of the* cloisters *(1198-1214), the best preserved in Rome. By this time figure sculpture was of less importance than mosaic and stone* intarsia. *The alternating inlaid and plain pairs of twisted pillars, the* coffered *arches and moldings set an architectural precedent.*

S. Maria in Cosmedin *The church was built during the 6thC on the ruins of a temple dedicated to Hercules. Enlarged in the 8thC, the church was given over to Greeks who settled in Rome after the Iconoclastic Revolt in the 8th and 9thC.*

S. Clemente *View of the* choir. *This interior is the only one in Rome that preserves something of the atmosphere of an early Christian bas-*ilica. *The nave is divided from the choir by 16 columns. Fine 12th-C mosaics decorate the* apse.

S. Sabina *View from the rear showing the* apse *and the* clerestory *down the length of the* nave. *Although it includes features of earlier buildings, in plan and projection the church shows the typical Roman basilica of the 5thC. The height of the nave is accentuated by its length and narrowness.*

Southern Italy

Religious buildings

Medieval southern Italy, particularly Sicily, was influenced by many diverse architectural styles from sources both far afield, such as the Aegean and Western Europe, and the Saracenic cultures closer at hand. The plan of **Palermo Cathedral** (1170-85) has both the dominant *nave* of Latin churches and a *Byzantine* configuration about the altar space. The classical pillars of the nave rise into pointed Arabic arches, and above these the magnificent ceiling is decorated with squares and stalactitic coves, a product of Muslim influence. Palermo Cathedral itself influenced a number of buildings, particularly **S. Spirito, Palermo** (*c.* 1179), with its decorative interior inlay work, and **Monreale Cathedral** (1174-82). The latter has a twin-towered *Norman* façade, a characteristic feature of Sicily since the 11th century, and a Sicilian style *choir articulated* externally with *blind arcading* and enriched with *polychrome* work. The interior, as at Palermo, is a blend of *basilica*-like main *aisle* with Byzantine altar space, separated by elegant columns. The Cathedral has an outstanding collection of 12th-century mosaics. A Benedictine monastery was once affiliated to the Cathedral, but only the vast 12th-century *cloisters* survive. Their beautiful rows of twin *colonnettes,* with *shafts* either inlaid with strips of mosaic or carved, show Norman art in Sicily at its best. At each corner there is a cluster of four columns sculpted in classical proportions. In the southwest corner there is a single column which forms a fountain.

    S. Cataldo, Palermo (12thC), is a *vaulted,* cruciform church which has Byzantine features with Apulian domes. The *squinch* arrangements between the domes and the bays the domes cover are of Islamic-Egyptian influence and a feature of Sicily. Oriental architectural details are apparent at **S. Giovanni degli Erimiti, Palermo** (12thC), although the church, with its two small domes over the nave and a tower over one of the three *apses,* is typical of Norman churches in Sicily. This church too has notable cloisters, with white marble pillars in pairs, each capped with carved leaf decoration. One side of the church has a wall from an older structure, possibly a mosque.

    In southern Italy, a similar amalgam of selected styles can be seen at **S. Cataldo, Táranto** (1071). It has a basilican plan, with a circular, Byzantine *drum* at the *crossing* decorated with blind arcading supported on slim half-columns. The church of **S. Leonardo, Siponto** (11thC), Fóggia province, has arcading and apses which are clearly Tuscan, and two hexagonal domes which are Aegean in influence. The *portal* is an amalgam of Apulian *Romanesque* and Byzantine decorative work.

    Stilo was the chief Basilian center in Calabria and the **Cattolica** (11thC) there is a delightful Byzantine structure. A more important Basilian monastery church is, however, **SS. Pietro e Paolo, Forza d'Agrò** (*c.* 1116), on the banks of the Fiumara d'Agrò. It has an imposing Norman structure, but there is a strong Byzantine feel evoked by the dome over the nave. A pair of partly ruined spires rise from the west side.

SS. Pietro e Paolo, Forza d'Agrò
This former Basilian monastery church was built of brick and lava and has fine polychrome decoration. The interior is lofty with stalactitic vaulting, a towering apsed chancel and a dome over the nave.

S. Cataldo, Táranto
Detail of a capital decorated with carved birds pecking among foliage, purely Byzantine in spirit. The interior is basilican in form, but with raised transepts. The nave is separated from the aisles by marble columns supporting round arches.

S. Leonardo, Siponto *A detail of the magnificent portal of the abbey church which shows a remarkable blend of Apulian-Romanesque form and Byzantine decoration. The Byzantine motifs and carvings in the door jambs are memorable.*

Monreale Cathedral
One of the richly decorated apses of this monumental building. The arcading and inlay work patterning the towering walls from ground to eaves are characteristic of the area.

Cattolica, Stilo *A provincial Byzantine structure, the roughly-hewn appearance of the construction is contrasted with the warm, reddish-brown of the brick and stonework, and the brickwork patterns of the* cupolas.

Ravello Cathedral *(1137). This beautiful marble and mosaic pulpit is the most remark-able feature of the Cathedral. Finished in 1272, it is an example of the final, most flamboyant phase of Romanesque sculpture in Apulia. The lions at the base are a feature found in other churches in southern Italy.*

Fóggia Cathedral *(1171). This section of 14th-C arcading with relief sculpture above one of the portals is of Pisan influence. The* crypt *and the lower external sections of the original Cathedral walls are Norman. The remainder of the building is a* Baroque *reconstruction undertaken after an earthquake in 1731.*

Tróia Cathedral *(12th-13thC) Detail of the massive doors (1119) of the Cathedral by Oderisio da Benevento, which were among the first bronze doors to be cast in Italy. The panel decoration across the face of the door showing serpents and beasts is Byzantine.*

S. Cataldo, Palermo *The large,* blind *windows which decorate the austere, cube-like exterior are a characteristic of Norman castle architec-ture in Palermo. The top edges of the walls of the building are crowned by a band of fine Arabic filigree work.*

Southern Italy

When the use of images was banned in the Eastern Church in 726, over 50,000 priests, monks and laymen of the Orthodox Church fled to southern Italy where they could pursue the monastic rule initiated by St Basil in *c.* 360. There were close on a hundred monasteries established in Calabria alone, spreading the influence of *Byzantine* art westward. To the north of southern Italy the chief Byzantine center was **Rossano.** Of particular interest near there is the monastery church of **S. Maria del Patir** (*c.* 1100), which has been restored. The church is *basilican* in form with a notable entrance *portal* that was added in the 15th century. The rest of this Basilian monastery is in a state of ruin.

With the end of Byzantine rule in southern Italy, the new stability of *Norman* control produced fine buildings such as **S. Nicola, Bari** (1081-1196), a prototype of Apulian-*Romanesque,* which was planned as a pilgrimage church. It has three portals in the main façade, the central one with its columns carried on the backs of lions. The *ashlar* masonry is particularly handsome. Also of interest in Bari are **S. Marco** (12thC), which was built by Venetian merchants, and **S. Gregorio** (11thC), a simple cube shape with *apses* on three sides and the main façade with the entrance portal on the other.

S. Margherita, Biscéglie (12thC), is one of the best preserved of smaller Romanesque churches, comprising an *aisleless nave* finished with an apse. Biscéglie, a small market town, also has a **Cathedral** (1073) with a lovely 13th-century façade which has a richly carved central doorway and Romanesque *corbel-table* and windows.

Bari Cathedral (1170) was built in place of an earlier Byzantine structure. It is basilican in plan with shallow *transepts*, the whole surmounted by an octagonal *drum,* a common Aegean feature. The Cathedrals at **Barletta** (*c.* 1156), Bitonto (see p.94) and the 12th-century examples at Ruvo di Púglia (see p.94) and **Bitetto** are similar. However, Barletta Cathedral has a chancel which is largely *Gothic.* Its nave has huge arches interspersed by pointed *vaulting.*

Otranto Cathedral (1080) has a beautifully simple façade with a fine 15th-century *rose window.* The *crypt* has fluted and carved columns with sculpted *capitals.* Much of the stonework was taken from Byzantine and ancient classical buildings and re-used.

S. Sabino, Canosa di Púglia (11thC), is predominantly Byzantine in style as it belongs to early Apulian-Romanesque building which was free of the northern Norman influences which were later to affect the Byzantine model. One of the most unusual of Apulian-Romanesque cathedrals is that at **Molfetta** (1150) which has twin eastern towers and three polygonal drums capped with pyramidal roofs at different levels which cover the *cupolas.* The interlaced *blind arcading* of the east end is Saracenic, while the projecting lion supports and columns of the central window are *Lombardic.*

The magnificent **Cathedral, Caserta Vecchia** (1113-53), has the typical Lombardic massing of high nave and lower aisles. The fine west façade has corbel-tables and a *gable articulated* by blind arcades of interwoven arches in the Sicilian manner. The *lantern* is an amalgam of Norman-Sicilian and Byzantine features.

Such Apulian and Calabrian church architecture spread to many provinces of the Byzantine Empire, along sea routes, so churches reminiscent of southern Italy in plan and form are found in Cyprus, Crete and parts of Turkey.

Otranto Cathedral
Detail showing one of the particularly fine sculptured capitals *that surmount the 14 columns separating* nave *and* aisles. *The church is built in the form of a* basilica.

SS. Trinita di Delia, Castelvetrano *(12thC). At the center of this cross-vaulted, cubic church is a cupola resting on four columns. Such a construction is typical of the Arab Byzantine architectural combination. The building was restored in the late 19thC.*

S. Giovanni degli Eremeti, Palermo *(12thC). Austerely plain inside and out, the church and* campanile *are crowned by reddish* cupolas. *While characteristic of Islamic architecture in Sicily, cupolas were a feature of Apulia from the 11thC.*

Matera Cathedral *(13thC). A fine example of late* Romanesque *architecture in Apulia, with a characteristic* Lombardic *construction of high nave with arched* corbel-table *flanked by lower aisles. Carved animals support many of the columns, particularly in doorways and windows.*

S. Sabina, Bari *(1170), above. The arched corbel-tables on the exterior of the nave, with carvings of grotesque animals at the joints of the arches, are Lombardic characteristics. The frieze above is a Byzantine feature.*

Erice Cathedral *(14thC). The Cathedral has a basilican plan with three aisles in the nave. The porch on the west side was built in 1426. The detached* campanile *was originally built as an Aragonese look-out tower. Its battlements and windows are typically late* Gothic.

S. Benedetto, Brindisi *(1080). This beautiful church has simple, small-scale cloisters surrounded by a portico with a low parapet. The slim, tapered columns have flat crutch capitals, some with carved Byzantine motifs.*

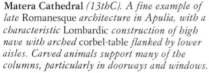

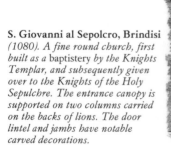

S. Giovanni al Sepolcro, Brindisi *(1080). A fine round church, first built as a baptistery by the Knights Templar, and subsequently given over to the Knights of the Holy Sepulchre. The entrance canopy is supported on two columns carried on the backs of lions. The door lintel and jambs have notable carved decorations.*

S. Nicola, Bari *Detail of a carved capital in the crypt. The basilica, with its wide transepts, nave, aisles and round apses, was the first of the great Norman churches to be built in Apulia and was a Romanesque prototype.*

Southern Italy

The most characteristically *Romanesque* religious building in Sicily is **Cefalù Cathedral** (1131), with its *Norman* structure of *basilican nave* with high *transepts* and *apsed* east end. The main façade (*c.* 1240) is flanked by two massive towers and enriched by a double row of arches on small columns and preceded by a 15th-century *narthex*. The fine interior has 16 columns flanking the *nave* with a mixture of *Byzantine* and ancient Roman *capitals*. Fine 12th-century Byzantine mosaics decorate the apse and the east end of the *presbytery*. **Bitonto Cathedral** (1175-1200) is an example of Apulian-Romanesque at its most accomplished. Heavy *pilasters* on the façade mark the nave from the side *aisles*. These pilasters are capped by a *cornice* checkered design, and the pattern is repeated above the arches of the *corbel-tables*. There is a magnificent *rose window* in the *gable* and the central doorway is edged in *Lombardic*, Saracenic and Byzantine carvings. Two slim columns supported on *consoles* flank the doorway. The interior is admirable with fine capitals on the pillars and pilasters. The cathedral of **S. Maria, Siponto** (11thC), Foggia province, was built over an earlier church which now forms the *crypt*. Many of the Byzantine and *Corinthian* capitals were taken from older buildings. Externally, the church is *articulated* by Pisan *blind arcading* with rounded arches supported on columns with richly ornamented capitals, while the square plan with a central *cupola* is eastern. The blind arcading of the exterior is repeated within the church.

The **Sanctuary of the Archangel St. Michael, Monte Sant'Angelo** (12thC), has a fine Romanesque doorway and beautiful Byzantine bronze doors made in Constantinople. The Sanctuary

S. Maria del Patir, Cosenza province *(11thC). Basilican in plan, the nave and aisles are terminated by semicircular apses, each enriched with blind arcading. Below many of the arches there are remains of a circular decorative motif. There are portions of very early pavement inside the church.*

Cathedral, Casserta Vecchia *(12thC), above. Detail of a carved lion in the entrance archway. Lions are characteristic elements of Roman-esque art, particularly in Italy. They are often found support-ing columns flanking porches and doorways.*

Cathedral, Ruvo di Púglia *Detail from the main portal framed in bands of carved Byzantine, Saracenic and classical motifs, surmounted by an archivolt spring-ing from two sphinxes. These are carried by columns which stand on lions and crouching human figures.*

S. Maria Maggiore, Monte Sant'Angelo, *left. The façade and its portal added in 1198. The doorway is decorated with bands of Byzantine and Saracenic decoration with Romanesque animals and figures. A fine lunette shows the Madonna and Child.*

became an obligatory stopping point on the way to the Holy Land at the time of the Crusades. There is a 13th-century belltower with octagonal plan. Monte Sant'Angelo has two other fine churches, **S. Maria Maggiore** (*c.* 1170) with its Pisan style façade of blind arcading and *lozenges,* and **S. Pietro** (12thC), which has a notable rose window.

Under Byzantine and, later, Norman rule, **Trani** was one of the most important harbors on the Adriatic coast. The **Cathedral** (1098-13thC), though reminiscent of S. Nicola, Bari, has a very individual appearance with a handsome façade decorated with blind arcades and bays and an imposing transept with carved *archivolt.* The nave is basilican. A similar basilican plan can be seen at the **Cathedral, Ruvo di Púglia** (*c.* 1237), a late Romanesque building with an unusual plain grey stone façade. This austere building material dramatizes the elaborate rose window, three doorways outlined with blind arcading, and the arched corbel-table. Such fine masonry detail is characteristic of Apulian churches.

The architectural interest of Apulia has much to do with the many small churches in the large towns. In **Matera**, for example, there are **S. Giovanni Battista,** with its beautiful Romanesque *portal* (1204), and **S. Pietro Monte Errone** (8thC), which has traces of Byzantine *frescoes,* as does **S. Maria de Idris**, the tiny church standing opposite. Standing in a courtyard beside Matera Cathedral is **S. Maria di Constantinopoli,** a Romanesque church with a fine doorway and 13th-century *lunette.* In **Andria, S. Agostino** (1230) was founded by the Teutonic Knights. The *Gothic* portal has remarkable jambs and arch formed by decorated bands of stone carved in shallow relief, producing a layered effect.

Bitonto Cathedral *Detail of relief work on the staircase of the pulpit (1229), probably depicting the three Magi before Herod. The background ornamentation is Islamic. The high narrow pulpit was made from fragments of an earlier tabernacle and high altar.*

Trani Cathedral
The Cathedral has a marvelous west façade with a central portal with bronze doors approached by a double stairway. The bold west tower engages the corner of the façade and has a stiking, lofty arch through its ground-level story.

Cefalù Cathedral *Detail of the Byzantine mosaics in the choir depicting saints, apostles and angels with a figure of the Virgin in prayer below Christ. The choir, together with the vaulted transepts, are the finest sections of the cathedral.*

Siponto Cathedral *The block-like massing of this building is Oriental. The façades are enriched by Pisan arcading which is repeated internally. The Lombardic portal has a deep archivolt which is carried on free-standing columns supported by lions carved in stone.*

Southern Italy

Castles & Palaces

In 1061 the Normans seized Sicily from the Moslems and began building a series of great monasteries, palaces and castles. The **Castle, Adrano** (*c.* 1100), is a Norman *keep* in the Western European style. Gradually, however, Norman court architecture in Sicily was influenced by the established, more sophisticated Muslim palaces, in particular the Fatimide castles of Egypt which became models for the four palaces of **Palermo**: di Favara, Menani, La Zisa and La Cuba. The **Palazzo di Favara** (997-1019) was built by the Emir Giafer and later converted by the Norman kings. Remains include a chapel and some *vaulted* chambers. **La Zisa** (*c.* 1166) is a massive building with flanking turrets. **La Cuba** (*c.* 1180) was built in imitation of it. The **Menani** (11thC) is a converted Saracenic palace. They were all built of poros, the rough local limestone. Externally these huge buildings were decorated with Muslim *arcading* and pattern work, and their interiors were rich in marble and mosaic designs.

The **Palazzo Reale**, or **dei Normanni, Palermo** (12thC), built by the Norman kings, was composed of several tower keeps. The Pisan tower has particularly fine mosaic decoration which is an amalgam of *Byzantine* and Muslim art. The **Castello Maniace, Syracuse** (*c.* 1232), is an impressive ruin, a 165 ft by 165 ft square-planned keep with cylindrical corner towers.

Many fortified towers were built in the region of Mount Etna starting in the late 11th century. A good example is at **Paterno** (14thC). Other examples in Catania are the **Motta d'Affermo, Motta Camastra** and the **Motta S. Anastasia**.

At **Lucera**, Frederick II settled a Muslim army and allowed them to build their own mosques. He built an enormous square-planned fortified **Palace** (1224-46) at one corner of the city. Its remains stand on a huge splayed base, 165 ft by 165 ft and this was encircled by *galleries* for archers.

Frederick's finest construction was the unique **Castel del Monte, Bari province** (1240), which had neither architectural precedent nor later imitators. Built on an octagonal plan with octagonal corner towers, the building anticipates the *Renaissance* with regular diagonal courses in the stonework, a Roman feature, and *egg-and-dart* patterning and moldings on the *consoles* off the main entrance. The **Castle, Bari** (1233-40), is another of Frederick's great castles. It was built on the foundations of a *Norman* and Byzantine fortress. The **Castel Ursino, Catania** (*c.* 1239), was also built by Frederick and partly destroyed by the lava flow from Mt Etna in 1669.

There are many fine palaces in the area. **Taormina** has several, characterized by limestone ornamentation with black and white oramentation with lava inlay. Of particular interest are the **Palazzo Corvaia** (14thC), **Palazzo Ciampoli** (1412) and the **Palazzo del Duca di S. Stefano** (12thC). The **Palazzo Arcivescovile, Palermo** (15thC), has windows with fine *tracery* work, while the **Palazzo Rufolo, Ravello** (11thC), has a galleried inner courtyard revealing a mixture of Norman and Saracenic ornamentation.

La Zisa, Palermo *Begun by William I, the palace consists of a tall, rectangular keep with great hall, joined at one side to a chapel by a long passage. The heart of the building is a small fountain-room.*

Palazzo del Duca di S. Stefano, Taormina *One of several stone-built palaces in the ancient city, all of which are characterized by pointed Gothic double windows. The larger windows have trefoiled heads.*

Palazzo Reale, Palermo *The Pisan Tower (1160-70) at the northern corner of the Royal Palace. Originally there were several tower-like blocks with two surrounding courtyards, as well as the Palatine Chapel.*

Castle, Paterno, *right. This three-story fortified tower has a chapel on the ground floor with an armory and living room above. The top story is lighted by wide Gothic windows.*

La Cuba, Palermo *One of the many castles built in the century following the* Norman *conquest of Sicily. The castle is surrounded on three sides by a lake. The structure is Norman but the decorative details show Islamic influence.*

Castel del Monte Bari province *Built by the Emperor Frederick II as a castle, palace and hunting lodge. The entrance gateway is an elegant blend of classical and Gothic influences and was once decorated in colored marble.*

Fortifications, Lucera *One of the two round towers which were added to the strategically important corner positions of the fortifications in the 13thC. The* scarped *platform was designed to protect the base of the tower from attackers.*

Castello Maniace, Syracuse *The castle consisted of a series of square rooms, geometrically arranged within the overall plan. The two* consoles *on either side of the imposing Gothic doorway originally bore bronze rams.*

Northern France

Religious buildings

The characteristic geometry of Cistercian architecture was rectangular, with *apse* or other curve in plan rarely intruding. **Bonport Abbey, Eure** (*c.* 1250), has a fine refectory; **Ourscamps Abbey, Aisne** (*c.* 1230), a magnificent infirmary built like a church with typical Cistercian windows, *vaulting* and *capitals,* and **Vauclerc Abbey, Aisne** (*c.* 1200), a *dorter* 230 ft long.

Typical of the Benedictine Order of the early Middle Ages was the traditional *basilican* plan of an *aisled* church with a triple apse and twin western towers, usually with another tower rising over the crossing of *nave* and *transepts*. The **Abbey, Jumièges** (*c.* 1065), is a fine example, with its giant western towers supporting the *gable* end of the nave. Also of interest are the **Abbaye-aux-Hommes** (1068-1115), begun by William the Conqueror, and the **Abbaye-aux-Dames** (1062-1110), both in **Caen.**

Amiens Cathedral (1220-88) is the largest *Gothic* Cathedral in France. The statuary over the porches was influential all over Europe. The interior is particularly spacious. The plan, typically French, has its volumes carefully organized around a central-axis with only slightly projecting *transepts* and a sweeping *chevet* of seven chapels. At **Laon Cathedral** (1160-1225) the magnificent central tower, and the open, airy design of the western towers, were extraordinarily influential throughout early Gothic architecture. The west front is *articulated* as two huge stories, the lower for the porches, the upper as a frame for a great *rose*

window. Before Laon, 12th-century façades were divided into vertical sections in *Norman* fashion. Other major churches in the area are **Noyon Cathedral** (*c.* 1145-1228), with its four-story nave; **Bayeux Cathedral** (13th-15thC), which has *Romanesque arcades* incorporated in the 13th-century nave; **Rouen Cathedral** (1202-30); **Senlis Cathedral** (1155-84), the southwest tower of which is the most elegant of all Gothic towers; the **Church of St Pierre** (1516), now a market-place, and the typically austere Cistercian church of **Le Val Abbey, Meriel** (*c.* 1200), in Seine-et-Oise.

Beauvais Cathedral (1247-1568) would have been the largest Gothic cathedral in Europe, but the plans were never fulfilled. The transepts and *choir* have the loftiest vaults in Europe, 158 ft high, the height of a 15-story office block. Such daring technological feats were beyond medieval expertise and twice the roof collapsed (1247 and 1284). There was also a spire over the *crossing* 495 ft high, the height of a 50-story office block, but this also collapsed (1573). Also of interest is **St Etienne, Beauvais** (12th-16thC), with a fine rose window in the north transept.

The **Abbey, Mont-St-Michel,** built on a huge rock in the bay between Avranches and St Malo, was the only stronghold to withstand the armies of Henry V when the rest of Normandy was overrun. From early times a place of pilgrimage, the Benedictines built a *Carolingian* church there in the 10th century and a Romanesque basilica in the 11th-12th centuries.

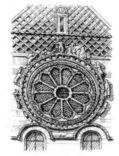

St Etienne, Beauvais *This example of a* rose window *set in the north* transept *depicts a Wheel of Fortune. It is one of the few sculptural innovations made in Augustinian church architecture.*

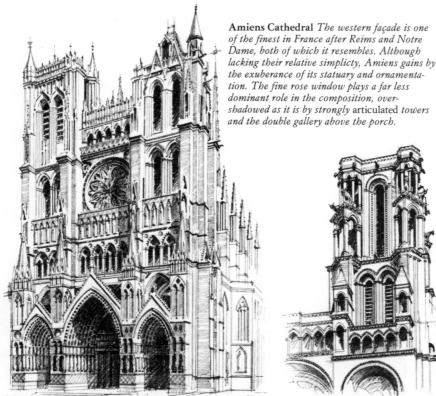

Amiens Cathedral *The western façade is one of the finest in France after Reims and Notre Dame, both of which it resembles. Although lacking their relative simplicty, Amiens gains by the exuberance of its statuary and ornamentation. The fine rose window plays a far less dominant role in the composition, overshadowed as it is by strongly* articulated *towers and the double gallery above the porch.*

Laon Cathedral *A feature peculiar to Laon Cathedral is the two-story turrets built diagonally into the corners of the towers. They frame the tall windows of the belfries, their lower story being rectangular in shape, the upper polygonal. Such mobility of volumes is extraordinarily baroque.*

Rouen Cathedral *View of the interior from the* ambulatory *of the* choir. *The cathedral has a double-story nave* arcade *and three fine towers. The south tower and part of the west front (1509-14) are masterpieces of late* Gothic *architecture.*

Coutances Cathedral *(1218-91). View along the nave, partially lit from the beautiful octagonal* lantern *centered over the crossing. Outside, the elongated openings and windows in towers and transepts are characteristic of the area.*

Evreux Cathedral *(1119-1531), above. This view into the* apse *shows how* compound piers *were chosen (round piers are more usual), matching those in the* nave. *The* triforium *has become a tier of windows, with* tracery *and glass playing a more dominant architectural role than does the masonry.*

Chapter-house, Fontaine-Guérard Abbey *(13thC), Eure. Although most* chapter-houses *had one portal, this one has three. The aisles are divided by small columns with* crocketed capitals. *Unusually, there is no change in floor level between the* cloisters *and the* chapter-house.

Chapelle des Templiers, Laon *(12thC), below. This octagonal church stands behind Laon Cathedral. The plan and design modestly echo the Dome of the Rock, Jerusalem. The porch and apsed chancel were added later.*

Church, Nouvion-le-Vineux *(12thC), Aisne. This village church has an extremely elegant and well preserved* Romanesque *tower. Each story is strongly articulated and the window surrounds are beautifully crafted.*

Northern France

Castles & Palaces

The earliest stone *donjons* were divided into three or four stories, lit by arrow slits on the lower floors and by small windows above. Later, a larger, fortified building, the castle, was added and this became the quarters of the lord or military governor. Additional defensive features, such as *machicolations,* were subsequently introduced. The peak of castle development was reached with the great fortress of **Gaillard Castle, Les Andelys** (*c.* 1196), now in ruins. The **Castle, Vitré** (14th-15thC), is one of the finest fortresses in Brittany, guarded by a sturdy *redoubt* flanked by two large, machicolated towers. **Fougères Castle, Ille-et-Vilaine** (12thC), is an outstanding medieval fortress, with 13 towers and some of the most massive walls in Europe. The **Castle, Josselin** (1490-1505), is half fortress, half palace and has numerous turrets on its particularly high walls.

Domestic buildings

By the late 15th century the future lay with the house rather than the castle. While some châteaux still had towers at the angles, such forms were largely symbols of wealth and importance rather than defensive in purpose. A fine example is the **Château, St Germain-de-Livet** (15th-16thC), Calvados, a delightful house surrounded by an ornamental moat. The main entrance gate has stone and brick decorations. Other examples include the **Hôtel de Bourgtheroulde** (*c.* 1475) and the **Château de Châteaudun** (1441).

Civic & Public buildings

There were few civic buildings in France to rival those of Flanders and Italy. Of particular interest, however, is the **Hôtel de Ville, Compiègne** (15thC), with elegant central tower, *mullioned* windows and corner turrets, and the **Hôtel de Ville, Arras** (1510), a large hall with *traceried* windows raised above an *arcade,* with a great belfry to one side.

Abbey church, Mont-St-Michel *(1022-1135), Manche, right. View of the* Romanesque nave, *showing a typical three-story* articulation *of the walls, with* triforium *and* clerestory *above. The* choir, *rebuilt 1456-1521 in the* Flamboyant *style, is surrounded by* aisles *and chapels.*

Cistercian Abbey, Royaumont *(c. 1250), Oise, left. The refectory of the abbey is an imposing, vaulted chamber. Cistercian austerity was largely kept for their churches, while their monastic buildings were invariably spacious and rather more elaborate.*

Village church, Bury *(12thC), Oise, right. Detail of a sculptured* capital. *In the 12thC the decoration of village churches was plain but by the late 13thC local craftsmen began to imitate the figure-sculpture of the great churches.*

Château de Martainville, Calvados *(1485), below. An elegant building, this has* mullioned windows *and sculptured* dormers, *with a handsome* oriel *projecting over the main entrance. Three of the corner towers have windows, the fourth being purely defensive.*

Abbey, Ourscamps *(c. 1230), Aisne. Cistercian infirmaries were particularly fine buildings. Most had their own chapel and great hall. The smaller row of windows at ground level has wooden shutters for ventilation.*

Château-Gaillard, Les Andelys
(c. 1196). Remains of the great fortress, built by Richard I of England to defend Rouen, then an English possession, against the French. The castle had a rectangular donjon, *protected by three lines of* outworks *and many almond-shaped towers.*

Château, Carrouges *(16thC).*
Many large houses had castle features, including moat, drawbridge, donjon and machicolations. *This château has an entrance pavilion instead of a gateway, a feature first introduced at the Castle at Martainville some 70 years earlier.*

Normandy farmhouse, Corbon
(16thC). A typical timber-framed farmhouse built of narrow studs *on a stone plinth, with panels of wattle and daub. The chimney has checkered stone and brick decoration on the stack.*

Duchess Anne's House, Morlaix
(15thC). The practice of building town houses with jettied *upper floors dates from the 14thC. Each projection increased the floor area so this construction was much used in crowded cities.*

Renan's House, Tréguier *(16thC).*
In storied houses, studding was necessary to support the wall plates and the infilling. Characteristic of this area of France are the diagonal timber braces.

Palace of Justice, Rouen *(1499-1500). Although largely rebuilt, it is nonetheless an impressive example of late* Gothic *architecture and has a finely sculptured turret. A shift from Gothic to* Renaissance *design is evident in the decorative detail.*

101

Northeast France

Religious buildings

The outstanding early *Romanesque* church in the area is the **Priory Church, Vignery** (*c.* 1050), a barn-like building with a windowless *apse.* There is an open gallery above the arches of the *nave* which casts light upon the walls. The nave and *aisles* and *choir* are all roofed with timber. Another outstanding Romanesque church is the **Cathedral, Langres** (12thC), a magnificent building with a great nave inspired by that at Cluny. Details hark back to the *Classical* style of Rome and include *Corinthian capitals* with traditional acanthus leaf moldings.

One of the smaller but most elegant of French *Gothic* cathedrals is that at **Soissons** (1180-1225). The *arcade, gallery, triforium* and *clerestory* are early Gothic, the remainder late Gothic. The major medieval building in the area is the **Cathedral, Rheims** (1211-90). It was the first to utilize window *tracery,* which was later to become a considerable feature of cathedral architecture. The west façade is lavishly detailed, with dominating porches and a beautiful *rose window,* 40 ft in diameter and flanked by high traceried openings.

One of the most memorable façades in northeast France is the west front of the **Cathedral, Strasbourg** (1230-1365). The apse, *crossing* and north *transept* are late Romanesque. Everything else, including the south transept and cliff-like west façade, is Gothic. The sculpture, influenced by that at Chartres, is exceptional, most notably the "Angels Pillar." The spire, completed in 1439, is 466 ft high and was the highest surviving structure in the world until those of the late 19th century in Chicago. The **Cathedral, Châlons-sur-Marne** (12th-14thC), has Romanesque towers between a 13th-century choir and a 14th-century transept, while the **Cathedral, Troyes** (1208-1429), has five aisles, a 13th-century choir and *chevet* and a 14th-century transept and nave.

Civic & Public buildings

The unifying symbol of a town was not its town hall but its principal belfry. Such belfries might be situated in the tower of a fortified church, over a gate within the town walls or in a tower over one of the gates, an example of the last being the **Dolder, Riquewihr** (1291), Haut-Rhin.

Dolder, Riquewihr *Haut-Rhin. A small town gate, this is a mixture of church tower and* donjon. *Four timber floors project in a series of* jetties *over the central arch. The roof is capped by a turreted belfry.*

Cathedral, Strasbourg *The west front, begun in 1277, has a recessed* portal, *richly carved with an elaborate* gable *of fretwork, surmounted by pencil-sharp pinnacles. The magnificent* rose window *was completed in 1291. Despite its complexity, it is a unified façade.*

Cathedral, Soissons *View of the three-story* nave *and* choir *and the tall windows in the* clerestory. *The choir has plain* lancet windows *in a semicircle. The south* transept *has clustered columns, narrow pointed arches and* shafts *supporting the* vaulting ribs.

Cathedral, Rheims *Detail of the vaulting in the* ambulatory. *The combination of both ribbed vault and pointed arch made it possible to cover irregular shaped bays. The* chevet, *with its ring of five chapels, influenced that of Westminster Abbey.*

Saint-Leger, Guebwiller *(12thC), Haut-Rhin. The west front is a particularly fine example of* Romanesque *architecture. Of note are the* Lombardic blind arcading, corbel table frieze *and the* pilasters.

Market Hall, Colmar *(c. 1480), Haut-Rhin. The hall has a* traceried *parapet,* mullioned *windows and high, steep roof with* dormer windows. *Diagonal tile patterning gives the roof individuality.*

Church, Chaource, *Aube. Entombment group panel, sculpted c. 1515. The medieval mystery plays had a great influence on 15th- and 16th-C religious inconography, of which this panel is an outstanding example.*

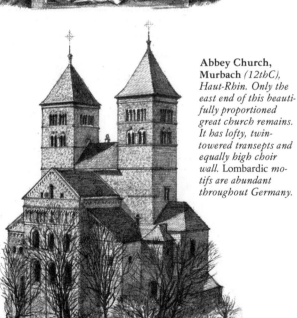

Abbey Church, Murbach *(12thC), Haut-Rhin. Only the east end of this beautifully proportioned great church remains. It has lofty, twin-towered transepts and equally high choir wall. Lombardic motifs are abundant throughout Germany.*

Porte des Allemands, Metz *(13thC). The gate, with its flanking turreted towers, was built over the River Seille and derives its name from the Knights of the Teutonic Order. Metz did not pass into French possession until 1552.*

Paris

Religious buildings

The major *Romanesque* building in Paris is the **Abbey of St Denis** (*c.* 1136-44), built by Abbé Suger to replace an earlier church. It is one of the few buildings in this style in the Ile-de-France. *Narthex, porch* and *apse* survive. There are also considerable Romanesque remains in the church of **St Germain-des-Prés** (11th-12thC).

Notre Dame was begun in 1163, the *choir* was completed in 1182 and the west front and twin towers between 1200 and 1250. It is the last of a group of early *Gothic* cathedrals to have galleries above the inner *aisles,* an example set by the Abbey of St Denis. The façade, the finest in France, was widely copied.

Most castle chapels of the early Middle Ages were as simple architecturally as were the fortifications themselves. They were usually on two floors, one for the master and his family, the other for retainers. The real development of castle chapels in France, however, dates from the reign of Saint Louis (Louis IX, r. 1226-70), particularly with the building of his private royal chapel in Paris, **Sainte Chapelle** (*c.* 1249), designed to house a relic from the Crown of Thorns. The architect, Pierre de Montreuil, one of the greatest of the 13th century, also built the **Refectory** (13thC), a remarkable *vaulted* hall in the priory of **St Martin-des-Champs** (12thC).

Domestic buildings

In the 13th century the Romanesque plan of ground floor *arcade,* multi-windowed *solarium* and *attic* was continued. The **Hôtel de Vaului-sant, Provins** (13thC), is a typical example.

In 15th-century Paris many houses had sculptured stair turrets, and often turrets were supported on *corbels* over the street to give extra house room. Of particular interest are the **Hôtel de Sens** (1475-1519), with turrets on corbels at the corners, and the late Gothic **Hôtel de Cluny** (1485-98), which has a first floor chapel with a fine *oriel window.*

Notre Dame *View of the exterior of the south transept. The transepts did not originally project beyond the outer aisles but* c. *1250-60 they were enlarged and two magnificent façades built in immitation of those at the Abbey of St Denis.*

Church, Arthies *(11thC), Val d'Oise, above. Detail of a decorated capital. Most village churches of the period were of great simplicity, and artistic expression took the form of sculpture, which often had little relation to the building.*

Franciscan Nunnery, Provins *(15thC). Franciscan houses are noted for their handsome cloisters, which are usually low pitched and with a multiplicity of columns (here alternately slender and thick) to support the rafters.*

Templar's Church, Rampillon *(c. 1240), Seine-et-Marne. The most striking feature of the churches of the Templars is the sculptured portals. The tympanum of the main door here shows Christ as a judge, with a magnificent series of apostles raised above a lesser arcade.*

Sainte Chapelle *View of the* apse, *situated in the upper floor, which served as the shrine for the Crown of Thorns, brought to Paris in 1239 by Saint Louis, and as an oratory for the king. The lower floor was reserved for retainers.*

Burgundy & Loire

Religious buildings

From the beginning of the Middle Ages the Benedictine houses which enshrined the remains of a saint became places of pilgrimage. The greatest of these churches were built between the 9th and 11th centuries and while lesser churches could not afford to rival them they nonetheless often copied one or more of their characteristic features. The Benedictine **Abbey of Fleurey** (*c.* 1607) followed the plan of the pilgrim churches in its *ambulatory* and adjoining *chapels*. Both these features and double *aisles* were adopted at the **Abbey of Cluny** (*c.* 1088). This was the largest and most sumptuous church of the period. It was also possibly the most influential, both in architectural and ecclesiastical terms. Its abbots advised kings and popes and it had more than 1400 foundations throughout Christian Europe, 10,000 monks living under its rule. The church interior was 580 ft in length, little short of that of St Peter's, Rome. The *nave* had 10 bays; in addition there were two *transepts,* five aisles and four great towers. It was much desecrated in later years, particularly during the Revolution, and little remains today. The **Abbey of Fontevrault** (*c.* 1119) has a long, spacious nave of four bays, which is aisleless and wider than the *crossing,* a characteristic feature of the Loire region. The four domes which cover the nave were rebuilt in 1910. All that remains of the original abbey buildings is the kitchen, built in the form of an octagonal tower, with a stone spire roof pierced by numerous chimneys.

Beautiful stonework is typical of the Loire area, often with decorative panel moldings or patterns of shaped *facing* stone. The **Church, Saint-Généroux** (*c.* 950), is a good example. Another interesting example is the **Church, St Aignan** (*c.* 1100), Loire-et-Cher, which is of large *basilican* plan with *apse,* ambulatory and adjoining chapels. The **Abbey Church, Pontigny** (*c.* 1150), Yonne, set in a vast field, has the provincial air of a handsome farm building. The church has short transepts, an angular east end, a generously proportioned nave and narrow side aisles. It is lit by a lofty *clerestory,* propped up by concealed *flying buttresses.*

Church, St Aignan *Detail of a decorated* capital. *There was a great revival of manuscript illumination in 11th-C France and the work of the scribe often served as a model for the sculptor. A recurring feature was initials decorated with twining foliage.*

Abbey Church, Pontigny *An elegant, uncomplicated building, it is constructed on the repetitive bay plan, so characteristic of Cistercian architecture. The façade is enhanced with lines of simple Gothic arcading.*

Abbey of Fontevrault, *right. View of the* ambulatory, *which has three adjoining chapels. It is a fine Romanesque church with four squat domes over the nave and with a well-lighted choir, which has unusually tall and slender columns.*

Church, Autrèche *(10thC), Loire-et-Cher, left. Churches of modest size with a nave and chancel type of structure and wooden roof are typical of the period. Walls were usually white, with ashlar blocks for the junctions. The buttresses of this church are uncommon in that they are semicylindrical.*

Burgundy & Loire

The most influential book on the architecture of the Middle Ages was the "Commentary of Beatus on the Apocalypse" (*c.* 780), particularly with its elaborate double page illustrations. Examples of where this influence may be seen include the Benedictine priories of **Saint-Julien-de-Jonzy, Saône-et-Loire** (*c.* 1160), **Montceau-l'Etoile, Saône-et-Loire** (*c.* 1115), and the **Abbey of Vézelay** (12thC), which has a particularly fine *portal.* Other examples showing Beatus's influence include the priories of **Saint-Bénigne, Dijon** (*c.* 1130), and **Perrecey-les-Forges** (*c.* 1120).

Bourges Cathedral (1195-1515) is famous for the arrangement of *nave* and double side *aisles,* similar to Notre Dame, Paris, but surmounted with *vaulted* galleries. The rounded *apse* is of archaic design and there is no *transept.* The west front is remarkable for its vastness of scale.

The **Cathedral, Chartres** (1194-1260), is the finest example of a cathedral which, instead of having galleries over the aisles, has tall windows in the *clerestory* and high vaults in the aisles. Such features later became the hallmark of high *Gothic.* Even by French standards, the Cathedral is outstanding for its abundance of exquisite 13th-century stained glass and for the many sculpted figures which adorn the doorways of the west front and elsewhere. The **Cathedral, Tours** (13th-16thC), is notable for its west façade, which is a magnificent example of the late Gothic *Flamboyant* style. The **Cathedral, Sens** (*c.* 1130), is the first of the Gothic cathedrals and has a finely proportioned west front. Unlike contemporaneous cathedrals, it does not have galleries above the aisles. The **Cathedral, Le Mans** (*c.* 1158), has an austere nave and an enormous *choir,* built in about 1217. The *Romanesque* **Cathedral, Autun** (*c.* 1132), is noted for its pointed arches and *blind triforium,* a device which was copied from the cathedral at Cluny.

Decorative sculpture, however, is the outstanding feature of Romanesque art in Burgundy. Notable examples include the "Eve of Autun," now in the Musée Polin, Autun. Autun Cathedral derived its importance and much of its wealth from being a place of pilgrimage. It has a nave covered with a pointed *barrel vault,* three apses at the east end and richly sculptured portals at the west front. The **Basilica, Paray-le-Monial** (11th-C), differs from other Clunaic examples in having a short nave. **Saint Andoche, Saulieu** (1115-1120), is notable for its magnificent carved Romanesque *capitals.*

The two-story elevation of the Benedictine **Priory, Anzy-le-Duc** (11thC), Saône-et-Loire, is thought to have been the model for the **Abbey, Charlieu** (11thC), and for the Abbey of Vézelay. The choir at Vézelay is exceptionally elegant, with *shafted colonette piers, water-leaf crockets* and a double-columned triforium. Another fine 12th-century building is the **Priory, La Charité-sur-Loire** (*c.* 1110), Nièvre. The church of **St Martin, Chablis** (1160), has a six-bayed nave with clerestory and two side aisles. It is one of the outstanding examples of early Gothic architecture to be found in France.

Parish Church, Bussy-le-Grand *(12thC). In small churches such as this, sculpture, expecially of* capitals, *was the work of local craftsmen and was usually unaffected by the prevailing styles of the larger, city churches.*

Bourges Cathedral *This great* Gothic *cathedral still retains its late* Romanesque *side doors, of which the south door, above, is by far the best preserved. The* choir *was completed in 1218 and the* nave *in 1260.*

Priory of Montceau-l'Etoile, *Saône-et-Loire. The tympanum of the west door. A section of the "Beatus Commentary" illustrating the Second Coming of Christ was the model for this carving of the Ascension. A copy of the book was included in most of the great monastic libraries in France.*

Abbey, Cluny *(1088-1120). The south* transept *is the only substantial part of the great church still standing. Three churches were built on this site. This, the third, was at once the largest Romanesque church, the largest French church and the largest abbey ever built.*

Cathedral, Angers *(1149-1274).*
The cathedral has an unusually tall west front with slender lateral towers and is a powerful example of late 12th- and early 13th-C architecture. The central tower, with cupola *and* lantern, *is* Renaissance *(c.1540). The long nave is aisleless.*

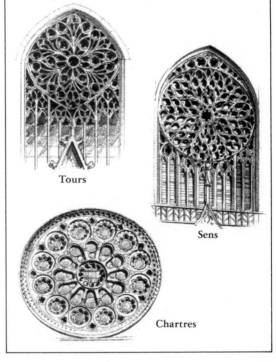

Abbey, Fontenay *(c. 1147), Saône-et-Loire. The Forge, above, was built in the early 13thC and was used as a smithy and metalwork shop. The Cistercians built many farm buildings, often masterpieces of wooden construction. Stone buildings such as this forge have a size unrivaled save by the monumental tithe barns of medieval England.*

Priory Church, Perrecy-les-Forges
Many of the church carvings of the period, such as the warrior angel on the corner of this capital, are examples of the profound influence exerted on church sculpture by the great third abbey church at Cluny.

Rose Windows

A characteristic of *Gothic* architecture is a circular or "wheel" window, filled with concentric or radiating *tracery*. The outstanding example is the rose window of the cathedral at Chartres. The flamboyant, late Gothic style incorporated rose windows within a wall of glass, as in Sens Cathedral. Another example is the window of the west façade of Tours Cathedral.

Tours

Sens

Chartres

Benedictine Abbey, Saint-Aubin
(12thC), Maine-et-Loire. The entrance to the chapter-house *is richly sculltured and the arch is painted with scenes depicting the story of the Magi. Most early Romanesque cloisters were built of wood, but often with stone arcades leading to the chapter-house.*

Burgundy & Loire

Castles & Palaces

When Henry II of England married Eleanor of Aquitaine in 1152 he acquired the wide regions of Aquitaine and Poitou in southwestern France as part of her dowry. He traveled ceaselessly through his domains and built numerous castles, both for administrative as well as military use. The most ambitious is the **Castle, Chinon** (12thC), which consisted of three castles on the spur of the River Vienne, each protected by a deep moat. Fort St-Georges is now demolished but to the west of it are the two other connecting castles — the Château du Milieu and the Château du Coudray, the latter having powerful towers on its walls. A later building, the **Château de Frazé, Eure-et-Loire** (1486), is quadrilateral in plan, with massive corner towers, *machicolations* and a strongly fortified entrance gate.

Domestic buildings

The **Hôtel Jacques Coeur, Bourges** (1443), is the most perfect example of a rich man's mansion in the 15th century. At a time when fortified mansions were still usual, this house was designed more for comfort than defense. The courtyard plan and fine sculptured turret of the **Maison des Echevins, Bourges** (15thC), follows the example set at the Hôtel Jacques Coeur, but on a much more modest scale.

Civic & Public buildings

Because of the feudal system, few town halls were built in medieval France. Of those that were, however, the **Hôtel de Ville, Bourges** (15thC), which was built in the *Flamboyant* style, and the **Hôtel de Ville, Dreux** (1502-37), are particularly well-preserved examples.

Saint-Philibert, Tournus *(c. 950). View of the two-story chapel, set between flanking towers. It is a largely* Romanesque *building, consisting of a nave with side aisles, a* crossing *with a massive tower (1120), and a* transept.

Maison des Echevins, Bourges *(1489-91). This finely sculptured turret shows the 15th-C practice of building town houses on a modest scale while keeping the plan and appearance of earlier and far grander mansions in the country.*

Château de Frazé, Eure-de-Loire *The entrance gate. While civil war remained endemic, large houses, as here, were fortified with drawbridge,* portcullis, machicolations *and battlements. The only refinement here is the addition of three* mullioned *windows.*

Château de Sully, Sully-sur-Loire *(14thC). The main building of the moated castle is a square stronghold with four corner turrets. The second floor is covered with an exceptionally fine keel-shaped roof, built of chestnut c. 1363.*

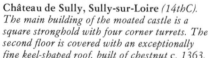

Houses, Place de la Poissonnerie *(14thC), Chartres. Many houses in towns and cities during the Middle Ages were built with over-*hang *upper floors as a means of providing extra floor space in congested areas. This, however, made the streets dank and dark and by the end of the 15thC many authorities prohibited them.*

Castle, Angers *(c. 1232). View of five of the 17 drum towers of the castle, which was an ad-vance post of the French kings on the border of Brittany. The striped pattern made with black shale bonded with limestone was probably inspired by the early 5th-C land walls of Con-stantinople, knowledge of which was brought back to western Europe by Crusaders.*

Castle, Chinon *(12thC). The for-tress consists of three strongholds, separated by deep moats. The Tour du Moulin, right, guards the western point of the Château du Coudray, one of the strongholds. The circular tower rises from an octagonal story which sits on a square base.*

Hôtel Jacques Coeur, Bourges *One of the three polygonal staircase turrets. Although primarily a domestic dwelling, it nevertheless had forti-fied features, such as defensible walls and a strongly built hexagonal* keep. *The mansion is built around a court.*

Medieval Street Corner, Arnay-le-Duc *(16thC). In many stone-built towns the influence of castle build-ing was strong, as with this corner turret on* corbels. *Other characteris-tic features are sculptured doorways to the plainer houses or stair turrets on houses without a courtyard.*

Southeast France

Religious buildings

Early monasteries were little more complex than farm buildings and remained plain even when later rebuilt in stone. Some abbey churches, however, such as **Montmajour, Bouches-du-Rhône** (11thC), with one of the finest *cloisters* of medieval Provence, are renowned for their *trefoil apses.* Many of these austere churches were without *aisles.* The **Abbey of Thoronet, Var** (12thC), is a Cistercian house in the purest Provençal *Romanesque,* built in a wooded, well-watered spot. It has impressive double-arched cloisters. The **Abbey Church, Cruas** (11th-12thC), is of particular interest for its *crypt,* lying beneath the *choir* and *transept,* with remarkably bold sculptured *capitals.* The tower over crossing of *nave* and transepts is also of particular note, rising up from a square base to an octagonal intermediate stage, then up to two circular stages.

The decorative simplicity of early Benedictine abbeys was dramatically changed during the 11th century. Both internally and externally, the early abbeys had few, if any, embellishments. Gradually apses were encrusted with sculptured *arcades* and *friezes,* while façades were covered with elaborate carvings or fronted with elegant *portals,* as at the **Abbey of Saint-Gilles, Gard** (1140). An interesting example of a medieval Benedictine abbey is that of **Saint Hilaire** (14thC), which has a wooden roofed cloister with coupled columns. **Saint Trophime, Arles** (12thC), is a masterpiece of Provençal late Romanesque, with fine sculptured *piers* and coupled columns in the cloister. The aisles are relatively narrow, matching the narrow nave, with *quadripartite vaults.*

Cloisters, where the monks read and, in some Orders, were permitted to speak, linked monastic buildings with the abbey church. The quadrangle concept was probably an influence from the East.

The **Cathedral, Maguelone** (*c.* 1030), in Hérault, is a fortified Romanesque church, where the Pope sought refuge in the 12th century. **Saint-Just, Narbonne** (1272), designed to be the city's cathedral, remained unfinished, with only the choir, two towers and the fortress-like entrance hall completed. The fortification of village churches, where they were the only place of refuge, became common during the Hundred Years War (1337-1453) between England and France.

The *Mozarabic* architectural style, prevalent in the south on both sides of the Pyrenees, was superseded by the *Lombardic* Catalan style, with characteristic vaults and *pilaster strips.* **St Martin-du-Canigou, Pyrénées-Orientales** (*c.* 1001-20), is a handsome example. Standing on a spur of the Canigou mountain, it was built on two levels. It has a magnificent *nave,* covered by three long *barrel vaults* and lighted at the *gable* ends only. Another imposing building is **Sainte-Eulalie, Elne** (11th-12thC). The nave has a semicircular banded barrel vault, carried on piers. The aisles have bays of quadripartite vaults, while externally shallow arcading decorates their walls. The **Augustinian Church, Serrabone** (12thC), Pyrénées-Orientales, has a porch decorated with elaborately carved animals.

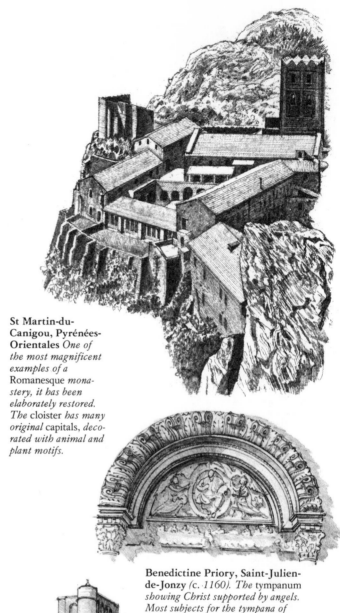

St Martin-du-Canigou, Pyrénées-Orientales *One of the most magnificent examples of a* Romanesque *monastery, it has been elaborately restored. The* cloister *has many original* capitals, *decorated with animal and plant motifs.*

Benedictine Priory, Saint-Julien-de-Jonzy *(c. 1160). The* tympanum *showing Christ supported by angels. Most subjects for the tympana of Benedictine churches were inspired by the finely illustrated pages of the "Beatus Manuscript."*

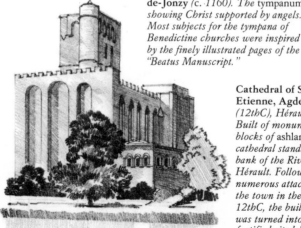

Cathedral of Sainte-Etienne, Agde *(12thC), Hérault. Built of monumental blocks of* ashlar, *the cathedral stands on a bank of the River Hérault. Following numerous attacks on the town in the 12thC, the building was turned into a fortified citadel.*

Castle Chapel, Simiane *(12thC), Vaucluse. The fine polygonal interior is of particular interest for the spiral structure of each of the 12 compartments of the vault. The chapel is a round, fortified building, intended to house a prince's tomb.*

Church of Sainte-Eulalie, Elne
Attached to the church is this fine cloister, a characteristic example of such structures in the southeast of France. Each of the superbly carved capitals illustrates a scene from the Old or New Testament.

Abbey, Saint-Gilles *The façade of the abbey church is one of the finest examples of Romanesque art in southern France. The richness and diversity of the sculptural ornamentation comes from the great number of medieval workshops which were employed on this project.*

Church, Thines *(12thC), Ardèche. A simple, granite church, it consists of an aisleless nave and an apse. The arcading and banding of the apse are features derived from northern Italy. Another decorative feature is the use of colored stone.*

Church, Montmajour Abbey *Situated on a medieval pilgrimage route, the church was founded in the 6thC and has a spacious crypt with a central rotunda, an ambulatory and radiating chapels. The fortified tower on the left is 14thC.*

111

Southeast France

St Nazaire Cathedral, Carcassonne (*c.* 1096), has a *nave* and *crypt* that were part of the former *Romanesque* cathedral, the graceful *choir* and *transept* being later rebuilt in the *Gothic* style of the Ile-de-France. The **Abbey of St Maximin, Bouches du Rhône** (13thC), is not the usual Dominican church of the characteristic two-*naved* plan that has the more general two *aisles*. There is a fine polygonal *apse* and Gothic nave 59 ft high. **Avignon Cathedral** (*c.* 1140-60) has a generously proportioned nave, covered by a pointed *tunnel vault* with transverse arches. There are no aisles. **Perpignan Cathedral** (14thC) is characteristic of the work of the medieval masons of this city, where rounded pebbles from the river were alternated with courses of red brick.

Castles & Palaces

In the 11th century many bishops had private residencies. These were mostly built within the fortifications of a town and could dispense with *keep,* turrets, moat and *ramparts.* Many had beautiful chapels, usually on two floors. The **Palace of the Popes, Avignon** (14thC), is a particularly grandiose example. Continually enlarged and enriched, it is one of the greatest Gothic secular buildings in France.

Civic & Public buildings

The *bastides* of southern France were uniformly planned. The walls and gates, church and market hall, were erected by the owner of the land, while the tenants were responsible for the building of their own houses, each of which was laid out on a rectangular plan. Older towns were fortified, often on a grand scale, as at **Carcassonne.** There the defenses, dating back to the 5th century, were strengthened with double walls, *barbicans* and 50 towers. Of particular note is the **Porte Narbonnaise,** built to protect the most vulnerable part of the city. In some cases fortifications were leveled and completely rebuilt, as at **Avignon** (1349-1370), where the exiled popes remade the walls on an imposing scale with *corbeled machicolations.* With the development of artillery in the 15th century, however, such defenses lost their military importance and were gradually succeeded by low, squat, massively thick fortresses, such as that at **Antibes** (15thC).

Church, Les-Saintes-Maries-de-la Mer *(1140-80), Bouches du Rhône. A fortress-like church, it has a stone tower built like a donjon and walls strengthened with battlements and machicolations. The roof vault is paved over and made into a terrace, surrounded by battlements. The turret over the sanctuary is backed by a boldly-stepped belfry wall.*

Villeneuve-les-Avignon, Gard *(c. 1300). The most striking architectural feature of French towns of the Middle Ages is their fortified gateways. The flanking towers shown here are part of the great Gate of St André, which dominates the town.*

Palace of the Popes, Avignon *Left, the exterior of the palace, one of the most imposing medieval monuments in western Europe. Outwardly it has the appearance of a grim fortress with its cliff-like walls and projecting towers, more than 148 ft high, but the interior was sumptuously furnished to accommodate the popes who resided there in exile from 1309 until 1376. Above, view of part of the Hall of Audience.*

Tower of Constance, Aigues-Mortes *(1241-50), Gard. The monumental round donjon has two entrances, one to the town, the other to open country, each protected by double doors and* portcullis. *The upper part of the main hall is surrounded by a corridor pierced by small windows, from which enemy penetrating the hall could be fired upon.*

Houses, Pérouges *(15th-16thC), Ain. View of some of the stone-built houses of this small, fortified medieval town. Most of the houses have* ashlar *work for the door and window surrounds. Many fell into decline during the 19thC but were subsequently extensively restored.*

Pont Saint-Benezet, Avignon *(1177-85). The usual method of crossing a river in medieval times was by ferry. Stone bridges were rare and, as here, often had a religious significance, there being a chapel at its midpoint. It was partly destroyed in the 17thC.*

Aigues-Mortes, Gard *(1272-1300). The town was founded by Saint Louis as a starting point for his crusade. A model of medieval military architecture, it has massive walls comparable to those at Carcassonne.*

Palace of Justice, Grenoble *(15thC). The façade of the building, once the seat of the parliament of Dauphiné. The central part consists of the main door and chapel, dating back to the 15thC. Later additions were made during the* Renaissance.

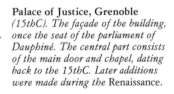

Citadel, Carcassonne *(13thC). Perhaps the most outstanding medieval fortress in France, it has a double ring of walls, battlements, a castle and towers, protected by a moat. It consists of an upper town, or fortress, and a lower town built on the fertile plain.*

Southwest France

Religious buildings

Medieval pilgrims went from shrine to shrine on their routes to Jerusalem, Rome and Santiago de Compostela. Monastic churches were unable to house the great numbers involved and many were radically modified or rebuilt. At **Sainte-Foy, Conques** (1035-1200), the rebuilt church was given an *aisled transept* and an *ambulatory* in order to accommodate processions within the church. The exterior is typical of Benedictine simplicity. Architecturally, however, the church is most remarkable for having a *vaulted nave*. **Saint-Sernin, Toulouse** (*c.* 1077), is another of the great pilgrim churches. It is 341 ft long, with double aisles, five radiating chapels and transept arms. During the 11th century the decorative simplicity of Benedictine abbeys gave way to a profusion of ornamentation. Exterior walls, once plain, were encrusted with *friezes* and sculptured *arcades,* while *portals* were turned into extravagant works of architecture. An example of such modifications is found at the **Abbaye-aux-Dames, Saintes** (1119-34), which has been much altered over the years, particularly in the 12th century when the main arcade was removed so that the nave and aisles became one and changes were made to the *crossing* so that it could carry a tower. The tower is shorter than that of Notre-Dame la Grande in Poitiers but is strikingly similar, standing on a square base with two stages above and flanked by a stair turret.

The **Cathedral, Angoulême** (*c.* 1105-28), has a long, wide nave without aisles, transepts with lateral chapels and a *choir* with four chapels. Stone domes cover the nave, while over the crossing there is a double dome raised on a *drum.* The present church is the fourth to be built on the

site and has itself been redeveloped over the years, most notably by restoration in the 19th century which changed the appearance of the west front. The **Abbey, Fontevrault** (1100-19), is not dissimilar in concept. The **Cathedral, Périgueux** (*c.* 1120-50), an almost exact copy of the plan of St Mark's, Venice, was a product of the *Byzantine* influence carried west along the trade routes by Venetian merchants. **Notre-Dame-la-Grande, Poitiers** (1130-45), has an imposing conical dome and flanking towers to the sculptured west façade. The nave is without direct lighting. It has square *piers* with *engaged columns* and is notable for its lofty arches. The building is *basilican* in plan and is important in being a prototype for *Romanesque* architecture in the area. The **Cathedral, Cahors** (*c.* 1120), is a massive building, as much castle as cathedral, with a cliff-like west façade. It is without aisles and crowned by two domes. The **Cathedral, Albi** (1282-1390), is a fortress-church built of brick and bristling with turret-like pinnacles, large semicylindrical *buttresses* and a bell-tower like a *donjon.* Windows are placed high and the monumental hall is *vaulted* inside. The particularly fine *Flamboyant* decoration of the choir was not added until late in the 15th century.

The **Collegiate Church, Bénévent l'Abbaye** (*c.* 1140), is typical of 12th-century collegiate churches, which exploit local building forms rather than impose a preconceived architectural style. The aisles are pierced by a passage and the nave has a plain vault. The **Church of the Jacobins, Toulouse** (1260-1304), built by the Dominicans, is unusual in having a line of columns down the center making, instead of a nave, two aisles side by side.

Fénioux, Charente-Maritime *(12thC). These "Lanterns of the Dead" are peculiar to the region and are found by many churches, particularly in Poitou. They are hollow columns with a pierced top, within which a light would illuminate the graves at night.*

Sainte-Foy, Conques *Built to house the remains of Saint Foy, this spacious Benedictine church stands on a pilgrimage route to Santiago de Compostela. It was remodeled to accommodate the numerous pilgrims, the traditional* basilican *plan being modified to incorporate* aisles *and additional altars.*

Cathedral, Angoulême *The detail illustrated, from the west façade, shows Christ surrounded by the symbols of the Evangelists. The tiered arcades of the façade are divided by lofty shafts into 5 bays. The church has one of the finest domes of the 12thC.*

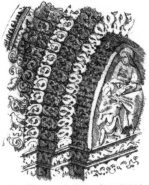

Saint Michel d'Aiguilhe, Le Puy *(11thC),* *Haute-Loire. The church, perched on top of a rock, is reached by a long flight of steps. The façade has the horseshoe arches of Mozarabic art, a style strong in northern Spain and along this section of the pilgrimage route.*

Saint-Pierre, Aulnay *(1119-35).* *Part of the* tympanum *of the* portal. *Considered to be one of the finest* Romanesque *churches of any small French town, with a* cruciform *plan, splendid* piers *and pointed arches, a deep* choir *and extremely handsome sculptural decoration, most especially over the entrance.*

Church, Lichères *(12thC),* *Charente-Maritime. Rural churches such as this, with their extremely rich façades, were often owned by monasteries. They had at first been stark, but from the late 12thC the more elaborate abbey sculpture was adopted for churches within their domain.*

Cathedral, Péri-gueux, *left. The nave which, with its aisles, acts as the entrance to the 12thC Byzantine church. Built in the form of a Greek cross, the arms and crossing are covered by huge domes resting on square piers cut through the arches. Save for mosaics, the church is unusually bare for this region.*

Notre-Dame-la-Grande, Poitiers *The west front, the most richly decorated Romanesque façade in France. In the* gable *Christ is depicted between the symbols of the four Evangelists. The other apostles are seated in the* blind *arcades. Above the portal there are scenes from the Old and New Testaments.*

Church, Saint-Michel d'Entraygues *(c. 1137), Charente. Built by the Augustinians, it is a fine octagonal Roman-esque church with a small* apse *in each side. It was probably used as a resting place for pilgrims on their way to Santiago de Compostela. In the 19thC it was con-siderably restored*

Saint-Pierre, Mozac *(c. 1130), Puy-de-Dôme. Detail of "The Three Marys," one of the many sculptured capitals in this Bene-dictine church. The designs a sculptor worked from came from illuminated manuscripts of his monastic patron.*

Southwest France

The crusading spirit of the late 11th century was symbolized by the Church of the Holy Sepulchre, Jerusalem, the goal of the greatest pilgrimage route in Europe. The *rotunda* and *basilica* plan of the Holy Sepulchre was imitated in both large and small churches. Examples include the Benedictine **Abbey, Charraux** (*c.* 1095), and the Benedictine **Abbey of Saint Pierre, Chauvigny** (1110), in Vienne. Town churches, lacking the endowments of the great abbeys and cathedrals, were invariably much more simple.

Few villages were fortified and, where there was no castle, the church became the place of refuge. Many were fortified, especially during the Hundred Years War (1337-1453), with defensive turrets and battlements. Such churches are found at **Charras, Charente-Maritime**, at **Compreignac** and at **Tarjac, Dordogne**.

Castles & Palaces

The 14th century marks the beginning of the era of luxury in France. Castles took on a domestic as well as defensive role and were built more like town houses, with sumptuous decorations and multiplicity of windows. The finest example is the Duc de Berri's **Palace, Poitiers** (*c.* 1386-95), of which the hall and a tower are all that remain.

Domestic buildings

The **House of Archambaud, Sainte-Antonin** (1120-25), Tarn-et-Garonne, has an attached tower, a typical feature of the town houses of the rich middle classes. It is three stories high and has a piano nobile, or principal floor, with sculptured *pillars* above an *arcaded* lower floor. Towns with a particular tradition of building in stone produced distinctive features, such as the fine 15th-century sculptured doorways at **Montferrand, Puy-de-Dôme**, showing the owners' crest or sign.

Civic & Public buildings

By the 9th century new towns were springing up around abbeys and castles, but it was not until the 13th and 14th centuries that the remarkable towns known as *bastides* were built in southern France, many of them erected by the English. They were uniformly planned and comprised a gridded rectangle with two wide streets crossing at right angles, their junction used as a market-place. The whole was enclosed by a defensive wall with fortified gateways. There are many examples, including those at **Villeneuve-sur-Lot** (*c.* 1253), at **Montauban** (*c.* 1144) and at **Castelsagrat** (*c.* 1270) in Lot-et-Garonne and at **Beaumont** (*c.* 1270) in Dordogne.

Priory of Montier-neuf, Poitiers *(c. 1085). Detail of a carved capital with elephants, inspired by a 10th-C silk in which were wrapped the bones of St Josse. Stone carvers, when departing from the traditional catalog, depended on patrons for choice of model.*

Abbey of Saint-Pierre, Chauvigny *Detail of a capital, depicting the Adoration of the Magi. The inspiration for such scenes is thought to have come from liturgical dramas enacted by the monks.*

Monastery of Saint-Pierre, Moissac *(12thC). The main doorway of the abbey church. Figures of St Paul and St Jeremiah adorn the sides. The doorway and the cloisters are all that remain but they are outstanding examples of early 12th-C Romanesque art.*

Church of Saint-Croix, Bordeaux *(10th-13thC). The 12th-C façade, with its tiered arcading and grand central door, was restored in the 19thC, when wide-eaved roofs were added. The walls of the nave are 10th-C, while the triple bays of the apse and transept chapels are of the early 12thC.*

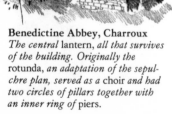

Benedictine Abbey, Charroux *The central lantern, all that survives of the building. Originally the* rotunda, *an adaptation of the sepulchre plan, served as a choir and had two circles of pillars together with an inner ring of piers.*

Castle, Tarascon *(c. 1400). The front of the castle, the only part with windows, stands on the edge of the River Rhône. A postern* gives access to boats. *The flanking towers are of the same height, to enable rapid movement of troops from one to another along the battlements.*

Porte Saint-Jacques, Parthenay *(13thC). Gates were a crucial part of a city's defensive system and were usually behind a moat and had corner towers and* corbeled machicolations. *This is a fine example from the early Middle Ages.*

Château de Cherveux, Deux-Sèvres *(15thC), left. While the fortified entrance is like a* donjon, *the building itself is more a manor than a castle. This transition from defensive buildings to those designed mainly for comfort, often compact in plan and finely proportioned, became possible with peace and stability.*

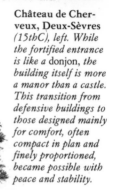

Fortified Mill, Barbaste *(15thC), right. The four square-angled towers dominate the mill bridge and rendered it unassailable. This is one of the few reminders of the everyday feudal life of Medieval France to survive intact.*

Hôtel de Ville, La Réde *(13thC), Gironde. Communal town buildings were usually built above the arcades of a market square or hall, as in this early example.*

Pont Valentré, Cahors *(c. 1308). Often a bridge formed part of a town's defenses and in the 14thC bridges were epecially heavily fortified. This, one of the best preserved of Gothic* fortified bridges, *has six arches and three gate towers.*

117

London

Religious buildings

The most important medieval building in Great Britain is **Westminster Abbey,** founded in 960, enlarged by Edward the Confessor and then entirely rebuilt by Henry III and his successors between 1245 and 1269. It has a magnificent *nave,* an octagonal *chapter-house vaulted* from a central clustered *pier,* and the only complete *chevet* in England. Of particular interest are the chapel and tomb of Henry VII and his queen, the finest example of late *Perpendicular* architecture in England. **Southwark Cathedral** (*c.* 1207) is, in comparison, a simple structure, although it has an imposing 165-ft-high tower in the Perpendicular style over the *crossing.* It was originally the church of the Augustinian Priory of St Mary Overie, and remains of *capitals* and *bases* from the early *cloister* are French in character, as too is the fine example of carved foliage.

The *choir* of Temple Church (*c.* 1185) is a rare example of the *hall church* design and is the supreme English structure of the Knights Templar, built in the circular plan characteristic of their churches. It has one of the earliest instances of marble *shafting,* a French device previously developed at Canterbury. The oldest parish church in London is **St Bartholomew the Great** (*c.* 1123-33), in Smithfield. It was originally the choir of the priory of Augustinian friars and its interior is distinguished by imposing columns and arches in the *Norman* style.

Castles & Palaces

The **Tower of London** (*c.* 1080) was at various times used as a fortress to subjugate London, as a palace for the kings of England and their courtiers and as a prison. The design of the hall and tower is thought to have been inspired by the palace at Rouen, long since destroyed. Many of its Norman and other medieval buildings are in an excellent state of preservation. Of especial note is the Castle Chapel. At **Hampton Court,** begun by Cardinal Wolsey in 1514, there is a magnificent Tudor gatehouse and Great Hall. Later additions were made by Sir Christopher Wren for William III at the end of the 17th century.

Henry VII Chapel, Westminster Abbey *(1503-19). Detail of the* fan-tracery *on one of the finest and most elaborate of the* pendant *vaults of the period. Masterly and extensive carving includes a series of 95 statues of saints.*

Temple Church, Inns of Court *Modeled on the Holy Sepulchre, Jerusalem, it has a circular* nave, *with* clerestory, *in the late* Norman *style, built by the Knights Templar. The Early English* oblong *chancel was added in 1240. The building was restored after being badly damaged in World War II.*

Tudor Gateway, St James's Palace *(c. 1532). A characteristic feature of domestic and collegiate buildings of the period was the quasi-military tower built astride a gateway. This one was built under Henry VIII and may have been designed by Holbein.*

The White Tower, Tower of London *(1086-97). This is the central* keep, *so named because it was at one time white-washed. It was built by William I and William II as a fortress from which to protect London. Two surrounding walls, equipped with towers, were added in the 13thC.*

Great Hall, Palace of Westminster *(1394-1402). Technological advances such as the* hammer-beam *enabled large floor areas to be roofed without the use of supporting* aisles. *This is among the finest timber-roofed buildings in Europe.*

Southeast England

Religious buildings

Some of the most important remains of the early Christian churches in Saxon England are found in Kent. Good examples are the churches of **St Peter and St Paul** (*c.* 604), **St Martin** (7thC) and **St Pancras** (10thC) in Canterbury, and the churches of **Reculver** (*c.* 664), **Lyminge** (*c.* 965) and **St Peter-on-the-Wall, Bradwell-juxta-Mare** (*c.* 660), in Essex. The typical plan consisted of the main body of the church, including the *chancel,* and surrounding chapels.

The masterpiece in the area is **Canterbury Cathedral** (1071-1503), where the shrine of St Thomas Becket drew pilgrims in the Middle Ages. The architect of the choir and *apse* was the master mason, William of Sens. It was as original and revolutionary to England as St Denis was to France. The cathedral has a magnificent late *Perpendicular* central tower (1490-1503). Among other imposing buildings are **Chichester Cathedral** (12thC), with double *aisles* and a fine spire; **Rochester Cathedral** (1179-1240) in Kent, with a plain *Norman nave* and beautiful Norman doorway on the west side; **St Albans Abbey** (11thC), which has the second longest nave in England, and **Waltham Abbey** (11thC) in Essex, famous for its Norman nave.

A product of the fine oak forests is a series of remarkable church belfries and towers in Essex, such as **St Lawrence, Blackmore** (12th-13thC), **All Saints Church, Stock** (13thC), and **St Andrew's, Greensted-juxta-Ongar** (*c.* 1013), which is the only surviving log church in England. In Buckinghamshire there is the impressive Norman church of **St Michael, Stewkley** (*c.* 1150-60), consisting of nave, tower and square-ended chancel. The west fronts of the tower arches are decorated with *beakheads.*

St Mary, Sompting *(11thC), in Sussex. The west tower, the only four-gabled spire left in England. Other features of the* Carolingian *style are the* pilaster strips *on the tower walls and the round-headed tower windows.*

Chichester Cathedral *Two large panels in the south aisle of the* choir, *one of which depicts the Raising of Lazarus, above, are examples of the medieval laws of "spiritual perspective," in which the scale of the figures is determined by their significance.*

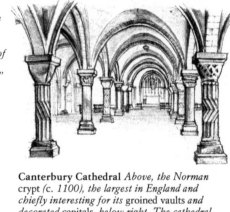

Canterbury Cathedral *Above, the Norman* crypt *(c. 1100), the largest in England and chiefly interesting for its* groined vaults *and* decorated *capitals, below right. The cathedral, below left, was the work of many builders, the* nave *being that of Henry Yevele, the outstanding architect of late medieval England.*

Southeast England

The Saxon church of **St Botolph, Hadstock** (*c.* 1020), in Essex, is Scandinavian in inspiration and notable for a door arch with carved and molded *imposts*. The *nave* and *transepts* are original but a west tower and north porch were added in the 15th century. **All Saints, Staplehurst** (11thC), in Kent, is a *Norman* church incorporating remains of an early Saxon church. **All Saints, Wing** (10thC and 14thC), in Buckinghamshire, has a fine seven-sided *apse* with *Carolingian pilaster strips* and *blind arcading*. In the raised *chancel* is to be found the largest Saxon arch in England.

The magnificent *rose window* on the east end of **St Nicholas, Barfreystone** (12thC), in Kent, is strikingly French. The mass of the church, comprising a nave and square-ended chancel with neither *aisles* nor towers, is pleasantly unsophisticated and contrasts with the fine decorative treatment of the façades. Among interesting churches in Sussex are **St Pancras, Arlington** (11th-14thC), built of flint and with largely *Early English* and Saxon details; the **Parish Church of Southease** (12th-13thC), also of flint and with a notable round tower, and **St Mary, East Guldeford** (*c,* 1505), which has a rectangular brick-

St Mary de Haura, New Shoreham *(12thC), Sussex. View of the interior of the* nave. *Originally the church was more than 197 ft long but the main section of the nave fell into ruin in the 17thC. Remains include the old* choir, *consisting of three equal* aisles.

St Lawrence, Blackmore *(12th-13thC), Essex. A massive timber church, notable for its wooden, three stage west tower. The church was built on the remains of the nave and* aisles *of a Norman* priory of Augustinian friars.

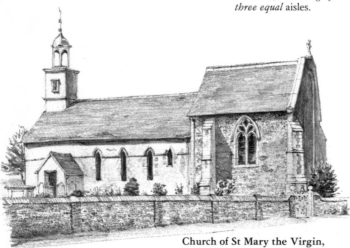

Church of St Mary the Virgin, Tilty *(13th-14thC), Essex. Originally a chapel outside a Cistercian abbey, it has a 13th-C nave and a 14th-C chancel, markedly different in form and detail. The east window is renowned for its fine* tracery.

St Peter-on-the-Wall, Bradwell-juxta-Mare *(c. 660), Essex. More like a fortified barn than a church, the walls are mostly of re-used Roman materials, supported by projecting* buttresses *at regular intervals.*

St Augustine, Brookland *(c. 1250), Kent. This parish church is remarkable for its octagonal, wooden-capped belfry, built in the 16thC. There is a 13th-C chancel with* piscina *and* sedilia *and a 14th-C north porch.*

built nave and chancel propped up by giant *buttresses*. Also of interest are **Holy Trinity, Colchester** (10th-15thC); **St Mary's, Chickney** (10thC), Essex, and **St Nicholas's, Worth** (11thC), Sussex.

Castles & Palaces

The early Norman castles were of the *motte-and-bailey* type. They were originally built of timber but most were rebuilt of stone in the mid-12th century. Examples of early stone castles include **Castle Hedingham, Essex** (*c.* 1140), and **Rochester Castle, Kent** (*c.* 1130). Stone castles of this period are usually one of two types. They either have a rectangular *keep,* as at **Colchester Castle** (11thC) and **Dover Castle** (1179-91), or a *shell keep* based on the earlier motte-and-bailey plan, such as **Arundel Castle** (11thC). Little of the shell keep remains at **Lewes Castle** (11thC), but there is a well-preserved 14th-century *barbican* built in front of the Norman gateway.

New fortified homes of the 14th and 15th centuries were generally either quadrilateral castles or tower houses. **Bodiam Castle, Sussex** (*c.* 1385), is the best example of the quadrilateral plan. **Herstmonceaux Castle, Sussex** (1444), is an elegant Flemish brick-built structure, protected by a moat and drawbridge and entered via an imposing gatehouse more than 82 ft high.

Domestic buildings

Most of the larger 14th-century manor houses were built around a central court. They, too, were entered via a gatehouse and were defended by a *portcullis,* drawbridge and moat. The main components were the hall and *solar* area. The hall, then at the peak of its development, was still the retainers' sleeping room. A typical example is the hall, **Penshurst Place, Kent** (1341-48). It has an open central hearth and smoke *louvre* in the roof. Other examples include **Horeham Hall, Essex** (1502-20); **Layer Marney Hall, Essex** (*c.* 1500-1525), which has a memorable entrance gate; **Ightham Mote** (14th-15thC), and **Hever Castle** (rebuilt 1462), both in Kent, and **Sutton Place, Guildford** (1524-5).

Castle Hedingham, Essex *(c. 1140). One of the most elegant of English hall-keeps, it is square in plan and built of rubble, faced in finely cut ashlar. The castle is primitive in comparison to French castles of the time, which already employed round or polygonal forms for greater strength.*

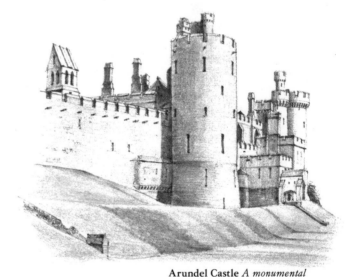

Dover Castle, *below. The earliest example of a* concentric *castle in western Europe and the most powerful in England. 12th-C* curtain walls *with flanking towers surround the great rectangular keep. Little remains of an outer line of walls.*

Arundel Castle *A monumental complex, comprising ramps, projecting towers and a great circular Norman keep, much restored in the 19thC. The mound and two baileys of the original castle survive. Of especial interest is the Barbican Tower (c. 1295) and the Bevis Tower (1170-90).*

Southeast England

Bodiam Castle, Sussex *(c. 1385).*
Typical of the quadrangular fort-
resses built in the 14thC, it is
perhaps the most celebrated of the
English moated castles. There are
two gateways with machicolations
and four corner towers.

Layer Marney Hall, Essex *(c. 1500-25). One*
of the most unusual of the 16th-C gatehouses,
being eight stories high and strictly symmetrical
in both design and detail. It was to have been
the dominating feature of a mansion but
nothing more was completed.

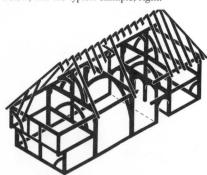

Ightham Mote, Kent *(14th-15thC). The quality*
of houses such as these lies in the simplicity of
the basic plan: a quadrangle surrounded by a
hall, a two-story block containing a chapel, and
a protective moat.

The Marlipins, New
Shoreham *(14thC),*
Sussex. A popular
decorative device for
houses in most of the
flint areas was the
combination of flints,
usually knapped,
forming a chessboard
pattern with squares
of ashlared *limestone.*

The Yeoman's House

The standard design for a prosperous farmer's
home in the Southeast was a house with a lofty
open hall, often two-storied, as in the diagram
below, and the typical example, right.

Old Bell Farm, Harrietsham (15thC), **Kent.**

Southern England

Religious buildings

Salisbury Cathedral (1220-*c.* 1260) is unique in being the only English cathedral to be built in the Middle Ages as a total conception, all the others having been erected piecemeal over many years. The sole addition is the spire, which is 404 ft high and the loftiest in England. The cathedral stands within a close and has quasi-monastic features, including *cloisters, chapter-house* and gateways, typical features of the 13th century. Cloisters were added at **Gloucester Cathedral** (1089-1100) during the 14th century. The last major addition to this *Romanesque* cathedral, apart from the Lady Chapel, is a tower, built in 1450 in the *Perpendicular* style. The three towers of **Wells Cathedral, Somerset** (12th-14thC), were added in the late 14th century. Of particular note in the interior are the inverted arches which support the columns, which in turn carry the massive weight of the central tower. **Winchester Cathedral** (1070-14thC), the long-est cathedral in Europe at 502 ft, was later redecorated in the Perpendicular style. **Exeter Cathedral, Devonshire** (11th-14thC), bears on its west front the largest array of 14th-century sculpted figures to have survived in England. **Oxford Cathedral** (13thC) now forms part of Christ Church college.

Sherborne Abbey Church, Dorset (12th-15thC), was originally a Benedictine foundation and is especially notable for its fine *fan vaulting.* In Gloucestershire, **St John the Baptist, Cirencester,** a *Norman* church, was greatly added to in the Perpendicular style by rich wool merchants in the 14th and 15th centuries. The south porch has three stories and is lavishly embellished with *tracery.* The church of **St Cuthberga, Wimborne Minster,** has twin towers and dates from Norman times with 15th-century additions. It houses many tombs and a chained library.

Salisbury Cathedral *The classic English cathedral, it was built without interruption, to a uniform plan and on a virgin site. The vaulting of the* chapter-house *is shown above, top. This superb, eight-sided building, erected between 1263 and 1284, is more than 56 ft in diameter and has 49 seats for members of the Chapter.*

Wells Cathedral, Somerset *Part of the chapter-house, begun in 1250. Thirty-two ribs, springing from the central column, are balanced by the decorative treatment of windows and wall* arcade.

Gloucester Cathedral *View of the* cloister, *rebuilt* c. 1370. *It is an elegant tunnel of* fan vaults, *on the south side of which the bay windows were divided into cubicles for use as writing areas for the monks.*

Winchester Cathedral *The* nave, *rebuilt* c. 1371-1450, *is the greatest transformation in the old church and is one of the most elegant examples of a fan-vaulted roof in Great Britain.*

Southern England

The planning of churches in the *Norman* period, such as the **Church of St Mary, Brearmore** (12thC), in Hampshire, was Celtic in origin. Characteristic is the squat tower, placed at the junction of *nave* and *chancel*. The Church of **St Lawrence, Bradford-on-Avon** (*c.* 700), in Wiltshire, was remodeled in the 10th century and has *blind arcades* with arches springing from broad, flat *pilasters,* a distinctly *Carolingian* influence. **St Mary, Iffley** (12thC), in Oxfordshire, has a magnificent west front, Norman in style, with a round window set in a rectangular panel, recessed centrally in the *gable.* The main entrance has superimposed orders of *beakheads* and *chevrons.* The nave, central tower and chancel formed the original church. **St James, Avebury** (11th-14thC), in Oxfordshire, is a mixture of many periods, having two Saxon windows, a Norman *portal* and *aisles* and a 14th-century chancel, while **St Mary, Langford** (11thC), also in Oxfordshire, is notable for its fine central tower.

Castles & Palaces

Carisbrooke Castle, Isle of Wight (11th-16thC), comprises remains of a Norman earthwork with a 14th-century gatehouse. In the 16th century *curtain walls, bastions* and *bulwarks* were built around the old castle to withstand artillery fire. In the upper story of the gatehouse there are ports for hand guns. The **Castle, St Mawes** (1540), in Cornwall, was built in the form of a clover leaf and was part of a network of fortifications constructed by Henry VIII as a defense against French invasion. Other castles in the network include **Pendennis Castle** (1544), also in Cornwall, consisting of a circular *keep* at the center of two rings of fortified walls, and **Portland Castle, Castletown** (1540), in Dorset, which is built like an open fan, its curved part facing the bay. **Compton Castle, Devonshire** (14th-16thC), which has been extensively restored in recent years, is one of the best examples of a medieval manor house fortified as a defense against possible French invasion.

St Lawrence's, Bradford-on-Avon
The outline of the gable is all that remains of the south porch. The church's narrow nave and square-ended chancel are more characteristic of northern Celtic churches than the basilican plan typical of the south.

St Mary's, Hartley Wespall *(14thC), Hampshire. Originally the church was built entirely of timber but later a stone and flint wall was added. Of note is the gable end of this framed building, strengthened by decorated braces and divided down the middle by a post.*

Tewkesbury Abbey, Gloucestershire *(c. 1123). View of the west front, which is more than 59 ft in height and is unique in its effect of recessed façade, reinforced by tall, unadorned shafts and molded arches.*

St Mary's, Brearmore *An architectural characteristic of this and many contemporaneous churches is that they appear to be an assemblage of rectangular boxes — nave, chancel, transepts and porches — connected by narrow openings.*

Domestic buildings

In Wiltshire, **Great Chalfield Manor** (*c.* 1470) is deliberately traditional in composition, but major innovations concern the hall, which was no longer open to the roof but covered over to make the house two-story throughout. **Cotehele House, Calstock** (1485-1627), in Cornwall, constructed around two granite quadrangles like an Oxford college, is notable as one of the least altered buildings of its period. **Ockwells Manor**, **Berkshire** (*c.* 1450) is remarkable for a timber-built house in that the large hall has a wall of windows. **Cothay Manor, Somerset** (*c.* 1470-80), is a handsome hall with an *oriel window.*

Commercial & Industrial buildings

There are many fine medieval barns in the area, including a timber barn at **Great Coxwell, Berkshire** (13thC), and stone barns at **Glastonbury** and **Pilton** in Somerset, **Abbotsbury** in Dorset and **Beaulieu** in Hampshire. They are typical of the domestic halls of Anglo-Saxon settlements in having the nave and aisles divided by timber columns and with doors in each gable end of the building. Other interesting buildings in the area include the **George Inn, Glastonbury** (15thC), Somerset; the **Guildhall, Cirencester** (15thC), Gloucestershire, and the **market cross.** Salisbury (14thC).

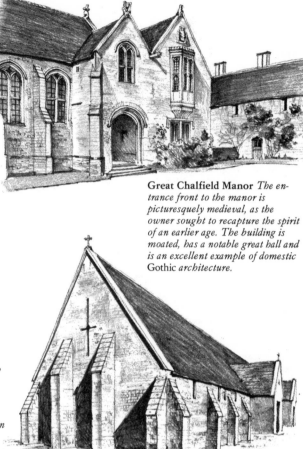

Great Chalfield Manor *The entrance front to the manor is picturesquely medieval, as the owner sought to recapture the spirit of an earlier age. The building is moated, has a notable great hall and is an excellent example of domestic Gothic architecture.*

Donnington Castle, Berkshire *(14thC), left. The ruined gatehouse is all that remains of the castle, otherwise destroyed in the Civil War. The gatehouse was built centrally on the east wall of a rectangular enclosure.*

Old Tithe Barn, Bradford-on-Avon, *(c. 1350), in Wiltshire, above. Tithe barns were built like churches, with nave and aisles, and strongly buttressed. They were designed to store a tenth of the produce of all land in England, levied under a tax first imposed in the 9thC.*

Barn, Great Coxwell *View of the interior. The barn was built by the Cistercians of Beaulieu after the site and adjoining manor and chapel of Great Coxwell had been given to them by King John.*

Cob Cottage, Ashton *(16thC), in Devonshire. Cob was the name used for mud buildings, such as cottages, particularly in Devonshire and Cornwall. Mud walls were usually built on a stone or pebble plinth, the base tarred and the roof thatched.*

Central England

Religious buildings

The classic Saxon building is **All Saints Church, Earls Barton** (*c.* 935), in Northamptonshire, with its *Carolingian pilaster strip* patterning and *long-and-short work* on the tower. Further examples of Saxon architecture are **St Mary and David, Kilpeck** (*c.* 1150), Herefordshire; **St Michael, Melbourne** (12thC), Derbyshire, and **All Saints, Walksoken** (*c.* 1146), Norfolk.

By the late 12th century, a preference developed for a widely spreading screen façade as an entrance *portico* to cathedrals, instead of the more characteristic twin towers, one at the end of each *aisle*. The **Cathedral, Peterborough** (1117-90), has a particularly dramatic screen, nearly 165 ft across, creating a marvelous layered effect. It has one of the finest *Norman* interiors after Durham Cathedral. **Lincoln Cathedral** (1185-1280) has a monumental screen front, but gone is the rich, layered quality of Peterborough Cathedral. Here the screen, with *blind arcading,* is more like a cliff. But the quality of the building as a whole is exceptional, with its grand *nave* and remarkable polygonal *chapter-house,* the first in England. Earlier chapter-houses were rectangular, although the circular chapter-house at **Worcester Cathedral** (1080-14thC) is an exception.

Of the other cathedrals in central England, **Ely Cathedral** (*c.* 1080) is highly individual, with its Norman nave and *transepts,* the 14th-century octagonal *lantern* and the huge, single tower at the west end. Also of interest: **Norwich Cathedral** (1096-1145), with narrow Norman nave and beautiful *Perpendicular* spire; **Lichfield Cathedral, Staffordshire** (*c.* 1190), with its remarkable screen front decorated with prominent statues, and **Hereford Cathedral** (*c.* 1079), which was largely redesigned after the original tower collapsed in 1786.

One of the major monuments of English medieval architecture is **King's College Chapel, Cambridge** (1446-1515), a huge space, beautifully crafted and covered by giant *fan vaults.* The rest of the college is of the 18th and 19th century.

Castles & Palaces

The majority of Norman castles began as *motte-and-bailey* earthworks, as shown by the remains at **Thetford** in Norfolk. But the great castles of the period had stone *keeps* rather than mottes. The earliest type was the rectangular hall keep, as at **Castle Rising, Norfolk** (*c.* 1140), or the tower keep, as at **Orford Castle, Suffolk** (*c.* 1166-82).

Domestic buildings

Stone-built Norman manor houses consisted of a first floor hall, often raised above an *undercroft.* Two remarkable examples are at **Boothby Pagnell, Lincolnshire,** and at **Hemingford Grey, Cambridgeshire** (*c.* 1150). Also of interest is the **Jew's House, Lincoln** (12thC). **Tattershall Castle, Lincolnshire** (1431-9), seems to revert to the 12th-century style with an isolated keep, but here it was not for defense so much as to separate served from servant and to provide a stronghold for valuables.

Peterborough Cathedral
The three huge arches of the west screen front, standing proud of the nave and aisles, were added as the nave neared completion. The ornamentation plays a secondary role to the architectural form.

St Margaret, Cley *(c. 1250), Norfolk. View through the* trefoiled *and* cusped ogee *doorway of the vaulted* porch *to the 15th-C, carved, seven-sacrament font.*

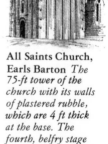

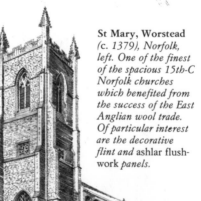

St Mary, Worstead *(c. 1379), Norfolk, left. One of the finest of the spacious 15th-C Norfolk churches which benefited from the success of the East Anglian wool trade. Of particular interest are the decorative flint and* ashlar *flush-work* panels.

All Saints Church, Earls Barton *The 75-ft tower of the church with its walls of plastered rubble, which are 4 ft thick at the base. The fourth, belfry stage has five decorated openings in each face.*

Holy Sepulchre, Cambridge *(c. 1130). This round church was largely rebuilt during restoration in the 19thC. The ambulatory roof is vaulted, and the oak roofs in the* choir *and north* aisle *were carved in the 14th and 15thC.*

Church Towers in Norfolk

A series of simple, beautiful church towers dominate the flat, lonely landscape of Norfolk. Dating from the 11th-15thC, many are round since it was easier to build them that way using local building materials such as pebbles.

St Lawrence, South Walsham *(15thC), left. This strong, buttressed tower survived a fire in 1827. There is a second 14th-15thC church in South Walsham, St Mary's, showing the abundance of churches in medieval Norfolk.*

Church, Potter Heigham *(11th-15thC). The church has an early circular tower with a 15th-C belfry added. Other round church towers are at Stody, Bawbergh, Colney, Threxton and Hales.*

St Gregory, Heckingham (11th-13thC), Norfolk. A simple but dignified thatched church consisting of nave and apse with an octagonal west tower that stands on a round base. The nave has a fine Early English chancel arch and north arcade.

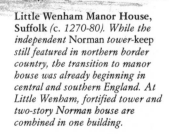

Tattershall Castle *Built on the site of an earlier castle by Ralph Cromwell, the Treasurer of England. What remains is a huge, square, brick-built, fortified manor house about 30 m high, containing a series of splendid state apartments.*

Little Wenham Manor House, Suffolk *(c. 1270-80). While the independent Norman tower-keep still featured in northern border country, the transition to manor house was already beginning in central and southern England. At Little Wenham, fortified tower and two-story Norman house are combined in one building.*

Central England

By the end of the 14th century the military importance of the castle had declined and fortified manor houses became a preferred alternative. These include **Stokesay Castle** (1285-1305), Shropshire; **Wingfield** (*c.* 1441-55), Derbyshire; **Maxstoke** (1346), Warwickshire, and **Oxburgh Hall, Swaffham** (1482), in Norfolk. Other established castles were radically modified at this time, such as **Kenilworth Castle** (*c.* 1160) in Warwickshire.

Under the Tudors ornamental brick patterning became fashionable. The earliest examples are at Tattershall Castle (see pp. 126-27), **Queens College, Cambridge** (15thC), and **Wallington Hall, Downham Market** (*c.* 1525), in Norfolk. Outstanding examples of raised brickwork decoration in Norfolk can be found at **East Barsham Manor** (*c.* 1500) and the **Rectory, Great Snoring** (16thC), and in Suffolk at **Giffords Hall, Stoke-by-Nayland** (*c.* 1500).

Town houses were usually built on long, narrow plots with limited frontages. Additional floors or rooms were added, properties amalgamated or subdivided and sometimes, as at **Lavenham** in Suffolk, frontages were built across two or more plots. At **Putley**, in Herefordshire, there is an example of a single-story *cruck* frame cottage. While the houses of the small freeholder or yeoman farmer were based on manor house prototypes, such cottages were restricted in width and height according to the size of timbers available. These restrictions were resolved by the development of the *box-framed* house.

Commercial & Industrial buildings

Guilds had strong religious ties, and sometimes pageants and miracle plays were performed in their halls. The **Guildhall, Lavenham** (*c.* 1529), is a particulary fine, timber-framed building. Other examples are the **Wool Hall, Lavenham** (15thC), and the **Guildhall, Norwich** (1407-13).

Medieval inns were the centers of town life. The **Angel, Grantham** (15thC), in Lincolnshire, was originally a pilgrim's inn supported by the church. It is stone-fronted with bay windows on either side of the central coaching gateway. Over the arch is an *oriel window*.

Cruck frame cottage, Putley *Primarily associated with medieval buildings, cruck construction was largely used in Wales, midwest and northwest England. Two curved tree trunks were joined at the top in the shape of a gable, spaced in bays and built on a plinth.*

Guildhall, Lavenham *A thriving center of the 16th-C wool trade, Lavenham had three guildhalls, of which this was the first to be built. It looks more like a richer version of its domestic neighbors than a major public building.*

House and shop, Lavenham *A fine timber-framed building with* jettied *upper story. The long frontage to the street was the product of joining several narrow plots behind a rebuilt street front, an amalgam of many parts behind a public street face.*

Ancient House, Clare *(1473), in Suffolk. Tudor and Jacobean houses originally had their timbers exposed. Here the decorative relief work,* pargetting, *added in the 17thC, became a distinctive feature of the area.*

128

Northern England

Religious buildings

The remains of stone churches dating from the last quarter of the 7th century are to be found at **Monkwearmouth Church, County Durham** (*c.* 675), and in the *crypts* at the **Abbey, Hexham** (*c.* 675), and **Ripon Cathedral** (*c.* 672-1522). **St John's Chapel, Escomb** (*c.* 700), County Durham, is one of the most complete of the Anglo-Saxon churches in England.

The Cistercians insisted on the exclusion of all superfluous ornament. One of the characteristics of their architecture is the pointed arch and, after Durham Cathedral, the first use of it in England was at **Rievaulx Abbey, Yorkshire** (*c.* 1131). Also of interest is **Fountains Abbey, Yorkshire** (*c.* 1132), one of the great monastic institutions and dominated by a 15th-century tower.

Durham Cathedral (1093-15thC) is the most important building of the Anglo-Norman style, both historically, since it is the earliest and most significant surviving example of a church constructed throughout with *ribbed vaults,* and aesthetically, for the fine proportions of the plan with its lengthy eastern limb and the outstanding quality of ornamentation. **York Minster** (13th-15thC) is the largest *Gothic* church in England with a *nave* second in height to that of Westminster Abbey. The beautiful polygonal *chapter-house* (1286-1307) and the *Early English transepts* have exquisite moldings. Also of interest are **Carlisle Cathedral** (12thC), badly damaged in the Civil Wars, **Chester Cathedral** (12thC), with its fine choir, and **Beverley Minster** (13th-15thC).

Rievaulx Abbey *Built on the left bank of the Rye, the ruined* nave *shows the characteristic austerity of 12th-C Cistercian architecture in England. The later* Gothic choir *and presbytery are more ornate.*

Monkwearmouth Church *One of a group of early Northern English churches. The porch is barrel-vaulted with some original decoration remaining. Intertwined beaked animals are surmounted by turned stone balus-ters. Above these are the remains of a carved frieze.*

York Minster *Fine* Perpendicular *towers dominate the largely* Gothic *complex. The cathedral has some unique stained glass, particularly the "Five Sisters," the elegant* lancet windows *of the north transept.*

Durham Cathedral *The most impressively sited of all the English cathedrals, towering above the river cliff. A giant of the English* Roman-esque, *it has the finest* Norman nave *in England with pillar shafts channeled with chev-ron, diaper and fluting decoration.*

Castle, Newcastle-upon-Tyne *(1175-8). In this view of the Castle Chapel, note the heavy zig-zag ornamentation on window and door frames. The castle, built by Henry II as an extra defense against the Scots, had a fine rectangular keep intended both for residential and for military use.*

Northern England

Castles & Palaces

The grander 12th-century *keep* castles were both military strongholds and self-contained houses complete with hall, chambers, chapel and kitchen. **Richmond Castle** (11th-12thC) is an example where a castle acted both as the residence of a feudal lord and the administrative center for the manors he held in vassalage. **Alnwick Castle** (*c.* 1157), with its magnificent stone *shell keep,* was built to replace the former wooden *motte-and-bailey* arrangement. The castle assumed its present form in the 14th century. The *barbican* is particularly fine. Other examples are **Bowes Castle, County Durham** (*c.* 1171), with its massive *Norman* keep built of stone quarried from Roman remains; **Carlisle Castle** (12thC), which was a stronghold of the border wars with an impregnable keep and 14th-century entrance gate; **Middleham Castle, Leyburn** (*c.* 1170), of which the rectangular Norman keep is one of the largest in the country, containing a particularly interesting three-story chapel, and **Conisbrough Castle, South Yorkshire** (*c.* 1185). This last example has perhaps the most magnificent keep in England. The circular, three-chambered, white tower is 85 ft high and has massive protruding spurs for added strength.

By the late 13th century, a complex of *curtain wall,* projecting towers and fortified gateways had taken over from the keep in castle design. Domestic accommodation was provided for in one of the towers, or in a range of buildings around the castle's courtyard. The keep became a model for the principal houses of the border country, as at **Langley Castle, Haydon Bridge** (*c.* 1350), **Haughton Castle, Northumberland** (14thC), and the ruins of **Belsay Castle, Northumberland** (14thC), which is considered one of the best examples of a *tower house* in the North.

Since builders of the time were unable to construct a widely spanning roof, the Norman hall usually had a high, narrow *nave* with side *aisles* like a church. **Rufford Old Hall, Lancashire,** is a 15th-century example which has a carved *hammer-beam* roof, short projecting screens built to reduce drafts and a unique paneled screen once used to shield the dais — the raised platform for the top table.

Domestic Buildings

Askham Hall, Lowther, in Cumbria, is an interesting 14th-century tower house with Elizabethan wings. **Aydon Castle, Corbridge** (14thC), is another fortified manor house, and so too is **Middleton Hall, Cumbria** (14th-15thC), which is a fine example of domestic architecture built about a courtyard.

In many houses a symbol of wealth was the lavish use of timber in the frame construction. At **Bramhall Hall, Greater Manchester** (15thC), *large framing* (the commonest form of framing before 1450) was used with close *studding* — the open frame being divided into narrow panels by vertical posts. This combination was the most expensive method of timber framing an architect could employ in the late Middle Ages.

Mortham Tower, Rokeby *(14th-15thC), in Yorkshire. The availability of building materials greatly affected architectural design. Here, roughly coursed* rubble *was used for most of the walls and larger blocks of ash-lared* gritstone *were used as* dressing.

Bramhall Hall, Greater Manchester *While dating from the 15thC, the form of the hall was much altered by the 16thC. Its numerous gables and the black and white work are characteristic of the area.*

Langley Castle, Haydon Bridge *(c. 1350). A fine example of a 14th-C battlemented tower house, restored in 1900. As the military strength of the* keep *dwindled, it became, instead, a model for fortified houses.*

Bamburgh Castle *(12thC). The nail-studded doorway to the keep. Covering about 9 acres, the castle was built of red sandstone. It consists of a 12th-C keep and three baileys which were extensively restored from 1894-1903. It was the first castle in England to be breached by cannon fire.*

Richmond Castle *Built in a commanding position on a cliff above the River Swale, the castle consists of a great, square keep, similar to the White Tower, London, and a triangular arrangement of curtain walls, a product of the awkward site. In the southern corner of the castle environs is the Norman Scolland's Hall with a first-floor hall.*

Conisbrough Castle, South Yorkshire, *above. Most of the wall encircling the inner bailey of the castle survives with its early round turrets. Within the huge, stark keep are the hall (on the first floor) and, above this, the solar and chapel, built into the thickness of the wall.*

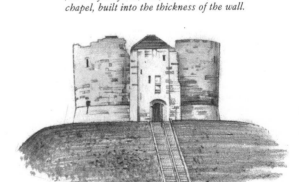

Alnwick Castle *The lead figures set on the battlements of the 15th-C gatehouse date from 1755 when Robert Adam was hired to Gothicize the castle. The original shell keep, begun in 1096, was rebuilt into a curtain wall with seven semicircular towers, the majority of which survive intact.*

Clifford's Tower, York *(c. 1244). Built on an 11th-C motte, the fortification is quatrefoil in plan. Originally, a rectangular tower, set between two of the curving walls, formed the entrance. The present gateway complex was built in the 17thC.*

Scotland

Religious buildings

Early Christian stone buildings in Scotland are rare. Remains of *bee-hive cells* are found in **Iona, Bute** and at **Aileach** in the Garvelloch Islands, and 10th-12th-century round church towers at **Restenneth** and **Abernethy** in Tayside, and **Brechin**. Of early sculptures, Celtic high crosses in **Iona** and **Islay** and the tomb shrines at **Jedburgh** and **St Andrews** are rich finds.

The 12th-century Benedictine, Cistercian and Augustinian monasteries adopted the standard European plan of church and living quarters grouped around *cloisters*. **Iona Abbey, Argyll** (13thC-1500), a Benedictine foundation, is virtually complete, having recently been restored. Others include, in Dumfries and Galloway, **Sweetheart Abbey** (*c.* 1273), a Cistercian foundation, **Melrose Abbey** (*c.* 1385) and **Jedburgh Abbey** (*c.* 1150-1200), and in Central region **Inchmahome Priory** (13thC).

Church architecture followed the English and continental model of *cruciform* plan with side *aisles*. Aisles were *vaulted* but *nave* roofs were timbered. Typical examples are **Kelso Abbey, Borders** (*c.* 1128); **Dunfermline Abbey** (*c.* 1150) and **Kirkwell Cathedral, Orkney** (12th-13thC). But perhaps the most individualistic in character is **St Rule's, St Andrews** (1070-93). Now a ruin, it was one of the longest churches in Britain with its massive walls pierced by small, double-*splayed* windows.

The typical parish church, such as the one at **Leuchars, Fife** (*c.* 1185), was an aisleless, two-chambered structure with round arches. They were often profusely decorated, usually with *chevron* molding, *corbels* carved as grotesque masks and elaborately carved *capitals*. Also of interest are **Dunning Church, Tayside** (12thC), and the remains at **Orphir, Orkney** (11th-12thC).

In the *choir*, Jedburgh Abbey, *Romanesque* round arches stand side by side with *Gothic* pointed arches, but with the construction of the choir of **Glasgow Cathedral** (13thC) the transition to Gothic is complete. Other Gothic examples are

Dunblane Cathedral *Although the Tower is* 12th-C Norman, *most of the building is* Gothic *dating from the 13th-15thC and has lovely pointed arches. There are fine* misericord *choir stalls (c. 1500).*

Nunnery Church, Iona *(13thC), above. The ruins of this church include the* nave *with an aisle and the adjoining Lady Chapel. The size of the church and the Nunnery as a whole is in complete contrast with the other, much larger Augustinian abbeys at Holyrood and Jedburgh.*

Melrose Abbey *One of the finest late medieval churches in Scotland, this red sandstone building was frequently sacked and rebuilt, and finally left unfinished. The eastern part of the nave, the south aisle,* transepts, *some of the tower and the chancel remain.*

Church of the Holy Rude, Stirling *(c. 1415-c. 1515). A good example of a town church with a fine west tower, aisled nave with massive round columns and a choir with a higher roof.*

Elgin Cathedral, Grampian (13thC), and the nave of **Dunblane Cathedral** (13thC). Late Gothic is seen best in the naves of the cathedrals at **Aberdeen** and **Dunkeld, Tayside**.

Castles & Palaces

The earliest Scottish castles, such as the **Mote of Urr, Dumfries and Galloway**, were constructed mainly of earth and timbers. **Rothesay Castle, Bute** (13thC), and **Loch Doon Castle, Dumfries and Galloway** (*c.* 1300), are typical of early stone castles with a *curtain wall* enclosing a large courtyard.

Several castles in Scotland were built with *keeps* and often, as at **Inverlochy Castle, Highland** (13thC), they were made by enlarging one of the angle towers. Other examples are **Bothwell Castle, Strathclyde** (13thC) and **Kildrummy Castle, Grampian** (13thC). Later, the gatehouse dwelling became a prominent feature, as at **Caerlaverock Castle, Dumfries and Galloway** (13th-15thC), **Tantallon Castle, Lothian** (14th C) and **Doune Castle, Central** (*c.* 1380).

The fortified hall-house is typical of the period, comprising an undercroft with spacious first-floor hall. **Rait Castle, Highland** (14thC), and **Morton Castle, Dumfries and Galloway** (13thC), are fine examples.

The great symbol of feudal Scotland is the tower house in which all the rooms, stacked vertically, were reached by one or more turnpike stairs. Good examples are: **Threave Castle, Dumfries and Galloway** (1369-90), **Neidpath Castle, Borders** (13th-15thC), **Blaynots Castle, Angus** (1569-88) and **Borthwick Castle, Midlothian** (1430).

The Late Middle Ages saw the extensive reconstruction of the royal palaces at **Linlithgow, Dunfermline, Holyrood in Fife, Falkland,** and the castles of **Stirling** and **Edinburgh**. They were transformed militarily to cope with the development of gunpowder, and domestically to include additional stories, elaborate wings and the application of *Renaissance* decorative details.

Hermitage Castle, Dumfries and Galloway *(14th-15thC). An aggressive looking castle surrounding a central courtyard. The upper openings originally gave access to a wooden gallery that projected out over any attackers. Two great* flying arches *connect the projecting towers.*

Mugdock Castle, Central *(c. 14thC), right. The southwest tower, shown here, is four stories high, with single chambers stacked one on another. Other remains include another tower and part of a fortified gatehouse.*

Tomb of Alastair Crotach, Rodel Church, Harris *(1528). A fine example of the Celtic tomb slab. It decorates the recessed tomb of a MacLeod clan chief.*

Castle Cary, Central *(15thC). This tower house has an east wing that was added in the late 17thC. The tower stands in a good defensive position on the edge of the Red Burn ravine. Each of its four stories has one chamber.*

Caerlaverock Castle *One of the most impressive of Scotland's 13th-C castles. Built on a curve of land near the Solway Firth, the 14th-15th-C defensive exterior is entered via a monumental double-towered gatehouse. Within are elegant* Renaissance *buildings, constructed around a triangular court.*

Wales

Religious buildings

The architecture of Celtic Wales was spartan and robust. A typical example is **Penmon Priory, Anglesey** (12thC), with its short-*aisled nave*, simple *transepts* and square-ended *chancel*. Even in the churches of the Cistercian Abbeys of **Aberconway** and **Clyn-y-groes** near Llangollen, interiors, with the exception of the *pier capitals*, are startlingly plain. In the rare instances where ornamentation was thought appropriate, *Norman* forms were freely adapted.

The Normans, following their conquest of southern Wales, began an intensive programme of church building, culminating in **St David's Cathedral, Dyfed** (*c.* 1180). Monasteries were of the standard continental type, comprising church, living quarters and *cloister.* Examples include **Caldy Priory, Dyfed,** and **Tintern Abbey, Gwent** (13thC).

The finest early Norman church in Wales is the Benedictine **Priory Church, Ewenni** (12thC) in Glamorgan. The Augustine **Priory, Llanthony** (12thC) in Gwent is unique in Wales, being the only cathedral having, in addition to a central tower, subsidiary towers at the west end of the nave. Towers were often added to early *Gothic* churches as lookouts or places of refuge. **St John's Cathedral, Brecon** (13thC), has one of the best examples, while another, added in 1506, is found at the great *Perpendicular* style church of **St Giles, Wrexham** (*c.* 1463). Sometimes these towers were detached, as at **Llandaf, Denbigh.**

Many churches were enlarged, usually by adding a wide aisle to one side of the nave, giving the appearance of a double-aisled church. There are numerous examples in **Clwyd.**

Castles & Palaces

The earliest castles were of the *motte-and-bailey* type, built of earth and timber. The more strategically placed of these, such as **Cardiff Castle** (*c.* 1090), were later rebuilt in stone. **Pembroke Castle** (13thC) was the first in Wales to have round towers, stronger and less vulnerable to missiles than angular towers. The most striking of all the early castles is **Chepstow Castle** (1067-1072), the first Norman castle to be built in Wales. The strongholds of the Welsh princes were largely demolished by the Normans but one of the most interesting of which there are remains is **Castell Carreg, Cennen** (13thC), Dyfed. The most formidable castles were those built by Edward I along the coast of northern Wales to control the occupied territories. Of the many concentric fortifications, **Harlech** (1283) and **Beaumaris, Anglesey** (1295), are especially notable.

Domestic buildings

Houses were generaly of the *cruck-frame* type, consisting of bays of timber trusses forming an "A" at their apex. The roof was usually thatched, the walls of *wattle and daub.* An example is the 15th-century farmhouse, re-erected in the **Welsh Folk Museum, St Fagans,** Glamorgan.

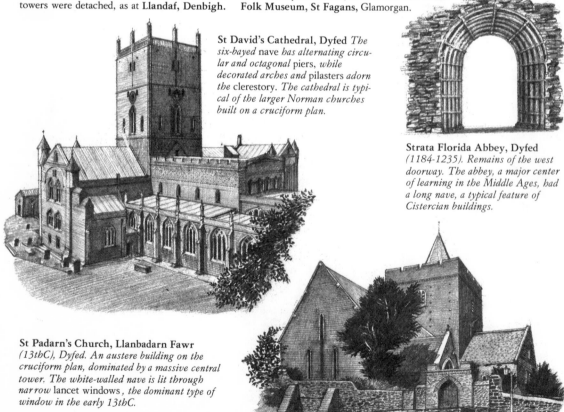

St David's Cathedral, Dyfed *The six-bayed* nave *has alternating circular and octagonal* piers, *while decorated arches and* pilasters *adorn the* clerestory. *The cathedral is typical of the larger Norman churches built on a cruciform plan.*

Strata Florida Abbey, Dyfed *(1184-1235). Remains of the west doorway. The abbey, a major center of learning in the Middle Ages, had a long nave, a typical feature of Cistercian buildings.*

St Padarn's Church, Llanbadarn Fawr *(13thC), Dyfed. An austere building on the cruciform plan, dominated by a massive central tower. The white-walled nave is lit through narrow lancet windows, the dominant type of window in the early 13thC.*

Beaumaris Castle *View of gate and bridge across the moat. The castle was built on a concentric plan, comprising an outer ring of defenses with 12 towers, two small gateways, each with an inner courtyard, and two more elaborate gatehouses, of which this is one.*

Pembroke Castle *An important fortress for Norman operations against Ireland, it was built on a strong defensive position at the end of a high ridge, surrounded on three sides by water. Of particular note is the round Great* Keep, *five stories high and with walls 20 ft thick.*

Caernarvon Castle *(c. 1285), below. A sophisticated example of a concentric castle, begun by Edward I. In addition to projecting towers (diagram, left), it has superimposed galleries between some of them to augment the castle's fire power.*

Harlech Castle, *left. Square in plan, with round towers at the four corners and a central gateway in the east wall, the castle stands on a rocky promontory, overlooking what was an inlet of the sea in the 13thC.*

Raglan Castle *(15thC), right. Once the castle consisted of a great tower — a self-contained fortified dwelling — standing within an encircling wall, complete with machicolations. It was restored and enlarged in the 16thC.*

Monnow Bridge, Monmouth *(1272). The route to Monmouth and south Wales across the Monnow is by this medieval fortified bridge. It is the only such fortified bridge still standing in Great Britain and one of the few remaining in Europe.*

Ireland

Religious buildings

The **Monastery, Skellig Michael** (12thC), Co. Kerry, is one of the earliest surviving Christian monasteries in Ireland. It consists of stone *beehive huts* and *oratories,* with characteristic rounded *corbel vaults.* Such vaults were also used in the rectangular **Gallarus Oratory, Dingle Peninsula** (12thC), in Co. Kerry. The **Church, St Macdara's Island** (12thC), Co. Galway, is equally plain, with a flat-headed doorway. The most characteristic feature of early Christian monasteries in Ireland, however, is the remarkable round towers, each often more than 98 ft high and capped by a conical roof. Their principal purpose was to serve as bell towers. Outstanding examples are found at **Glendalough, Co. Wicklow** (11thC), **Scattery Island, Co. Clare** and **Devenish Island, Co. Fermanagh.**

Romanesque work, while small in scale, was often lavishly decorated, notably with the *chevron* molding borrowed freely from the Normans. An extreme example of a decorated element is the doorway of **Clonfert Cathedral, Co. Galway** (12thC), which has numerous motifs, including foliage and animal and human heads. The most influential of all Irish churches, however, is **Cormac's Chapel, Cashel** (1127-34), in Co. Tipperary. Small in comparison to continental models, it is however a giant among contemporaneous Irish buildings. Many of its features were adapted elsewhere, such as the stone roofs of **St Kevin's Kitchen, Glendalough** (12thC), and **St Flannan's Oratory, Kellaloe** (12thC), and the *blind arcading* found along the interior walls of the *nave* in the church at **Kilmalkedar, Dingle Peninsula** (12thC).

The arrival of the continental monastic orders inspired the building of numerous abbeys, among them **Mellifont Abbey** (13thC), **Jerpoint Abbey** (*c.* 1400), and **Monasteranenagh, Co. Limerick** (1170-94). Further change came with the advent of the Normans at the close of the 12th century. The Dublin cathedrals of **Christchurch** (13thC) and **St Patrick's** (1220-54) are both early *Gothic,* while the *Transitional* style is seen best in **St Mary's Cathedral, Limerick** (*c.* 1180-95). Among other 13th-century buildings of interest is **St Canice's Cathedral, Kilkenny** (1251-80), which is a notable Cistercian reconstruction of the abbeys of **Holycross, Co. Tipperary** (1169), and **Tipperary** (12thC).

Castles & Palaces

The Normans built strong fortresses in the 12th and 13th centuries, as may be seen at **Carrickfergus,** (1180-1205) and **Trim Castle,** (13thC). Peculiar to Ireland is the rectangular *keep* with round towers at the corners, a good example of which is **Terryglass Castle, Co. Tipperary** (13thC). **Enniscorthy Castle** (1586-95) was built on the site of an earlier, 13th-century castle and has a four-story keep, again with a strongly-built round tower at each corner. There are also numerous *tower houses,* as there are in Scotland, of which **Dunguaire, Co. Galway** (16thC), is among the best preserved.

Round Tower, Glendalough *(11thC). The door is more than 10 ft above the ground. The roof was rebuilt in the 19thC, but the original stones were used. Once there were more than 100 of these towers in Ireland.*

St Kevin's Church, Glendalough *(12thC), Co. Wicklow. This modest-sized church is known as St Kevin's Kitchen. The monastery St Kevin founded there in the 6thC developed over the next two centuries into a large community.*

Trim Castle, Co. Meath *View of the* keep *and part of the* curtain wall *of Ireland's largest castle. It was built by the Normans and is square in plan. Its extensive wall is reinforced with turrets, gate-towers and a moat.*

Church, St Macdara's Island *A small rectangular church, measuring 20 ft x 13 ft, with gable ends built of carefully hewn blocks of stone, the larger being at the base and the smaller higher up. A characteristic of these early churches is the extension of the side walls and roof over the two ends.*

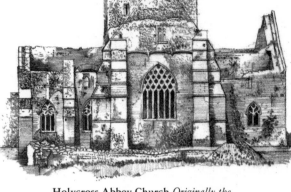

Holycross Abbey Church *Originally the church of a Cistercian abbey, it has recently been restored for use as a parish church. It is remarkable for the quality of its masonry work, most notably the rib-vaulting of the chancel and transepts.*

St Patrick's Cathedral, Dublin
The nave of this early Gothic cathedral, the largest in Ireland and rivaling some of its English counterparts in size. It is cruciform in shape and was largely rebuilt during the second half of the 19thC.

Tower House, Dunguaire
Fortified chieftains' dwellings such as this usually had rectangular towers, although a few, especially the earlier ones, are cylindrical and pointed. The windows have square drip mouldings.

Cormac's Chapel, Cashel *The outstanding* Romanesque *building in Ireland, it is distinguished for the elegance of its* blind arcading, *use of ornamentation and elaborate stone roof. It is spacious for its time.*

Stone sculpture

The predominant symbol of early Christian Ireland is the stone cross, with a circle surrounding the intersection of shaft and arms. Many had sculpted scenes of biblical themes.

Flann's Cross, Clonmacnoise, Co. Offaly

North Cross, Ahenny, Co. Tipperary

Muiredach's Cross, Monasterboice, Co. Louth

East Germany

Religious buildings

The **Abbey Church, Gernrode** (*c.* 959), has a central space in the *Byzantine* style, with a ladies' gallery and remarkable plaster relief work in the *nave*. The west façade (*c.* 1100), built by *Lombardic* craftsmen, has a wall of *arcades* flanked by two handsome round towers. The **Liebfrauenkirche, Halberstadt** (12th-13thC), has important plaster work in the *Romanesque choir screen* (*c.* 1200).

The **Convent Church, Quedlinburg** (1129), has an exterior of smooth, solid masses and an interior of uncluttered simplicity, held together by the square geometry of the *crossing*. Elegant twin towers frame the west front, *articulated* by *pilasters* and *corbel tables*. The **Abbey Church, Paulinzella** (1112-60), the finest of the houses of the reformed Benedictine abbey at Hirsau, has a narrow *narthex* which is southern German in its proportions. The **Cathedral, Freiberg** (*c.* 1230), Karl-Marx-Stadt, was originally a Romanesque church but was rebuilt in the *Gothic* style as a hall church. All that remains of the first building is the Golden Portal, so named from the lavish gilding which at one time covered it.

Since there was little high quality building stone in north Germany, brick construction work was common and, under Lombardic influence and Burgundian patronage, spread along the Baltic coast into Poland and parts of Russia. Good examples of the German bricklayers' craft are found in the *basilican*-planned Premonstratensian **Church, Jerichow** (*c.* 1150), and the **Cathedral, Brandenburg** (*c.* 1165). While the church at Jerichow has exposed brickwork, that at the **Abbey Church, Lehnin** (1180-1270), is largely plastered over. The articulation is generally more complex, while the nave and its *vaults* are in the transitional style from the Romanesque to the Gothic sytle. At **Wismar** there are two good examples of brick churches: **St George** (14th-15thC) and **St Mary's** (15thC). Another example worth note is **Zinna Monastery, Potsdam** province (15thC). It was built by the Cistercians and has brick *gables* which are Flemish in influence.

The **Cathedral, Magdeburg** (1209), replaced a 10th-century Romanesque building. The new building, though badly damaged during World War II, has traces of the more mature French Gothic, while most contemporaneous buildings, certainly until 1250, were still predominately Romanesque. The 12th-century *cloisters* are particularly notable.

Many churches have the characteristic Saxon façade, where the end of the nave might be as high or even higher than the twin towers at their sides. Examples are found at the **Church, Tangermünde,** and the **Cathedral, Havelberg** (13thC).

Civic & Public buildings

Interesting civic works include the **New Town Gate, Tangermünde** (1420). The town was an important center for river traffic on the Elbe. The magnificent brickwork fortifications are typical of the rich towns of the Altmark and northeast Germany. Other notable 15th-century gates are found at **Salzwedel** and at **Jüterbog**.

Premonstratensian Church, Jerichow *View toward the raised* choir, *which dominates the interior. Although built over a short period of time, the church is nonetheless a fine example of the art of brickwork, notably in the round columns with their trapezoidal capitals.*

Zinna Monastery, Potsdam *province. The four-story buildings, of which two stories are in the roof, have beautifully paneled stepped brick gables. One is crowned with a fine timberframed belfry.*

Cathedral, Magdeburg *The two-story* cloister *of the church, built of field stone. Of particular note is the two-story "Tonsur," which has a turreted stone roof similar to a Bronze Age bee-hive hut. It projects into a courtyard and has an arcaded ground floor, once the monks' washing place.*

Convent Church, Quedlinburg *Above left, view of the* nave *and side* aisles *of this* cruciform basilica. *The church is perched on a rock, where once a prehistoric fortress stood, and dominates the town below. Entrance to the building is via a* narthex. *Above the narthex is the so-called Nuns' Gallery, opened by arches to the church. Above, detail of a capital, which shows a close link with the work of Lombardic craftsmen. Here, however, the carving is more complex and of a higher quality.*

Abbey Church, Lehnin *View of the apse of this brick church. The lower part is divided into panels with elaborately interwined corbel tables, which were inspired by those at the Premonstratensian church of Jerichow. The windows above were added at a later date.*

Lutherhaus, Eisleben *(15thC). The late Gothic house where Martin Luther died in 1546. Town houses usually had high roofs and were built either parallel to a street with dormer windows or at right angles to it with gables.*

Town Gate, Jüterbog *One of the three surviving gates of the medieval town walls. The brick blind arcades, panelling and angled shields are similar to the articulation of the façades of nearby Zinna Monastery.*

Fortified Gate, Salzwedel *The city grew in importance during the 15thC and was protected by strong gates and bastions, designed to withstand artillery fire. Of particular interest are the gabled battlements and the entrance with blind arcading.*

Northern Germany

Religious buildings

The massive **Cathedral, Bremen** (11thC), was rebuilt in the 16th century and again in the 19th but retains its original proportions. Outstanding remains of the original building include the 11th-century *crypt,* the fine 13th-century bronze font and the *fan vaulting* above the north *aisle.*

St Michael's, Hildesheim (*c.* 1001), rebuilt since World War II, is a typically early *Romanesque* church with *basilican* plan and two aisles, but with west and east ends terminated by *transepts.* galleries and slender staircase towers. The **Cathedral, Hildesheim** (11thC), has likewise been rebuilt since 1945. The use of alternating single pillars and double columns in the *nave* is characteristically Saxon. Of particular note are the great bronze doors within the cathedral.

Twelfth-century churches include the Benedictine **Monastery, Königslutter am Elm** (1135), a Romanesque basilica with three aisles and five *apses,* and the **Cathedral, Brunswick** (1173-95), which was the first large, *vaulted* building of medieval Saxony to be erected without interruption. The church is a *cruciform* basilica with its choir and *crossing* over a vast crypt.

There are a number of fine country churches of the late Romanesque style in northern Germany. Examples include **St Alexander's, Wildeshausen** (13thC), the **Church, Huntlosen** (12thC), Weser-Ems, which was considerably enlarged in the 13th and 14th centuries, and the **Church, Schobull** (13thC), Schleswig-Holstein, which is brick built and a typical example of the church architecture of the area. The **Church, Ratekau** (*c.* 1168), Schleswig-Holstein, is a one-aisled church with a huge round tower on the west end, the only one of its kind remaining.

Castles & Palaces

The **Imperial Palace, Goslar** (*c.* 1050), was restored in 1132 and then rebuilt in 1879, but originally it consisted of a raised, two-naved, wooden-roofed main hall. The central throne room was delineated by parallel *arcades.* The imperial apartments at the south end include the fine two-story chapel of St Ulrich.

Domestic buildings

Domestic buildings of the 14th, 15th and 16th centuries were characterized by lofty roofs, frequently with more stories above the façades, lighted by *dormer windows.* Usually a lower story of masonry supported a timber upper section. Examples exist at **Goslar, Hildersheim** and **Brunswick.** The city of **Lüneburg** also has some fine medieval houses, many with brick-stepped *gables* with a pulley hoist at the top.

Civic & Public buildings

The rise of the middle classes in the late Middle Ages caused the building of many fine town halls. Outstanding among them is the **Town Hall, Goslar,** with arcaded ground floor opening on to the market. The council chamber is on the upper floor and is crowned with decorative *balustrading* of six straight-sided gables.

Cathedral, Brunswick *The wooden, painted figure of Christ on the Cross (c. 1173) is the work of the sculptor Imerwald. It is more Italian than German in spirit and resembles an allegedly miraculous crucifix, the "Volto Santo," in the cathedral of Lucca.*

Monastery Church, Bursfelde *Originally the church consisted of the east part only; the west part, with its high central space, galleried* arcade *and side aisles, was added in 1135. There are a number of fine frescoes, all of which show oriental influence.*

Benedictine Monastery, Königslutter am Elm *Detail of the north* cloister *walk, built between 1150 and 1170. The decorated columns support an upper story. The fine foliage and animal* capitals, *classical in inspiration, are of great richness.*

Cathedral, Bremen *The three-aisled* crypt, *built in 1068, has particularly fine carved capitals. The two sides depicted above show, on one panel, a wolf fighting with a winged snake and, on the other, a rosette of the sun.*

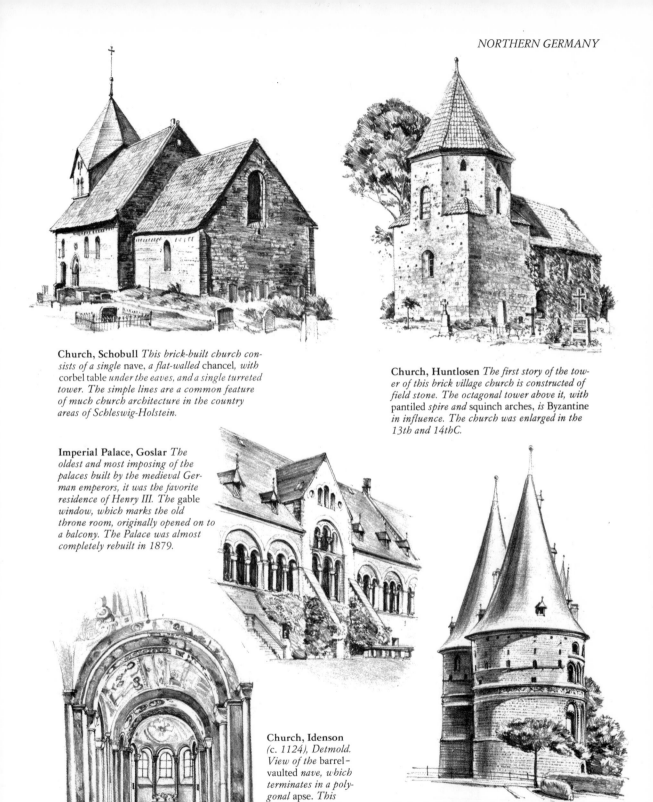

Church, Schobull *This brick-built church consists of a single nave, a flat-walled chancel, with corbel table under the eaves, and a single turreted tower. The simple lines are a common feature of much church architecture in the country areas of Schleswig-Holstein.*

Church, Huntlosen *The first story of the tower of this brick village church is constructed of field stone. The octagonal tower above it, with pantiled spire and squinch arches, is Byzantine in influence. The church was enlarged in the 13th and 14thC.*

Imperial Palace, Goslar *The oldest and most imposing of the palaces built by the medieval German emperors, it was the favorite residence of Henry III. The gable window, which marks the old throne room, originally opened on to a balcony. The Palace was almost completely rebuilt in 1879.*

Church, Idenson *(c. 1124), Detmold. View of the barrel-vaulted nave, which terminates in a polygonal apse. This diminutive building is constructed of large sandstone blocks and is especially notable for its fine frescoes in the Byzantine style.*

Holstein Gate, Lübeck *(1477). A city gate, fortified by a pair of enormous turreted towers. The outer faces of the towers are plain, while those facing inwards towards the city have ornamental ceramic friezes. The striped brickwork pattern is a Byzantine influence.*

141

Central Germany

Religious buildings

The **Cathedral, Trier** (*c.* 1035), has a gigantic west front of two square towers flanked by staircase turrets straddling the first bays of the *aisles*. On either side, at the base of the towers, are enormous *blind* arches with two stories of shallow galleries. There is a semicircular *apse* at the end of the *nave*. The **Cathedral, Speyer** (1031-61), an impressive *Romanesque basilica* with four towers and two domes, has an elegant *eaves gallery* running around the nave and *transepts*, and magnificent *groined vaults* over the nave and aisles. The **Cathedral, Mainz** (*c.* 1009-12thC), is another vast church, with the exterior of the east apse *articulated,* as at Speyer, by windows framed by molding and by an eaves gallery. Less magnificent but nonetheless distinctive is the **Cathedral, Worms** (11th-12thC). It has an apse at both ends, each flanked by towers, and a low, octagonal tower over the *crossing*. The entrances are in the aisles, a characteristic of both English and German cathedrals.

The **Cathedral, Minden** (13thC), a beautiful Romanesque basilica, has a handsome *westwork* enriched by a porch and blind *arcading*. The tiered blind arcading of the *chancel* interior is a familiar feature of the Rhineland. Another typical Rhineland Romanesque church is that of **St Mary, Gelnhausen** (13thC), a ponderous limestone building with spires and *gables* externally, while internally blind arcades and elaborately carved *consoles* decorate the chancel. The **Cathedral, Naumberg** (1044), was rebuilt in the 13th century on a considerably larger scale but in an unpretentious, late Romanesque style. Despite the four towers, it is an austere building with small windows and sparse molding. The extremely handsome west *choir,* built in the new style, was added in the late 13th century. Its striking unity of form is emphasized by the continuation of the wall arcading along the sides of the choir over the windows of the choir end.

The collegiate church of **St Patroclus, Soest** (1200-20), exemplifies the medieval conflict between the sacred and the profane, with the eastern portion belonging to the archbishop of Cologne and the western section, including the monumental tower, belonging to the town. Soest was one of the most important Hansa towns of the interior and the tower was a symbol of the town's power and independence.

St Pantaleon, Cologne (10thC), a huge church with deeply projecting transepts, wide aisles and alternating pillars and columns, has a Romanesque façade. The **Abbey Church, Münstereifel** (11thC), is similar to St. Pantaleon but has its façade flanked by towers with round bases and octagonal tops.

A distinctive feature of the *Carolingian* period is the rare type of round or polygonal church, such as the **Palatine Chapel, Aachen Cathedral** (792-805). The interior of the westwork of the **Minster, Essen** (1039-56), was closely modeled on the Palatine Chapel. The columns of the tiered arcading are notable for their particularly fine *Corinthian capitals.*

Convent Church, Freckenhorst *(12thC). Detail of the lower section of the basin of the font (1129), showing an imaginary creature from hell. The upper section of the basin depicts episodes from the life of Christ.*

Cathedral, Mainz *Detail of some* capitals *in the southeast porch. Representations of fiendish creatures were mainly the work of* Lombardic *masons, whose influence can be traced from the Po valley to the cathedrals of Germany.*

Palatine Chapel, Aachen Cathedral *Originally this was the chapel of Charlemagne's palace. The octagonal central space is covered by a* domical vault *and the area is ringed by an* ambulatory *at ground level. Above the ambulatory is a* gallery *on the floor level of the palace.*

Cathedral, Worms *The late* Romanesque *west* chancel. *The molded blind arcades and round, segmented window in the center were probably the work of Lombardic stonemasons. Two circular towers flank both west and east* apses.

Cathedral, Speyer
View of the tower over the crossing, with two taller, square towers flanking the choir end. This is the best preserved section of the cathedral and is notable for its Lombardic details.

St Mary of the Capitol, Cologne *(c. 1040-65). View of the* crypt, *which is among the finest in Germany. It has three* aisles, *separated by columns with massive cushion capitals supporting groin vaults.*

Abbey Church, Münstereifel *(11thC), Köln. The* westwork, *which consists of a rectangular structure crowned by a heavy square tower. The church is in the shape of a Greek cross. The western arm forms the entrance, while the* nave *is in the eastern arm.*

St Patroclus, Soest *The westwork breaks from the traditional concept and consists of a massive square tower decorated with* rose windows *and capped by an elegant Rhenish spire. There is an open* loggia *below it instead of a* portal.

Minster, Bonn
(c. 1150-1218). The building was erected in two phases and is an amalgam of French, Norman and German architectural styles. The arcades *of the 12th-C cloisters are recessed into the thickness of the wall.*

Abbey Church, Vreden *(11thC). Detail of the crypt (1014-44). It has three aisles with varied columns and capitals: the square columns have* clustered *shafts and simple capitals, the round columns lightly marked panels and carved capitals.*

Central Germany

Churches with two *chancels* are characteristic of *Carolingian* architecture in Germany. The west chancel was usually built as part of the *westwork,* forming a massive tower to which the *nave* was attached. An outstanding example is the **Abbey Church, Corvey** (12thC).

The **Abbey Church, Maria Laach** (1093-1152), is reminiscent of the cathedrals of Worms, Speyer and Mainz. Additional richness, however, is given by the use of basalt for the *Lombardic blind arcading* and columns, contrasting with the red stone walls. The **Church of the Apostles, Cologne** (*c.* 1190), is one of a series of *trefoil* churches in the city. Instead of a splendid *portal,* as is common in France, the west end has a single, vast tower, flanked by staircase turrets and crowned by a typically Rhenish roof, a pyramid rising from the steep *gables* on each face. Other trefoil churches in Cologne include **St Martin** (1185) and **St Gereon** (11thC). The latter has a magnificent east end in which the round *apse* is enhanced by an *eaves* gallery and a plattenfries, or *frieze* of rectangular sunk panels, a characteristic feature of the Cologne region. The **Cathedral, Cologne** (1248), the largest *Gothic* cathedral in northern Europe, has an imposing 500-ft, twin-towered west front. The high Gothic influence of the Ile-de-France and Picardy is particularly strong in the *choir.* Alterations to the cathedral continued to be made until 1880.

Castles & Palaces

The exaggerated character of medieval German castles was caused by the restricted mountainous sites on which they were built. Concentric defenses were almost impossible to construct and the problem was resolved by a great variety of ground plans, with each sector cut off from the others by ditches and accessible only by drawbridge. Behind such strongly defended approaches stood fine residential quarters. A good example is the **Castle, Eltz** (12thC), which was restored in 1920. It is a typical ganerbenburg, or castle which had multiple ownership, with four separate dwellings opening onto the courtyard, rather like later medieval town buildings. Another example is the **Castle, Schönburg** (14thC), Niederbayern, while the best preserved of the Rhineland castles is the **Marks-burg, Braubach** (*c.* 1231-15thC).

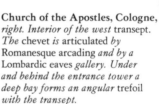

Palace, Gelnhausen *(c. 1200). The colonnade, part of the ruins of Emperor Frederick Barbarossa's castle. Other surviving structures include the entrance hall, chapel and watchtower. The decoration shows the influence both of southern France and of Normandy.*

Church of the Apostles, Cologne, *right. Interior of the west* transept. *The* chevet *is* articulated *by* Romanesque arcading *and by a* Lombardic eaves *gallery. Under and behind the entrance tower a deep bay forms an angular* trefoil *with the transept.*

Jakobkirche, Coes-feld *(1248). The west* portal, *all that remains of this fine Romanesque hall church, which was largely destroyed in World War II. The portal is unusual in having a clover leaf arch over the door instead of the more traditional* tympanum.

Abbey Church, Maria Laach *A monumental Romanesque* basilica *of three aisles. The* narthex *was added in 1220 and was finely carved capitals. The dour interior was originally poorly lighted but in the 1950s new stained glass windows were introduced.*

Abbey Church, Corvey *The west-work, a magnificent example of* Carolingian *architecture. The upper parts of the towers and intermediate structure are 12thC. The church is one of the oldest Benedictine buildings in Germany.*

Marksburg, Braubach *View of the gatehouse. A characteristic of German castles built on strong hill sites was that defense was deliberately concentrated on the gates. The Marksburg consists of a central tower, with the palace and other buildings constructed around it.*

St Michael, Fulda *(820-22). The rotunda, the original chapel of the abbey cemetery, is one of the earliest German copies of the Holy Sepulchre, Jerusalem. It has a fine ambulatory and above a gallery covered with a flat roof.*

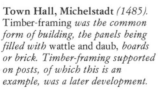

St Peter, Fritzlar *(1085-13thC). View of the* crypt *which, together with the west face and the lower parts of the towers, is all that remains of the 11th-C church. A typical Rhineland feature externally is the eaves gallery.*

Town Hall, Michelstadt *(1485). Timber-framing was the common form of building, the panels being filled with wattle and daub, boards or brick. Timber-framing supported on posts, of which this is an example, was a later development.*

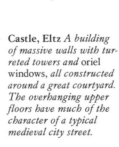

Castle, Eltz *A building of massive walls with turreted towers and oriel windows, all constructed around a great courtyard. The overhanging upper floors have much of the character of a typical medieval city street.*

145

Southern Germany

Religious buildings

Little remains of the Benedictine **Abbey, Hirsau** (1059-71), save the *Romanesque* Owl Tower but the influence of the Hirsau style of monastic architecture was widespread and an impressive survivor is the **Abbey Church, Alpirsbach** (11th-12thC), which is distinctive for its austerity and painstaking craftsmanship. The standard monastic layout of the Cisterician buildings is a sign of their innate conservatism. Even when their monasteries were altered or enlarged, as at **Maulbronn** (*c.* 1147-14thC), the basic plan of *cloisters* at the heart of the complex and church on the north side was retained.

The 13th-century porch at Maulbronn is the earliest German example of the transition from Romanesque to *Gothic,* while the monks' refectory is an amalgam of Romanesque grandeur and Gothic proportions and construction. The **Cathedral, Regensburg** (1275-1534), with a façade flanked by *Flamboyant* towers, is regular in plan with three eastern *apses* without an *ambulatory,* a typically German feature. The **Chapel of All Saints** (*c.* 1150-60), built as a bishop's burial place, opens off the Gothic cloisters of the cathedral. Its classical harmony of forms is unusual for German Romanesque. **St Jakob, Regensburg** (1150-1230), was built for the monks of the Irish church in Germany. It has a finely sculpted Romanesque north *portal.* Other interesting Romanesque buildings include **St Waltereich Chapel, Murrhardt** (15thC), a limestone building, **St Gallus, Brenz,** with fine *westwork,* and the *crypt* of the **Church, Oberstenfeld** (1016).

The **Cathedral, Bamberg** (1185-1237), on the other hand, is traditional Gothic in style. Romanesque exuberance is absent and there is no tower over the *crossing.* The octagonal upper parts of the west towers, with their superimposed corner tabernacles, are copies of those at Laon.

The power of the burghers grew during the late Middle Ages and was symbolized by the large and lavishly decorated churches which they built. These minsters invariably had a huge, single west tower. Those at **Freiburg** and **Ulm** are *basilican* in plan, while **St Martin's, Landshut** (14th-15thC), is a hall church. Another distinctive feature is the single portal instead of the triple portal characteristic of French cathedrals. The hall church, already in evidence in Westphalia during the Romanesque period, made a major contribution toward German late Gothic. The *aisles* were the same height as the *nave* and separated from it by tall columns. The church had, in fact, become one vast room. Examples are found at the **Cathedral, Munich** (13thC), the **Church of St George, Dinkelsbühl** (1448-1492), and the **Church, Altötting** (15thC).

Civic & Public buildings

Well-preserved fortifications of the period are found at **Ingolstadt,** notably the **Cross Gate** (1383), a stepped tower gate with turrets at the corners of each stage and with a *shingled* spire at the crown. There are well preserved medieval town halls at **Ulm, Regensburg** and **Amberg.**

St Michael, Altenstadt *(c. 1200), Oberbayern. The best preserved* Romanesque *church in Bavaria, it is built of* tufa *and has fine details typical of the* Lombardic *style. There is a chancel* apse *as well as two smaller apses closing the side aisles.*

Stadtkirche, Freudenstadt *(17thC). Detail of the 12th-C carved lectern, thought to have come from the monastery church of Alpirsbach. The figures of the four Evangelists supporting the book rest were carved from a single piece of lime wood.*

Cathedral, Freising *(1159-1205). Detail of the Bestiensäule, a column covered with carvings of imaginary creatures, in the* crypt. *The groin vault of the crypt is carried on three rows of alternating round and square columns.*

Cistercian Abbey, Maulbronn *The lay brothers' refectory is an early example of the transition from Romanesque to* Gothic. *The capitals foreshadow the Gothic while the proportions, construction and use of double columns are typically Romanesque.*

Houses in Market Place, Miltenberg *(c. 1500), right. Characteristic Franconian features here are the* oriel window *and the interlocking* braces *between the posts and rails.*

Dürer's House, Nuremberg *(15thC). A gabled house which has been extensively restored. Many Nuremberg houses have lower stories of stone with timber-framed upper stories. When built at road junctions, such houses were usually finished in a half-hip rather than with a gable.*

House, Wertheim *(16thC), left. Many of the panels between windows in timber-framed houses were elaborately carved, while houses of jettied construction had ornamental brackets, often with numerous carved figures.*

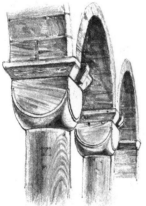

St Aurelius, Hirsau *(1059-71). The* arcade, *altered* c. 1120, *is typically Swabian, with ponderous cushion capitals that have no intermediate collar and so rest directly on the columns. St Aurelius is the smaller and older church of the Benedictine monastery at Hirsau.*

Baier Gate, Landsberg *(1425). Town gates in the Middle Ages were often decorated with Christian figures or symbols. This gate is well preserved and has fine sculptures and* outworks *flanked by tiny turreted towers.*

Monastery, Bebenhausen *(12thC). The main hall. Ponderous ribs, slightly pointed in the style of early Burgundian Gothic, spring from heavy capitals on short, round columns. The capitals are sculpted with entwined torch motifs.*

147

Switzerland

Religious buildings

The architectural influence of northern Italy was strong in 5th-century Switzerland. *Baptisteries* with an octagonal plan had developed in 4th century northern Italy, especially in Milan, with the building often encircled by an octagonal or a square *ambulatory*. In Switzerland a good example of the octagonal version is the Baptistery of **Riva San Vitale, Ticino** (5thC). Its interior is decorated with fine 14th- and 15th-century *frescoes* which have been recently restored.

The beautiful *Romanesque* **Abbey Church, Schaffhausen** (11thC), is *basilican* in plan with a flat-ended *chancel* and a long plain *nave* with a wooden ceiling carried on tall columns. Built by the Hirsan movement, which promoted a life and liturgy closely modeled on those at the great Abbey at Cluny in France, the church has all the simplicity and serenity of Cluniac architecture.

The **Church, Roumainmôtier** (*c.* 1180), Vaud, was built in pale Jura stone and has the quality and character of Burgundian Romanesque. Its plan was based on the design of the second Abbey at Cluny. The church is entered by a 13th-century *Gothic* porch and a two story *narthex* built early in the 12th century and decorated with fine 13th century frescoes. The **Priory Church, Payerne** (*c.* 1040-1100), is similar, with a *barrel vaulted* nave which, again, followed the Cluny model. Recently restored, it is considered the finest Romanesque church in Switzerland. The **Church, Saint Sulpice, Vand,** is a sturdy Romanesque building, with a semicircular chancel and a massive tower over the *crossing*.

The **Abbey Church, Hauterive** (12thC), Fribourg canton, was altered and extended in the 14th and 18th centuries, but has the pure rectangular geometry typical of Cistercian architecture. The *cloisters* are particularly characteristic, with *arcades* of twin *colonnettes* resting on a continuous *plinth*.

The Emperor Henry II built a cathedral at Basel, but it was destroyed by fire in 1185. The present **Minster** (12th-15thC) was built in warm red sandstone. The lofty west façade has slim Gothic towers and *open-work* spires. On the north side there is a magnificent Romanesque *portal* with sculpture decoration and surmounted by a *rose window* depicting the "Wheel of Fortune".

The finest Gothic building in Switzerland is **Lausanne Cathedral** (1175-1275). It has a lofty, narrow nave, simple and ordered, an east end *articulated* by two turreted towers, and a crossing surmounted by a massive tower with a spire that dominates the whole building. The south portal is enriched by a series of 13th-century sculptures.

Of the other fine cathedrals in Switzerland, **Fribourg Cathedral** (1283-17thC) is outstanding for its monumental Gothic tower crowned by an elegant pinnacled octagon. **Chur Cathedral** (12th-13thC) is an amalgam of Romanesque and Gothic styles. Unusually, the nave is off-axis to the chancel. The nave has finely carved *capitals* and there is a magnificent carved 15th-century triptych in the chancel. **Zürich Cathedral** (11th-13thC) has a tall twin-towered façade and a high, austere nave. The raised chancel is terminated by a relatively flat series of chapels forming the *chevet*.

Minster, Basel *Detail showing the fine carved* capitals *in the* nave. *The* triforium *is* Romanesque *and the* nave *has two side* aisles *on each side.*

Church, Müstair *(10thC).* One of the oldest *churches in Switzerland and part of the Bene- dictine Monastery of St John the Baptist. Originally the church had a* basilican *plan, but the nave was converted, redividing it into a two- aisled design in the 15thC.*

Chur Cathedral *Detail of a sculptured capital on the south side of the* choir *de- picting Daniel enthroned between two lions. To the right is a king seated between the Devil and a dragon and a serpent.*

Abbey, Hauterive *View of the* cloisters *which are modeled on those at Fontenay, in France, but here there are three arcades instead of two. The twin* colonnette *arrange- ment and the capitals are copies*

Church, Roumainmôtier *This lovely stone-built church has a high,* barrel-vaulted *nave dominated by an elegant central tower with a needle spire. The façades of the tower and the* gable ends of the transepts *are enriched by carved* Lombardic *decorative motifs.*

Notre-Dame-de-Valère, Sion *(11th-15thC). A magnificent fortress-church commanding a hill top with a view of the valley below. The church has a polygonal tower, fortified with battlements, and a defensive north wall complete with a wall walk.*

Riva San Vitale, Ticino *This view of the* baptistery *shows the lofty octagonal core which is surrounded by a lower, square-planned* ambulatory.

Zürich Cathedral *The northwest corner of the cathedral showing the fine main* portal *with its* articulated *Romanesque surround. The aisles have* galleries *above them, running the length of the* nave.

Abbey Church, Reichenau *(11thC). The magnificent west tower of this Benedictine abbey church. Built to replace a* Carolingian *structure, it has small round-arched windows. The tower is articulated vertically by* pilaster strips, *and horizontally by a frieze of arches.*

149

Switzerland

Geneva Cathedral (10th-13thC) has a very tall, narrow *nave,* austerely decorated with handsome *compound piers* and a lofty *choir* enriched with a *triforium. Gothic* architecture in Switzerland is Germanic in form but very much plainer, particularly internally where the chief architectural quality is clear, simple structure. **Bern Cathedral** (1421-16thC) has a simple lofty nave with side *aisles* and an equally tall choir divided from the nave by a soaring, unadorned arch. The building has no *transepts* but a huge square tower punctuates the junction of nave and choir rising to an octagonal stage and an *open-work* spire.

Castles & Palaces

In the 14th and 15th centuries many castles were made more exaggeratedly Gothic in appearance with high pitched roofs, stone flanking towers, *corbeled* corner turrets and stone *machicolations.* A superb example is the **Castle, Aigle** (13th-1475), with its elegant turreted towers. These are as much for defense as appearance because a steeply pitched roof is better able to deflect projectiles. Another magnificent castle is that at **Chillon** (13thC), which stands on an islet by the banks of Lake Geneva. The position of the castle, perched on the water's edge, is a defense in itself, following Germanic prototypes that relied on natural defenses such as cliffs and rivers.

The **Château, Vufflens-le-Château** (15thC), stands high on a plateau overlooking the River Morge. The monumental square-planned *keep* has a high *lantern* roof and four smaller towers around its base for added protection. The rectangular domestic quarters are detached from the keep by the entrance courtyard. These are flanked by circular corner towers and capped by a huge, *hipped* roof. The distinctive machicolations of the towers and the upper floors lend a strong medieval aura. The **Castle, Thun** (14thC), is also of interest with its massive keep with turreted corner towers that dominate the town from a rocky perch.

Domestic buildings

A characterisitc of the Engadine area (the upper valley of the River Inn) is the beautiful floral, geometric or heraldic patterns enriching their exterior walls. The decorative effect is achieved either by painting the white walls or, as at the **Padrun Mansion, Andeer** (16thC), by covering a grey plaster base with limewash which is then scraped away to give the desired decorative effect — a technique known as sgraffito.

Civic & Public buildings

The **Town Hall, Fribourg** (16thC), is particularly interesting for its exterior, double staircase under a canopy and for its turreted belfry. While the form of the building is still very much Gothic, the style of the *mullioned* windows, the stone *balustrading* of the staircase and the arches beneath it, is classical. The wooden columns supporting the canopy are traditional. Other town halls of note in Switzerland are the **Town Hall, Bern** (15thC); the **Town Hall, Basel** (16thC) and the **Town Hall, Sursee** (16thC).

Geneva Cathedral *Detail of the* capitals *on the south side of the* nave. *The carvings are reminiscent of both Burgundian and* Lombardic Romanesque. *The Cathedral has a series of carved capitals ranging from Romanesque to* Gothic *in style.*

Bern Cathedral, *above. Detail from the carvings that cover the jambs and central pillar of the main* portal. *They depict the Wise and Foolish Virgins wearing contemporary clothes and bridal crowns. These figures and the* tympanum *decoration were carved by the master sculptor Erhard Küng in the 16thC.*

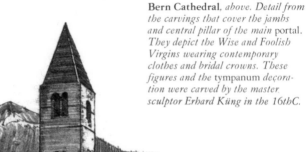

Church of Mont, Tiefencastel *A tiny Romanesque church with a tall turreted tower characteristic of the mountain churches of the Bünder Oberland.*

Castle, Aigle *A magnificent late Gothic castle with massive* drum *towers each with a conical roof. A covered wall walk runs along the inside of the* curtain walls. *The keep is a large turreted building at the center of the complex.*

Castle, Chillon *Built on an islet site projecting from the banks of Lake Geneva, the castle controlled an important trade route across the lake. The oldest part of the castle is the tall, central Tower of Alinge (10thC). A moat protects the castle on the bank side.*

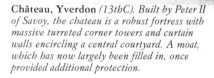

Château, Yverdon *(13thC). Built by Peter II of Savoy, the chateau is a robust fortress with massive turreted corner towers and curtain walls encircling a central courtyard. A moat, which has now largely been filled in, once provided additional protection.*

Padrun Mansion, Andeer *A fine example of the large gable-ended houses in the Engadine area. The walls are decorated by sgraffito, a regional decorative craft in southern Switzerland.*

Ramparts, Morat *(14th-15thC). This impressive fortified city still has its medieval* ramparts *intact with covered wall walk, shown here, and projecting towers. These towers present a flat face toward the city, and a curved defensive face outward. A 13th-C castle guards the entrance to the city to the southwest.*

Spreuerbrücke, Lucerne *(1408). In the middle of this covered bridge there is a tiny chapel, added in 1568, where a series of painted panels fixed in the triangular roof supports depicts the Dance of Death. Much of the bridge was heavily restored in the 19thC.*

151

Austria

Religious buildings

The oldest Cistercian monastery in southern Austria is the **Abbey of the Holy Cross, Heiligenkreuz** (1135-87). It has an austere and lofty *Romanesque nave* with side *aisles* and a *Gothic choir* (1288-95) of the *hall-church* type, lighted by huge, soaring windows. Placed near the entrance to the monks' refectory is a beautiful fountain pavilion, added in the late 13th century, where the monks washed before meals. The **Abbey, Zwettl** (1138-14thC), is a classic Cistercian work with lovely *cloisters* and *chapter-house* and with a magnificent 14th-century abbey church with lofty hall-type interior and soaring *compound* columns.

Gurk Cathedral (1140), despite later additions, is a comparatively unspoilt Romanesque building with a high, narrow *nave* and low side aisles terminated in the west by two tall, square towers which flank the recessed porch. There is a plain *chevet* with shallow *apses* and the *transepts* do not extend beyond the aisles. The **Bishop's Chapel**, incorporated in the *tribune* behind the west front, is decorated with handsome murals, painted in about 1230.

The major Gothic building in Austria is **St. Stephen's Cathedral, Vienna** 1304-1491). It is largely adapted from an earlier Romanesque building, the main addition being a huge new choir itself like a hall-church, terminated by three polygonal apses. The outstanding feature, however, is the south tower, part Italian *campanile* and part north European belfry, a lofty obelisk with filigree ornamentation. The majority of Gothic churches in Austria are of the hall type, with nave and side aisles of equal height. Good examples in Vienna include the **Church of the Augustinians** (14thC), the court church built within the imperial palace; the **Church of Our Lady on the River Bank** (13th-14thC), with *Flamboyant* west front and

Karner, Petronell *One of the oldest and finest of the karners, it consists of two engaged drums. The larger, the main body of the chapel, is windowless. Below the turret roofs are corbel table friezes and slim shafts.*

Parish Church, Schögrabern *(13thC). The semicylindrical* apse *is* articulated *in the characteristic* Lombardic *manner with arched* corbel table *and elegant, slender shafts standing on a molded* plinth *and held to the apse by an encircling stone sill.*

Cathedral, Gurk *The* Romanesque crypt *of the cathedral. It covers a large area, originally designed to accommodate the numerous pilgrims who flocked to the tomb of St Emma. The many columns supporting the* groin vault *have fine* cushion capitals, imposts *and* moulded bases.

Church, Wiener Neustadt *(1194). View of the* portal, *one of the outstanding Romanesque works in Austria. The arcaded screen wall on either side of the portal is reminiscent of Maria Laach Abbey, in Germany, and is a feature of the Bamberg School.*

ponderous seven-sided tower crowned with a pierced dome, and the **Church of the Minorities** (14thC), with a nave divided into three. But a more favored concept was that of paired naves, best seen in the **Parish Church, Schwarz** (15thC), and the **Church, Feldkirch** (15thC), which has a double nave and high *fan-vaulting,* typical of late Gothic churches in the Alps.

One of the more unusual building types of medieval Austria is the karner, a small, circular or polygonal funerary chapel, usually built over a charnel house. Outstanding examples include the round chapel at **Petronell** (12thC) and the polygonal chapel at **Tulln** (*c.* 1250), the latter having a handsome *blind arcade.*

Castles & Palaces

There are many fine 12th-century castles in Austria, their picturesque quality derived from the need to accommodate them on mountainous sites. One of the most notable is that at **Heidereichstein** (12thC), which has a massive circular tower. Other examples include the castles at **Rappottenstein** (*c.* 1157) and at **Salzburg** (11th-15thC).

Domestic buildings

Attractive 15th-century mansions include the **Bulmerhaus, Steyr,** with a *gable* and a *jettied* upper floor, and the **Kornmesserhaus, Bruck an der Mur,** of which the first two floors have elaborately decorated *galleried arcades* with fine Flamboyant style rosettes, *traceried balustrades* and elegant *ogee* arches.

Abbey of the Holy Cross, Heiligenkreuz *Left, the* nave *with Burgundian* rib vaulting *springing from the* engaged columns *of the arched corbel table. Right, the interior of the* chapter-house *looking toward the* cloisters. *The cross ribs bear* Baroque *paintings.*

St Stephen's Cathedral, Vienna *Detail of the* traceried gables, *designed by Hans Puchsbaun, which externally arti-culate the scale and proportions of the* nave. *They are an adaptation of the traceried work above the main portal and* rose window *of Strasbourg Cathedral.*

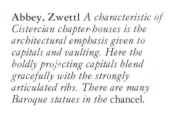

Abbey, Zwettl *A characteristic of Cistercian chapter-houses is the architectural emphasis given to capitals and vaulting. Here the boldly projecting capitals blend gracefully with the strongly articulated ribs. There are many Baroque statues in the* chancel.

Little Golden Roof, Innsbruck *(1500). This attractive structure, a combination of* loggia *and* oriel window, *was added to a quite plain building to give it distinction. The first floor balustrade has an unusual frieze consisting of coats of arms.*

Belgium

Religious buildings

Romanesque architecture in Belgium is divided into two distinct types. The earliest is the Mosan, or Meuse Romanesque, style that lasted until the mid-12th century. Churches are usually of great simplicity and were frequently built over a *crypt* with timber *vaulting* carried on square pillars. They often have a formidable west front and a bulky tower. A good example is the collegiate church of **Ste Gertrude, Nivelles** (10thC), a Romanesque *basilica* with 12th-century west front and 14th-century tower flanked by turrets. The remainder was built in the 19th century.

The Scheldt-Romanesque style (*c.* 1150-1250) followed the Mosan style and is characterized by churches with a central tower and main entrance in the west on axis, and with greater elaboration of the *nave* and more ornate decoration than hitherto. The major example is **Tournai Cathedral** (*c.* 1110-1213), with its four-story nave and *transepts* and monumental *crossing.* The polygonal *choir* with radiating chapel was added in the 13th century. It is pierced by large windows divided by slender pillars. The rich exterior is crowned by *gables* and *pinnacles* which are carried up above the *eaves* line.

The stone church at **Hamoir** (12thC) has a particularly interesting *apse,* decorated externally with a band of niches under the eaves, while *blind* arches on *imposts* carried on *pilasters articulate* the lower part. A high, stone *plinth* surrounds the building. The church of **St Barthélemy, Liège** (13thC), has a magnificent west front, distinctly German in influence. The rest of the church was remodeled in the 18th century. Inside there is an outstanding bronze font (1107-18). The **Church, Tourinnes-la-Grosse** (11th-12thC), is notable for its huge stone-built west tower embellished with a projecting staircase turret.

The more modest country churches of Belgium often have the appearance of a barn. An example is the church of **Saint-Eleuthaire, Esquelmes** (11thC), a plain church which was restored in the 19th century and after World War I. It has a high nave extended by a *presbytery* and semicircular apse. A belltower was added later. The **Church, Chièvres** (12thC), consists of a rectangular nave with a polygonal apse. The entrance, with elegant *archivolt,* is at the center of one side. Three arched windows, their sills extending the length of the wall, enrich the façade and a *corbel table* articulates the eaves.

Church of Guvelingen, Saint-Trond *(12thC). A pleasant rural church, it was restored in 1938 and has a high* nave *with low flanking* aisles *and a fine belfry with a* broach spire. *External decoration is in the form of an irregular checkered pattern of brick and stonework.*

St Pieter, Herent *(c. 1425). Detail from the surviving 11th-C crypt. The angles of the crossing are* articulated *by clustered columns with a continuous* frieze *for the* capitals, *decorated with vegetation, foliage and figures, a combination of* Romanesque *and early* Gothic *forms.*

Oratory of the Order of St John of Jerusalem, Chièvres *(12thC). A barn-like church, it stands in a field outside the town and consists of two parts, nave and* sanctuary, *with a simple belfry spire. The austere stone walls have blind arches.*

Cathedral, Antwerp *(1352-1411). The west front, with its single, monumental tower 403 ft high. The cathedral is the largest church in Belgium and has a magnificent nave with seven aisles and narrow transepts.*

Church, Aubechies *(11thC). A fine stone church whose character stems from the fact that it was never completed, hence the severity of the ponderous crossing tower articulating the junctions of nave and choir. There were to have been transepts and a flanking aisle.*

Parish Church, La Hulpe *(13thC). Entrance to the nave is via this fortress-like stone belfry tower. It has a* broach spire, *a characteristic of Mosan country churches. Access to the* vaulted *upper story of the tower is by the staircase tower projecting from the side wall.*

St-Hermès, Renaix *(12thC). This Roman-esque crypt, partly restored in the Gothic period, extends under the choir and tran-septs of the church. Of particular note are the alternating round and octagonal columns and the heavy cushion* capitals.

St Barthélemy, Liège *(12thC). The fortress-like west front of the church, which consists of* helm-roof *towers and a three-story* narthex, *articulated by blind* arcading, pilasters, engaged columns *and* corbel table. *The Rhineland Romanesque influence predominates.*

Church, Bois-et-Boursu *(12thC). A fine country church of stone, with a sanc-tuary with* apse, *a high nave and simple west tower. The walls of the sanctuary are articulated externally with Lombardic paneling, the earliest example to be found on a Mosan church.*

Belgium

Gothic buildings in Belgium took on distinctive regional characteristics. In Schledt the churches often have corner towers, a central *crossing* and double *ambulatories,* while in the district of Kempers and along the coast, simple hall-like churches are common, built of brick and occasionally with alternating courses of sandstone. In the district around Bree, Limbur, the many fine 15th-century churches, such as those at **Neeroeteren** and **Beek**, are a product of the prosperous wool trade of the 14th to 16th century. Walls are of local marl stone and towers are often polygonal.

Other Gothic buildings of interest include the church of **Saint-Nicolas, Tournai** (13thC), a modest building with a strong, *gabled* front flanked by tall, turreted towers which *articulate* the junction between the high *nave* and the low side *aisles.* An open gallery, the height of the *clerestory,* runs around the building. The cathedral of **SS Michel and Gudule, Brussels** (13thC), has an early Gothic tower (1226) and two magnificent west towers, added at about the same time as the west façade (1525-75).

Apart from religious houses such as abbeys and monasteries, there are a series of beguinages, which are self-contained buildings surrounded by a wall, for lay sisters devoted to charitable work. These beguinages took the form either of a village of small cobbled streets and brick houses, often surrounded by canals, as in **Louvain** (14th-18thC), or of a group of buildings formed around a court or green, as in the 13th-century example at **Bruges**. There was usually a church or chapel in addition to the communal rooms.

Castles & Palaces

The **Château des Comtes, Ghent** (1180), is a fine example of a castle utilizing a river or lake to protect one or more of its flanks. Many castles were built near the richer towns for purposes of administration and taxation. The castle here was built in order to control the rich merchants who had themselves constructed elaborate fortified tower-houses within the city. The idea of building a palace within the walls as well, separate from the *donjon,* was in emulation of contemporaneous German examples. Another chateau is that at **Beersel** (14thC), which consists of three giant towers connected by walls and surrounding a circular court. The **Donjon Ter Heiden, Rotselaar** (16thC), while retaining the castle form is also concerned with domestic functions.

Domestic buildings

The stone built **Maison de l'Etape, Ghent** (12thC), is a rare example of a *Romanesque* house in Belgium. The style is not dissimilar to that found in Tournai but the stepped gable is more typical of Flanders. There are three handsome houses in **Jerusalemstraat, Bruges** (16thC), with two brick-stepped gables for the two end houses, linked half way up their parapets by two *crenellated* bays which make up the third house. The façades are articulated by tall, slender, double-recessed arches, in which the *mullioned* windows and floors of the various stories are found.

Church, Wezeren *(12thC). An outstanding stone village church with a solid west tower which has heavy* buttresses *and a handsome spire. The internal decorative motifs include some of the finest* Romanesque *sculptures in Belgium.*

Cathedral, Tournai *(c. 1110-1213). One of the enormous* apses, *flanked by twin towers, which terminate each arm of the* transepts. *A central* lantern *crowns the* crossing. *The four tiers of narrow arched openings was a German device for bringing richness and color to large wall surfaces.*

Nôtre Dame, Lissewege *(13thC). A magnificent brick church, it is of a Latin cross plan with a* nave *and side* aisles, *transepts with polygonal ends and a choir flanked by two* apses. *The major feature, however, is the giant belfry tower, a characteristic of Flemish marine churches, enriched with tiers of blind* arches.

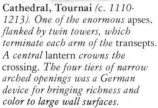

Nôtre Dame, Tongeren *(13th-16thC). The church is planned on a Latin cross scheme with the transept arms contained within the boundary of the aisle façades. The nave, with its high* clerestory, *and the south transept date from the mid-13thC, while the elaborately decorated tower and recessed entrance were added in 1441.*

Château des Comtes, Ghent *A magnificent example of a fortified medieval castle, it consists of a huge four-story* donjon *surrounded by a battlemented outer wall. It stands on a bank of the River Lys and has its entrance on the land side protected by an elaborate gatehouse with octagonal towers.*

Donjon Ter Heiden, Rotselaar *A brick tower-house, it consists of a hexagonal core with three projecting wings. Diagonal coursing is given to the brickwork at the* gable parapet *and decorative bands of stonework on the main façade.*

Abbey, Bijloke *(14thC), Ghent. Detail of the brick gable of the refectory of the abbey with its elaborate decorative brick moulding and blind arches. The walls are adorned internally with some outstanding examples of 14th-C frescoes.*

Château, Beersel *This red brick fortress, consisting of three enormous towers, apse-shaped on the outside and gabled on the inside face, is surrounded by a deep moat. The towers are pierced with gun* loops *and connected to each other by high walls with a defensive gallery.*

Belgium

Civic & Public buildings

Early civic buildings in Belgium owed much to the architecture of castles, palaces and domestic buildings. A fine example is the **Hôtel de Ville, Aalst** (13thC), which has a fortified appearance reminiscent of the 13th-century Hôtel Echevinal, Vilvorde. The **Hôtel de Ville, Damme** (15thC), is also indebted to castle architecture. A rectangular building with *corbeled* corner turrets, it has a high basement with the main hall above. The façade is symmetrical around central steps and entrance porch and is accentuated by the hexagonal belltower on the roof. On either side are three large windows, their sills encircling the building. There is an ornate parapet with tri-lobed arches and raised *pinnacles* with stepped *gabling*. The **Hôtel de Ville, Louvain** (*c.* 1425-75), is a lofty, three-story building encrusted with statuary and crowned on the gable ends by high pinnacles and a decorative battlemented parapet enriched with *open-work* floral motifs. The **Hôtel de Ville, Oudenaarde** (16thC), borrows from the Louvain Hôtel de Ville's decorative gable ends but its three-story main façade concentrates all its elements on a lavishly decorated central tower.

One of the most handsome of the town halls is that at **Bruges** (14th-15thC), which has a façade of tall, slender windows alternating with stone *piers*. There are tiers of ornately decorated statuary. Octagonal turrets *articulate* the corners and center while the ridge of the roof has floral motifs.

Civic power was most forcefully expressed in giant belfry towers, such as that at **Bruges** (13th-14thC), which dominates the town's medieval market buildings. The **Belfry, Ghent** (1321-80), also acts as a focal point for a whole group of public and civic buildings.

Commercial & Industrial buildings

The **Cloth Hall, Ypres** (1200-1309), restored in the 19th century and rebuilt after destruction in World War I, is one of the most magnificent examples of medieval commercial building. The **Halles and Belfry, Nieuport** (14thC), also rebuilt after World War I, is an unpretentious building, lacking the monumentality of those of Flanders. The main façade consists of two stages surmounted by a parapet with simple pinnacles and handsome corbeled corner turrets.

Hôtel de Ville, Aalst *This town hall is quadrilateral in plan and has circular corner towers with turrets and stepped* gables *on the lateral ends. The plain stone façades are articulated by tiers of tri-lobed windows and are enriched with arches,* colonnettes, *and* crocket capitals

Halles and Belfry, Bruges*. For many centuries this was the main market of the town. It consists of buildings planned around a central courtyard, dominated by a magnificent belltower. The tower was built in two stages (13th and 15thC).*

Hôtel de Ville, Louvain *A lavishly decorated* Flamboyant *building, it has octagonal pinnacled turrets articulating the corners and high gabled ends with pinnacles crowning the apex of roof and gable parapet. The elaborate sculptures in the niches and consoles depict biblical scenes.*

Abbey, Ter Doest *(c. 1275), Lissewege. A brick barn, part of the abbey complex. Monumental in proportions, it is typical of monastic farm buildings in having a high centre portion with side aisles. The decorative brick blind windows of the gables contrast effectively with the functional simplicity of the oak roof inside, supported on stone bases.*

Guild of Masons House, Ghent *(1526). The façade of the building. Although built of stone it continues the tradition of timber-frame buildings with its vertical panels enriched with decorative horizontal bands between the head and sills of the windows.*

Hôtel de Ville, Oudenaarde *A fine late Gothic town hall, built by Henri van Pede. It is reminiscent of many of the buildings in the Grand Place, Brussels, in having an ornate central tower, crowned by a stone coronet, which dominates the main façade.*

Cloth Hall, Ypres *The main façade, 433 ft long, is of simple plan and has rectangular openings on the ground floor with two stories of arched openings above. Each floor is distinguished by a continuous sill. Pinnacled turrets articulate the lateral ends and central emphasis is given by the monumental belltower.*

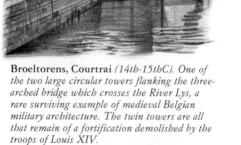

Broeltorens, Courtrai *(14th-15thC). One of the two large circular towers flanking the three-arched bridge which crosses the River Lys, a rare surviving example of medieval Belgian military architecture. The twin towers are all that remain of a fortification demolished by the troops of Louis XIV.*

Guild Houses, Grand Place *(16thC), Antwerp. The Gothic tradition remained strong in Belgium even at this late date. The façades of this and similar buildings are designed in bays, separated by slender piers surmounted by arches. Decorative pinnacles adorn the gables.*

Holland

Religious buildings

The major *Romanesque* buildings in Holland are both in **Maastricht**, a prosperous mercantile city in the 12th century. The finer of the two, **St Servaaskirk** (12thC), has an *apsed* east end *articulated* by *blind arcading* and *eaves gallery,* flanked by twin towers in the manner of Rhineland cathedrals. The west end has three towers with *helm roofs,* a spacious *narthex* and a first story chapel. The **Vroumekirk** (*c.* 1150) is renowned for its *westwork* with cliff-like central section flanked by slim, round turreted towers. At the east end is an apse articulated by blind arcading and flanked by twin towers with Rhenish helm roofs. The *vaulting* of both churches is *Gothic.*

The **Abbey, Middelburg** (1128-16thC), was dissolved in 1559 but is a magnificent walled complex with a huge central courtyard, irregular in shape, containing two churches, the **Nieuwe Kerk**, a modern reconstruction in the *Flamboyant* Gothic style, and the **Koorkerk**, which incorporates parts of the old *choir.* French influence is seen at its strongest in the Gothic **Cathedral, Utrecht** (1254-14thC). The *nave* collapsed in 1674 but the remaining choir and 14th-century tower are outstanding.

By the late 13th century outstanding examples of brick-built architecture were appearing in Holland. Characteristic features include wooden *barrel-vaulting* and a single high tower. Two such churches are the **Grote Kerk, Brouwershaven** (1350-1450), and the **Oude Kerk, Amsterdam** (*c.* 1306-16thC). **St Peter, Leyden** (1294-1426),

is another fine brick church with well-defined columns. **St Jan's Cathedral, Hertogensbosch** (1419-1529), is a particularly handsome church with a lofty and spacious choir and rich decorative work, in contrast to the generally more austere Dutch church architecture. An equally ornate church is the **Groote Kerk, Breda** (13thC), with a 15th-century tower.

Many 14th- and 15th-century Dutch churches have fine towers, often with elaborate octagonal *lanterns.* Examples include **St Jan, Maastricht** (*c.* 1450); **Nieuwe Kerk, Delft** (15thC), with a tower built in 1396; the **Cathedral, Haarlem** (1400-90), and **Martinskerk, Groningen** (13th-15thC), which has a Gothic base combined with a handsome *Renaissance* tower.

Castles & Palaces

Notable castles include that of **Radboud, Medemblik** (1288), a brick castle with stepped *gables* which have been restored; the **Knights' Hall, The Hague** (1288), a fine brick building with huge gabled façade flanked by round turreted towers, and **Muiden Castle** (1205-15thC).

Civic & Public buildings

As in Belgium, the wealth of Dutch cities of the Middle Ages is reflected in numerous town halls. Good examples include the **Town Hall, Middelburg** (1412-1599), which was a prosperous center of the wool trade, and the **Town Hall, Veere** (1474-1599), which has a tall façade crowned with six gables and flanked by corner turrets.

St Servaaskerk, Maastricht *Detail of a* Romanesque *column and* capital *found in the chapel. A former cathedral,* St Servaaskerk *is a handsome* Romanesque basilica, *resembling churches typical of the Rhine area.*

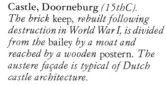

Castle, Doorneburg *(15thC). The brick* keep, *rebuilt following destruction in World War I, is divided from the* bailey *by a moat and reached by a wooden* postern. *The austere façade is typical of Dutch castle architecture.*

Cathedral, Utrecht *View of the choir. The noble, spacious interior was influenced by the* Gothic choir *of Amiens, begun 18 years earlier. The* nave *collapsed in 1674, was rebuilt, then restored from 1921 to 1935. The stained glass windows date from this recent restoration.*

Grote Kerk, Brouwershaven *The* choir, *which was built in the 14th C. Of particular interest is the skillful use of different building materials, with stone for the columns and red brick for the arches and the* blind arcading.

Vroumekirk, Maastricht *The cliff-like westwork, reminiscent of the Abbey Church at Freckenhorst, was built c. 1000. The flanking round towers are a characteristic feature of many Rhenish cathedrals.*

Town Hall, Middelburg *A large brick building, it has pinnacled gables, elaborate corner turrets, open-work parapet and geometrical paneling above the main windows. The walls between the windows are enriched by pinnacled niches, which are embellished with statuary.*

Koppelpoort, Amesfoort *(1440). This water-gate is part of a heavily fortified bridge-gate, straddling the river Eem. It was designed to control access to the town, which was by both road and water.*

Castle, Genhoes *(14thC), Oud Valkenburg. This fine castle is one of many to be found in the area around Valkenburg. It is more ornate than most Dutch castles, being built of mellow stone with elegant decorative brick bands encircling the base.*

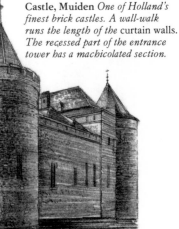

Castle, Muiden *One of Holland's finest brick castles. A wall-walk runs the length of the curtain walls. The recessed part of the entrance tower has a machicolated section.*

Northern Spain

Religious buildings

Santiago de Compostela was one of the three great pilgrimage cities of the medieval world, the others being Rome and Jerusalem. The **Cathedral** (1077-1128) has a two-story elevation. Designed to accommodate the great number of pilgrims who came to venerate the remains of the apostle St James, it has an *ambulatory* surrounding the *apse* which continues in the form of *groin-vaulted aisles* around the *transept* and down the *nave,* connecting the seven chapels of the *chancel* with the transept.

Many churches were built on the pilgrimage routes to Santiago de Compostela. **León,** an important city in the Middle Ages, was a stage on the road and the fine church of **San Isidoro** (1054-1188), a *basilican* building, was built into the medieval ramparts. All that remains of the 11th-century portion is the *narthex.* Another example of a pilgrimage church is **Santo Sepulchro, Torres del Rio** (*c.* 1200), an unusual octagonal chapel, clearly derived from the Holy Sepulchre, Jerusalem. Of particular note is the influence of Islamic architecture on the pattern of the *ribs* and in the octagonal *lantern* crowning the building. The **Cathedral, Burgos** (1221-1457), the third largest in Spain after those at Seville and Toledo, is among the most beautiful in the country. Its distinctive exterior has two western towers with spires, reminiscent of Cologne Cathedral, and an ornate central lantern. Internally, the octagonal Constable's Chapel has outstanding *Gothic* features. The walls and altar were later decorated by *Renaissance* sculptors.

Other notable buildings include the **Cathedral, Lérida** (1203-78), with an abundance of fine 13th-century *Romanesque* sculpture, and the **Cathedral, Barcelona** (1298-1448), which was built to replace a Romanesque church and has an exuberantly decorated interior.

Cathedral, Burgos
El Sarmental Portal, the main entrance to the cathedral, with a tympanum depicting the Evangelists at their writing tables. This and other features of the exterior are reminiscent of French and Rhenish styles, while the elaborate interior is much more Spanish in character.

San Pedro, Besalú *(12thC). Detail from the* capitals, *which are richly decorated with representations of stories from the Gospels. San Pedro has a notable* ambulatory, *with radiating apsidal niches and a* vault *carried on four pairs of columns.*

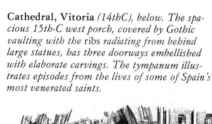

Cathedral, Vitoria *(14thC), below. The spacious 15th-C west porch, covered by Gothic vaulting with the* ribs *radiating from behind large statues, has three doorways embellished with elaborate carvings. The tympanum illustrates episodes from the lives of some of Spain's most venerated saints.*

Cathedral, Santiago de Compostela, *(see also p. 278). Detail of the Portico de la Gloria (1168-88), the masterpiece of Spanish* Romanesque *sculpture, with carvings of the Last Judgement and a huge figure of Christ in the central tympanum.*

Cathedral, Huesca *(1497-1515). Detail of the tympanum, with reliefs depicting Christ with Mary Magdalene and the Magi. The elegant main façade is divided by a gallery and a* portal. *The cathedral has the late Gothic square plan comprising nave and two aisles.*

Cathedral, Avila *The fortified* apse, *built of granite on the eastern side of the city walls. Crowned with a double row of battlements, it formed a* bastion *in the ramparts. The austere appearance is mellowed by* pilasters, *Romanesque windows and Gothic pinnacles.*

Cathedral, Barcelona *The* cloisters, *the lower story of which is Romanesque (12thC) while the upper story, with its late Gothic arches and* tracery, *was added in the 15thC. There are 22 chapels at the back of the* cloisters *together with an enclosed fountain.*

Cathedral, Jaca *(11th-12thC). Detail of a capital in the south porch depicting King David with his musicians. The cathedral, one of the oldest in Spain, was the first example of Romanesque architecture in the Pyrenean region and its style influenced many of the buildings on the pilgrim ways.*

Cathedral, Lérida *Detail of the south doorway, showing the finely sculptured multiple* archivolts, *with dogtooth ornament,* chevrons *and scrolls of foliage. Carvings of fantastic beasts enrich the capitals.*

Santa Maria, Aranda de Duero *(15thC). The façade, a typical example of the* Isabeline *style with exuberant decorative work of lace-like carvings, heraldic motifs and free forms covering the entire face. The style was extensively used on civic as well as religious buildings.*

San Juan Bautista, Baños de Cerrato *(661), Palencia. This triple-arched church is one of the best preserved monuments of Spain. The aisles, here, are covered with timber vaulting and have arches on marble columns.*

163

Northern Spain

Spain is especially rich in religious buildings, quite apart from those built along the pilgrimage routes to Santiago de Compostela. The **Cathedral, Tarragona** (12thC), a late *Romanesque* building, was completed in the early *Gothic* period and has a fine 13th-century *lantern* tower and a 14th-century *apse* on the north *transept*. **Santa Maria, Ripoll** (12thC), was rebuilt in the late 19th century after a disastrous fire but has the remains of a beautiful *portal,* one of the finest of Catalonian Romanesque sculptures. The doorway is framed on all sides by bands of carving, dominated by the figure of God surrounded by the symbols of the four Evangelists.

There are outstanding wall paintings in the 12th-century Catalonian churches of **Santa Maria** and **San Clemente, Tahull**. The latter has a magnificent belfry modeled on a Lombardic campanile. Notable churches in **Segovia** include **San Esteban** (13thC), a Romanesque building with a particularly fine tower with five tiers of *arcades* on each face, and **San Millán** (12thC), which has well-rounded apses *articulated* with half columns, a *porticoed* gallery with carved *capitals* and *modillions,* and a tall *Mozarabic* belfry of the 11th century.

Other outstanding buildings include the church, **San Martin, Frómista** (*c.* 1060), an example of the austere pilgrimage hall church with a tall octagonal lantern at the *crossing,* and **San Tirso, Sahagún** (*c.* 1145), an amalgam of Catalonian Romanesque and early *Mudejar* brick architecture. The old **Cathedral, Salamanca** (12thC), a handsome Romanesque building with a vast central dome, is intact but masked by the new **Cathedral**

(1530-60). Further buildings of note in Salamanca include **San Martin,** a Romanesque church with a *Plateresque* gallery, and the **Ursuline Convent** (16thC), which is renowned for its exquisitely carved, low relief tomb sculpture.

Castles & Palaces

A characteristic of Spanish castles is the extremely tall tower, rising above elaborate lengths of *curtain walls,* with loop-holes and built to withstand artillery fire of the time. A good example is at **Peñafiel** (15thC), known as the gran bruque or great ship, with two lines of curtain walls running along the crest of a hill, the inner being studded with round towers and having a continuous wall walk. The **Castle, Coca** (15thC), is a magnificent example of Mudejar architecture and is built of brick rather than of stone. The **Castle, La Mota** (1440), Medina del Campo, is another battlemented brick castle, with a massive square *keep* at one corner, with four pairs of twin turrets at its corner angles as additional fortification.

Civic & Public buildings

The **Walls** (11thC) of the city of **Avila**, which remain complete, are an outstanding example of fortifications in the Middle Ages. They are 40 ft high for much of their 1.5 mile length. Strengthened in the 14th century, the walls are *buttressed* by 88 granite block towers and *bastions* and have eight gateways. The **Colegio de San Gregorio, Valladolid** (1488-96), is one of the most superb examples of the *Isabeline* style, with an opulent entrance and some fine Moorish carvings.

Cathedral, Gerona *(1312). Detail of 12th-C relief work in the* cloisters. *The church was founded by Charlemagne in 786 and was rebuilt in the 11th and 14thC. The piers of the south walk have* friezes *depicting the Book of Genesis.*

San Román, Cirauqui *(13thC). This simple village church is remarkable for its magnificent* portal. *Instead of framing the door, the portal falls short of it and disguises its true shape. The* archivolt *has alternating plain and ornamental banding.*

San Salvador, Leyre *(11th-13thC), Navarre. View of the* crypt, *which has high* vaulting *and ponderous* capitals *supported by short columns of irregular height and design. The abbey is one of the great Roman-esque works of Spain, built when Leyre was a center of monastic life.*

Casa de las Conchas, Salamanca *(15thC). The patio is decorated with multilinear arches and pierced* balu-strades *with sculptured heads and coats of arms. The façade is en-riched with carved scallop shells and* Isabeline *windows with wrought iron grilles at ground level.*

Isabeline style

The style was named after Isabel the Catholic (r. 1474-1504) and was the last to evolve before the *Renaissance*. It is characterized by extreme ornamentation, often contained in panels and covering whole façades, but with decorative emphasis given to entrances.

Church of San Pablo, Valladolid (1463)

Torre del Clavero, Salamanca *(c. 1450). The massive polygonal tower* keep is *all that remains of the castle, which was once the main citadel of the city. The sentry turrets, resembling fortified* oriel windows, *are decorated underneath with fine* Mudejar *trelliswork.*

Colegio de San Gregorio, Valladolid (1488-96)

Castle, Valencia de Don Juan *(15thC), left. The castle has a cluster of exceptionally tall and thin round towers on its keep and* curtain walls *and is an outstanding example of medieval castle architecture in northern Spain.*

Castle, Coca *A vast brick fortress, it is a major example of Mudejar military architecture. It has three concentric battlemented perimeters together with a monumental keep at its center.*

Castle, Fuensaldaña *(15thC), Valladolid. One of the many castles built by the nobility during the civil wars of the 15thC. This example was neither finished nor occupied but has an imposing keep with corner towers rising from the ground and* outworks *of rectangular plan.*

Central Spain

Religious buildings

For many centuries Toledo was inhabited by a mixture of peoples, including Christians, Jews and Moslems. Under Christian rule, *Mudejar* architecture attained its finest expression in palaces, churches and synagogues. A characteristic was the use of brick construction, *blind arcading* and belfries faced with *azulejos* and geometrical *strapwork*. An outstanding example is the church of **Christo de la Luz** (1000), which was built as a mosque but was converted in the 12th century to a Mudejar church. **Santa Maria la Blanca** (12thC) was Toledo's oldest synagogue until it, too, was converted into a church in 1405. The **Cathedral, Toledo** (1227-1493), has five *aisles* and a range of side chapels. It is also notable for housing many outstanding religious paintings.

Unlike Mudejar architecture, which was carried out by Muslim craftsmen under Christian rule, the *Mozarabic* style was, on the whole, executed by Christian craftsmen and enriched with Moorish features. Interesting examples of Mozarabic architecture include **Santa Maria de Melque, Toledo province** (*c.* 900), a small *cruciform* church with horseshoe arches and window heads.

The monastery of **Santa Maria, Guadalupe** (1340), is a richly endowed place of pilgrimage comprising a strongly fortified group of buildings complete with battlemented towers and turrets, while the **Cathedral, Murcia** (1394-16thC), is a large *Gothic* structure, encrusted externally with *Renaissance* and *Baroque* decorative work.

Civic & Public buildings

The **Puerta del Sol, Toledo** (*c.* 1200), is a particularly fine Mudejar gate, with two horseshoe arches, decorative brick blind arcading and sculptured panels. The **Puerta de Serranos, Valencia** (1349), has *traceried* wall paneling above two gateways and flanking polygonal towers encircled by a *corbeled* gallery.

Santa Maria, Guadalupe *The fountain building of the monastery, erected in 1405 in the center of the* cloister. *Built in the* Mudejar *style, it is an extreme example of the adoption of Moorish forms and motifs in a Christian building.*

Puente de San Martin, Toledo *(13th-14thC), below. The bridge forms the western approach to the city across the Tajo river and is on the site of an earlier one, destroyed by flooding. It is a slim structure of five spans, with a fortified tower at each end.*

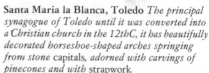

Cathedral, Murcia *The octagonal Capilla de los Vélez (15thC), a splendid late* Gothic *edifice built off the ambulatory of the Cathedral. The star vaulting and wall decoration are subtle mixtures of several Renaissance motifs.*

Santa Maria la Blanca, Toledo *The principal synagogue of Toledo until it was converted into a Christian church in the 12thC, it has beautifully decorated horseshoe-shaped arches springing from stone capitals, adorned with carvings of pinecones and with strapwork.*

Castle, Manzanares el Real *(15thC). During the years of struggle between Christians and Moslems in New Castile many castles were built, of which this is one of the most handsomely decorated examples. The interior is notable for a fine* Isabeline *gallery.*

Castle, Calatrava la Nueva *(c. 1216), Ciudad Real. View of the chapel and its magnificent rose window. The Castle, built for the Order of the Knights of Calatrava, is now mostly in ruins but remains include, in addition to the chapel, monastic buildings, double curtain walls and a keep.*

Casa de los Golfines, Cáceres *(15thC). The palace has the appearance of a fortress but is embellished with a splendid Isabeline-style cornice, an elegant stepped panel, articulated by molding, embracing windows and entry portal, and a spacious patio.*

La Lonja de la Seda, Valencia *(1482-98). The east wing of the building, with its large gateway and side windows, contains the old exchange hall of the silk merchants. The west wing has square-headed Gothic windows together with an open gallery on the upper floor.*

Puerta del Sol, Toledo *Moorish influences are evident in most secular buildings of the Middle Ages in Toledo, but are particularly strong in this Hospitallers' gate with its horseshoe arches, intersecting arcades, pyramidal battlements and corbeled sentry balconies.*

167

Southern Spain

Religious buildings

Andalusia was under the control of Islam from the mid-8th to the 15th century. Moorish architectural influences are much in evidence, such as horseshoe-shaped arches, ornamental brick relief work, *cupolas* supported on *ribs* and entrances crowned with *blind arcading*. One of the finest examples of Muslim work is the **Cathedral, Córdoba** (785), which was a mosque until adapted in the 16th century. It is a monumental building with a massive pillared interior. The plan is the standard Muslim one of crenellated square perimeter enclosing a forecourt, with basin for ritual ablution, a covered gallery and a prayer hall. The east front has particularly fine Moorish relief ornamentation. The **Cathedral, Seville** (1402-1520), the largest medieval cathedral in Europe, also owes its form and monumental scale to the mosque which it was built to replace.

Castles & Palaces

Many Moorish features were incorporated in *Mudejar* work. Examples include the major palace complex in the area, the **Alhambra, Granada** (13thC), and the **Palace, Seville** (14thC), which has *artesonado* ceilings and *azulejos* decoration. The courtyard of the **Casa de Pilates, Seville** (15th, 16thC), is another fine example of the Mudejar style, with azulejos work and an abundance of *stucco* ornamentation. Another outstanding castle is the **Alcazaba, Almeria** (8thC).

Cathedral, Córdoba, *left. The interior, with its abundance of granite and marble pillars. The two tiers of arches are made of alternating bands of white stone and red brick. The Cathedral was once a mosque, the largest save for the Ka'ba in Mecca.*

Castle, Almodóvar del Rio *(16thC), Córdoba, below. An imposing Moorish castle, it was rebuilt in the 14thC and is a fine example of the highly decorated nature of* Mudejar *military architecture.*

Cathedral, Seville *View of the 12th-C minaret, which was not demolished in 1401 when the mosque was pulled down but was incorporated in the new Christian building. The four sides are relieved by recessed panels of filigree work, flanked by panels of* diapered *brickwork. The belfry was added in the 16thC.*

Alcazar, Seville *(12thC). View from the Moorish arched Patio de las Munecas, with its carved stucco and azulejos decoration, to the Salon de Embajadores, which has a remarkable cedarwood cupola. Most of the present building of the Alcazar dates from the Christian era.*

Alhambra, Granada *(1338-90). The Court of the Myrtle Trees, leading to the audience chamber of the Moorish rulers. This courtyard, together with the Court of the Lions, forms the heart of the complex. The Alhambra is among the most decorated of Islamic palaces.*

Portugal

Religious buildings

The **Cathedral, Lisbon** (12thC), was originally a fortress church and has battlements and two towers flanking its façade. The **Cathedral, Coimbra** (1162), with its battlemented walls and turret-like *buttresses*, is another such. Of particular note is the large *nave* window designed like a door, with *machicolated* sill to defend the main door beneath. Other examples of fortified churches are the cathedrals of **Oporto** (12thC) and **Evora** (12th-13thC). The latter has a façade flanked by massive towers and has monumental *cloisters,* built in the 14th century.

The **Templars Church** in the **Convent of Christ, Tomar** (12thC), was modeled on the Holy Sepulchre in Jerusalem. The outside wall has 16 sides, and the central sanctuary is octagonal. The *Manueline* style nave (1510-14) is one of the last great architectural works in Portugal to be entirely free of *Renaissance* influence. The earliest important building in the Manueline style is the **Church of Jesus, Setúbal** (1491). It is late *Gothic* in plan and structure and has elaborate Manueline decorative work, consisting of rope molding enriching *piers, apse* and window surrounds, and a profusion of vegetable motifs and twisted, spiral forms.

Castles & Palaces

The **Tower of Belém, Lisbon** (1515-19), built of white limestone, is a robust fortress, five stories in height. The battlemented platform jutting out toward the water was for artillery. The **Castle, Vila de Feira** (11thC), reconstructed in the 15th century, has a huge rectangular *keep* with square angle turrets, each crowned by conical, brick spires, a characteristic more of southern than of northern Portugal. Other examples of massive keeps are found at the **Castle, Guimarães** (10thC), which was reinforced in the 15th century by seven square towers and encircling walls, and the **Castle, Braganza** (1187), where the keep is 88 ft high and flanked by watchtowers.

Church of the Conceicão Vella, Lisbon *(16thC). The south face of the transept, with its magnificent portal, is all that remains of the original church. It is, nonetheless, an outstanding example of the Manueline style.*

Templar Church, Convent of Christ, Tomar, *below. West window of the monastery church, one of the most celebrated examples of Manueline predeliction for naturalism combined with exotic and highly decorative forms.*

Monastery, Batalha *(1398-16thC). Detail from the chapels, which were never finished. They were designed by Mateus Fernandes the Elder, the most Gothic of the Manueline architects. Work was discontinued on the chapels when King João III abandoned them in favor of a cathedral in Lisbon.*

Tower of Belém, Lisbon *This Manueline tower, standing by the River Tejo, has balconies and two arched windows of Moorish design. Internally there are royal quarters with a fine Gothic ceiling. The tower has extensive Moorish decoration.*

Hieronymite Monastery, Lisbon *(1502). View of the Jeronimos cloister, two stories high and overlaid with heavy, layered ornamentation. The Monastery was one of the first to be financed by the wealth brought to Portugal from South America.*

Denmark

Religious buildings

Ribe Cathedral (c. 1130) and **Viborg Cathedral**
(c. 1140) are strongly influenced by earlier German
and Italian prototypes. At Ribe the southwest
tower is capped with a Rhenish *helm roof* and the
apse is *articulated* in typical *Lombardic* manner.
The *crossing* is domed, a feature more typical of
southwest France. Viborg has twin west towers,
while at the east end smaller towers flank the apse.

The **Church, Kalundborg** (c. 1170), a Greek
cross plan with five towers, functioned as a
fortified stronghold as well as a church, for it is
strategically placed between northern Denmark
and southern Sweden. Numerous other centralized
churches were built along the shores of the Baltic
during the Middle Ages to act both as religious
and defensive centers, notable examples being the
round churches at **Bjernede Kirke** (c. 1160-80).

In Denmark, as in Norway, many small, stone
parish churches were modeled on the Anglo-
Saxon plan of rectangular *nave* and *chancel*.
Windows were few and small and a narrow arch
connected nave and chancel. Examples are found
at **Hover** (11thC) and **Gudrum**. Royal churches
were more elaborate versions of these simple
parish churches. Many have semicircular apses at
their eastern ends and towered west fronts.

Roskilde Cathedral (1190) is a fine brick
church with a twin-*aisled* plan modeled on French
Gothic and has west towers with needle-like
spires. The *choir* is reminiscent of that at Tournai,
a result of the commercial links between the two
cities. Another outstanding building is **Odense
Cathedral** (c. 1247). Aahus Cathedral has a
hall-type choir and an enormous west tower with
fine spire. Both examples have decorative stepped
gables, which embellish the ends of the aisles at
Odense and the *transepts* at Aahus. Other notable
brick churches include the **Abbey Church,
Logumkloster** (1173); **Söndresogn Church,
Viborg** (13thC), a *rib-vaulted hall-church,* and
that at **Norre Alslev** (14thC), which has a
handsome tower with gables.

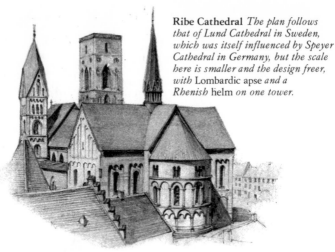

Ribe Cathedral *The plan follows
that of Lund Cathedral in Sweden,
which was itself influenced by Speyer
Cathedral in Germany, but the scale
here is smaller and the design freer,
with* Lombardic apse *and a*
Rhenish helm *on one tower.*

Church, Venge
*(12thC), Jylland. A
simple cruciform
church, it consists of
a single aisle, two-
story* transepts *and
three semicircular
apses. Narrow arches
connect the columns
of* nave, *transept arms
and* choir. *The tower
is a later addition.*

Round Church, Bjernede Kirke
*The upper section is built of brick, the
lower of small granite blocks. Four
large stone columns support the
conical roof. The form of such
churches appears to be an amalgam
of Templar church with castle* keep
and chapel.

Church, Kalundborg
*Designed in the form
of a Greek cross,
it has a square central
tower, with four
octagonal towers
pinning down the
four arms of the cross.
The church was almost
entirely rebuilt in the
late 19th century
and then extensively
restored between 1917
and 1921.*

Norway

Religious buildings

The *Romanesque* stone churches of Norway, such as **Stavanger Cathedral** (*c.* 1130), have the massive cylindrical *piers* and bold spatial quality of those of *Norman* England. The influence of English medieval architecture was remarkably strong in Norway, largely due to Norway's geographical position. Since access to Sweden was made virtually impossible by the formidable mountain barrier, its most accessible neighbor was England across the sea. One result of such contact is the English appearance of **Trondheim Cathedral** (1130-1290), which bears strong similarities in plan and internal spatial arrangement to some of the cathedrals of central England, such as that at Lincoln. It has central and western towers, a lofty *nave,* eastern *chapels* in each arm of the *transepts,* a *choir,* bordered by a stone screen, with an *ambulatory* behind, and an elegant *triforium.*

Some of the earliest churches in Norway were, like the 6th-century Irish churches, no more than a single rectangular room, in which a *chancel* might later be included. Good examples include the 11th-century parish churches at **Moster** and at **Alstarhoug.** The royal church, with a similar origin, was yet another type. While the former was a product of the local community, the latter was erected by the royal court. They are found in many parts of Sweden, Denmark and Norway and consist of a nave and chancel. Following Norman practice, the square eastern end was later abandoned in favor of a semicircular apse, as may be seen at **St Halvard, Oslo.** Some had towers to provide accommodation for the king and his court.

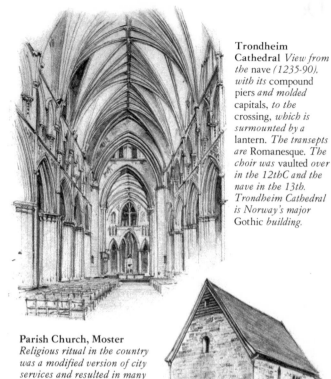

Trondheim Cathedral *View from the* nave *(1235-90), with its* compound piers *and molded* capitals, *to the* crossing, *which is surmounted by a* lantern. *The transepts are* Romanesque. *The choir was* vaulted *over in the 12thC and the nave in the 13th. Trondheim Cathedral is Norway's major* Gothic *building.*

Parish Church, Moster
Religious ritual in the country was a modified version of city services and resulted in many simple churches. This one comprises a nave and chancel *connected by an arch.*

Stave churches
Unique to Norway, Stave churches developed (11th-16thC) from simple timber buildings with the bases of the wall posts buried in the earth to more refined structures where the bases were joined to a ground sill frame. Plans followed the Anglo-Saxon tradition of rectangular *nave* and *chancel.*

Decorative detail from Stave church, Urnes

Detail from Stave church, Hyllestad

Stave church, Urnes (1125-40)

Stave church, Borgund (c. 1150)

Sweden & Finland

Religious buildings

Swedish abbey churches of the 12th century, such as those at **Nydala, Småland,** and **Roma, Gotland,** were modeled on French prototypes, especially that at Fontenay, in having a plan with a clearly defined *module* throughout. The **Abbey Church, Varnhem,** which was rebuilt in the 13th century, has a semicircular *sanctuary* ringed with chapels, as at Fontenay. The major *Romanesque* building in Scandinavia is **Lund Cathedral** (1080). Radically altered in the 12th century and extensively restored in the 19th, it is a *basilican* church with *nave* and side *aisles, transepts* and an *apsed chancel.* An Italian stonemason from Speyer in Germany supervised the work and introduced the *Lombardic* style of *vaulting,* the lively exterior decoration characteristic of the Rhineland and the monumental and richly decorated interior typical of continental architecture. The building played a dominant role in introducing German and Italian ideas to Scandinavia, spread by the artists and masons trained in its workshops. The churches in **Gotland,** such as **St María, Visby** (1225), and the churches at **Dalhem** and **Oja,** were especially influenced by Lund Cathedral. A characteristic feature was the hall form with west tower, often including galleries.

Romanesque stone churches in Sweden are characterized by lofty nave and *choir,* tall towers and semicircular eastern *apses.* A magnificent example is the fortified church of **Husaby,** which has an immense square tower flanked by small circular turrets added in 1057. German influence is strong but the plan of nave without transepts, and choir or chancel with a semicircular apse, is a distinctively English influence.

The major *Gothic* buildings in Sweden are the cathedrals of **Uppsala** (*c.* 1270-1315), **Skara** (*c.* 1300) and **Linkoping** (*c.* 1130-13thC). Uppsala started with an English plan but in 1287 a French mason was appointed supervisor and gave the building an apsidal end with an *ambulatory* and chapels around the choir, typical of French cathedrals. Skara has a Latin cross plan with west towers and lofty English style nave. Linkoping was originally an Anglo-Norman church with transepts and semicircular apses. Considered too small, the choir was rebuilt with an ambulatory and in the mid-13th century English builders were commissioned to construct the magnificent nave, which is *hall-church* in its form.

The hall-church type of 14th-century building, such as **St Mary's, Sigtuna,** the **Convent Church, Ystad,** and the **Church of the Holy Trinity, Uppsala,** were strongly influenced by prototypes in Holland and north Germany. Some, like that at Ystad, have beautifully decorated *gabled* brick façades. Hall-churches on a vaster scale are the cathedrals at **Strängnäs** and **Värsterås, Lake Mälar.** The former is renowned for its outstanding brick interior.

Sculptured ornamentation was rare in the brick churches of central Sweden, vaults decorated with *frescoes* and painted wooden ceilings being the dominant decorative features. Good examples are the east vaults at **Strängnäs** and the wooden ceilings at **Dädesjö, Smaland** (14thC), and at

Abbey Church, Roma *(12thC), Gotland, Sweden. Ruins of the* nave arcade, *all that remains of this extremely simple and austere stone-built abbey church. It has plain* piers *and* columns, *the sole function of which is to* articulate *the separate parts of the abbey.*

Linkoping Cathedral, *Sweden. South door of the nave. A curious collage of elements, it is thought to have been made up of parts from elsewhere because of the disparity between the thickness of the side columns and those on the arch above, and between the ornateness of the tympanum* compared *with the plain frame.*

Church, Dalby *(11th-13thC), Sweden. A royal church of great size, which also functioned as a cathedral. It was a* basilica *with nave and two* aisles *but later additions include a* transept, *a new choir and much brick* vaulting.

Södra Rada, Värmland (1323). The peak of medieval mural painting was attained in Uppland in the 15th and 16th century, notably in the decoration of the vaulting of the **Church, Täby.**

One of the oldest stone churches in Finland is the church at **Jomala** (12thC), **Aland Islands,** which contains the remains of lovely 14th-century paintings which at one time decorated the whole interior. A characteristic Finnish feature, save in the churches of the Aland Islands, is the free-standing belltower, often added many years later. **The Church, Inkoo** (13thC), Uusimaa, has a fine brick patterned gable as well as a stepped wooden belltower on a stone base (18thC). Another example is at **Siuntio, Uusimaa** (15thC), which has outstanding decorated gables and a belltower added in the 19th century.

The only major Gothic cathedral in Finland is the one at **Turku, Turku Pori** (13th-16thC), much rebuilt but still retaining its medieval aura in the brick-built interior. Of the larger churches, the characteristic feature is their hall-church form, usually with three *aisles* and beautifully painted vaults. A good example of this form is **Porvoo Cathedral, Uusimaa** (*c.* 1415).

Church, Skanella *(11thC), Sweden. In the late 11thC the semicircular* apse *replaced the hitherto straight east wall. Another dominant characteristic was the central tower, a fashion first set here and later adopted in many churches at Sigtuna.*

Church, Tryde *(12thC), Sweden. Detail of the carved font (c. 1160), the sides of which are enriched by figure sculptures. There was little ornamentation in early churches, the emphasis being mainly placed on their baptismal fonts.*

Kalmar Castle, Sweden *(14thC). The massive castle was built around a* circular *tower house. Standing on a promontory on the east coast, it is one of the strongest fortresses in Sweden. Its defenses comprise* ramparts, *four corner towers, a moat and a drawbridge.*

Parish Church, Tyrvaa *(14th-16thC), Finland. A simple* hall-church *built of large blocks of crudely dressed stone, it is typical of 14th-C churches in Uppsala, north Sweden and Finland. Of particular note are the brick decorations of the gables (1513-15).*

Olavinlinna Castle, Finland *(1475). A fortress guarding the border with Russia. The traditional* keep *and* curtain walls *were abandoned for aggressive corner towers, which are part of the castle residence.*

Yugoslavia

Religious buildings

The large cathedrals of the Adriatic, such as that at
Poreč (*c.* 550) and **St Maria Formosa, Pula**
(6thC), are wholly western in plan but some
eastern architectural elements, such as the cross-
shaped *martyrium* of the latter, are frequently used.
The major influences on the Balkans were Salonica
and Constantinople. **St Pantaleon, Nerezi**
(*c.* 1164), for example, drew heavily on models in
Constantinople, with its octagonal central *drum*
contrasting with four square drums.

The centrally-planned church was common in
9th-century Dalmatia and was either cross-shaped,
trefoil or round with projecting niches. A good
example of the last is **St Trojce, Split** (9thC), while
St Donat, Zadar (9thC), is circular with surrounding *ambulatory* galleried above. There is a
narthex to the west and three *apses articulated* by
blind arches to the east. *Hall-churches,* such as **St
Sophia, Ohrid** (9thC), were equally common
during the 9th and 10th centuries, as were single-
nave, barrel-vaulted churches such as **St Lukor,
Kotor** (*c.* 11thC). The exterior walling of most
late *Byzantine* buildings was profusely enriched.

The elongated *quincunx* church remained the
basic form for 14th-century architecture in central
and southern Yugoslavia. Good examples are at
Staro Nagoričane (1313), where a *basilican* plan
was remodeled, and at **Gračanica** (1321), which
is not dissimilar in plan but has extremely tall
drums to the domes. The walls of early 14th-century
Serbian churches are comparatively simple brick or
cloisonné work, with the occasional meander or
herringbone pattern. By the middle of the 14th
century the decoration of walling had become
richer and more profuse, but the characteristic
feature of corner domes and drums, seen at
Gračanica, gradually disappeared.

In the Morava Valley the traditional Byzantine
forms and textures, enriched with *Romanesque*
twisted *colonettes* and the pointed *tracery* windows
of the *Gothic,* produced a series of extremely
elegant churches, fine examples being those at
Ravanica (1375-77), **Kalenić** (1407-13) and at
Rudenica (1402-27). The plans consist of three
semicircular niches with half domes built around
an adapted Greek cross or quincunx form.

Church, Gračanica
*One of the finest
examples of medieval
Serbian architecture, it
has four corner domes
and drums arranged in
the form of a pyramid
topped with a high
drum and embellished
with semicircular,
pointed gables.*

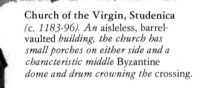

Church of the Virgin, Studenica
*(c. 1183-96). An aisleless, barrel-
vaulted building, the church has
small porches on either side and a
characteristic middle Byzantine
dome and drum crowning the crossing.*

St Kliment, Ohrid
*External detail of the
apse, showing the
checkered pattern
of the brickwork,
cloisonné bands and
tall recessed niches
which articulate the
sides of this section of
the building.*

Church, Kalenić *The
effect of loftiness is a
dominating feature,
achieved by an elon-
gated cupola and by
vertical division of the
façades. Alternating
bands of brick and
stone and the distinc-
tive silhouette are
reminiscent of
many buildings on
Mount Athos.*

Bulgaria

Religious buildings

Among the most remarkable examples of early *Byzantine* church architecture in Bulgaria is the **Old Metropolis, Nesebâr** (5thC). The ruins are an impressively austere version of an *Hellenistic basilica,* with a *naos* of nave and side *aisles,* a single trilateral *apse* to the east and a three-sectioned *narthex* to the west. The only decorative work seems to have been murals, traces of which are to be found in the apse.

Early church architecture involved minor modifications to the basic basilican plan by the use of *vaulting* and more ponderous supports. The *hall-church* terminated by three powerful apses, which was developed in the 9th century, was a unique departure. A good example is **St John the Baptist, Nesebâr** (*c.* 900). From the late 9th to the 11th century large basilican churches were built, often with galleries. Examples include **St Achill, Prespa Lake** (9thC), and the church at **Staro Nagoričane** (1067-71), which now forms the lower portions of the 14th-century church.

The characteristic *quincunx* church plan of middle and late Byzantine architecture is rare in Bulgaria. Here the most common church is an aisleless, *barrel-vaulted* nave with a central dome raised high on a *drum* and with a second and lower drum crowning the narthex. **St Martyrs Church, Târnova** (*c.* 1230), has a beautiful west façade, rich in the decorative motifs characteristic of the area, such as *blind* arches with windows above, recessed within a larger arch. The **Church of the Archangels, Nesebâr** 14thC), is an example of the elongated, aisleless church with a dome.

Old Metropolis, Nesebâr *Ruins of the once monumental church, with its great walls built of alternating bands of stone and brick work. The church body is divided into a* nave *with side* aisles *by rows of solid pillars.*

Church of the Archangels, Nesebâr *View of the richly decorated exterior, with alternating bands of brick and* cloisonné. *The* archivolts *of the* blind arcading *are* articulated *by triple lines of decorative rosettes.*

St John Aleiturgitos, Nesebâr *(14thC). Irregular bays of blind arcading, wide above the sides, narrow on the main apse and even narrower on the minor* apses *encircle the lower storey. A corbel-table frieze, enriched with* polychrome *decoration, articulates the apse.*

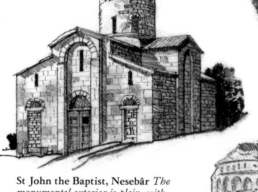

St John the Baptist, Nesebâr *The monumental exterior is plain, with none of the decorative enrichment of later church architecture in Nesebâr. Four massive pillars form the cross of this domed cruciform church, while above the cross rises a huge* drum *dominating the whole.*

Greece

Religious buildings

Church building in northern Greece and the Balkans in the 5th and the 6th centuries usually comprised a *basilica* with cross *transepts*. An outstanding example is the basilica of **St Demetrios, Salonica** (5thC). One of the most impressive churches of the Aegean coastlands, it has a *nave* 180 ft long and fine carved *capitals* with *imposts*. **St Sophia, Salonica** (6thC), a transitional form between domed basilica and domed cruciform church, has a spacious interior with *arcaded* walls pierced by small windows. Only the *apse* and center bay are lighted. It is a squat, plain cube crowned by a square *drum*. The 9th- and 10th-century mosaics of the *vaults* enliven what would otherwise be a sombre marble interior.

The most common plan for a middle *Byzantine* church was the *quincunx* or cross-in-square plan. **Panaghia Chalkeon, Salonica** (1028), is a fine example, extended to the east by three apses and to the west by a *narthex*. The central dome has an octagonal drum with *cornice,* while the arms of the cross have triangular *pediments*.

St Katherini, Salonica (13thC), differs little in plan from Panaghia Chalkeon, but the basic scale is one of loftiness with a higher dome, and apse and *barrel vaults* over the cross arms accentuated by a low narthex. Four drum sites at the corners of the narthex balance the drum over the center of the building.

The most impressive church ground plan of the Middle Ages, however, is the Greek cross-octagon arrangement, which is usually on a small scale. The outstanding example is the magnificent **Katholikon, Hosias Lukas** (1020), a simple cube crowned by a low octagonal drum and shallow dome. The **Theotokus, Hosias Lukas** (*c.* 1040), is modeled on similar lines. The influence of Constantinople is powerful, but the overall effect is original and was to influence middle Byzantine building in Greece for many years to come. The apses project on this multi-angled building and are distinguished by their many elegant windows, which are almost all of either two or three parts, divided by plain *mullions*.

The church of the **Holy Apostles, Salonica** (1312), has higher corner drums than is usual with late Byzantine architecture. The interiors by the 14th century were generally wider and loftier than hitherto and the texture of the walls much richer. Another characteristic of late Byzantine architecture is the opening up of the narthex front by arcading.

While church building was often innovatory, monastic complexes remained conservative. They usually comprised a wide courtyard and enclosing walls lined with storerooms, stables and workshops. To one side of the courtyard, and almost always sited opposite the church itself, was the refectory.

St Basilios, Arta
(13thC). Typical of the smaller churches of the time, it has strong Byzantine forms and rich exterior decoration with checkered design, unusual brick-work fans in the window spandrels, *saw tooth bands and broken hook* friezes.

Katholikon *and* **Theotokos, Hosios Lukas** *(c. 1020 and c. 1040), Corinthia. The Katholikon, above, is a Greek cross-octagon, one of the finest middle Byzantine church plans. Detail below, of the central* drum *of the Theotokos, with colonettes articulating* the angles.

Church, Ayioi Anaryiroi *(11thC), Kastoria. The form of this church, as with so many others in the area, is similar to the* hall-churches *and* basilicas *to the north in Bulgaria, while the masonry technique and ornamentation are characteristic of buildings in southern Greece.*

Basilica B, Philippi *(c. 540), Macedonia. Remains of the basilica, which was originally designed to compete with the great churches of Justinian's early years. It was a blend of timber-roofed basilica with the elaborate construction of the domed churches of Constantinople.*

Church, Panayia Koubelidike *(11thC), Kastoria. This tiny trefoil church with its high central drum is, like many of the numerous basilican churches in northern Greece, uncomplicated in plan. There are many fine frescoes dating from 13th-16thC.*

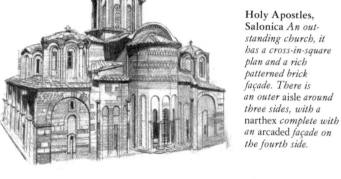

Holy Apostles, Salonica *An out-standing church, it has a cross-in-square plan and a rich patterned brick façade. There is an outer aisle around three sides, with a narthex complete with an arcaded façade on the fourth side.*

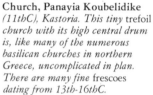

St Demetrios, Salonica *(5thC). The nave, 40 ft wide, ends in an apse and is flanked by double aisles with round arches supported by columns of green, red and white marble.*

Panaghia Chalkeon, Salonica *(1028). The powerfully articulated west façade, with brick half-columns supporting three huge arches. The cornices of the two west domes follow the rounded lines of the windows, a typical Athenian decorative feature.*

Church, Daphni *(c. 1080), Attica. A fine example of a Greek cross-octagon church, consisting of a domed central space expanding into a cross and overlapping subsidiary spaces around. The inspiration for churches such as this was the numerous cross-domed churches of Byzantium.*

Greece

From the late 11th century, much of wall ornamentation such as interlace patterns and geometric and foliage forms was reduced or eliminated. By the mid-12th century, however, three *quincunx* churches in **Argolis** at **St Moni, Mérbaka** and **Chonika**, and a Greek cross chapel at **Plataniti**, had again been given decorative richness on the walls. The first three churches are identical, with triple projecting *apses, drums articulated* by *colonettes* and with *blind* arches framing the windows.

There are many small churches in **Kastoria**, *basilican* in plan with high *naves* and small *clerestory* windows. Nave and *aisles* are *barrel vaulted,* while a *narthex,* often surmounted by a gallery, usually precedes the nave. **Ayioi Anaryiroi Varlaam** (1018) has exceptionally fine *frescoes* and the earliest example of *groined vaulting* in Greece. It is an aisled basilica with a single apse. Examples of churches built of colorful *cloisonné* masonry with *cufic* motif inserts include the **Taxiarkhai of the Metropolis** (11thC); **Ayois Stefanos** (11thC), with tall nave and hexagonal apse, and **Ayios Nikolaos Kasnitsis,** a rectangular church with round apse and beautiful frescoes.

Kapnikarea, Athens (11thC), is typical of the craftsmanship of the classical phase of middle *Byzantine* architecture in Greece and is marked by elegant heart-shaped foliage on the *capitals* of the window columns. **St Theodorio, Athens** (1060-70), is similar in that both look back toward more classical and purer work.

Mistra Cathedral (*c.* 1309) and the **Aphentiko** or **Panayia Hodegetria, Mistra** (*c.* 1310), are amalgams of Byzantine basilican plans with galleries, together with the *transept* arms of a Greek cross plan with open galleries. The latter church has four small *cupolas* and a central dome with a fine belltower. In many ways the Aphentiko is an innovation in building plans, for the original Greek cross scheme was modified. The ground floor, as with a basilica, was divided into nave and vaulted aisles, the whole preceded by a narthex of two stories. Four of the galleries' corner bays are domed and covered outside by drums. The blend of longitudinal and central plan elements was an original conception and was much emulated locally, where it became the prototype for what is known as the Mistra style. One of Mistra's most beautiful churches is the **Pantanassa** (1365). It is similar to the Aphentiko in plan but finer and more slender in its proportions. There are side aisles and there is a gallery over the narthex. A handsome flight of steps leads to a *loggia,* which was sited to provide a view over the Eurotas Valley.

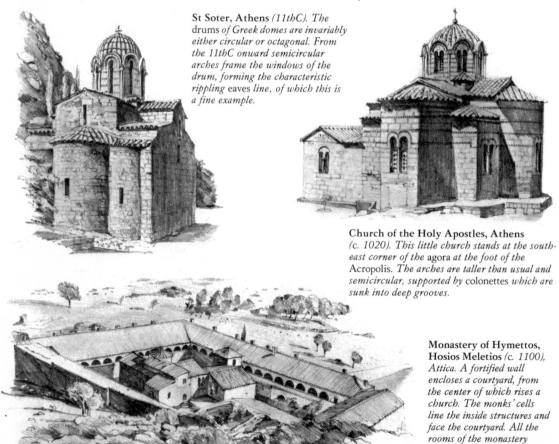

St Soter, Athens (11thC). The drums of Greek domes are invariably either circular or octagonal. From the 11thC onward semicircular arches frame the windows of the drum, forming the characteristic rippling eaves line, of which this is a fine example.

Church of the Holy Apostles, Athens *(c. 1020). This little church stands at the southeast corner of the* agora *at the foot of the Acropolis. The arches are taller than usual and semicircular, supported by* colonettes *which are sunk into deep grooves.*

Monastery of Hymettos, Hosios Meletios *(c. 1100), Attica. A fortified wall encloses a courtyard, from the center of which rises a church. The monks' cells line the inside structures and face the courtyard. All the rooms of the monastery are vaulted.*

Katholikon, Great Lavra *(11thC), Macedonia. The church stands at the center of the enclosed courtyard of the monastery. The triconch plan of three semicircular niches, each surmounted by a half-dome, was thereafter frequently copied elsewhere on Mount Athos.*

St Theodoroi, Mistra *(c. 1296). The last of the churches to be built in Greece with a central octagon. The Greek cross-octagon, widely revived in the late 13thC, had last been employed in the church at Daphni c. 1080. The church was restored in 1932.*

Aphentiko *or* **Panayia Hodegetria, Mistra** *(1310). View of the* nave, *looking east. The church is built to a composite plan, comprising a combination of Byzantine basilica together with Greek cross plan with domes.*

Panayia Paragoritissa, Arta *(1282-89). An interesting variant of the 8th- and 9th-C church plans in Constantinople, it has a triple tier of arcades between the corner piers of a central, domed space, which screens the bay from the surrounding ambulatory.*

Church, Mérbaka *(12thC), Argolis. Part of a group of buildings with the austere wall patterns which had been usual since the late 11thC. Simple* cloisonné *walling is enlivened with dog-tooth and meandering brick* friezes *and with inserted ceramic bowls.*

St Yoannis, Lindos *(c. 1100), Rhodes. The use of small* ashlar *masonry and narrow window slits set in recessed double frames are influences from Asia Minor, while the fusion of* chancel *with the east bays of the* nave *is taken from examples on the Greek mainland.*

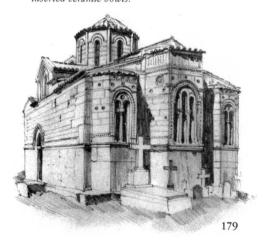

Turkey

Religious buildings

The oldest major church building to survive in Constantinople (Istanbul) is **St John Studios** (*c.* 463). The remains of its short *nave* and side *aisles* demonstrate the continuing strength of the classical tradition in the post-Constantinian empire. The most architecturally important building in Constantinople, however, is **St Sophia** (532-537), now a mosque. Built on a scale and with a lavishness previously unattempted, it is the most noble product of Justinian's reign. Instead of the traditional master builder, the Emperor selected Anthemios of Tralles and Isidorus of Miletus, scientists and inventors who could apply their expertise to both engineering and building practice. Their bold structural system consists of a vast rectangle, 230 ft by 250 ft, inside which are four giant *piers* defining the side aisles and from which spring arches carrying the enormous central dome. North and south of the four piers are great *buttresses,* 25 ft wide and 60 ft long, which take the full thrust of the great central dome.

Alternating bands of stone and brick masonry were a characteristic feature throughout the Byzantine Empire from the 5th to the 9th century. In the upland areas of Turkey during the same period builders adhered to a few basic plans. In Lycaonia, southeast of Konya, there are remains of *vaulted basilicas* and *hall-churches,* while around Kayseri in Cappadocia cross-planned churches, such as **Kizil Kilise, Sivrihisar** (9thC), are more usual.

From the 6th century until the middle *Byzantine* period, the religious buildings in the interior and north of Turkey were either cross-shaped churches, hall-churches with nave and flanking aisles or vaulted chapels without aisles. Examples include **Nakip Cami, Trebizond** (9thC), a *barrel-vaulted* hall-church, and **St Anne, Trebizond** (*c.* 884), a *basilica* with nave and aisles. It was these same traditional plans that monks followed when hollowing out the caves of Cappadocia at **Goreme** and **Sogandere** in the 10th and 11th centuries.

A great variety of churches were built in Armenia during the 6th and 7th centuries. They are generally aisleless nave churches, cross-domed hall-churches or cross-in-square structures. From the 7th century, however, the church with an octagonal center area crowned by a large dome and with the interior forming a cross-octagon became the dominant Armenian type. Good examples are **St Hripsime, Vagharshapet** (618), the **Church, Avon** (7thC), and the **Holy Cross, Aghtamar** (915-921). Middle Byzantine architecture frequently adopted traditional building types, as in the **Kahrie Cami, Constantinople** (11th-14thC), which consist of a central bay with four extremely shallow arms. The building is renowned for its beautiful *frescoes.* The **Fetiyeh Cami, Constantinople** (*c.* 1315), is typical of late Byzantine work, with emphasis on a highly decorated exterior with multiple window recesses, brickwork meander *friezes* and an abundance of checkerboard stonework.

St Sophia, Constantinople (Istanbul).
The church, one of the most original buildings of the period, has a magnificent lofty space under the great central dome. The vast complex is entered via a noble atrium *consisting of outer* narthex *and a two-story main narthex.*

South Church, Fenari Isa Cami (1282-1304), Constantinople. Detail of the apse *walling. This decoration is typical of late 13th-C work in Constantinople, with its rich brick ornamentation and alternating bands of brightly colored brick and ashlar work.*

Kalenderhare Cami, Constantinople (c.850). One of the few cross-domed churches to have survived. It was built on Roman remains, and the core is intact. Later Byzantine additions were made in the 13th and 15thC.

Kizil Kilise, Sivrihisar, right. Cross churches are typical of central and eastern Cappadocia. This has strongly projecting wings and an apse, which is polygonal without and horseshoe-shaped within, balancing a short nave *and a tower over the* crossing.

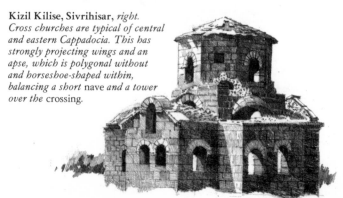

St John Studios, Constantinople
Remains of the nave *and* aisles. *The aisles had large windows but it is believed that there was no* clerestory *so that the nave would have been comparatively dark. In 5th-C Constantinople* basilicas *were usually equipped with* galleries.

Tekfus Sarayi, Constantinople *(14thC).*
Remains of the three-story palace, built on top of the city walls and projecting out toward the open country. The groin-vaulted *ground floor rests on two rows of columns and was modeled on the* keeps *of* Gothic *Europe.*

Holy Cross, Aghtamar *Characteristic of Armenian church building are four* transepts, *terminated by apses, which spring from an octagonal centerpiece. Other typical features are large, well-cut* facing *stones and simple decorative bands.*

Rock chapels, Cappadocia
The main features of these 10th- and 11th-C chapels—floors, walls, *piers*, columns, altars and *chancel* screens—were hewn out of rock in the hillside. They are small, always terminated with an apse and often richly decorated with *frescoes*. The majority are of the standard basilican plan.

Toqualé Kilise, Goreme
(10th-11thC). This is among the largest of the rock churches. The comparatively spacious nave is entered via a square porch. A five-arched screen wall, decorated with numerous icons, divides the nave from the chancel.

Rock caves, Goreme *Small groups of hermits and monks lived in these caves at Goreme, which they carved out of the hills as they did their chapels. Many hundreds of monks lived in the area at one time but by the 11thC their number had been greatly decreased.*

Russia

Religious buildings

Christianity spread through Russia in the 10th century and with it came *Byzantine* church architecture. Onion-shaped domes were developed to help counteract the effects of rain and snow.

Much of the Byzantine architecture of Kiev, planned as a city to rival Constantinople in excellence, was destroyed during the Tartar invasion of 1239. The most interesting building that survives in the area is the **Cathedral of St Sophia, Kiev** (1037-61), a cross-planned brick *basilica* and the first great Byzantine building in Russia. It was rebuilt in the 17th and 18th centuries, but the nucleus of five *aisles* and *apses* remains. The **Cathedral of the Transfiguration, Chernigov** (*c.* 1036, rebuilt 18thC), is a domed basilica with a two-story *narthex.*

At Novgorod, an artistic and cultural center, a typical 10th-century church plan evolved characterized by a central high *drum* and dome, three eastern apses and white-painted stucco walls. Good examples are the **Cathedral of the Monastery of St Anthony** (1117-19) and the **Cathedral of St Nicholas** (1113-36). The **Paraskeva-Pyatnitsa Church, Novgorod** (1207), is a delightful brick-built church, almost square in plan with a wide central apse flanked by smaller apses and striking *barrel-vaulted* vestibules. Towards the 14th century, designs were made even simpler with only one shallow central apse and a simple *gable* on each façade. **St Theodore Stratilates** (1360-61) is an exceptionally fine example.

Although the architectural influence of Kiev remained, the Moscow area became the center of power in the 12th century. The **Cathedral of the Assumption,** or Uspensky Cathedral, Vladi-mir (12th C), is an elaborate, double-aisled building modeled on St Sophia, Kiev. The Cathedral of **St Demetrius, Vladimir** (1194-97), was built at the center of a 12th-century palace which has since been demolished. The lofty nave is divided into three aisles.

One of the most elegant of early Russian buildings, the **Church of the Protection and Intercession of the Virgin,** Bogolyubovo (1165), is rectangular in plan with a single, central dome. The façade has three vertical divisions and has rounded gables. Four square-sectioned pillars support the central drum and dome of the **Cathedral of St George, Yuryev-Polsky** (1230-15thC). External decoration mixes *Romanesque* and Byzantine motifs with local forms of folk art.

The **Cathedral of the Assumption, Moscow** (1475-79), a five-domed building partly designed by an Italian, blends Russian Byzantine and Italian *Renaissance* architecture. In many cases the multiple domes were graded to produce an attractive pyramidal effect, as at the **Cathedral of the Annunciation, Moscow** (1482-16thC).

The Cathedral of **St Basil the Blessed, Moscow** (1555-17thC), embodies the final phase of Byzantine architecture in Russia. The plan resembles an eight-pointed star, each point a chapel with its own handsomely domed tower.

Cathedral of St George, Yuryev-Polsky *Detail of the lavish sculptural decorations that enrich the entire south façade.*

Cathedral of St Demetrius, Vladimir *Detail taken from the* corbel frieze *and* blind arcading *which decorate the* apse *exteriors. The upper part of the external walls is covered with elaborately carved masonry relief work.*

Cathedral of the Transfiguration, Pereyaslavl-Zalessky *(1152-57). A beautifully simple building with a cube-like nave, surmounted by a lofty* drum *and dome. A band of saw-tooth and zig-zag molding enriches the* cornice.

Cathedral of the Annunciation, Moscow *The two tiers of* ogee gables *encircling the central dome are a purely decorative device to hide the arches that step up the side of the high* drum *on the inside.*

Pyatnitsa Church, Chernigov
(12thC). Originally part of a nunnery, this church is a fine interpretation of the domed cruciform design. Above the simple ground plan the roof has an elaborate section, stepping up like a pyramid to the high central drum.

Cathedral of St George, Novgorod *(1119-30), above. The body of the church is like the keep of a castle. Three of the façades are articulated by heavy lesenes. Each of the three aisles of the lofty interior has an apse at the east end. The drums are positioned asymmetrically.*

Paraskeva-Pyatnitsa Church, Novgorod *The chief decorative effect of this church is achieved by the clustered pilasters which project at the corners of the structure. The drum and tiny dome were rebuilt in the 14thC, the gabled roof in the 16thC and the cupola in the 18thC.*

Kremlin, Novgorod
(15thC). A tower in the south-east section of the Kremlin fortifications. The oval-shaped fortress had 13 towers, each different in scale and decorative detail, of which nine survive.

Cathedral of St Basil the Blessed, Moscow
Built to celebrate Ivan IV's final victory over the Tartar armies, the cathedral presents a kaleidoscopic impression of color and form at the southern end of Red Square. Each of the eight, brightly painted onion-shaped domes has contrasting decoration.

Czechoslovakia, Romania & Hungary

Religious buildings

The **Deanery Church, Plzeň** (14thC), in Czechoslovakia, is a monumental *hall-church*, Germanic in its great size and with the *nave* divided into three, the central section being terminated by a lofty *chancel*. Another hall-church in Czechoslovakia is the **Deanery Church, Kolin** (13thC). The chancel was added in the 14th century and was the work of Peter Parler, a member of a family of builders from Cologne. His greatest talent lay in the shaping and *vaulting* of individual spaces within a conventional plan. Of particular distinction is his vaulting of the chancel of **Prague Cathedral** (*c.* 1352-85), many ideas for which had first been developed in English cathedrals, notably those at Wells and Lincoln. Other churches of interest in Czechoslovakia include **Holy Trinity, Kutná Hora** (14thC), a small, elegant hall-church with simple vault supported on slim round columns, and the **Parish Church, Vetla** (14thC), Lower Labe, which has a small square *nave* with the *ribs* of its vaulting springing from a round, central column.

In Romania **Alba Iulia Cathedral** (13thC) consists of a nave and flanking *aisles* with *transepts* and tower over the *crossing*. The sculptural decoration is outstanding, especially the foliage on the *cornice* of the *apses,* which is comparable to that of the Benedictine abbey at Jak.

St Stephen's Church, Nagybörzsony (13thC), in Hungary, a simple rural church, consists of a west tower, nave and half-domed apse. Of particular interest is the fine decorative work, including a *corbel-table* of the apse enriched with sculptured heads. The **Benedictine Abbey, Jak** (13thC), is renowned for its rich sculptural decoration and beautiful *frescoes,* remains of which are found in the main apse and lower part of the southwest tower. The plan consists of a nave and side aisles, all three terminated by apses. The west façade is flanked by two towers. The **Abbey Church, Pannonhalma** (13thC), was the first Benedictine monastery to be built in Hungary and became one of the richest. A *basilican* church, it has a chancel raised high above the *crypt* and many features favored by the Cistercians, such as the *sexpartite vaulting* of the nave and the clustered columns from which spring the vaulting ribs. The **Provostship Church, Felsöörs** (13thC), has a plain nave and side aisles with handsome west tower, square on the lower stage and octagonal above the turret, *articulated* by *Lombardic* corbel-table, *pilasters, portal,* and windows framed with *arcading.*

Castles & Palaces

The **Castle, Karlštejn** (*c.* 1348), in Czechoslovakia, extensively restored in the 19th century, was built on rising ground and consists of a huge *keep,* containing the Emperor's quarters and chapel, surrounded by a group of lower buildings. The *gabled* **Castle, Horšovský** (*c.* 1275) is notable for its lofty, rib-vaulted chapel. The **Royal Castle, Esztergom** (12th-13thC), Hungary, has a polygonal keep, several stories in height at its center. Attached to this are the remains of a palace wing. The chapel is connected to the keep by a narrow corridor and a *chantry chapel.*

Castle Chapel, Esztergom *The entrance to the chapel is flanked by pairs of ornately carved columns and capitals. This detail from one of the capitals depicts a man and a beast fighting each other, an allegory of the struggle between good and evil.*

Castle Chapel, Cheb *(c. 1180), Czechoslovakia. View of the upper part of the two-storeyed chapel of the castle. The ribs of the vaulting spring from four slim pillars. Carved capitals and alternating octagonal and round pillars appear in many 12th-C churches.*

Cathedral, Pecs *(11th-19thC), Hungary. The main façade was remodeled in the late 19thC, when the greater part of the church was rebuilt. It is a basilican church with Lombardic aisles. The square towers at the west and east ends were added in the 12thC.*

Cistercian Abbey, Osek *(c. 1240), Czechoslovakia. The chapter-house, a remaining section of the original abbey, with ponderous rib vaults springing from corbels. The proportions and the ornamentation, particularly of the capitals, are Burgundian in influence.*

Church, Densis *(13thC), Romania. An outstanding example of Transylvanian architecture, the church is constructed of monumental stones quarried from Roman buildings, some with their original carvings, and is dominated by a tower.*

Abbey Church, Jak *Hungary. The portal, which projects from the main façade. The decorative motifs and chevron and leaf patterns are a Norman influence, while the two decorated columns are Italian Romanesque.*

Abbey Church, Pannonhalma, *Hungary. View of the crypt, which consists of a nave and side aisles. The ribs of the groin-vaulting spring from corbels on ponderous capitals and short, fat columns, which divide the nave from the side aisles.*

Abbey Church, Deaki *(13thC), Diakovce, Czechoslovakia. The building consists of an upper and lower church, each having nave and aisles, with apses closing the east end of each aisle. Barrel-vaulting covers the lower church and, in turn, carries the floor of the upper church.*

Church, Karsca *(11thC), Hungary. The original church consisted of a rotunda, built in the 11thC. To this was added a nave and side aisles, and the rotunda was converted into a chancel. The façade, with its corbel-tables and pilasters, is Lombardic in character.*

Church, Odorhei *13thC), Transylvania, Romania. Centrally-planned churches of the 13thC are common in Hungary but rare in Transylvania. The quatrefoil plan adopted here is similar to that of the chapel of St James at the Abbey Church, Jak.*

185

Modern Classical World

During the eight centuries following the sack of Rome (455), the church dominated intellectual life. Philosophical enquiry, scientific research and, indeed, all European thought took place within the confines of an accepted Christian doctrine.

Renaissance architecture

In the extraordinary explosion of literary, artistic and cultural life in 14th-century Italy, which is known as the Renaissance, or rebirth, and which lasted until the 16th century, scholars questioned and sometimes rejected these hitherto inviolable assumptions. The medieval church had believed in the transience of man and his unimportance in this life. Renaissance scholars, writers and artists, on the other hand, though they were not hostile to Christianity, believed in the importance of the individual here on earth. They questioned what Man was and had been, finding in the classical Roman world both the inspiration and the models for their humanist beliefs. Italy, its ruins still witness to that former humanism, was the center of this rebirth, the influence of which spread throughout Europe during the next two centuries.

The first signs of the Renaissance are found in the writings of Dante, Petrarch and Boccaccio, in the paintings of Giotto and in the buildings of Filippo Brunelleschi, the first great architect of the Renaissance. His buildings, such as the Pazzi Chapel, Florence (1429), take more from Tuscan and Romanesque styles, however, than those of the ancient world.

The discovery in 1414 of the treatise on architecture by Vitruvius, the Roman architect and engineer, was the greatest single influence in stimulating the development of the Renaissance style. Italian Renaissance architects and their successors all over Europe relied heavily on this and later publications for inspiration.

These books, which eventually became available in printed editions, spread much more quickly than had been possible in the Middle Ages.

The architect's place in society also changed with the advent of the Renaissance. He was no longer working purely in the service of the church and chiefly concerned with technical problems. His status and income improved and his services were now sought by princes and by rich merchants and bankers, as well as by the church. Within the artistic world itself attitudes also changed, artist and architect now often becoming one. Brunelleschi, besides practising architecture, was a goldsmith and sculptor; Leone Alberti a mathematician, writer and scholar, and Michelangelo Buonarroti a painter and sculptor. Renaissance artists rarely specialized and believed that their work gained thereby.

Mannerism

The balance and harmony of the Renaissance was gradually superseded by Mannerism, a style developed by 16th-century Italian architects. They sought variety and excitement, so much so that they treated the rules laid down by classical architects in a cavalier manner, using decorative pictorial effects, deliberate discord and elaborate, frequently fussy ornamentation to achieve an immediate visual sensation. The work of Michelangelo, Giacomo da Vignola and Giulio Romano show the style at its best. In less capable hands it was characterized by façades layered with elaborate carvings, strapwork frames and gables crowned by obelisks.

The regional variations on the mannerist style were particularly rich and its interpretation in Elizabethan England and plateresque Spain was distinctly different from that of Flanders or Germany. Outside Italy the style was marked chiefly by applied decoration and lacked the boldness of frame that was the key to the magnificent Baroque buildings of 17th-century Italy.

Palladianism

The buildings of Andrea Palladio of Vicenza are the purest interpretation of the humanist ideals of the classical world. His handsome villas with their temple porticos raised high above a basement story are the epitome of the Virgilian dream. Palladio's architecture and writings were based on a close study of antiquity and had an enormous influence on the 18th-century exponents of classical architecture in England, where Chiswick House, London (1725), by Lord Burlington, is a notable example, and in North America in the 18th and 19th century. One of the chief English architects of this style was Inigo Jones, as witnessed by his Queen's House, Greenwich (1616-35).

Renaissance details
Decoration, which was increasingly designed to be seen from the front, was based on classical examples. Carving was executed on all elements, including capitals, friezes and pilasters. Ornament was based either on classical mythology or on pagan examples.

Rustication

Window pediment

Volute

Villa Capra, Vicenza, and Chiswick House, London, plans *The former has the main entrance on one side but with all four entrances given equal weight, while in the latter there are only two entrances and the principal one is more commanding. The façades of both buildings are like Greek temple porticos.*

Chiswick House

0   230ft

Villa Capra

Baroque

While the rest of Europe was still adopting Renaissance forms, Italian architects had already in the 17th century moved to the dramatic concave and convex forms of the Baroque, which was to dominate architecture until 1720. The Baroque's marvelous theatricality reflected a religious attitude to life, a shift from the secularism of the Renaissance. The style was bold and unconventional, the interiors startlingly lighted. Good examples are Francesco Borromini's S. Ive della Sapienza, Rome (1642-50), and Bernini's Colonnade, St Peter's, Rome (1506-1612).

Rococo

During the final phase of the Baroque in the early 18th century, a more decorative variation, rococo, developed. It began in France and spread to Germany, Belgium, the Netherlands and Scandinavia, where it remained the dominant style until 1770. A characteristic feature was decorative stucco surrounds to windows, mirrors and ceiling paintings. The whole spirit of the style was lighter and gentler than Baroque, and the Orders, which had been used to such dramatic effect in the Baroque period, now played a distinctly minor role.

Neoclassicism

The Neoclassical movement of the second half of the 18th century represented architecture's contribution to the prevailing spirit of rationalism, and was in large measure popularized by the artist David, court painter to Napoleon, to lend grandeur to his master's empire. Inspired less by ancient Greek buildings, architects rejected the elaborate density of the Baroque and rococo and moved to a purer, more severe style. The Orders once again became part of the structure of a building and decoration became less important.

Construction

The first great achievement of Renaissance architecture was the dome added by Brunelleschi to Florence Cathedral between 1420 and 1436. Centralized churches, often crowned with a dome raised on a drum, were a characteristic feature of Renaissance architecture. The dome was the major device to regulate interior space and as a primary element in external composition, as in St Peter's, Rome. Vaulting was generally semicircular and without ribs, and timber roofs, which Byzantine and medieval architects had left exposed, normally had a plaster ceiling. Walls were generally constructed of ashlar masonry or coursed brickwork.

Dome, Florence Cathedral
The Renaissance prompted the building of a new giant dome on Florence Cathedral. A circular Byzantine type of dome (a) could be built ring-by-ring without temporary support, but the direction of thrust exerted by such a dome would have crushed the existing octagonal drum. A ribbed dome (b) would direct its thrust in a more suitable direction but would have required too complex temporary support during construction. Filippo Brunelleschi solved the problem with (c), which combines the advantages of round dome construction with the direction of thrust exerted by a ribbed dome.

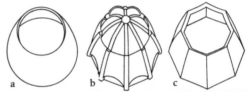

a   b   c

Design

The major characteristics of Renaissance buildings are axiality and frontality, both in plan and elevation. Pediments were pitched low, in the classical manner, and the volute, as in S. Maria Novella, Florence (*c.* 1455-60), became a device for making the transition from low to high elements. Basements and ground floors were often rusticated, as were the wall angles, to give the appearance of strength. Openings were arranged symmetrically, doors and windows being framed with a classical molded architrave, sometimes finished with a triangular or segmented pediment. Horizontality was emphasized by deep cornices, balustrading and molded string courses. The Orders were used either to articulate façades or as a structural element in the portico. The columns were rusticated, fluted or carved. The pillared and gabled temple front attached to façades is a characteristic feature, particularly of the Anglo-Palladian school.

Decoration

During the Renaissance, frescoes were used to decorate the interiors of domes and decorative stucco work was applied to the ceilings of timber roofs. Ornamentation was based on classical examples. Statues, increasingly designed to be seen from the front, were frequently set in niches. Often architectural pattern books provided the basic designs for ornamentation.

Features of mannerist ornamentation include grotesques and cartouches, and plant forms which wreathe around chimneys, portals and gables. Decorative obelisks were often used to crown gables. Later, interior paneling was covered with gilt and stucco work and by the 18th century boundaries between structure and decoration had dissolved, as in the Baroque churches of southern Germany.

Italy

Although the two main centers of the Renaissance were Florence and Rome, the early Renaissance style was marked by numerous regional interpretations. By the early 16th century, however, a national style had evolved, known as the High Renaissance.

In Florence the palazzo, or palace, was developed. This was a rectangular block with an arcaded central courtyard, its cliff-like walls often rusticated and having boldly projecting cornices. An outstanding

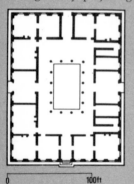

Palazzo Strozzi, Florence, plan *The archetypal Renaissance palazzo, it has entrances on all four sides, the main entrance facing the street, and a great central courtyard. The façade of the palazzo is rusticated uniformly and the building is capped by a great cornice.*

example is the Palazzo Strozzi (1489). The columned arcade, as in the Foundling Hospital (1419), became a distinctive feature of Florentine architecture.

It was not until the High Renaissance that Rome embarked on major building programs, as in the Palazzo Farnese (1541-46) by Antonio da Sangallo, and the Tempietto (1499-1502) by Donato Bramante. The mannerist and Baroque period are represented by Michelangelo's work on the Campidoglio (1561-84) and St Peter's, by Giacomo da Vignola's Il Gesu (1568-84), by Gianlorenzo Bernini's S. Andrea del Quirinale (1658-70) and by Borromini's S. Carlo alle Quattro Fontane (1638-41). The palaces generally had astylar façades and here, too, huge walls were common.

The mercantile tradition of Venice and her medieval heritage led to a different style of building. Key features were a central range of windows, articulation by Orders, balconies and a crowning entablature, and a rusticated ground story, as in the Palazzo Corner Spinelli (*c.* 1480). Most palaces were compact because of their cramped sites.

Campidoglio, Rome, plan *The first example of Baroque use of space. Michelangelo Buonarroti transformed the medieval civic center of Rome by adding façades to buildings on three sides of the square and by building an elegant flight of steps to reinforce the axial line running through the square.*

The characteristic features of Palladio's fine palaces and villas are the raised piano nobile, axiality and frontality, centralized space, often crowned with a dome, and a temple portico on the main façades. A good example is the Villa Capra, Vicenza (*c.* 1550), which two centuries later strongly influenced architecture in both England and North America.

The Baroque style erupted in monumental proportions in and around Turin, most notably in the buildings of Guarino Guarini and Filippo Javarra. In southern Italy the Baroque was extravagantly ornamental, reflecting the Spanish heritage of the region.

France

The Italian Renaissance had little impact on France until the late 15th century, and then its effects were noticeable chiefly in details, as in the wing added by François I to the Château, Blois (1498-1638), with its magnificent spiral staircase. The first important Renaissance project in France was Gilles Le Breton's modernization of the medieval castle at Fontainebleau (*c.* 1528), followed by Ancy le Franc (1546) by Sebastiano Serlio, and the Bridge Gallery at Chenonceaux (1576). The golden age of French classical architecture was from 1589 to the late 17th century. Clarity and simplicity of individual parts were its hallmarks, complemented by a bold, totally co-ordinated design. Key buildings were the Palais du Luxembourg, Paris (1615-24), by Salomon de Brosse, the Château de Maisons-Lafitte (1642) by Francois Mansart and the Vaux le Vicomte (1657-61) by Louis le Vau. In the 17th century state patronage produced architecture on a grand scale, notably at Versailles (1661-1756), where architecture became an expression of the pomp and ceremony of the court of Louis XIV. Landscape was also made an integral part of the whole composition.

The 18th and early 19th century were characterized by numerous fine town houses, modestly proportioned and decorated in an exuberant rococo style. The late 18th century brought monumental Neoclassical works, such as the Pantheon (1757-90) and the Madeleine, Paris (1806-42), as well as the works of Nicolas Ledoux, among them the industrial estate, Arc-et-Senans (1772-75).

United Kingdom

The Elizabethan age (1558-1603) was the age of great mansions. Despite their somewhat mannerist form, they had Gothic features and Renaissance details. Characteristic elements were towers, gables, decorative parapets and balustrading, large mullioned windows and a long gallery. The houses of the Jacobean period (1603-25) were equally imposing but the style was more refined. Classical columns and entablatures provided articulation. The internal decoration, especially the carving, was lavish.

Stuart architecture (1603-1714) was dominated by two men, Inigo Jones and Sir Christopher Wren. Jones was an ardent disciple of the Italian Renaissance, Wren of the French Renaissance. The vertical Elizabethan gables were now replaced by straight walls, crowned by the strong horizontal line of the cornice. Roofs were hipped and sometimes hidden by parapets. Vast built-up windows were abandoned for small rectangular ones set in a large wall space. Wren used classical features such as domes and columns for architectural emphasis. Good examples are St Paul's Cathedral, London (1675-1710), Queen's House, Greenwich (1616-35), and the outstanding Sheldonian Theatre, Oxford (1663-69).

Georgian architecture (1714-1830) was heralded by an explosion of brilliant Baroque monumentality, as in Blenheim Palace, Oxfordshire (1705-20), by Sir John

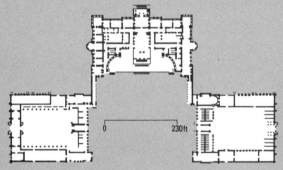

Blenheim Palace, Oxfordshire, plan *The last great Baroque building in the United Kingdom, the plan shows its monumental scale and how frontality is emphasized by a recessed center.*

Vanbrugh. English Baroque was comparatively short-lived, however, and was superseded by the harmonious proportions and refined detail of the Anglo-Palladian school, led by architects such as Lord Burlington, William Kent and Colen Campbell, who had all made a careful study of the exquisite classicism of Palladio's architecture in Italy.

In the Gothic Revival of the late 18th century and early 19th century, literary taste began to influence architecture. Strawberry Hill, London (1747-63), by Horace Walpole, was the first of the great Gothic Revival works. It is characterized by the irregular plan and flamboyant medieval decorative details and forms

that were developed in later, more refined works, such as Sezincote, Gloucestershire (1803-15), and the Royal Pavilion, Brighton (1815-21), both being extravagant interpretations of the Indian style. The latter, by Nash, also included Chinese motifs.

The Regency Style (1810-30), with its magnificent terraces and squares, brought a profusion of wrought iron work in windows and balconies, seen at their best in Cheltenham, Bath and Brighton and in Nash's urban projects, such as Regent Street, London. With the end of the Napoleonic Wars in 1815, the Greek and Gothic Revivals dominated building. Examples are the British Museum, London (1823-47), by Sir Robert Smirke, and the works of Augustus Pugin.

Spain

Architecture of the early Renaissance in Spain (1492 to the mid-16th century) was austere. Long, plain walls were, however, marked by elaborately ornamented windows and doorways in the plateresque style, a continuation of the Gothic work of the Isabeline period. The Renaissance period (mid-16th century to mid-17th century) was reflected in buildings such as the Palace of Charles V, Granada (1527-68), where rusticated masonry, superimposed Orders and a handsome circular patio, reminiscent of part of Hadrian's Villa, Tivoli, clearly refer to Italian Renaissance architecture. Later works, such as the Escorial, Madrid (1562-84), by Juan de Herrera, are vast with massive walls. Their rigid formalism was replaced by the brilliance of Baroque (mid-17th to mid-18th century), as in the façades of the Cathedral, Murcia (1730-49), and of Santiago de Compostela (1738-49).

Germany

The Renaissance arrived late in Germany and references were generally from Flemish copy books. The style was predominantely mannerist and decoration included scrollwork, obelisks, pilasters and statuary. A purer Renaissance style, seen at its finest in the Town Hall, Augsburg (1615-20), by Elias Holl, soon replaced this early flamboyance. The outstanding Renaissance church is St Michael, Munich (1582-97). Sixteenth-century domestic buildings were characterized by tall, multistory gables.

In the early 18th century Italian Baroque buildings proliferated. In the middle of the century, however, the bold native Baroque of Bavaria and southern Germany emerged. Characteristic exterior features are strong articulation by columns and pilasters and handsome twin-towered façades. The interiors are a seemingly miraculous fusion of structure and decorative stucco work. Pillars took over from walls and the vaults themselves dissolved into a world of stucco, created by architects and artist-craftsmen working in collaboration. The style, which transcended national boundaries, is also found extensively in Austria, Czechoslovakia, Switzerland and in Poland.

In the late 18th century, the Baroque gave way first to the French rococo style and then to the Neoclassical style, when palaces and town houses were modeled on the courtly life at Versailles.

Belgium & Holland

In many ways the Renaissance in the Netherlands was merely a reaction against the Gothic style. Restraint replaced flamboyance, horizontality replaced verticality, and Renaissance details were applied to traditional forms. The books of architectural ornament by Vredeman de Vries (1527-1606) were a major influence.

The first important building in the mannerist style was Antwerp Town Hall (1561-65) by Cornelius Floris. A purer classical style was developed by Lieven de Key in the Town Hall, Leyden (1597), and by Hendrik de Keyser, who designed the terraced houses of Amsterdam with their handsome gables with flanking scrolls and decorative strapwork.

The refined Palladian style, with its central pediment and hipped roof is characteristic of many buildings in 17th-century Holland.

In Belgium an extremely bold Baroque form with sumptuous decorations and exaggerated effects dominated architecture in the 17th century. A fine example is the church of St Carolus Borromeus, Antwerp (1615-21). The early 18th century brought the French rococo style but from about 1750 the symmetrical severity of the Neoclassical style predominated.

Scandinavia

The Renaissance had little impact in Scandinavia except in Denmark. There the earliest Renaissance buildings are the castles built by Frederick II in the 16th century, such as Kronborg, Elsinore (c. 1570), and Frederiksborg, Hillerod (1602). They had a Dutch style, with curvilinear gables and handsome spires. The Dutch Palladian school was particularly strong in the late 17th century, as may be seen at Charlottenburg Palace, Copenhagen (1672-83). This gave way to the French classical style in the mid-18th century. By about 1800 Neoclassicism was taking a strong hold.

Dutch architectural influences were equally strong in Sweden in the late 17th century. In Norway, however, classical influences were felt largely in applied elements, such as pilasters, quoins and pediments built of wood.

Eastern Europe

The inherited tradition of the Byzantine world remained dominant in Russia, and Renaissance influences are found mainly in classical details, such as superimposed Orders, entablatures and classical molding applied to Byzantine forms. The major Renaissance building is the Cathedral of the Archangel Michael (1505), in the Kremlin, Moscow, designed by an Italian. The Baroque had more effect in the magnificent palaces of St Petersburg (Leningrad), built largely by foreign archi-

tects and characterized by their vast scale and extreme regularity. In Czechoslovakia and Poland the mannerist style was strong in the early 17th century, but then it was superseded first by Italian Baroque and then by the Baroque of southern Germany.

North America

Early colonial architecture tended to resemble the styles of the settlers' homelands, so that Spanish styles are evident in the missions of southern California, Georgian elegance in 18th-century Virginia. The first buildings in New England were mainly timber-frame, weather-boarded houses. Major architects whose influence is apparent include Sir Christopher Wren, as in the Governor's House, Williamsburg (1706-20), Virginia, and James Gibbs, whose church of St Martin-in-the-Fields, London (1722-26), became the prototype for most of the major churches from Charleston in the south to Vermont in the north. The Anglo-Palladian school also produced many fine buildings, such as the Redwood Library, Newport (1749), Rhode Island, by Peter Harrison.

The major styles were the Colonial Style in the 17th and 18th century, when buildings were of red brick with medieval gables and massive chimneys; the Georgian Style, also of the 18th century, which was characterized by a symmetrical plan and elevation, a pedimented central bay and a clean brick façade with a handsome portal, and the fairly austere Federal Style of the late 18th and early 19th century, with doors crowned by fan lights and flanking side lights. Thomas Jefferson made the Neoclassical Style popular in the late 18th century and early 19th century. Modeled on ancient Rome, it made use of the Tuscan and Corinthian Orders, and the temple portico usually had a pediment enclosing a lunette and a raised podium. After 1820 the Greek Revival came into favor. The three Greek Orders, with a full entablature and a low pitched pediment, were employed. The Gothic Revival, in vogue from the 1830s, had an irregular plan,

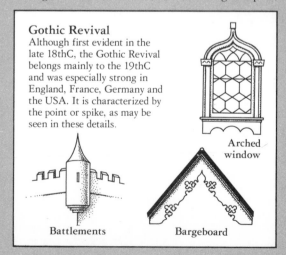

Gothic Revival
Although first evident in the late 18thC, the Gothic Revival belongs mainly to the 19thC and was especially strong in England, France, Germany and the USA. It is characterized by the point or spike, as may be seen in these details.

Arched window

Battlements   Bargeboard

numerous gables with decorative barge boards in an openwork or gingerbread pattern, large pointed windows and, occasionally, towers and battlements. Many examples were built of timber and finished in board and batten.

Religious buildings

Renaissance architects preferred to build churches on a centralized plan, usually circular, polygonal, octagonal or Greek cross in form. Most were free-standing, their center crowned by a dome. The circle itself was regarded as the perfect geometric form, and its absolute harmony was equated with the perfection of God. The churches of the Renaissance, unlike those of the Middle Ages but like the temples of antiquity, were regarded as monuments and memorials and their central quality and crowning dome were key elements, even though the circle had little architectural use.

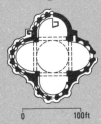

S. Maria della Con-solazione, Todi, plan
A typical Renaissance centralized church, with the altar space beneath the great dome. Based on the Greek cross plan, its apses form the four arms.

The main church of the High Renaissance is St Peter's, Rome, a monumental exposition of the classical principles outlined by Vitruvius. The key mannerist building is the Jesuit church of Il Gesu, Rome (1568-84), by da Vignola. It has a cruciform plan with a three-bay nave and dome over the crossing. The aisled nave and dome became a distinctive feature of Baroque churches. Many churches of the late 17th and early 18th century have twin-towered west façades with pedimented centers.

Castles & Palaces

During the Renaissance secular buildings became as important as religious buildings. The archetypal Renaissance palace, first developed in Florence, was a rectangular block, generally without columns but with a central, arcaded courtyard.

The increasing·use of artillery in the 15th century made the medieval fortified castle obsolete. Although French châteaux, such as Chambord (1519-47), retained their traditional form, their façades were of the Renaissance style and their skyline mannerist. This mixture gave way to a long, monumental façade punctuated by pavilions crowned with segmented gables and with elaborate roofs, or to a balustraded parapet with the roof hidden behind. Outstanding examples are Fontainebleau and Versailles. The monu-mental axiality of Versailles, reinforced by grand avenues, water canals and gardens adorned with fountains, terraces and arbors, was the epitome of a totally coordinated design.

Projecting wings flanking an immense entrance court and bold domes crowning the main hall, which was placed along the axis, were characteristic features of 18th-century palaces. When size and cost made such gigantic houses obsolete, they were replaced by a more refined Palladian style of house.

Domestic buildings

In most of Europe the Gothic or medieval tradition was so strong that the new ideas were adopted slowly. Houses were still built to medieval plans and only the details began to show the influence of Renaissance ideas, as in Gothic Belgium or Holland, where gables crowned with pinnacles were replaced with obelisks and cornices to give a horizontal emphasis. Where the tradition of building in timber persisted, most houses were simply larger, more decorative versions of earlier buildings; often, since timber roof technology was limited, roofs were of standard shapes, set side by side with a gutter running between them.

Civic & Public buildings

Most Italian Renaissance town halls are simple rectangular blocks with a horizontal emphasis. One of the great projects of 16th-century Italy was Palladio's scheme for encasing the medieval Town Hall, Vicenza (1571), in an encircling two-story classical loggia. Gothic verticalism gave way to classical horizontality for the first time in the Town Hall, Antwerp (1560-65). Characteristic of northern Europe were long, steeply-pitched roofs with a pedimented or gabled central section and often a crowning cupola. In Belgium and Holland, rich and powerful guilds built magnificent guild houses in the 17th and 18th century, as in the Grande Place, Brussels (17thC). In England during the same period town halls were compact, multipurpose buildings with an arcaded ground floor used as a market.

Urban Design

In contrast with Hellenistic and Roman cities, the civic centers of medieval cities were not designed as a whole but as separate and individual elements. During the Renaissance, however, architects reverted to the classical prototype, as in the center of Pienza, Italy (1460-62), where a vernacular village was transformed into the first ideal city of the Renaissance. Another example is the Campidoglio, Rome (1561-84), an irregular agglomeration of buildings which Michel-angelo transformed into a grand civic center. The key to such works was their axiality, terminated by a palace or a church, with space itself becoming a matter for design. The ultimate purpose of the Renaissance designers—the city as a coherent structure—was finally achieved by Vincenzo Scamozzi at Palma Nova, Italy (1593), which was in fact a distant, fortified outpost of Venice planned·as a nine-sided polygon with a hexagonal central piazza.

Northern Italy

Religious buildings

The Carthusian **Certosa di Pavia, Pavia province** (1396-16thC), is a remarkable example of early *Renaissance* architecture in Lombardy. The richly carved, classical façade of the church was added in the 15th century. Other remodelings include **S. Satiro, Milan** (1474), a domed church rebuilt by Donato Bramante on the site of a 9th-century building. The intriguing *chancel* was built to appear larger than it is by accentuating the real perspective. There is also a fine octagonal *sacristy*. **S. Maria della Grazie, Milan** (1493-97), is an abbey church to which *choir, transepts* and dome were added by Bramante.

A great ecclesiastical building program in 16th-century **Milan** included the restoration of the early Christian *rotunda* of **S. Lorenzo** (1573) by Martino Bassi. It also included work by Pellegrino Pellegrini, notably **S. Fidele** (1569), which has a bright, spacious interior with *vaults* carried on giant, semicircular walls, and **S. Sebastiano** (*c.* 1576), a delightful, round church which re-interprets the traditional centrally planned churches. By the early 17th century, Milan was a stronghold of strict architectural classicism. Since it was by working on the **Cathedral** (1387-1483) that artists and architects sought to establish themselves, the *Gothic* form was gradually and subtly transformed, the classical façade of the Cathedral dating from 1616 onward. Other significant Renaissance churches in Milan are **S. Maria della Passione** (*c.* 1550) and **S. Maria presso S. Celso** (16thC).

The **Madonna di Campagna, Verona** (1559), by Michele Sanmichele, epitomizes Leone Alberti's ideal of a free-standing round church. The austere exterior is complimented by the complex interior.

Sigismondo Malatesta, although a notorious ruler of Rimini, tried to establish a center of humanistic culture there to rival those created by the Medici family in Florence and the Este family in Ferrara. One of his most extravagant ventures was the transformation of **S. Francesco, Rimini** (1446), his ancestral burial place, into an elaborate pantheon, renamed the Tempio Malatestiano. The new façade was designed by Alberti and brought Renaissance architecture closer to that of the ancient classical world. The façade remains incomplete, and an enormous dome was to have crowned the east end.

Both Guarino Guarini, one of the most inventive architects of the period, and Fillipo Juvarra worked in Turin in the 17th and early 18th centuries. Guarini designed **S. Lorenzo** (1668-80), which is basically octagonal in plan, and the **Sidone Chapel** (1668-90) in **Turin Cathedral** (1491-98), with its superb use of marble. Juvarra's masterpiece is the **Superga, Turin** (1717-31), which encapsulates the climax of Italian *Baroque* and shows the preoccupation of Italian religious architecture of the period with the centralized church crowned by a huge dome. Other impressive works by Juvarra in Turin are the **Chiesa del Carmine** (1732-35), the façade of **S. Christina** (1715-28) and **S. Fillipo Nevi** (1714).

S. Simone Piccolo, Venice *(1718-38). Designed by Giovanni Scalfurotto, this church on the Grand Canal has a Byzantine dome and plan amalgamated with a portico modeled on Palladio's work at Maser and the Pantheon, Rome.*

Milan Cathedral *The Renaissance façade, with its window and doorway pediments, was begun in 1616 and completed c. 1813. Many architects were involved in the design of the façade, but it was based largely on the original scheme by Carlo Buzzi. The style recalls the wide spreading gable façades of Romanesque churches.*

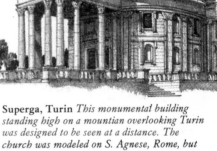

S. Maria di Caragnano, Genoa,
left. A centrally planned church by Galeazzo Alessi which commands a hill site above the city. The entry façade is generously wide with a central pediment flanked by elegant belltowers. The large dome over the crossing is surrounded by four minor domes.

Superga, Turin *This monumental building standing high on a mountian overlooking Turin was designed to be seen at a distance. The church was modeled on S. Agnese, Rome, but the proportions are more vertically orientated to show off its mountain site.*

S. Zaccaria, Venice *(1456-1515), left. By Antonio Gambella and Mauro Codussi, this church has a fine, orderly façade in which partiality for surface ornament has been controlled by a particularly neat decorative scheme.*

Certosa di Pavia, Pavia province *The giant portal with its ponderous coupled columns by Benedetto Briosco. The Gothic style church was given its outstanding classical marble façade by Giovanni Amadeo in 1492.*

S. Francesco, Rimini *Leone Alberti transformed what was once a modest friary church into a magnificent monument for Sigismondo Malatesta, who had secured the lordship of Rimini from rivals within his family.*

S. Lorenzo, Milan *(rebuilt 1573). The Early Christian quatrefoil plan of this church remains but Martino Bassi added a classical domical vault supported by massive Doric piers, and a projecting cornice which gives the interior the appropriate monumental quality.*

Northern Italy

Mantua has two churches, **S. Andrea** (1472-1512) and **S. Sebastiano** (*c.* 1460, both by Leone Alberti, which were greatly to influence church building. S. Andrea has a Latin cross plan and S. Sebastiano a Greek cross in square plan so they represent the two main types of church building. The entrance *portico* of S. Andrea was modeled on an ancient Roman triumphal arch and leads into a fine *aisleless nave*.

A characterisitic feature of *Lombardic* architecture in the late 15th century is the elaborate decorative reliefs that appear to transform the shape of the various components of a building. This can be seen in the **Colleoni Chapel, Bergamo** (1470-73), by Giovanni Amadeo, where the simple spaces of the interior were enriched by applied ornament. Decoration plays a similar role at **S. Maria dei Miracoli, Brescia** (1488).

S. Maria della Croce, Crema (1490-1500), by Giovanni Battaglio, is a round church with *Baroque* projections in the form of a Greek cross. The main *drum* is *articulated* by tiers of *arcading* and the ornamentation is the characteristic terracotta *polychrome* work of Lombardy.

The design of the priory of **S. Orso, Aosta** (1494-1506), was influenced by French *Gothic* as can be seen particularly in the turreted corner tower and the decorative banding of the windows. The church of the **Abbey of S. Benedetto, Po** (1540), was remodelled by Giulio Romano, with monumental palazzo-style façades.

S. Maria dei Miracoli, Venice (1481-89), by Pietro Lombardo, has an aisleless rectangular plan and a *barrel-vaulted* roof. The exterior of the building has an exquisitely articulated marble casing. The classical details are restrained although the qualities of the materials used, such as *porphyry* and *verd-antique* paneling, are emphasized. **S. Giorgio Maggiore, Venice** (1566-1610), by Andrea Palladio, stands on an island in the lagoon, presenting a magnificent silhouette of dome, turrets and tall *campanile*. The giant façade was completed by Vincenzo Scamozzi and incorporates the *Classical Orders*. **Il Redentore, Venice** (1577-92), is similar in plan but with side chapels in place of aisles and dwarf-like in comparison.

One of the most important Venetian architects of the 17th century was Baldassare Longhena. He built the extravagant Baroque **S. Maria della Salute, Venice** (1631-82), which stands on a stepped *podium* above the Grand Canal. The church is in the shape of a regular octagon, with a high drum crowned by a huge dome over a surrounding *ambulatory*. The chief difference internally between this and earlier *Renaissance* models is that the columns within the octagon, instead of continuing up into the drum, stop at its base, making room for the huge figures that crown the projecting *entablature*. Other examples of late Baroque churches in Venice include the **Chiese dei Gesuiti,** (1715-29), by Domenico Rossi, which is pure and sober in style compared with the bizarre "Christmas cake" ornamentation of **S. Moisè** (*c.* 1660), by Alessandro Tremignon, and described by John Ruskin as "the basest example of the basest school of the Renaissance".

S. Francesco, Ferrara *(1494). By Biagio Rossetti, a major architect of 15th-C Italy. While the interior of this church is a synthesis of diverse models, the exterior is an example of sober classicsm, which owes much to Alberti.*

S. Maria dei Miracoli, Venice
This beautiful tiny church has a marble façade articulated by refined blind arcading and a wheel-type rose window which recalls earlier Italian Romanesque traditions.

S. Lorenzo, Turin *(1668-80). Interior of this imaginative building by Guarino Guarini showing the complex layering of geometric shapes which characterizes the building both inside and out. The church is basically an octagon.*

S. Giorgio Maggiore, Venice
The crossing beneath the dome. The plan is cruciform and an apse finishes each arm. The enormous piers of the interior are articulated vertically by Corinthian columns and pilasters.

Turin Cathedral *(1491-98). Much building work in Italy at this time followed various regional traditions. Here the style is Roman, as seen in the wide spreading façade and the coupled pilasters.*

Il Redentore, Venice *The building is best seen from a distance so that the dome over the crossing is not hidden by the* portico *at the front of the long arm of the* nave. *The façade shows the results of years of adapting the ancient temple portico to a church front in Italy.*

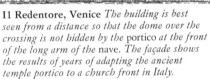

S. Andrea, Mantua, *right. The magnificent entry façade, based on ancient classical prototypes, consists of a huge porch flanked by four giant pilasters which support the* bold cornice *and* pediment. *Above is a curious canopy which projects from the central window of the higher, recessed* gable *at the end of the nave proper.*

Colleoni Chapel, Bergamo *The façade of the chapel showing its lavish decoration, including both re-cessed sculptured figures and repeated carved shapes.*

S. Maria della Salute, Venice, *left. The main dome is balanced by a secondary one flanked by turrets over the* chancel. *Decorative details cascade down from the magnificent domes on to scrolled buttresses and radiating chapels.*

S. Francesco alla Vigna, Venice *(c. 1570). The church was designed by Jacopo Sansovino, but the façade is by Andrea Palladio and is a tiny version of the S. Giorgio Maggiore façade.*

195

Northern Italy

Castles & Palaces

One of the earliest examples of the use of *faceted* masonry is on the monumental circular corner towers added to the **Castello Sforzesco, Milan** (1455). This type of decoration is associated with the great Italian fortresses of the Middle Ages. The entire façade of the **Palazzo dei Diamanti, Ferrara** (1493), by Biagio Rossetti, is covered in faceted masonry blocks. The long façade has carved corner *pilasters,* a *scarped* base and a fully elaborated *cornice* dividing the two stories.

The **Palazzo Marini, Milan** (1553-58), is a monumental mansion designed by Galeazzo Alessi and shows his free use of *stucco* ornamentation, merging *Renaissance* classicism with local Italian traditions of elaborate decoration. The *Ionic Order* is used for many of the classical elements of the building, but it is often replaced with grotesque carved stone decoration.

The *Loggia* and the *Odeion* are all that remain of the **Palazzo Cornaro, Padua** (1524), by Giovanni Falconetto. The buildings of the square created a *forum,* which was largely based on the ancient classical Roman model.

Andrea Palladio built a number of Palazzi in **Vicenza,** including the **Palazzo Thiene** (1556), the **Palazzo Valmarana** (*c.* 1565) and the **Palazzo Chiericati** (*c.* 1580). The last example is a ponderous building, almost top heavy, but interesting for the *colonnaded* loggia introduced into the standard palazzo façade. The design, with its *rusticated* lower story, was made 30 years before the palazzo was built.

The **Castle, Stupinigi** (1729-33), Torino by Filippo Juvarra, is in the Italian Renaissance star-shape with wings grouped symmetrically around a central core, which here incorporates a beautiful *Rococo* hall. The immense scale of the building is without parallel in northern Italy.

The **Palazzo Madama, Turin,** was originally a castle (13th-15thC), then restyled (1718-21) with Versailles, in France, as a reference for the overall form. The boldly drawn façade by Juvarra is, however, distinctly Italian, in stone blockwork rather than the brick of the eastern section.

Rich and festive façades are characteristically Venetian. An early Renaissance example fronts the **Pallazo Corner Spinelli, Venice** (*c.* 1480), which follows the medieval tradition of central *portico* facing the Grand Canal and balconies at the large, symmetrically arranged windows, but has a classical monumentality. The **Palazzo Dario, Venice,** is a *Gothic* house which had its rich classical façade added in 1487. The proportions are early Renaissance, while the decorative details and use of materials are in the Venetian tradition. The more flamboyant **Palazzo Vendramin-Calergi** (16thC) is like the Palazzo Dario, having twin windows with each pair set in a single arch and a round window in the *tympanum* formed by the arch. The **Palazzo Corner della Ca'Grande** (1532-56), by Jacopo Sansovino, and the **Palazzo Pesaro** (1663-79), by Baldassare Longhena, both have a similar monumentality, but here the verticality of the façades is stressed by the bold columns above the rusticated basements.

Castle, Stupinigi *This monumental country palace was designed as a "hunting lodge," hence the statue of the stag at bay on the highest point. Barrack-like wings project from the* Baroque *body of the building like crab claws.*

Palazzo Vendramin-Calergi, Venice *Detail of the* fenestration *from the classic Venetian palazzo façade. The ground floor is relatively subdued, being* articulated *vertically by* pilasters, *while the two upper floors have a strong horizontal emphasis.*

Palazzo dei Diamanti, Ferrara *Following Biagio Rossetti's design the* faceted *blocks of each story were cut to different angles to create a chiaroscuro effect — a contrast of light and shade.*

Palazzo Martinengo, Venice *(16thC). A patrician's house, this palazzo is extremely simple and traditional in form. The design is more typical of* Byzantine *Venice than the* Renaissance. *The façade was once covered in* frescoes.

Bridge of Sighs, Venice *(c. 1595), right. Although the bridge is nobly decorated with* rusticated *pilasters, heraldic devices and ornate bars at the windows, it earned its name for being part of the route between the Doge's palace and the prison.*

Palazzo Thiene, Vicenza *(c. 1550-56). Although an enormous project was planned, only this corner of the palazzo by Andrea Palladio was built. A* pedimented *central block was to have faced the main street.*

Venetian staircases

Some give access to the splendid halls of the celebrated 15th- and 16th-C schools, as at the **Scuola di S. Giovanni Evangelista.** Some are monumental, such as the **Scala dei Giganti** in the courtyard of the Doge's Palace, but most typical are the simple open courtyard stairs.

Scala del Bovolo

Traditional open staircase

Scala dei Giganti

197

Northern Italy

The **Palazzo Grimani, Venice** (1556-75), was Michele Sanmichele's masterpiece. The plan fits into an irregular site, stretching back at an angle from the Grand Canal façade. He also designed the **Palazzo Pompeii, Verona** (1530), a handsome building with *rusticated* basement and elegant *piano nobile articulated* by *fluted Doric* columns linked by *balustrading*. The **Palazzo Bevilacqua, Verona** (*c.* 1530), again by Sanmicheli, has a boldly articulated design with alternating wide and narrow bays. In comparison, the **Palazzo Canossa, Verona** (*c.* 1532), is extraordinarily gentle with bays of equal width and *pilasters, entablatures* and window moldings delicately drawn. The three central bays, the focal point on the ground floor, are reminiscent of the **Palazzo del Tè, Mantua** (1525-*c.*1534),by Guilio Romano, an enormous suburban villa built around a large square courtyard. Unusual in proportion, this palazzo has the appearance of a low, single-story block although it is articulated by giant Doric pilasters on tall *plinths*. The porches and windows are heavily rusticated while the entrance is via an elegant triple *arcade*.

The **Palazzo Ducale, Mantua** (*c.* 1539), is part of the Castello dei Gonzaga. It has an elaborate terrace, the Estivale, which has strange rustication and twisted Doric columns. The **Palazzo Contarini delle Figure, Venice** (1504-46), has a piano nobile articulated by a bold *pediment* carried on antique *fluted* columns that foreshadow later Venetian classicism. The story above the piano nobile has round-arched windows reminiscent of Lombardy. Other important palazzi in Venice are the **Palazzo Loredan** (*c.* 1536), a *Gothic* building remodeled by Antonia Abbondi: the **Palazzo Mocenigo Nero** (*c.* 1579), with its main rooms lighted by triple windows and façade reminiscent of that of the **Palazzo Papadopoli** (*c.* 1560), by Giangiacomo Grigi; the **Palazzo Balbi** (1582-90), by Alessandro Vittorio, and the restrained **Palazzo Guistiniani-Lolin** (1623) by Baldassare Longhena.

Domestic buildings

Andrea Palladio, in his design for the **Villa Capra**, or **Rotonda, Vicenza** (*c.* 1550), was the first architect since those of the ancient classical world, who thought to build a temple façade on the side of a domestic house. The design of the villa adheres strictly to the *Classical* rules of architecture and puts into practice Palladio's interpretation of *harmonic proportions*. The Villa Capra caught the imagination of 18th-century English aesthetes such as Lord Burlington and Colen Campbell, inspiring Chiswick House and Mereworth Castle in England.

Palladio's villas, unlike Roman or Florentine examples, were usually surrounded by fields and vineyards worked by the owner, and included outbuildings such as laborers' houses, barns and grain stores. The main house, usually built on rising ground, was invariably two-story. Examples include the **Villa Pojana Maggiore, Vicenza** (*c.* 1550-55), which has a pediment rising above the roof line like a *gable*.

Palazzo Rezzonico, Venice *(1667-1756). The architect was Baldassare Longhena but the palazzo was completed after his death. The* rusticated *ground floor has a triple water-gate and is simple compared to the* bold piano nobile *above with its* arcade-*like window units.*

Palazzo da Porto-Breganze, Vicenza *(c. 1570). One of the last of Palladio's palazzo projects, the Palazzo da Porto-Breganze was intended to be the dominant element of a large square. The* giant, *engaged Composite* columns *are reminiscent of those used at the Loggia del Capitano, Vicenza.*

Palazzo Pessaro, Venice *(1663-79). This is an exuberant and eclectic building by Longhena. The fine windows resemble those of Jacopo Sansavino's Library of St Mark, and the double-arched water entrance and semicircular sweep of steps recall the Palazzo Corner della Ca'Grande.*

Palazzo Raimondi, Cremona *(1496-99). left. The only known work by Elviso Raimondo. The façade is stylistically refined and harmonious and achieves subtle patterns of light and shade in sunshine.*

Palazzo Grimani, Venice, *right. The powerful façade gives great emphasis to the triple-arched water gate. Behind it the plan is distorted to fit an extremely awkward corner site, the main axis running at an angle to the façade.*

Palazzo Canossa, Verona *A building of well defined proportions by Michele Sanmicheli. The bays of the façade, outlined by low relief pilasters, are no longer independent but part of the façade wall, an effect achieved by carrying the base and imposts of the windows across the whole wall front.*

Palazzo Sforza, Venice *(c. 1460). Detail of the faceted masonry on the façade of this palazzo by Benedetto Ferrini or Antonio Filarete. The architect's project, to modernize an older Venetian building, was not completed.*

Palazzo Carignano, Turin *(1679). The building, by Guarino Guarini, was left unfinished until the 19thC. The convex and concave elements of the façade are framed by the straight wing sections.*

Villa Capra, Vicenza *The plan is a composition of square, circle and rectangle, which is bilaterally symmetrical. This symmetry is emphasized by the giant porticos. The villa was described by Goethe as "habitable but not homely."*

Northern Italy

In **Genoa**, significant domestic buildings are the **Villa Cambiaso** (1548), by Galeazzo Alessi, which has a three-bayed *loggia* flanked by projecting wings, and the **Strada Nuova** (1558), which consists of two rows of houses with palazzo-style frontages engaging the street.

The **Villa Foscari, Malcontenta** (*c.* 1560), Venezia, by Andrea Palladio, has a tall basement story, a precaution against flooding, and imposing *portico* and staircases. While the Villa Capra became a model for 18th-century English classicism, this villa has its equivalent in the 20th-century Maison Stein in France. The **Villa Barbaro, Maser** (*c.* 1560), also by Palladio, reflects the architect's (and his clients') interest in the Villa Guilia, the most spectacular new building in Rome at the time.

Artists and architects often designed their own houses. The **Casa Guilio Romano, Mantua** (*c.* 1540), is a two-story building with a palazzo style façade comprising a *rusticated* ground floor and an elegant *arcaded piano nobile* with *pedimented* window frames curiously embedded in the *blind* arches. Also of interest are the **Casa Mantegna, Mantua** (15thC), and **Casa Rosetti, Ferrara** (*c.* 1490).

The **Villa Manin, Passeriano** (*c.* 1738), in Venezia province, by Giovanni Ziborghi, is monumental in scale with villa, stables and farm buildings surrounding a colossal forecourt the size of the piazza in front of St. Peter's, Rome. The elaborate loggias running the length of the stables and farm buildings are typically Venetian.

The **Villa Pisani, Strai** (*c.* 1735-1756), Padova province, is set in a large park-like garden. Its various elements form a *Baroque* ensemble, but the villa, begun by Girolanio Frigimelica and completed by Francesco Preti, still has *Palladian* undertones. The house is separated from the stable block by a long canal which also divides the formal gardens behind the house.

The **Villa Cicogna, Bisuschio** (16thC), Varese province, was originally built as a hunting lodge in the 15th century, but was completely remodeled and redecorated by the Campi brothers. The house has beautiful gardens and one of Italy's finest water staircases.

At the **Villa d'Este, Cernóbbio** (1570), much of the *Renaissance* garden has gone, but of particular interest is the double water staircase framed in an avenue of cypresses, perhaps one of the most beautiful sights in any Italian garden. The **Villa Carlotta, Cadenabbia** (1747), Como province, is also famous for its magnificent gardens which rise in terraces from the lake to the house.

Civic & Public buildings

The **Loggia, Brescia** (*c.* 1490-1560), has an arcaded ground floor with a huge hall above. This upper story is *articulated* by *half-columns* with unusually ornate *capitals* and decoratively carved *pilasters* and encircling *frieze*.

The **Basilica, Vicenza** (*c.* 1550), is Palladio's brilliant remodeling of the medieval senate house of the city by the addition of a two-story loggia that encircles the buildings.

Casa Guilio Romano, Mantua
View of the portico *showing the curious way in which the* string-course *turns up over the entrance forming a pediment which flattens the arch below it.*

Casa Mantegna, Mantua, *left.*
The circular courtyard. The house was not conceived solely as a dwelling place but as a "casa dell' artista," a place of retreat and for artistic exhibitions.

Casa Rosetti, Ferrara, *above. A sober building, the major embellishments being the characteristic Ferrarese twin windows which pierce the* piano nobile.

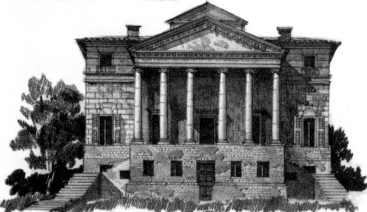

Villa Foscari, Malcontenta, *left. The villa stands on the banks of the River Brenta, a short boat trip from Venice, and has, like Venetian palazzi, its façade facing the water.*

Villa Badoer, Rovigo *(c. 1556). By Andrea Palladio, it is the only one of a group of villas to have minor porticos flanking the central block (one of which can be seen in the drawing, left) completed. The podium and portico of the building express the prestige of the owner.*

Loggia, Brescia
The most significant Renaissance *building in the town. The lower story is the work of Fromentone, and the upper story was added by Jacopo Sansovino.*

Basilica, Vicenza
An arch of the loggia showing the half-columns facing each pier and the free-standing columns in front. The entablature *of the half-columns creates the* imposts *of the round arches.*

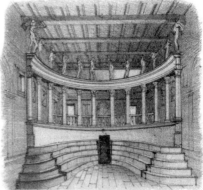

Rialto Bridge, Venice *(1588-91), above. Da Ponte produced this graceful, single-arched stone bridge to accommodate trade along the Grand Canal, as well as to provide for shops on the bridge itself*

Teatro Olympico, Vicenza *(1585). The theatre was begun by Palladio and finished after his death by Vincenzo Scamozzi. The structure was built ingeniously into an older building. The stage wall is pierced.*

Theatre, Sabbioneta *(1588-90). Designed by Scamozzi, it is the first theatre of modern architecture. The theatre has three imposing,* Palladian *style façades. The auditorium is narrow with seating planned in a horseshoe shape and backed by an elegant* colonnade.

Northern Italy

The charitable foundations of Venice known as scuole were housed in buildings which were partly hospitals and schools, as well as serving as meeting places for the religious fraternity. Architecturally important are the **Scuola Grande di S. Marco** (1485-95) and the **Scuola di S. Rocco** (1517-60), a *Renaissance* building with a graceful façade. The great hall houses 56 Tintoretto canvases.

The **Library of St Mark's, Venice** (1537-53), is Jacopo Sansovino's masterpiece. Built facing the Doge's Palace, it is a boldly *articulated* building three bays wide and 21 bays long. Such proportions create great horizontal emphasis and this is reinforced by the massive *cornices* and *entablatures*. The upper entablature is particularly dominant with its wide, windowed *frieze*.

The **Loggia del Capitano, Vicenza** (1571-72), by Andrea Palladio, was designed to unite the hall of the residence above with the public *loggia* below, as well as to create a distinctive building. To do this, Palladio utilized a giant *Classical Order* to decorate the public façade.

The façade of the **Collegio Elvetico, Milan** (1608), was added by Francesco Ricchino in 1627. The concave sweep that marks the center of the façade is a *Baroque* feature. Another great Baroque complex is the **University, Genoa** (1630), planned by Bartolomeo Bianco.

The **Palazzo della Gran Guardia, Verona** (1610), was designed by Domenico Curtoni for public meetings. A monumental building, it is long and narrow with an imposing *rusticated* ground floor of round-arched openings and the upper floor ponderously articulated by coupled sets of *Doric* columns.

The **Teatro Farnese, Parma** (1618-28), is Giovanni Aleotti's best known work. The theatre is a significant improvement on the Teatro Olympico in Vicenza in that it was the first to employ a single *proscenium* arch to frame a deep space where flats could be used. Constructed in a hall on the first floor of the Palazzo Pilotta, the theatre is a post-World War II reconstruction using salvaged original materials.

Scuola Grande di S. Marco, Venice *One of several scuole in Venice, this notable example has a façade of two stories articulated by* Corinthian pilasters *and rising to a semicircular* pedimented *skyline. The ground floor is decorated with panels of reliefs carved in perspective.*

Porta S. Giovanni, Padua *(1528), left. The town gate, by Falconetto. The high* attic story *and the base articulated by four columns on high pedestals are reminiscent of an ancient Roman triumphal arch.*

Loggia del Capitano, Vicenza, *left. A building that cleverly offered both public meeting place below and a hall of residence above. The design is coordinated by the giant* columns, capitals *and the* entablature *that crowns the façade.*

Library of St Mark's, Venice *Detail of the two-story* arcade, *its* piers *faced with* Doric *half-columns on the ground floor and* Ionic *columns above. A barrel-vaulted* loggia *runs along the ground floor of the library.*

Central Italy

Religious buildings

Florence Cathedral (1296-1436) has been much altered over the years, additions including a new façade added at the end of the 16th century to replace one which had been destroyed. The interior is on a vast scale and has high *Gothic vaulting*, supported in the *nave* by only four arches. The dominating feature, however, is the great dome (1420-36), which is 348 ft in height. It was the work of Filippo Brunelleschi, considered to be the first architect of the *Renaissance* and certainly among the greatest. Brunelleschi produced one of the most intriguing technical solutions in the history of building: a method of covering a huge space with a great dome. For this he relied more on the mechanical arts of the medieval cathedral builders, whose knowledge of *Classical* mechanical techniques was considerable, than on contemporaneous Renaissance theories. His solution was simple: since the use of scaffolding for such a vast project would have been time-consuming and expensive, he devised a method of erecting the dome in a series of rings, each of which he made self-supporting before he commenced work on the next. The final structure combines a hemispherical dome within an octagonal rib cage. Three chains of linked sandstone blocks bind the dome, giving additional strength. The interior is decorated with a huge *fresco* of the Last Judgement.

At **S. Lorenzo, Florence** (1421), work enlarging the existing church on the model of the great monastic churches had already begun when Brunelleschi was appointed advisor in 1421. The traditional *basilica* was transformed into an elegant, centralized church, its planning *module* evolving from the square of the *crossing*. It is an outstanding example of his genius for accommodating existing work with his own original plans and adapting plans to awkward sites. The inspiration here is Tuscan *Romanesque* formality and the Gothic spaciousness of earlier centuries. Of particular note is the *sacristy*, which is cube-shaped and roofed with a dome with central *lantern*. Brunelleschi's design for **S. Spirito, Florence** (1436), while employing the centralized basilican plan of S. Lorenzo, was far more expressive of the new Renaissance spirit. The *Orders*, for example, were designed purely for aesthetic effect.

The new green and white marble façade added to **S. Maria Novella, Florence** (*c.* 1455-60), was the work of Leone Battista Alberti, who was the epitome of the Renaissance man, being not only an architect but musician, playwright, painter and scientist. The major problem facing him in the renovation of the façade was how to unify the basilican section of high nave and low side *aisles*. For this he employed both *pilasters* and *engaged columns* but his real innovation was in using a geometric curved form, the *volute*, to make a smooth transition from low to high externally on the façade. Thereafter the volute was to become one of the key elements of Renaissance and *Baroque* façade design. Another important work in Florence by Alberti is the **Shrine of the Holy Sepulchre, S. Pancrazio** (*c.* 1455-60), which is simple in form but decorated in many colors.

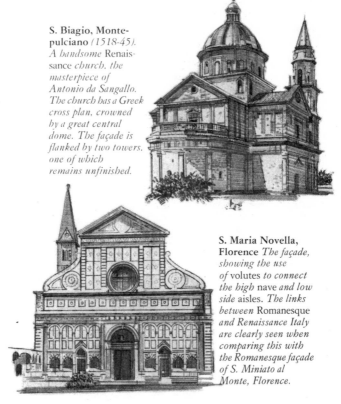

S. Biagio, Monte-pulciano *(1518-45). A handsome Renaissance church, the masterpiece of Antonio da Sangallo. The church has a Greek cross plan, crowned by a great central dome. The façade is flanked by two towers, one of which remains unfinished.*

S. Maria Novella, Florence *The façade, showing the use of* volutes *to connect the high* nave *and low side* aisles. *The links between Romanesque and Renaissance Italy are clearly seen when comparing this with the Romanesque façade of S. Miniato al Monte, Florence.*

Florence Cathedral *View of the dome, the work of Filippo Brunelleschi, which took almost 16 years to complete. Ghiberti worked with him on the project until 1426. The* lantern *was added between 1445 and 1467, after Brunelleschi's death.*

Central Italy

Among the most elegant examples of Filippo Brunelleschi's art in Florence is the **Pazzi Chapel** in **S. Croce** (1429). It consists of an oblong hall divided into three parts, with a central square crowned by a dome and flanked by *tunnel-vaulted* bays. A later addition is the fine entrance porch, which is also probably by Brunelleschi. Another of his works, **S. Maria degli Angeli, Florence** (1434-37), is the first instance in the *Renaissance* style of a completely centralized church. with the altar at the center. It became a prototype for many later Renaissance churches.

    S. Maria Maddelena de' Pazzi, Florence (15thC), by Guiliano da Sangallo, has a magnificent classical *atrium* in the *Ionic Order* with an arched entrance in the center, cutting into the *entablature*. **S. Maria delle Grazie**, Pistoia (*c.* 1452), is an austere church by Michelozzo di Bartolommeo. It is in the *Byzantine* square shape with a central dome and with smaller chapels, also domed, at the four corners. **Pienza Cathedral** (1460-62), by Bernardo Rossellino, who was primarily a sculptor, is most unusual for Italy in that it is a *hall-church*.

Castles & Palaces

The **Palazzo Ducale, Urbino** (1444-82), is a colossal complex with picturesque skyline of turreted round towers and an irregularity of massing which utilizes the spectacular site to the most dramatic effect. The complex has two main fronts: the east façade with *loggia* flanked by towers faces the countryside, while a townside façade on the west forms two sides of a piazza. There is a magnificent *arcaded* Central Court.

S. Spirito, Florence *(1436). For this church Filippo Brunelleschi employed a* basilican *plan, as he did at S. Lorenzo, but the overall effect is more expressive of the essential* Renaissance *spirit. The* volutes *were to be a reference for Leone Alberti.*

S. Maria della Conzolazione, Todi *(1508-1609). This church is of the Greek cross design with a round drum rising from a flat roof, a simplified version of Bramante's plan for St Peter's, Rome. The bold massing is articulated by* pilasters *and by deep cornices.*

Basilica, Loreto *(1460-c. 1495). A pilgrimage church, which was modified from 1481 under the supervision of Guiliano da Maiano, who vaulted the nave and fortified the east front. Numerous artists were employed here, including Donato Bramante and Francesco di Giorgio.*

S. Croce, Florence. *View of the porch of the Pazzi Chapel, seen from the Great Cloister. The interior decoration has bold arcs and Corinthian pilasters. The building's concept owes much to the sculptural treatment of architectural forms in many ancient Roman buildings.*

S. Lorenzo, Florence, *left. The interior of the church, which is by Brunelleschi and is on the medieval monastic plan of nave and side aisles. The* transepts *are bordered by five chapels, the central one continuing the nave. Far left, view of the tomb (1421) of Lorenzo de' Medici by Michelangelo Buonarroti. The magnificent sculptures form an integral part of the architectural composition of the square, domed chamber in which they are situated.*

Palazzo Ducale, Urbino *The west façade. The medieval buildings of the palace were remodeled and extended during the Renaissance. The point from which both old and new buildings spring is a spacious courtyard, surrounded by elegant arcades.*

S. Francesca al Monte, Florence *(15thC-1504), below. An* aisleless *church with side chapels by Cronaca. It is an amalgam of Roman sensibility of space, in the simplicity and robustness of forms, and Tuscan* articulation.

S. Bernardino, L'Aquila *(1454-72). View of the magnificent Renaissance façade, added by Cola dall' Amatrice in 1525-27. It is boldly drawn with coupled columns and lofty* pedestals *for the ground floor.*

Central Italy

Florence in the 15th century was among the most affluent of the city states, and many magnificent early *Renaissance* palaces were built. An outstanding example is the colossal **Palazzo Pitti** (1458). The original palace comprised the row making up the façade; two wings, projecting back toward the gardens and forming a central courtyard, were added by Bartolomeo Ammannati and are boldly *rusticated* with a masonry technique reminiscent of a Roman aquaduct.

The *astylar* façade was characteristic of many of the palaces, including the **Palazzo Strozzi, Florence** (1489), by Benedetto da Maiano, Guiliano da Sangallo and others. Possibly the finest privately owned palace of the time in the city, it has a large *arcaded* courtyard and rusticated masonry like giant fieldstones. An astylar façade as on the Palazzo Strozzi is found on many other palaces in the city. These include the **Palazzo Medici-Riccardi** (1444) by Michelozzo di Bartolommeo, which has a *cortile* around which are planned the various rooms as in ancient Pompeii, an arrangement which became the principal Renaissance palace prototype; the **Palazzo Pazzi-Quaratesi** (1460-72), probably by Guiliano da Maiano, and the **Palazzo Gerini-Neroni** (*c.* 1460). The **Palazzo Rucellai, Florence** (*c.* 1455-60), designed by Leone Alberti, was one of the first Renaissance palaces to be *articulated* by *pilasters* and this became a model for much palace building that followed. The **Palazzo Pandolfini** (*c.* 1518), by Raphael and others, is unlike the usual Florentine type (which is of three stories and is generally rusticated throughout) in having two stories and rustication only at corners and door surrounds, in the manner of a Roman palace. In all other respects, however, it is in the Florentine tradition.

One of the great monuments of Renaissance palace design is Giacomo Barozzi da Vignola's **Palazzo Farnese, Caprarola** (1559), a huge fortress-like construction, pentagonal in shape and built on a mountain site. It is of symmetrical plan, with *portal,* stairs, and elaborate ramp.

Domestic buildings

The **Villa del Poggio a Caiano, Florence** (1480-85), by da Sangallo, an engineer and notable sculptor in addition to being an architect, is an early example of a Renaissance villa in a mixture of Roman and Tuscan styles. It has a *piano nobile* raised above an arcaded basement and articulated by a decorative *frieze* and sculptured *pediment.* The **Villa d'Este, Tivoli** (*c.* 1565-72), a former Benedictine monastery, is by Pirro Ligorio, who began his career as a painter. It is a vast complex standing on a cliff-like terrace at the top of a hill. The main emphasis, however, is on the elaborate fountains, one of which is by Gianlorenzo Bernini, and gardens that descend the slopes below.

The villas of **Frascati** often have magnificent gardens equal to those of Florence. Oustanding examples are the **Villa Aldobrandini** (1601), by Giacomo della Porta, which has one of the finest *Baroque* gardens in Italy, the **Villa Mondragone** (16thC), with a *loggia* by da Vignola, and the **Villa Garzoni Collodi** (17thC).

Palazzo Pitti, Florence, *left.* *To enrich the division of the three-story façade, a series of elements was applied, such as molded* string courses, *fan-shaped* vaussoirs *around openings and decorative masonry facing.*

Rocca Pia Castle, Tivoli *(c. 1458-64). The round tower was the chief defense against cannon fire since, unlike a square tower, cannon balls would glance off the surface. Another defensive device was the addition of strong* bastions.

Palazzo Farnese, Caprarola *The core of the pentagonal-shaped palace is this elegant circular courtyard of two* arcaded *stories, finely* articulated *with a* rusticated *lower story and coupled* Ionic *columns in the upper. The palace itself is of five stories, including basements, with rooms for priests, servants and nobles.*

Palazzo Tarugi, Montepulciano *(16thC), left. A handsome* Renaissance *building with the two lower stories articulated with giant Ionic columns and the top story with* pilasters. *The ground floor is arcaded. Of note are the openings, to the left and above the doorway, which were used for identifying callers in the street beneath.*

Palazzo Medici-Riccardi, Florence *A traditional palazzo, it is given order and clarity by molded string courses and the grading of masonry texture for each of the three floors, from rusticated blocks on the ground floor to a fine,* ashlar *top story.*

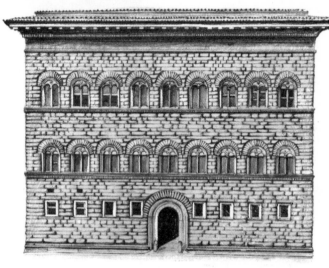

Palazzo Strozzi, Florence *The giant block, detached on three sides, is the most classical of the* astylar *palaces, with the blockwork graded story by story. Each façade is punctuated by a central entrance, symmetrical* fenestration *on all three stories and a* cornice.

Renaissance gardens

An outstanding feature of the 16thC Renaissance was the combination of art and nature in gardens, which were often terraced and were embellished with elaborate fountains, water jets, statuary and decorative grottoes.

"Gate of Hell", Sacro Bosco (1550-70), *Bomarzo*

Boboli Gardens, Florence (1550)

Palazzo Gerini-Neroni, Florence *A characteristic of early Florentine palaces such as this is the simplicity of design in both the proportion of windows to façade and in the texture of walling, usually with rusticated ground story and* stucco *or ashlar work above.*

Central Italy

Civic & Public buildings

Filippo Brunelleschi's first public building was the **Foundlings' Hospital, Florence** (1419). The traditional medieval hospital plan, consisting of *cloisters,* dormitories and entrance *loggia,* was here given a façade which was built solely for its aesthetic effect, its forms being taken from those of *Romanesque* Tuscany. The building was sited so as to form a public square in front of the Church of the Annunciation.

Michelezzo di Bartolommeo was the architect of the monastery of **S. Marco, Florence** (*c.* 1438), which included the first *Renaissance*-style library. The room was divided into *nave* and *aisles* and became a prototype for numerous others. Another magnificent library is the **Library of S. Lorenzo** (1525), designed by Michelangelo Buonarroti to be incorporated in the west cloister of S. Lorenzo, Florence. It is a long, low room without aisles and is entered via a lofty vestibule.

One of the major civic works of the Renaissance in Florence was the transformation, under the direction of Bernardo Rossellino, of an untouched village into **Pienza** (1460-62), a grand episcopal seat for Pius II. It became the first ideal Renaissance city. The main elements are grouped around the principal piazza and include the **Palazzo Vescovile** and the **Palazzo Piccolomini,** the latter being reminiscent of the Palazzo Rucellai, Florence, on which the architect had worked.

Government buildings of today were often originally buildings such as bishops' palaces which had themselves been designed to serve a number of purposes. The monumental complex of the **Uffizi, Florence** (1560-*c.* 1585), was designed by Georgio Vasari to house, under one roof, the various administrative departments which had hitherto been scattered throughout the city. The core of the new complex is an elegant street, terminated at one end by the **Palazzo Vecchio** (1299-1314), a massive *Gothic* building, and at the other by a fine arched screen. The street between is *articulated* by a ground story loggia and flat wall strips dividing the *fenestration.*

Library of S. Lorenzo, Florence *View of the elaborate triple staircase which ascends from a lofty vestibule to the first story library. The area is* articulated *by coupled columns recessed in the walls and carried by* consoles.

Ospedale del Ceppo, Pistoia *(13th-14thC). The hospital, which cared for lepers among other sick people, had this elegant* loggia *added in the 14thC. It was enriched by an enameled terracotta* frieze *and medallions by Giovanni della Robbia and others.*

Foundlings' Hospital, Florence *The entrance loggia, with* Corinthian *columns and semicircular arches. The terracotta medallions on the* spandrels *were models for those on the hospital in Pistoia.*

Uffizi, Florence *This great complex of administrative offices, four stories in height, is grouped around a street. Typical of Renaissance space is the strong axial line running the length of the street and terminated by a round arch.*

Rome

Religious buildings

S. Maria del Popolo (1472-80), like many of the city's churches of the 15th century, was built in the reign of Pope Sixtus IV. Classical style columns were employed to transform the *Gothic basilica* (as exemplified by S. Maria Minerva, Rome) and create a handsome façade. The second major religious building of the period is **S. Agostino** (1479-83), more monumental in scale and with a boldly *articulated* façade and a curious *attic* story with sides sloped like a *pediment*.

The **Sistine Chapel, Vatican City** (1473-81), by Giovanni de Dolci, has a formidable bastion-like exterior. The fame of the building rests on the beautiful *frescoes* painted by Michelangelo Buonarroti on the *barrel-vaulted* ceiling (1508-12) and across the altar wall (1534-41).

St Peter's (1506-1612) gave Donato Bramante the opportunity to design a three-domed centralized church on the lines of the Pantheon, liberating church design from the cruciform plan. Bramante was succeeded by Raphael and others who greatly altered the design, but Michelangelo resumed Bramante's plan, spending the last 30 years of his life completing the monumental church with its great dome. Carlo Moderno extended the plan to form a Latin cross and added the palatial façade between 1606 and 1612.

S. Maria degli Angeli is Michelangelo's ingenious transformation of the *tepidarium* of the Thermae of Diocletian into a church in 1561-62. The cavernous sense of space is much exaggerated by the placement of the altar not on the axis of the hall but on the transverse axis. Michelangelo's design for the Sforza Chapel of **S. Maria Maggiore** (*c.* 1560-73) has a similar simplicity and purity but on a much smaller scale. The monochrome coloring of both works is an essential ingredient.

The work by Francesco Borromini to transform **S. Giovanni in Laterano** (1646-50) into a major *Baroque* building was constrained by Pope Innocent X's wish to preserve the old basilica. Alternate bays of the existing *nave* were turned into wide *piers,* articulated at the edges by giant *pilasters* the height of the nave. Each pier is enriched at its base by a colored marble tabernacle niche, and in between the high bays he inserted low arches in a lighter colored stone. Borromini had planned to vault the interior but was forbidden to do so by his patron. In the remodeling of the façade of the **Oratorio di S. Filippo Neri** (1637-40), Borromini countered restrictions on his using columns that might clash with the existing church by bending the façade inwards fractionally, so creating a tremendous sense of tautness which is emphasized by the elegant *pediment* crowning the façade.

S. Giovanni in Laterano *The magnificent* portico *in the eastern façade by Alessandro Galilei. The Cathedral of Rome, this* basilican *church was mostly rebuilt in the 17th and 18thC.*

S. Marcello al Corso *(1682-83). The concave façade by Carlo Fontana enriched by coupled columns, an ornate broken* pediment *and a circular picture frame above the door. The theatricality of the design marks the advent of late* Baroque *classicism.*

Oratorio di S. Filippo Neri *The* oratory *added to the Oratorians' church by Borromini, which includes a library and accommodation for the priests. The façade has a gentle concave curve* articulated *by* pilasters.

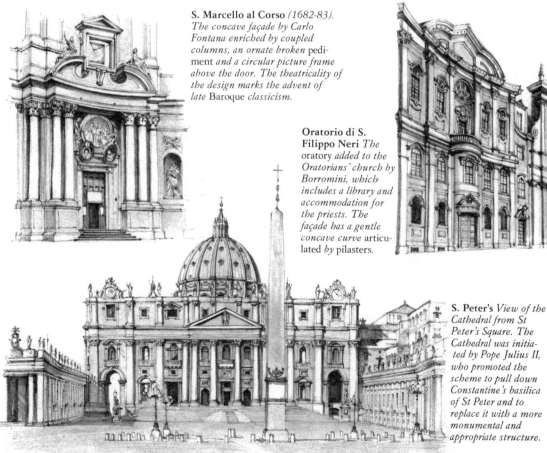

S. Peter's *View of the Cathedral from St Peter's Square. The Cathedral was initiated by Pope Julius II, who promoted the scheme to pull down Constantine's basilica of St Peter and to replace it with a more monumental and appropriate structure.*

Rome

S. Carlo alle Quattro Fontane (1638-41) was the first church built in Rome by Francesco Borromini. The plan is basically a Greek cross with an undulating wall line. The whole is crowned by an oval dome on *pendentives*. The design is an accumulation of geometric forms rather than the multiplication and division of a basic unit of measurement, which is the basis of *Classical* planning. S. Ivo della Sapienza (1642-50), also by Borromini, is the church of the University of Rome. The building is enclosed at one end of a magnificent, two-story *arcaded* courtyard which itself has a concave screen façade. Major and minor spaces of the church, created by the unusual hexagonal plan with its six surrounding lobes, overlap. The geometry of the structure is composed of two interlocking triangles forming a star. The *cupola* supports a hexagonal *lantern* crowned by a corkscrew spire.

S. Agnese (1652-55) was begun by Carlo Rainaldi as a Greek cross plan, but the design was awkward and restricted with an overpowering dome. The commission was given to Borromini who transformed the plan, skilfully building over the existing interior and remodeling the façade, making it wider and more powerful looking with flanking towers either side of a taut, concave center section with *pedimented portico*.

SS. Martina e Luca (1635-50), by Pietro da Cortona, has a Greek cross plan with *apses.* The church is crowned with a boldly drawn dome on a high *drum* pierced by windows. The most impressive feature of the building is the façade, which is two stories in height and seemingly squeezed outward by the projecting *piers* at either end. The piers themselves are *articulated* by coupled *pilasters* and the center section of the façade with engaged columns. In S. Maria della Pace (15thC-1657) da Cortona created an even more fluid design with a two-story pedimented *portal* of concave and convex sections which appears detached from the main body of the church, and two-story cloisters.

SS. Vincenzo e Anastasio (1646-50), a massive *Baroque* building, is the one major building by Martino Longhi the Younger. The two-story façade has triple columns flanking the portal, each stepped slightly forward in plan and linked at both stories by bold pediments. S. Andrea del Quirinale (1658-70) is a small, simple church by Gianlorenzo Bernini. The *nave,* a domed ellipse, has a projecting vestibule with a handsome pedimented façade. The semicircular porch is flanked by columns and is enclosed by an archway which is itself framed by giant *Corinthian* pilasters.

The siting of the twin churches S. Maria di Monte Santo and S. Maria dei Miracoli (1662-79), both by Rainaldi, is particularly skilful in the way they separate the three main streets entering the Piazza del Popolo. S. Maria del Priorato (1764-6), by Giovanni Piranesi, was a chapel for the Priory of the Knights of Malta. The ancient Roman and *Etruscan* motifs of the design make this church one of the more exotic and picturesque works of the city.

S. Maria della Pace
A 15th-C church given a new façade by Pietro da Cortona. The interplay of convex upper story, which is articulated *by* projecting piers, *and the semicircular* portico *below is characteristic of* Roman Baroque.

S. Agnese *A church which was extensively remodeled by Francesco Borromini. The long façade is brought alive by the concave center section and the flanking towers that act as a magnificent foil to the bold dome and* drum.

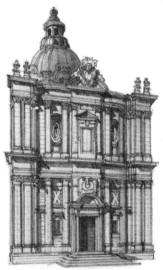

SS. Martina e Luca *One of the first great high Baroque churches. The similarity between internal and external features is remarkable, as if the internal spaces were used as a mold for the external forms.*

S. Carlo alle Quattro Fontane
The upper story of the magnificent façade. The concave and convex curves are restrained by the engaged columns and belt-like entablature. *The oval medallion is carried by angels.*

Il Gesu *(1568-84). Interior of the principal church of the Jesuits in Rome. Designed by Giacomo Vignola, it has the prototypical Jesuit aisleless plan to give more of the congregation a good view.*

Tempietto, S. Pietro in Montorio *(1499-1502), right. This church, by Donato Bramante, has a 16-columned, Doric peristyle. It is the closest Renaissance interpretation of the spirit of ancient classical building.*

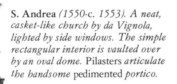

S. Andrea *(1550-c. 1553). A neat, casket-like church by da Vignola, lighted by side windows. The simple rectangular interior is vaulted over by an oval dome. Pilasters articulate the handsome pedimented portico.*

S. Susanna *(1597-1603). The outstanding building by Carlo Maderno. Unlike many mannerist buildings, the façade has remarkably well proportioned bays, with the Orders and other decoration graded in size toward the center.*

Scala Regia, Vatican *(1663-66). Gianlorenzo Bernini was asked to create a new entrance to the Vatican City while accepting the length and angle of the original. He planned this ceremonial staircase covered by a barrel vault. The far end of the corridor has a false perspective.*

Rome

Castles & Palaces

The **Palazzo Venezia** (1455-71), a cardinal's residence by Leone Alberti, is a monumental complex with a huge two-story *arcaded* courtyard. The plan includes an "L"-shaped section, which wraps around the courtyard with a tower in the angle, and a church. The **Cancelleria Vecchia** (1458-62) is most typical of 15th-century palazzi in its large scale and its use of the style of *articulation* found in the façades of the ancient Roman *insula*. The façade is much altered, but the courtyard is original.

The **Cortile del Belvedere** (1503) by Donato Bramante was designed to bridge the saddle of land between the old papal palace and the detached villa (1485-87) built for Pope Innocent VIII. A simple but monumental design in the spirit of Hadrian's Villa, Tivoli, it has a long rectangular courtyard lined with barrack-like blocks which cut into the rising ground.

The **Palazzo Farnese** (1541-46) was the first of a series of papal palazzi in the city. Originally a 15th-century cardinal's residence, the palazzo was conceived as a free-standing block with a central *cortile* with arcades and a monumental façade with unbroken *string courses* and rows of identical windows. The *cornice* was designed by Michelangelo Buonarroti, who took charge of the building program in 1546.

The chief interest of the **Palazzo Borghese** (*c.* 1560), by Giacomo Vignola and others, lies in the handsome courtyard with two of its three stories arcaded with double columns. The **Quirinal Palace** (16th-17thC), a summer residence of the popes, has a handsome two-story *loggia*, oval staircase and handsome *belvedere* added by Ottaviano Mascanno. The **Palazzo Barberini** (1628-33) shows a change from the traditional block concept to an "H"-shaped plan, first developed in the Villa Farnesina, Rome. The third story of the façade has its window frames built to accentuate perspective.

Other palazzi of interest in Rome are the **Palazzo di Montecitorio** (1650) and the **Palazzo Chigi-Odescalchi** (1664), both by Gianlorenzo Bernini, and the magnificent **Palazzo Doria-Pamphili** (1732-35) by Gabriele Valvassori.

Domestic buildings

The **Villa Papa Guilio** (1550-55), by Giorgio Vasari and Giacomo Vignola, has an inspired ground plan. The entry façade, with its triumphal arch motif, opens out to the rear in an elegant semicircular loggia which embraces the grand cortile. Beyond that are formal gardens and a sunken court, lined with summer rooms and approached by two curving flights of steps which appear to mirror the entrance loggia behind.

Palazzo Farnese, *above. Designed by Antonia Sangallo and completed by Michelangelo Buonarroti, it is one of the finest palazzi of the period. The façade was the model for the Reform Club building, London.*

Villa Papa Guilio *The distinctive entrance with its* rusticated *block-work through which the columns of the* portal *and flanking pilasters are threaded. The effect resembles triumphal arches of ancient Rome.*

Palazzo Zuccari *(c. 1590). Bizarre designs are a feature of late 16th-C Tuscan garden architecture. The garden entrance of this Roman house is a huge, grotesque jaw. The flanking windows and front façade are similar.*

Palazzo Massimo dell Colonne *(1532). View of the courtyard, with the entrance passage to the right. A complex building by Baldassare Peruzzi, the rooms are arranged around the courtyard. The façade, curving with the street, is drawn on to the neighboring building.*

Palazzo Spada *(1652-53), above. Of the few domestic commissions which Francesco Borromini undertook, this was one of the most interesting with its deceptive* colonnade *built to increase perspective.*

Porta Pia *(1561). The size of this small gateway by Michelangelo is exaggerated by the heavy frame of pilasters supporting first a segmented pediment, then a triangular one above.*

Colonnade, St Peter's *(1655-67). Gianlorenzo Bernini's purpose was to use this colonnade to link the ceremonial precincts, the Piazza and the Cathedral itself, with the surrounding districts.*

Spanish Steps *(1723-26). One of the masterpieces of urban design by Francesco de Sanctis, the Spanish Steps continued Pope Sixtus V's concept of a Roman city plan, a movement system along a series of straight avenues joined by architectural features.*

213

Rome

The **Villa Farnesina** (1509-11) by Baldassare Peruzzi, has a "U" plan with an *arcaded loggia* in the center, palazzo-style façades and decorative interiors painted by Raphaelo Raphael and his pupils. The fascination of Raphael's **Villa Madama** (*c.* 1516) lies in its unfinished state. The design was for a more monumental work of which this deceptively simple structure on a terrace is but a fragment. The heart of the **Casino de Pio IV, Vatican City** (1559), is an oval terrace on a hillside with the three-story house on rising ground opposite.

Civic & Public buildings

One of the more remarkable public buildings of the 15th century is the **Hospital of S. Spirito** (1474-82), an enormous complex commissioned by Pope Sixtus IV with a monumental façade *articulated* by arcaded loggias. It became a prototype for hospital building.

A revolutionary architectural concept of late 16th-century Italy was that space itself is an element of design. Michelangelo Buonarroti transformed the **Campidoglio**, the medieval civic center of Rome, into the first great *Baroque* space between 1561 and 1584. The equestrian statue of Marcus Aurelius had already been positioned at the center of the group of the existing buildings. Michelangelo added the elegant flight of steps that reinforces the axial line running through the statue and the Palazzo del Senatore. The rest of Michelangelo's plan includes the refronting of the façades of the Palazzo del Senatore and the Palazzo Conservatori with giant Orders of Pilasters, and the design for the oval piazza around the central statue linking the three buildings.

Roman Fountains
The fountain wall, such as the **Fontana di Trevi** (1732-62), was either carved from an embankment, built as a free-standing wall, or as an enrichment for a palazzo façade. Other fountains are sculptures in the round, such as the **Fontana dei Fiumi** (1652) and the **Fontana della Barcaccia** (17thC).

Fontana dei Fiumi

Fontana della Barcaccia

Fontana di Trevi

Campidoglio *View of the Piazza del Campidoglio in front of the Palazzo del Senatore, which in its earlier castellated form had been the civic center of Rome from medieval times. Michelangelo Buonarroti's transformation of the area, centered on an equestrian statue, is the first great piece of* Baroque *planning.*

Acqua Paola (1612). A magnificent fountain wall, built with marble salvaged from the ancient Forum of Nerva and granite columns from the old church of St Peter. The fountain was once supplied by Trajan's aqueduct, which brought water from Lake Bracciano 30 miles away.

Southern Italy

The *Renaissance,* founded in humanism, had little effect on southern Italian architecture outside Naples. The new style came primarily in decoration mixed with more traditional *Gothic* forms. A good example is the tall *campanile* of the **Cathedral, Soleto** (15thC), which looks almost Islamic with its applied ornament.

Spanish rule led to the more richly ornamented buildings of southern Italy and Sicily, distinguishing them from the *Baroque* buildings of Rome and northern Italy. This amalgam of Italian vernacular building with Spanish *plateresque* in the south is best seen in the church of **S. Croce, Lecce** (16thC-1644). The architecture of Sicily was always more conservative but nevertheless fantastic decorative effects were achieved at this time, such as in the paneled façade of **S. Maria della Scala, Messina** (15thC). The *faceted* masonry of the lower story is an unusual feature for a church. The general form of the ornamentation is reminiscent of late Gothic in Spain.

S. Sebastian, Acireale (1693-1705), built following the earthquake of 1693, has a façade which is an amalgam of Spanish and Italian Baroque. It is alive with decorative details: statuary in elegant niches, grotesque masks enriching the corbels of molded *pilasters* and a line of cherubs that dance along the *cornice* of the ground floor. Despite such extravagance the main lines are still conservative. The earthquake also destroyed the medieval façade of **Syracuse Cathedral** (7thC). A magnificent late Baroque façade was built (1728-57) to replace it. The exuberant forms are held together by powerful-looking, free-standing columns flanking the main *portal.* A feature peculiar to Sicilian architecture is that the façade also serves as a bell-tower.

Noto Cathedral (1710-1770) was completely destroyed by the earthquake and had to be rebuilt. The work was mostly done by Vincenzo Sinatra. The generous, broad façade has a central *pediment* and flanking towers and is *articulated* by free-standing columns, creating a beautiful chiaroscuro effect in strong sunlight.

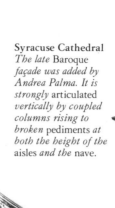

Syracuse Cathedral *The late* Baroque *façade was added by Andrea Palma. It is strongly* articulated *vertically by coupled columns rising to broken* pediments *at both the height of the* aisles *and the* nave.

S. Croce, Lecce *To one end of a 17th-C Celestine convent by Giuseppe Zimbalo rises the façade of S. Croce which, unusually, has a* Romanesque rose window *and medieval-style stone brackets in its design.*

S. Pietro, Modica *(18thC), left. Despite the richness of ornamentation and the magnificent flight of approach steps, the façade is quite flat, in the classical manner. The articulation is reminiscent of S. Croce, Lecce.*

Noto Cathedral *Although this cathedral has such an imposing façade, palatial proportions and the ornamental richness of Roman Baroque, its planning was constrained by the conservative classicism of Sicily.*

Southern Italy

The bell-tower façade is seen at its best in the churches of **S. Giorgio** (1744-75) and **S. Giuseppe** (18thC) in **Ragusa**. Both were designed by Rosario Gagliardi, one of the most creative architects of the period in Sicily. The tower-like character of the façades is more marked here than at Syracuse Cathedral, (see p.215).

The *Baroque* architecture of Apulia is relatively restrained. Façades are more often than not flat, the convex and concave curves that give so much vitality to Roman Baroque being rare. Remoteness from the north and Rome delayed the development of architectural styles to the extent that the sculptural decorations which are such a distinctive feature of the churches of **Lecce** are fashioned on 16th-century models. Good examples include **S. Angelo** (1663) and the *Romanesque* church of **SS. Nicola e Cataldo,** which had its decorative Baroque façade added *c.* 1716. **S. Matteo, Lecce** (1700), is more completely Baroque but is clad in scale-like tiles. The **Cathedral of S. Oronzo, Lecce** (1659-70), is by Giuseppe Zimbalo.

The former Carthusian monastery of **S. Martino, Vomera,** now a museum, has a fine *cloister,* an amalgam of *Renaissance* style and Baroque, which was begun in the late 16th century. The **Church of the Annunciation, Naples** (1761-82), by Luigi Vanvitelli, has a two-stage, concave façade and Latin cross plan.

Castles & Palaces

The **Palazzo Sylos Labini, Bitonto** (15thC), is a rare example of the early Renaissance in southern Italy. It has a fine courtyard with a triple, round-arched *arcade* and *loggia* with a carved Renaissance *balustrade* on one side. The former **Royal Palace, Caserta** (1752-74), by Vanvitelli for the Bourbon King, Charles III, is one of the largest palaces in Europe and is a monumental rectangle in plan divided into four courtyards by cross wings. The grand façades are colonnaded and each is pierced by about 250 windows. The effect is reminiscent of Versailles, in France, as was intended. A gargantuan passage way cuts axially through the block. At the center of the plan is an octagonal vestibule from which a grand ceremonial staircase ascends at right angles.

The **Palazzo Villadorata, Noto** (1737), designed by Paolo Labisi helped by Vincenzo Sinatra, consists of a long, low façade, with a plain main entrance flanked by ponderous *Ionic* columns. The real delight of the building is the sculptural ornamentation which brings the curving balconies and window *pediments* to life.

Domestic buildings

The **Villa Valguanera, Bagheria** (*c.* 1713), by Tommaso Napoli, was the first of many late Baroque villas to be built in the countryside around Palermo. It has an imposing approach, flanked by vases and statuary, and an elegant oval courtyard enclosed by farm buildings. The area became a popular summer resort. The **Villa Palagonia** (1715) is similar. The picturesque amalgam of buildings, landscape, and often ornamental gardens, is the key to their quality.

S. Giorgio, Ragusa, left. The magnificent, three-stage belfry façade. The center section has a gentle convex curve and is flanked by two tiers of triple Corinthian columns, stepped in plan. The façade is articulated horizontally by window sill, cornices and balcony, and vertically by columns.

S. Spirito, Agrigento Detail of the early 18th-C Baroque stucco work in the apse of this Romanesque church. The way the carving overlaps the frame is characteristic.

Porta Capuana, Naples *(1485), below. This gate is one of the finest monuments of the 15thC in Naples. Part of the replanning of the city, the gate consists of a single arch articulated by a carved band and framed by Corinthian pilasters.*

Palazzo Aiutamicristo, Palermo *(1490-95). Much palace and domestic building was an amalgam of southern Italian and Spanish models. The two-story arcaded courtyard here arose from Spanish-Angevin connections.*

Trulli houses

These simple Apulian dwellings, mostly around Alberobello and Locorotondo, were built from the early 16thC by herdsmen and farmers with stones cleared from the fields. They rarely consist of more than one story and are often used as barns and byres as well as for domestic quarters.

Street, Alberobello
Both exteriors and interiors were lime plastered from the late 19thC and whitewashed.

House near Laureto, *left. The roofs were built up in horizontal rings to a capstone.*

Royal Palace, Caserta
Section of the façade of the former royal palace, which is the epitome of the last phase of Italian Baroque. The palace is a monumental complex of 1200 rooms, austerely planned in a rectangular block 820 ft by 984 ft. There are 34 staircases in all.

Castel Nuova, Naples *(1279-82), above. The Arch of Alfonso, the* Renaissance *gatehouse of the castle which served as the official residence of the Angevin, Aragonese and Spanish Viceroys.*

Villa Valguanera, Bagheria *This is one of many late Baroque villas built near Palermo. Standing on top of a small hill, it has a concave façade which embraces an elaborate double staircase. This type of façade is a characteristic feature of other villas in the Palermo area.*

Northern France

Religious buildings

The temple *pediment* became the primary motif for French church façades in the mid-18th century, while internally there was a search for greater lightness of decoration. A notable example is **Saint-Vaast, Arras** (*c* 1755), which is an amalgam of the *Gothic* proportions and forms of the local *hall-church* tradition, together with columns, *entablatures* and an *architrave* based on classical antiquity.

A common feature of the smaller towns and villages of Brittany is the parish close, which is often of magnificent proportions. A cemetery forms the center of the complex with access through a triumphal arch, signifying the entry of the virtuous into Paradise. Around the sides of the cemetery are usually a church, charnel house and Calvary. The Calvaries, carved out of granite, depict Christ's Passion and scenes from his life. Many are intricately carved since villages rivaled each other in their attempts at magnificence, but others are the somewhat crude work of local craftsmen. There are numerous examples in Brittany, notably at **Lampaul-Guimiliau**.

Castles & Palaces

The **Château, Gaillon** (1502-10), Eure, rebuilt by Cardinal Amboise, is largely medieval in form with *Flamboyant* wings. The influx of craftsmen and artists, however, gradually transformed the remainder of the building with the application of classical details, this being one of the earliest attempts in northern France to accommodate the *Renaissance* style. At the **Château, Fère-en-**

Tardenois (1552-62), Jean-Jacques Bullant built a handsome gallery carried on a bridge spanning a valley, the monumental arches referring back to the aqueducts of ancient Rome. **Le Petit Château, Chantilly** (*c.* 1560), also by Bullant, is a fine *mannerist* building but it revives a late Gothic feature of *dormer windows* cutting through the roof *cornice*. At the **Château, Blérancourt** (1612), the concern is for mass in preference to surface decoration. Standing on a rectangular site surrounded by a moat, the house, built at one end, was planned as a rectangular block with four corner pavilions, an open court in front with the entry side defined by two detached pavilions, and a free-standing arch in the center. The traditional high-pitched roof was here abandoned for square domes on the pavilions.

The **Château, Balleroy** (*c.* 1626), Calvados, by François Mansart, is wholly dependent on the relationship between three side wings of three stories each and a four-story central structure. Each volume is defined by its own high-pitched *hipped* roof. There is a handsome forecourt on a raised terrace, with the corners on the open side defined by elegant pavilions in the manner of Blérancourt. The **Château, Maison-Lafitte** (1642), by Mansart, is a classic building of the Louis XIV period, "C"-shaped in plan with each part delineated by a separate, high roof. The façades are *articulated* by coupled *pilasters* and pedimented central bays, front and back, which enhance the axial line drawn from the street front to the gardens at the rear. The interior decor is a synthesis of painting and sculpture.

Church, St Thégonnec *(1587), Finistère. Of particular interest in the late Gothic and Renaissance period is the Flamboyant decoration found on village churches, such as this.*

Château, Gaillon
The château was medieval in concept but was transformed by the application of classical details on the entrance, such as Lombardic pilasters.

Fontaine-Henri, Calvados *The steeply pitched roofs, turreted towers and narrow dormer windows are Gothic in tradition, while the façade is Renaissance.*

Saint Vaast, Arras *The interior of this church by Pierre d'Ivry, comprising a vast, lofty space, articulated by rows of giant columns and bold architrave and entablature. The light, spatial quality is reminiscent of medieval hall-churches.*

Domestic buildings

Houses such as **Fontaine-Henri, Calvados** (1537-44), and the **Hôtel d'Ecoville, Caen** (1535-38), are largely traditional in plan and form. The whole of the latter and the north wing of the former are by Blaise le Prestre and introduce a new element, the notion of linking windows and niches in vertical panels by means of super-imposed pilasters or columns. These panels are taken up beyond the *eaves* lines in the form of gabled dormer windows.

Civic & Public buildings

There was a great increase in urban building in the early 18th century with the opening up of the old town walls, which were no longer necessary with peace and stability reigning in France. Long, straight streets were built through many of the medieval districts, forming spacious squares which inspired monumental buildings. Such buildings were seen as a means of enhancing the beauty of towns. **Rennes,** for example, had been destroyed by fire in 1720. Jacques-Ange Gabriel planned two new squares. In the Place Louis le Grand there was already an appropriately monumental building, the **Palais de Parlement** (1618) by de Brosse, which had escaped the fire. It is a boldly out-lined, highly defined building anticipating much that is later associated with Mansart. For the other, the **Place Louis XV,** Gabriel planned the great **Town Hall** (1736-44) with a central tower which houses a large clock. The **Mordelaise Gate, Rennes,** is all that remains today of the city's 15th-century ramparts.

Château, Chantilly (*c. 1560), Oise, above. The Petit Château, designed by Jean Bullant in his typically mannerist style. It comprises a long, low central block of six-bays, linking two pavilions which have high pitched roofs.*

Hôtel d'Ecoville, Caen *A magnificent, picturesque mansion with largely tradi-tional ornamentation. Of particular note is the strategy of linking the windows in a ver-tical panel. The court-yard, although it has been partly rebuilt, is especially fine.*

Town Hall, Rennes, *left. A finely modeled building with wings tied back by concave ends and* hipped *roofs to an elegant central tower. The scheme is entirely for visual effect, related to the square in front, since entry is at the sides.*

Place des Hêros, Arras *(17thC). One of the stone and brick houses with ornamen-tal gables and rusticated pilasters which sur-round this handsome square and La Grande Place, which were reconstructed in the Flemish manner.*

Palais de Parlement, Rennes *The "C"-shaped plan is sharply defined by its con-tinuous high-pitched roof, straightforward wall with bold* rusti-cated *ground story and articulation by strong cornice lines and pilasters. The façade was altered in the 18thC.*

Northeast France

Religious buildings

The *hall-church* tradition was popular in Northeast France, for the lightness and spaciousness of the form lent itself to elaborate *Baroque* designs. These are often an amalgam of southern German and Roman Baroque styles. Good examples are **Saint-Sébastien, Nancy** (1720-31), and **Saint-Jacques, Lunéville** (1730-47). Unlike the center of France, which was dominated by Parisian taste, these buildings had local individuality.

Castles & Palaces

The **Château, Lunéville** (1702-06), by Gabriel Boffrand, is modeled on the layout of Versailles and is dominated by the controlling axial line to which both buildings and gardens are subordinate. Instead of the buildings pinning down the axial line, they are treated more like detached wings, parallel to each other but joined by a *corps de logis,* which in this case is a giant *portico.* An interesting feature is the wall surface which, instead of being *articulated* vertically, is expressed horizontally by bold *cornices.* In the **Château, Haroué** (1712-13), Boffrand incorporated medieval towers with clean-lined wings and a corps dè logis, in front of which is another layer consisting of elements such as *colonnades* and portico based on *Palladian* originals. The **Château des Rohan, Strasbourg** (1731-42), was the magnificent town residence of the prince-bishop. The major work of Robert de Cotte, it has a superb river façade whose dominating feature is a columned portico, which lends appropriate grandeur. The chateau has the aristocratic boldness and elegance associated with the court style.

Civic & Public buildings

One of the few urban projects to be completed outside Paris in the 18th century is the **Place Stanislas,** or **Place Royale,** and the **Place de la Carrière, Nancy** (1752-55), by Emmanuel Héré. Rivaled only by the squares of Baroque Rome, it is a magnificent sequence of spaces inserted into an existing context. The Place Stanislas, which became the new center of the city, is a large rectangular space, dominated by the **Town Hall** (1752-55). An axial line runs away from this via a triumphal arch, reminiscent of the Arch of Severus, Rome, through the long, central gardens of the Place de la Carrière. The axis is terminated at the far end by the **Fer du Cheval,** a space enclosed laterally by two hemicycles to the sides and by the **Hôtel de l'Intendance** (1751-53) to the front.

Saint-Jacques, Lunéville
Probably by Gabriel Boffrand, the outstanding French rococo *architect, it is a* hall-church *with a magnificent* Baroque *façade with twin, round towers and* articulated *by giant* Corinthian *columns and* pedimented portico *crowned by a large clock.*

Salt Works, Arc-et-Senans
(1775-79). This block of offices by Claude-Nicolas Ledoux, with its rusticated Doric *columns, was at the center of an ambitious industrial complex. It was one manifestation of a revolutionary movement in 18th-C France which stipulated that utilitarian architecture should also be of aesthetic excellence.*

Château, Moncley *(1778), Francne-Comté, above. The handsome central structure, which is "C"-shaped in plan and has projecting wings emphasized by pyramidal roofs and joined to the main block by a sweeping concave façade which is drawn behind the* Ionic portico.

Château, Saverne *(1779-89), below. The immense garden façade by Nicolas Salins. It is articulated by giant Corinthian* pilasters, *slightly projecting pedimented ends, a bold central section with its* columns, *and by a raised* attic.

Town Hall, Nancy *This monumental building by Emmanuel Héré de Corny has a rusticated ground storey and pedimented central section and dominates the Place Stanislas. The building terminates the axis between this square and the long and spacious Place de la Carrière.*

Château des Rohan, Strasbourg *A bold Baroque building, it has a rusticated ground story and pedimented central section with domed roof and massive Corinthian columns. It is the work of Robert de Cotte, one of the earliest and most gifted of the French rococo architects.*

Town Gate, Langres *(17thC). This elegant, domed pavilion was built over the town gate in 1647. Of particular note is the way the two forms, old and new, are joined by the broken entablature. The whole building is given coherence by the crowning pediment.*

Château, Lunéville *This imposing portico carried on giant columns allows the central axis, around which the gardens and buildings are planned, to be channeled through the corps de logis.*

Fer du Cheval, Nancy *With its square plan and two attached hemicycles, the building acts as a connecting link between the earlier urban works and the grandiose developments of Nancy, of which this is itself a part, conceived by Emmanuel Héré.*

Central Square, Charléville *(1608-20). Clement Métezeau laid out the town on a grid-iron plan, which revolved around this, the main square, of which one side is shown and five much smaller squares.*

Paris

Religious buildings

In many 16th-century churches and chapels *Gothic* structure, combined with classical decoration, persisted. An example is **St-Etienne-du-Mont** (1517-1618), where the front façade is an amalgam of Gothic style *rose window,* classical *portico* and *pediment* and *mannerist gable* and obelisks. Inside there is a magnificent *rood-screen.*

Church architecture of the early 16th century in France, however, was primarily concerned with alterations and additions. **St-Eustache** (1532) is the one exception in Paris. Then a completely new building, it has a Gothic plan and structure layered in *Renaissance* detail. One of the most interesting of the early 17th-century ecclesiastical projects was the addition of a new façade by Solomon de Brosse to the late Gothic church of **St-Gervais** (1494-1657). The first classical façade of any importance in France, it has a high pedimented central section, *articulated* by superimposed *Doric, Ionic* and *Corinthian* columns, a device taken from examples found in chateau architecture. **St-Paul-St-Louis** (1625-34), like St-Gervais, has a façade with a three-story central section articulated by coupled columns. The *Baroque portal* was added by Père Martellarge. The **Church of the Sorbonne** (1635-42), designed by Jacques Lemercier for Cardinal Richelieu, has all the formal grandeur of Baroque Rome but the ornamentation is restrained, as on so many French churches of the period, in order to accentuate the architectural composition. The plan is unusual in having a *nave* and *choir* of equal length around the *crossing,* while the shallow *transepts* are repeated by flanking chapels. There are two main façades, the one of the north transept, facing the college court, being *articulated* by a central, free-standing classical portico. The **Church of the Val de Grace** (1645-67), by François Mansart and completed by Lemercier, has a façade resembling

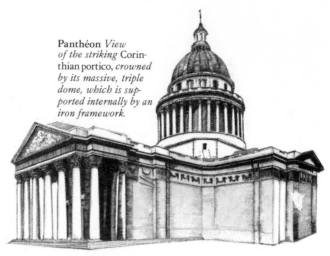

Panthéon *View of the striking* Corinthian portico, *crowned by its massive, triple dome, which is supported internally by an iron framework.*

The Madeleine *A magnificent church in the style of a Roman temple, it has a surrounding peristyle of Corinthian columns and stands on a podium 23 ft high. The entrance is reached by a flight of 28 steps. Windows piercing the drums of three domes provide lighting.*

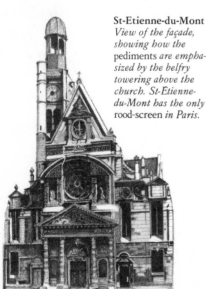

St-Etienne-du-Mont *View of the façade, showing how the pediments are emphasized by the belfry towering above the church. St-Etienne-du-Mont has the only* rood-screen *in Paris.*

St-Paul-St-Louis *The archetypal Jesuit church and one of the earliest examples in France, it is the work of François Derand. The classical façade, taken from 16th-C Italian examples, masks the dome, a Jesuit innovation never repeated.*

that of the Church of the Sorbonne but here it is bolder, with an elegant projecting portal, scrolled *volutes* marking the transition from low side *aisles* to high *nave,* and a magnificent dome which stands on a high *drum* articulated by *pilasters.* The great number of *piers* accentuate the verticality, an effect which is continued by the crowning statuary and candelabra of the drum.

The **Church of Les Invalides** (1679-91), by Libéral Bruant and Jules Hardouin-Mansart, has a Greek cross plan with circular chapels in the outer angles, but the general assembly of elements, from the magnificent portico to the central dome, is Baroque. This famous dome is derived from St Peter's, Rome, but the innovations are intriguing. Usually a window marked the axis but here a solid form, that is the coupled columns and buttress of the drum and dome, is employed.

Work on most of the bigger Parisian churches had started in the 17th century and all that remained for many 18th-century architects was their completion, often by the addition of a façade. **St Roch** is an interesting example. Begun by Lemercier in 1653, the Baroque façade was added by Jules-Robert de Cotte in 1736. **St-Sulpice** was begun in 1645, remodeled by Louis Le Vau in 1655 and given its two-story *colonnaded* screen façade with flanking towers by Giovanni Servandoni between 1733 and 1749.

The **Panthéon** (1757-90), by Jacques Soufflot, has a handsome exterior. Greek cross in plan, the main entrance has a portico of six elegant Corinthian columns drawn slightly past each side of the front arm and counterbalanced by austere, windowless walls. The building is crowned by a triple dome on a high drum in the manner of Les Invalides. The **Madeleine** (1806-42) by Pierre Vignon is an imitation Roman temple, the epitome of late 18th-century academic preoccupation with all aspects of *Classicism.*

Church of Les Invalides *View of the* Renaissance *dome, one of the outstanding examples in France of 17th-C ecclesiastical architecture. The dome is covered with lead sheeting on a wooden frame, the surface being decorated with gold leaf.*

St-Eustache, *right. The nave, flanked by double* aisles, *is reminiscent of Notre Dame in plan but the pillars are* articulated *by classical* pilasters. *The church plan, however, is largely medieval rather than Renaissance. The* vaulting *of* nave *and* chancel *is in the* Flamboyant *style. The chapels have many fine frescoes.*

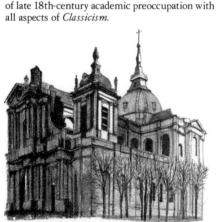

St Louis, Versailles *(1743-54). One of the most* Baroque *of all French churches, it is the work of Jacques Hardouin-Mansart de Sagonne. The play of forms includes a boldly articulated front façade, flanking columns and angled pilasters and curved ends to the* transepts.

St-Gervais *View of the façade, with its superimposed* Doric, Ionic *and* Corinthian *columns. The main part of the building is* Flamboyant *Gothic. The elm in the forecourt marks the place where medieval citizens congregated and where courts of justice were usually held.*

Paris

Castles & Palaces

France led western Europe in the building of magnificent city and country palaces. The **Palais de Fontainebleau, Seine-et-Marne** (1528-40), by Giles Le Breton, and subsequently altered and added to by others, has an irregular plan, the main interest lying in the various courts encircling part of the Court of Honour, and the superb terrace, gardens and lakes which combine to create vistas radiating from the various parts of the complex. The asymmetrical assemblage was the result of alterations to the medieval château, a task complicated by the fact that existing parts had already been incorporated into some of the wings. The **Louvre** (1546-1878), begun by Pierre Lescot for François I, consists of a monumental square courtyard built by Lescot, Louis Métezeau, Jacques Lemercier and others, with long, flanking wings on the east side. Together with the **Tuileries,** which was destroyed by the Commune in 1871, it formed a mammoth palace complex. The magnificent east façade was added by Louis Le Vau, Claude Perrault and Charles Lebrun between 1667 and 1670. Raised above a smooth ground story, it has projecting end bays, each with a recessed center, a *pedimented* center and a giant *Corinthian colonnade* between. The **Château, Grosbois** (1597-1617), Seine-et-Marne, is a handsome building with two-story wings and a three-story main block with concave center, crowned by a pedimented *attic.* The **Palais de Luxembourg** (1615-24), by Salomon de Brosse, has the archetypal French hôtel plan of three-story *corps de logis,* with projecting corner pavilions, and two-story wings, forming a court with a one-story entrance screen punctuated by a *porte-cochère.* Built for Marie de' Medici, it was originally intended to be an imitation of the Palazzo Pitti, Florence, but all that remains is the

Palais de Luxembourg *View of Salomon de Brosse's central court, which is enclosed on the entrance side by a one-story rusticated screen and handsome porte-cochère, which is crowned by a large dome.*

Palais de Versailles

Begun by Louis Le Vau for Louis XIV, it consists of a monumental palace complex built around the old hunting château. It was later extended by the addition of north and south wings, together with the Gros Pavilion and the Petit Trianon.

Chapel

Galerie des Glaces

Petit Trianon

Palais de Fontainebleau, Seine-et-Marne *Detail of the Cour du Cheval Blanc, one of the numerous courts making up the palace. An outstanding feature is the horseshoe-shaped staircase, sweeping down into the courtyard.*

quality of boldness, but without any extraneous surface decoration, and the fine *rustications*. **Vaux-le-Vicomte, Seine-et-Marne** (1657-61), a magnificent château designed by Louis Le Vau, has an extremely bold design with corner pavilions on the front façade and a recessed concave center with a superimposed *portico*. The garden façade is punctuated by slightly projecting pavilions with high roofs, while the center is a huge domed oval projection, the Grand Salon. Such extravagance was not to be exceeded until Louis XIV begun to build the **Palais de Versailles** (1661-1756). This great complex is dependent on a single controlling idea, a strong axial line linking forecourt, palace buildings and formal gardens. Begun by Le Vau and extended by Jules Hardouin-Mansart and Jacques-Ange Gabriel, it is the most *Baroque* of all French buildings. Among many outstanding features are the **Galerie des Glaces** by Hardouin-Mansart and the **Petit Trianon** (1762-68) by Gabriel. The Petit Trianon, built in the gardens, is renowned for its delicate classicism. The magnificent gardens, with their canals, fountains and terraces, which are inseparable from the overall plan, are by André Le Nôtre.

The **Château, Champlâtreux** (1733), has a magnificent garden façade, designed in a manner reminiscent of the stable block at Chantilly. The **Palais Royal** (1752-70) is an interesting remodeling of the earlier palace by Contant d'Ivray, a brilliant eclectic who re-used François Mansart's garden façade at Versailles to considerable effect here. The palace was originally known as the Cardinal's Palace, since it had been commissioned by Cardinal Richelieu, Louis XIII's first minister, in 1624. Richelieu left the mansion to the king and shortly afterward the royal family moved there from the Louvre and the palace was re-named.

Château, Grosbois *The main block, which is of interest for its simplicity of style and boldly articulated* volumes, *is punctuated by a concave bay. Unlike other buildings of the period, where brick was used for surfaces and white for the quoins*, *the surfaces here are of white plaster, the quoins of brick and stone.*

The Louvre *View of one façade of the square court, which was designed by Pierre Lescot and was the first part of this vast palace. Once the largest royal palace in the world, the Louvre is now a museum.*

Palais Royale *A handsome staircase by Contant d'Ivry, which is lighted from above. The palace was built for Cardinal Richelieu, who bequeathed it to Louis XIII. The garden façade was modeled on that at Versailles.*

Hôtel Lamoignon *(1584). The work of Baptiste du Cerceau, it is one of the best preserved of the late 16th-C Parisian houses. Of note is the use of* giant *pilasters and the cutting of* the *entablature by* dormer *windows.*

225

Paris

Domestic buildings

The **Hôtel Cârnavalet** (*c.* 1545) by Pierre Lescot is unique in being the only surviving Parisian building of the mid-16th century. It was given *Renaissance* features by François Mansart and handsome carved lions at the entrance by Jean Goujon. The **Hôtel Lamoignon** (*c.* 1584) by Jean du Cerceau the Younger has one of the earliest examples of a courtyard façade *articulated* by giant *Corinthian pilasters,* and is equipped with *gabled dormer windows* crowning the *cornice.*

The **Place des Vosges** (1605-12), probably by Claude Chastillon, is a fine *arcaded* square made up of elegant town houses, each with its own distinctive yet uniformly high-pitched roof. Many have been rebuilt in their original form since the 17th century. Designed for Henri IV, it is the oldest of the Parisian squares and was at one time notorious as a duelling ground. The **Hôtel de Sully** (1624-29) by du Cerceau is traditional in plan with a center *corps de logis,* and with flanking wings and pavilions joined by a low screen with a *porte-cochère.* It is a handsome building with novel decorative enrichment, particularly in the central courtyard. The **Hôtel Lambert** (1640) by Louis Le Vau is a brilliant piece of architecture, utilizing its river site to the full. Access to the courtyard and building is via two vestibules, one octagonal and the other oval. The corners of the courtyard are curved and at one of them a staircase, at right angles to the main axis, leads to a corridor which in turn gives access to a long gallery running to the river's edge. The building is given dramatic impact by the elegant use of classical *Orders.*

The **Hôtel d'Evreaux** (1707) by Pierre Bullet, is an unassuming but handsome house, built on an awkward corner site in the Place Vendôme with entry on an angle into a central courtyard in which symmetry is re-established by a concave façade at one end and a ground-story *peristyle* at the other. The **Hôtel de Soubise** (1705-09) has an outstanding *colonnaded* courtyard of coupled columns. The columns run along the face of the main block as well, acting as supports to a bold *cornice* and in that way tying the main block and flanking colonnades together.

Other 18th-century Parisian hôtels of interest include the **Hôtel de Mâtignon** (1722-24), which was the home of the diplomat Talleyrand from 1808 to 1811 and is now the Paris residence of the prime minister; the **Hôtel de Biron** (1728-31) by Jacques-Ange Gabriel the Elder, which is now a museum and houses many of Rodin's works and was once a convent, during which time the mother superior had much of the paneling destroyed as being vainglorious ostentation, and the **Hôtel de Toulouse** (1713-19) by Robert de Cotte, now the Banque de France, which contains the handsome Galerie Dorée. *Neoclassical* town houses of note include the **Hôtel de Gallifet** (1775-96), with a *balustraded portico* seemingly detached from the building as if it were a separate artefact, and the **Hôtel de Salm** (1784) by Antoine Rousseau, which was destroyed by fire in 1871 but rebuilt in 1878.

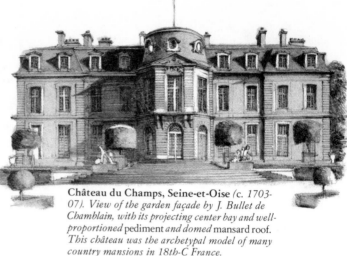

Château du Champs, Seine-et-Oise *(c.* 1703-07). *View of the garden façade by J. Bullet de Chamblain, with its projecting center bay and well-proportioned* pediment *and domed* mansard roof. *This château was the archetypal model of many country mansions in 18th-C France.*

Château, Rosny *(c.* 1610-20), *Seine-et-Oise. A handsome red-brick château, with low central block and high flanking pavilions. The horizontality is emphasized by the bold string courses and the verticality by the stone quoins and by the window bays of the main block.*

Place Vendôme *(1698). A huge square, it has its principal axis marked by openings at either end and the lateral axis by pedimented bays, of which this is one. The square was originally conceived as an imposing site for a monumental statue of the so-called Sun King, Louis XIV.*

Château, Maisons-Lafitte *(1642). The pedimented central section of the façade of the chateau, which, as a whole, is of simple composition, "C"-shape in plan, built around an axial line extending from the street front.*

Hôtel Amelot de Gournay *(1712). View of the handsome oval courtyard of Germain Boffrand's Baroque house. The high main block and low flanking wings are articulated by pilasters as well as ground-story arcading.*

Château, Ecouen *(c. 1560). Part of the château was designed by Jean Bullant and includes this pavilion, built in the court of the south wing. The use of the superimposed Order of giant Corinthian columns is one of the earliest examples in France.*

Hôtel de Soubise *(1705-09). By Pierre-Alexis Dalamair, it has a handsome façade facing the Court of Honor with a pedimented center articulated by two stories of coupled Corinthian columns. The bold cornice is carried on coupled columns.*

Vaux-le-Vicomte, Seine-et-Marne *(1657-61). Built by Louis Le Vau for Fouquet, Louis XIV's treasurer, it is a chateau on the most lavish scale. The axiality of the plan and gardens centers on the huge oval of the Grand Salon, a bay which breaks forcefully out of the main block.*

Hôtel Cârnavalet *The only surviving example of a Parisian town house of the mid-16th C. It is by Pierre Lescot and has a particularly fine courtyard with elaborate allegorical figures in relief between the windows and handsome pedimented gable dormer windows crowning the cornice.*

Hôtel Lambert *Detail of the courtyard, showing the curved corner giving access to one of the vestibules flanking the main staircase. The walls are articulated by pilasters, with the entrance defined by two tiers of columns.*

Paris

Civic & Public buildings

One of the few public buildings to be erected in 17th-century Paris is the **Hall of the Marchands-Drapiers** (*c.* 1655-60) by Jacques Bruant. The only surviving part is the façade, which is now in the Cârnavalet Museum, Paris.

The **Place Vendôme** (1698) is a magnificent urban project by Jules Hardouin-Mansart, a huge square with two openings *articulating* the main axis and with *pedimented* bays articulating the lateral axis. It is grand scenic architecture in the manner of *Baroque* Rome. The provision of housing around the square was of secondary consideration. In the center of the square is a tall column, covered with bronze taken from cannon captured by Napoleon at the Battle of Austerlitz. The column was torn down in 1871 by the Commune but was later re-erected by the Third Republic. The **Place de la Concorde** (1753-75) was finally completed by the addition of two monumental palaces on its north side. Designed by Jacques-Ange Gabriel, they have magnificently bold designs with *rusticated* ground story, pedimented end pavilions and recessed centers with *colonnades* of giant *Corinthian* columns. It is the first of the great *Neoclassical* projects in France in which the detailed study of classical buildings is clearly evident. The square was the scene of many executions by guillotine between 1793 and 1795. When the slaughter ceased, the square was incongruously renamed "Concorde." The **Odéon** (1778-82) is a handsome Neoclassical building. A severe rectangle, it relies for liveliness on the rustication of the walls and the bold, eight-columned *portico* with its crowning balustrade. The entrance to its horseshoe-shaped auditorium is via a magnificent double staircase.

The **École de Chirurgie** (1771-76) by Jacques Gondoin is a Greek-style building and has a temple façade of six *Ionic* columns and an *attic* story. Behind this is a semicircular lecture theatre. The **École-Militaire** (1768-73) by Gabriel is a handsome *Palladian*-style building with pedimented windows and bold temple-style portico with square attic story crowned by a dome. It was built at the instigation of Mme de Pompadour, a favourite of Louis XV, as a military academy where young but impecunious gentlemen might be trained as officers. The **Hôtel des Monnaies** (1771-75) by Jacques-Denis Antoine has a rusticated ground story and *arcaded* center section with *balustraded* portico and attic story. Later in the 18th century Louis XV had the mint transferred to the mansion, when it was given its present name. The **Palais de Justice** (13thC) was rebuilt by Antoine and others between 1776 and 1785. The legal laws of France were changed during the Revolution and new courts were designed within the building.

One of the most challenging commissions an architect received in late 18th-century France was Claude-Nicolas Ledoux's project to build a series of toll houses around the new city walls. Amalgams of fortress and temple, they controlled the various entrances and were designed to impress people approaching the city.

Hôtel de Salm *(1784). A magnificent town house by Antoine Rousseau, it has a main block of* rusticated *walls with ground story* pedimented *windows with circular niches above containing busts. The* domed central *rotunda with its curving outer wall* articulated *by massive* Corinthian *columns brings the building to life.*

Hôtel de Sully *(1624-29). One of the great Parisian houses of the early 17thC, it was designed by Jean du Cerceau. The façades of the courtyard are handsomely ornamented by sculptured friezes and pediments and by allegorical figures in the niches. The building has been faithfully restored to its original splendor.*

Hôtel de Gallifet *(1775-96). Detail of the courtyard façade. The outstanding feature is the manner in which the* balustraded portico *is designed as if detached from the main building, lika a* stoa *with a building behind.*

Hall of the Marchands-Drapiers
View of the centerpiece of the façade, showing two caryatids *supporting a broken pediment, within which is seated the figure of Paris.*

Chambre des Députés *(1724). The massive and extremely wide Corinthian portico, shown here, was added in 1807. The style of the building is reminiscent of ancient Roman architecture at its most monumental and severe, with rusticated windowless walls. The angles of the main block are articulated by* pilasters.

Place de Vosges
(1605). One of the houses in what was known originally as the Place Royale, a fashionable center of 17th-C Paris. Plots around the square were let at nominal rents provided the buyers built to an agreed format. On the north and south sides of the square are two ornate pavilions.

Place de la Concorde *One of the twin palaces designed by Jacques-Ange Gabriel to close the north side of this most handsome of Parisian squares with a monumentality appropriate to the power and grandeur of 18th-C France.*

The Odéon *A magnificent rectangular block, it has a bold portico and balustrade, and rusticated walls and galleries along the ground floor. The theatre was originally built for a company of French comedians. It was destroyed by fire in 1807 but was rebuilt in the same style.*

Barrière de la Villette *(1785), right. One of the four surviving tollgates of Paris. Originally there were 40 such tollgates ringing the city, forming an extremely varied catalogue of architectural styles which were based on those of classical buildings.*

229

Burgundy & Loire

Castles & Palaces

The châteaux of the early *Renaissance* are characterized by traditional forms layered with Italian decorative detail. In France they are found mainly in the Loire Valley. The **Château, Chaumont** (1465-1510), Loir-et-Cher, is more a medieval fortified castle than a domestic home, despite the fact that the Renaissance was already well established by the time the château was completed. Peace was a prerequisite of the Renaissance but the owners of this château, having had their previous castle razed on the orders of Louis XI, were as much concerned with defense as they were with elegance and so replaced it with a stronghold of massive walls, *machicolations* and battlements protected by moat and drawbridge. The outer west façade, the oldest side, is entirely military in purpose, while the other façades, although having defensive capabilities, show Renaissance influences. The château is one of the most famous in France and has numerous romantic associations with the history of the country and the many famous people, including Catherine de' Medici, widow of the French King Henri II, who at one time or another resided there.

The **Château, Amboise-sur-Loire** (1490), is now incomplete but the remains are those of the first royal residence in France. It is a collage of styles from the purest French *Gothic* of the castle chapel to the 16th-century *mannerist* addition of tall *filials* and *dormer windows* which crown the *cornice* of the main building. The **Château, Blois** (1498-1638), is a picturesque building but is so more by accident than design, having undergone a series of transformations, including the greatest extension of all in the 17th century

Château, Amboise-sur-Loire *The increasing use of artillery rendered the medieval fortified castle redundant. Many, like this, retained traditional features, such as the round tower, when they were transformed in the 16thC.*

Château, Chaumont *An outstanding feature of the château is its picturesque outline of turreted towers, high-pitched roofs and staircase towers. Built by Pierre d'Amboise, it is in the transitional style between* Gothic *and* Renaissance.

Ducal Palace, Nevers *(1475-16thC). Now a court of justice, it is a handsome Renaissance building with a symmetrical façade which has a tall, octagonal staircase tower on axis with flanking corner towers.*

Château, Chenonceau *The original building comprised the portion on the left. It is notable for the clustered conical turrets, which are reflected in the water. In 1576 the arched bridge was added.*

when François Mansart was engaged to improve it. Mansart designed a monumental palace with *corps de logis*, pavilion and wings, but only a fragment was built engaging the existing building. In so doing he formed an irregular courtyard. The greater concern with the parts rather than with the whole was not altogether ineffective for, although the result was not what had originally been intended, this very fact created a remarkable amalgam with the first building. One of the outstanding features of the château is the superb staircase which was added to the façade and was intended for receiving guests at great receptions.

The **Château, Chenonceau** (1515), as originally built, consisted of a simple square block with a central passage, *corbelled* corner turrets and high-pitched roof. It was then extended by a covered, five-arched bridge between 1556 and 1559, and in 1576 Jean Bullant built on top of the bridge an ornate gallery. This château is small in comparison to royal residences for it was commissioned by a private patron. Another château built for a member of the rich bourgeoisie is the **Château, Bury** (1511-24), which is now in ruins. While it appeared traditional, with its huge round corner towers, it was in fact revolutionary for its buildings were grouped around a court with the corps de logis at one end, punctuated by a high central section, and with a low screen wall at the other. It was to become a prototype for French château building for the ensuing hundred years. Both this, the château at Chenonceau and that at Azay-le-Rideau (1518-27, see p.232), which was also built for a private citizen, have a common feature, a new regularity of strictly rectangular plan.

Château, Brissac *(c. 1606-21), Maine-et-Loire. Built on medieval foundations, only this part was completed. It is picturesquely sited between medieval round towers and is articulated by rusticated voussoirs and pilasters.*

Château, Rigny-Ussé-sur-Loire *(15thC-17thC), Indre-et-Loire. This striking château seems, when viewed from a distance, to erupt on the skyline with its profusion of turrets and chimney stacks. The decorative details are mannerist.*

Château, Blois (1498-1638)

From the 13thC onward a succession of buildings was erected around a central, irregular courtyard. These include an elegant wing for François I with a magnificent staircase tower, medieval in form but classical in design, and another wing by François Mansart, *articulated* by deep *cornices* and superimposed *Orders*. Mansart's wing, known as the Gaston d'Orléans wing after the prince for whom it was built, is in the classical style in startling contrast to the earlier parts of this enormous palace.

Gaston d'Orléans wing

François I wing

St Michael, Dijon *(15thC). The church is an amalgam of Gothic and Renaissance styles. Typical of French classicism of the period, the façade with its triple porch was added between 1537 and 1540 and has more in common with the Romanesque than the Gothic.*

Burgundy & Loire

Both the form and decoration of the French château were simplified over the years. An outstanding example is the **Château, Villandry** (1532). Only the great fortress *donjon* of the original building survives but it is now surrounded by elegant classical wings. The fine gardens were remodeled in the 19th century in imitation of a landscaped English garden. The **Château, Valençay** (12thC), is another example, having been rebuilt in the 16th century.

The **Château, Ancy-le-Franc** (*c.* 1546), is a refined classical building by the Italian architect Sebastiano Serlio. A large rectangular block with central courtyard, square corner towers with pyramidal roofs and a continuous *cornice*, it is free of the interruptions of earlier French châteaux where panels of windows had continued beyond the *eaves* into elaborate *gabled dormer windows*. The high-pitched roof is characteristically French. The **Château, Anet** (*c.* 1548-52), by Philibert de l'Orme, was one of the first French buildings of the *Renaissance* in which Italian and French forms and details were successfully integrated. Although largely destroyed during the Revolution, two key features remain intact—the five-domed chapel with its twin towers and pyramidal roofs, and the monumental entrance gate consisting primarily of a series of rectangular blocks culminating in the central clock tower.

The **Château, Tanlay** (16thC), is a graceful, moated Renaissance building with domed towers and handsome wings grouped around a court of honor, which is entered across a stone bridge and through a monumental entrance porch. The **Château, Chambord** (1519-47), with a plan reminiscent of a medieval concentric castle, has a square donjon with round corner towers and elaborate turreted skyline. The donjon is built along the center of one side of a large rectangular courtyard, surrounded by one-story buildings on three sides and backed by a long three-story block with projecting wings and flanking round towers on the fourth. It was designed by the Italian architect Domenico da Cortona and is a strange amalgam of Italian classical details and *Flamboyant* forms, a mixture due primarily to modifications made by French masons.

Other châteaux of interest include the **Château, Villegongis** (1530), Indre, which is thought to be by da Cortona because of the

Maison Milsand, Dijon *(c. 1561). One of the decorated windows of this house, which is an example of the indulgence in surface effects that characterized many provincial houses at this time.*

Château, Chambord *The main façade of this monumental château of 400 rooms, built for François I. Based on the plan of a fortified castle, it is an amalgam of contradictory styles, with elaborate mannerist roofscape and uncluttered* Renaissance *walls articulated by* cornices *and* pilasters.

Château, Azay-le-Rideau *(1518-27). As with many buildings of the period, this château retains its medieval appearance both in plan and detail, such as the bold,* machicolated *cornice and corner* turrets. *The* gabled dormer windows *articulated by narrow columns and pilasters are decorated in the new style.*

Château, Villandry *This handsome château is grouped around a court of honor and consists of three elegant wings, incorporating a medieval donjon. The flanking towers are emphasized by the high-pitched roofs over the end bays. The wall surfaces are articulated by bold cornices.*

similarities in detail to the château at Chambord; the **Château, Talcy** (16thC), which is traditional in appearance, and the **Château, Lude** (15thC), Sarthe, a fortified château with angle towers built in 1457 and which was transformed in the 16th century by the application of Renaissance decorative work. The **Château, Cheverny** (1634-36), is a fine classical building, rigorously symmetrical, with flamboyant skyline and magnificent interior of the Louis XIII period.

Civic & Public buildings

Cardinal Richelieu commissioned Jacques Lemercier to build a country mansion for him near Paris, but little remains. However, he also commissioned Lemercier to build a town nearby to house his court, and the result, **Richelieu, Indre-et-Loire** (1631), is a small but intriguing town composed on a gridiron plan contained in a large rectangle, like a Roman military camp. The town is terminated at either end by a spacious square. Since it was a new town and not a transformation of one already in existence, it needed a thriving economy to prosper. This, however, never materialized and the town did not develop.

Château, Ancy-le-Franc *A fine Renaissance château, it has square towers at the angles and a central courtyard. The high-pitched roof is in the French style, but other elements, including the refined articulation of the pilasters, cornices and niches, have the aura of a northern Italian villa.*

Hôtel Pincé, Angers *(1523-33). Many 16th-C houses still retained traditional medieval features, such as these* mullioned *windows. Other medieval features include corner turrets and high-pitched roofs.*

Château, Beaumont-sur-Vingeanne *(1724). One of the smallest of the châteaux, it has slightly projecting wings, a central* pediment *carried on* consoles *and an elegant curving double staircase to the main floor, which is raised above a low basement.*

Old Town Hall, Orléans *(1503-13). Numerous town halls of this period were rebuilt in the Renaissance style. In this example the 14th-C belfry was preserved when a new building, with Italian articulation and decorative work, was built in front of it.*

Hôtel de Ville, Beaugency *(1526). A more humble building than that at Orléans, it is nonetheless a fine example of the municipal architecture of the time. The delicate-looking façade is an amalgam of* Gothic *turrets and filigree work with classical cornices and arches.*

Southeast France

Castles & Palaces

The **Château, La Tour d'Aigues** (1560), Bouches-du-Rhône, is an adaptation of the Pavilion du Roi by Pierre Lescot at the Louvre. The most remarkable feature is the main entrance (1571), a giant *pediment* carried on huge *Corinthian pilasters* with a horizontal *frieze* midway and a large central arch flanked by columns and niches. This scheme is repeated above but on a smaller scale and with pilasters instead of columns and small arches in place of niches. The design is based on reconstructions of ruins of ancient Roman remains in the area. Another interesting building is the **Château d'Ansouis, Vaucluse,** which is a medieval fortress with many 17th-century additions.

Domestic buildings

The fashions of early 18th-century Paris were quickly emulated in the provinces. There are outstanding town houses at **Avignon,** such as the **Hôtel de Villeneuve-Martignan** (1741) and the **Hôtel de Caumont** (1720-21), both by Jean-Baptiste Franque. Other interesting town houses include the **Hôtel de Cambacéres, Montpellier** (18thC), by Jean Giral, and in **Aix-en-Provence** the **Hôtel de Boyer d'Eguilles** and the **Hôtel d'Espagnet.** The reason for the wealth of Aix-en-Provence and the grandeur of its houses is that the town was the capital of Provence as well as being the seat of the area's supreme court of justice from 1501 until 1790. Avignon also has many fine 17th- and 18th-century houses, notably the **Musée Calvert.**

Civic & Public buildings

The **Town Hall, Toulon** (1656), is of particular note for its elaborate entrance *portal.* It was the work of Pierre Puget, who had studied in both Rome and Florence. The carved figures show the influence of Gianlorenzo Bernini but with bizarre nautical touches, such as a ship's figurehead. Puget had previously been commissioned to decorate warships and this influenced his later work. At the **Hôtel de Ville, Arles** (1675-84), Jules Hardouin-Mansart utilized elements from the garden façade at Versailles by Louis Le Vau. Other Hôtels de Ville of interest include those at **Aix-en-Provence** (17thC), with fine entrance gate, and at **Marseilles** (17thC), which has an outstanding façade. The **Hôtel de Ville, Lodéve** (17thC), Hérault, was the former bishop's palace, the town being the seat of a bishop from the 4th century until 1790. The bulk of the building is of the period of Louis XIV. The **Hôtel Dieu, Lyon** (1741-48), which established the reputation of Germain Soufflot, is Italianate in appearance. The architect had studied in Rome and developed a sense of the monumental and its concern with mass and regularity. The main façade is punctuated by regular bays *articulated* by columns. The **Château d'Eau, Montpellier** (1753-67), is a brilliant example of public works architecture. The termination of an aqueduct, it is a pavilion articulated by Corinthian columns and forms part of the Promenade du Peyrou.

Hôtel Dieu, Lyon *A building by Germain Soufflot, the leading French Neoclassical architect, it has contemporaneous Italian monumentality, expressed by clearly defined masses accentuated by attic stories and articulated by Ionic columns.*

Château, La Tour d'Aigues *The most remarkable part of the château is the elaborate triumphal arch entrance (1571). Of particular interest is the unbroken entablature over full pilasters, which was modeled on ancient Roman remains found in the vicinity.*

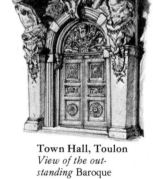

Town Hall, Toulon *View of the outstanding Baroque portal which was added to the façade by Pierre Puget. Carved figures, in the manner of Baroque Rome, carry the exceptionally heavy balcony.*

Château d'Eau, Montpellier *The town landmark, it was designed by Antoine and Etienne Giral and is an impressive terminal to an aqueduct. The aqueduct, which is reminiscent of the Pont du Gard, has two tiers of arches and is ½ mile in length and 65 ft in height.*

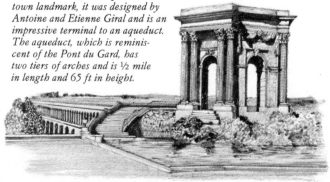

Southwest France

Castles & Palaces

Southwest France is rich in fine *Renaissance* mansions. An outstanding example is the **Château de Montal, Lot** (1523-34), a medieval stronghold which was transformed by its owner following his return from Charles VIII's campaign in Italy into a splendid Renaissance castle. The **Château, Dampierre-sur-Boutonne** (10thC), was largely rebuilt in the 16th century and is notable for its double galleries, one on top of the other, their ends terminated by circular towers. The **Château de Bournazel, Aveyron** (1545-1500), by Giullaume Philander and possibly Giullaume de Lissorgues, has a magnificent double-arched external screen added in about 1550. An interesting feature is the way the lessons of the Italian Renaissance have been creatively adapted to a more irregular form, such as the column spaces which have an alternating rhythm set by the arches and slender wall niches.

Domestic buildings

Considerable architectural activity took place in **Toulouse** in the mid-16th century. The old quarter is particularly rich in Renaissance houses, many of which were old buildings reconstructed in the new style. Good examples include the **Hôtel de Bagis** (1538), with an elaborate sculptured *portal* in which *hermes,* standing on *plinths,* hold up the *architrave,* which in turn carries a coat of arms decorated with angels.

Civic & Public buildings

The **Town Hall, La Rochelle** (1595-1607), had its spacious court yard refaced with a *galleried* Italian Renaissance façade. Another fine building in La Rochelle is the **Palais de Justice** (18thC).

The **Grand Theatre, Bordeaux** (1772-88), by Victor Louis, is an outstanding building, consisting of two parts, concert hall and theatre, linked by a grandiose staircase which rises to a high level to give access to the stalls of the theatre. The stairs then split into two flights ascending to galleries with access to the concert hall and the upper section of the theatre auditorium. The building is a masterpiece of technique and ordered planning.

Hôtel d'Assézat, Toulouse *(1552-62). View of the entrance courtyard, which is traditional in form but which has been given a highly picturesque layering of Italianate motives decorating the wall surfaces.*

Grand Theatre, Bordeaux *Detail of the staircase. The first flight of stairs ascends to a landing from where a door,* articulated *by* caryatids *and flanked by niches decorated with statuary, leads into the stalls. Two further flights ascend to upper galleries.*

Town Hall, La Rochelle *The courtyard of the Town Hall. The architectural style here was gleaned from pattern books of the three Greek Orders but with innovations, such as the fat columns of the ground story arcading with the fluting wrapped by plain bands.*

Hôtel de Bernuy, Toulouse *(1530). The galleried courtyard of this town house is articulated by* Corinthian *columns and bold cornices. Among the classical details are* Gothic *elements, such as the* mullioned *windows.*

Château, Bournazel *This handsome screen of double arcades was added to the château c. 1550. The detail is Italian but the* module *of the Orders is more irregular, as was frequently the case in French buildings.*

London

Religious buildings

Inigo Jones, a genius who was by far the first to introduce the Italian *Renaissance* to *Gothic* England, built the **Queen's Chapel, St James's Palace** (1623-27), and **St Paul's, Covent Garden** (1631-33), a handsome barn-like building with a Tuscan *portico* and wide overhanging eaves.

St Paul's Cathedral (1675-1710), Sir Christopher Wren's masterpiece, formed the hub of his Renaissance building in London after the Great Fire of 1666. St. Paul's was the largest building of its period to be completed as its architect intended and encompasses considerable structural ingenuity. The double dome is the focal point of the building and its relation to the proportions of the rest of the building, both inside and out, was one of Wren's chief concerns. He built 51 churches in the City of London, all in the Renaissance style, with fine steeples and plain Protestant *naves*. Of those surviving, the best examples are **St Mary-le-Bow** (1670-73); **St Stephen's, Walbrook** (1672-77); **St Bride's** (1671-78); **St Mary Abchurch** (1681-86), and **St Swithin's** (1677-85).

Nicholas Hawksmoor, Wren's protégé, produced a series of fine *Baroque* churches similarly characterized by distinctive and original steeples and by their plans with intersecting axes. Examples include **St Alphege** (1712-14); **Christ Church, Spitalfields** (1723-29); **St George-in-the-East** (1715-23); **St Anne's, Limehouse** (1714-30); **St Mary Woolnoth** (1716-24), and **St George's, Bloomsbury** (1716-31), the last being the most classical of all his churches.

James Gibbs was a brilliant technician who took up the classicism first developed by Wren. He designed **St Peter's, Vere Street** (1721-24), and **St Martin-in-the-Fields** (1722-26). The latter, his most famous work, shows the combination of steeple and classical temple portico which was a prototype for church building for years to come.

John Nash and Sir John Soane were the two major architects at the end of English classicism. The beautiful façade of **All Souls', Upper Regent Street** (1822-25), is the only surviving Regent Street building by Nash. Soane's most original **St John's, Bethnal Green** (1825-28), and **Holy Trinity, Marylebone** (1824-28), have a Baroque concern for the play of solids and voids.

Castles & Palaces

The **Banqueting House, Whitehall** (1619-22), is Jones's most celebrated work. The hall is a double cube in form and follows *Palladian* ideals closely. It was originally designed for the performance of court masques.

Wren planned the extensive rebuilding of **Hampton Court**, but only the south wing and the Fountain Court were completed (1689-95).

Domestic buildings

The first truly classical building in England was Jones's **Queen's House, Greenwich** (1616-35). It was originally two rectangular blocks flanking the main road to Dover and connected by a bridge. The gap was later joined by John Webb, Jones's protégé, when the road became disused.

St Mary-le-Bow *As with all Sir Christopher Wren's churches, the spire, here added in 1680, is the focus of attention. A square-planned lower stage is topped by several ever smaller, colonnaded circular stages.*

St Paul's Cathedral *The west façade flanked by two belltowers and showing the use of the* Corinthian Order *for the lower colonnade and the* Composite *for the upper one. The upper level is continued as sham wall hiding flying-buttresses on the north and south sides.*

St Mary Woolnoth, *right. A square-planned church by Nicholas Hawksmoor, particularly charming for its monolithic twin-towered façade. The ground story is articulated by giant Doric columns.*

St Martin-in-the-Fields *A prototypical building, James Gibbs's most important church was much copied. The exterior is* articulated *by a giant Corinthian Order and is culminated by the magnificent* pedimented portico. *The steeple appears to pinion the building.*

Orangery, Kensington Palace *(1704-5). The interior of this elegant brick building, probably by Hawksmoor and Sir John Vanbrugh. The large windows of the orangery give a quality of lighting that enhances the restrained classical features.*

St Mary-le-Strand *(1714). Another of Gibbs's steeple churches, St Mary-le-Strand has particularly fine proportions with its* Ionic *portico and delicately* articulated *steeple of three stages.*

Christ Church, Spitalfields *A strikingly individual church by Nicholas Hawksmoor. The dominating steeple, with its incorporated spire, is stepped forward in plan on to four tall, supporting columns.*

Queen's House, Greenwich, *left. The nucleus of the complete Greenwich Palace complex, the Queen's House, with its rusticated ground story and Ionic colonnade, marks Jones's first use of Palladianism.*

Banqueting House, Whitehall *The fine façade of the hall, enriched with Corinthian and Ionic Order columns over* rusticated *walls. John Webb included the hall in plans for a monumental palace complex — the Palace of Whitehall — but this was unfulfilled.*

Hampton Court *The east façade of the south wing, showing Wren's controlled design with an unbroken* parapet *and applied portico. The low ground story emphasizes the* piano nobile *with its upper mezzanine floor lighted by circular windows.*

237

London

The major influence on the English *Palladian* school was Lord Burlington, who traveled extensively in Italy. His chief work in London was for himself, **Chiswick House** (1925-36), which he completed in collaboration with William Kent. The two most influential architects of the late 18th century were Sir William Chambers and Robert Adams. Chambers's **Albany, Piccadilly** (1770-74), was altered and extended by Sir Henry Holland in 1803-4. His Palladian **Manresa House, Roehampton** (1760-68), is now a Jesuit college. Adam remodeled **Syon House, Brentford** (1761-73), and designed **Osterley Park** (1761-80). He was also one of the architects who advised Horace Walpole on his fairy-tale house, **Strawberry Hill, Twickenham** (1750-70).

Sir John Soane was one of the most original of British architects. His own house at **13, Lincoln's Inn Fields** (1812-14), is now a museum. He also rebuilt **Pitzhanger Place, Ealing** (1801-3).

Civic & Public buildings

Sir Christopher Wren's many fine buildings include the **Royal Observatory, Greenwich Park** (1875-76), a handsome octagonal building, and **Chelsea Royal Hospital** (1682-91), which is large-scale, red-brick Dutch-style architecture and became a prototype for other projects in Europe and North America. The **Royal Naval Hospital, Greenwich** (1696-1702), has a grand *Baroque* plan, taking its position from the apparently modest Queen's House which it frames in the most dramatic manner. Another memorable London landmark is **Horse Guards, Whitehall** (c. 1748-59), by Kent. A Palladian complex, it has striking Venetian-style windows and *pedimented* wings.

One of the most original of urban projects was John Nash's plan to connect St James's and Westminster with Regent's Park. The architecture of **Regent Street** (1818) was replaced from 1907 to 1927, but its quality was comparable with the grandiose terraces addressing the park itself, such as **Park Crescent** (1812), **Chester Terrace** (1825) and **Cumberland Terrace** (1826). Also by Nash are the **Royal Opera House Arcade** (1816); the **Theatre Royal, Haymarket** (1920-21), and **Carlton House Terrace, The Mall** (1827-33), his last major urban project.

Sir Robert Smirke's finest building is the **British Museum** (1823-47), which shows his enthusiasm for Greek *Neoclassicism*. His other works include **Canada House, Trafalgar Square** (1824-27), and the **King's College** (1830-35) extension to **Somerset House** (1776-80), the palatial government offices by Chambers.

Chiswick House *Attached by a low wing to an early 17th-C house, Chiswick House was conceived as a place for entertaining. It was modeled on Palladio's Villa Rotunda but lacks the villa's warmth, as is shown by the heavy* Baroque *entrance stairway.*

13, Lincoln's Inn Fields *An interior of Sir John Soane's house, which has survived as the museum he founded. Soane created a remarkable sense of space by making ingenious use of the limited room available. He had previously built number 12, and some Soane interiors also survive there.*

Eltham Lodge, Eltham *(1663-65). Hugh May designed this building with its Dutch-style hipped roof and handsome pedimented entrance façade. The style became a prototype for several later Georgian houses.*

Strawberry Hill, Twickenham *Originally the residence of Horace Walpole, who rebuilt the house in a fantastic* Gothic *style with turrets and battlements. Robert Adam designed the round room ceiling.*

Dulwich Art Gallery and Mausoleum *(1811-14). This design by Sir John Soane consists of a long* gallery *built of London stone, attached centrally behind the mausoleum. The whole has a simple massing which foreshadows much late 19th- and early 20th-C architecture.*

Park Crescent *The first of John Nash's buildings for Regent's Park, the Crescent was originally to have been the southern half of a complete circus. The forms are calm and ordered and* articulated *by coupled* Ionic *columns. The chief rooms have large arched windows.*

Royal Naval Hospital, Greenwich *View from the Thames-side lawns of the complex, which is now the Royal Naval College. Beyond the coupled* colonnades *and twin domes of Sir Christopher Wren's design is the* Palladian *Queen's House by Inigo Jones.*

Chelsea Royal Hospital *Two sides of Wren's rather austere design, which encloses three sides of a courtyard. The brick body of the building contrasts subtly with the stone used for the* porticos. *The central element houses the Great Hall.*

Cumberland Terrace *The most monumental of the Regent's Park terraces, comprising three enormous blocks linked by triumphal arches. Raised above plain basements, the buildings are articulated by giant* Ionic *pilasters and projecting porticos. The central block has an enormous pediment and* arcade.

Woolwich Arsenal *(1716-20). The old foundry building, one of a series of monumental buildings making up the arsenal which anticipate the buildings of the 19th-C engineer builders.*

Southeast England

Domestic buildings

An outstanding feature of Elizabethan mansions is the long gallery, such as that of **Penshurst Place, Kent** (1340-16thC), which has molded *quatrefoil* and square-shaped paneling and a beautiful plastered ceiling. Elizabethan houses derive much of their picturesque quality from additions and extensions made during subsequent periods. The facade of medieval **Knole House, Kent** (*c.* 1450), was enriched with obelisks, heraldic beasts, shaped *gables* and *mullioned* windows in the late 16th century, while the hall was remodeled in about 1605 with a flat, decorative ceiling and a profusely carved screen. Another major Elizabethan building is **Hatfield House, Hertfordshire** (1607-12), which has the traditional "E"-shaped plan, vast in scale, with domed corner towers at each wing and a magnificent two-story classical *loggia* occupying the center of the south front. The magnificent Jacobean mansion of **Audley End, Essex** (1603-16), has also preserved the traditional "E"-shaped manor house plan and on an equally monumental scale. It has an imposing turreted river façade with richly *articulated* porches and elegant bay windows. **Petworth House, Sussex** (1688-96), has a west front 322 ft long and is noted for the Carved Room, decorated by Grinling Gibbons, a prolific craftsman, in 1692.

Baroque additions are found in many large houses, such as **Moor Park, Hertfordshire** (1620), which was restored in 1720 by Giacomo Leoni and has gardens by Capability Brown, as has **Stowe Park, Buckinghamshire** (17-18thC). The 18th century witnessed the building of numerous *pedimented* and columned mansions, such as **West Wycombe Park, Buckinghamshire** (*c.* 1760), which has a huge main *portico*.

Of interest in Essex are 17th-century *timber-framed* buildings with ornamental plasterwork. Good examples are the **Garrison House, Wivenhoe**, and the **Crown House, Newport**, both with relief work, the former in floral *strapwork* and the latter with simple molded panels. By 1700 brick had become the predominant building material and many 16th- and 17th-century timber houses were given brick façades.

Civic & Public buildings

After the Dissolution of the Monasteries, when monks could no longer care for the sick, many hospitals and almshouses were built by private benefactors and were usually constructed around courtyards and included a hall and chapel. Examples include the **Abbot's Hospital, Guildford** (1619), a magnificent brick building with Flemish *gables;* **Whitgift Hospital, Croydon** (1596-99), Greater London, and **Sackville College, East Grinstead** (1619), Surrey.

Commercial & Industrial buildings

Sir John Vanbrugh created the storehouse, **Chatham Dockyard, Kent** (*c.* 1720), which rivals in scale those of the 19th-century engineer builders. The gateway is of particular interest, for it emulates medieval fortified town gates and their heraldic decoration.

St Peter's, Brighton *(1823-28), Sussex. Sited to close the north end of the Steyne, a spacious green, this beautiful* Gothic Revival *church was designed by Sir Charles Barry. The elegant two-story arch, recessed porch and pinnacled buttresses layered in front of the fine tower, form a miniature screen front, a notable feature of a great many of the English cathedrals.*

Mereworth Castle, Kent *(1722-25). Built by Colen Campbell and modeled on the Villa Capra, Vicenza, it is square in plan with a dome and circular central hall, lavishly decorated with plasterwork. The main rooms are planned around the hall.*

Royal Pavilion, Brighton *(1815-21), Sussex. Originally a small house, it was remodeled by John Nash for the Prince Regent (George IV) in an amalgam of Indian and Chinese motifs, creating a bizarre building with a great dome, roofs like tents and numerous decorative pinnacles.*

Stowe Park Buckinghamshire. *The north portico (1720), by Sir John Vanbrugh. Many distinguished architects and artists contributed to the rest of the building, notably Robert Adam, William Kent and Grinling Gibbons.*

Moor Park, Hertfordshire, *below. The magnificent lofty portico of the west front. The original house was built c. 1620 but a later owner had the façades restyled in stone and the building restored in 1720.*

Sissinghurst Castle, Kent *(16thC). The detached gatehouse, originally one of the four sides of this mansion. This quadrangular plan with gatehouse on one side was a typical building scheme of this period.*

Mathematical tile cladding

Introduced in the southeastern counties in the 18thC, mathematical tiles provided a cheap means of giving a fashionable appearance to timber-framed buildings. Their uniform appearance, for which they are named, gives shallow window *reveals,* as at Westgate House, Lewes, below.

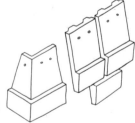

Mathematical tiles, particularly popular in the coastal regions, have a fine brick face and were hung on battens in the same way as other tiles.

House, Smarden *(16th-19thC), Kent. There are many examples of weatherboarding in the southeast, especially on cottages and barns, for it was an economic alternative to tile-hung or brick-faced walls. Oak and elm boarding was usually left bare, but softwoods were tarred or painted.*

House, Sedescombe *(17thC), Sussex. A building practice of the southeast, particularly Sussex, is a covering of plain tiles hung on timber-frame houses to protect the walls from rain and wind. The earliest, as here, were plain but later shaped tiles were used.*

241

Southern England

Religious buildings

One of the outstanding classical churches in southern England is **All Saints, Oxford** (1706-08), designed by Dean Henry Aldrich. It is reminiscent of Sir Christopher Wren's St Lawrence Jewry, London, but is more elaborately *articulated* with rich coupled *pilasters* and a *Baroque* tower. Other churches of interest include **St Mary, Avington** (1779), Hampshire, with a classical interior and fine west tower, and **St Peter's, Wallingford** in Oxfordshire, which has a *Gothic Revival* tower and spire erected in 1777.

Castles & Palaces

Of the great houses, **Longleat, Wiltshire** (1567-80), is perhaps the outstanding example of Elizabethan architecture. It was built to the "H"-shaped plan, with one section forming the house and the other enclosing a courtyard. The façades are articulated by fine bay windows. The master mason was probably Robert Smythson. **Montacute House, Somerset** (*c.* 1588-1601), is another handsome Elizabethan house, with projecting wings with curved *gables* and a slim bay-windowed entrance porch at the center of one side of the "H." **Wilton House, Wiltshire**, had its south front remodeled between 1649 and 1653 following a fire in 1647. Its corners are taken up in one story gabled towers above the height of the roof. The magnificent state rooms are the work of Inigo Jones. **Blenheim Palace, Oxfordshire**

(1705-20), Sir John Vanbrugh's masterpiece, is a huge building in the Baroque style, comprising two stories built around three sides of a vast courtyard. The Great Hall has an arch in front of the entry to the Salon, with the flanking stairs screened by arched walls. **Windsor Castle, Berkshire** (11th-19thC), is a magnificent royal palace enclosing more than 12 acres. Many monarchs added to the fortification over the years.

Domestic buildings

King's Weston, Avon (1711-14), is one of Vanbrugh's most attractive houses, even the entrance *portico,* despite its great size, being delicate in appearance. Vanbrugh's influence is strong in a number of provincial houses, such as **Widcombe Manor, Bath** (*c.* 1727), which has a richly articulated south front with coupled, *fluted pilasters,* carved *keystones* and a *pedimented* central section with channeled *ashlar.* **Ditchley Park, Oxfordshire** (1720-25), designed by James Gibbs, has a serene classical front, three stories in height, with projecting sides and center bay. The salon has rich plasterwork decoration. **Sezincote, Gloucestershire** (*c.* 1803), has an English plan combined with oriental arches, corner turrets and onion domes. It was the first English building to be modeled on Indian styles and has notable gardens landscaped by Humphrey Repton. **Luscombe Castle, Devon** (1800), designed by John Nash, also has handsome gardens landscaped by Repton.

House, Cheltenham *(c. 1820), Gloucestershire. Detail of a wrought iron balcony, of which there are many examples in the town. Decorative wrought iron was a characteristic feature of the* Regency *period and was often used on balconies and verandahs.*

Church Cottage, Swindon *(c. 1700), Wiltshire.* Small framing *was used in the construction of this house, with vertical and horizontal timbers dividing the frames into small squares. This was a feature of larger houses but spread to smaller houses during the 17th and 18thC.*

St Candida and Holy Cross, Whitechurch Canonicorum *(12th-13thC), Dorset, left. Detail of a tomb (c. 1612) in the north chancel. The tomb is Italian Renaissance in spirit, overlaid with Flamboyant style Jacobean carving and molding.*

Sezincote, Gloucestershire *This Indian-style architecture has extended eaves, elaborate corner pavilions and central onion dome. It was designed by Samuel Pepys Cockerell, from drawings made in India, for his brother, a nabob who had made his fortune working for the East India Company.*

Manor House, Upper Slaughter *(16thC), Gloucestershire. A gabled Elizabethan house built of rubblestone, with a porch of ashlar work added in the Jacobean period. The combination of rubblestone and elegant porch is an effective mixture of building and architecture.*

Dairy, Blaise Hamlet *(1802), Avon. Built by John Nash at Blaise Castle, it was the first utilitarian building on the estate to be disguised as a cottage. The hamlet itself (1810-12) was an attempt to group such buildings within a village.*

Yew Tree Cottage, Launcells *(c. 1800), Cornwall. Cob, a mixture of mud and straw, was common in the 18th and 19thC for the humbler country buildings, such as cottages, small farm houses and barns. It was a laborious process in which walls were built up in layers without shuttering. Roofs were invariably thatched.*

Arlington Row, Bibury *(16thC), Gloucestershire. A splendid row of Cotswold cottages, a product of the golden age of cottage building (1530-1660), when the wattle and daub houses of medieval England were replaced in limestone areas with stone walls and roofing slates.*

Model villages

Distinct from traditional villages, which grew up in a haphazard way over the centuries, are model villages, which landowners built in the 18th and 19thC as self-contained units for their employees and pensioners. Villages were also built for factory workers, as at **Street, Somerset** (1829), where a factory village was financed by a Quaker family of leather manufacturers.

East Stratton, Hampshire *(1806). The village comprises nine pairs of cottages, with brick and thatch in the vernacular tradition of the area.*

Nuneham Courtenay, Oxford-shire *(1773). Landscaped by Capability Brown and planned by Sir William Chambers, the village comprises 19 pairs of cottages, one and a half stories in height and with dormers in the roof.*

Southern England

Queen's Square, Bath (1728-36), by John Wood the Elder, is reminiscent of contemporaneous squares in London but his later work in Bath drew on Imperial Roman architectural features to emphasize the Roman origins of Bath. The **Circus** (1754) completed by his son, John Wood the Younger, is a large structure comprising ordinary town houses surrounding a central garden. The younger Wood's greatest achievement, however, is the **Royal Crescent** (1767-75). Semielliptical in shape, it has a great sweeping wall of *engaged columns* standing on a one-story *plinth,* the plinth being the entrance level of the houses.

Numerous almshouses were built in the 17th and 18th centuries. Some were simple rows of cottages, as in the *cob* example at **Cheriton Fitzpaine, Devon** (17thC), and the *gabled* examples at **Chipping Campden, Gloucestershire** (1612) and **Somerton, Somerset** (1626). More elaborate examples are the *arcaded* buildings at **Mortonhampstead, Devonshire** (1637), and the **Penrose Almshouses, Barnstaple** (1627).

Civic & Public buildings

The genius of Sir Christopher Wren lay in his ability to adapt his designs not only to the site but also to produce the best results from the resources, financial and otherwise, available to him. An outstanding example is the **Sheldonian Theatre, Oxford** (1663-69), which has a fine *pedimented* and gabled south façade. It was modeled on the Theatre of Marcellus, Rome, but was roofed over because of the harsher English weather.

Queen's College was the major building project of the late 17th and early 18th century in Oxford. The medieval buildings were in poor condition and were replaced with an ambitious program of buildings designed by Nicholas Hawksmoor. This included a fine **Library** (1692-95), much influenced by Wren, and the **North Quadrangle, All Souls** (1716-35), with a *Gothic* veneer and classical interior.

Commercial & Industrial buildings

Blandford Town Hall, Dorset (1734), by John Bastard is an elegant *Palladian*-style building, with a pedimented façade and an open, three-arched ground floor. In contrast, **Abingdon Town Hall, Buckinghamshire** (1678-82), by Christopher Kempster is a *Baroque* building of the most extravagant kind.

Town Hall, Abingdon *A bold design, two stories in height, with an open arcaded ground floor. The hall, much influenced by Sir Christopher Wren, adapts the grander domestic architecture of the period to a civic building. Its outstanding feature is the row of giant pilasters.*

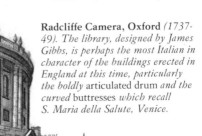

Radcliffe Camera, Oxford *(1737-49). The library, designed by James Gibbs, is perhaps the most Italian in character of the buildings erected in England at this time, particularly the boldly articulated drum and the curved buttresses which recall S. Maria della Salute, Venice.*

Tom Tower, Christ Church *(1682), Oxford. Wren designed this tower to complete the north side of the quadrangle at Christ Church. To harmonize with the Tudor hall behind, Wren vaulted the archway and surmounted it with a domed octagonal tower.*

Clarendon Building, Oxford *(1711-15). Originally the university printing house, designed by Nicholas Hawksmoor, it has a Doric portico and pedimented gable ends with bold bands articulating the windows, which are sunk in shallow recessed panels.*

Central England

Religious buildings

St Philip's, Birmingham (1710-25), is among the finest of 18th-century churches and is now the city's cathedral. Its simple plan consists of a *nave* and galleried *aisles,* to which a *chancel* was added in the 19th century. **Sts Peter and Paul, Cherry Willingham** (*c.* 1753), Lincolnshire, is a simple, classical cube with *pedimented* front crowned by an elegant *lantern.* **St John the Evangelist, Shobdon** (1753), Herefordshire and Worcestershire, has a fine *Gothic* interior, while **St Mary, Ingestre** (*c.* 1676), Staffordshire, is a lovely parish church with west tower and nave.

Domestic buildings

Chatsworth House, Derbyshire (1686-96), is a complex stone building of enormous scale and set in magnificent grounds landscaped by Thomas Archer. Unlike most great houses, which have a distinct front and back, Chatsworth House has four different yet harmonious fronts. **Castle Ashby, Northamptonshire** (1572), is a mixture of Elizabethan and late *Renaissance* styles. It is asymmetrical in plan with a central court closed on the south side by a raised long gallery which links the bedroom wings. **Burghley House, Cambridgeshire** (1552-85), has the clean lines of Elizabethan architecture but the form is innately conservative, modelled on the more traditional concept of high turreted gate house.

Kirby Hall, Northamptonshire (1570-1638), is an amalgam of traditional quadrangle plan and frame to which classical elements, such as the elegant projecting porch, have been added. **Wallaton Hall, Nottinghamshire** (1580-85), built by Robert Smythson, is a massive building with high square corner towers and a huge central block crowning the main hall. **Drayton Hall, Northamptonshire** (1702-03), is a largely medieval building in which the central courtyard was given a new façade and elegant flanking *colonnades.* Other buildings of interest are **Hanbury Hall, Herefordshire and Worcestershire** (*c.* 1701), by William Rudhall; **Boughton, Northamptonshire** (1690), with a French style north wing with large *mansard* roof; **Easton Neston, Northamptonshire** (1702), an impeccably proportioned two-story house, and **Hardwick Hall, Derbyshire** (1590-97).

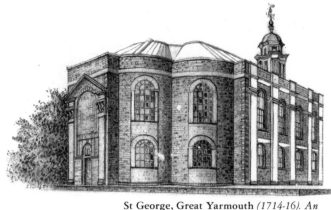

St George, Great Yarmouth *(1714-16). An ungainly yet handsome* Baroque *church, it has an exterior articulated by giant* Doric *pilasters and with the four corners of the building lobe-shaped. The interior of the church was modeled on prototypes by Sir Christopher Wren.*

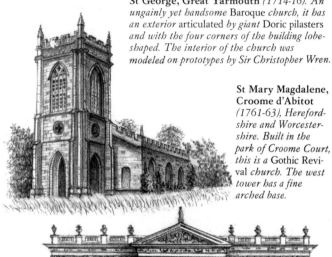

St Mary Magdalene, Croome d'Abitot *(1761-63), Herefordshire and Worcestershire. Built in the park of Croome Court, this is a* Gothic Revival *church. The west tower has a fine arched base.*

Chatsworth House, Derbyshire *The monumental west façade, boldy articulated with giant* Ionic *columns and projecting* pedimented *centre. A typical feature of the* Baroque *is different designs and aspects for each façade.*

Martello tower, Suffolk *(1810-12). One of many Martello towers which line the shore between Bawdsey and Shingle Street. Modeled on the Torre della Martella, Corsica, they were built as defenses against Napoleon.*

Kedleston Hall, Derbyshire *(1757). The hall comprises a central block with projecting wings on the north façade, connected by curved corridors. The Adam brothers added the Baroque south front.*

245

Central England

There are many handsome country houses in central England. **Blickling Hall, Norfolk** (1616-27). built by Robert Lyminge in rose-red brick, is a fine Jacobean house with domed corner towers and a three-*gabled* front *articulated* by elegant *oriel windows*. **Raynham Hall, Norfolk** (1622), a brick house in which the traditional "H" plan has been modified to accommodate the *Palladian* style, has notable Flemish gables. **Sudbury House, Derbyshire** (1613-c. 1670), a Jacobean house, was modified in 1670 by the addition of a distinctly classical two-story porch and by *balustrading, dormer windows* and *cupola*. **Stoneleigh Abbey, Warwickshire** (1714-26), is an impressively scaled building by Francis Smith and has cliff-like façades. His masterpiece is **Sutton Scarsdale, Derbyshire** (1724), a *Baroque* building now in ruins. Other notable country houses include **Houghton Hall, Norfolk** (1721), by Colen Campbell, one of the earliest Palladian houses in England; **Holkham Hall, Norfolk** (1734), a magnificent Palladian mansion designed by William Kent with a frontage of 104 m and with various elements strongly articulated, and **Heveningham Hall, Suffolk** (1778), by Sir Robert Taylor, another Palladian building with a great pillared center block rising from an *arcaded* basement.

The prosperous agricultural economy of Norfolk in the 18th century attracted a growing labour force and with it housing problems. One solution was the building of estate villages, such as that at **Holkham** (c. 1760), a group of superior Tudor style cottages built at the park gates. The idea of estate villages was not new, however, for one had been built in about 1702 at **Chippenham, Cambridgeshire,** which consists of pairs of one-story cottages with a half-story above the ground floor. Each pair is linked by outhouses, with their brick walls color washed and their roofs tiled. Another example is found at **New Houghton, Norfolk** (1729), where there are 10 cottages and almshouses built by the gates of Houghton Hall.

Civic & Public buildings

Late 17th-century work at Cambridge was dominated by the genius of Sir Christopher Wren, who designed **Pembroke College Chapel** (1663), a tall and elegant building with pedimented fronts. Another of his works is the **Chapel, Emmanuel College** (1668-73), a boldly articulated building in the Baroque manner, with a large pediment broken by a lofty cupola and with ground floor arcading linking it to the other college buildings. Wren's masterpiece in Cambridge, however, is the **Library, Trinity College** (1676-84), a long rectangular, two-story building with interior carvings (c. 1695) by Grinling Gibbons.

James Gibbs, the pre-eminent English architect of the early 18th century after Wren, was involved in work at Cambridge University from 1722. His projects there include the **Senate House** (1722-30), a great, single room with its façades articulated by giant *pilasters* and *engaged columns* and with a central pediment on each face, and the **Fellows' Building, King's College** (1724-49), to a great extent constructed of portland stone.

Thorpe Hall, Cambridgeshire *(1653-56). A lavish rectangular block, one of the few great houses to be built during the Commonwealth (1649-60). Emphasis is given to the first floor rooms by their alternating window pediments.*

Madeley Court, Shropshire *(16thC). Remains of an early Elizabethan house which, with its polygonal towers flanking the gabled entrance, harks back to the great gatehouses so typical of earlier Tudor England.*

Sparrowe's House, Ipswich *(c. 1567), Suffolk. View of the main façade, which was enriched with pargetting in 1692. The decorative panels of the oriel windows depict the extent of the then known world.*

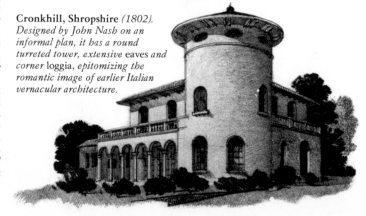

Cronkhill, Shropshire *(1802). Designed by John Nash on an informal plan, it has a round turreted tower, extensive eaves and corner loggia, epitomizing the romantic image of earlier Italian vernacular architecture.*

Black-and-White houses

A characteristic feature of the Welsh border counties and of Worcestershire and Warwickshire is *timber-framed* houses with their timbers painted black. It was largely decorative since a permanent blacking was not available until the 19th century.

Reader's House, Ludlow *(17thC), Shropshire. View of the two-story porch. The black woodwork offset against the white stone is a particularly effective decorative device. Elizabethan and Jacobean houses were often painted, usually with lamp black in a water paint.*

Salwarpe Court, Herefordshire and Worcestershire *(16thC). View of the façade, which is embellished with water paint. The lamp-black had often to be reapplied to the timber.*

Black Daren, Llanveynoe *(16thC). Hereford-shire and Worcestershire. Stone long-houses, such as this, consist of a byre at one end and domestic quarters at the other, with a con-necting passage. Long-houses are the most common early form of sheltering.*

House, Sleaford *(c. 1800), Lincolnshire. Pantiles, as in this example, are a common feature of village building in Lincoln-shire, Leicestershire and Nottinghamshire. They are a product of local commercial ties with Holland and were first imported in the 17thC.*

The Gables, Honeybourne *(17thC), Hereford-shire and Worcestershire. Many small, gabled houses were built of coursed rubble in the Middle Ages. Masonry was the most prestigious material of the time, but was available only to the richest until the 17thC, when stones became available from quarries.*

Ickworth House, Suffolk *(1796-1836). A huge, circular classical building from which the rooms are reached by two curved corridors. It was designed by Francis Sandys but work was interrupted by the Napoleonic Wars. The gardens were landscaped by Capability Brown.*

Custom-House, King's Lynn *(1681), Norfolk. Designed by Henry Bell, it is, like Kempster's Town House at Abingdon, Oxfordshire, an adap-tation of domestic architecture in the construction of civic and market buildings. It is lightly articulated with pilasters, blind arches and panels.*

Northern England

Castles & Palaces

The architecture of the northern counties was less affected by current fashions than elsewhere in England due to the area's distance from London and the continent. The great houses of the 18th century were few but many were of exceptional quality. Sir John Vanbrugh's plans for **Castle Howard, Yorkshire** (1699-1712), broke with tradition in having wings on both south and north fronts and a great central dome, which provides light to the hall. **Seaton Delaval Hall, Northumberland** (1720-28), also by Vanbrugh, is a magnificent building, its dramatic effect enhanced by its bleak setting on a cliff above the sea. **Bramham Park, Yorkshire** (c. 1715), is a plain house but is given a dramatic appearance by the giant *Doric colonnades* connecting the central block to the wings. **Wentworth Castle, Yorkshire** (1710-14), stands on top of a hill and has the monumental elevations of European late *Baroque*. **Duncombe Park, Yorkshire** (1713), by William Wakefield, has the character and quality of a Vanbrugh building with its magnificent west front with high *pedimented* center and projecting wings, which have giant coupled Doric *pilasters* at the two ends adding to the monumentality.

Domestic buildings

In the early 17th century local stone replaced timber for building, but the plans were traditional and usually comprised a central block containing the hall, two stories in height, and projecting wings. Good examples are found in the cloth-manufacturing districts, such as **East Riddlesden Hall, Yorkshire** (c. 1640). Characteristic features include broad, low proportions and the combination of vernacular structures with architectural details. Stone buildings in the north are commonly more austere than those in the south.

Until the 19th century most laborers lived in cottages of one room. Many smallholders, however, lived in a dwelling known in Yorkshire as a coit, in which domestic quarters and cattle shed were combined under one roof, carried on four wooden pillars. The prosperous farmer began to separate the byre from the domestic part of the house in the 17th century. This new type of house developed from the traditional long-house and appeared in Lancashire and Yorkshire in the 18th century. They were fairly spacious, two-story dwellings with an attached barn.

Before the concentration of the clothing industry in towns, weaving was carried out in the worker's home. The weavers' cottages included a workroom for the looms, which was usually on the first floor and was lighted by a long row of windows.

Civic & Public buildings

The outstanding public building in the area is the **Assembly Room, York** (1731-32), a brilliant evocation of classical antiquity. Lord Burlington based the complex—a large room for dancing, a room for cardplaying and another for refeshments —on an ancient Egyptian arrangement.

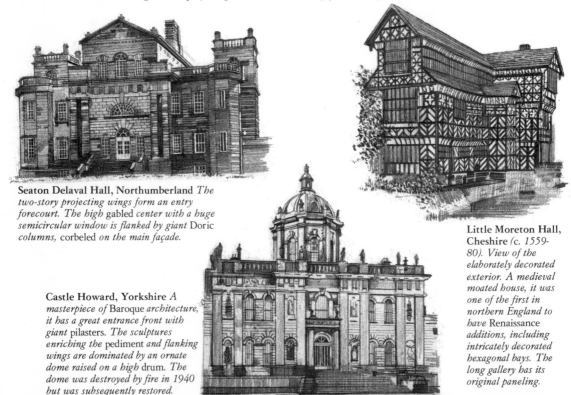

Seaton Delaval Hall, Northumberland *The two-story projecting wings form an entry forecourt. The high* gabled *center with a huge semicircular window is flanked by giant* Doric *columns,* corbeled *on the main façade.*

Castle Howard, Yorkshire *A masterpiece of* Baroque *architecture, it has a great entrance front with giant* pilasters. *The sculptures enriching the* pediment *and flanking wings are dominated by an ornate dome raised on a high* drum. *The dome was destroyed by fire in 1940 but was subsequently restored.*

Little Moreton Hall, Cheshire *(c. 1559-80). View of the elaborately decorated exterior. A medieval moated house, it was one of the first in northern England to have* Renaissance *additions, including intricately decorated hexagonal bays. The long gallery has its original paneling.*

New villages for laborers

Numerous model villages were built in the north, outstanding examples in Yorkshire being those at **Fulneck** (1748), the first Moravian settlement in England, and at **Ripley** (1780-1860). Other examples include **Barrow Bridge, Lancashire** (1830), a mill village, and **Low Moor** (1785), a factory village in Lancashire.

Belsay, Northumberland *(c. 1830). The village consists of a line of cottages in an austere* Greek Revival *style, with a somewhat out-of-context urban arcade. It was designed by John Dobson.*

Harewood, Yorkshire *(1760), left. A village designed for estate workers, it is an amalgam of vernacular and contemporaneous architectural taste.*

Assembly Rooms, York *View of the Great Ballroom and its surrounding* aisle. *It was based on a design by Andrea Palladio which, in turn, followed a description by Vitruvius of an ancient Egyptian hall, used as a place for entertaining in large houses.*

Art Gallery, Manchester *(1824-34). A building in the* Greek Revival *style, designed by Sir Charles Barry. The various parts are boldly* articulated, *particularly the entry façade with its projecting* portico.

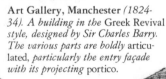

Bastle, Bellingham *(18thC), Northumberland. These fortified farm houses were built in the 16th and 17thC along the troubled borders with Scotland. The living quarters are on the first floor while the ground floor was used to house animals and fodder.*

Smith's Farm, Dalton *(1689), Lancashire. A single-story barn with a two-storey south end, the first story being living quarters. It is an example of the ingenuity of the vernacular builders, who used different combinations to meet their particular needs.*

Scotland

Religious buildings

Most ecclesiastical work after the Reformation consisted of modifications to medieval buildings; even new buildings followed traditional forms, with simple rectangular plans and *Gothic* details, although the **Chapel Royal, Stirling Castle** (1594), and the **Church, Dairsie** (1621), show *Renaissance* influences.

The addition of an *aisle* in the *transepts* produced the characteristic Scottish "T"-shaped plan, as at **Ayr** (1635) and the **Tron Kirk, Edinburgh** (1633), one of the most ambitious of the type. An unusual plan in Scotland is the centrally planned church, as at **Burtisland, Fife** (1592), which is square in plan, and **Lauder, Lothian** (1673), a Greek cross church. **Canongate Church, Edinburgh** (*c.* 1690), has an aisled Latin cross plan and a handsome façade. Interesting churches from the Georgian period include **St Nicholas West Church, Aberdeen** (18thC), by James Gibbs, who was a native of the city, and the **Parish Church, Hamilton** (1732), by William Adam, which is another centrally planned church.

Castle & Palaces

The earliest attempts at Renaissance design are the new façades of the royal palaces of **Falkland** (1502), which was added between 1537 and 1542, and **Stirling** (1540-42). Their influence, however, was minimal since traditional Scottish forms remained more popular throughout the country. The final development of the *tower house*

building was the baronial style of the late 16th and early 17th century. The style is interesting for the profusion of decorative classical detail, such as *corbeled* upper stories with their purely decorative *machicolated parapets* and pepper-pot turrets, *pedimented dormers* and *balustrading*. Nostalgia is also evident in the angle turret, originally a French device which had been adapted by the medieval builders. Good examples are found at **Claypotts, Angus** (1569-88), with *gabled* round-towers; **Crathes Catle, Strathclyde** (1553-96), and **Craigievar Castle, Grampian** (1610-26), the finest of all having been spared alterations. Another example is **Glamis Castle, Tayside** (1650-96), which has a tower dating from the 15th century.

After the Restoration (1660) Sir William Bruce founded the Classical School in Scotland. He designed a *Doric* entrance and the west façade of **Holyroodhouse, Edinburgh** (1671-79).

Domestic buildings

The many domestic buildings by Bruce include **Prestonfield House, Edinburgh** (1687), and **Hopetoun House, Lothian** (1698-1702). The last was his most exuberant project. The dominant figure in Scottish architecture in the early 18th century was William Adam, the father of the architects John and Robert. He designed a series of modest country houses in the Anglo-*Palladian* tradition, such as **Duff House, Banff** (*c.* 1720-45), which has strong overtones of Vanbrugh.

Crichton Castle, Lothian *(14thC). View of the Italianate façade, which was added* c. 1590 *to the tower house by the Earl of Bothwell following his extensive travels in Italy.*

Craigievar Castle, Grampian. *A handsome example of the Scottish baronial style, which reached its peak during the early 17thC. It is "L"-shaped, seven stories in height and has a line of* corbeled *turreted towers.*

Church, Burntisland, *Fife. A centrally planned church, crowned by a large square tower, with an octagonal turreted top which was added in 1749. The church is galleried internally and has a central floor space to accommodate the long communion table of the reformed rite.*

Canongate Church, Edinburgh *Designed by James Smith on a* basilican *plan, it is reminiscent of European Catholic churches with flamboyant* ogee *styled gable* parapet *for the main façade.*

Drumlanrig Castle, Dumfries and Galloway
*(1679-90). A monumental building by James
Smith with corner towers five stories high and
a front raised above an arcaded terrace and
reached by a Baroque flight of stairs. The castle
is an amalgam of Heriot's hospital in Edinburgh
and the classicism of Holyroodhouse.*

House, Forebank
*(1757), Lothian. A
development of the
late 17thC was a
medium-sized house,
two stories in height,
with symmetrical
plan, central entrance
and staircase on axis
flanked by the main
rooms of the house.*

Bellevue Crescent, Edinburgh *(c. 1820). The
plan for the new town of Edinburgh was devised
at the same time as John Wood and his son
were redesigning much of Bath. Open space was
moulded on geometric figures of crescent,
circle, oval and square, their centres occupied by
extensive, and lush gardens.*

Tower houses

The standard plan for these houses, built in
Scotland between the 14th and 17thC, was a
simple rectangle. Wings were often added and
some had additional buildings within, forming a
courtyard. By the late 16thC the *tower house*
was developing into a purely domestic building
and by the 18thC the Scottish baronial style was
pre-eminent throughout much of the country.

**Kirkhope Tower,
Borders** *(c. 1600).
Built of uncovered
rubble, it is four
stories in height with
a garret above and is
virtually intact. It
was originally built
into the north side
of the outer defenses
of a castle.*

**Dryhope Tower,
Borders** *(1613), left.
Originally the tower
was of four stories,
the ground floor being
a vaulted storehouse.
Immediately above the
storehouse was the
hall, which was
reached by means of a
newel staircase.*

Wales

Domestic buildings

The Industrial Revolution in the 18th century destroyed the simple pastoral economy of Wales and caused a rapid increase in cottage building. Many of the new cottages were erected in scattered, rural settlements where miners and quarrymen could supplement their earnings by small-scale farming. In Dyfed they were mostly sturdily built stone homes with huge side chimneys. Another feature in Dyfed was decorative thatching with bands of twisted rush encircling the *gable, eaves* and ridges. The thatch was usually taken up in a cone around the gable chimney, creating a distinctive outline. Walls were usually of *cob* or stone construction with rounded corners. In Gwynedd, an area of igneous rock, many cottages were built of large, roughly-trimmed boulders. A distinctive feature of early 19th-century cottages here was the *hipped dormer window*.

Cottages of the 18th century were either traditional in form, with high-pitched thatched roofs and small, irregularly spaced windows, or the more regularly designed cottages of the Industrial Revolution, often with low-pitched slate roofs and more generous windows. Examples of the former are found in older settlements such as **Hawarden, Flintshire,** far removed from the new industrial centers. In the northeast timber cottages were common. Most were traditional in construction, with heavy oak frames and clay-daubed panels. During the 18th century lighter frames, covered with *weatherboarding* or sometimes with lathe and plaster, were introduced.

Civic & Public buildings

The most impressive of the public buildings of the period is the **Shire Hall, Monmouth** (1724), which is *articulated* by giant *Ionic pilasters* and elegant central *pediment* with an *arcaded* ground floor and hipped roof. The **Market Hall, Llandiloes** (1609), is a magnificent timber building with an arcaded ground floor. The design is largely traditional with two tall vertical timbers and heavy oak arches.

Numerous model villages were built in the early 19th century. **Tremadog, Gwynedd** (*c.* 1800-11), was planned as a port and ferry point between the Welsh coast and Ireland and consisted of a central area reminiscent of an Italian piazza, complete with arcaded market hall. **Morriston, Monmouthshire** (*c.* 1768), was planned with a grid as the core of a sizable town. The intention was to attract colliery and copper workers.

Commercial & Industrial buildings

The most memorable engineering works of the period are by Thomas Telford. He built the monumental aquaduct **Pont Cysyllte, Ruabon** (1794-1805), Clwyd, to carry the Shropshire Union Canal across the Vale of Llangollen, and the cast iron **Waterloo Bridge, Betws-y-Coed** (1815), across the River Conway. Among his other works are the **Menai Bridge, Gwynedd** (1820-26), and the **Conway Road Suspension Bridge, Conway** (1826), which has castellated towers designed to harmonize with the eight massive towers of the 13th-century castle.

Cottage, Rhoscolyn *(18thC), Gwynedd. A typical cottage of the Industrial Revolution, characterized by larger and more symmetrically sited windows than hitherto and evenly constructed walls. A common internal feature is the* gabled *fireplace.*

St Fagan's Castle, *(1560-80), South Glamorgan. Built within the thick* curtain walls *of a medieval castle, it is a hall house with an* axial *entrance and through passage. The high-pitched roof and steep gables of Tudor England persisted longer in Wales than elsewhere.*

Talgarth, Trefeglwys *(c. 1660-70), Powys. A three-unit building with a central chimney dividing the staircase from the lobby entrance, a typical arrangement for many of the larger houses in Powys during the late 17thC.*

House and byre

The house and byre homesteads of Wales were similar to the long-houses of southern England, with house and byre usually under one roof. Often the living quarters were given a different color from the byre, which was in most cases painted white.

Cefn Buarddau, Llanaelhaearn *(18thC), Gwynedd. This single-story cottage is characteristic of most small holdings. If a barn or byre was needed, the house was usually extended at the gable end. The dormer windows are an addition of a later period.*

Blaen-Ilain, Llanennog *(18thC), Powys. An example of a homestead with entry to the house through the byre. This is the traditional plan for long-houses in England.*

Pont Fawr, Llanrwst *(1636). This is the first bridge in Wales to break with the vernacular tradition and utilize clean, classical proportions. It may have been designed by Inigo Jones. Several buildings in the town are attributed to him as he was believed to have been born there.*

Menai Bridge, Gwynedd *(1820-26). The work of Thomas Telford, it was the longest suspension bridge of the time and spans the Menai Straits. It is constructed of cast iron and is more than 2600 ft in length with a central span of 578 ft.*

Treowen, Woanstow *(c. 1627), Gwent. View of the fine* Renaissance *porch, with elaborate coupled pilasters, molded string-courses. decorative bargeboards and mullioned windows. The Renaissance style came to Wales some 50 years after it was common in England.*

Cottage, Llangorwen *(17thC), Powys. A single room cottage with chimneys on the gable ends and entry door at one side. Such cottages usually had a high-pitched roof, which was the most suitable shape for thatching, and small irregularly placed windows.*

Ireland

Religious buildings

The Greek temple served as a model for many civic, public, commercial and religious buildings in Ireland. The façade of **Holy Trinity, Kircubloin** (*c.* 1840), was modeled on an engraving of a *Doric* temple at Sunium, while the **Pro-Cathedral of St Mary, Dublin** (1815), has a lofty Doric *portico* added in 1840. Catholic churches, on the other hand, usually turned for inspiration to Catholic Europe, *Renaissance* and *Baroque* architecture in France and Italy in particular, largely because many of the clergy were educated in Europe and most had traveled there. An example is **St Mel's Cathedral, Longford** (1840-93).

Presbyterian Church, Portaferry *(c. 1840), Co. Down. View of the façade of this ponderous,* Neoclassical *church by John Millar. It stands on a high base and has heavy* Doric porticoes *at both front and back.*

Castles & Palaces

Following the supression by the English of an uprising in 1536, English influence became predominant. **Ormond Castle, Carnick-on-Suir** (15thC), Co. Tipperary, was remodeled in the late 16th century by the addition of a *gable*-fronted mansion, the finest Elizabethan house in Ireland. Examples of 17th-century additions to earlier fortified houses include **Donegal Castle**, the *keep* of which was built in 1505 and the manor house added in about 1623, and **Lemaneagh Castle, Co. Clare**, which has an original keep of about 1480 and was remodeled in 1643. A number of 17th-century buildings, such as **Kanturk Castle, Co. Cork** (*c.* 1610), and **Burntcourt Castle, Co. Tipperary** (1640), still incorporated some defensive features after they had been remodeled.

Ormond Castle, Carnick-on-Suir, *Co. Tipperary. This Elizabethan mansion, the first example in Ireland of a large house in which the primary concern was not defense, was added to a 15th-C castle.*

Domestic buildings

Rothe House, Kilkenny (1594), is a typical example of the fine merchants' houses which were at one time found in all the large towns. These houses were usually of two or three stories and had high gables and *mullioned* windows. The Dutch-inspired house of Restoration England became a model for a number of homes built from the middle of the 17th century, such as that at **Beaulieu, Co. Louth** (1660-67). One of the first of the *Palladian* style houses was built at **Bellamont Forest, Co. Cavan** (*c.* 1730), by Thomas Coote, with *pedimented* Doric portico and *piano nobile* raised above a *rusticated* basement. At **Furness, Co. Kildare** (*c.* 1740), the principal house was probably designed by Francis Binsdon. It has a tall central block of three stories linked to two-story wings by single-story walls.

Burntcourt Castle, Co. Tipperary. *Even when defense ceased to be the main consideration, many of the larger houses, such as this, still incorporated corner towers in case of attack. The symmetry of plan was an early attempt to emulate* Renaissance *architecture.*

Commercial & Industrial buildings

The first major classical building in Ireland was the **Royal Hospital, Kilmainham** (1680-84), Dublin, by Sir William Robinson, built as a home for retired soldiers. It consists of buildings around a large courtyard, articulated by pedimented centers with the principal façade punctuated by a square tower crowned with a spire. The **Old Parliament House, Dublin** (1729-39), now the Bank of Ireland, was the earliest application in England and Ireland of the Palladian style to public buildings. The architect, Sir Edward Pearce, gave it a lofty, colonnaded *Ionic* façade with projecting wings. The *peristyle* around the sides was added later.

Carton House, Co. Kildare *(1739-45). Detail of the salon, part of the magnificent state apartments. The house was remodeled by Richard Castle. The* stucco *ceiling of the salon is by Paul and Philip Francini.*

Beaulieu House, Co. Louth. *By the mid-17thC a taste for the latest architectural fashion resulted in the building of many fine classical houses, such as this, but few survive. The new style was characterized by* hipped *roofs,* dormer windows *and wide brick eaves to provide architectural detail.*

Marino Casino, Dublin *(1758). A small garden house, one of the outstanding examples of 18th-C Irish building, by Sir William Chambers. Doric columns support a heavy* entablature. *The house is in the form of a Greek cross.*

Custom-house, Limerick *(1765-69). A handsome* Palladian *building by Davis Duckart of five bays with a* rusticated *ground floor. The three center bays are* articulated *by tall* Corinthian pilasters *and elegant* cornice *and* arcading.

Dwyer-MacAllister Cottage, Derryna-muck *(18thC), Co. Wicklow. This cottage is characteristic of the two-roomed cottage in having a steeply pitched, thatched roof.*

Custom-house, Dublin *(1781-91). A long, low building, the work of James Gandon. The dome, carried by a high* colonnaded *drum, was inspired by Sir Christopher Wren's dome at Greenwich Hospital, London.*

Farmhouse, Warrington *(18thC), Co. Down. A typical example of the houses built for English farmers in parts of Ulster between 1660 and 1720. Many incorporate building techniques and facilities found in 17th- and 18th-C English homes.*

East Germany

Religious buildings

The **Hofkirche, Dresden** (1738-51), by Gaetano Chiaveri, is a magnificent example of late Roman *Baroque* architecture, but although the source is clearly Italian the single spire on the front façade is a German innovation. As with many German buildings, it was rebuilt after suffering damage during World War I.

Castles & Palaces

Schloss Hartenfels, Torgau (1470-1544), by Konrad Krebs, is among the finest examples of early *Renaissance* architecture in Germany. The first large secular building in the country since the *Romanesque* palaces and one of the last German castles to be built on a mountain peak, it is a legacy of medieval defensive strategy. Its most spectacular feature is the external staircase, which is carried on decorative *pillars*. Another handsome building is the **Albrechtsburg, Meissen** (15th-16thC), by Arnold von Westfalen, which is also notable for a spiral staircase.

Mannerism came later to Germany than elsewhere and was modeled on the more ornate north Italian examples. An outstanding example is the **Fürstenhof, Mecklenburg** (1550-55), which is Italian in scale but with greater wealth of ornamentation, in particular decorative *friezes* and triangular *pediments* above the windows. The **Zwinger, Dresden** (1711-22), is Mattaeus Pöppelmann's masterpiece. It was built as part of a huge plan for a palace but what remains is like a stage backdrop, with an orangery on the east and west with semicircular wings, north and south, punctuated by elaborate pavilions at their vertices.

Civic & Public buildings

The **Arsenal, East Berlin** (1695-1717), largely the work of Andreas Schlüter, has a splendid central courtyard with examples of Baroque sculpture around the doors and above the entrance *Portico.* The **Brandenburg Gate, East Berlin** (1788-91), by Gotthard Langhans, is in the *Greek Revival* style in imitation of the Propylaea, Athens. The **New Guard House, East Berlin** (1816-18), by Karl Schinkel, is a bold design, a solid box with tower-like corners and a bold *Doric* pedimented portico. Another notable building is the **State Opera, East Berlin** (1741-43), by van Knobelsdorff, which was rebuilt as a museum.

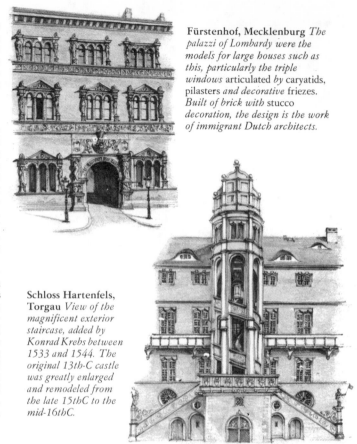

Fürstenhof, Mecklenburg *The palazzi of Lombardy were the models for large houses such as this, particularly the triple windows* articulated *by* caryatids, pilasters *and decorative* friezes. *Built of brick with* stucco *decoration, the design is the work of immigrant Dutch architects.*

Schloss Hartenfels, Torgau *View of the magnificent exterior staircase, added by Konrad Krebs between 1533 and 1544. The original 13th-C castle was greatly enlarged and remodeled from the late 15thC to the mid-16thC.*

Hofkirche, Dresden *This Roman Catholic church is a* basilica *with a* wide *nave,* choir *gallery and a handsome tower of four stages over the entrance. The two top stages of the tower are of open-work.*

Zwinger, Dresden *The Royal Gate of the palace, with its abundance of columns and pilasters. The palace, badly damaged during World War II but subsequently restored, was designed in the 18thC as a residence where the royal court might hold their pageants and elaborate tournaments.*

Northern Germany

Religious buildings

The **Stadtkirche, Bückeburg** (1611-15), a synthesis of *Gothic* and *Renaissance* styles, has a Gothic hall form with *rib* and panel *vaulting* carried on Renaissance columns and *capitals*. The heaviness of the sculptured façade is a *mannerist* feature. The round-headed windows with early Gothic *tracery* are a curiosity. Another important building is **St Michael, Hamburg** (1751-61), by Johann Prey and Ernst Sonnini.

Castles & Palaces

Bückeburg Castle (16th-17thC) has some fine Renaissance work, including a monumental gateway and the Golden Room (1606), an outstanding mannerist interior in which every part of the wall surface is encrusted with elaborate carvings and decorative work. The **Castle of Charlottenburg, West Berlin** (1695-1712), was begun by Arnold Nering and extended by the Swedish architect Eosander von Göthe who, following a visit to France where he was greatly impressed by Versailles, added the orangery and tower.

Domestic buildings

A characteristic of the *timber-framed* houses in the region of Weser, Lower Saxony, are panels decorated with rows of sun motifs, rosettes or *strapwork friezes,* which cover the framework between the sill and the middle rail. In stone buildings the most elaborate work is found on the gables. Mannerist decoration, as in the **Essighaus, Bremen** (1618), often covered the entire façade and included strapwork and scroll work and an obelisk crowning the gable.

Castle, Ahrensburg *(c. 1594), Schleswig-Holstein. A handsome manor house, it is traditional in plan with a classical façade with octagonal corner towers, crowned with* cupolas, *and decorative triple* gables.

Cloth-workers' Hall, Brunswick *(1591). A long building by Balthasar Kircher, with fine decorative gables, particularly on the east end where the gable itself is* articulated *by double* cornices. *The gable steps are softened by brackets, statuary and numerous* pinnacles.

Stadtkirche, Bückeburg *The* mannerist *façade of this great hall-church. The verticality of the boldly sculptured* buttresses *break through the cornice lines and* balustrading *by the addition of numerous spikey pinnacles.*

Farmhouses, Altes Land
Outstanding examples of *timber-framed* buildings are found in the marshland of Altes Land, between Hamburg and Stade. They are characterized by decorative brick *gables* or half-*hipped* roofs. The entrance for warehouse and domestic unit is in the center of the façades.

House, Jork   **Farmhouse, Steinkirchen**

Northern Germany

A characteristic of vernacular buildings around **Goslar** and **Celle** is *timber-framing*, with large carved plates beneath the windows and painted brick walls. In Lower Saxony, the large hall-houses of the 18th century combine both farm buildings and domestic accommodation under one roof. The large *gable* ends often have stories supported on *jetties* over the entrance to the central *aisle*. Inscriptions, sometimes religious in origin, were frequently carved along the frame.

Civic & Public buildings

A typical *mannerist* building of the Weser *Renaissance* is the **Town Hall, Hannoversh-Münden** (17thC), Kassel. It is adorned with an Egyptian obelisk, rather like a *Gothic finial*, a common feature on gables and entrance porches in the area. A characteristic of mannerist interiors is the use of *cartouche panels*, grotesque figures and *strapwork*, derived from fantasy rather than nature. The **Great Council Chamber** of the **Town Hall, Lüneburg** (1566-84), is a good example, being a paneled room enriched with elaborate wood sculptures by Albert of Soest. Outside, the boldly *articulated* market façade was not added until 1720.

Commercial & Industrial buildings

The **Schütting, Bremen** (1536-38), the merchants' guild hall, is an elegant building with tall *mullioned* windows divided by an encircling *stringcourse* and crowned with carved crests and relief panels. The *balustrading* above the *cornice* and axial *portal*, the double flight of stairs and bracketed columns framing the door and flanking windows were additions made in the late 16th and early 17th century.

Willmann House, Osnabrück *(1586). Decorative wood carving followed traditional forms well into the late 16thC. The example here shows German plaitwork bands, and* Roman- *esque billets and rosettes which are oriental in origin.*

House, Lüneburg *(16thC). A typical house of the prosperous in Lüneburg at this period, it has a handsome stepped* gable, *with twisted brick banding around the windows, plain columns and many decorative medallions.*

Town Hall, Hannoversch-Münden, *left. The main entrance. The building, typical of the* Weser *Renaissance, has triple gables decorated with scrollwork, statuary and pyramids. The obelisk, a key part of the design, gives the* square *portal a suggestion of verticality.*

Town Hall, Lüneburg *(13th-18thC), right. Detail of the great Council Chamber, a Renaissance masterpiece carved by Albert of Soest. The plaitwork is purely decorative although in earlier years it was thought to be capable of warding off evil spirits.*

Town Hall, Einbeck *(1550-93). An outstanding example of the decoration of a timber-frame building on the grand scale. The German plaitwork bands and sun motifs are similar to those on the Willmann House and are found extensively in Lower Saxony.*

Central Germany

Religious buildings

The outstanding *Baroque* building in the area is the church and hospital of **St Clement, Münster** (1745-54), designed by Johann Schlaun for the Brothers Hospitaller, in which a domed tri-*apsidal* church engages a corner of the quadrilaterally planned hospital. Another fine church is that of **St Paulinus, Trier** (1734).

Castles & Palaces

The **Castle, Vischering** (16thC), Westfalen, is a typical example of a nobleman's residence, being a picturesque composition of stone wall and tiled roof standing on an island site. Other imposing buildings include the **Castle, Gemen** (15thC), Westfalen, which was remodeled and extended in the 17th century; the **Castle, Raesfeld** (1643-58), and the **Castle, Brühl** (1725-28), which has a magnificent Baroque staircase added (1740-48) by Neumann in which a single flight of stairs climbs to a landing which is punctuated by a tomb-like monument against the wall and framed by coupled columns.

Schlaun built an outstanding series of buildings in Westphalia in which awkward sites and modest means nevertheless produced remarkable effects, as in the palace of **Erbdrostenhof, Münster** (1753-57), in which the constraints of an oblique angled corner site produced a simple triangular forecourt and bold concave façade with a projecting *pedimented* central section. Another building of note is the **Redenzschloss, Münster** (1767-84).

Domestic buildings

It was not until the end of the feudal system that *timber-framing* was employed on simple buildings. By the 16th century standard units had evolved for the building of houses in European towns and cities, providing maximum flexibility to accommodate diverse uses and providing an outlet for artistic expression. The typical house consisted of a ground story of workshops and stores, with living quarters on the upper floors. Good examples in Hessen are found in **Fritzlar, Marburg an der Lahn** and **Alsfeld**. A characteristic of parts of Hessen, as at **Holzburg** and **Heidelbach**, are farms in which the house is at the front, with barn and byre grouped behind.

Farmhouse, Enger *(18thC). A series of giant farmhouses is found in the country-side around Enger. They are usually* timber-framed *buildings with brick* nogging *and have a large roof, often covering four stories, with domestic quarters at one end.*

Town Hall, Alsfeld *(1512). A handsome timber-framed building, it has an* arcaded *ground floor built of stone. The two-story bay windows are supported on* corbels *above the arcaded ground floor and are covered by unusually elegant slate-covered needle spires.*

Town Hall, Berg-strasse *(1557), Heppenheim. Of special note is the way the* braces *between the posts and rails are decorative rather than purely structural, as they would have been at an earlier date.*

Houses, Fritzlar *(16thC), Hessen. One of the features of half-timbering is that a series of buildings, all using uniform lengths of timber, may be given individuality by accommodating diverse elements, such as the oriel window on the right of this view.*

Hexenburgermeisterhaus, Lemgo *(1571). A fine example of a patrician's house it has a gabled* façade *with cornices delineating each story and articulated* with *fluted* columns. *The gable is bordered by elaborate* voforms *which have shell motif decoration.*

Southern Germany

Religious buildings

Italian influence was particularly strong in southern Germany, as may be seen in the Fugger family's funerary **Chapel, Augsburg** (1509-18). Its sculptured pictures framed by *blind arcading* are thought to be the earliest example of the Italian *Renaissance* style in Germany. Here the arcading is used for purely decorative purposes. **St Kilian's, Heilbronn** (13th-15thC), is a *Gothic* church with a magnificent Renaissance tower, added between 1513 and 1529, which is an amalgam of *Romanesque* imagery and classical forms. The **Theatine Church, Munich** (1663-90), completed by Enrico Zuccalli, is also Italian in character, owing little to its surroundings. Indeed, the façade might stand in an Italian piazza. The richly *stuccoed* interior was much copied in southern Germany. The **Stift Haug, Würzburg** (1670-91), is a monumental and austere Italianate church, unusual in that the *transept* is placed midway upon the longitudinal axis. **Neumunster, Würzburg** (1711-16), by Joseph Greising and possibly Johann Dientzenhofer, has one of the most beautiful of *Baroque* façades with a brilliant play of convex and concave forms. The interior decoration is largely the work of Dominkus Zimmermann and his brother Johann. The **Church, Aldersbach** (1720), is a monumental yet unpretentious building. Its interest lies in the brilliance of interior stucco work by the brothers Cosmas and Egid Asam. The parish and pilgrimage **Church, Steinhausen** (1727-31), by Dominikus Zimmermann, is an amalgam of Baroque oval plan with Gothic hall-choir. The *ambulatory* is divided from the nave by 10 pillars *articulated* by clustered *pilasters* and decorative *capitals*. The *frescoes* in the nave *vault* are by Johann Zimmermann. The pilgrimage **Church, Weis** (1746-54), Dominikus Zimmermann's masterpiece, consists of a *rotunda* with an elongated *apsidal choir* at one end with a convex façade layered in front of the rotunda at the other. The picturesque outline is greatly enhanced by surrounding meadowland. Zimmermann, reluctant to leave his greatest work, spent the last years of his life near the church.

Weltenberg Abbey (1717-21) is remarkable for its setting, built as it is on a loop of the Danube opposite huge white cliffs. The Baroque church was designed by Cosmas Asam and consists of a *narthex* and nave, both oval in shape. Externally the church is of modest proportions but the inside, lighted by a magnificent window above the high altar, is an outstanding example of Baroque art. **St John Nepomuk, Munich** (1733-46), is a tall, narrow building by the Asam brothers, its unity of style arising from their absolute control of all phases of design and construction throughout. The **Church, Vierzehnheiligen** (1743-72), by Balthasar Neumann, the master of German Baroque, is a complex and contradictory building. It has a magnificent west façade of *pedimented* convex and concave center, framed by twin towers, while the multiplicity of windows and jutting *cornice* gives it the appearance of a castle façade. The interior, with its transepts and choir with apses, is in complete contrast to the bold exterior.

Church, Steinhausen
Detail of the highly decorated capitals *of the 10 large pillars which divide the oval* nave *from the surrounding* ambulatory.

Church, Vierzehnheiligen, *left. The twin-towered west façade, one of the masterpieces of German* Baroque *art. Above the* pediment *are statues of Christ, Faith and Charity.*

Monastery, Ettal *(1710-48). A Benedictine monastery was founded here in 1330 and was rebuilt by Enrico Zuccalli. It is a monumental complex in a magnificent Alpine setting, with a high Baroque church at its center.*

St Michael, Berg am Laim *(1737-43), Munich. The lavishly molded façade with its convex central section was intended to terminate the vista from a grand avenue, a typically Baroque gesture.*

Church, Kappel *(1685-89), Oberfranken. The work of the master builder Georg Dientzenhofer, it is a handsome pilgrimage church, distinctly oriental in design, with each of the three apses of the ground plan punctuated by slender towers.*

Church, Wies *Detail of the pillars and capitals of the nave, in which the architecture seems to dissolve into the stucco of the vault. It is the outstanding example of Bavarian rococo art.*

St Michael, Munich *(1582-97), left. The three-story gabled mannerist façade, the work of Wolfgang Miller and Friedrich Sustris. Built for the Jesuits, the church is Italian in style and is enriched with sculptures and blind windows.*

Cathedral, Passau *(17thC). The original Gothic church was destroyed by fire and was rebuilt by Carlo Lurago in the Baroque style. This view of the west front shows how the tall, pedimented central part is linked by the low façades of the side aisles to flanking towers.*

Theatine Church, Munich *Despite the absence of convex or concave forms, this façade by Enrico Zuccalli is exceptionally powerful, with pedimented central section and flanking towers with helmet roofs carried on volutes.*

Southern Germany

Freising Cathedral (12thC) is a notable example of a *Baroque* modification to an older church. The rebuilding was carried out by Cosmas and Egid Asam between 1723 and 1724, transforming the *nave* with plaster and *fresco* into a coherent piece of plastic decoration on a cavern-like scale. Other Baroque buildings in the area include the **Benedictine Abbey, Regensburg** (1722-33), by the Asam brothers; **St Georg, Amberg** (1718-23), by *stucco* artists from Wessobrunn and with frescoes by students of Cosmas Asam; the **Church, Andechs** (1751-55), decorated by Johann Zimmermann, and the **Parish Church, Rottenbuch** (1737-47), a late 15th-century *basilica* remodeled and given a handsome interior in which *Gothic* structure and Baroque stucco work blend harmoniously.

Three families dominated architecture in the district of Vorarlberg on the borders of Austria and Germany—the Moosbruggers, the Beers and the Thumbs. Outstanding churches by Michael Thumb include those at **Schönenberg** (1682-95), **Obermarchtal** (1686-92) and **Grafrath** (1686-94). The **Church, Birnau** (1746-58), by Peter Thumb, is notable, not only for the harmony created by the separate elements of clergy house, church and tower, but also for the *rococo* façades. The single, graceful tower is unusual at a time when twin towers were especially popular. Memorable frescoes decorate the interior. The **Abbey Church, Weingarten** (1715-23), by Kaspar Moosbrugger and others, is cruciform in plan and has a central dome over a magnificent façade with a protruding convex central section tied back to low flanking towers by narrow concave bays. It is one of the largest Baroque churches in Germany.

The Beer family worked chiefly in Switzerland but the most gifted member of the family, Franz Beer, produced a number of churches in southern Germany, the most notable examples being those at **Irsee** (1699-1704), with a monumental twin-towered façade, and **Holzen** (1696-1704), which is memorable for its extremely rich stucco ceiling.

One of the last of the great Baroque church builders of southern Germany, as well as one of the most productive, was Johann Fischer. His major buildings include the **Church, Osterhofen** (1726-31), which forms the north side of a monastic complex and utilizes the existing plan of an earlier Gothic church as well as incorporating an earlier *choir*. The richly decorated interior is by the Asam brothers. The **Church, Diessen** (1731-39), another of his buildings, has a plain façade but a majestic interior by various artists, including Franz Schmutzer, which is an amalgam of the French style and vernacular ornamental tradition. Fischer also built the **Church, Zwiefalten** (1740-65), which, together with that at **Ottobeuren** (1748-92), are his largest and most imposing works. The latter is a cruciform church with a tall, *pedimented* convex façade, *articulated* by engaged columns.

Dreifaltigkeits-kirche, Munich *(1711-14). The main entrance, which is polygonal and* articulated *by* engaged columns *and bold* Baroque cornices.

Abbey Church, Osterhofen *The artistry of the interior lies in the way the architectural forms dissolve into the decorative areas, an outstanding example of Cosmas and Egid Asam's genius for ornamentation.*

Abbey Church, Weingarten *View of the interior, with* stucco *work by Franz Schmutzer and* fescoes *by Cosmas Asam. The galleries are concave and are carried on pillars articulated by clustered* pilasters. *The handsome Baroque façade is constructed of sandstone.*

Schleissheim Castle, Oberbayern *(1701-27), below. A monumental building by Joseph Effner, it has a 1080 ft cliff-like façade, which is distinctly French in style. The castle is augmented by formal gardens in the French style, which was popular in Germany at the time.*

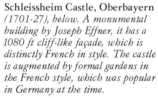

Castle, Aschaffenburg *(1605-14). A monumental building by George Ridinger. The closed courtyard plan with huge corner towers is reminiscent of the Escorial, Madrid. The* gables *articulating each side are in the* mannerist *style.*

Residenz, Munich *(1569-19thC). The Antiquarium, the first part of the palace to be built (1569-71). It was designed to house Albrecht V's collection of classical antiquities and was modeled on the state rooms of Italian palaces.*

Castle, Pommersfelden *(1711-18). One of Germany's finest Baroque castle-palaces, the work of Johann Dientzenhofer. An outstanding feature is the free-standing staircase which is surrounded by galleries and enclosed in a handsome pavilion.*

Residenz, Würzburg *(1737-50), left. Detail of the ceremonial staircase designed by Balthazar Neumann. It is covered with a vaulted ceiling which is decorated with frescoes by Tiepolo.*

New Palace, Bayreuth *(1753-54). One of several buildings erected for Princess Wilhelmina, who strove to transform the city into another artistic center like Potsdam. The interior is handsomely decorated in the rococo style.*

Castle, Tübingen *(16thC). Founded in the 11thC, the castle was rebuilt in the Renaissance. Most of the structure is starkly simple but enriched by isolated elements, such as the portal.*

Southern Germany

Castles & Palaces

Many castles and palaces were built in southern Germany during the 16th and 17th century and others were extended. An outstanding castle is that at **Heidelberg** (14thC-1632), which had a splendid *Renaissance* wing added between 1556 and 1559. The largest of the town palaces is the **Residenz, Munich** (1569-19thC, see p. 263). Built for the Bavarian court, it is an irregular grid of buildings and courtyards locked at an angle to the earliest part, the Antiquarium, in the southeast corner. Other castles in the area include that at **Plassenburg, Kulmbach,** which was rebuilt (1559-69) by Kaspar Fischer with handsome *arcaded* Renaissance courtyard enriched with *Lombardic*-style bas-reliefs. The **Castle, Ansbach** (14th-18thC), was transformed in the *Baroque* style by Jacques-Ange Gabriel, the Viennese court architect, between 1713 and 1714 after a disastrous fire. The Baroque interior is notable for the particularly fine Princes' apartments. The **Nymphenburg Castle, Munich** (1663-18thC), begun in the style of an Italian palazzo, was transformed in the spirit of Versailles with the addition of four lateral pavilions linked by galleries. One of the pavilions, the Amalienburg, was a hunting lodge with a magnificent circular Hall of Mirrors by the accomplished *rococo* architect François Cuvilliés. Another pavilion, the Badenburg (1718-21), by Josef Effner, was the bathing pavilion and is a forerunner of the imposing summer cottages of 19th-century New England. The banqueting hall was decorated by Johann Zimmermann with *stuccoes* in the rococo style and with rich *frescoes*. The castle faces on to a handsome park, which was greatly enlarged in 1701, and formal gardens, also dating from the early 18th century. The decorative rococo style, first used at Versailles in about 1700, was developed elsewhere in southern Germany by numerous French architects who had settled in many of the princely courts. Italian influence is also strong, since most German architects and decorators had trained in Italy or had certainly traveled there.

Civic & Public buildings

The town halls built in southern Germany during the 16th and 17th centuries, such as that at **Heilbronn** (1535-96), are generally of an unpretentious kind. Somewhat grander and more picturesque is the **Town Hall, Rothenburg ob der Tauber** (c. 1570). The angled turret on the *gable* end is 14th-century *Gothic*, while the part facing the marketplace is of the Renaissance period. The most magnificent of all town halls in southern Germany, however, is that at **Augsburg** (1615-20). An enormous *astylar* building in the manner of Renaissance Florence, it is by Elias Holl. The *pediment,* adorned with a pine cone, a fruit which appears on the city's coat of arms, is framed by two towers. Holl, the city architect of Augsburg, was Germany's leading Renaissance architect and the town hall, which has German verticality in its central section contrasting sharply with the classical bays, is his masterpiece.

Castle, Heidelberg *The Otto-Heinrich wing, added between 1556 and 1559, introduced a* Renaissance *element into this medieval castle. Such* cornices *and* pedimented *windows divided by* Orders *gave a new harmony to German architecture of the period.*

Alte Hofhaltung, Bamberg *(1576). Only this fine courtyard and its massive scale distinguishes this former episcopal palace from the vernacular farmhouses common in the area.*

Hercules Fountain, Augsburg *(1596-1602), left. One of three bronze Renaissance fountains by Adriaen de Vries which adorn the Maximilianstrasse, a street of burghers' handsome mansions.*

Town Hall, Nördlingen *(16thC), right. This elaborate Renaissance stone staircase with its decorative* balustrading *and fluted* pillars *was added to the building in 1618.*

Town Gate, Endingen *(18thC).*
Entrance to the marketplace is via
this fine gatehouse, which is a
combination of vernacular building,
in the simplicity and utility of its
volumes, and architecture in the
articulation of the façades.

Nuremburg Gate,
Ellingen *(17thC).*
The gate comprises a
massive octagonal
tower astride a square
base with a central
arch flanked by two
towers. The bold rusti-
cations of the archway
are like giant boulders.
The building's charm
lies in the simple mass-
ing of the various parts.

Town Hall, Rothenburg ob der Tauber *An*
earlier Gothic *structure was transformed into*
this magnificent Renaissance building by the
addition of a fine gable *end, elegant* oriel
window *and turreted staircase tower.*

Swabian farmhouses

Huge farmhouses are a distinctive feature of
Swabia and are a combination of house and
byre, with roofs reaching almost to the ground
and *gable* ends decorated with frames. Farther
to the southwest around the Black Forest many
of the houses have *hipped* roofs.

Farmhouse,
Winterstettenstadt

Farmhouse,
Oberessendorf

Town Hall, Esslin-
gen *(1586). Detail of*
a carved column and
capital in the entrance
hall. The hall is a
timber-frame building,
traditional in form but
with numerous Renais-
sance details.

265

Switzerland

Religious buildings

Medieval ecclesiastical architecture lasted well into the late 16th century in Switzerland and it was not until the Jesuits began building their numerous churches that any profound changes occurred. The first example, the **Jesuits' Church, Lucerne** (1666-73), has a simple *barrel-vaulted* interior, with *frescoes* in the vaulting of the *nave,* expressed externally by a semicircular *pediment* flanked by tall twin towers, over which are domed belfries.

Among many works by Franz Beer, the most gifted member of the Beer family of architects, is the **Abbey Church, Rheinau** (1704-11), with a handsome twin-towered façade. The **Monastery, Einsiedeln** (1719-51), by Cosmas and Egid Asam and Franz Kraus, is a magnificent *Baroque* complex with only the façade of the giant Abbey Church, by Caspar Moosbrugger, breaking out of the huge monastic enclosure into the square beyond. It is a *wall-pillar* church with a nave of three bays. There is an impressive twin-towered façade with a high, convex center, with side bays beneath, set slightly back and curving behind the plane of the towers. Flanking the façade are *rusticated colonnades,* one story high, giving the building the appearance of a monumental palace by curving out around the entrance piazza. Other churches of note by Moosbrugger are at **Muri** (1694-98), an interesting but complex building where the existing twin-towered *Romanesque basilica* was extended, and at **Ittingen** (1703), which is memorable for its Baroque interior.

The last of Europe's great Baroque churches is the **Abbey Church, St Gallen** (1748-70), largely by Peter Thumb but with a twin-towered east façade (1761-68) by Johann Beer. It is a wall-pillar church consisting of a large central *rotunda.* The great length of the church is counterbalanced by the twin-towered east façade, which boldly stresses verticality through the strong line of *pilasters articulating* the corners, the elegant *cupolas* of the domes, and by the double curves of the façade with the concave center articulated by giant columns. The **Cathedral, Solothurn** (18thC), designed by architects from Ticino, is an outstanding example of a Swiss church in the Italian Baroque style. It replaced a Gothic cathedral. It has a vast nave, the columns of which have pilasters adorned with floral decoration. There is little further decoration save for a fine pulpit of pink marble.

Monastery, Einsiedeln *The handsome monastic buildings are grouped around the* Baroque *church, which dominates the vast square in front of it. The Great hall (18thC) is on the second floor of the monastery.*

Abbey Church, St Gallen *One of the last great Baroque churches in Europe. The east façade is stressed vertically by the high twin towers and the section between them. The original abbey was founded in 612.*

Von Roten Mansion, Rarogne *(1702), right. A fine vernacular building, to which certain architectural elements, such as stone quoins and window surrounds, have been added.*

Farmhouse, Hutwil *(18thC), Lucerne, left. Typical of the district around Lucerne are three-story homes with attached barns, as in this example. Roofs are invariably massive, often reaching almost to the ground, usually half-hipped and with a bell-bottom gable.*

Austria

Religious buildings

The *Baroque* style materialized slowly in Austria.
The signs were already there in the early 16th
century in buildings such as **Salzburg Cathedral**
(1614-28), but Italian influence remained strong.
Baroque churches in Austria are generally less
flamboyant than those of southern Germany and
the Baroque appears mainly in large town churches
and abbeys rather than in parish churches. The
outstanding architects were Fischer von Erlach,
Jakob Prandtauer and Johann von Hilderbrandt.

The **Monastery, St Florian** (1685-1715),
Upper Austria, begun by Carlo Carlone and
completed by Prandtauer after 1708, is one of the
largest abbeys in Austria. It comprises a huge
rectangular block with a large courtyard at one
end and two smaller ones at the other. The
church forms one corner of the complex, with its magnificent twin-towered west façade facing outward.
The library, marble hall and staircase block are
especially fine. One of the most majestic of the
Baroque projects is Prandtauer's additions to the
Monastery, Melk (1702-14), which turned the
existing buildings into a monumental and dramatic
whole, dominated by the church with its striking
twin-towered west façade. It is a *wall-pillar* church
with a *drum* and dome crowning the crossing of
nave and shallow *transepts*. The church, as with
all the buildings of the abbey, is bound to another,
a feature necessitated by the narrowness of the
rocky site. **Peterskirche, Vienna** (1702-08), by
von Hilderbrandt, is of a long oval plan with
crowning drum and dome and twin-towered
façade, but the design is compact. Also of interest
in Vienna is the **Piaristenkirche** (1716-53) by
von Hilderbrandt and the **Alte Jesuitenkirche**
(1662) by Carlone. The outstanding work of
Austrian Baroque architecture, however, is the
Karlskirche, Vienna (1716-37), von Erlach's
masterpiece. The plan is a large, extremely long
axial oval, crowned by a huge drum and dome.
The *choir* is square inside and rounded without.
The most interesting feature is the monumental
façade, with its reference to both the ancient
classical world and to Baroque Rome.

Karlskirche, Vienna
*The bold façade is an
amalgam of diverse
elements, such as the
Greek pedimented
portico, the columns,
reminiscent of
Trajan's column in
Rome, and the dome,
which is typical of
Baroque Rome.*

Cathedral, Salzburg
*A monumental Italian
Renaissance building
by Santino Solari, but
with elements of the
Baroque, such as
crowning domes on
the towers and the
highly decorative
central pediment.*

Monastery, Melk *A
Benedictine abbey in which
medieval and Renaissance
buildings were woven
together to majestic effect.
The monastery is greatly
enhanced by its superb
setting on a bend of the
Danube above Metz.*

**Monastery, St
Florian** *The hand-
some Baroque entrance
portal by Prandtauer.
It leads into the main
courtyard which has
superimposed balco-
nies, carved columns
and many statues.*

Austria

Castles & Palaces

Baroque art was essentially a religious art, designed to provide the Counter-Reformation with heavily decorated churches in contrast to the frugal and unadorned buildings of the Lutheran Church. The style was introduced into the Habsburg Empire by Charles V, and it was soon adopted for private houses and other buildings. The **Schloss Schalla-burg** (1572-1600) is particularly interesting for the transformation which took place to the Italian palazzo style, seen in many castles. Here the two-story *arcaded* courtyard is German in character with rows of *caryatids* on the top story and stone elements against the *stucco* background.

Many medieval castles were remodeled in the 16th century and later, such as **Ambras Castle**, near **Innsbruck** (1571), which was given an elaborately carved and gilded room known as the Spanish Room. The **Hofburg, Vienna** (*c.* 1220), was the imperial palace of the Habsburgs, built from the 13th century onward around a medieval nucleus. A more monumental and palatial version of Hadrian's villa, it was added to over the centuries. Remarkable Baroque additions include the **Imperial Library** (1723-26), now the National Library, by Johann Fischer von Erlach, the court

architect, which is in the tradition of the great monastic libraries, such as that at Melk. His son, Josef Fischer von Erlach, built the **Spanish Riding School** (1729-35), a magnificent indoor riding school surrounded internally with two stories of galleries supported on columns, and also designed the **Imperial Chancellery Wing** (1729), a monumental building with a *rusticated* two-story lower level and an upper level *articulated* by *Corinthian pilasters*. The **Palace of Schönbrunn, Vienna** (1696), is another building by the elder Fischer von Erlach. It was the summer palace, built on the edge of the city, but has been much altered. The **Belvedere, Vienna**, comprises two palaces: the Upper Belvedere (1721-24), designed for ceremonial occasions, and the Lower Belvedere (1716), a residential complex built for Prince Eugene of Savoy by Johann von Hilderbrandt. The two are linked by magnificent terraced gardens. Other palaces of interest include the **Schwarzen-berg Palace, Vienna** (1705-20) by von Erlach; **Lobkowitz Palace, Vienna** (1685-87), and the **Schloss Mirabell, Salzburg** (1721-26), which was remodeled by Von Hilderbrandt but much of it was destroyed by a fire in 1816. Of the surviving parts, the Great Staircase is outstanding.

Servitenkirche, Volders *(1620-24). The clock tower, with its elaborate dome and red and white decorative panels, was added c. 1735 to the church, which is a fine example of Baroque art.*

National Library, Vienna, *right. Formerly the Imperial Library, it was built as part of the Hofburg, the Habsburg's imperial palace. It is a two-story building with a domed oval center and barrel-vaulted arms. The handsome interior frescoes are by Daniel Gran (1730).*

Palace of Schönbrunn, Vienna, *below. The Great Gallery, with its magnificent stucco work framing the ceiling frescoes. The palace was built for the emperor Leopold I, who wished for a residence to rival Versailles itself. The palace has outstanding rococo interiors.*

Town Hall, St Veit an der Glan *(18thC), above. View of the decorative Baroque stucco façade, with its Corinthian pilasters, molded window surrounds and crested pediment, all added to the building in 1754.*

Upper Belvedere, Vienna, *right. Detail of one of the massive figures with military trophies above, which support the arches carrying the vaults of the lobby opening out onto the gardens.*

Landhaus, Graz *(1557-65). Built by an Italian architect, it was originally the seat of the Diet of Styria. It is a fine* Renaissance *building with an* outstanding *arcaded courtyard of three stories with pillars carrying the arches which are themselves* articulated *by pilasters.*

Schloss Porcia, Spittal an der Drau *(1527), above. The central courtyard, three sides of which are lined by elegant Renaissance galleries which have handsome decoration, such as medallions and balustrade pillars. The Italian palazzo-style courtyard, such as this, is rare in Austria.*

Dawn-Kinsky Palace, Vienna *(1709-13), right. The heavily sculptured portal with two giant figures standing on round shafts and flanked by two free-standing columns. The portal is the focal point of a magnificently decorated* Baroque *façade.*

Rokokohaus, Innsbruck *(c. 1730). Many traditional town houses have façades such as this, enriched with stucco work. The rococo-style example here has a particularly elaborate form of ornamentation applied to the building façade.*

Farmhouse, Fischbachau *(18thC), right. Decoration on domestic country buildings was usually by frescoes and was designed for the broad gable ends of the houses. The low-pitched roof is a characteristic feature of the Tyrol.*

Belgium

Religious buildings

The change from *Gothic* to early *Renaissance* styles in Belgium is well illustrated by the ornate *flèche* added to the medieval tower of the **Cathedral, Antwerp** (1352-1411). While the tower has some of the shape found in many town hall spires, the forms are here united by vertical bands. With the early Renaissance the various stages of a tower became expressed horizontally by *entablatures, balustrading* and *cornices*. The Renaissance style developed in Belgium from the mid-16th century, later than elsewhere, and was largely a reaction against Gothic, with the horizontal replacing the vertical and restraint replacing flamboyance. Much ecclesiastical work consisted of interior additions, such as the *rood-screen* in **Tournai Cathedral,** added between 1570 and 1573 by Cornelis Floris.

Notre Dame, Montaigu (1609), by Wenceslas Cobergher, was one of the first centrally planned domed churches in the Low Countries. **St-Charles Borromeo, Antwerp** (1616-21), is a fine *Baroque* church with a magnificent tower which has square lower stages and a circular top stage with a dome and crowning *cupola*. The west façade, with its superimposed *Ionic* and *Composite* columns and *Flamboyant volutes,* has the boldness and monumentality of Baroque Rome. **St-Loup, Namur** (1621-45), is notable for its boldly *articulated* Baroque façade, with the giant columns and *pilasters* tied to the façade by a series of stone bands. The large flanking volutes are capped by urns. The façade of the **Church of** the Augustinians, Brussels (1620), now incorporated in the Church of the Trinity, has a magnificent design with coupled columns, broken *pediments,* and long, bold scrolls making the transition from the broad, lower stage to the upper stage. Crowning the façade is a flamboyant crest capped by a triangular pediment.

The **Church of the Grand Béguinage, Malines** (1629-47), has an imposing interior and exterior. The façade is similar to that of the Church of the Augustinians, Brussels, but with three horizontal stages and with the façade broken vertically into five bays and *articulated* by bold pilasters, except for the central bay which has single attached columns.

St-Michel, Louvain (1650-66), is another church with an outstanding Baroque façade, more decorative than most in Belgium, with carved *friezes* and Flamboyant volutes, the volutes being enriched with foliage work. The same elaboration continues into the crowning pediment, in which the central sections are recessed while the supporting pilasters undulate frontally. The church of **St Jean-au-Béguinage, Brussels** (1657-76), has a *gabled* façade, with a high central section having a triangular pediment and low flanking gables with elaborate scrolls, broken pediment and crowning vases. The scroll work here is repeated in miniature over the entrance *portal*. The same arrangement of three gables is seen on the façade of **Notre Dame, Lebbeke** (18thC), but the design is simpler in outline, with these convex and concave gables but little other articulation.

Cathedral, Antwerp
This slender and extremely ornate spire was added to the medieval tower in 1507-15 and is an example of the transitional style between Gothic *and* Renaissance *forms.*

Notre Dame, Montaigu *The church was designed by Wenceslas Cobergher. It is one of the first examples of the* Baroque *style in Belgium and, with its huge dome, has all the monumentality of Baroque Rome.*

Saint-Aubain, Namur *(1750-72). The church has an elegant dome and* cupola *on a drum articulated by coupled columns. The magnificent front façade has two low but taut straight ends with a center bay pressed outward, the center of the bay being accentuated by a semicircular curving* pediment *and bold* cornices.

Chapel of St Anne, Antwerp *(1540). View of the superb Baroque portal which was added to the chapel in the 17thC. Of interest are the pediments in the center, one articulating the keystone, the second framing the niche which crowns it, the whole framed by a swan-neck pediment.*

Church of the Trinity, Brussels *(1620). View of the magnificent Baroque façade of the church. The façade was originally designed for the Church of the Augustinians but when the sanctuary was demolished the façade was incorporated in the Church of the Trinity.*

St Jacques-sur-Coudenberg, Brussels *(1776-87), right. The church has a Neo-classical façade, the main portico of which is crowned by a pediment which, at its apex, is level with a horizontal cornice lined with balustrading.*

St-Michel, Louvain *The façade of this exuberant Baroque church is extremely tall, with a projecting central section articulated by two columns either side. Pilasters articulate the sides, while two bands of stone tie the Orders back to the wall.*

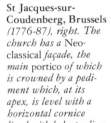

St Jacques, Liège *(1558-60). The Renaissance portal to the church. A refined classical design by Lambert Lombard, it was based on a triumphal arch with a recessed center containing entrance, medallion and crowning niche. The projecting sides are articulated by slim capitals.*

Belgium

Castles & Palaces

Medieval building traditions in Belgium lingered on well into the *Renaissance* period. An example is the **Château de Beauvoorde, Wulveringen** (1573-1617), a fortified house complete with gun loops, encircling moat, *mullioned* windows and *gabled dormers* and façades. The classical influence is seen only in the windows of the gables, which have semicircular arches and shell *tympana*. The triangular *pediment* above has the verticality of the *Gothic* style. Other examples of houses combining medieval and classical features include the **Château Jehay, Liège** (16th-17thC), the **Château de Cleydael, Aartselaar** (14th-16thC), and the **Château de Bossestein, Broechem** (14th-17thC), which has a fine *arcaded* entry court to which access is via an *axial* gatehouse.

Of the early Renaissance-style chateaux a good example is the **Château d'Ooidouk, Bachte-Maria-Leerne** (16thC), which has an elegant arcaded *portico* with gallery above in the central courtyard. The **Hospital of Notre Dame, Oudenarde**, is largely medieval but has a fine chapel (13th-14thC) and 16th-century *cloisters*. To these was added a handsome Renaissance building, the **Episcopal Residence** (1623-29), where the bishop stayed when visiting the hospital. While it is a contemporary of the first *Baroque* buildings, it has all the restraint and classical harmony of early 16th-century Italy. The **Château de Beaulieu, Machelin** (1654), by Luc Faidherbe, is an amalgam of Renaissance and Baroque styles and has corner towers flanking the main façade. The façade has an elaborate pediment of concave, convex and triangular geometry, and a boldly *articulated portal* with giant *Ionic pilasters*. The **Château, Soiron** (1749), is a Baroque mansion raised above a *rusticated* stone basement, with polygonal bays projecting at the sides and stone *quoins* and window surrounds. The whole is symmetrical and is crowned by a huge *mansard roof*. The architecture is extremely refined, in stark contrast to the **Château, Poeke** (17th-18thC), which is strikingly flamboyant with elaborate turreted and gabled skyline and decorative bays and windows with molded hoods and some with wrought-iron balconies. The **Château, Leeuwergem** (1745), a rectangular block with pedimented center bays, Baroque dormer windows and mansard roof, is a handsome building in the Louis XV style, articulated by lightly drawn pilasters and paneling. The **Château, Attre** (1752), is concerned with both architectural and landscape designs and has an *axial* main block with high-pitched roof, high pedimented center and low projecting wings reinforced by flanking garden pavilions. The **Château, Seneffe**, has an outstanding **Theatre** (1770-90) by Charles de Wailey, with a *barrel-vaulted* corridor lined with columns and designed to distort perspective in the manner of Francesco Borromini's gallery in the Palazza Spada and the Scala Regia in the Vatican.

The *Neoclassical* style in Belgium is represented by the **Château, Wannegam-Lede** (1786), which owes much to the Petit Trianon, and the **Château de Duras, Saint-Trod** (1789).

Episcopal Residence, Hospital of Notre Dame, Oudenarde. *A two-story building by Simon de Pape, it has an* arcaded *ground story leading on to a monumental staircase. The façade is divided by wide horizontal zones incorporating* plinths *for the* Doric *and* Ionic *columns.*

Château de Beauvoorde, Wulveringen *View of the south façade. The high roofs have decorative stepped gabling. The château, with its* saddle-back roof, *is a rare and handsome example of a 16th-C fortified country house.*

Château de Duras, Saint-Trod *The château comprises an austere main block with projecting wings, while the entrance is* articulated *by an* Ionic *peristyle, repeated inside by the curving wall of the entrance hall. Crowning the entrance is* balustrading *surrounding a domed room.*

Château Jehay, Liège *An "L"-shaped building, it has the horizontality of the early* Renaissance *but* Gothic *features, such as the* corbel table frieze, *the decorative* ogee *arches articulating the window frames and the round corner tower with its decorative* polychrome *work, still predominate.*

Château, Modave *(1649). A magnificent* Baroque *mansion, it stands on a high cliff above a river. The entry façade is asymmetrical, with a subtle withdrawal and projection of volumes, articulated by* pilasters *and separate roofs in the French manner.*

Château, Soiron, *left. View of the main façade. This château is a fine example of a building in the Louis XV style, with a broad* pedimented *center,* mansard roof *and elegant curved steps leading up to a Baroque portal.*

Château, Poeke *A Baroque mansion in the French style, it has a flamboyant turreted and gabled skyline. The château is designed on a picturesque plan, with curved and straight edges, projecting and receding, which are symmetrical on the front and asymmetrical along the sides.*

Château de Cleydael, Aartselaar *A moated château, it has an "L"-shaped main block with the courtyard in the angle marked by the onion-domed square corner tower. The turreted skyline and asymmetrical plan give the aura of a Renaissance manor house.*

273

Belgium

Domestic buildings

Timber was the principal material used for the façades of late *Gothic* houses. From the *Renaissance* onward it was gradually replaced by brick and stone. An early timber Renaissance house is the **Maison du Diable, Malines** (*c.* 1530). The **Musée Plantin-Moretus, Antwerp** (1550), originally the house of a printer, is a fine classical style house. The **Chancery, Bruges** (1535), on the other hand, is less restrained. Indeed, its flamboyantly decorated *gables* and carved *friezes,* seem to foreshadow the *Baroque.* Most domestic buildings in Belgium are small, narrow-fronted town houses. Other examples can be seen in Tournai and Brussels. Of the larger town houses a good example is the **Maison de Jacques Jordaens, Antwerp** (1641), a fine Baroque building with a façade divided by horizontal bands but given vertical emphasis by its entry bay. The **Maison de la Bellone, Brussels** (1697), by Jean Cosyn, is another handsome Baroque house with the front divided by *pilasters* into seven narrow window bays, which are enriched with panels and *fluting* and stand on carved *plinths.* The whole center is crowned by a bold *pediment* adorned with sculptures. The **Maison des Ducs de Brabant, Brussels** (1698), by G. de Bruyn, is a monumental Baroque building in the Grand Place. It has lofty pilasters and a huge semicircular pedimented center crowned by *balustrading.* The *piano nobile* is *articulated* by balustrading. The **Maison de la Rue Royale, Ghent** (1746), by David't Kindt, is an elegant *rococo*-style house.

Civic & Public buildings

The **Hôtel de Ville, Antwerp** (1560-65), by Cornelius Floris, was a prototype for the early Renaissance in Belgium, with its *rusticated* ground story, *galleried* top story and bold gabled central bay which contrasts with the comparative plainness of the main building. The **Hôtel de Ville, Lierre** (1740), is a magnificent rococo building, in many ways a civic reinterpretation of the Maison de la Bellone, Brussels, except that it has nine bays and a raised attic story.

Commercial & Industrial buildings

The **Maison du Saumon, Malines** (1519), was built for the Fishmongers' Guild and had a new façade added in 1530. The only sign that it might have been anything other than a domestic house is the carved salmon surmounting the door. In this building the traditional bands of windows have been broken up and a more elegant vertical accent given by the slender *engaged* columns and projecting *entablatures* and *cornices.*

There are numerous fine guild houses in the **Grand Place, Brussels,** built in the 17th century. Examples include that of the **Carpenters** (1697), the **Printers** (1697), and the **Shipmasters** or **Maison des Bateliers** (1697). The **Cloth Hall, Tournai** (1610), by Quentin Ratte, was rebuilt after being damaged in World War II. There are a number of Guild Houses in the **Grand Place, Antwerp,** built during the latter part of the 16th century, that are fine examples of northern European Renaissance design.

Maison du Diable, Malines *View of the fine gabled, timber façade. The gable is jettied and is supported by carved wooden figures. Windows are organized in bands.*

Maison de Jacques Jordaens, Antwerp *A superb* Baroque *building which was designed for the painter Jacques Jordaens. The entry bay has been given greater vertical emphasis by the molded* pilasters *and the flamboyant* pediments *over the windows and gables.*

Gables

The predominance of roof ridges gave rise to a remarkable series of decorative *gables,* which are excellent examples of false fronts. The areas of greatest interest are not the main façades, which apart from minor modifications are fairly standard, but these gables which are purely symbolic elements.

House, Grand-Place, Brussels (17thC)

Maison de la Demi-Cure, Antwerp (*c.* 1750)

Maison du Pigeon, Brussels (1697)

Maison du Flûtiste, Ghent *(1669). The façade is crowned with an elaborate gable with the bust of a flautist placed in the central oval. This is flanked by bold* volutes *and enriched with garlands and with statuary.*

Maison du Saumon, Malines *The façade, which was added by Willem van Wechtere. Built for the Fishmongers' Guild, it has a sculpted salmon placed over the entrance.*

Guild House, Grand Place, *Brussels. The central façade of the Maison des Bateliers has its gable modeled on the stern of a ship. The over-elaboration of these façades, with their decorative* corbels, *carved columns and pilasters and ornate crowning gables, is typical of the Baroque period in Brussels.*

Hôtel de Ville, Antwerp *The original building was burnt down in 1576 but was rebuilt on identical lines in 1579. The façade is articulated by superimposed* Orders.

Maison de la Bellone, Brussels *The house was designed for Prince Eugene de Savoie-Carignan. The portal is crowned by a coat of arms in bold relief and is surrounded by urns and foliage.*

Béguinager, Diest *(1671). The elaborate Baroque entrance arch. It is boldly* articulated *by the columns, the rusticated jambs of the arch, the bold* cornice *and the curving pediment, which is crowned with a niche in which there is a sculpture of* The Virgin and Child. *This upper half of the entrance arch is united to the lower part by the side scrolls.*

Holland

Religious buildings

The *Renaissance* developed comparatively early in Holland, but the *Gothic* influence lived on for some time. The major innovation in ecclesiastical architecture was the addition of handsome towers to churches. A good example is the tower of the **Oudekerk, Amsterdam** (1565-66), by Joost Jansz. The **Zuiderkerk, Amsterdam** (1606-14), by Hendrik de Keyser, is a mixture of late Gothic-style form with Tuscan detail. **Westerkerk, Amsterdam** (1620), also built by de Keyser, is a six-bay *basilican* church with a single west tower and fine, spacious interior with handsome classical columns. Dutch classical architecture favored centralized churches and a good example is the **Nieuwe Kerk, Haarlem** (1647), an elegant church, cross in plan with equal arms, and a handsome interior *articulated* by *Ionic* columns and *pilasters*. It has a tall, austere brick façade with central columned *portal* and a high, round, arched window set in triple, recessed frames.

Castles & Palaces

The **Royal Palace, Amsterdam** (1648), is a fine classical building on a monumental scale with narrow projecting wings, while the **Royal Palace, The Hague** (1633-44), is an Italianate-style building with a *pedimented* main building, flanked by long wings with *arcaded* ground stories.

Domestic buildings

The **Trippenhuis, Amsterdam** (1662), by Justus Vingboons, is two houses combined to form one elegant, pedimented building articulated by giant, *fluted Corinthian* columns carried on a bold, first-story *cornice*. The **Château, Middachten** (1695), by Steven Vennecool, is a remarkably refined building with a finely articulated entrance with the crowning cornice turning up into a semicircular pediment. **Het Paviljoen, Haarlem** (*c*. 1785), by Leendert Viervant, is a handsome suburban villa designed on an awkward site in which two wings meet at right angles.

There are many fine 17th-century and early 18th-century *gabled* terrace houses along canals, such as **Herengracht, Keizergracht** and **Prinsengracht** in **Amsterdam** and also around the **Market Square, Maastricht**.

Civic & Public buildings

The **Old Town Hall, The Hague** (1564), is a civic building on a corner site with *cantilevered balustrade* and arcaded gallery above with crowning gable. The **Royal Theatre, The Hague** (*c*. 1765), formerly the Nassau Weilburg Palace, designed by Pieter de Swart, is a refined Louis XVI-style building with concave center and pedimented ends articulated by *rusticated* corners.

Commercial & Industrial buildings

The **Butchers' Guild Hall, Haarlem** (1602), is a fine *mannerist* building with stepped gables and gabled *dormers* enriched with obelisks and *strapwork*. The **Cloth Hall, Leyden** (1640), is a handsome Dutch *Palladian* building, the work of Arent van's-Gravensande.

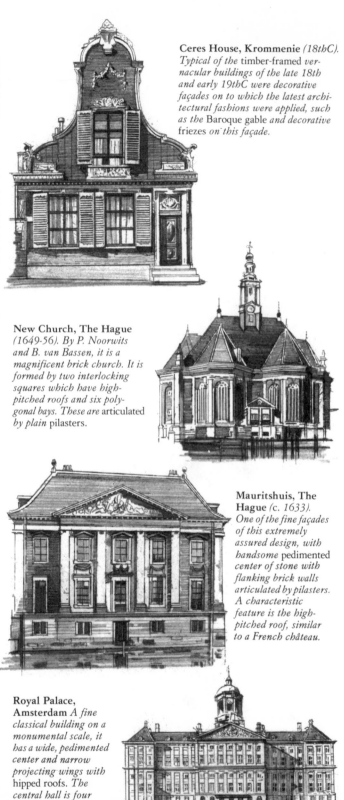

Ceres House, Krommenie *(18thC). Typical of the timber-framed vernacular buildings of the late 18th and early 19thC were decorative façades on to which the latest architectural fashions were applied, such as the* Baroque gable *and decorative friezes on this façade.*

New Church, The Hague *(1649-56). By P. Noorwits and B. van Bassen, it is a magnificent brick church. It is formed by two interlocking squares which have high-pitched roofs and six polygonal bays. These are* articulated *by plain pilasters.*

Mauritshuis, The Hague *(c. 1633). One of the fine façades of this extremely assured design, with handsome* pedimented *center of stone with flanking brick walls articulated by pilasters. A characteristic feature is the high-pitched roof, similar to a French château.*

Royal Palace, Amsterdam *A fine classical building on a monumental scale, it has a wide, pedimented center and narrow projecting wings with hipped roofs. The central hall is four stories in height.*

Dutch post mills
This example at **Retranchement, Zealand,** shows how the working parts are contained in the body, which was always made of wood and which stands on a post. The body can be rotated on the post to face the prevailing wind, an exercise that is made easier by the addition of a wooden vane which itself catches the wind.

Steps and pushing post

Sails facing the wind

Town Hall, Gouda *(1449-59). A handsome building which is an amalgam of late* Gothic-*style form with its vertical emphasis and early* Renaissance-*style decorative details. The Renaissance staircase was added in 1603.*

Town Hall, Enk-huizen *(1686-88), right. By Steven Vennecool, it is a remarkably brave design which relies for its quality on the scale of its façade, the proportion of its windows and its extremely shallow central projection.*

Royal Library, The Hague, *(1734-61), below. Formerly the Hôtel Huguetan, it is an elegant* rococo-*style building by a French architect, Daniel Marot.*

Town Hall, Leyden *(1597-1603). By Lieven de Key, it is an outstanding Renaissance build-ing, of special interest for the decorative* strapwork *and* fretwork *which had been made popular by the books of Vredeman de Vries.*

Northern Spain

Religious buildings

During the 16th century religious building continued on a grand scale, largely financed by the new riches taken from South America, where the Spanish had established an empire. **San Esteban, Salamanca** (1524-1610), by Juan de Alava, is a *Gothic* monastery with a *plateresque* façade *articulated* by superimposed *pilasters* and richly ornamented half-columns. The monastery of **San Marcos, León** (1524-49), by Juan de Badajoz, has a fine plateresque façade with flanking towers, articulated by lightly drawn decorative panels and pilasters. The Jesuit monastery of **San Ignacio de Loyola, Azpeitia,** is renowned for its magnificent domed *Baroque* church, designed in 1681 by Carlo Fontana, an Italian. A *cupola* crowns the dome and *mannerist* obelisks punctuate the curving, *buttressed* walls. The *pedimented* front façade of the ground story is *arcaded* and articulated by coupled columns.

Castles & Palaces

Two palaces in the area are of special note. The **Palacio de Monterrey, Salamanca** (1540), is a symmetrical building with low flanking towers crowned with a decorative *parapet,* a typical *Renaissance* plan. Between the two towers is a long gallery on the top floor, articulated by an *open-work balustrade.* The **Royal Palace, La Granja de San Ildefonso** (18thC), was built by Philip V, a grandson of Louis XIV, in imitation of the palace of Versailles, in France.

Domestic buildings

Salamanca has many plateresque domestic buildings of the 16th century, such as the **Casa de la Salina** and the **Casa de las Muertes,** the latter being one of the first examples of plateresque art. Other examples of plateresque work include the **Casa de Miranda, Burgos** (1543), which has an elegant two-story arcaded courtyard with *fluted* columns and plateresque paneled balustrading, and in **León** the **Casa de los Guzmanes** (*c.* 1560), with a notable façade, low flanking towers and an arcaded top story between. The proportions are *Classical,* the ornamentation restrained.

Civic & Public buildings

Universities thrived in 16th-century Spain. That at **Salamanca** (1514-29), a celebrated seat of learning, has a great entrance with twin doors crowned by an elaborate decorative *attic* and flanked by giant twin columns.

Cathedral, Santiago de Compostela *(11th-13thC, see also p. 162). View of the west façade, the finest example of Spanish late* Baroque, *added between 1738 and 1749 by Fernando Casas y Novoa. The façade acts as a screen in front of the lavishly sculptured Portico de la Gloria (1183).*

Royal Palace, La Granja de San Ildefonso *View of the center portion of the main façade. This section, with its giant* Corinthian *columns and story with* caryatids, *was designed by Filippo Juvarra, an Italian. The style is a flamboyant form of Italian Baroque.*

San Esteban, Salamanca *View of the* portal *of the monastery, which is of a somewhat subdued plateresque style with chiseled relief panels on the* pilasters *and with decorative medallions and frieze.*

University, Salamanca *The main entrance gate, which is encrusted with elaborate bas-reliefs and paneled Italian-style pilasters with a Gothic frame. The university complex covers a vast area and at the height of its fame in the 16thC its students at any one time numbered as many as 12,000.*

Street, Santillana del Mar *(11thC), Santander. The 16th-18thC houses of this small town have balconies and upper rooms supported on corbels. Some have ground floor arcading, top story loggias and coats of arms.*

Palacio de Monterrey, Salamanca *One of a number of palaces built by aristocratic families for their sons when they came to Salamanca University to study. It has fine plateresque ornamentation, a style prevalent in the city, and Italian forms, notably the window frames.*

Casa de las Conchas, Salamanca *(1512-14), left. A handsome yet unusual façade, enriched with carved scallop shells. Below the windows of the main rooms are heraldic motifs.*

Casa de los Picos, Segovia *(c. 1500), right. The interest of this building lies in the bold, simple detailing of door and windows, which is accentuated by the faceted blockwork of the surround.*

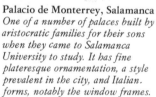

Hospital Real, Santiago de Compostela *(1501-11). Elaborate decoration above the plateresque portal. One of the many buildings surrounding the Cathedral, it was founded as a hospital for pilgrims.*

Horréo, Galicia *(18th-19thC). A common sight in the province of Galicia are stone corn cribs, which are long gable-ended barns with tiled roofs, raised on high stone piles topped with circular stones. The cribs were designed to protect corn from both rain and vermin.*

Central Spain

Religious buildings

Murcia Cathedral (14thC) has a magnificent *Baroque* façade added between 1730 and 1749 by Jaime Bort Milia. The elaborate ornamentation is a revival of the *plateresque* work of the early *Renaissance,* but the deep curve of the main niche, the broken *pediment* over the central entrance and the flanking columns are bold baroque forms. Another outstanding cathedral in central Spain is that at **Toledo** (1227). The original style was French *Gothic* but many additions and alterations were made before its completion in about 1500. Of particular interest is the Transparente (1732) by Narciso Tomé, an extravagant *reredos* consisting of a single concave bay, the same height as the *ambulatory,* flanked by superimposed columns and statuary.

Castles & Palaces

The **Palacio del Infantado, Guadalajara** (1480-92), by Juan Guas, is a late Gothic building in which the incorporation of classical windows and composition of the façade make it a hybrid between the medieval and Renaissance periods. The **Alcazar, Toledo** (1537-53), originally a Moorish and Gothic building, was remodeled for the Emperor Charles V by Alonso de Covarrubias. He added the elegant *arcaded* courtyard as well as a new façade with a central entrance flanked by *Ionic* columns and crowned with an oval coat of arms, itself framed by columns and a pedimented *entablature.* The Alcazar was restored following its destruction during the civil war of 1936-39.

The **Escorial, Madrid** (1562-84), begun by Juan Bautista de Toledo for Philip II, is an austere rectangle with monastery, college and palace, each with its own courts, flanking the *axial* line. The complex is entered via a *portal,* leading into an enormous rectangular courtyard which is terminated by a church in the Italian-style. The church is Greek cross in plan, with a handsome *Doric* façade and high central dome. The **Palacio Real, Madrid** (1738-64), by the Italian architect Giovanni Sacchetti, is Italian in style and incorporates a single courtyard with projecting corner pavilions, the whole raised above a high, *rusticated* basement.

Civic & Public buildings

The **Collegio de San Ildefonso, Alcala de Henares** (1537-53), Madrid, is a fine plateresque building, but Gothic influence is much in evidence. **Tavera Hospital, Toledo** (1542-79), by Bartolomé de Bustamente, is a stark, rectangular block, *astylar* in the Italian manner, but with the characteristic Spanish *portico* with the entrance door reaching the height of the façade. There is a central courtyard in the Florentine style.

Spanish Baroque of the early 18th century is characterized by the synthesis of architecture and decoration, particularly in altars and doors. The main elements are *Salomónica* columns and *Estípite pilasters,* and geometrical and *cartouche* panels. An outstanding example is the door of the **Hospicio de San Fernando** (1722) by Pedro Ribera, Spain's leading Baroque architect.

Escorial, Madrid *View of the south façade. The massive complex comprises monastery, college, church and palace, grouped around a series of courtyards and encased in an enormous rectangle of five-story, cliff-like walls pierced by windows and massive corner towers.*

Palacio del Infantado, Guadalajara *This palace by Juan Guas has Italian windows and* faceted *block work walls with* Isabeline *ornamentation. The buildings comprising the internal courtyard, which have been restored, are in the Gothic style.*

Palace of the Marqúes de dos Aguas, Valencia *(1740-44). View of the principal door, which has the flamboyance of a Roman Baroque wall fountain. The façade was originally painted and the entire palace was the work of Hipólito Rovira y Brocandel.*

Palace of the Marqués de la Conquista, Trujillo *(17thC). A corner of the palace, facing the main square. The palace was built by Hernando Pizarro, brother of the conquistador, and has an arcaded ground floor, elaborately decorated with molded corner pilasters.*

Alcazar, Toledo *View of the vast central courtyard, with its two stories of arcading. The early Italian influence is evident in the lightness of proportion and in the restraint shown in the ornamentation, both internal and external.*

Cathedral, Murcia *The richly decorated portal, an outstanding example of Baroque design with its elaborate play of convex and concave curves flanked by two tiers of coupled columns, which in turn support a half dome.*

Hospicio de San Fernando, Madrid *The main entrance (1722). Some of the most imaginative examples of Spanish Baroque architecture are the numerous 18th-C altars and doors, such as this with its decorated pilasters which are broken up by secondary capitals.*

Collegio de San Ildefonso, Alcala de Henares *(1537-53), Madrid, below. View of the finely proportioned* plateresque *façade. The ornate central section is characteristic of the 16thC, while the richly decorated windows of the middle story are Isabeline in style.*

Casas Colgadas, *or* Hanging Houses, Cuenca *(17th-19thC). Built above a deep ravine, these houses are a solution to overcrowding adopted in many tightly packed medieval towns, since balconies provide much needed working and living space. Balconies also afford relief from the intense heat.*

Palacio Real, Aranjuez *(1567-18thC). View of the great outer square, framed by the principal building and its wings. It is in the Classical style and is built in a mixture of brick and stone.*

Southern Spain

Religious buildings

One of the finest *Renaissance* churches in southern Spain is **Granada Cathedral** (1528). Begun in the *Gothic* style by Enrique de Egas, it was transformed by Diego de Siloye into a classical building by the addition of *Orders* applied to the great *piers* and by a west front designed by Alonso Cano, which has three tall recessed arches the same height as the building. The **Cathedral, Jaen** (1540), is largely a classical building in both form and detail but it has a notable *Baroque* west front with flanking towers. The five-bay center is *articulated* by giant *Corinthian* columns and a bold *cornice,* crowned with *balustrading* and statuary. Above is another story, with *pedimented* center and *pinnacled parapet*. Other outstanding buildings include the **Cathedral, Malaga** (1528), a great *hall-church,* and the **Chapel, College of San Telmo** (1724-34), Seville, by Leonardo de Figueroa, which has a Baroque façade with a three-story central section flanked by coupled columns. The ground-story columns are elaborately carved with figures and medallions.

Castles & Palaces

The **Palace of Charles V, Granada** (1527-68), financèd by a tax on the Moors, was designed by Pedro Machuca to be a majestic imperial residence. It is square in plan with a central, circular courtyard with *colonnading* of superimposed *Doric* and *Ionic* Orders. The façades are boldly drawn with each bay defined by coupled columns. The *cornice* line between the two floors is projected to accommodate the line of columns, since verticality was of prime importance. The ground floor is *rusticated* throughout, save for the three central bays.

Domestic buildings

Diego de Iano's Casa de Ayuntamiento, Seville (1527-64), is a long, two-story building with a central section of three stories. The façade, divided by bays in the manner of the Lombard Renaissance, is articulated by *pilasters* on the ground story with elaborate columns above. The ornamentation is a good example of the *plateresque* style.

Cathedral, Granada
View of the Baroque façade which, with its lofty recessed arches, has much in common with a medieval cathedral screen front. The building, begun in 1528, was not completed until the 18thC and illustrates architectural development in Granada during those centuries.

Cathedral, Almeria
(1524). View of a portal, of which the cathedral has two. Because of raids by Barbary pirates, the church, which replaced a mosque, was fortified, an uncommon necessity at this period. The mixture of military and classical elements is intriguing.

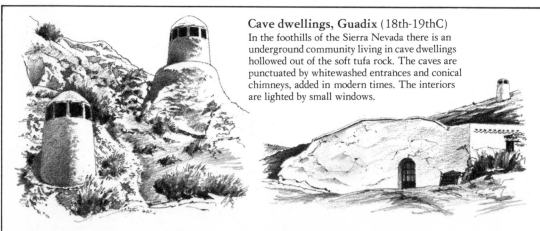

Cave dwellings, Guadix (18th-19thC)
In the foothills of the Sierra Nevada there is an underground community living in cave dwellings hollowed out of the soft tufa rock. The caves are punctuated by whitewashed entrances and conical chimneys, added in modern times. The interiors are lighted by small windows.

Portugal

Religious buildings

There are two outstanding pilgrimage churches in northern Portugal, the **Nossa Senhora dos Remédios, Lamego** (1750-60), a fine *Baroque* building, and the church of **Bom Jesus, Braga** (1784), which is *Neoclassical.* The siting of both is impressive, since they stand at the top of a steep flight of steps. The interior of the church of **San Francisco, Oporto**, a *Gothic* building, was re-modeled in the 18th century with elaborate carved and gilded woodwork. The church of **Santos Passos, Oporto** (1767-98), by Andre Ribiero Soares, has a handsome twin-towered façade, the dark stone of the architectural elements highlighted by the use of *azulejos.* Another interesting church is that of **São Pedro dos Clerigos, Oporto** (1732-50), by Nicolau Nasoni, with a curious elliptical *nave,* a product of the small site, and Baroque façade in the manner of 17th-century Italy.

Castles & Palaces

The **Convent of the Palace, Mafra** (1717), was designed by the German architect Johann Ludwig and others for King João V. It is a monumental complex, flanked at the ends by projecting wings crowned with domes and with a *basilica* punctuating the center. The architectural style is reminiscent of Carlo Fontana's buildings in Rome. The **Royal Palace, Queluz** (1747-60), Lisbon, is by Mateus Vicente de Oliveira. The façade, with its smaller number of pillars and general clarity of design, is French in style, but the flamboyant *pediments* above the windows are distinctively Italian Baroque.

Civic & Public buildings

The **University Library, Coimbra** (1716-20), designed by Gaspar Ferreira and decorated by Claudio de Laprada, consists of a basic plan of three rectangular rooms, which act as a frame for the elaborately carved and gilded decoration.

A particular feature of the Baroque buildings of northern Portugal is the use of dark granite for architectural elements which contrasts with the lighter wall surrounds. Good examples are found in the 18th-century town halls at **Braga** and **Guimarães**, where the dark brown local stone brings the curving pediments and particularly the decorative window frames alive.

Royal Palace, Queluz. *The garden façade comprises seven bays,* articulated *by giant* pilasters *springing from the ground, instead of* plinths, *while a pediment crowns the three central bays. The windows are embellished with curved pediments.*

Church, Tavira *(17thC). This ambitious façade is unusual for so small a church, since its nave plan and absence of a tower make it one of the most basic of church types. It is little more than a decorated shed, with all attention reserved for the articulation of the entrance façade.*

Church of Bom Jesus, Braga. *This* Neoclassical *church, completed in 1837, stands at the top of magnificent criss-cross flights of steps built in 1723 and enriched with sculptures and numerous fountains.*

Lobo-Machado House, Guimarães *(18thC). Of special interest on the façade are the flamboyant hoods to the windows and the bold curving pediment springing from pilasters at the sides of the façade.*

283

Denmark

Religious buildings

An outstanding example of the centralized churches of 17th-century Scandinavia is **Frelserkirke, Copenhagen** (1682), by Lambert van Haven. It is square in plan with projecting rectangles on each side, one of which, the entrance, is punctuated by a tall tower. Another interesting church is **Trinislatis Church, Copenhagen** (1637-56), which is largely traditional in form despite its *Baroque* styling. **Frederikskirche,** or the **Marble Church, Copenhagen** (1756-19thC), was designed by Nicolas-Henri Jardin, a French architect, as part of the urban design for the Place Royale. In the spirit of the monumental Baroque churches, it has a projecting temple front, behind which is an enormous dome on a high *drum* which is laid on top of a shallow inner dome. In between is a third dome, which can be seen through openings in the lower one. The inner dome is carried on two tiers of columns, which in turn form the *ambulatory.* One of the major *Neoclassical* buildings in Scandinavia is the **Var Frue Kirke, Copenhagen** (1810-29), by C.F. Hansen. It is a Roman temple in plan with Greek-style ornamentation.

Castles & Palaces

Castles were still being built in the early 16th century but they were more spacious and imposing than hitherto. The political and commercial ties with Holland are evident in such buildings as the **Castle, Hesselagergård** (1538), a rectangular block, built of brick and having corner towers and arched *gables.* The *Renaissance* spirit reached Denmark from Germany and England as well as Holland. Several castles, such as **Kronborg, Helsingør,** the model for Shakespeare's Elsinore, were remodeled in the 1570s. Another example is **Fredericksborg, Hillerod,** which was remodeled and extended in 1602 by two Dutch architects. It is the classic Dutch-style building in Denmark, with long, high-pitched roofs.

Frederikskirche, Copenhagen *The church was designed to terminate the main axial line of the plan of the palace square at Amalienborg. The chief consideration in the design was the great elevation of the dome and the* articulation *of the façade.*

Raad-og-Domhus, Copenhagen *(1803-15). The façade of this amalgam of town hall and courthouse. It is a handsome* Neoclassical *building by C.F. Hansen, notable for its fine proportions and also for its sharp articulation.*

Kronborg, Helsingør *Rebuilt in the 1570s for Frederick II, it stands at an inlet of the Baltic and was intended to symbolize Denmark's power. Built by Flemish master masons, it was the first* Renaissance *palace in Denmark and is the largest castle in Scandinavia.*

Hermitage, Dyrehaven *(1734-36). A hunting lodge, it is a masterpiece of the late* Baroque *by Laurids Thurah. The main rooms on the first floor are articulated by projecting end bays with segmented* gables, *while* pilasters, *sculptured niches and garlands provide added richness.*

The architecture of 17th-century Denmark was dominated by the Dutch *Palladian* style, with its comparatively plain façades and tall, broad roofs. A good example is the **Charlottenburg Palace, Copenhagen** (1672-83), designed by Evert Janssen, a Dutch architect. The **Castle, Clausholm** (1699-1723), consists of a high central block with long, barrack-like wings forming an entrance courtyard. The *axiality* is emphasized by a large *pedimented* central section. The style shows French influence, which is even more evident in the elegant brick house at **Christianssaede** (1690) by Nicodemus Tessin the Younger.

Fredensborg, near Copenhagen (1720), was a pleasure palace, built for Frederick IV. A domed building, it recalls the spatial sensibility of the Italian Renaissance villa but the character of roof and façade are distinctly Nordic. **Frederiksberg Castle, Copenhagen** (1697-1734), was one of a series of buildings that began a Danish classical architectural tradition. The model for the building was the Roman palazzo, while the gardens were shaped on those at Versailles.

Domestic buildings

The mansion, **Rosenholm, Jylland** (16thC), was heavily influenced by French architecture, with accentuated corner pavilions and central gateway. The *articulation,* however, with stepped gables and steep roofs, is Dutch. The **Manor House, Ledreborg** (1740), is a two-story building articulated by plain *pilasters, balustraded* end bays and a central bay with a segmented pediment. The building is given its grand appearance by wings and lodges projecting into magnificent gardens in the spirit of French classicism.

House, Kongens Nytorv *(18thC), Copenhagen. Built by the architect C.F. Harsdorff as a residence for himself, it is an unusual Neo-classical house with the scrolls rather than the volutes of the* Ionic capitals *emphasized.*

Farmhouse, Dannemore *(18thC), Lolland. View of the thatched gateway, leading into the farm-yard. Characteristic of the area is the court-yard arrangement formed by house, barn and cowsheds.*

Windmills

A characteristic of the island of Laesø in the 18th century were numerous post-mills, their name derived from the big vertical post around which the mill is turned according to the direction of the wind. Post-mills were later superseded by the so-called Dutch windmill.

Post-mill, Laesø

Post-mill, East Zealand

Farmhouse, Jordløse *(1735), Fyn. The complex comprises a rectangular range of buildings, including barns, byre, store-houses and domestic accommodation, wrapped around a central courtyard. The north side, illustrated above, is the house and has a centrally-placed porch.*

Norway

Religious buildings

Most 17th-century churches were cruciform in plan, often crowned with needle spires. At the same time the *stave* church was replaced by log construction or board and batten work. A good example is the **Church, Kvikne** (1652), North Østerdal. By the mid-18th century the *Baroque* influence was strong, particularly on interiors, as at the **Church, Sør-Fron** (1786-92), Gudbrandsal. Octagonal in plan, it is crowned by a central *lantern.* The Baroque interior has an elegant gallery, which is carried on columns and extends around the church. It was designed by Sven Aspaas, who built the elongated octagonal church at **Røros** (1784). The **Church, Kongsberg** (1740-61), is a Lutheran brick building with a flamboyant Baroque interior of carved timber with two tiers of galleries. It has a *pedimented* central section, crowned by a tall tower and *cupola.*

Domestic buildings

In the valleys of Norway, such as Hallindal, Telemark and Numedal, log construction plays a key role in vernacular building. Most farmhouses are less complex than those in the Alps and consist of a domestic unit, with loft, warehouse and storage areas. Rooms were built on a unit plan, based on the average length of a log, which was usually 20 ft. Unlike Danish farmhouses, which were planned around courtyards under one main roof, Norwegian versions were composed of separate elements arranged either in linear plan or forming spacious enclosures.

Civic & Public buildings

Following the Swedish-Norwegian Union (1814-1905), towns such as Oslo, which were provincial under Danish rule, became gradually transformed into cities of importance with Norway's greater independence. The first public works were of a monumental kind, such as the major urban project in Oslo which was formed by the **Palace** (1824-48), counterbalanced by the **Magistrates' buildings** and the **University** (1841-52), designed by C.H. Grosch. The University building has an imposing *Ionic portico.* Grosch was also responsible for the *Doric* **Exchange** (1826-28), a fine building with widely spaced columns. Buildings such as this are hybrids between the end of *Neo-classicism* and the beginnings of modern architecture.

Loft, Brøstrud *(18thC), Numedal. The farms of the mountainous midlands of Norway usually have elaborate lofts, generally in regionally distinctive forms. In this example the loft is built on high ground away from the homestead. The second floor has flanking galleries.*

Loft, Torpo *(18thC), Hallingdal. Decorative stave lofts, with elaborate fretwork galleries on the upper floor, are typical of the valley of Hallingdal. The combination of applied decorative work and simple log construction provides an attractive form of vernacular building.*

Damsgard, Bergen *(1770-95), above. A symmetrical building on a small scale, with gabled end bays, a tall pedimented central bay and a high roof crowned with a cupola. The plan is French Renaissance while the detail and decorations are pure Baroque.*

Exchange, Oslo *(1826-28). One of a series of buildings which transformed Oslo from a small provincial town into Norway's capital. It was designed by C.H. Grosch, who was probably advised by the great German architect, Karl Schinker.*

Sweden

Religious buildings

Numerous centrally planned *Baroque* churches were built in the 17th and 18th century in Sweden. Good examples are **St Katarina, Stockholm** (1656), by J. de la Vallée and Goran Adelcrantz, **Hedvig Eleonora, Stockholm** (1656), by de la Vallée, which is crowned by a high dome and was not completed until 1868, and the **Cathedral, Kalmar** (1660-1703), by Nicodemus Tessin the Elder. **Caroline Mausoleum, Stockholm** (1671), another work by Tessin the Elder, is a Greek cross in plan with a boldly drawn façade *articulated* by coupled, free-standing *Ionic* columns on a high *plinth* with a plain *attic*. The dome was added in the 1740s. **Lars Kagg Mausoleum, Floda Church** (1661), in Södermanland, is a more spacious Greek cross plan by Eric Dahlberg, with lighter elevations articulated by shallow *pilasters* and *pedimented* arms.

There are many fine village churches in Sweden. **Habo Church, Västergötland** (1720), the only timber-built church with *aisles* which have galleries, has a characteristic detached belltower with a *helm* roof. **Alvros Church, Härjedalen** (16thC-1741), is cruciform in plan with a high-pitched roof and belltower, also with a helm roof.

Castles & Palaces

The **Royal Palace, Stockholm** (1690-1753), by Nicodemus Tessin the Younger, is the largest palace in Scandinavia. The cliff-like walls are articulated on the north side by an entrance *portal* flanked by columns with a balcony above. The other façades have slightly projecting central bays, articulated by giant half-columns.

Riddarhuset, Stockholm *(c.1642-c.1656), left. View of the façade of one of the finest Dutch Palladian buildings in Sweden. The building is of particular note for its giant* pilasters, *their smoothness finely balanced by the richly ornamented bays between them.*

Kina Slott, Drottningholm, *right. This small palace was designed in a Chinese Rococo style, with rippled eaves line, decorative ridges, a polygonal center bay and curving wings, to which are attached small pavilions.*

Cathedral, Kalmar *A fine, centralized church with an elongated Greek cross plan. The four sides are* articulated *by tall towers, a pedimented main entrance, Palladian in style, and with pediments over the apses at the transverse ends. The church has an outstanding* Baroque *interior.*

Belltowers

A characteristic of late 17th- and early 18th-C rural Sweden and Finland is the detached belltower, many of which were added to medieval churches. They are usually several stories in height, either square or octagonal in plan and are crowned with a *cupola*.

Fröso,
near Östersund

Jukkasjärvi,
near Kiruna

Sweden

Dutch architectural influence was strong in Scandinavia in the late 17th century. One of the best examples is the Nobles' Assembly building, the **Riddarhuset, Stockholm** (*c.* 1642-*c.* 1656, see p.287). By Simon de la Vallée, and continued by the Dutch architect, Joost Vingboons, who remodeled the façade in the most handsome Dutch *Palladian* style and gave it a central *pediment* and detached wings.

Civic & Public buildings

The **Botanicum, Uppsala** (1788), has a plain main block which is brought sharply alive by the addition of a powerful *Doric* temple front. Ancient Greek architecture belongs essentially to the more solid temple where mass, rather than space, was of primary importance and this dramatic play between mass and space is also to be seen in the **School, Härnösand** (1790s).

Commercial & Industrial buildings

The **Exchange, Stockholm** (1767-76), by E. Palmstedt, has a projecting center bay with a pedimented *portico* set within it. The ground floor is *arcaded* and *rusticated*, with delicate molding for the first story windows. Coupled columns *articulate* the ends of the central bay, which is Doric on the ground floor and *Ionic* above. The **East Indian Company Building, Gothenburg** (*c.* 1740), by Carl Harleman, is a monumental edifice with pedimented central bay, while the flanking sides are each articulated by small projecting bays with segmented pediments.

School, Härnösand *A fine* Neoclassical *building of simple geometry with bold pillars in the porch, somewhat like a domed* rotunda, *which forms a protruding semicircular addition to the main part of the building block.*

Town Hall, Sigtuna *(18thC). A utilitarian structure but with concern shown for symmetry, which is emphasized by the central* pedimented *door and the* cupola *crowning the roof. Simple buildings such as this influenced the immigrant carpenters in North America.*

Botanicum, Uppsala *View of the front façade by L. J. Deprez showing how the wide, dominating* Doric *temple front adds monumentality to an otherwise plain block. The low pitched pediment adds to the overall effect of vast scale.*

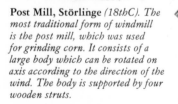

Post Mill, Störlinge *(18thC). The most traditional form of windmill is the post mill, which was used for grinding corn. It consists of a large body which can be rotated on axis according to the direction of the wind. The body is supported by four wooden struts.*

Storehouse, Alvros *(16thC). Farm buildings in Sweden are either of the courtyard type, with half-timber construction, or are separate log constructions in which individual buildings, such as storehouses and barns, are clustered together to form a more adjustable arrangement.*

Finland

Religious buildings

A characteristic of country churches of the province of Ostrobothnia is their steep, *shingle*-covered pointed roofs. A good example is the **Church, Tornio** (1684-86), by Matti Härmä. The interior has a decoratively painted and *vaulted* timber ceiling. The detached belltower, the oldest in Finland, was built in 1687. Another church of note in the province is that at **Nurmo** (1772), which has a giant, timber belltower in three stages, standing on the edge of the village street.

The **Church, Lapua** (1827), Ostrobothnia, is a huge timber building, cruciform in plan and with an octagonal dome on a high *drum*. Designed by C.L. Engel (and possibly by Heikki Kuorikoski), it has a characteristic three-story belltower. It was the first of a series of churches of this type designed by Engel, who also built the **Cathedral, Helsinki** (1830-40).

The last great *Neo-classical* building in Finland is the **Orthodox Church, Turku** (1846), also by Engel. It has a circular dome with a *cupola* and a bold *Doric portico*. It owes much to the **Church, Hämeenlinna** (1798), by L.J. Desprez, which was the first church in Finland to be built in the Neoclassical style.

Domestic buildings

One of the most interesting of the country houses is that at **Viurila**. The main house, a simple *pedimented* two-story building (1804-11), was by C.F. Bassi. The most interesting section, however, is the stables, added by Engel in about 1840, which are *articulated* by extremely bold pedimented Doric porticos. Engel was also responsible for the **Manor House, Vuojoki** (1836), Ostrobothnia, a fine Neoclassical building three stories in height, with *rusticated* ground story.

Civic & Public buildings

The **Town Hall, Hamina** (1798), by Carl Brockman, is an elegant classical building with a rusticated basement and projecting center bay crowned with a pediment. The fine tower was added by Engel in 1840. The beginnings of the Neoclassical style in Finland took place with the **Old Academy** (1802-15) by C.C. Gjörwell and C.F. Bassi, and the **New Academy** (1829-33), by Bassi, both in **Turku**. The former is a monumental block, relieved on the main façade by a projecting pedimented central bay with a rusticated ground story. The New Academy has a restrained two-story façade with projecting central bay, and a rusticated ground floor supporting a monumental *colonnaded* portico without a pediment. The colonnade is enriched with a decorative *frieze*.

The major civic project is the **Senate Square, Helsinki** (1816-40), which marks the transformation of the city into the nation's capital in 1812. Designed by Engel, the focal point is the **Cathedral** (1830-40), which stands on a high, stepped terrace on one side of the square. Cruciform in plan, each arm is articulated by porticos. The center has a tall drum with half-columns and dome, while two pavilions mark the edge of the terrace facing the square.

Belltower, Ruoko-lahti *(1752). With the development of the cruciform church in Sweden and Finland in the 18thC, the traditional belltower was replaced by a three-story tower. A characteristic of eastern Finland is the octagonal belltower.*

University Library, Helsinki *(1836-45). The building has a domed central room, two stories in height, with recessed entrance porch on one side and with offices on the other. Flanking it are two reading rooms, with* vaulted *roofs carried on plain* Corinthian *columns.*

Church, Hämeenlinna *A bold,* stucco-*faced* Neoclassical *building, it has a massive dome, intended to resemble the Pantheon, Rome. The recessed portal, with its flanking columns, is Egyptian in style, a popular form at the time. The tower and* cupola *were added in 1837. The church was enlarged in 1892.*

Loft, Vanaja *(18thC), Karelia. A feature of northern Karelia is a detached farmhouse with a loft built of square-shaved logs with a galleried upper floor. The loft was both a repository for valued objects and a summer house with sleeping accommodation.*

Russia

Religious buildings

The *Renaissance* style was introduced into Russia in the late 15th and early 16th century by north Italian architects, who had been invited primarily as consultants for military projects. While the new style affected buildings in **Moscow**, such as the **Cathedral of St Michael the Archangel** (1504), it had little influence elsewhere in Russia. Even in Moscow, however, innovations usually comprised ornament applied to existing structures rather than new structures themselves, for *Byzantine* forms remained general.

The *Baroque* style first made its appearance in a series of city churches, such as the **Church of the Nativity of the Virgin, Moscow** (1649-52). These Baroque churches were usually built by the guilds. The architecture gradually became more sculptural and extravagant, but the basic Byzantine forms persisted. Late 17th-century Baroque replaced sculptural and asymmetrical buildings with more refined and wholly symmetrical buildings. A good example is the **Church of the Virgin of the Intercession, Moscow** (*c.* 1690-93), symmetrical in plan and consisting of a cube with *apses*. It stands on a high terrace and flights of steps in the Baroque style ascend on three sides of the building. The crowning tower is built in octagonal stages. Numerous monasteries, such as the medieval **Monastery of the Holy Trinity, Zagorsk** (15thC), had new buildings erected within their walls during the late 17th and early 18th century. Most of these monasteries, such as **St John the Baptist, Zagorsk** (1693-99), were Baroque in style, an influence derived from Moscow.

Cathedral of St Michael the Archangel, Moscow
Designed by a Venetian architect, the elegant three-bay façade is articulated by classical pilasters, with great shell motifs decorating the lunettes of the end bays. The basic form, however, is Byzantine.

St John the Baptist, Zagorsk, *right. The monastery from the south east. The church was built over the main east gates of the city and is an outstanding Baroque building with a simple geometry of rectangular blocks, built one on top of the other.*

Monastery of the Holy Trinity, Zagorsk *The five-stage belltower is in the Baroque style and is articulated by pilasters and by coupled columns. The tower was added to the main building between 1741 and 1770 and it seems to foreshadow James Gibbs's London church towers.*

Church of the Nativity of the Virgin, Moscow *(1649-52), left. The roofs and façades of 17th-C Baroque church buildings, as in this example, became much more highly decorated, unlike smaller medieval churches.*

Church of the Archangel Michael, Moscow *(1690-1739), right. Standing in the Monastery of the Savior, it is a tower church with square lower stages and octagonal upper stages and is articulated by pilasters.*

Castles & Palaces

Many monasteries, kremlins and towns were extended and remodeled on *picturesque* lines in the late 17th century. An outstanding example is the **Kremlin, Rostov** (*c.* 1670-83), a monumental palace complex which had decorated round towers added to its walls. Within the walls numerous ecclesiastical and domestic buildings were built and arranged in a distinctly asymmetrical form. In most cases decorative emphasis was given to the exterior rather than the interior of buildings and often included tile and brick patterns.

In the 18th century many fine places were built for the aristocracy in **Leningrad**. Most of the architects were from western Europe. Examples include the vast **Winter Palace** (1732-36) by Rastrelli, which is the most important work in the city and has a monumental river front, boldly *articulated*; the **Marble Palace** (1768-85) by Antonio Rinaldi, an Italian architect from Rome, and the **Stroganov Palace** (1747-53), another work by Rastrelli.

Civic & Public buildings

The major public buildings in **Leningrad** are *Neoclassical* in style and include the **Academy of Sciences** (1783-89), a *Palladian*-style building by Giacomo Quarenghni. Other important works include the **Admiralty** (1806-23), a basically *Greek Revival* building on to which are piled *Gothic* and *Baroque* elements, and the **General Staff Headquarters** (1819-29), which consists of a monumental three-story building in a wide crescent shape into which a giant Roman-style triumphal arch was inserted.

Church of the Virgin of the Intercession, Moscow *A magnificent composition representing the last of Baroque Russian architecture. Pyramidal in form, it stands on a high terrace with an* arcaded *base.*

Church of the Twelve Apostles, Kremlin *(1635-56), Moscow, right. Part of the Palace of the Patriarch, it is of cruciform plan crowned by five decorative domes, of which these are two, as in medieval examples. The church stands on a plinth above two ceremonial entrance gates.*

Kremlin, Rostov, *below. The round towers added to many kremlins, monasteries and town walls, such as in this example, were by the late 17thC more for decoration than for defense. The exuberant decoration of the Baroque style was eminently suitable for such embellishments.*

St Nicholas, Suzdal *(1766), above. A pleasantly uncomplicated church built of wood, it has a* cantilevered *gallery and steeply-pitched plank-covered roof with* gabled *ends. The axiality of the church is emphasized by the central, covered staircase.*

291

Czechoslovakia

Religious buildings

The early churches, such as **Svatý Mǒric, Olomouc** (1412-1540), were largely traditional in plan. Most of the later churches of interest belong to the late 17th century and to the 18th century, with Italian *Baroque* represented by examples such as the **Piarist Church, Kroměřiž** (1737). French Baroque is seen in many churches, notably the **Church of the Crusader Knights, Prague** (1679-88), by Jean-Baptiste Mathey, a handsome building elegantly *articulated* with *pilasters* in low relief. It is cruciform in plan with a central oval shape, crowned by a dome. By the early 18th century, however, the major influence in Czechoslovakia was the Baroque of Austria and southern Germany, particularly in the many buildings by the Dientzenhofer family, such as the **Schloss Church, Smirice** (1699-1713), by Christopher Dientzenhofer. **St John Nepomuk, Prague** (1730-39), by Kilian Dientzenhofer, Christopher Dientzenhofer's son, has a magnificent twin-towered façade with a convex center articulated by two giant columns. His design for **St Nicholas, Prague** (1703-52), is more monumental. A centrally-planned church, it has an unusual façade with raised center flanked by coupled columns, each with its own *pediment,* while low pedimented bays link the façade to flanking twin towers. He also designed the **Magdalen, Carlsbad** (1733-36).

Castles & Palaces

Early castles, such as that at **Kostelec** (1549-60), which has a central courtyard and round corner towers, were traditional in form. Many later castles, however, have Italianate *arcading,* for when the *Renaissance* came to Czechoslovakia it was dominated largely by Italian artists and architects. Examples include those at **Jindřichuv Hradec** (*c.* 1580), **Litomyšl** (1568-73) and at **Bučovice** (1567-82). Of the Baroque buildings the **Schloss Troja, Prague** (1679-96), by Mathey, is a particularly handsome building with remarkable classical wall surfaces which are enriched with elaborately sculptured *capitals,* main *portal* and flamboyant double staircase.

Piarist Church, Kroměřiž *A particularly fine* Baroque *church, it consists of a domed* rotunda *and twin-towered main façade with a convex center. The exterior of the entire building is* articulated *by* pilasters.

Svatý Mǒric, Olomouc, *right. A handsome* hall-church, *it has a single central* nave *with flanking* aisles. *The molded pillars are traditional in concept while the overall spatial quality of the interior with its decorative geometry has a classical simplicity.*

Schloss Church, Smirice, *left. This church by Christopher Dientzenhofer has an elaborate play of convex and concave curves, giving rise to startling* pediments *and unusual roofing. The stuccoed body of the church stands on an elegant,* rusticated plinth.

Schloss Troja, Prague *An outstanding Baroque building, it has a high central structure with low, flanking wings. The main building is articulated by giant pilasters standing on high plinths, while an elaborate curved double staircase ascends to the main entrance of the building.*

House, Slavonica *(16thC), right. Numerous houses in Bohemia and Moravia, such as the example here, have this type of* gable parapet, *in which units with semicircular and segmented tops are built up in steps.*

Poland

Religious buildings

Poland is rich in religious buildings. The **Sigismund Chapel, Cracow** (1519-33), one of the finest of east European chapels, became the prototype for a series of centralized chapels of the Polish *Renaissance*. Designed by Bartolommeo Berecci, it is a stylish classical building with a windowless, cube-shaped base crowned by an octagonal *drum*. Round windows in the drum light the interior. The Jesuits's Church of **SS Peter and Paul, Cracow** (1605-19), by Giovanni Trevano, is the outstanding *Baroque* church in Poland. Roman Baroque in style, it has a handsome *pedimented* façade and a dome over the *crossing*.

Wawel Cathedral, Cracow *(16th-C). View of the Vasa Chapel and the Sigismund Chapel, on the southside of the cathedral. These two centralized buildings are arranged symmetrically around the principal entrance to the cathedral.*

Castles & Palaces

The **Royal Castle, Cracow** (*c.* 1502), by Franciscus Florentinus, had a north and west wing added between 1507 and 1536. The castle also has a magnificent *arcaded* court façade in the Italian style. Many castles were given additions in the form of classical gates in the 16th century. An example is the **Castle, Legnica** (16thC), which had a monumental Italianate gate added in 1532. The **Castle, Brzeg** (*c.* 1530), also has a handsome sculptured gatehouse, added in 1552. The decorative style is that of Renaissance Lombardy. Many of these gatehouses were enriched with sculptured portraits of their owners or of allegorical figures.

Celejowski House, Kazimierz Dolny *Many 17th-C private houses such as this in Kazimierz Dolny were characterized by elaborate ornamentation, including mannerist obelisks with Flemish-style strapwork and fretwork.*

Domestic buildings

One of the most attractive houses in **Danzing** is the **Golden House** (1609-18), which was designed by Abraham van den Blocke and is *articulated* by decorated *pilasters* and sculpted *friezes*. There are some fine Renaissance houses in the port town of **Kazimierz Dolny**, including **St Christopher** (1615) and the **Celejowski House** (*c.* 1635). Their façades are brought alive by elaborate *mannerist* ornamentation and often by fine pedimented and *pinnacled parapets*.

Arsenal, Danzig *(1600-05). A monumental building, it is entered by way of two impressive portals, of which this is one. The façade and roof-line are embellished with statuary, examples in this building of how architectural ideas were absorbed from northern Europe.*

Golden Gate, Danzig *(1612-14). Part Roman triumphal arch and part Italian palazzo, the gate is modeled on classical examples and has a large central arch and flanking pedestrian passages. The verticality is emphasized by free-standing columns on high plinths.*

293

New England

Religious buildings

The New England meetinghouse is a unique architectural contribution of the British colonies. The Puritans rejected the Anglican church plan with the altar at the end of the *nave* for a centralized plan with the pulpit as the key element. This more spacious and flexible design also served as a meeting place for civic affairs. The oldest surviving example is the **Old Ship Meetinghouse, Hingham** (*c.* 1681), Massachusetts. Other examples include the meetinghouse at **Sandown, New Hampshire** (1774), and **Rocky Hill Meetinghouse, Amesbury** (1785), Massachusetts. The most important of these churches to be built in New England prior to the Revolution (1776) was the **First Baptist Meetinghouse, Providence** (1774-75), Rhode Island, by Joseph Brown, based on the design of James Gibbs's London churches.

The **Old North Church, Boston** (1723), Massachusetts, by William Price, was the first church in the British colonies to adopt the rectangular block form, punctuated by an attached west tower, established by Sir Christopher Wren in London. The marvelous interior is a simplified version of Wren's St James's, London.

The **Touro Synagogue, Newport** (1759-63), Rhode Island, by Peter Harrison, was the first synagogue to be built in America. The plain, almost *Neoclassical* exterior cloaks one of the finest interiors of 18th-century America. The architecture is not distinctively that of a synagogue, but more an elegant room adapted for the purpose. Harrison also designed **King's Chapel, Boston** (1749-58), Massachusetts. It was the first church to be built of stone in America, a rectangle with a *hipped roof* and an unfinished tower surrounded by a giant *Ionic portico* in timber. Also of interest by Harrison is **Christ Church, Cambridge** (1761), Massachusetts.

Meetinghouse, Sandown *Such buildings were both the civic and religious centers of community life. This one is a simple square hall with doors on axis. The classical elements were modified to accommodate local carpenters' skills.*

Old Ship Meetinghouse, Hingham *Originally square in plan, this meetinghouse was extended in the mid-18thC. Of particular technical interest is the construction of the roof, which is carried on three huge trusses. Ships' carpenters probably built the church.*

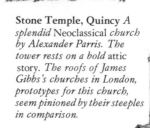

Stone Temple, Quincy *A splendid Neoclassical church by Alexander Parris. The tower rests on a bold attic story. The roofs of James Gibbs's churches in London, prototypes for this church, seem pinioned by their steeples in comparison.*

Round Church, Richmond *(1813), Vermont. The church is a novel interpretation of the classic centralized church type by a carpenter and builder, William Rhodes. The only concession to style are the* pilasters *and* pediments *of the entrances and the crowning* cupola.

Church of Christ, Lancaster, *left. A masterpiece of early American architecture, by Charles Bulfinch. The building has a geometry of squares, triangles, cubes and cylinders beautifully combined together and enriched by Flemish bond brickwork.*

Asher Benjamin, the author of the first American handbook for carpenters and builders, "The Country Builder's Assistant" (1797), built several fine churches, including **Old West Church, Boston** (1806), Massachusetts, in brick, and the **Old South Church, Windsor** (1798), Vermont, in timber. The latter was a reference for the **First Congregational Church, Bennington** (1806), Vermont, by Lavius Fillmore, the focal point of a beautiful New England green. It is typical of many provincial churches with a handsome geometry built up like a set of children's blocks. The **Congregational Church, Middlebury** (1809), Vermont, considered to be Fillmore's masterpiece, was greatly influenced by Benjamin.

The **Church of Christ, Lancaster** (1816), Massachusetts, is a masterpiece by Charles Bulfinch. The play of solids and voids has a simplicity matching orthodox modern architecture where each element retains its own individual form.

The change of building materials from timber to stone brought increased scale and use of texture. The monumental quality of the **Stone Temple, Quincy** (1828), Massachusetts, would have been impossible to emulate in wood. **St Paul's Cathedral, Boston** (1820), Massachusetts, by Alexander Parris, is a fine *Greek Revival* building with a lofty Ionic temple façade raised on a high *podium* reached by steps running the whole length of the façade.

The **First Parish Congregational Church, Brunswick** (1845-46), Maryland, is interesting, not only for its highly unorthodox interior with a *hammer-beam roof* but also because its architect, Richard Upjohn, had a great understanding of the nature of building materials and his designs help to express their qualities.

In a bizarre vein, the **Grove Street Cemetery Lodge, New Haven** (1845-46), Connecticut, is an Egyptian revival curio.

First Congregational Church, Bennington *Lavius Fillmore, the architect of this church, was inspired by Asher Benjamin's handbook for carpenters and builders, "The Country Builder's Assistant" (1797). He utilized vernacular skills to weld together the elements of his designs.*

Touro Synagogue, Newport *Considered the masterpiece of Peter Harrison, the synagogue is basically a rectangle sited at an angle to the street. The austerity of the design is complemented by an* Ionic *porch.*

First Parish Congregational Church, Brunswick *One of the sharp* lancet *windows of the church, which were designed by Richard Upjohn to enhance the qualities of carpentry.*

Trinity Church, Brooklyn *(1771), Connecticut. An Anglican church, broadly in the form of a meetinghouse but more rectangular and with an* aisleless nave. *The building is simple with a stark pediment.*

Grove Street Cemetery Lodge, New Haven, *right. The Egyptian style was much in favor for entrances to cemeteries such as this. Its design combines* temple, propylon *and portico.*

New England

Domestic buildings

The prominent siting of **Parson Capen House, Topsfield** (*c.* 1683), Massachusetts, on the common near the meetinghouse, shows that the parson was held in as high regard in North America as he was in the Old World. The house itself is a fine example of European medieval *timber-framing* techniques, combined with some aspects of the hall house of 14th- and 15th-century England.

The **Hunter House, Newport** (1748), Rhode Island, is an outstanding example of colonial American architecture. The distinctive gambrel roof, a form of curved *mansard roof* with a *ridge gable,* is characteristic of many 18th-century houses in Newport. Other good examples in Newport are found in **Washington Street** and **Pelham Street.** The designs of such houses as the **Wentworth-Gardner House, Portsmouth** (1760), New Hampshire, are more concerned with architecturally fashionable features, even to the extent of imitating in wood the projecting *quoins* and *rusticated* masonry of some late 17th-century stone-built English houses. **Moffat-Ladd House,** Portsmouth (1763), New Hampshire, a fine timber-frame building, has an elegant porch and swan-neck *pediments* to the first floor windows. The **Old Manse, Deerfield** (1768), Massachusetts, is another timber-frame building with bold wooden quoins. The **Williams House, Deerfield** (1756), Massachusetts, has a swan-neck pediment above the door. Also of interest is the **Otis Residence, Boston** (1796-97).

By the late 18th century the *Federal Style* emerged from the early *Colonial Style,* which was largely vernacular, rather like the *Adam Style* emerging from English *Palladianism.* Characteristic features of the Federal Style are low-pitched roofs, smooth façades, large glazed areas and *portals* with elliptical fanlights and flanking side lights. Providence, Rhode Island, was one of the main architectural centers during the Federal Style period. The **Brown Residence, Providence** (1786-88), designed by Joseph Brown, the brother of the owner, is a good example. Another Federal Style house is the **Ruggles House, Columbia Falls** (1818), Maine, by Aaron Sherman.

Shortbridge House, Portsmouth *(c. 1770), New Hampshire. An outstanding feature of many houses in Portsmouth is an entrance with* pilasters *and* swan-neck *pediment.*

Parson Capen House, Topsfield, *above. This is an impressively large wooden house, which is medieval both in structure and plan with the hall and parlor divided by the chimney and lobby. The overlaps at first floor* jetty *and eaves increase its grandeur.*

Vassall House, Cambridge *(1759), Massachusetts, right. Enlarged by Henry Wadsworth Longfellow in the 19thC, this house has a handsome façade with a pedimented section* articulated *by a deep* cornice *and giant* Ionic *pilasters.*

Wentworth-Gardner House, Portsmouth *A typical New England house of the 18thC clearly modeled on the characteristic small house of 17th-C England. Although the house is built in wood, the details are designed to simulate the quality of stone.*

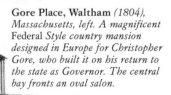

Gore Place, Waltham *(1804), Massachusetts, left. A magnificent* Federal *Style country mansion designed in Europe for Christopher Gore, who built it on his return to the state as Governor. The central bay fronts an oval salon.*

Like the Adam Style in England, the Federal Style came into its own in interior decoration. One of the finest exponents of the style was a wood carver, Samuel McIntire, who brought a new delicacy and sensitivity to the restrained geometry of Federal interiors. He spent his whole life working for the wealthy merchants in the seaport of **Salem**. Good examples include the **Pierce-Nichols House** (1782) and the **Pingree House** (1805). The latter was a prototype for many houses in the coastal communities of New England, such as the **Nickels-Sortwell House, Wiscasset** (1807-12), Maine, and the **Thomas Poynton Ives House, Providence** (1806), Rhode Island. In rural New England the traditional house was restyled with applied ornamentation, as in the **Sloane House, Williamstown** (1801), Massachusetts, in imitation of those along the coast. Interesting variations on the Federal Style are to be found in houses such as **Sears House, Boston** (1816), Massachusetts, by Alexander Parris, and the **Larkin House, Portsmouth** (1815), New Hampshire, with its ancient Greek-style details.

Dowley House, Worcester *(1842), Massachusetts. Built for a leather merchant by Elias Carter, this mansion evokes the style of a plantation house of the South. The sides are boarded and the timber front imitates* rusticated *masonry.*

Pingree House, Salem. *The simple brick façade of this house has a finely proportioned, semi-circular* portico *with an elliptical fanlight engaging the house at the junction of cornice and* string-course.

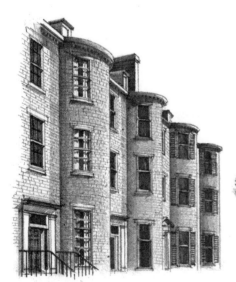

Louisburg Square, Boston *(c. 1840), Massachusetts. The concept of the bow-fronted* Regency *town house, as in Brighton, England, was used to provide an urban elegance to the cities of New England, as here in Boston.*

Hunter House, Newport *(1748), Rhode Island. An elegant,* gambrel-*roofed house with a decorative* Baroque *portal. The fine proportions of the main façade are enhanced by the horizontal boarding, just as a stone wall might have been enhanced by* rustication *in Europe.*

Kingscote, Newport *(1838), Rhode Island. This building by Richard Upjohn is an outstanding example of the American early* Gothic *villa, with its broken roof line, decorative* gables *and asymmetrical plan. The wing to the left of the illustration was added by McKim, Mead and White in 1880.*

New England

Many 19th-century houses in New England reflect a strong interest in the ancient classical world. The admiration for Greece is epitomized by such buildings as the **Russell House, Middletown** (1828-30), Connecticut, which is in the form of a giant *prostyle Corinthian* temple. The pure ancient temple form was usually modified by the addition of wings which provided both additional accommodation and a more flexible design, as in the **Brown House, Old Mystic** (1835), Connecticut. This impressive building with its elegant *Ionic portico* became a prototype for many houses in the expanding sections of the country, as seen in the **Wilcox-Cutts House, Orwell** (1843), Vermont, and the **Alsop House, Middletown** (1836-40), Connecticut, a fine *Greek Revival* villa with deep *eaves* and decorative *frieze*. Other Greek Revival houses include the **Ransom House, Castleton** (*c.* 1840), Vermont, by T. R. Drake, and **Gale House, Newport** (1834), Rhode Island.

The picturesque movement in late 18th- and early 19th-century England, with its emphasis on irregularity in form and outline, had considerable effect on the architecture of the New World via various publications. Cottage villas in the rural *Gothic* style became fashionable. Good examples are the **Rotch House, New Bedford** (1843), Massachusetts, by A. J. Davis, the author of "Rural Residences," published in 1837, and **Roseland Cottage, Woodstock** (1846), Connecticut, by Joseph Wells. Characteristic features are molded hoods to the windows, the pointed arch and curvilinear *gingerbread* trim along gables and eaves. Many timber houses, including the latter, were finished in board and batten. **Soper House, South Royalton** (*c.* 1850), Vermont, is an example of simple carpenters' Gothic.

Civic & Public buildings

The **Old Colony House, Newport** (1739), Rhode Island, designed by Richard Munday, a master carpenter, is an amalgam of vernacular vigor and classical restraint. The central *portal* with balcony and broken *pediment* above add a *Baroque* flourish. The **Connecticut State House, Hartford** (1793-96), now the City Hall, by Charles Burchfield, has an *ashlar* ground story and is crowned by an elegant Baroque *cupola*.

The major building project of the period in New England was the **State House, Boston** (1795-98), by Charles Bulfinch. Although a monumental building, it is less boldly *articulated* and substantial than its *Neoclassical* models in London, especially Somerset House.

The **Redwood Library, Newport** (1748-50), Rhode Island, was designed by Peter Harrison, a prominent architect of colonial America. A Yorkshireman, he had seen the buildings of Lord Burlington and William Kent in England. The library was his first building and his use of the temple form was the earliest in America.

College buildings of interest include **Connecticut Hall, Yale University** (1750-52), New Haven, Connecticut, and **University Hall, Brown University** (1770), Providence, Rhode Island, by Joseph Brown. **Bulfinch Hall, Phillips**

Russell House, Middletown *A mansion for a rich trader by Ithiel Town and Alexander Davis. The social aspirations of the owner seem to be symbolized in the giant* Corinthian *temple form.*

Cowles House, Farmington *(1780), Connecticut. This elegant Venetian-style window with a superimposed balcony crowns the columned portico of this beautiful example of colonial architecture in wood by William Sprats. The entrance is articulated by pilasters.*

Roseland Cottage, Woodstock *This summer house by Joseph Wells for a wealthy silk merchant is a timber-built* Gothic *patchwork of oriel windows, decorative bargeboards and verandahs supported by ornamented trellises. The entrance has a cantilevered canopy with a surmounted crest of fleurs-de-lis.*

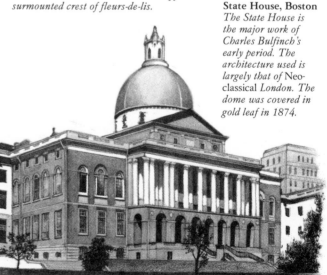

State House, Boston *The State House is the major work of Charles Bulfinch's early period. The architecture used is largely that of Neoclassical London. The dome was covered in gold leaf in 1874.*

Academy (1818-19), Andover, Massachusetts, is a handsome brick building by Bulfinch, with pedimented central bay and crowning *cupola*. Nearby is **Pearson Hall** (1817-18), also by Bulfinch, with a shallow central recess and a *balustrade* above the eaves. The **Atheneum, Nantucket** (1847), Massachusetts, is a *Greek Revival* building in wood. The double pedimented façade has a recessed porch articulated by two Ionic columns and flanking *pilasters*.

Commercial & Industrial buildings

The **Market House, Newport** (1761-62), Rhode Island, based on an engraving of Old Somerset House, London, was Harrison's last project. His intention was to revitalize his native architecture, taking inspiration from Colen Campbell's "Vitruvius Britannicus," a treatise on Neoclassicism. **Quincy Market, Boston** (1825), Massachusetts, by Alexander Parris, is a long horizontal, two-story block with a temple portico at each end and a raised central section covered by a low dome. The building was cleverly converted into a shopping mall in the 1970s. The **Arcade, Providence** (1828), Rhode Island, is one of the earliest enclosed shopping streets in New England, a forerunner of the enclosed shopping malls of modern North America.

Examples of early 19th-century industrial communities are the **Merrimack Company Buildings, Lowell** (*c.* 1825), Massachusetts, and the textile community of **Harrisville** (*c.* 1830-*c.* 1840), including two surviving mills and brick housing around an elegantly spired church and pond. In textile villages the mills dominated rather than the meetinghouse, as shown at **Amoskeag Mills and Housing, Manchester** (*c.* 1840), New Hampshire.

State Capitol, Montpelier *(1838), Vermont. The giant Doric portico of the Capitol building was based on a reconstruction of the Thesion, Athens (465 BC). Originally by Ammi B. Young, the Capitol was rebuilt in 1859 following a fire.*

Old Colony House, Newport, *below. Once the seat of state government, this building's charm lies in its provinciality. The façade is punctuated by a truncated pediment and the roof has a central cupola.*

Redwood Library, Newport, *right. A wooden building by Peter Harrison that imitates the nature of stone, both in the scale of the Doric temple portico and the decorative rustication.*

Market House, Newport *An elegant building by Harrison, heavily indebted to an engraving of Old Somerset House, London, from which he took the ground story* arcading *and the articulation above.*

Barn, Hancock *(1826), Massachusetts, right. A barn built by Shakers (an extreme Puritan sect) around stalls for horses and cows, with a manure pit below and a circulation ramp for wagons.*

Mid-Atlantic States

Religious buildings

Christ Church, Philadelphia (1727-54), Pennsylvania, a handsome *Colonial Style* church, was based on English architectural pattern books. **St Paul's Chapel, New York City** (1766 and 1794), by Thomas McBean, is one of the finest examples of the style in the city. Also of similar date is **St Mary's Chapel, Baltimore** (1806), Maryland, by Maximilien Godefroy, a strange amalgam of ancient classical features and a small *Gothic* chapel.

Baltimore Cathedral (1804 -*c.* 1818), Maryland, by Benjamin Latrobe, has a classical Roman design. A traditional Latin cross plan, covered by a large dome, which has an internal *drum* reaching the floor of the church with alternating small and large arched openings. The façade is a giant *Ionic portico* pushed in front of twin towers with a circular top stage. **Christ Church, Washington** D.C. (1808), by Latrobe, is an early American *Gothic Revival* building, but despite the Gothic detail the simplicity of forms has much in common with the architect's *Neoclassical* buildings. **St Paul's Episcopal Church, Troy** (1826-28), and **St Luke's, Rochester** (1824-28), both in New York, are notable early Gothic Revival churches.

Trinity Church, New York City (1846), is a Gothic Revival church by Richard Upjohn, who was born in Dorset, England, trained as a carpenter, surveyor and draftsman and emigrated to America in 1829. His mechanical arts education suited the requirements of the Gothic Revival, and his use of decoration was inspired by the influential works on church design by Augustus Pugin. Other notable buildings by Upjohn include **St Thomas's Episcopal Church, Amenia Union** (1849-51), New York, a simple, brick vernacular building; **St John in the Wilderness, Copake Falls** (1851-52), New York, similarly simple but of board and batten with a side entrance porch, and the Gothic Revival **St Mary's, Burlington** (1846-48), New Jersey.

Domestic buildings

In contrast to the delicate, *timber-frame* buildings of New England, the brick and stone houses built in and around **Philadelphia**, Pennsylvania, are more boldy *articulated,* in a manner reminiscent of James Gibbs, whose work was published in America. Examples are **Mount Pleasant** (1761-62) and **Clivedon** (1761), both in Philadelphia.

The **White House, Washington D.C.** (1792-1800), by James Hoban, is a monumental rectangle raised above a *rusticated* ground story, with a large, circular Ionic *colonnade* surrounding a semicircular bay. The **Octagon, Washington** D.C. (1800), by William Thornton, is a handsome building designed to fit an awkward plot.

In 1836, in **Andalusia, Pennsylvania,** Thomas U. Walter undertook a project to encase an existing 18th-century house in a Greek *Doric* temple. Such classicism was popular and there are numerous *Greek Revival* mansions in New York. Good examples are **Rose Hill, Geneva** (1839); **Hyde Hall, Cooperstown** (1811-13), and the **Hunting House, Sag Harbor** (1845).

Whalers' Church, Sag Harbor *(1844), New York. This strange Egyptian-style building by Minard Lafever is rather like a temple pylon. Originally it had a steeple like a spyglass, but this was demolished by a hurricane-force wind in 1938.*

St Thomas's Episcopal Church, Amenia Union, *above. An attractively simple building by Richard Upjohn, with the section of the* nave *displayed externally by a gable. The chimney-like belfry and the projecting porch emphasize the main axis.*

Trinity Church, New York City *The epitome of the romantic era in America, Trinity Church is a handsome* Gothic Revival *building now dwarfed by the multi-story buildings of Wall Street. Even so, the* crocketed *spire retains its grandeur.*

St Mary's Chapel, Baltimore *By Maximilien Godefroy, the church curiously combines* Gothic *chapel with* blind arcading, *a triumphal Roman arch articulated by engaged columns, and a deep cornice with an* attic *story.*

Hyde Hall, Coopers-town, *above. An impressive* Neo-classical *building by Edward Hooker. The hall is one story except for the projecting* Doric portico, *which has a* pedimented *upper story set back in line with the main façade.*

Rectory, Grace Church, New York City *(1847), right. By James Renwick Jr, it is based largely on the works of Augustus Pugin, the English Gothic Revival theorist. Features to note are elegant* oriel windows, *and* pinnacled *gables.*

Christ Church, Washington D.C. *This is one of the earliest Gothic Revival churches in America, by Benjamin Latrobe. The Gothic style is, however, relatively austere, with each volume simply expressed and the details arranged in as plain a way as possible.*

Mount Pleasant, Philadelphia, *above. A fine classical building with a brick* string course, quoins, *and a bold, pedimented central section to the façade. The* hipped roof *is dominating and has a surmounting* balustrade.

House, Andulasia *The huge* Doric peristyle, *made of timber, was wrapped around an existing 18th-C farmhouse to complete a Neo-classical design by Thomas U. Walter and the owner of the house, Nicholas Biddle, himself a classicist.*

Delamater House, Rhinebeck *(1843), New York, right. A board and batten house by Alexander Davis which exemplifies the theories of rustic cottage design which Davis recorded in "Rural Residences," published in 1837.*

Hammond-Harwood House, Annapolis *(1774), Maryland, above. This elegantly detailed entrance is the central feature of the façade of a fine Georgian house by William Buckland.*

Mid-Atlantic States

Civic & Public buildings

The **United States Capitol, Washington D.C.** (1793-1865), was originally a *Palladian* building with a central *rotunda* designed by William Thornton. After being damaged in the War of Independence, the Capitol was rebuilt, mostly by Benjamin Latrobe, William Thornton and Charles Bulfinch, and completed by Thomas U. Walter.

Some state capitol buildings are on a domestic scale, such as the **Old State House, New Castle** (*c.* 1732), Delaware. The body of **Independence Hall, Philadelphia** (1731-52), Pennsylvania, by Andrew Hamilton, is similarly of relatively small scale. Other notable civic centers include the **Old Town Hall, Wilmington** (1798), Delaware; **City Hall, New York City** (1811); the **Albany Center, Albany** (1816), New York, and **Federal Hall, New York City** (1833-41).

Robert Mills was commissioned to build a fire-proof **Treasury Building, Washington D.C.** (1838-42), following his Fireproof Building, Charleston. The Treasury Building is monumental in scale with alternating *groin-vaulted* bays and *barrel-vaulted* corridors.

Commercial & Industrial buildings

One of the centers of *Greek Revival* architecture was **Philadelphia,** Pennsylvania. Of note are the **Second Bank of the United States** (1818-24), with a *Doric portico* based on the Parthenon, Athens, and the **Merchants' Exchange** (1832-34), with its *lantern* like the Choragic Monument of Lysicrates, Athens.

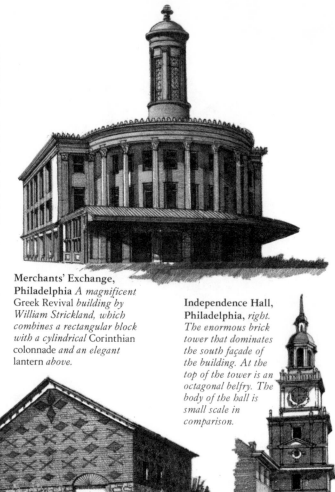

Merchants' Exchange, Philadelphia *A magnificent* Greek Revival *building by William Strickland, which combines a rectangular block with a cylindrical* Corinthian colonnade *and an elegant* lantern *above.*

Independence Hall, Philadelphia, *right. The enormous brick tower that dominates the south façade of the building. At the top of the tower is an octagonal belfry. The body of the hall is small scale in comparison.*

Barn, near McAlisterville
(1861), Pennsylvania. Like medieval English barns, a characteristic of many barns in the area is the decorative brick-patterned gable ends, with patterns ranging from purely geometric to figurative designs. The holes of the design ventilate the barn.

Pennsylvania barns

In the southeastern part of Pennsylvania barns are built into the hillsides so that the upper story, the threshing floor, can be entered directly from the hillside. Underneath is the cow barn, entered from the other side of the barn.

Doors to the threshing floor

Forebay and cow barn

Great Lakes States

Religious buildings

The section of **Ohio** around Akron was part of the Western Reserve set aside by Connecticut for its emigrants. When they first arrived their important buildings were, understandably, fashioned to resemble those of home. A good example is the **First Congregational Church, Tallmadge** (1825), built by Lemuel Porter, a typical New England, carpenter-built church. In comparison, **St John Chrysostom, Delafield** (1851-53), Wisconsin, by Richard Upjohn, is a new departure. In the *Gothic Revival* style, it was designed to be built using the limited mechanical means available on the frontier. The decorative *bargeboards* were not cut with the comparatively sophisticated jig saw, but the decoration was built up so that basic carpentry tools could be used.

Domestic buildings

Although the **Turner House, Milan** (*c.* 1828), Ohio, was originally on the frontier, it is like many smaller houses built at roughly the same time in Connecticut and Virginia and was obviously influenced by the same pattern books. The **Cotton House, Green Bay** (1840), Wisconsin, is a notable *Greek Revival* timber building.

Civic & Public buildings

For major civic buildings it was inevitable that the newly developing states should rely on architects from the East, such as Ithiel Town and Alexander Davis who built the **Old State Capitol, Springfield** (1840), Illinois. The **State Capitol, Columbus** (1838-60), Ohio, by Henry Walters, Davis and others, is a rationalist composition. A long horizontal rectangle forms the body, and this is crowned by a huge *drum.*

First Congregational Church, Tallmadge *A handsome timber-frame church which resembles similar earlier examples in New England. This resemblance is no accident as the Tallmadge church was built by Connecticut settlers soon after their arrival in Ohio.*

Turner House, Milan, *below. The architect of this handsome* Ionic-style *house is unknown. The two-story central block is offset by one-story wings with colonnades. The building was probably designed from* Classical *pattern books.*

Old State Capitol, Springfield, *right. Ithiel Town and Alexander Davis designed this* Greek Revival *building with its* Doric porticos *front and back, and the bold, domed lantern with its encircling colonnade.*

St John Chrysostom, Delafield *A board and batten church by Richard Upjohn. The rough planks used in construction still carry the marks of the circular saws used, showing how the* Gothic Revival *details were designed to compensate for the limited means of the frontier.*

State Capitol, Columbus, *right. The capitol building is a huge rectangular block capped by a cylindrical* drum *and articulated by* Doric *pilasters. Each façade has a recessed center and above the entry recess is a triangular* pediment.

The South

Religious buildings

In contrast to the masonry churches of the old
world the early churches of Virginia were timber,
but none remains. Three are known to have been
built in brick, of which **St Luke's**, near **Smithfield** (1632), Virginia, is the only one still intact.
It is the oldest surviving church in America and
has, like English parish churches, internal *truss-
work, tie beams* and a *rood-screen*. **St Paul's,
Edenton** (*c.* 1760), North Carolina, has a similar
plan with its tower attached to the *gable* end, but
the architecture is a simple, elegant *Georgian*
style. **Christchurch, Kilmarnock** (1732), Virginia, a handsome barn-like church, has a Greek
cross plan with each arm covered by a huge
hipped roof. **St Michael's, Charleston** (1752-61),
South Carolina, like all the major churches in
the colonies, was modeled on James Gibbs's St
Martin-in-the-Fields, London, details of which
were profusely illustrated in Gibbs's "A Book of
Architecture." The main body of the church is
stuccoed brick, the *portico* and steeple, wood.
Monumental Church, Richmond (1812), Virginia, by Robert Mills, is a bold *Neoclassical* building,
octagonal in plan, with a domed roof pierced by a
glazed *lantern*. The **Centenary Methodist Episcopal Church, Charleston** (1842), South Carolina,
is one of a series of *Greek Revival* churches in
Charleston. If it were not for the obviously
ecclesiastical windows along the *nave,* this *prostyle
Doric* temple, by E. B. White, could well be a civic
building.

Domestic buildings

One of the oldest surviving brick-built houses in
America is the **Adam Thoroughgood House,
near Norfolk** (1636-40), Virginia. A one-story
house with chimneys at each gable end, the plan
is reminiscent of the smaller English medieval

St Luke's, *near*
Smithfield *A* Gothic-
*style, brick-built
church with entry via
the attached tower.
The curious pediment
over the entrance and
the round arch are
classical in origin.*

St Paul's, Edenton,
*below. A slender,
shingled spire crowns
the elegant brick
tower of this church.
Within, the spacious
nave is aisleless, con-
forming to the simple
Georgian style of
the building.*

Governor's Palace, Williamsburg *A brick-
built Georgian mansion with a five-bay plan
rebuilt by John D. Rockefeller, Jr. The hipped
roof with dormer windows has a balustrade and
a cupola, flanked by chimneys.*

St Michael's, Charleston *A
survivor of the Colonial Style.
The giant Doric portico is
itself dominated by a lofty
spire, with its octagonal top
three stages rising from a
square base. The tower rises
from the main body of the
church, as in James Gibbs's St
Martin-in-the-Fields, London.*

houses. **Bacon's Castle, Virginia** (*c.* 1665), is a high, *Jacobean*-style brick-built manor house, with Flemish-style curved gables and angled chimneys.

Probably the most distinguished architecture of 18th-century America was to be found in Williamsburg, Virginia. The town was restored between 1928 and 1934 to its state as a busy colonial capital. Most of the houses are frame buildings with applied ornamentation, but the **Governor's Palace** (1706-20) is a fine brick-built Georgian mansion. The architecture of Williamsburg greatly influenced buildings such as **Westover, Charles City** (*c.* 1730-1734), Virginia, and **Stratford Hall, Stratford** (*c.*1725-1730), Virginia. **Gunstanton Hall, Lorton** (1755), Virginia, has a high-pitched roof with *dormer windows* and a *piano nobile* raised above a low basement. Entry is via an elegant porch.

The major domestic buildings of the South in the late 18th century were invariably *Palladian* in style with a central *pedimented* block flanked by pavilions, often attached to the central structure by curving corridors, as at **Mount Airy**, near **Richmond** (*c.* 1758-62), Virginia. Here, the decorative use of contrasting building materials, limestone for pediment and window surrounds and dark sandstone for the walls, gives a sense of the *Baroque*. The earliest English-style Palladian houses in the South were those like the **Miles Brewton House, Charleston** (*c.* 1765-69), South Carolina. Such buildings were a century and a half behind the comparable architectural development in the old world.

Monticello, Charlottesville (1770-1809), Virginia, the house of Thomas Jefferson, is reminiscent of the English Palladian tradition, but warmer, with a less strict *axiality*. The design is sculptural, to be seen from a variety of angles on its spectacular mountain site.

Waverley, *near* **Columbus** *(1855), Mississippi. A magnificent timber-frame mansion with a central hall flanked by curving flights of stairs with the main rooms on either side. The deep recess in the façade indicates the central hall.*

Westover, Charles City, *right. One of the portland stone portals,* Baroque *in contrast to the clean brick façades, which emphasize the entrances of this mansion. The building has an axial plan.*

Stratford Hall, Stratford *This brick-built Georgian mansion was the birthplace of Robert E. Lee. It has an "H"-shaped plan with a* piano nobile *raised above a polychrome basement. The chimneys enclose roof decks.*

Owens-Thomas House, Savannah *(1819), Georgia, right. The verandah of this Regency-style house by William Jay, an Englishman, has beautifully decorated columns and wrought iron work. The important rooms are raised above a rusticated basement and are above the dampness and dirt of the busy street.*

Mount Airy, *near* **Richmond** *Thought to be by John Ariss, who had studied architecture in England, the mansion is* Palladian. *The portico, the windows and* quoins *are cream colored, while the walls are a dark contrasting sandstone.*

Monticello, Charlottesville, *right. Thomas Jefferson often remodeled his house, influenced by Lord Burlington, the 18th-C English Neoclassicist, and Andrea Palladio, the 16th-C Italian architect.*

The South

Drayton Hall, near Charleston (1738-40), South Carolina, is one of the finest *Georgian* mansions in America. Standing on the banks of the Ashley River, the main entrance has a handsome two-story *portico* raised above the ground story and reached by a double staircase. Another brick-built Georgian mansion is **Tyron Palace, New Bern** (1770), North Carolina, with a high *pedimented* central structure. The first *Adam Style* building in South Carolina was the **Joseph Manigault House, Charleston** (1790-97), built by Gabriel Manigault.

One of the most elegant town houses in the South is the **Nathaniel Russell House, Charleston** (*c.* 1809), South Carolina, three stories in height, with an octagonal bay projecting on the garden side and containing a spacious oval room.

Handsome examples of pre-Civil War Louisiana architecture are houses such as **Shadows, New Iberia** (1834), and **Rosedown Plantation, Saint Francisville** (1835). The former has an elegant galleried façade with giant *Doric* columns running the full height of the building, emphasizing verticality. The latter has separate columns for each story emphasizing horizontality.

The more traditional Louisiana architecture of low *hipped roof,* as can be seen at Shadows, was abandoned in houses such as **Madewood Plantation** (1844-48), in which the dominant feature is the *Ionic* portico with columns rising, not from *pedestals,* but from a *stylobate* as in a Greek temple. The celebrated plantation house, **Oak Alley, Vacherie** (1839), is in the form of a magnificent Doric temple, eight bays by seven bays, with wide galleries under an enormous hipped roof. The house stands by the Mississippi.

In Tennessee, **Rattle and Snap, Columbia** (1845), is one of the most elaborate *Greek Revival* houses in America, with a lofty *Corinthian* portico and projecting center bay. Other Greek Revival houses include **Milford Plantation,** near **Pinewood** (1850), South Carolina, a grandiose mansion with a giant portico in which the columns have curious Egyptian-style bell *capitals;* **Belle Meade, Nashville** (1853), Tennessee, thought to be by William Strickland; **Berry Hill, Halifax County** (1845), Virginia; **Gaineswood, Demopolis** (1842-60), Alabama; **Bellevue, La Grange** (1853), Georgia; **D'Evereux, Natchez** (1840), Mississippi; **Rosalie, Natchez** (1821), and **Bellamy House, Wilmington** (1859), North Carolina.

Just like the Mississippi river boats that once passed its façade, **San Francisco, Reserve** (*c.* 1853-56), Louisiana, is an amalgam of classical, *Gothic* and Victorian elements welded together. **Longwood, Natchez** (1860), Mississippi, by Samuel Sloan, was never finished. It is a huge octagonal brick structure of basement and three main floors. A striking feature of the house is the tall *cupola* containing a *solarium* and observatory covered by an onion-shaped dome. *Gothic Revival* houses of note in the South include **Afton Villa, Saint Francisville** (1849), Louisiana, with its picturesque *barge boards* and pointed arches, and **Staunton Hill, Charlotte County** (1848), Virginia, a castellated house by John Johnson.

Houmas House, Burnside *(1840), Louisiana. A magnificent plantation house of stuccoed brick with three sides colonnaded with giant Doric columns. The roof has dormer windows and is crowned by a square cupola.*

San Francisco, Reserve, *above. A plantation house built by the planter Edmond B. Marmillion for himself and restored in 1975. Apart from the decorative detail, of particular interest are the enormous roof, ventilated by a band of louvres on the attic floor, and the water cisterns flanking the house.*

Longwood, Natchez, *right. Detail of one of the covered balconies. The house is a delightful Oriental-style folly by Samuel Sloan. Construction work was stopped by the Civil War and the house was never finished. The architect had planned to solar heat the house, as well as devising an elaborate system of ventilation for the long summers.*

Shadows, New Iberia *Commissioned by the plantation owner David Weeks, this is a galleried town house with the gallery included under the roof of the house itself. An external stairway leads to the gallery.*

Shirley Plantation, Hopewell *(c. 1769), Virginia, above. A square-planned, three-story mansion with French-style mansard roof and two-story Palladian portico front and rear. The arrangement of outbuildings forms a French-style entry courtyard.*

Miles Brewton House, Charleston *(1765-69), South Carolina, above. A luxurious town house by an unkown archi-tect, with an imposing galleried portico. The sophistication of the English Palladian style is advanced for a build-ing of this period in the South.*

Madewood Planta-tion, Louisiana, *below. The house consists of the central body, with its giant Ionic, pedimented portico, and low side wings which are smaller versions of the main structure but with flat pedi-mented façades.*

Nathaniel Russell House, Charleston, *right. A characteristic of the Federal Style is a circular or oval stair-case, inspired by the work of Robert, John and James Adam in England. This example is lighted by triple windows on the prin-cipal floor.*

Drayton Hall, *near* **Charleston** *(1739-60), South Carolina. An amalgam of Palladian-style portico with the low, Sir Christopher Wren-style proportions of the main block. Columns of the Tuscan and Ionic Orders support the porch and balcony.*

Gallier House, New Orleans *(1857-60), Louisiana. A characteristic of New Orleans during the early 19thC are houses with street façades enriched by balconies supported on slender cast-iron columns with grill work above. The style is reminiscent of Regency England.*

The South

Civic & Public buildings

When Williamsburg superseded Jamestown as
the capital of Virginia in 1699, it was quickly
enlarged into an elegant colonial town with a
central avenue terminated at one end by the
Capitol (1751-53), a handsome "H"-shaped
building, and at the other by **William and Mary
College** (1695) by Sir Christopher Wren. Both
buildings have elegant *cupolas* which emphasize
the axial line linking the two buildings.

  Chowan County Courthouse, Edenton
(1767), North Carolina, is a distinguished-looking
two-story building with a *pedimented* central bay
and a cupola crowning the *hipped roof*. The
architecture of the building is very English, with
its Wren-style proportions. After the War of
Independence it became fashionable for American
architects to break away from such traditions.

  Thomas Jefferson, who succeeded Benjamin
Franklin as United States Ambassador in Paris in
1784 and later became third President of the
United States, was an accomplished architect
utilizing knowledge based on both his architectural
reading and the observations made during his
European travels. His use of the ancient Roman
temple style was an attempt to establish an
American architecture independent of British
models. The **University of Virginia, Charlottesville** (1817-26), was based on French *Neoclassical* plans which Jefferson had seen while he
was in Paris. The pavilions, which line the central
lawn, represent the 10 schools of the university,
and the Rotunda contained the library and the
lecture rooms, with gymnasia in the wings. The

**Cruck-frame church,
Jamestown** *(17thC).
Interior of a cruck-
frame church, one
of a collection of
reconstructed buildings
from the period 1607
to 1698 when James-
town was the state
capital of Virginia.
Other buildings
include a fort and
timber-framed houses.*

**Capitol, Williams-
burg** *Largely rebuilt
in c. 1927, the
Capitol building has
an "H"-shaped plan.
The projecting wings
are finished with round
bays like church
apses. The roof is
enhanced by dormers
and a tower.*

Town House, Charleston *(19thC),
South Carolina. Single-fronted town
houses, such as this, are common in
Charleston. The gable-end faces the
street and the entrance is along one
side via a galleried porch-verandah
which runs the length of the house.*

University of Virginia, Charlottesville

Thomas Jefferson's architectural theories were
realized in the building of Virginia University.
The lawn is the heart of the complex, originally
being open to the mountains at one end, and
closed to the town at the other by the Rotunda,
which was based on the Pantheon, Rome.

Rotunda

Colonnade along the lawn

diversity of the pavilion façades forms an encyclopaedia of architecture drawn from engravings of ancient Rome and *Palladian* buildings.

The prevalence of wood in American building posed the problem of fire. One of the most innovatory buildings of the period is the **County Record**, or **Fireproof Building, Charleston** (1822), South Carolina, by Robert Mills. The building is a two-story block built entirely of masonry. The contrasting colored basement rises well above ground level. Inside, two *barrel-vaulted* passages link the central *porticos* at the front and the back. At the center is an oval stair well.

The **Capitol, Raleigh** (1831-33), North Carolina, largely by Ithiel Town and Alexander Davis, is a handsome Neoclassical building with a bold *Doric* portico raised above a high, *rusticated* ground floor. The **Hibernian Hall, Charleston** (1835), South Carolina, was built for the social and charitable Hibernian Society by Thomas U. Walter. The building is an elegant *prostyle Ionic* temple with a portico reminiscent of the Erechtheion, Athens. Another *Greek Revival* building is the **Old City Hospital, Mobile** (1830), Alabama, with its two-story Doric portico and projecting pedimented central section. More spectacular is the **Actors' Theatre, Louisville** (1837), Kentucky, originally a bank by Gideon Shryock. The entrance is monumental with side walls tapering inward and a horizontal *architrave* and *cornice* carried on two giant Ionic columns. The same architect designed the **Old State House, Little Rock** (1842), Arkansas, which is another handsome Doric building.

Capitol, Richmond *(1785-92), Virginia. This giant* Ionic *temple-style building by Jefferson is an enlarged version of the design for the Maison Carrée in France, and was the first application of a pure* Classical *temple form in America.*

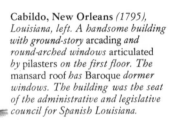

Cabildo, New Orleans *(1795), Louisiana, left. A handsome building with ground-story* arcading *and round-arched windows* articulated *by pilasters on the first floor. The mansard roof has Baroque dormer windows. The building was the seat of the administrative and legislative council for Spanish Louisiana.*

State Capitol, Nashville *(1854-59), Tennessee. A magnificent Greek Revival-style building by William Strickland, with a bold Ionic portico raised above a rusticated basement. The cupola was modeled on the Choragic Monument of Lysicrates, Athens.*

County Record, *or* **Fireproof Building, Charleston** *A simple block,* Neoclassical *in its plainness and in the simple* Doric *porticos front and back. The interior of the building is a series of alternating groin- and* barrel-vaulted *bays up to the second floor where there are flat plaster ceilings.*

Market Hall, Charleston *(1841), South Carolina, right. This is a handsome building in Roman temple form. It is raised on a high* rusticated, podium-like *basement story, the portico being reached by an elegant double staircase.*

309

The West Coast

Religious buildings

There were 21 Franciscan missions constructed along the coast in California between San Diego in the south and Sonoma in the north. Much of the building was by Californian Indians or by craftsmen from Mexico. The buildings were simple structures relying on primitive decorative details outside and *frescoes* inside. The standard mission consisted of a church, priests' quarters, workshops, barracks for soldiers, guest rooms, a convent, storerooms and a kitchen with ancillary rooms. A mission had to be planned around a central open court for defense.

The chief building of a mission was the church. **San Diego de Alcala**, near **San Diego** (1774-1813), was the first to be built, but the most important of the early mission churches of California was **San Carlos de Borromeo, Carmel** (1793-97). The church has a *Baroque* façade with different-size flanking towers. The bold and simple form is characteristic. Inside, the long, narrow *nave* is covered by a *barrel vault* carried on a series of stone *ribs*. Other early missions of note are the ruins of **San Juan Capistrano** (1797-1806), with its giant arch and *groin vault* reminiscent of ancient classical ruins, and **San Gabriel Arcángel, San Gabriel** (1771-1800), a long, high rectangular block with massive *buttressed* walls and a simple nave.

The later missions, built in the early 19th century, were more classical and refined, as at **Santa Barbara** (1815-20), **La Purísima Concepción Mission, Lompoc** (1818), and **San Luis Rey de Francia**, near **Oceanside** (1815).

San Carlos de Borromeo, Carmel *This was the second in a series of missions to be built along the west coast of the United States. It is a strongly-built stone church with a vaulted nave roof. The mannerist-style central door has a Baroque window set above it.*

Santa Barbara *Later mission churches of the early 19th-C, such as this, have refined classical features. Here, the twin-towered façade is strictly symmetrical with a superimposed pedimented portico.*

Kawaiahao Church, Honolulu *(1842), Hawaii. This church was built of coral blocks and replaced a thatched church built in 1820 by the first Protestant missionaries. The tower, in the Gothic style, and the somewhat ponderous Doric portico both give emphasis to the main axis of the church.*

San Luis Rey de Francia, *near* **Oceanside** *The long nave of this mission church was built with 6 ft thick adobe walls. The elegant gabled façade has a single belltower attached to one side.*

San Gabriel Arcángel, *San Gabriel* *The striking feature of this mission church is the long, high nave with the ceiling carried on exposed beams supported by decorative corbels. The walls are painted with notable murals.*

The Southwest

Religious buildings

With the colonization of the southwest by Spain, Franciscan missionaries began to build a whole series of mission churches and buildings which were an amalgam of indigenous Pueblo Indian building construction with Catholic European architecture. The building material at hand, *adobe,* had been used for centuries.

San José de Gracia, or the **Church of the Twelve Apostles, Las Trampas** (*c.* 1760), New Mexico, was built like a fortress with a recessed entry façade framed by twin belltowers. **San José de Laguna, Laguna Pueblo, New Mexico** (1706), is simpler in both form and detail, but has stepped *gables* pierced by a twin belfry. The interior is decorated with Indian wall paintings.

San Xavier del Bac, near **Tucson** (1783-91), Arizona, is the grandest of the Spanish-style churches in the southwest. Externally the forms of the church are bold and monumental. Twin towers with octagonal belfries of painted white *stucco* flank the elaborately carved red-brick *portal,* and there is a high dome over the *crossing.* The plan is cruciform, with *nave, chancel* and *transepts* covered by shallow oval domes.

The monumental **San José de Tumacácori,** near **Nogales** (1796-1822), Arizona, is now in ruins. The magnificent *Baroque* portal consists of a round-arched door flanked by coupled columns with a second, smaller stage above framing a rectangular window. Other notable missions include **El Santuario de Chimayo, Chimayo** (1816), and **San Francisco de Asis, Ranchos de Taos** (*c.* 1772), both in New Mexico.

San José de Gracia, Las Trampas, *above. An* adobe *church of simple solids and voids, with the massive side walls turned up to form the twin belltowers of the façade. The recessed section of the façade is painted white and has a prominent balcony over the doorway.*

San Xavier del Bac, *near* Tucson *The* Baroque *portal of this fine church, which is the height of the nave and has decorative columns and ornate scroll work made of carved red brick. These details are in stark contrast to the white* stucco *walls of the church itself.*

San Estéban Rey, Acoma *(c. 1629-c. 1642), New Mexico. The monumentality of early mission churches is due to the slab-like adobe walls. Here, the twin-towered façade has sloped walls.*

San José de Tumacácori, *near* **Nogales** *The Baroque façade. A notable feature of the decoration above the portal is the way in which the* gable *is tied to the flanking towers by a molded band.*

San Francisco de Asis, Ranchos de Taos, *right. The abstract geometry of such adobe churches has a striking effect. Here, the belltowers and walls of the church are supported by massive buttresses.*

The Southwest

The religious buildings of Texas were generally more sophisticated in construction than those of New Mexico. A good example is the mission church at the **Alamo, San Antonio** (1744-57). Built of stone instead of *adobe*, its forms and decorative details are crisper and more exact. Another is **Nuestra Señora de la Purísima Concepción de Acuña, San Antonio** (1731-55), a massive stone church with walls more than 3 ft thick.

The architectural heritage of Spanish Franciscan missionaries found a remarkable outlet in the decorative stone façades of the churches of Texas. **San José y San Miguel de Aguayo, San Antonio** (1720-31), has an elaborate *portal* which would have suited the *Baroque* façades of early 18th-century Madrid.

Civic & Public buildings

The Pueblo Indian tribes occupied the whole area of the upper Rio Grande. Unlike the nomadic Indian tribes with their tepees, the Pueblos built elaborate villages of terraced communal dwellings, often several stories in height. The walls were built of adobe, the roofs of closely set logs embedded in the tops of the walls, as at **Taos Pueblo, Taos** (*c.* 1700), New Mexico.

Many of the early buildings of **Santa Fé, New Mexico,** once the capital of the Spanish southwest, are built of adobe. A good example is the **Governor's Palace** (1610-14). The form and construction are in the traditional Pueblo Indian manner, while the long *loggia* of the façade is a distinctly Spanish feature.

San José y San Miguel de Aguayo, San Antonio
The church has a boldly carved Spanish Baroque portal, with a decorative doorframe layered in front of the door itself, and a balcony above reached from an ornately carved oval window opening.

Taos Pueblo, Taos *The dwellings of this Indian village, or pueblo, are grouped around a large central area of common ground. From the early 16thC, the traditional pueblo building consisted of simple cube-like living units, often piled one on top of the other so the upper terraces had to be reached by ladders.*

Adobe houses

The native building material of the southwest region was adobe—sun-baked blocks made of mud mixed with straw or manure. The blocks were usually made in a wooden mold and, once the walls were constructed, they were covered with a rendering of clay.

Adobe houses, Santa Fé

Alamo, San Antonio *The most famous of a group of missions built by the Spanish in the region of San Antonio. The domed church has a stepped and curved gable façade which includes this story-high portal flanked by decorative columns on plinths and niches.*

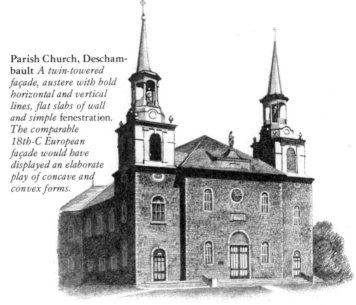

Canada

Religious buildings

The typical Quebec church of the late 18th and early 19th century has a plain, barn-like exterior combined with a rather *Baroque* interior, as shown by the **Parish Church, Lacadie** (1801), and the **Second Parish Church, Cap Santé** (1754-1807). The **Anglican Cathedral, Quebec City** (1804), however, was built by English workmen and has a James Gibbs's-style steeple. Other churches in the style of early 18th-century London are **St John's, Belfast** (1825), Eldon; **Greenock Church, St Andrew's** (1824), New Brunswick, and **St Andrew's, Niagara-on-the-Lake** (1831), Ontario.

Notre Dame, Montreal (1824-43), Quebec, by James O'Donnell, is a fine *Gothic Revival* building with a twin-towered façade and a giant screen of three arches joining them in a manner reminiscent of Peterborough Cathedral in England.

The great architect of Canada's classical period was Thomas Baillairgé. Working in Quebec he added the unique triple spires to the **Parish Church, Sainte-Famille** (1843), and built the **Church, Les Bequets** (1836). The finest of all his churches is **St-Joseph, Lauzon** (1830-32). The *nave* was lengthened in 1954 and the original façade re-erected. Another of his churches, the **Church, Deschambault** (1838), is Baroque in comparison, particularly the twin-towered façade with protruding central bay. Baillairgé produced the design for a new façade to the **Basilica, Quebec City** (1844), but after a year the work was abandoned and the remainder of the original late 17th-century façade was incorporated with the new work that had been completed.

Sharon Temple, Holland Landing (1825), Ontario, was built in timber by an extreme Protestant sect. The plan, a simple geometry of squares, and the form, dominated by a central square tower crowned by a *lantern,* are an attempt to initiate a new church architecture.

The beginnings of Victorian Canada are to be seen in many small, classically planned churches with *Gothic Revival* ornamentation, as at **St John's, Lunenburg** (*c.* 1840), Nova Scotia, and the **Church, Burritts Rapids** (1831), Ontario.

Parish Church, Deschambault *A twin-towered façade, austere with bold horizontal and vertical lines, flat slabs of wall and simple fenestration. The comparable 18th-C European façade would have displayed an elaborate play of concave and convex forms.*

St John's, Lunenburg *The church is an illustration of the beginnings of* Gothic Revival *in Canada, which here consists of the application of pinnacles, buttresses and pointed arches to what had become a traditional North American church structure.*

Old Meeting-house, Barrington *(1765). A simple structure, more building than architecture, built by New Englanders from Cape Cod and Nantucket. Classical details, such as the corner* pilasters, *were simplified in the hands of the local carpenters who built it.*

West Dumfries Chapel, Paris Plains *(c. 1845), Ontario. This unusually elegant cobblestone building is a hybrid, with its simple classical broken* pediment *and rusticated quoins offset by pointed Gothic Revival windows and door.*

Canada

Domestic buildings

A number of settlements in Nova Scotia were settled by boat builders, fishermen and lumbermen from Cape Cod. Not surprisingly, houses such as **Simeon Perkins House, Liverpool Ferry** (1766), and the earlier **Amberman House, Granville Ferry** (18thC), show strong New England influences.

Both the European and the American classical vernacular tradition influenced early Canadian architecture, as shown by the now derelict **Woodruffe House, Saint David's** (*c.* 18thC), the **Alpheus Jones House, Prescott** (*c.* 1820), and **Bertie Hall, Fort Erie** (1826), all in Ontario. The last is a rectangular block with the roof drawn forward over the façade to form a *portico* of giant square columns, which is reminiscent of early 19th-century classicism in Virginia. The **Barnum House, Grafton** (*c.* 1817), Ontario, has an elegant engaged temple façade of white painted pine *articulated* by giant *Doric pilasters.*

The *Regency,* British colonial-style house is another distinctive architectural type in Canada. The Canadian interpretation of the style, however, included a somewhat random *picturesqueness,* as at **Dundurn, Hamilton** (1832-35), with its flanking Italianate towers, and bold treatment, as at **Rockwood, Portsmouth** (1842), both in Ontario.

Elizabeth Cottage, Kingston (*c.* 1845), Ontario, is an eccentric amalgam of *Gothic* elements, a picturesque building but Regency in spirit. More typically Regency is **Riverset, L'Orignal** (1833), Ontario, with its elegant *loggia,* chimneys and projecting bays which punctuate the sides of the building.

Civic & Public buildings

Province House, Halifax (1811-19), Nova Scotia, is prototypical of Canadian architecture for administrative buildings, with its porticoed façade, Venetian-style side windows, *rusticated* ground story and *Adam* interiors. The **Old Government House, Fredericton** (1828), New Brunswick, has a fine semicircular porch, low projecting wings and *mullioned* bay windows. **Osgoode Hall, Toronto** (1829-45), Ontario, consists of three sections built at different times. The earliest part, the east wing, was influenced, as was English architecture of the period, by a nostalgia for 16th-century *Renaissance* Italy.

Crysler Hall, Upper Canada Village *(1846), Ontario. The house is an example of strictly applied American-style classicism, a result of the immigrant's pursuit of the architectural ideals of the country from which he had emigrated.*

Osgoode Hall, Toronto *The building was originally the home of the Law Society of Upper Canada and consists of a high central section with slightly lower projecting wings. The center of each section is punctuated by a* portico *raised above an arcaded* ground story.

Sir William Campbell House, Toronto *(1822), Ontario. The façade, with its broken pediment and oval window which, despite the fashionable* Greek-Revival *porch, is reminiscent of early 19th-C Virginia.*

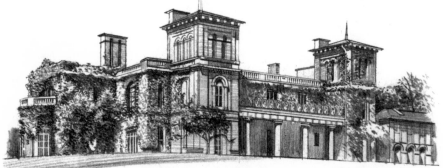

Dundurn, Hamilton *This Regency-style house is charming for its rambling and somewhat confused architectural form. Prime features are the Italianate towers, added some years after the body of the house was completed.*

Early Canadian barns

These buildings are a marvelous example of form following function. Because of the need to provide an easy approach for hay wagons to the *dormer* loading bays, barns such as this at **St Pierre, Quebec,** were built against high ground on one side, any gap being bridged by ramps.

Front of barn

View from the back

Mount Uniacke House, Mount Uniacke *(1813), Nova Scotia. This house was restored in 1949 and shows how Regency-style mansions, complete with* pilaster-*framed outline and* piano nobile *raised above a stone-built basement, were part of a cultural fashion for the early colonists in Canada.*

Barn, Nassagaweya *(19thC), Ontario, below. The three-bay barn, found on many small farms, was introduced by the English first to New England, then the midwest of the United States and Canada. It consists of a central through passage with livestock on one side and storage space on the other.*

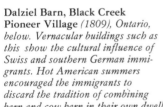

Dalziel Barn, Black Creek Pioneer Village *(1809), Ontario, below. Vernacular buildings such as this show the cultural influence of Swiss and southern German immigrants. Hot American summers encouraged the immigrants to discard the tradition of combining barn and cow barn in their own dwelling.*

Barn, St Charles *(19thC), Quebec. Such magnificent farm buildings as this seem to grow out of the ground. The arrangement of the barn being a raised story over the cow barn was a form that suited many farmers and is found throughout Pennsylvania as well as parts of Canada.*

Modern World

In the last quarter of the 18th century the established order of the Western World faced a severe challenge. The American and French Revolutions eventually led to a radical change in political and social structures. Nor did the upheavals stop there. The consequences of a technological revolution were equally far-reaching. The invention of the steam engine broke the dominance of wind and water power and started the change to a society which was largely industrial and urban from one which had been principally agricultural and rural. Steam power caused large factories to replace small isolated workshops. The promise of employment and higher wages drew farm laborers from outlying rural areas to the new industrial areas.

These changes had an immediate impact on the techniques and materials used by architects and builders. The development of the railways meant that builders no longer depended on local materials. In England, with the invention of the Hoffman Kiln in 1858, bricks were mass-produced and transported throughout the land. The uniform Victorian red brick became a dominant feature of every industrialized town. Old, well-tested craftsmanship gave way to mass-production and assembly by semiskilled labor.

The tremendous exuberance and optimism of the Victorian adventure – initiated in Great Britain but soon adopted by the rest of western Europe and North America — brought with it, simultaneously, unparalleled social problems. The new factories gave wealth to a few powerful individuals and birth to an industrial workforce which before long began to demand its share of the spoils. Political and economic oppression drove many to seek a new life overseas, in America, South Africa, Australia and New Zealand. The greatest number sailed to the United States, a promised land of opportunity and hope, where every man had a chance to win the privileges once confined to the few.

Architecture reflected the prevailing tensions. At one end of the scale styles of what at this time might be called uncertainty and doubt arose. These looked back to both the Greek and Gothic worlds. At the other end a style based on functionalism and engineering techniques appeared. This dichotomy was visible throughout the 19th century. Later, in revulsion at industrial squalor, William Morris and John Ruskin attempted to make architecture an instrument of social reform. Their reliance on the skill of the individual craftsman, and his consciousness of his own responsibilities, however, gave way at the turn of the 19th century to standardization of house plans and to large-scale mass production of decorative motifs. Science and technology raised early 20th-century expectations to unforeseen

heights as change became even more rapid, expectations that in the West were fulfilled in material terms. Rebellion against tradition and the established ways of doing things led to social and moral standards that would match the enormous and extraordinary developments in science and technology. In architecture, the International Style of the 1920s and 1930s was an attempt to match the discoveries of the day. New materials and more sophisticated techniques made it seem as if any structure could be achieved. An inevitable reaction set in, resulting, in the 1970s, in a return to eclecticism and the revival of vernacular styles.

Construction

The development of new materials was crucial for the creation of new styles. In the early 19th century cast iron, in the form of girders, beams and columns began to be used extensively, as in St. Katherine's Dock, London (1824-28), by Thomas Telford. Previously it had been employed only in chains and tie-bars for arches and vaults. The first major innovation in techniques of construction was the balloon frame. Originally known as Chicago construction, it was invented in the 1830s by George W. Snow, a surveyor and civil engineer, and provided both a more economical and a speedier system of construction than had the mortise and tenon frame of posts, girts, beams and

Balloon frame *The cheap manufacture of nails revolutionized traditional timber-frame construction in the USA. A large number of mass-produced upright members (studs) run from the base of the house to the eaves and all horizontal members (plates) are nailed to them, making a dense wooden frame.*

braces. Balloon framing uses a skeleton of thin plates and studs nailed together and running the entire height of the building, past the floor joists. This method of construction (which is still in use today), made possible by the cheap manufacture of nails, converted an expensive and complex craft into an industry, and unskilled labor replaced skilled craftsmen. Later developments in the manufacture of iron, such as the industrial production of puddle iron in the 1840s and the development in 1856 of the Bessemer converter for making steel, had profound consequences. Equally significant progress was made in glass manufacturing.

The results of both advances were combined in the Crystal Palace, London(destroyed), designed by Joseph Paxton to house the Great Exhibition of 1851, in which a skeletal structure of thin iron members displayed a delightful alternative to massive buildings of brick and stone. In the Eiffel Tower, Paris (1889), the use of cast-iron components and frame building structural methods was perfected.

In the late 19th century frame construction was developed further in Chicago after the great fire of 1871. With this type of construction the load of the building was no longer supported by the external walls but by cast-iron columns and beams which run through the interior. Buildings could now soar beyond the five or six stories to which they had been, in general, limited. Techniques of steel framing, yet stronger than iron, began to be developed in the early 20th century in the United States, as in the Woolworth Building, New York City (1912).

Reinforced concrete — that is, concrete reinforced by the insertion of iron, and later steel bars — was first used toward the middle of the 19th century, but was not employed to any great extent until the early years of the 20th century.

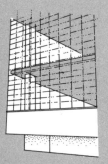

Bauhaus, Dessau *A major feature of Walter Gropius's design for the group of buildings for the Bauhaus, Dessau (the school of craftsmanship, building and design), is the non-loadbearing, all-glass curtain walls of the workshops wing. The loadbearing corner posts are inset so that even at the corners glass butts against glass.*

A major innovation of the 20th century was the non-loadbearing curtain wall. Its development went hand in hand with that of frame construction. The modern curtain wall is composed of mass-produced modular elements. As frame structures were perfected, ever improved techniques of glass manufacture allowed larger areas to be glazed. Windows were gradually transformed into glass walls, no longer carried within the frame but applied to it. A particularly good example is the Bauhaus, Dessau (1925-26). It was only in North America in the late 1940s, however, that curtain walls were first used on a vast scale, as in the UN Secretariat (1947-50), and the Lever Building (1952), both in New York City.

English Eclecticism

In the 1830s and 1840s the classical tradition continued, accompanied by the Gothic Revival, which was at first a peculiarly English development. Good examples of buildings in the classical tradition are the Reform Club, London (1837) by Sir Charles Barry, and St. George's Hall, Liverpool (1840) by H. L. Elmes. The Gothic Revival first emerged in the 18th century, when Horace Walpole began to gothicize Strawberry Hill, but the building that made it a national style, however, was Barry's reconstruction of the Palace of

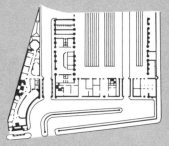

St Pancras Station, London, plan *The Gothic Revival station frontage and hotel were by Sir George Gilbert Scott. The great train sheds stretching behind Scott's building were by W. H. Barlow, the civil engineer.*

Westminster, London after a fire in 1834. The Revival reached its peak between the 1850s and 1880s, with buildings such as the Law Courts, London (1874-82), by Edmund Street; Keble College Chapel, Oxford (1873-76), by William Butterfield, and Sir George Gilbert Scott's masterpiece, the frontage buildings of St. Pancras Station, London (1865).

Alongside these backward-looking styles, however, radical changes were taking place in more utilitarian structures. In Sir Joseph Paxton's Crystal Palace, Isambard Kingdom Brunel's railway engineering and many industrial schemes, the new techniques involving prefabricated steel and glass units were being used. Architecture was never to be quite the same again.

Arts & Crafts Movement

Repelled by the squalor of industrial development, and by the ugliness of both the materials and the style of much 19th century urban building, William Morris and his followers tried to combat the whole idea of mechanical production by returning to an idealized though not wholly accurate version of medieval methods. Morris found inspiration in the tranquility and simplicity of the vernacular buildings of the English countryside. His ideas on architecture were contained in the Red House, London(1859-60), designed for him by Philip Webb. The vernacular references of the Red House were further developed and enriched by Norman Shaw, C. F. A. Voysey, Charles Rennie Mackintosh and Sir Edwin Lutyens. The houses which these architects designed were for the affluent few, however, and Morris's belief that architecture could be an instrument of social reform was not put into practice until 1933, when the first garden city, at Letchworth, Hertfordshire, was built by Raymond Unwin and Barry Parker, with its emphasis on housing, not houses.

Art Nouveau

In the final years of the 19th century, a remarkable and original style developed, first in Brussels in the work of Victor Horta, and then in Paris under the leadership of Hector Guimard. It also emerged in Germany, where it was called *Jugendstil,* and in Italy, where it was named the *Stile Liberty* after the London store. Art Nouveau was essentially decorative, and its expressed aim was to highlight the ornamental value of the curved line in sinuous, undulating and asymmetrical forms. It was the first modern style to be free of historical precedent. A good example is the Tassel House, Brussels (1892), by Victor Horta, in which he exploited the potential beauty of metal and glass in marvelous curving lines and forms.

North America (1870-1940)

The two outstanding architects in the United States in the 19th century were Thomas Jefferson, who closed the chapter on the modern classical world, and Henry Hobson Richardson, who opened the next, on the modern world. Jefferson embodied the humanistic and classical inheritance, Richardson the new romantic and utilitarian ideas. Richardson produced an heroic architecture, conveying continuity, permanence and security in bold monolithic block walls, turreted towers and grand sweeping arches, as in Trinity Church, Boston (1873-77), and the Crane Memorial Library, Quincy (1880-83). This somewhat medieval style which he so enthusiastically developed was superseded by the Italian palazzo style of McKim, Mead & White, to be seen in such buildings as the Public Library, Boston (1888-92), which precipitated academicism with its deliberate imitation of the past. Other references were sought in English Queen Anne architecture and its New England counterpart, the Colonial Style.

In complete contrast were the Chicago School's experiments with its new forms and techniques which eventually resulted in the development of skyscraper construction. Chicago was the thriving capital of the Midwest and had to be rebuilt cheaply and quickly after the great fire of 1871 which had left much of the city in ruins. The masonry construction of the Auditorium Building (1887-89), by Louis Sullivan, maintained the bold style established by Richardson. A prototype skyscraper with its skeletal steel frame and curtain walling was the Reliance Building (1890-94) by Daniel Burnham, in a style which culminated in the Carson Pirie Scott Store (1899-1904), by Sullivan. The light frame and the broad bands of windows anticipated the International Style.

The heir to the Chicago School was Frank Lloyd Wright, who in the early years of the century was responsible for an astonishing number of domestic buildings. Wright abandoned the conventional concepts of providing a room for every use and turned floors into free, open, flowing spaces which were arranged around huge, open fireplaces, the like of which had not been seen since colonial times. Windows were no longer mere holes in walls, but became continuous bands of glass wrapped around the corners so as to integrate inside and outside space. The long, low horizontals seemed to hug the ground, and the sense of shelter was reinforced by great oversailing roofs. Wright, who always strove for organic simplicity, began his work with houses such as the Arthur Heurtley House (1902) and the Robie House, Chicago (1909), and it culminated in Fallingwater, Mill Run (1935), Pennsylvania. The influence of these houses on American domestic architecture was enormous.

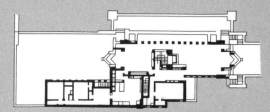

Robie House, Chicago, plan *The first floor of Frank Lloyd Wright's classic prairie house which wheels around the central fire-place.*

Early 20th-century Germany

German architecture, aided by the new methods of construction, was characterized by a utilitarian style. The Turbine Factory, Berlin (1908-9), by Peter Behrens, and the Fagus Factory, Alfeld (1911), by Walter Gropius, are typical. The first was a large shed of massive concrete walls, its modernity lying in its simplicity rather than its structure. Unlike William Morris, who had opposed mass production, German architects valued standardization. Their ideas were represented by the Bauhaus School of Design which was established at Weimar in 1919 by Walter Gropius and then moved to Dessau in 1925, where Gropius designed the premises. The fundamental aim of the school was to re-educate the artist to a new role in an industrial and democratic society and persuade him to design for industrial production rather than to combat it. The Nazis, who found such notions degenerate, closed the school, but the ideas which were formulated there were soon absorbed in the United States, where Gropius eventually settled.

19thC American Eclecticism
The illustrations below show Mckim, Mead & White's Boston Public Library in comparison with its Parisian prototype, the Bibliothèque Sainte-Geneviève (1843-50), by Henri Labrouste.

Boston Public Library

Bibliothèque Sainte-Geneviève

De Stijl

De Stijl, a movement founded by a group of Dutch painters, architects and sculptors in 1917, aimed to abolish all styles and liberate art from representation and individual expression. They wanted to avoid the arbitrary, the casual and the accidental and create a universally valid style. De Stijl took Frank Lloyd Wright's ideas of advancing and receding planes and floating horizontals, combined them with Cubist references, and transformed all these borrowings into a new architecture which was based on such elementary means of expression as vertical and horizontal lines, and primary colors with black, white and grey. An example is the Schröder House, Utrecht (1924), by Gerrit Rietveld.

Schröder House, Utrecht *Gerrit Rietveld's design, with its interlocking concrete plains giving a complex three-dimensional form, epitomizes the de Stijl movement.*

Expressionism

Expressionism, unlike De Stijl, did not amount to a cultural program. It was an ambiguous movement that sought, after the holocaust of World War I, to produce something lyrical and poetic. Its themes were various and ranged from Art Nouveau to a form of surrealism, and from a somewhat blind, Romantic Nationalism to a strict, objective rationalism. The National Romantic element is seen at its best in the Eigen Haard Estate, Amsterdam (1921), by Michael de Klerk. This has strong Art Nouveau as well as vernacular revival elements. The rationalist theory is best represented by the Chilehaus, Hamburg (1922-23), by Fritz Hoger, in which the structural elements are clearly defined. Other expressionist buildings are the almost surreal Einstein Tower, Potsdam (1920), by Erich Mendelsohn, and the Goetheanium, Dornach (1925-28), by Rudolf Steiner.

Constructivism

Constructivism was developed in Moscow after World War I by two brothers, Naum and Antoine Pevsner. Both were sculptors. In the field of architecture it manifested itself in a style which emphasized construc-

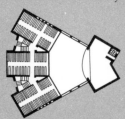

Russakov Workers' Club, Moscow, plan *The individual shape of this structure by Konstantin Melnikov was dictated by the 1400-seat auditorium with its daring cantilevered sections.*

tional expression through the use of industrial material and so had links with De Stijl. Architects also looked to the incorporation of features which carried information and propaganda. Good examples include the Russakov Workers' Club, Moscow (1927-29), by Konstantin Melnikov, the Zuyer Club, Moscow (1928), by I. P. Golosov, and the Cineac Cinema, Amsterdam (1934), by Jahannes Duiker.

International Style

The International Style dominated architectural development in the 1920s and 1930s and remained the foundation on which much of the world's architecture was based until the late 1960s. Its roots lay in the work of Adolph Loos, an Austrian, Auguste Perret's industrial buildings in France, the work of Behrens and Gropius in Germany and the pioneering work of Dutch architects such as Jacobus Oud and Gerrit Rietveld. The style took shape in the 1920s and reached the classical purity with which we now associate it during the following decade. It combined ideological and social criteria with aesthetic considerations and sought to give the impression of volume rather than mass and axial symmetry rather than regularity. Applied decoration was avoided. Characteristic features were white stuccoed walls, long horizontal bands of windows and flat roofs. Major examples are Maison Cook (1926), and the Maison Stein, Garches (1927), both in Paris by Le Corbusier, the Lovell Beach House, Los Angeles

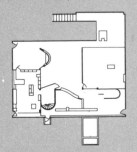

Maison Stein, Garches, plan *The first floor of this luxurious villa by Le Corbusier which includes a terrace, the living room, the dining room and the kitchen.*

(1926), by Rudolf Schindler; the Lovell House, Los Angeles (1929), by Richard Neutra and the Tugendhat House, Brno (1930), Czechoslovakia, by Ludwig Mies van de Rohe. By the 1950s axial symmetry, a higher degree of volumetric control and a concentration on centralized space, became dominant features in both high-rise and low-rise buildings, as in the Apartments Lake Shore Drive, Chicago (1951), and Crown Hall, Illinois Institute of Technology, Chicago (1956), both by Mies van der Rohe.

Architecture of Reinforced Concrete

Early major buildings to use reinforced concrete were the Unity Temple, Oak Park, Chicago (1904), by Wright, and the Church, Le Raincy (1922), near Paris, by Auguste Perret. The latter is a magnificent hall church with flattish vaults carried on slender concrete columns. The wall surface consists of a continuous

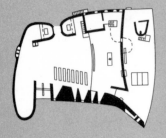

Notre-Dame-du-Haut, Ronchamp, plan *Le Corbusier's sweeping use of concrete is very evident in the curving wall line of this small pilgrimage church. The church can hold no more than 200, but its site allows for large out-door congregations.*

concrete grill filled in with stained glass. The superb plastic qualities of the material were best developed in a series of magnificent buildings by Le Corbusier. This started with such romantic white villas as the Villa Savoye, Poissy (1927), and his apartments for the Weissenhof Estate, Stuttgart, (1927), with their ocean liner feel, and culminated in the Unité d'Habitation, Marseilles (1947-52), and Notre-Dame-du-Haut, Ronchamp (1950-54), with its extraordinary curving forms and irregular, splayed windows that break all the rules of the International Style. While many architects used the medium with the restraint required by stone, Le Corbusier demonstrated its great possibilities for making symbolic forms and for molding space. Examples include the TWA Terminal, Kennedy Airport (1956-62), New York, by Eero Saarinen, and the Philharmonie, Berlin (1956-63), by Hans Scharoun.

Palazzo dello Sport, Rome *(1956-77). Detail from the magnificent shell-structure of this building by Pier Luigi Nervi, one of the great exponents of reinforced concrete architecture. The "Y"-shaped structures transmit the entire weight of the domed roof to the legs of the building while also providing an ample lighting area.*

Architecture with Steel

From the late 1940s onward the works of Mies van der Rohe brought the steel frame developed by the

Suspended roof *The use of steel with its great tensile strength allowed new structural techniques and so new forms in architecture. This detail shows a section of the roof of a steel-frame building suspended from a girder above the roof line.*

Chicago School to its purest form and culminated in the Seagram Building, New York City (1956-58). His stripped-down aesthetic has the precision and perfection of proportion associated with the temples of Classical Greece. His buildings are variations on a theme, the theme of the Seagram Building being the framed rectangle. This formula was soon taken up by others, among them Skidmore, Owings & Merrill in, for example, the Lever Building (1952) and the Manufacturers' Trust Company (1953-54), both in New York City, and by Eero Saarinen in the General Motors Technical Center, near Detroit (1951-55).

Humanism

In buildings such as the Villa Meira (1938-39) and the Town Hall, Säynätsalo (1950-52), Alvar Aalto reacted against the functionalist tradition of the International

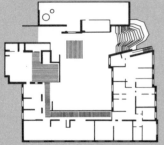

Town Hall, Säynätsalo, plan *The central courtyard of this civic center in Finland is reached by irregular grassed steps which have deteriorated. The harmony of the whole complex results from the careful arrangement of its elements of different shapes.*

Style which he had helped to introduce in Finland. His buildings of this period, like Wright's prairie houses, encourage and dramatize the ordinary and everyday with smaller scales, receding and advancing planes and the use of natural materials such as timber and brick. Aalto also began to exploit the juxtaposition of disparate parts. A good example of this is the Finlandia Hall, Helsinki (1971). His ability to handle disparate parts and the generosity with which he allows asymmetrical spaces to evolve profoundly influenced the work of contemporaries such as Hans Scharoun, for example his Maritime Museum, Bremerhaven (1969-75).

Regionalism & Brutalism

In the 1950s the young English avant garde — chiefly Alison and Peter Smithson, James Stirling and James Gowan — reacted against the limitations of the International Style and promoted a regionalist style. They believed that it was more practical and appropriate to use traditional methods of construction using natural materials rather than sophisticated, experimental ones. They were also interested in both the Mediterranean tradition of domestic buildings, constructed of rough masonry, and in the simplicity and utility of the factories and commercial buildings of the Industrial Revolution. The works of Voysey and Mackintosh, as well as by some of Le Corbusier's, such as the Villa, Les Mathes (1935), and the Maison Jaoul, Paris (1954-56), were a further stimulation. At the same time there evolved a similar but more rationalist style, labeled Brutalism and exemplified by the School, Hunstanton, (1954), Norfolk, by Alison and Peter Smithson, with its uncompromising exhibition of materials and starkness of form. The flats at Ham Common, London (1955), by James Stirling and James Gowan, synthesized the two trends. Stark geometry, with its dependence on International Style aesthetics, was later distorted for topographical considerations in schemes such as Park Hill Housing Estate, Sheffield (1955-61), by the City Architect's Office.

Architecture & the American Experience

The awareness of a national consciousness uninfluenced by European ideas, and of the uniqueness of the American experience, have become crucial considerations for American writers, artists and architects in the 20th century. In architecture, Richardson began to tackle industrial phenomena such as railroad stations and office buildings and, in 1936, Henry Russell Hitchcock, the American architectural historian, wrote that the combination of strict functionalism and bold symbolism in the best roadside buildings provided the most encouraging signs for mid-20th-century architecture. Schindler achieved such an architecture in the Tischler House, Bel Air (1949-50), California, and the Janson House, Hollywood, (1949). Both were uninhibited by the cultural constraints of Europe, and both forged a rare link between the architectural history and the everyday exuberance of roadside America.

In the 1960s and 1970s Robert Venturi and his colleagues went still further. Arguing that mainstreet America was almost alright they did not ignore it but set about civilizing it, not with motifs snatched from the past but with elements inspired by the ordinary and everyday world. Examples of their architecture are the Trubeck and Wislocki Houses, Nantucket (1971-72), Massachusetts, the Brant House, Vail (1976), Colorado, and among civic buildings, the Dixwell Fire Station, New Haven (1970-73), Connecticut.

American versus European Architecture

The American East Coast architects, Michael Graves, Richard Meier and Peter Eisenman, regard architecture as something which should be of pure form and independent of external considerations such as social problems. Their points of reference are the white villas of the 1920s and 1930s found in Europe, particularly

Trubeck House, Nantucket, elevation *A modest, wholly American style produced by Robert Venturi and John Rauch. The house displays New England traditions and in particular the shingle style.*

those by Le Corbusier. These references they transformed into handsome boxes, exposing both the structure and skin at key points in a manner reminiscent of Edward Hussey's 19th-century work on Scotney Castle, Kent, where parts of the old 17th-century building were carefully dismantled in such a way as to retain features of interest and to increase the romantic character of the scene. A good example is Meier's Smith House, Darien (1965), Connecticut.

The European approach was very different. There formal quality was less important than fulfilling social functions. Architects were concerned not with houses but with housing programs, not with the private but the public realm and not so much with art as with life. This approach can be found in the work of Aalto and Scharoun and was developed by German architects such as Gunter Behnisch in his Housing for the Elderly, Reutlingen (1973-76), by Faller & Schröder in Housing, Tapachstrasse, Stuttgart (1965-68), in the works of Edward Cullinan & Partners, such as housing at Highgrove, Hillingdon (1972-77), and in the work of Erskine in Sweden. Their work is characterized by the use of materials as found, such as asbestos or other sheet materials. They are able to utilize awkward sites, produce occasional deliberately unexpected geometry in both section and plan, and to serve the requirements of life within a building rather than attempting to impose a rigid form upon it.

The American approach by contrast is concerned primarily with the ability to quote architectural precedent and handle pure form. It is a product of an architectural education in which ideas and theories are developed, just as they were in 18th-century England. European architects tend to follow the Bauhaus in their concern to create a functional architecture and they seek new materials and techniques for pragmatic rather than philosophical reasons. Their philosophy allows architecture to find its own particular shapes and forms, depending on external factors, particularly those concerned with environment.

There is now a complete split in the architecture of the western world, not just a time-lag as one school is superseded by another. This division between the formalistic outlook and the more pragmatic approach was expressed succinctly by Leonardo da Vinci some 500 years ago. Humanists tended to despise him because of his knowledge of the mechanical arts. "Because I am not a literary man," he wrote, "presumptuous persons will think that they may reasonably blame me by alleging that I am an unlettered man. Foolish men... they say that because I have not letters I cannot express well what I want to treat of."

Clearly, Americans and Europeans must go their own way if they are to continue to be involved in the architectural interpretation of their own experience. A healthier dialogue between the two, however, would provide a fresh perspective by which each could review that experience.

Northern Italy

Domestic buildings

Italian *Art Nouveau* was particularly extrovert. It can be seen in the **Palazzo Castiglioni, Milan** (1901-3), by Giuseppe Sommaruga, a strongly massed building enriched with bold, sculptural decoration, including pairs of putti which crown the second story windows. Early housing schemes in Milan include the **Apartment House, Via Moscova** (1923), by Giovanni Muzio. It consists of one main block overlaid with a series of forms. The modern movement in Italy was instigated by the Futurist architect Antonio Sant'Elia, who believed that a new architecture could shape an ideal society. After his death in World War I Giuseppe Terragni took up his ideas and founded Gruppo 7, a group which sought to create an architecture based on clarity, order and an honest use of materials. Terragni abhorred the eclecticism which he saw around him and his projects in **Como,** such as the **Novecomun Building** (1927) and the **Casa Frigerio** (1939), owed a great deal to Berlin and constructivist Moscow.

Ignazio Gardella's work employs simple planes and shows a keen regard for the simplicity and utility of the vernacular tradition. A good example is his **House, Broni** (*c.* 1951). The **Casa Quaglio, Sutrio** (1953-54), which has a large umbrella roof carried on massive brick *piers,* and the **Casa Migotto Ora, Pozzi** (1953), are both by Gino Valle and are designed in a similar vein. The **Casa Apollonio, Galliato** (1965), Varese, by Enrico Castiglioni, is built like a huge spiralling *volute* with bands of windows cut, like a pattern, into the walls. The somewhat bizarre quality of this building is typical of many contemporary Italian designs.

The design of the scheme of **Housing, Gescal Quarter, Milan** (1972-75), was co-ordinated by Piero Sartogo and Gianni Colombo. Individual buildings are arranged quite freely but they are bound together by a band which is drawn around the lower floors of the separate blocks so that each is linked to its neighbors. It is the complete antithesis of the **Housing, Gallarateze Quarter, Milan** (1969-74), by Carlo Aymonino and others, in which the rationalist principles of Terragni are continued on a vast and monumental scale. It was conceived as a series of long blocks arranged around a small, open-air auditorium. Interest is added by the round staircase towers, the projecting balconies and the giant *colonnades.* The **Olivetti Social and Residential Center, Ivrea** (1968), by Iginio Cappaia and Pietro Mainardis, is a steel-frame building clad in aluminium. It consists of an hotel and pedestrian street in the middle around which are arranged a cultural center, swimming pool and restaurant.

Palazzo Castiglioni, Milan *The building represents the transitional phase between vernacular architecture and* Art Nouveau. *The simple basic form has been enlivened through the addition of sculptures and decorative molding.*

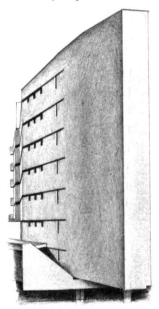

Apartments and Offices, Via Rugabella, *(1950-51), Milan. The building consists of shops on the ground floor, offices on the first floor and apartments above. Designed by Luigi Moretti, it is in a free and informal manner.*

Novecomun Building, Como *This block of flats, with its bull-nosed corner, crisply cut windows and stark wall surfaces, epitomizes Italian architecture of the 1920s and the following decade.*

Housing, Gescal Quarter, Milan *The scheme consists of a series of standard blocks, arranged according to functional rather than aesthetic needs. Visual coherence is provided by the light bands which are drawn across the separate blocks.*

Housing, Gallarateze Quarter, Milan *One of the blocks designed by Aldo Rossi. This particular example is painted white in order to contrast with the red plaster of the other blocks, the yellow footbridges and blue corridors.*

Olivetti Social and Residential Center, Ivrea *The different parts of the center have their own distinct architectural forms. It has an imposing front facing the street, with living units and terraces here at the rear stepped down to the park.*

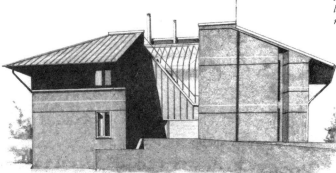

Casa Manzano, Udine *(1965-66). Though this house by Gino Valle has a conventional front and sides, it has been split on the rear elevation. The space has been glazed and stairs lead up to a roof terrace.*

Youth Hostel, Cervinia *(1950s). By Franco Albini, it is a fine* timber-frame *building located on the side of a hill and supported by huge tapering brick-work pillars, in the vernacular Alpine tradition.*

House, Broni *A bold utilitarian design, it has a butterfly roof and massive walls pierced with crisply cut windows. At the front there is a large, two-story glazed section from ground to roof, which is reinforced by the balcony projecting from the living room.*

School, Fagnano Olona *(1972), right. This school by Aldo Rossi has a crisp, rational design, consisting of three parallel blocks which flank a central courtyard. The courtyard is punctuated by this* rotunda, *which is the school library.*

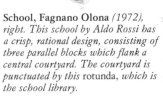

Northern Italy

Civic & Public buildings

The **Casa del Popolo, Como** (1936), was designed by Giuseppe Terragni as a center for the Italian Fascist party. It is a rectangular, concrete building faced in marble. Despite the powerful front with its exposed frame and the play of solids and voids, it was probably not to Mussolini's liking, for to him power was best expressed by the forms, rather than the details, of Roman classicism. A more typical example of Fascist architecture is the **Railway Station, Milan** (1931), a massive building by Eugenio Montuori.

The use of extravagant forms was a characteristic of Italian architecture in the 1960s. A good example is the **City Hall, Segrate** (1962), Milano, by Michele Achilli and other architects, in which the extremely bold forms are superimposed with mammoth columns.

Commercial & Industrial buildings

Italian architects have designed some magnificent buildings in iron and glass, such as the **Victor Emmanuel II Gallery, Milan** (1865-67), by Giuseppe Mengoni, a magnificent shopping arcade which can still compete today, in terms of scale and grandeur, with the enormous precincts built in the United States during the 1970s. The first large-scale work designed in a more modern idiom was the **Fiat Works, Turin** (1919-27), in Lingeretto, by Giacomo Matte-Trucco. It is typical of the rationalist trend which was then influencing European architecture. On the roof is a ¾ mile

City Hall, Segrate *The whirling forms of concrete seem to draw the spectator toward and into the building. While interesting on a formal level, the building lacks the necessary imposing civic imagery.*

Casa del Popolo, Como *One of the most outstanding buildings of pre-war Italy, it consists of offices which are built around a central courtyard. The structural frame is exposed along the front.*

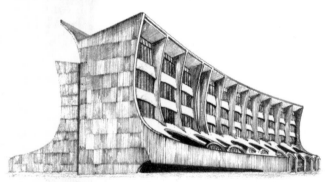

Technical Institute, Busto Arsizio, *(1960). Enrico Castiglioni's building is typical of many of his works in which spaces are encompassed in complex shell constructions. The design has an intuitive quality in contrast to some of the more rationalist buildings which were being constructed at the time.*

Palazzo del Lavoro, Turin *(1960). The roof, which is almost 165 sq ft, is carried on 16 concrete columns, 80 ft tall, which have ribbed mushroom capitals, such as that illustrated, left.*

Victor Emmanuel II Gallery, Milan *This shopping arcade was influenced by 19th-century English architecture, notably the Crystal Palace and the giant sheds of railway stations. The roof covers two intersecting streets, one of which links the Opera House with the Cathedral Piazza.*

test track. The ingenuity is typical of the work of architects who believed that the roof of a building should be adapted to diverse uses.

Some of the most remarkable works in modern Italy were designed by the structural engineer Pier Nervi, whose works rank with those of Maillart, the Swiss engineer. Good examples include the **Exhibition Hall, Turin** (1948-49), one of the finest exhibition halls in Europe, and the **Palazzo del Lavoro, Turin** (1961), in which the huge roof is divided into 16 separate sections, each carried on a vast mushroom column.

Patronage was a notable feature of Italian architecture. Two particularly generous industrialists were Adriano Olivetti and his son Roberto, who commissioned, among other buildings, the **Olivetti Headquarters, Via Clerici** (1954), Milan, by G. A. Bernasconi, A. Fiocchi and M. Nizzoli. The latter two also designed the **Flats, Ivrea** (1952), for Olivetti workers, while Ignazio Gardella designed their **Community Hall, Ivrea** (1959). Other interesting commercial buildings include the **Newspaper Offices, Milan** (1964), by Alberto Roselli. It is constructed of an exposed steel frame with the printing machines visible behind diffused glass on the lower floors. The editorial offices are above and are glazed from floor to ceiling. The magnificent **Pirelli Building, Milan** (1959), was designed by a group of architects led by Gio Ponti, with Nervi employed as the principal consulting engineer. It comprises 34 stories with its ground plan shaped as an ellipse.

Torre Velasca, Milan *(1957). The architects of this tower were Ludovico Belgiojoso, Enrico Peressutti and Ernesto Rogers. Some of the architecture of the mid-1950s in Milan was characterized by a Liberty revival (the Liberty style was fashionable in the* Art Deco *period) of which this building, with its overhanging upper stories, is an interesting example.*

Instituto Marchiondi Spagliadi, Milan *(1957). By Vittoriano Vignano, it is one of the few examples of Brutalist architecture in Italy. Its stern and aggressive aesthetic is lightened by undertones of Giusseppe Terragni's work.*

Newspaper Offices, Milan *This is a modern palazzo-style building in which the architect has incorporated both the printing and the editorial departments under one roof.*

Olivetti Factory, Ivrea *(1952). By Luigi Figini and Gino Pollini, the design of this building follows the formal simplicity and the structural clarity of Terragni's work.*

Offices, A. Zanussi Rex Factory, Pordenone *(1961). This building by Gino Valle represents a bold answer to problems including eliminating traffic noise with a heavy, deep-set concrete exterior.*

Rome

Domestic buildings

Antonio Sant' Elia, the Italian, said in 1914 that no architecture had been produced in Italy since the 18th century. He overlooked, however, some of the magnificent structures which were built at the end of the 19th century, most notably the Railway Station and the Galleria in Milan. In Rome the palazzo tradition had become so strong that few had either the courage to break out of the straight-jacket or even make refinements to the basic pattern. Of the earlier projects of this century the most interesting is the popular housing of the **Gino Coppede Quarter** (1919-23), which has a certain picturesque monumentality and gives the impression of a series of Italianate villas piled one on top of the other.

The first domestic buildings designed in the modern idiom did not appear before the late 1940s. 4, **Via Magna Grecia** (1949), by Angelo di Castro, and 10, **Via Fratelli Ruspolli** (1949), by Ugo Luccichenti, are typical. A key element in them is the play of geometry along the main façades and the use of solids and voids, as well as advancing and receding planes. At the **Casa Roma, Viale Bruno Buozzi** (1949-50), by Luigi Moretti, the whole façade has been treated like a broken *pediment*, the void occupied by a stairway. Moretti was also the architect of the **Casa della Cooperativo, 27, Via Jenner** (1949), where he again treated the façade as a decorative motif. Mario Ridolfi employed a simple play of geometry in his **Palazzina Mancioli, Via Lusitania** (1952-53), where the long terraced walls are multi-faceted. In his **Apartment, 38, Via Paisiello** (1948-49), he extended the upper floors in order to create the appearance of two separate parts and managed to retain a comfortable balance between the old and the new. The idea of actually defining the different functions of a building was not new but within the context of the traditional Roman palazzo it took on an interesting form in the **Palazzina, San Maurizio** (1962). Via R. Roma, by Moretti, and the **Apartments and Offices, Via Campania** (1962-65), by the Pasarelli brothers. In the latter building there are three separate parts: shops, offices and apartments, the function of each individually expressed. Not since the courtyard homes of ancient Ostia had the palazzo form been so dramatically reinterpreted. Other buildings of interest include the **Palazzino Zaccardi, Via G.B. de Rossi** (1950-51), by Ridolfi, and the **Quartiere INA Casa, Triburtino** (1949-54), by L. Quaroni, Ridolfi, and others.

Civic & Public buildings

The **Victor Emmanuel Monument, Piazza Venezia** (1888-1911), is perhaps, after St. Peter's, the most forceful monument in Rome. Designed by Count Giuseppe Sacconi, it stands on the slopes of the Capitol. It was constructed lavishly of white marble, in a distinctly *Neobaroque* design. Sacconi borrowed quite freely and unashamedly from the past, notably in the handsome *quadrigas* on the corner pavilions, and was most certainly attempting to recreate that extravagant aura which must have been so evident in Imperial Rome.

Casa Baldi, Via Flaminia *(1960). The plan of this building by Paolo Portoghese is hexagonal. Each room and corner window is expressed externally by carved walls, which are in turn* articulated *by a* bold *string-course and by a deep eaves.*

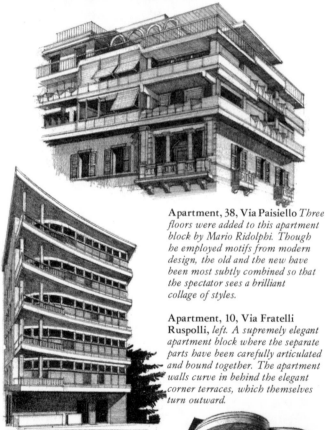

Apartment, 38, Via Paisiello *Three floors were added to this apartment block by Mario Ridolphi. Though he employed motifs from modern design, the old and the new have been most subtly combined so that the spectator sees a brilliant collage of styles.*

Apartment, 10, Via Fratelli Ruspolli, *left. A supremely elegant apartment block where the separate parts have been carefully articulated and bound together. The apartment walls curve in behind the elegant corner terraces, which themselves turn outward.*

Palazzina San Maurizio, 35, Via R. Roma *The sweeping curves of the apartment terraces,* Baroque *in feeling, are contrasted and balanced by the sharply deliniated wall below. While the terraces are arranged as a series of semi-circular layers, the wall is plain.*

Popular housing

In Rome there are several magnificent housing complexes which were built at the turn of the century. All of the structures are enriched by the addition of extravagant detail, applied with considerable panache.

Gino Coppede Quarter

Gino Coppede Quarter, entrance

S. Saba Quarter

Casa Roma, Viale Bruno Buozzi *One of Luigi Moretti's finest buildings, it is of particular interest for its split façade. The overall design is one of symmetry but the roof-line is strangely asymmetrical.*

Apartments and Offices, Via Campania *In this building the architect has devised very different forms for the three separate functions of the building. The smooth, elegant office block is here surmounted by intricately articulated apartments.*

Victor Emmanuel Monument, Piazza Venezia *The monument comprises a vast platform on which sits an enormous colonnaded structure. Before this there is a terrace surmounted with an equestrian statue of the king. Around the terrace, steps cascade down to the level of the street.*

Rome

Nothing more was built on so grand a scale as the Victor Emmanuel Monument, but monumental characteristics remained the norm for the remaining civic and public buildings which were erected in the early decades of the century. Traditional forms, bold *rustication* and a profusion of decorative molding and sculptured *keystones* and *pediments* were common. A good example is the **Palazzo di Giustizia, Piazzo Cavour** (1888-1910).

Little else of note was built until the 1930s and then a whole series of civic buildings were produced in which the major characteristics are the play of solids and voids, the exposing of the interior structures, and bare wall surfaces, sometimes used with excessive regularity. Among good examples are the **Post Office Building, Via Marmorata** (1933), by Mario Ridolfi and Mario de Renzi, many buildings by Luigi Moretti, such as the **Casa delle Armi** (1934), the **Sala al Foro Italico** (1936), the **Piazzale** (1936), and the **Casa della Gioventu, 1, Via Induno** (1933), and the **University** (1935) by Giovanni Michelucci, Marcello Piacentini and others.

The major works by Pier Luigi Nervi in Rome are the **Palazzetto** (1957) and the **Palazzo dello Sport** (1959). The former was designed to seat 4,000 and is the more handsome of the two structures. Its dome is supported by 36 concrete struts which transmit its weight to an underground concrete ring. The latter seats 16,000. Here an *aisle* encircles the supports of the dome, while the entire façade is glazed.

Commercial & Industrial buildings

The **Stazione Termini** (1947-50), by E. Montouri and L. Salini, is one of the finest modern structures in Rome. It consists of a booking hall and entrance foyer housed under an enormous curving roof. Behind and above this is a block of offices with shops and cafés underneath. These open out onto a broad mall leading to the station platforms. **Leonardo da Vinci Airport** (1950-57) was designed by A. Luccichenti, V. Monaco, R. Morandi and A. Zariteri. However, it is without the fine quality and simplicity of the station. The **Rinascente, Piazza Fiume** (1959-61), by Franco Albini and Franca Helg, demonstrates the adaptability of the palazzo. It consists of a six-story department store, its façade *articulated* by the exposure of the steel frame and the *cornices*.

Casa della Cooperativo, 27, Via Jenner *(1949). By Luigi Moretti, this is one of his most interesting designs in Rome and is a key building in the development of modern architecture in Italy for the way the façade is treated as a decorative motif, with vertical layers appearing to have been peeled away.*

Rinascente, Piazza Fiume *This detail from the store shows the exposed steel frames as well as the service ducts, which are accommodated in the corrugations of the cladding and are balanced by* cornices.

Offices of the Ordine dei Medici, Via G. B. de Rossi *(1970). By Piero Sartago and others, this building is composed of very distinct volumes, each one layered on top of the other. The design combines elements of work by Moretti and Mario Ridolfi.*

Palazzetto dello Sport *The smaller of two sports stadiums built by Pier Luigi Nervi. The building has a remarkable structure. Most noticeable is the hemispherical shell roof and its "Y"-shaped supports.*

Zoological Gardens *(1911). One of two arched entrances, by A. Brasini and G. Berluzzi, which flank the main drive. The elephant's head keystone appears as a somewhat bizarre feature, nestling as it does among classical motifs such as* capitals *and stepped* entablature.

Central & Southern Italy

Religious buildings

S. Giovanni, Autostrada de Sole (1961), Florence, is one of the most interesting buildings in the region. Designed by Giovanni Michelucci and constructed of coarse rubble block with a tent-like roof, its swirling, plastic forms have diverse sources and origins, notably Le Corbusier's Ronchamp roofscape and the designs of Hans Sharoun. The church of **S. Franco, Francavilla al Mare** (1959), near Pescara, by Ludovico Quaroni, has a huge *nave* with a high ceiling, and an elegant, detached *campanile.* The church represents a modern interpretation of the traditional theme of a giant church and campanile, built so as to dominate the immediate environs.

Domestic buildings

In the late 1960s and the early 1970s there was a reaction against the somewhat inhuman qualities of modern architecture. At one level this resulted in a vernacular revival and on another to the proliferation of intricate schemes characterized by broken, irregular plans and skylines and a general picturesqueness of composition. Good examples are projects by Paolo Portoghesi and S. Gigliotti, such as the **Casa Andreis, Scandriglia** (1965-67). The **Students' Apartments, Urbino** (1963), by Giancarlo de Carlo, marked the beginning of this more organic kind of architecture with their juxtaposition of circular and rectilinear elements which are carefully positioned along a gentle and undulating hillside.

Civic & Public buildings

The **Stadium, Florence** (1930-32), established Pier Luigi Nervi as a designer of concrete structures. The building's importance lies in the way the design was reduced to merely structural elements, arranged in a manner which made them both decorative and functional. The influence of Robert Venturi, the American architect, is discernible in some later Italian architecture in details, such as eccentric window shapes. Examples can be found in the work of V. de Feo and F. Ascione, such as the **Library and Cultural Center, Torre del Greco** (1969), and an earlier building, the **Technical Institute, Terni** (1968).

Commercial & Industrial buildings

The juxtaposition of craftsmanship with modern, sophisticated motifs is found in the buildings of Paolo Soleri. He was an admirer of Antoni Gaudi and worked, for a time, under Frank Lloyd Wright. His **Solimene Ceramics Factory, Vietri-sur Mare** (1954), near Salerno, is a five-story hall in which the floors are connected by a continuous spiral ramp. The façade is made up of giant panels and triangular areas of glazing.

The desire to draw tourism has resulted in a considerable amount of vernacular revival work in this region as well as some bizarre and unusual buildings. An outstanding example is the **Shop, S. Felice Ciceo** (1970s), which fits into the tradition starting with the Maison Batelliers in Brussels.

S. Giovanni, Autostrada de Sole *The church was dedicated to the memory of those who lost their lives during the building of the Autostrada. The architect sought to blend the different elements so that the walls and the dome became one.*

Library and Cultural Center, Torre del Greco *The building was conceived as a simple shed design but it has acquired a greater vitality through its stepped section and the incorporation of asymmetrical shapes, which cut into the roof of the building.*

Shop, S. Felice Ciceo *This seaside building combines the venacular with nautical, and even classical motifs. The portal, for instance, is displayed as the stern of a ship and yet it nevertheless incorporates a broken pediment at the top.*

Galleria Umberto I, Naples *(1887-91), right. By Emanuele Rocco and other architects, this magnificent shopping hall consists of an arcade designed in the form of a cross. The dome, which is glazed, is the main source of light for the arcade.*

Northeast France

Religious buildings

Many of the churches built during the 20th century have been influenced by the forms and structural techniques developed for contemporary commercial and industrial buildings. However, the pilgrimage church of **Notre-Dame-du-Haut, Ronchamp** (1950-55), was a reaction both against this influence and against the rather restrictive formal style of the postwar modern architecture. It was designed by Le Corbusier and was his first venture into ecclesiastical architecture. With its gently rounded towers and huge shell-like roof which projects out over the battered walls, the building is both massive and compact. The interior is a mass of convex and concave curves, the thick white rough-cast walls being pierced by deep-set splay windows of differing shapes and sizes that are filled with colored glass. The primary colors of the door and window openings offset the white concrete and produce a striking effect. Additional light is funneled into the interior by the church's three towers. Although initially the building appears rather primitive, it is a highly sophisticated and quite original piece of work, without any historical precedent.

Domestic buildings

Nancy was one of the main centers of *Art Nouveau* in Europe and had a flourishing cultural milieu in which the decorative arts and architecture thrived. Perhaps the best example of Art Nouveau architecture in Nancy is the **Villa Marjorelle** (1898-1900). Designed by Henri Sauvage, it has four related but different façades and is particularly interesting for the successful integration of a variety of different building materials.

Commercial & Industrial buildings

The introduction of new structural techniques at the beginning of the 19th century utilizing steel, combined with the development of reinforced concrete in the mid-19th century, produced a series of novel, frame buildings, such as the **Chocolate Factory, Noisiel-sur-Marne** (1871-72), by Jules Saulnier. It is part of a company village established well in advance of its English counterparts. The main factory building has a steel frame with brick infill, a method to be used in Chicago some 12 years later. Another interesting industrial building is the **Duval Factory, Saint-Dié** (1946), Vosges, by Le Corbusier. The factory was built after his original plans for the reconstruction of Saint-Dié (destroyed in World War II) had come to nothing.

Notre-Dame-du-Haut, Ronchamp *Designed by Le Corbusier, it replaced a 13th-C pilgrimage church destroyed in 1944. The dominant features are the shell roof and the three round-topped towers.*

Villa Marjorelle, Nancy *A fine example of* Art Nouveau *architecture, it was designed by Henri Sauvage who was one of the major exponents of Art Nouveau architecture in France.*

Duval Factory, Saint-Dié *The southeast façade of this millinery factory, rebuilt after World War II by Le Corbusier. The louvers projecting from the window-frames provide shade. Originally, ceilings, woodwork and pipes were painted in bright colors to contrast with the concrete.*

Lock, Kembs-Niffer, Haut-Rhin *(1958). Designed by Le Corbusier, it contains offices for customs and pilots. The various parts are clearly* articulated *under one large shell roof.*

Paris

Religious buildings

Church architecture of the late 19th century tended to follow the *Gothic* style with the occasional use of *Romanesque* or *Byzantine* styles. The most memorable example of the Byzantine influence is the church of the **Sacré-Coeur** (1875-1914), one of the best-known landmarks in Paris. This handsome eclectic church, designed by Paul Abadie, was undertaken after the Franco-Prussian War.

Innovations in church building were wholly structural and reflected the changing use of building materials elsewhere. The church of **S. Eugene** (1854-55), designed by Louis-Auguste Boileau, is notable for being the first iron-framed church. **S. Jean-de-Montmartre** (1892-1900), by Anatole de Baudot, was the first church to be built using reinforced concrete, but not until Auguste Perret designed **Notre-Dame, Le Raincy** (1922-23) was reinforced concrete used in any radical way. At Le Raincy, the shallow vaulted roof is held like a canopy on slender reinforced concrete columns. The walls are no more than glazed grills providing an abundance of light, so the building has become a classic lantern church.

Domestic buildings

Hector Guimard was the most gifted architect of the French *Art Nouveau* movement. Although little remains of the movement as a whole, there are some memorable examples of Guimard's work in Paris. These include **Castel Orgeval, Villemoisson** (1904-5); **Castel Béranger, 14 Rue la Fontaine** (1897-98); **Jassedé Building, 142 Avenue de Versailles** (1903-5), and **Chalet Blanc, Rue du Lyceé, Sceaux** (1908). While Guimard produced some public works, particularly his imaginative entrances to the Paris Metro with their curving, organic forms, Art Nouveau was given little official encouragement after the turn of the century and so to continue with the style he had to work exclusively for private clients.

Sacré-Coeur, Paris *One of the major landmarks of Paris, it stands on the heights of Montmartre, its cluster of white domes having a distinct* Byzantine *quality. Its other notable features include a tall belltower and the richly decorated interior.*

Notre-Dame, Le Raincy, *below. A pioneer building by Auguste Perret. The entire structure is of concrete, the shallow,* vaulted *roof being held like a canopy on slender reinforced concrete columns. Stained glass windows stretch the full height of the walls.*

Castel Béranger, 14, Rue la Fontaine, *above. The work of Hector Guimard, this flamboyant use of plant forms in the arch and columns of the* portal *and in the decorative ironwork of the entrance gate is a characteristic of much of his work.*

Castel Orgeval, Villemoisson *With its mixture of brick and unhewn stone, turreted roofs, timber* corbels *and decorative balcony, this is a classic* Art Nouveau *building. It was designed by Hector Guimard, who was one of the most outstanding exponents of the French Art Nouveau movement.*

S. Jean-de-Montmartre *By Anatole de Baudot, this was the first church built using reinforced concrete. The arches crowning the low flanking wings and those of the high westwork are decorated with mosaic.*

Paris

Paris contains memorable work by some of the leading architects of the period. One such architect was Henri Sauvage, a contemporary of Hector Guimard. He was a talented designer in both *Art Nouveau* and *Art Deco* styles before World War I, but he produced his most radical work in the 1920s. He experimented with prefabrication, low-cost housing and *International Style* modernism and in 1923-25 designed the **Stepped Building, Rue des Amiraux**. In principle this is a tent-like structure with apartments and overhanging terraces stepped back on the outside. The building was a remarkable innovation and became a major reference for buildings in Britain, Germany and Switzerland during the 1960s and 1970s. A similar but smaller version of his idea can be seen in one of Sauvage's earlier projects, the **Stepped Flats, 26, Rue Vavin** (1912).

Auguste Perret was one of the earliest exponents of modern architecture and the first to use reinforced concrete creatively in architecture. A major example of his work is the **Apartment Building, 25, Rue Franklin** (1903). Here the concrete frame *articulates* the receding and advancing planes as clearly as *pilasters* or columns did in the buildings of the modern classical world. The walls are completely glazed and internal pillars carry the floor loads, rather than loadbearing walls.

Other early 20th-century buildings include the **Hotel, 21, Rue Octave Feuillet** (*c.* 1907) by Charles Plumet, and the **House, Boulevard Murat** (1906), by P. Guddet. This last has a completely glazed façade divided into six vertical bays, three stories in height.

Adolf Loos designed the **House, Avenue Junot** (1925-27), for Tristan Tzara. It is a remarkably refined and austere six-story building with the lower three stories in blockwork with *rendering* for the upper story. A tall, deep balcony recess is cut into the top two stories.

Jassedé Building, 142, Avenue de Versailles, *(1903-5). Detail of the boldly curving balconies. This striking apartment building is one of the few remaining examples of French Art Nouveau architecture and was designed by Hector Guimard.*

La Roche-Jeanneret House, Auteuil *View of the double-height picture gallery with its curved wall and high clerestory window and balcony on the left. The chief façades of the house by Le Corbusier face east and north.*

Maison Coo Boulogne-sur-Seine *An elegant town house by Le Corbusier. With its use of pilotis in particular, it demonstrates characteristic features of Le Corbusier's proposed new architecture.*

Apartment Building, 25, Rue Franklin *This was a revolutionary building for its time and was the first occasion on which a reinforced concrete frame was used for a domestic building. It was designed by Auguste Perret who reveled in the novelty of large balconies and glazed areas.*

Stepped Building, Rue des Amiraux *Designed by Henri Sauvage, this was one of the most radical apartment buildings of the period. Conceived as a tent-like structure, its stepped section and overhanging terraces were to influence numerous architects in the 1960s and 1970s.*

The simple and *Cubist* style of Loos's architecture had a great effect on the **Apartments, Rue Mallet-Stevens, Passy** (1927), by Robert Mallet-Stevens. These dwellings consist of a series of overlapping cube-like volumes stepping up to the roof.

From the 1920s however French architecture was largely dominated by Le Corbusier. An example of his work is **La Roche-Jeanneret House, Auteuil** (1923). Originally two houses joined at right angles, it is now the Foundation Le Corbusier. The Roche House, with the large curving wall of the double-height picture gallery, was designed around the collection of cubist paintings assembled by the Swiss banker, Raoul La Roche. The whole is a picturesque ensemble of white walls, long bands of windows flush with the façade and projecting bays and balconies. The building by Le Corbusier which ultimately had the most universal application was **Maison Cook, Boulogne-sur-Seine** (1926). This is a remarkable building in which Le Corbusier clearly demonstrated points that became characteristic of his new architecture. The building is raised on *pilotis* — free-standing concrete columns. Because of this use of columns for the structure of the buildings, there are no load-bearing walls allowing the façade to be designed without concern for its structural role, especially allowing long bands of windows. In addition a roof garden is created by using the flat roof slab. The overall effect is one of a cube-like house on stilts, a haunting Le Corbusier theme.

The **Villa Savoye, Poissy** (1927-31) is one of the most influential of all Le Corbusier's work of the 1920s and 1930s. It is an elegant white box raised on pilotis above garaging, staff rooms and entrance hall. The main rooms are on the first floor opening out onto a terrace. A parallel example of Le Corbusier's work is the **Maison Stein, Garches** (1929). Here, the double-height garden terrace is the main feature.

Maison, Rue Belliard *(1913). The work of H. Deneux this tall and visually impressive building stands on an awkward corner site. To overcome the problem, two flat planes are angled toward each other and joined by a five-story window panel. The wall surfaces are enriched by mosaics.*

Villa Savoye, Poissy *This elegant white Le Corbusier villa stands upon pilotis with its piano nobile raised above the center of a great field. The main floor is reached by a ramp rather than a traditional staircase.*

Art Nouveau

Shown here are two good examples of *Art Nouveau* work in Paris. While often merely surface decoration, Parisian Art Nouveau was extremely bold and *Baroque* in feel with its elaborate use of sculptured foliage around *portals,* balconies and windows.

Detail from Apartments, Place Félix Faure (*c. 1905)*

Doorway, Maison de Rapport, Avenue Rapport (1900-01)

Chalet Blanc, Sceaux *(1908). Detail of the Art Nouveau wooden gate. The house itself has a rather romantic almost fairytale appearance and was designed by Hector Guimard, the most gifted architect of French Art Nouveau.*

Paris

The **Maison de Verre, 31, Rue Saint-Guillaume** (1927-32), by Pierre Chareau and Bernard Bijvoet, is one of those rare buildings that seem to have few if any architectural precedents. It was the private house and surgery of a Dr Dalsace and his wife and presented a number of design problems. The family owned the lower two floors of a three-story apartment block. There was limited space so the architects inserted an additional floor, first pinning the third story on a steel frame and then rebuilding three new floors below. Because of of the need for light as well as privacy, the façade facing the entry court has a glass block wall, while the garden façade has large areas of glass and glass block. The steel frame was left partially exposed inside and its strength rendered the façade simply a cladding, a radical innovation that was not to be fully developed until much later.

During the 1940s and early 1950s Le Corbusier began to move away from the restrictions of *International Style* architecture. His interest in the primitive simplicity and utility of Mediterranean buildings expressed itself in the two **Jaoul Houses, Neuilly** (1954-56). They are rectangular in plan with massive load-bearing walls dividing the plan lengthwise into one small and one large bay on each floor. The roofs are *vaulted* and the rough concrete of the *vaults* is left exposed externally. The massive brick walls are pierced by small openings, the main *gabled* ends being paneled.

Civic & Public buildings

Henri Labrouste was one of the major architects of 19th-century Paris. He designed the **Bibliothèque Saint-Geneviève** (1843-50), the first French library to be designed as a separate building. Despite its classical façade, it is structurally radical with a complete iron frame and a metal double roof. Labrouste also designed part of the **Bibliothèque National** (1862-68), which has a magnificent reading room covered by nine terra-cotta domes carried on slender iron columns. The crowns of the domes are pierced to allow natural light into the reading room from above.

The **Opera House** (1861-75) by Charles Garnier is a bold, *Neobaroque* building. It has a long, sumptuous foyer and magnificent grand staircase enlivened with statues. In much the same way, the **Petit Palais** (1897-1900) by Charles Girault is a civic building in the grand design tradition. It has a domed central pavilion *articulated* by a giant arch framing the entrance *portal* and is flanked by domed pavilions with *pedimented* façades, the whole raised on a *rusticated* basement.

The late 19th-century also saw the construction of the **Eiffel Tower** (1887-89). Built by Gustave Eiffel for the Paris Exhibition of 1889, it is one of the most monumental examples of frame building. At the time its boldness and novelty caused considerable controversy.

During the 1920s the International Style influenced the design of various civic buildings. Two outstanding examples are **Cité de Refuge, 12, rue Cantagrel** (1929-33), and the **Maison Suisse, Cité Universitaire** (1930-32), both of which were designed by Le Corbusier.

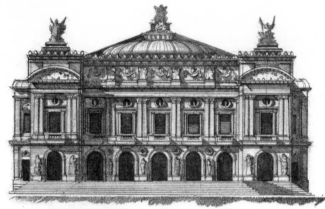

Opera House *This is a magnificent* Neobaroque *building with a highly ornate and sculptural façade that echoes the opulence of Imperial Rome. It was designed by Charles Garnier, who was attempting to create a Napoleon III style, and is considered by many people to be the masterpiece of the Second Empire.*

Ozenfant Studio, 15, Avenue Reille *(1922-23). This is a marvelous four-story house by Le Corbusier with a two-story studio at the top. Built on an awkward corner site, its simple geometric forms, glazing, open-planning and outer staircase combine to produce a striking example of the* International Style.

Jaoul Houses, Neuilly *These two detached houses by Le Corbusier, stand on one rectangular site sharing a drive and entrance fore-court. They make bold use of rough brick and raw concrete.*

Apartments, 24, rue Nungesser-et-Coli *(1933). An eight-story apartment building by Le Corbusier. The top two stories were his apartment where he lived until his death in 1966.*

Petit Palais *An art gallery designed by Charles Girault for the the International Exhibition of 1900. It was influenced very much by the tradition of grand design and with its domed pavilions and arched* portal *is a magnificent Neobaroque building.*

Bibliothèque Saint-Geneviève *With its classical façade* articulated *by a broad* cornice, *round-arched windows and* pilasters, *this is a marvelous* Neoclassical *building in the Place du Panthéon, designed by Henri Labrouste.*

Maison Suisse, Cité Universitaire *View of the entrance to the hostel with the dormitory block behind. Designed by Le Corbusier, this is a four-storey block raised on* pilotis *with a small, windowed north façade. The south façade has a* curtain wall *of glass.*

Eiffel Tower *This famous Parisian landmark was built by Gustave Eiffel in collaboration with the Swiss engineer Maurice Koechlin. When it was originally built this monumental iron-frame building was the tallest in the world but since then, despite the addition of a further 65 ft for a television transmission aerial, it has been exceeded by skyscrapers elsewhere.*

Museum of Modern Art *(1937). This plain and rather stark building with its almost Neo-classical style was a forerunner of the rationalist movement of the 1970s. It was designed by a number of architects, including J. C. Dondel and A. Aubert.*

335

Paris

There are a number of very interesting and fairly recent examples of modern architecture in Paris. The **Brazilian Students' Hostel, Cité Universitaire** (1956-59), by Le Corbusier, consists of a five-story slab block raised on *pilotis* with ancillary accommodation, such as the dean's quarters and communal facilities, collected in a collage on either side of the open ground story.

The **Pompidou Center** (1977), designed by Renzo Piano and Richard Rogers as a new cultural center, is another remarkable building. The intention behind it was to give Paris an architectural complex worthy of 20th-century achievement. An architectural competition was held for the design in 1969 and it was specified that there should be six floors and that the center should be able to house 10,000 visitors daily.

Other interesting modern public buildings include the **UNESCO Headquarters, Place de Fontenoy** (1953-57), by Marcel Breuer, Pier Luigi Nervie and Bernard Zehrfuss; the **Communist Party Headquarters, Boulevard de la Villette** (1971), a snaking glass-walled building by Oscar Niemeyer, and the **Australian Embassy** (1978) by Harry Seidler & Associates.

Commercial & Industrial buildings

Paris contains some fine 19th-century railway stations. Of particular interest are the **Gare de L'Este** (1847-52), the **Gare du Nord** (1862-63) and the **Gare d'Orsay** (1898-1900). In addition there are still a number of Hector Guimard's *Art Nouveau* entrances to the Paris Metro, one being that to the **Porte Dauphin** (1900).

Pompidou Center *This remarkable complex was designed by Richard Rogers and Renzo Piano. When completed, its exposed frame led some to describe it as an unfinished structure with the scaffolding left in place. In scale and technique, however, it is comparable to the medieval cathedral.*

Porte Dauphin *Entrance to the Metro, the underground railway of Paris. This striking work is one of a series of imaginative Art Nouveau entrance pavilions in glass and iron designed by Hector Guimard. There are now few examples of fine Art Nouveau work in Paris.*

Brazilian Students' Hostel, Cité Universitaire *View of the east façade of the building. The low building in front of the hostel is the office and living quarters of the dean. Designed by Le Corbusier, the hostel is notable for its use of rough-cast concrete, an innovation that influenced many other architects.*

Newspaper Office, Rue de Reaumur *(1903). The offices of "Le Parisien" by G. Chedanne show something of the impact of the structural and aesthetic advances made in building the Eiffel Tower. Here the architecture similarly depends on the external expression of the structure of the building.*

Australian Embassy, Rue Jean Rey *By Harry Seidler and others, this consists of a chancery block and an apartment block with ancillary accommodation, including a theatre. This is contained in two wedge-shaped counter curves which are linked by a two-story glass entrance and by a first-floor bridge.*

Southeast France

Religious buildings

The **Monastery of Sainte-Marie de la Tourette, Eveux-sur-l'Arbresle** (1952-59), Rhône, is one of Le Corbusier's greatest works. The Dominicans of Lyon, who had already commissioned work from 20th-century artists such as Jean Lurcat, Jacques Lipchitz and Fernand Léger, approached Le Corbusier to design their new monastery. To some extent he followed the layout and themes of the old Cistercian monasteries, in which each part of the complex was laid out in a uniform manner at right angles to another part.

Standing on a hilltop above the village, Le Corbusier's monastery is quadrangular in plan with the central space occupied by *cloisters.* To the north of the cloister is the church. Everything else, such as chapels, *atrium* and *oratory,* is grouped at right angles around the cloister and quadrangle. Particular points of interest are the curving walls of the lower church and chapels, and the pyramid-shaped roof of the oratory. The monastery is raised on stilts in the southwest corner, and added drama is provided by the way the ground falls away at this point, and by the sweeping views out to the hills beyond. Today the monastery is the Thomas More Center for theological research.

Domestic buildings

The **Unité d'Habitation, Marseilles** (1947-52), designed by Le Corbusier, was the first of a series of such structures where whole communities, together with shopping areas, recreational facilities and ancillary accommodation, were to be housed within one coherent unit.

Raised on massive *pilotis,* the unit consists of an immense rectangular block. In the main structure there are some 350 single- and two-story apartments with one shopping story situated half way up the structure. On the roof there are recreational and other communal facilities.

The Marseilles Unité made a considerable impact at the time and five others were built along the same lines. Four of these were in France and one was built in Charlottenberg, West Berlin.

Unité d'Habitation

Designed by Le Corbusier, this was his answer to the problem of low-cost mass housing. His idea was to create a community of some 1600 people living in one coherent structure that contained not only homes but also a shopping street and a communal roof with recreational facilities.

Roof terrace

West façade and shopping street

Unité d'Habitation, Marseilles

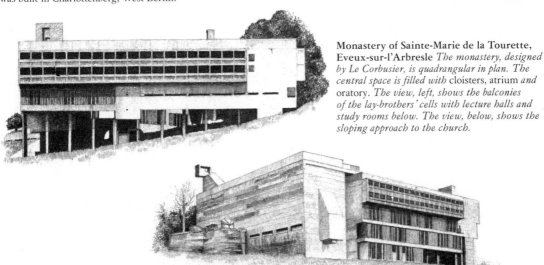

Monastery of Sainte-Marie de la Tourette, Eveux-sur-l'Arbresle *The monastery, designed by Le Corbusier, is quadrangular in plan. The central space is filled with* cloisters, atrium *and* oratory. *The view, left, shows the balconies of the lay-brothers' cells with lecture halls and study rooms below. The view, below, shows the sloping approach to the church.*

Southeast France

Civic & Public buildings

The **Youth Center, Firminy-Vert** (1963-65), is yet another influential building designed by Le Corbusier and was originally intended as part of a much larger complex. It is a long, linear building standing on rising ground with a high, sharply inclined west façade over the downward slope and a lower, more gently inclined east façade. This incorporates an entrance canopy and ramp to one side. The concrete paneled roof is supported on steel cables, hence the gentle curve *articulated* on the *gable* ends. The inclined façades and hung roof subsequently appeared in numerous buildings around the world.

Commercial & Industrial buildings

The pressure of tourism is one of the key elements that has shaped the environment in this part of France. The effects could be said to have begun in **Monte Carlo** with the creation of the world-famous **Casino** (1878). This imposing and elaborate building was designed by Charles Garnier, although its northwest wing was added by another architect at a later date.

By the 1960s and 1970s, however, architects were facing two opposing problems. One was to provide an environment for tourists wishing to escape from the brashness of much tourist development, and the other was to cater directly for mass tourism. The tourist village of **Port Grimaud** (1965-69), conceived by François Spoerny, aimed to fulfil the first need. Its crooked streets and differing house styles provide a nostalgic reminder of traditional Provençal architecture. **La Grande Motte, Hérault** (1963-75), designed by Jean Balladur, caters entirely for mass tourism. With its artificial pyramids of apartments and hotels, it is part of the continuing tourist development along the 100-mile coastline of Languedoc and Rousillon.

Youth Center, Firminy-Vert
This was part of the recreational and cultural complex proposed for the industrial town, which was largely destroyed during World War II. It was designed by Le Corbusier. The long, inclined façade was intended to open out onto a stadium with an open-air stage and small amphitheatre.

Palais de Justice, Lyons
(1836-41), below. This is a Neo-classical building with a handsome colonnade of composite columns. It was designed by Louis-Pierre Baltard and with its clear-cut lines is a rather late example of this style, which continued to be fashionable in France until the 1830s.

La Grande Motte, Hérault *Illustrated here is La Grande Pyramide, a striking example of the work of Jean Balladur, the architect of La Grande Motte. The project, which forms part of the tourist development on the southeast coast, was designed primarily to serve the needs of mass tourism.*

Port Grimaud *Above, a Provençal-style building; right, view over Venetian-style waterways. Both of these nostalgic elements form part of the tourist village of Port Grimaud, which was created by François Spoerry. The success of the village has made it the model for similar projects elsewhere in Europe.*

Southwest France

Domestic buildings

There are some interesting examples of Le Corbusier's work of the 1920s and 1930s in this region. One is the **House, Lège** (1920), near Pessac. This is one of a group of 10 houses built for M. Frugès, an industrialist. From it developed the much larger and better-known **Frugès Housing Estate, Pessac** (1924-26), near Bordeaux. The estate was originally planned for 200 houses although only 50 were actually built.

Both projects were built as workers communities and Le Corbusier was given free rein to experiment with his ideas for mass housing, a problem that absorbed him for most of his career. The basis of the architecture was standardization, and the concept behind the layout was a garden city in the early 20th-century English tradition.

Speed and economy of construction being of paramount importance in mass housing, Le Corbusier provided a variety of units based on one standard *module,* with flat roofs, large terraces and horizontal bands of windows. Of particular interest is the way in which the original houses had, by the 1960s, been radically transformed by the occupants with the addition of pitched roofs, terraces, *cornices* and *pilasters.* Unwittingly, Le Corbusier had provided a basic structure, which was enriched and extended by the occupants. The concept has influenced architects of the 1960s and 1970s. During the 1930s Le Corbusier became increasingly interested in the more primitive building styles found in such areas as North Africa and southern Europe. The simplicity and utility of the buildings, together with the use of raw materials, greatly appealed to him. Using such materials as rough stone, bare-faced brick, raw concrete and rough timber, he constructed a series of houses of which the **Holiday House, Les Mathes** (1935), near Marennes, is a notable example. Le Corbusier built the house in three separate operations: first the stone walls were erected, then the timber framework and corrugated asbestos roof, and finally the prefabricated elements such as window frames and partition walls.

Holiday House, Les Mathes
Because he could not provide continuous supervision, Le Corbusier erected the house in three separate stages. The stone walls were put up first, then the timber framework and finally the window frames and partition walls.

House, Lége, *near* **Pessac** *One of a group of 10 houses built by Le Corbusier near the dockyards. They are notable for the way in which the original flat-roofed houses have been transformed by pitched roofs and terraces.*

Covered market, Royan *(1956). An elegant, reinforced concrete roof, it is typical of the structures developed in the post-war period.*

Frugès Housing Estate, Pessac (1924-26)

Originally planned as an estate of 200 houses, only 50 were built. Conceived as a workers' community by Le Corbusier, the project comprised standard units to which the occupants later made additions on the façades.

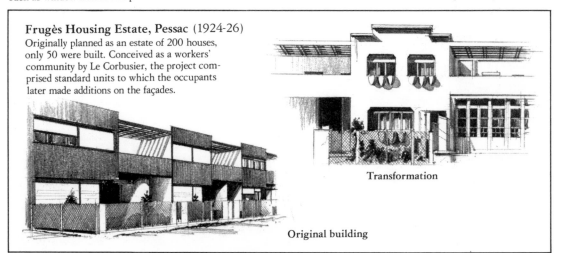

Transformation

Original building

London

Religious buildings

Westminster Cathedral (1897-1903), by John Francis Bentley, is one of the best-known landmarks in London. It is a huge red and white striped building and with its elegant *campanile* and shallow domes is a fascinating mixture of medieval Italian and *Byzantine* influences: Other interesting churches include **All Saints, Margaret Street** (1849-59), by William Butterfield; **St Jude's, Hampstead Garden Suburb** (1903-13), by Sir Edwin Lutyens, and the rather bizarre **Mosque, Regent's Park** (1970s), by Sir Frederick Gibberd.

Domestic buildings

During the last part of the 19th century there was a shift away from the heavy Victorian styles to a lighter architecture called "Queen Anne." Norman Shaw was one of the leading architects in this field and he built a series of residential houses characterized by clearly *articulated* volumes, tall red-brick chimneys, *dormer windows* and *gables*. These include **Lowther Lodge, Kensington Gore** (1872-75), and **Swan House, 17, Chelsea Embankment** (1875-77).

The influence of C. F. A. Voysey's approach can be seen in the **Totterdown Fields Estate, Tooting** (1903-11), built by the London County Council. This so-called cottage estate was a reaction against the rather drab mass-housing of the time. Probably the most interesting and courageous of the housing estates is **Hampstead Garden Suburb** (1907-15). By Barry Parker and Raymond Unwin, it also contains fine examples of work by Lutyens.

During the 1930s many talented architects fled from Germany and settled for a while in London, bringing the *International Style* with them. One was the Russian-born Berthold Lubetkin who worked with a group called Tecton. They built **Highpoint I** (1933-35) and **Highpoint II** (1936-38). These two blocks of flats stand on adjacent sites in Highgate, where they are well-known landmarks. The first block consists of a double cross-shaped plan, with parts of the building carried on columns; the second is a more conventional slab with long bands of windows.

Council housing, too, was affected by the International Style, most notably in **Churchill Gardens, Grosvenor Road** (1950-62), Pimlico. This was designed by A. J. Philip Powell and John Hidalgo Moya and is possibly the best post-war housing scheme in London. Another pioneering development was **Alton Estate, Roehampton** (1952-59), which is the nearest the English avant-garde got to the principles of Le Corbusier.

The **Flats, Ham Common** (1955), Richmond, by James Stirling and James Gowan, marked a radical change in direction for British architecture. The flats were influenced by the work of Le Corbusier and are a fine example of the *Brutalist* style. An interesting and fairly recent example of mass-housing is **Housing, Highgrove** (1972-77), Hillingdon, designed by Edward Cullinan & Partners. The simplicity of elevations and crisp, horizontal bands of windows hark back to the early modern movement, while the back-to-back housing is reminiscent of the 19th century.

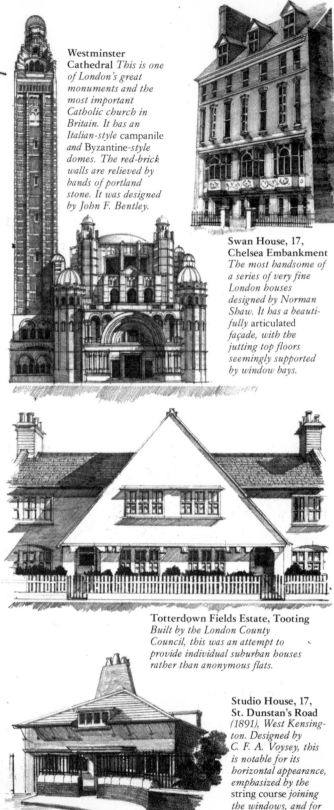

Westminster Cathedral *This is one of London's great monuments and the most important Catholic church in Britain. It has an Italian-style* campanile *and Byzantine-style domes. The red-brick walls are relieved by bands of portland stone. It was designed by John F. Bentley.*

Swan House, 17, Chelsea Embankment *The most handsome of a series of very fine London houses designed by Norman Shaw. It has a beautifully articulated façade, with the jutting top floors seemingly supported by window bays.*

Totterdown Fields Estate, Tooting *Built by the London County Council, this was an attempt to provide individual suburban houses rather than anonymous flats.*

Studio House, 17, St. Dunstan's Road *(1891), West Kensington. Designed by C. F. A. Voysey, this is notable for its horizontal appearance, emphasized by the string course joining the windows, and for its deep eaves.*

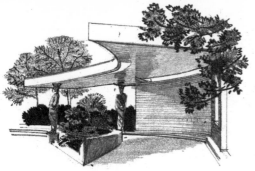

Highpoint II, Highgate *Detail of the entrance canopy, with its striking use of* caryatids *instead of steel columns. Designed by the Tecton group, Highpoint I and II are major landmarks in the development of modern British architecture.*

Sun House, Frognal Way *(1935). This is one of the first truly modern houses in England. It is interesting for its use of reinforced concrete walls, steel column supports to the projecting balconies and long horizontal windows. The design was by Maxwell Fry. The gallery to the left of the top floor is now glazed.*

Churchill Gardens, Grosvenor Road *Designed by J. Philip Powell and John Hidalgo Moya, this is part of a council housing scheme on a 30-acre site. Interest lies in the structural frame articulating the façade.*

Flats, Ham Common *An interesting example of the* Brutalist *style by James Stirling and James Gowan, the flats consist of these three-story terraces plus two two-story pavilions. They were influenced by the work of Le Corbusier and are interesting for their use of raw concrete.*

Housing, Trafalgar Road *(1968), left. Here small blocks have been stacked onto large ones and connected by access galleries. The result is a departure from the typically flat façade of traditional terrace housing.*

Housing, Highgrove *The work of Edward Cullinan & Partners, this consists of 113 houses in five parallel rows on a triangular plan. An interesting feature is the use of prefabricated plastic coated metal roofs.*

London

By the 1970s domestic architecture was experiencing a reaction against the often monotonous impersonality of the 1960s. To some extent there was a return to individuality and to craftsmanship. Examples include **Lillington Street, Pimlico** (1961-70), and **Housing, Marquess Road** (1976), Islington, by Darbourne & Darke, and **World's End Housing, Chelsea** (1977), by Eric Lyons.

But the scale of work was often enormous. The **Barbican, City of London** (1959-79), by Chamberlain, Powell & Bon, contained housing for 5000, and **Brunswick Center, Brunswick Square** (1973), by Patrick Hodgkinson, which is a giant structure with terraced housing on either side of a shopping mall. There have been various attempts to incorporate some individuality into mass-housing schemes. Two of the most successful examples are **Housing, Tufnell Park** (1968-71), by M. Gold, with its elegant crescent of *stuccoed* walls, oversailing top stories and crisp windows, and **Alexandra Road Housing, Camden** (1969-79), by Neave Brown.

Civic & Public buildings

The *Classical* style predominated during the early part of the 19th century, such as the **Reform Club** (1838-41) by Sir Charles Barry, a fine Italianate palazzo, but from about 1840 it gave way to the *Gothic Revival,* which reached its peak in the period 1855-86. The **Houses of Parliament Parliament Square** (1835-52), by Barry and Augustus Pugin, was the first great example of English Gothic Revival.

The **Law Courts, Strand** (1874-82), by Edmund Street, is a particularly fine Gothic Revival work. Also of interest are the *Romanesque* **Natural History Museum, Cromwell Road** (1873-81), by Alfred Waterhouse, the **Dean's Yard, Westminster** (1853), and the Italianate-style **Foreign Office, Whitehall** (1861-73).

During the late 1880s there was a move away to a more *Baroque* style, as seen in **New Scotland**

Alexandra Road Housing, Camden *A curving four-story terrace, it faces a communal garden. Parallel to the back of this terrace, and on the other side of the street, is a six-story wall of terraces.*

Foreign Office, Whitehall *Detail of the very fine staircase showing the* vaulted *and domed vestibule. The work of Sir George Gilbert Scott, this striking building is a magnificent 16th-C Italian Renaissance-style design.*

Law Courts, Strand *This picturesque outline epitomizes the Victorian* Gothic Revival *and is part of one of the finest buildings of the time. Particularly notable are the corbeled* turrets, pointed arches *and* gabled *façades.*

Mary Ward House, Tavistock Place *(1895-98). This is a fine* Arts and Crafts *building which, with its mixture of* stucco *and brick, influenced some of the early council housing schemes. Architects were Dunbar Smith and Cecil Brewer.*

New Scotland Yard, Victoria Embankment *The work of Norman Shaw, this is an imposing mixture of* corbeled *turrets in the Scottish baronial style and* Baroque *elements. Its upper brick section is* articulated *by bands of portland stone, while the lower section is of granite.*

Yard, Victoria Embankment (1887-90), by
Norman Shaw, and the **Palace Theatre, Cambridge Circus** (1890), by T. Colcutt.

By the turn of the century the trend was
toward a simpler, freer style, personified in the
work of various *Arts and Crafts* architects. One
of the most notable of these was Harrison Townsend, who designed the **Horniman Museum,
London Road** (1900-10), Forest Hill. This is a
handsome building that combines *Byzantine* and
Arts and Crafts elements. Townsend also designed the **Whitechapel Art Gallery** (1887-99),
a simpler and bolder building and one of the rare
examples of *Art Nouveau* architecture in England.

With the exception of some Art Nouveau
works, architecture in England until 1914 tended
to be eclectic. Edwardian Baroque characterized
many of the buildings of the early 20th century.
Examples are **Deptford Town Hall, New Cross
Road** (1902-04), by the firm of Lanchester,
Stewart & Rickards, and the more monumental
Government Buildings, Parliament Square
(1898-1912), by John Brydon.

Although traditional styles continued, by the
1920s the influence of the European modern
movement was being seen in such buildings as the
**Royal Horticultural Society Building, Vincent
Square** (1923), and the **Royal Masonic Hospital,
Ravenscourt Park** (1930-32). *International Style*
modernism first made its mark on public buildings such as the **Pioneer Health Center,
Peckham** (1936), by Sir Owen Williams.

From the 1950s there was a reaction against
the restrictions of the International Style. James
Stirling in particular designed a series of crisp,
brick buildings most notably the **Children's
Home, Putney** (1960), and the **Old People's
Home, Blackheath** (1960).

Of post-war buildings on the South Bank the
Royal Festival Hall (1951-64) by Robert Matthew
for the London County Council is certainly one of
the finest. It is a grand, but functional building.

**Horniman Museum,
Forest Hill** *With its
memorable clock tower,
this is a remarkable
free-style design by
Harrison Townsend
that combines both
Byzantine and Arts
and Crafts influences.
It was built to house
the collection of F. J.
Horniman M.P.*

**Deptford Town Hall, New Cross
Road** *This is a classic example of
Edwardian Baroque and was the
work of Lanchester, Stewart &
Rickards. Outstanding features are
the Tuscan columns, sculptured
panels and pedimented center.*

Penguin Pool, Regent's Park Zoo
*(1938). By the Tecton group, this
was one of the earliest wholly
modern projects in London. As well
as providing good viewing angles,
the curved ramps and walls were
based on a study of penguins' habits.*

Whitechapel Art Gallery *This is
one of the rare examples of English
Art Nouveau architecture. It was
designed by Harrison Townsend and
is particularly interesting for its
boldly arched entrance and
assymetrical composition.*

London

Commercial & Industrial buildings

Throughout the 19th century iron and glass were used extensively in building. Some of the most interesting work includes arcades such as **Burlington Arcade, Piccadilly** (1818-19); **Royal Opera Arcade, Pall Mall** (1816-18), and the much later **Leadenhall Market** (1881).

The 19th century was also the great railway age and many fine stations were built. Among them are **St. Pancras** (1865-70), a masterpiece of *Gothic Revival* by Sir George Gilbert Scott and one of his best-known works; **King's Cross** (1850-52), by Lewis Cubitt, and **Paddington** (1852-54), by Isambard Kingdom Brunel and Sir M. D. Wyatt. With the railways came hotels such as **Hotel Russell, Russell Square** (1898).

Gothic Revival predominated until well into the 1880s, so much so that when **Tower Bridge** (1886-94) was built it was still clothed in traditional stonework despite being an early instance of a steel-frame structure. There was a multiplicity of styles. The **Albert Buildings, Queen Victoria Street** (1871), by F. J. Ward, is an example of Venetian Gothic. It broke away from the idea of a completely co-ordinated façade and, by providing bold *cornices,* enabled each floor to be treated in a separate manner. **The Prudential Assurance Building, Holborn** (1899-1906), with its romantic terracotta *gables* and spires was one of the last of the great Gothic Revival buildings. It was designed by Alfred Waterhouse and was also one of his last buildings.

The turn of the century saw the construction of a number of interesting offices by some of the leading architects of the day. They include

Royal Exchange, Bank *(1834-44). A bold* Corinthian *temple* portico *leads into this impressive day-lighted space. The Exchange. modeled by Sir William Tite on a Roman* basilica, *was originally open to the sky. the glass roof being added in 1880.*

Economist Building, St. James's Street *The complex contains three quite separate elements—a bank, offices, and flats. They are housed in three differing towers which are linked by a terrace. The architects were Alison and Peter Smithson.*

Hillingdon Civic Center, Uxbridge *(1976-78). Part of the modish vernacular brick disguise of this complex, designed by Robert Matthew, Johnston-Marshall & Partners. Points of interest are the* hipped *roofs and multi-faceted walling.*

Variety in commercial buildings

Examples shown here give an idea of the differing historical styles used during the late 19th and early 20thC. Below is the neo-*Georgian* **Headquarters of the North Eastern Railway Co., Cowley Street**, by Horace Field; right, is a *Gothic Revival* office building, Eastcheap.

Office building, Eastcheap.

North Eastern Railway Co. H.Q.

Sanderson's Wallpaper Factory, Chiswick (1902-3), by C. F. A. Voysey; **Mappin House, 158 Oxford Street** (1906-8), by John Belcher and J. J. Joass; **Adelaide House, London Bridge,** by Sir John Burnet and T. S. Tait, and two magnificent buildings by Sir Edwin Lutyens, the **Midland Bank, Poultry** (1926-30), and the eight-story **Britannic House, Finsbury Circus** (1924-27).

Genuinely modern styles started in the 1930s. *Art Deco* flourished along the Great West Road in buildings such as the **Hoover Factory** (1932-35). It was designed by Wallis Gilbert & Partners, who also designed **Victoria Coach Station** (1932). **Arnos Grove Underground Station** (1932), by Charles Holden, is also interesting as an example of the *Functionalist* style. And likewise **Simpson's, Piccadilly** (1936), by J. Emberton, and **Peter Jones, Sloane Square** (1938), by Slater, Moberley, Reilly & Crabtree, were also heavily influenced by modern European trends.

From the 1950s there was a great deal of commercial building in London. Initially much of it was influenced by the work of Le Corbusier, notably in the **Offices, Albermarle Street** (1957), by E. Goldfinger.

The Economist Building, St. James's Street (1960-64), by Alison and Peter Smithson, was an interesting project. Three separate elements—a bank, offices, and flats were housed in three towers of differing height and scale connected by a raised terrace. The intention was to blend the new style into the existing environment. Contextual constraints also affected the **Offices of the Chartered Accountants, Moorgate Place** (1970), by William Whitfield.

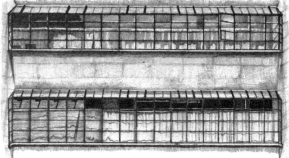

Hay's Wharf, London Bridge *(1928-32). A warehouse in Southwark by H. S. Goodhart Rendel in the typical* Art Deco *style. The glazed windows of the bay illustrated, light the administrative offices which are set between tower-like wings which contain the staircase and ancilliary accommodation.*

Albert Buildings, Queen Victoria Street *One of a number of Venetian* Gothic-*style offices by F. J. Ward. It is notable for the way in which each floor is treated as a separate band on the façade. A bold corbel table frieze gives coherence.*

Beaufort House, St Botolph Street *(c. 1935). P & O offices designed by E. Schaufelberg. The building's notable features include the symbolic ship's bridge, and a south façade in which simple, white cubes cascade to the street frontage in the Parisian style of Robert Mallet Stevens.*

Glass Warehouse and Showroom, Hailey Road, Thamesmead *(1973). A striking modern building by Norman Foster Associates. Essentially it consists of a sophisticated shed of blue corrugated metal sheeting wrapped around a steel frame. Interest lies in the taut glass gable end of the building.*

Daily Express Building, Fleet Street *(1933). This fine concrete-framed building with its horizontal bands of windows and striking polished black glass facing is a well-known landmark. It was designed by Ellis & Clark in collaboration with Sir Owen Williams.*

Southeast England

Castles & Palaces

Scotney Castle, Kent, is the epitome of the picturesque. Edward Hussey, having had a new house built for him between 1837 and 1842, demolished the old structure but retained its most interesting features to create a romantic ruin. Also of interest is **Mentmore Towers, Buckinghamshire** (1851-54), by Sir Joseph Paxton.

Domestic buildings

The **Red House, Bexleyheath** (1859-60), was designed by Philip Webb for William Morris. It is a particularly fine work in the *Arts and Crafts* style and epitomized Morris's concern with the need for a more human and romantic approach in architecture of the time.

From the 1860s a number of architects, most notably Webb, Norman Shaw, C. F. A. Voysey and Sir Edwin Lutyens, moved toward a greater simplicity. Outstanding houses by Shaw include **Willesley, Cranbrook** (1864-65), Kent; **Glen Andred, Groombridge** (1866-67); **Houndswood, Harper Lane, Radlett** (1871-72), and **Chigwell Hall, Essex** (1875-76). All of these houses are larger than hitherto and are characterized by the use of *gables*, tall decorative chimneys and brick and tile hanging for walls.

Interesting works by Voysey are **Norney**, near Shackleford (1897), Surrey; **New Place, Haslemere** (1887); the **Orchard, Chorley Wood** (1899); **Tilehurst, Bushey** (1904); the **Homestead, Frinton-on-Sea** (1905-7), and **Vodin, Pyford Common** (1903), Surrey. In all of these houses the characteristic features are roughcast brick walls, large gables and horizontal bands of *mullioned* windows.

Lutyens was the dominant figure in early 20th-century English architecture. He produced a series of large-scale houses, one of the best of which is the brick-built **Tigbourne Court, Witley** (1899), Surrey. The Arts and Crafts movement also affected popular housing, such as in **Welwyn Garden City** (1916), Hertfordshire.

Le Château, Silver End (1927-28), Essex, by T. S. Tait, with its flat roofs, horizontal bands of windows, and white walls provides a complete contrast. It was the first of the British *International Style* buildings. One of the most poetic and lyrical of the modern movement buildings is **High and Over, Amersham** (1929), by Amyas Connell. Subsequently Connell went into partnership with Basil Ward and Colin Lucas and together they designed **Dragons, Woodmancote** (1935-36), Sussex, and **Potcroft, Sutton** (1938). Both are interesting houses that make pleasing use of timber. The use of timber occurs in other buildings of the period, notably **Bentley Wood, Halland** (1935-36), by Serge Chermayeff; **Wood House, Shipbourne** (1937), by Walter Gropius and Maxwell Fry, and **High Spindle, Woldingham** (1938-39), Surrey, J. W. M. Dudding.

Much English architecture during the late 1960s and the 1970s was both monotonous and unimaginative. Exceptions, however, include **House, King's Walden** (1969-71), Hertfordshire.

The planned city of **Milton Keynes, Buckinghamshire**, also contains some interesting examples of 1970s' architecture. These include **Eaglestone Housing** (1975) by Ralph Erskine, the housing scheme at **Calverton End** (1974) by Cliff Nicholls and the **Sheltered Housing Coffee Hall** (1974) by MacCormac & Jamieson.

Scotney Castle, Kent
View of the Ashburn-ham Tower. From 1837 Edward Hussey began the work of slowly eroding the old castle to create a picturesque ruin in the landscape.

Suburban House, Brighton *(1905). A typical example of the more popular housing of the time. Houses such as these were also affected by the* Arts and Crafts *movement but this one is particularly interesting for the mock Tudor elements.*

Vodin, Pyford Common
View of the arched porch. The house was designed by C. F. A. Voysey and is a fine example of his work. The main points of interest include the roughcast brickwork and angled walls.

Red House, Bexley-heath *The house was designed for William Morris by Philip Webb. With its irregularity of plan and vernacular forms, this house is the epitome of the Arts and Crafts movement.*

6, Temple Gardens, Moor Park *(1936-37), Hertfordshire. A typical example of the work of Amyas Connell, Basil Ward and Colin Lucas. Interesting features are the curving stairs, dining room bay, and roof terrace canopy. These soften the more angular shapes.*

House, King's Walden, Hertfordshire, *below. This is a remarkable Italian-style building designed by Raymond Erith. His complete understanding of the rules of Classical architecture has resulted in a* purely Georgian *building.*

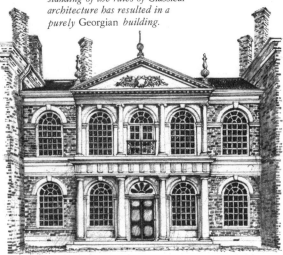

Dragons, Woodmancote, Sussex *An interesting house by Connell, Ward and Lucas. Essentially it is an* International Style *building but the use of timber cladding, added later, produces a more personal and warmer appearance.*

Housing, Calverton End, Milton Keynes *These houses are of interest for their lean-to roofs projecting above the boundary walls. Designed by Cliff Nichols, they are grouped informally around a communal area.*

Housing, Milton Keynes

Shown here are two examples of housing at Milton Keynes. **Netherfield Housing,** below, consists of a number of highly formal buildings, the layout creating the effect of a long, continuous and regular vista. By contrast, **Eaglestone Housing,** right, represents a concern for picturesque irregularity.

Eaglestone Housing

Netherfield Housing

347

Southeast England

Civic & Public buildings

Multipurpose structures providing various forms of entertainment or recreational facilities have been a notable phenomenon of 20th-century England. Classic examples are the seaside piers, such as the **Palace Pier, Brighton** (1891-1901). Originally designed for 19th-century visitors embarking by boat, they were later developed into elaborate promenades on cast-iron stilts and decked with exotic pavilions. Other examples of interest are the **West Pier, Brighton** (1863-66), and piers at **Margate** (1853-56, 1900). **Hastings** (1869-72), **Eastbourne** (1866-72) and **Clacton** (1870-1901). Piers are less popular than they were and are today often left unrepaired.

Of the pavilions built on land the most notable is the **De La Warr Pavilion, Bexhill** (1935), by Eric Mendelsohn and Serge Chermayeff. This consists of long, low volumes broken on the sea side by a glazed, semicircular bay enclosing a spiral staircase. By the 1970s such multipurpose structures had mushroomed into elaborate leisure centers, such as that at **Bletchley, Buckinghamshire** (1974). Also of interest are the **Royal Corinthian Yacht Club, Burnham-on-Crouch** (1931), by Joseph Emberton, and the **Festival Theatre, Chichester** (1962).

Commercial & Industrial buildings

The **Pantiles, Tunbridge Wells** (19thC), is one of the most brilliant blends of architecture and building. Consisting of a gently curved *colonnade* of shops and mainly 19th-century houses, it combines perfectly elements of the vernacular and the grand Italian design tradition. Of interest, too, are the more modern **Shopping Center, Netherfield** (1973-76), Milton Keynes, by Ed Jones, and the small **Brighton Square, The Lanes** (1966), Brighton, by Fitzroy Robinson & Partners.

The **Olivetti Training School, Haslemere** (1969), by James Stirling, is an interesting mixture of 19th- and 20th-century influences. It consists of a large addition to an existing house, the connecting link being a wedge-shaped glazed hall in the 19th-century conservatory tradition.

De La Warr Pavilion, Bexhill *A striking example of 1930s' architecture by Eric Mendelsohn and Serge Chermayeff. Interesting features are the curving balconies articulating an elegant circular staircase at the restaurant end.*

Bletchley Leisure Center, Buckinghamshire *View of the free-form pool which is covered by a huge pyramidal steel roof, glazed with faceted acrylic sheets. This is a typical example of the multipurpose structures built in the 1970s.*

Oast Houses, Toy's Hill *(19thC), Kent. These fine buildings are characteristic of Kent and Sussex and are used for drying hops. A circular cowl turning in the wind provides ventilation. Most are of the 19thC.*

Pantiles, Tunbridge Wells, *left. This gently curving* colonnade *was originally laid out in 1638. It consists of a number of shops and houses, most of which date from the 19thC. Many of the buildings are local builders' interpretations of current architectural fashions.*

Olivetti Training School, Haslemere, *Surrey, right. The glazed link with ramps that connects the classroom wings to the old house. This structure follows the 19th-C conservatory tradition, while the classrooms themselves are very much of the 20thC. The architect was James Stirling.*

Southern England

Domestic buildings

There are several fine late 19th-century houses in the area. They include **Bryanston, Blandford Forum** (1889-94), a refined classical building by Norman Shaw; **The Barn, Exmouth** (1895-96), a fine *Arts and Crafts*-style building by E. S. Prior, and **White Lodge, Denchworth Road** (1898-99), Wantage, by B. Scott. By contrast, **42, Sinah Lane, Hayling Island** (1933-34), is a beautiful *International Style* house by Amyas Connell and Basil Ward.

Civic & Public buildings

From 1945 there was a great deal of university building in England. **Oxford** contains many examples that are interesting for their attempts to blend with the city's historic past. The most notable examples are **St. Catherine's College** (1964) by A. Jacobson, and the **Wolfson Building, Somerville College** (1966), by Arup Associates.

Commercial & Industrial buildings

There are a number of fine modern commercial buildings in southern England. They include the **Electronics Factory, Swindon** (1965), by Norman Foster and Richard Rogers; the **IBM Offices, Havant** (1970), by Foster Associates, with its mirror glass façades and umbrella roof; the **Herman Miller Factory, Bath** (1976), by Farrell & Grimshaw, and **Gateway House, Basingstoke** (1976), by Arup Associates, with its elegant landscaped terraces and central courtyard.

St. Hilda's College, Oxford *(1970). This is a fairly recent example of university building in Oxford. Designed by Alison and Peter Smithson, its main points of interest are the* splayed *corners and applied timber screen.*

Keble College Chapel, Oxford *(1867-83). This is a magnificent red-brick building designed by William Butterfield. In style it captures the spirit of medieval Oxford, although the use of brick distinguishes it from the stone buildings.*

Queen's College, Oxford *(1966). A notable example of the work of James Stirling. The stairs are* articulated *externally while the structure is shored up by great concrete posts. In plan the college is an irregular, sloping crescent wrapped around a quadrangle on the edge of the river.*

Deanery Gardens, Thames Street, Sonning *(1901). This is a charming brick house built by Sir Edwin Lutyens, the leading architect of the time. With its* Arts and Crafts *style, it is typical of his early country house work.*

Clifton Suspension Bridge, Bristol *(1830-63). This remarkable piece of engineering was designed by Isambard Kingdom Brunel. The principal span of 250 ft across the deep Avon Gorge is suspended on chains held by Egyptian-like pylons.*

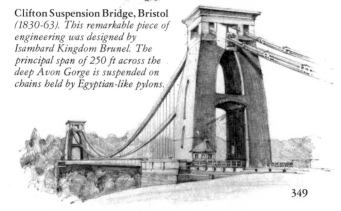

Central England

Religious buildings

The **Cathedral, Coventry** (1952-62), by Sir Basil Spence, is significant for its synthesis of building and works of art. It was built at right angles on to the ruins of the old cathedral, the linking element being a lofty entrance porch.

Domestic buildings

Pastures, North Luffenham (1901), Leicestershire, is a bold *Arts and Crafts*-style building by C. F. A. Voysey and is an early forerunner of the modern movement. **New Ways, Northampton** (1926), by Peter Behrens, however, is one of the first truly modern buildings. Another, later example, is the *International Style* **Shawn's, Cambridge** (1938), by Justin Blanco White.

The vernacular tradition was remarkably strong in housing groups. An early instance is **Edensor, Chatsworth** (1838), by Joseph Paxton, with its houses designed in *picturesque* style.

Civic & Public buildings

Despite a massive rebuilding project in Birmingham, there are still a number of 19th-century buildings of note in the city. They include the **Town Hall** (1832) by J. A. Hansom, a fine *Neoclassical* building, and the **Law Courts** (1886-91) by Aston Webb and Ingresco Bell.

From 1945 there was much new building, particularly of schools and colleges. An important project was the **Secondary School, Hunstanton** (1950-54), by Alison and Peter Smithson, with its crisp steel and brick volumes.

The **Engineering Faculty, Leicester University** (1969), by James Stirling and James Gowan consists of a large shed lighted from above and two highly *articulated* office blocks. In the **Cambridge History Faculty** (1964) by Stirling, the façades become virtually redundant, attention being concentrated on the huge glazed section which leans against the "L"-shaped interior. Other interesting modern buildings in **Cambridge** include **Cripps Building, St. John's College** (1964), and **Clare Hall** (1966), by Ralph Erskine.

Other notable modern universities include **Loughborough** (1967), by Arup Associates, and **East Anglia, Norwich** (1969), by Sir Denys Lasdun, which has stepped terraces zig-zagging along the edge of parkland. The latter university includes the **Sainsbury Center** (1978), by Foster Associates, a gleaming shed-like building with finely machined proportions and a disregard of context that gives an alien quality.

Commercial & Industrial buildings

The **Boots Chemical Works, Beeston** (1930-38), Nottingham, by Sir Owen Williams, is one of the most remarkable British buildings of its time. An enormous complex, it uses the mushroom pillar construction developed by Swiss engineer Robert Maillart. Another notable commercial building is the **Willis Faber and Dumas Offices, Ipswich** (1976), by Foster Associates, a three-story, brown-colored building with a concave and convex plan. The structure of the building is faced with a glass skin.

Edensor, Chatsworth
A house from the model village *designed by Joseph Paxton. The village itself consists of a number of stone, detached houses built in a variety of styles and grouped in an irregular and* picturesque *manner.*

Pastures, North Luffenham
The particularly striking feature here is the bold semicircular arch of the loggia *on the south side. The house was designed by C. F. A. Voysey and with its unpretentious* Arts and Crafts *style foreshadows the modern movement that followed.*

Uplands, Blythe Bridge *(1937-38), Staffordshire. This is a remarkably flamboyant and individualistic design. Of particular interest are the bold rounded bays, long curving windows and irregular levels. The architect was A. Glyn Shewin.*

Cornford House, Cambridge *(1966). Essentially, this consists of a simple set of brick volumes of one- and two-story height. The outside angle of the living space is eroded by the garden terrace. The architects were C. St. John Wilson and M. J. Long.*

House, Walford Road, Ross-on-Wye *(1975).
An interesting design by Clive Plumb. The main
part of the house is on two stories within the
wedge-shaped section. This section contains
various features, including raised living space.
The remainder of the house is one story,
arranged under the lean-to roof which can
subsequently be extended to accommodate
additional rooms.*

**Engineering Faculty, Leicester
University** *Designed by James
Stirling and James Gowan, it is the
most important of their buildings.
The style of the building is an
amalgam of 19th-C industrial architecture found in Britain and Russian
constructivist architecture.*

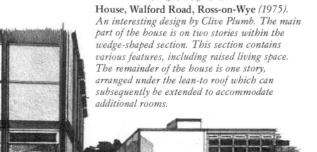

**Secondary School,
Hunstanton** *View of
the gymnasium. This
was an extremely
influential post-war
building, designed by
Alison and Peter
Smithson. The main
points of interest are
its beautifully* articu-
lated *set of steel and
brick volumes.*

**Studlands Park,
Newmarket**
*(1970-76). One of
the detached houses
in a large modern
village designed by
Ralph Erskine. It is a
simple, utilitarian
building that incor-
porates some of the
vernacular tradition.*

**Willis Faber and Dumas Offices,
Ipswich,** *right. Glass is the predominant feature in this striking
building by Foster Associates. It
is a three-story building with a
concave and convex plan and entirely
wrapped in glass. Inside, banks of
escalators rise up to a staff restaurant
and roof garden.*

Boots Chemical Works, Beeston
*This large building incorporates the
mushroom pillar construction first
used in 1908 by Robert Maillart.
Loading bays on the north side are
covered by a long, one-story band
of glass while the offices above are
articulated like pavilions. Despite its
size, it is a light, transparent building.*

Northern England

Religious buildings

The most important church buildings in the area are the two cathedrals at **Liverpool**. The first, the **Anglican Cathedral** (begun 1904) by Sir Giles Gilbert Scott, is a magnificent *Gothic Revival* building of red sandstone. It has a cruciform plan with a high tower and has particularly boldly *articulated* volumes. By contrast the **Roman Catholic Cathedral** (1960-65) by Sir Frederick Gibberd is highly bizarre. Built on a circular plan, it is distinguished by a huge conical roof topped by a stained-glass *lantern*.

Domestic buildings

Cragside, Rothbury (1870-85), was designed by Norman Shaw for Lord Armstrong, the armaments manufacturer. It has a multitude of *gables* and turrets and is a delightfully picturesque building. The later **Chesters, Chellerford** (1891), also by Shaw, is much more subdued. As the result of incorporating an existing house in the design the overall plan is irregular, but the chief façades are symmetrical and articulated with *Ionic* columns, bold *cornice* and *rusticated* window frames.

Other buildings of the 1890s include two marvelous houses by C. F. A. Voysey. They are **Broadleys** (1898-99) and **Moor Crag** (1898-99), both in **Gill Head, Windermere**. Built a little later, the more flamboyant **Heathcote, Ilkley** (1906), and **Gledstone Hall, Skipton** (1923-27), are both by Sir Edwin Lutyens and both show the exploration of *Renaissance* ideals.

Post-World War II housing schemes include the simple brick-built **Terrace Housing, Preston** (1957-61), by James Stirling and James Gowan; **Byker Housing, Newcastle** (1970-80), by Ralph Erskine, a community for 10,000 people, and

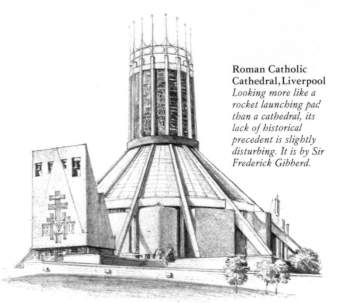

Roman Catholic Cathedral, Liverpool *Looking more like a rocket launching pad than a cathedral, its lack of historical precedent is slightly disturbing. It is by Sir Frederick Gibberd.*

Housing, Runcorn New Town *(1967). View of street façade which is* articulated *by staircase towers and entrance canopies. The* Brutalist *influence can be seen in the rough block and in the raw concrete.*

Chesters, Chellerford *Originally this was an 18th-C house that was considerably altered and extended by Shaw. With its* Baroque *details, this is a classical house in contrast to Shaw's earlier work.*

Cragside, Rothbury, *above. This large, picturesque country house was designed by Norman Shaw. Its memorable features are its* crenellated *tower and its multitude of* gables *and turreted roofs.*

Forge, Ford, Northumberland *Detail of the forge doorway, which is in the shape of a huge horseshoe. The forge is part of a* model village *which was built from the 1860s onward.*

Park Hill, Sheffield (1957-61), built by the City Corporation, in which cliff-like walls of apartments are linked by a network of raised streets.

Civic & Public buildings

St. George's Hall, Liverpool (1841-56), by Harvey Lonsdale Elmes and Charles Robert Cockerell, is a boldly articulated *Neoclassical* building containing among other things a large central hall and oval concert hall. The **Town Hall, Leeds** (1853-58), was subsequently rebuilt to reflect the new civic splendors of Liverpool. It is an Italianate *Baroque*-style building designed by Cuthbert Broderick who produced other memorable work in the area.

Of more recent interest are **Dunelm House, Durham University** (1964), by Architects Co Partnership, with an elegant bridge by Ove Arup, and **Palmerston School, Liverpool** (1976), by Foster Associates.

Commercial & Industrial buildings

The **Oriel Chambers, Liverpool** (1864-65), by Peter Ellis, is a masterpiece of early commercial architecture. Although essentially Gothic Revival, it is interesting for its cast iron frame.

The **Corn Exchange, Leeds** (1861-63), is another fine building by Broderick. Oval in plan, it is covered by a huge iron and glass dome. Broderick also designed the **Grand Hotel, Scarborough** (1865-67), a monument to the growth of the seaside town in the 19th century.

Recent post-World War II buildings include the **Bus Station** and **Car Park, Preston** (1969), in the *Brutalist* style by Building Design Partnership, and the **Cummins Engines Factory, Darlington** (1972), by Kevin Roche and John Dinkerloo.

Byker Housing, Newcastle *View of the main feature of the scheme — a huge, snaking wall of building between three and eight stories in height, with balconies on the residential side. Housing 10,000 people, it was designed by Ralph Erskine.*

St. George's Hall, Liverpool *View of the interior of the public hall by Charles Robert Cockerell and Harvey Lonsdale Elmes, the leading* Neoclassicists *of the time.*

Town Hall, Leeds *This Italianate Baroque-style building consists of a boldly articulated square block with a lofty clock tower masking the high roof of the Great Hall. It was designed by Charles Broderick.*

Oriel Chambers, Liverpool *The façade of one of the most influential of 19th-C British office buildings. It was designed by Peter Ellis, using a cast iron frame, which anticipated the construction of the Chicago skyscrapers by some 20 years.*

City Library, Manchester *(1929-34). This imposing building, a well-known landmark in Manchester, was modeled on the Pantheon, Rome, although the proportions of* rotunda *and* portico *are very different. It was designed by Vincent Harris, one of the traditionalist architects of the time.*

Scotland

Domestic buildings

The simplicity and austerity of the vernacular tradition was continued by architects into the late 19th and early 20th century. The best examples are **Melsetter House, Holy Island** (1898-1902), Orkney, by William Lethaby, and **Windy Hill, Kilmalcolm** (1899), Strathclyde, and **Hill House, Helensborough** (1902-4), both by Charles Rennie Mackintosh.

Civic & Public buildings

Typical of the early 19th century were monumental *Greek Revival* buildings, such as the **National Gallery of Scotland, Edinburgh** (1850-54), by W. H. Playfair. The most remarkable buildings in the late 19th and early 20th century are those by Mackintosh. The **Scotland Street School, Glasgow** (1904-6), is a three-story structure with a rectangular plan. Staircase towers project, in semi-circular bays, at right angles to a central corridor. Another of his buildings is the **Glasgow School of Art** (1897-1909) which emphasizes mass and clearly *articulated* volumes, and has considerable tautness generated by Mackintosh's use of stone, glass and metal.

Commercial & Industrial buildings

One of the more extravagant commercial buildings is the **Templeton Carpet Factory, Glasgow Green, Glasgow** (1889), by William Leiper, with its *Gothic*-style windows and parapet. Equally interesting are the **Olivetti Offices, Dundee** (1969-71), by Edward Cullinan & Partners, which has an irregular crescent-shaped rear elevation.

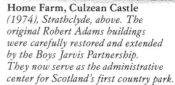

Home Farm, Culzean Castle *(1974), Strathclyde, above. The original Robert Adams buildings were carefully restored and extended by the Boys Jarvis Partnership. They now serve as the administrative center for Scotland's first country park.*

Glasgow School of Art *Detail of the library oriel windows of Charles Rennie Mackintosh's most famous building. Iron window frames were later replaced by bronze ones. The library was added to the School of Art in 1907-9. The façade of the school displays the disturbed symmetry of Art Nouveau.*

Hostel, St Andrews University, *(1964). Key features of these study-bedrooms by James Stirling include the* multifaceted *façades, giving each room a view over the surrounding countryside, and the glazed promenade, which forms the main corridor of the building.*

Melsetter House, Holy Island, *right. A powerful yet simple building designed by William Lethaby, in which he incorporated the stepped* gable *façades and roughcast rendering of the vernacular tradition.*

Bridge, Firth of Forth *(1881-89), right. Designed by Benjamin Baker and John Fowler, it was one of the remarkable technical achievements of its day. Some 1½ miles long, it has an unsupported span of 1706 ft.*

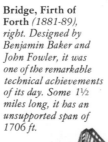

Wales & Ireland

Castles & Palaces

During the 19th century a number of castles were reconstructed in an extravagent manner in Wales. A leading architect in this field was William Burges who built **Castell Coch**, near **Cardiff** (1875-89). Only the foundations and some of the walls were extant when Burges began the task of building this medieval-style castle of three round towers with conical roofs. He also executed additions and new decoration to **Cardiff Castle** (1868-85), giving it Arab and Greek motifs. Both here and at Castell Coch he introduced strong *Gothic Revival* elements.

Domestic buildings

French *Renaissance* château architecture influenced the design of great Welsh houses, such as **Wynnstay**, near **Ruabon** (1861), by Benjamin Ferreray, and **Kinmel**, near **Abergele** (1871-74), by W. Eden Nesfield. The vernacular tradition was strong in both Ireland and Wales well into the 20th century, so much so that the modern buildings seem quite stark in contrast.

Civic & Public buildings

A Renaissance revival was much in evidence in Wales in the mid 19th century. The **Royal Institution of South Wales, Swansea** (1841), by F. Long, has a bold *Ionic portico*. Later Cardiff buildings also reflect the classical influence, an example being the **National Museum of Wales** (1910-27) by D. Smith and C. Brewer.

A more *Baroque* style was fashionable in Ireland, such as the **Old City Hall, Belfast** (1906), by A. B. Thomas. The **Library, Trinity College, Dublin** (1961-67), by Ahrends, Burton & Koralek, is an impressive modern building.

Several estate villages were built in 19th- and early 20th-century Wales. One of the most curious is **Portmeirion**, Gwynedd, a resort village built by the architect Clough Williams-Ellis from the 1920s onward.

Castell Coch, Cardiff, *Wales, right. A remarkable* Gothic Revival *reconstruction by William Burges. An authentic touch is the inclusion of a working drawbridge and portcullis. Castell Coch is the Welsh for "Red Castle"*

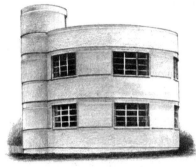

Parkes House, St Davids *(1967), Wales. A cylindrical weekend retreat, designed by James Gowan. Simple recessed bands* articulate *the façade, and a staircase tower projects above the rest of the house.*

Geragh, Sandycove, Dublin *(1937), Ireland, above. This striking house, designed by Michael Scott, is a free-form variant of the* International Style. *Its proximity to the sea is reflected in the nautical lookout terraces and the windows in the stepped section of the house.*

Broadstone Station, Dublin *(1850), Ireland, above. By John Skipton Mulvany, this building is designed in an amalgam of Greek and Egyptian styles including projecting* bays and bold cornices.

Guildhall, Swansea *(1930-34), Wales, right.* A handsome Neoclassical *building by Sir Percy Thomas. The ground story is* rusticated, *and a tall archway is cut into the tower block.*

East Germany

Domestic buildings

East Berlin contains several fine *International Style* housing schemes by Bruno Taut. They include the elegant crescents at **Grellstrasse, Prenzlauer Berg** (1927), and **Erich-Weinert-Strasse, Prenzlauer Berg** (1929-30); three handsome parallel blocks of apartments, stepped in plan, at **Normannenstrasse, Lichtenberg** (1928), and the project at **Trierer Strasse, Wiezensel** (1926-28). In the same area, at **60, Oberseestrasse** (1932), there is an elegant "L"-shaped house by Ludwig Mies van der Rohe.

The **Schminke House, Löbau** (1932-33), by Hans Scharoun, is clearly a reaction against the more orthodox *Functionalist* tradition. Rather than imposing a rigid plan, he allowed each function to determine its own particular form. The plan itself consists of a basic rectangle with wedge-shaped ends opening out into projecting balconies.

Civic & Public buildings

The work of Karl Friedrich Schinkel in East Berlin can be seen either as the end of the modern classical world or as the beginning of the modern world for, despite his *Neoclassical* style, his work has a reductive quality that belongs to the modern world. Good examples are the **Schauspielhaus** (1819-21), although it was extensively damaged during World War II, and the **Altes Museum** (1824-28), with its memorable façade.

The **Einstein Tower, Potsdam** (1920-21), by Erich Mendelsohn, was one of the first finely molded designs that could have made real use of the developments in reinforced concrete. Due to post-war shortages, however, it was built of brick and concrete and was *rendered* to give it its homogeneous quality.

The **Bauhaus, Dessau** (1925-26), by Walter Gropius, is of great importance in the Functionalist movement. It is an asymmetrically-planned complex consisting of three parts: a school of design with classrooms, a students' hostel, and workshops. The façades were designed purely for their functional purposes.

Hermann Mattern House, Bornim *(1934), near Potsdam. By Hans Scharoun, the building is essentially another Functionalist construction, but the curved wall defining the living area and recessed dining area is an attempt to provide visual satisfaction as well as the usual practical requirements.*

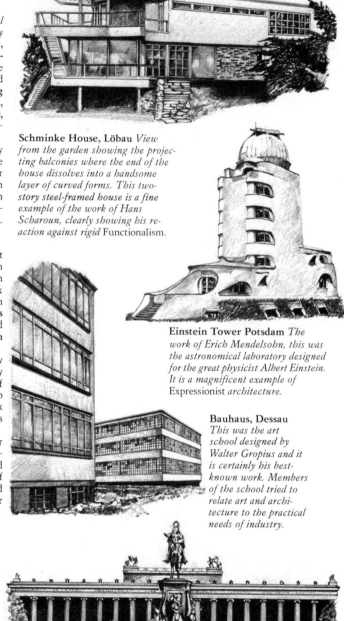

Schminke House, Löbau *View from the garden showing the projecting balconies where the end of the house dissolves into a handsome layer of curved forms. This two-story steel-framed house is a fine example of the work of Hans Scharoun, clearly showing his reaction against rigid* Functionalism.

Einstein Tower Potsdam *The work of Erich Mendelsohn, this was the astronomical laboratory designed for the great physicist Albert Einstein. It is a magnificent example of* Expressionist *architecture.*

Bauhaus, Dessau *This was the art school designed by Walter Gropius and it is certainly his best-known work. Members of the school tried to relate art and architecture to the practical needs of industry.*

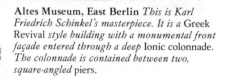

Altes Museum, East Berlin *This is Karl Friedrich Schinkel's masterpiece. It is a Greek Revival style building with a monumental front façade entered through a deep* Ionic *colonnade. The colonnade is contained between two, square-angled piers.*

Northern Germany

Religious buildings

The **Parish Church, Wolfsburg** (1960-62), is the principal element in a group of three buildings designed by Alvar Aalto for the center of the parish. The other buildings consist of a parish hall and accommodation for the clergy, together with clubrooms and other facilities for young people. The buildings enclose a square. The interest centers on Aalto's mastery of handling quite disparate elements, such as tower and *aisles.*

Other interesting churches include the **Kreuzkirche, West Berlin,** (1930), an *Expressionist* design by Gunther Paulus; the nearby **Kirche am Hohenzollerndamm** (1931-33), by Fritz Hoger; **St Norbert-Kirche, West Berlin,** (1961-62), by Hermann Fehling and Damel Gogel, and the **Kaiser Wilhelm-Gedachtnis-Kirche, West Berlin,** (1955-63), by Egon Eiermann.

Domestic buildings

Interesting early 20th-century houses in **West Berlin** include the **Freudenberg House, Nikolassee** (1907), by Hermann Muthesius, who was greatly influenced by Charles F. Voysey and his English contemporaries; **13-14, Burknerstrasse, Neukölln** (1910), by Bruno Taut, and **Pension Westend, 32, Kastanienallee** (1912), a particularly fine building by Auguste Endell.

The **Gross-Siedlung, Onkel-Toms-Hutte, West Berlin** (1926-31), is one of a series of fine housing estates within West Berlin and includes work by Bruno Taut, Hugo Häring, Hans Poelzig and others. Much of it is in an uncompromisingly modern style but the work by Paul Schmitthenner, such as **4, Am Fischtal** (1929), and the terrace housing of Heinrich Tessenov, **58-60, Am Fischtal** (1929), have conceded to traditional tastes of the day with their pitched roofs and great concern with symmetry.

By contrast the **Garden Suburb, West Berlin** (1914-17), in Staaken, also by Schmitthenner, has picturesque *gable* façades and an irregular plan. This garden suburb is an excellent example of the new *National Romantic* movement.

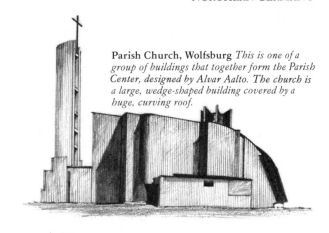

Parish Church, Wolfsburg *This is one of a group of buildings that together form the Parish Center, designed by Alvar Aalto. The church is a large, wedge-shaped building covered by a huge, curving roof.*

Kreuzkirche, West Berlin *A detail from the elaborately decorated* portal. *The over-elaboration of the façade, while well handled, was clearly a reaction against the functional* New Architecture *ushered in by the* Bauhaus.

House, Onkel-Tom-Strasse, West Berlin, *(1923). This is one of a whole series of notably modern houses in Zehlendorf. This particular house was designed by Richard Neutra and Erich Mendelsohn. Both of these men were leading proponents of the* International Style.

Terrace Housing, Staaken, West Berlin. *By Paul Schmitthenner, the terraces are part of a garden suburb. The Dutch-style gable and irregular plan are typical of* Expressionist *work of this period in Northern Europe.*

4, Am Fischtal, West Berlin *Designed by Paul Schmitthenner, the house makes various concessions to traditional tastes that must have placated many of the critics of the New Architecture. Nevertheless, for all its almost* Dutch Palladian *style it is still an outstanding example of a* Functionalist *house.*

Northern Germany

Domestic buildings

Most of the modern architects working in early 20th-century Germany, such as Erich Mendelsohn, Bruno Taut and Hans Scharoun, had gone through an *Expressionist* phase. All this changed with the setting up of the *Bauhaus* and the experimental work developed by the avant-garde, particularly in **West Berlin.** Of particular interest are a series of detached houses in Zehlendorf, characterized by simplicity of volumes, front façades with a sparsity of windows, and garden façades with floor to ceiling windows, often opening onto terraces. They include 66, **Wilskistrasse** (1932) by Ludwig Hilberseimer, **85, Onkel-Tom-Strasse** (1932) by Richard Neutra and Erich Mendelsohn, and 42, **Sophie-Charlotte-Strasse** (1928), a fine building by Adolf Reading.

This mixture of Expressionism and *Functionalism* can also be seen at **55, Heerstrasse, West Berlin** (1928), Charlottenberg. The work of Hans Luckhardt, Alfons Anker and others, it is a steel-frame building with *rendered* concrete cavity walls.

The **Siemensstadt Estate, Charlottenberg Nord** (1929-31), is one of the most interesting housing projects in West Berlin. It is a vast housing scheme for workers from the Siemens Company and became a prototype for others in Europe. It includes designs by Otto Bartning, Scharoun, Hugo Häring and Walter Gropius.

The **Ziegler House, West Berlin** (1936), in Steglitz, is a fine design by Häring. He created a novel plan with receding and extended planes which break away from the strict orthogonal geometry of other houses in Steglitz, such as **17, Schmidt-Ott-Strasse** (1932) by Erich Richter and **19, Dietrich-Schafer-Weg** (1935).

The work of Scharoun in the 1930s moved further and further away from the Functionalist tradition of the Bauhaus. Key elements were the use of traditional materials, such as bricks and timber, as in the **Pflaum House, Falkensee** (1935), near Berlin, and the **Mohrmann House, 10, Falkensteinstrasse** (1939), West Berlin. His shift from rigid Functionalism is perhaps seen most clearly, however, in the **Dr. Baensch House, Gatow** (1934-35), Berlin-Spandau.

There are also some interesting houses by Egon Eiermann in West Berlin. They are characterized by clearly defined parts and precision of detail. Good examples include the **Hesse House, Lankwitz** (1933), and the **Dr. Steingroever House, Charlottenberg** (1937).

55, Heerstrasse, Charlottenberg, West Berlin *Designed to a* Functionalist *plan, the house has terraces rotating out from the principal façade.*

Ziegler House, 112, Lepsisstrasse, West Berlin *This house, which was designed by Hugo Häring, is a masterfully handled free-form plan composed of individual parts arranged in a fan around the living and dining areas.*

Dr Baensch House, 19, Hohenweg, West Berlin *The house has a free plan, with the convex façade of the living room overlooking a sloping garden. Designed by Hans Scharoun, it shows his shift from rigid Functionalism.*

Mohrmann House, 10, Falkensteinstrasse, West Berlin *For this house Scharoun used natural materials, such as brick and timber. Its traditional appearance indicates the constraints that are felt in Scharoun's work during the Nazi era.*

66, Wilskistrasse, West Berlin *This powerful building, designed by Ludwig Hilberseimer, probably represents the extreme example of the reductive architecture of the International Style. The result is a remarkably bold and forceful image.*

High Rise Flats, Zabel-Krüger-Damm, West Berlin *These flats, designed by Scharoun, were based on a similar scheme of his in Stuttgart in the early 1960s. The undulating plan and obvious visual complexity were an attempt to reintroduce architectural attractiveness into the urban environment.*

Swimming Stadium, Olympischer Platz, West Berlin, *(1934-36). The work of Werner March, the stadium takes its inspiration from the great amphitheatres of Imperial Rome. It is an example of the* Neoclassicism *that, with the advent of the Nazis, replaced the* New Architecture.

Neue Vahr Apartment Building, Bremen *(1958-62). This building was designed by Alvar Aalto. The undulating form that characterizes it was the result of the small apartments being planned in a fan shape, so that each was provided with a long band of window.*

Philharmonie, West Berlin

Designed (1956-63) by Hans Scharoun, this concert hall was conceived as a huge valley, at the bottom of which sat the orchestra, while up the sides were placed the seats. The roof was thought of as that of a large tent. The result is a magnificent cavern for musical performances.

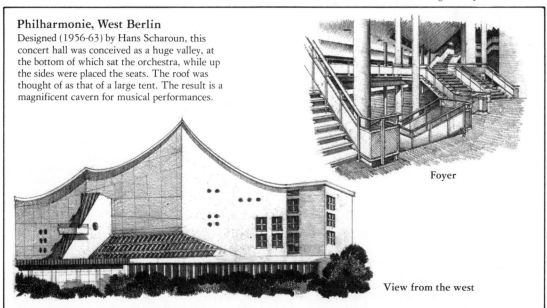

Foyer

View from the west

359

Northern Germany

Civic & Public buildings

The advent of the Nazi regime effectively brought the *New Architecture* to a standstill and a monumental *Neoclassicism* began to take its place, as exemplified by the **Olympic Stadium** and **Swimming Stadium, West Berlin**, (1934-36, see p.359), designed by Werner March.

Many of the notable buildings erected after World War II were designed by Hans Scharoun. They include **The Philharmonie, West Berlin** (1956-63, see p.359), with its vast auditorium, and the **Theatre, Wolfsburg** (1965-73). The latter has an original plan consisting of three parts: the main auditorium and two delicate wings laid out in a linear fashion following the contours of its hilly site. By contrast the **Cultural Center, Wolfsburg** (1958-63), designed by Alvar Aalto, is much more controlled and the various elements more obviously harmonized.

The **State Library, West Berlin** (1964-78), was Scharoun's last work. In this he handled disparate parts better than in any of his other works. The **National Gallery, West Berlin** (1962-68), is the antithesis of Scharoun's free-form philosophy. Designed by Ludwig Mies van der Rohe, everything is concentrated on *axiality* and centralized space. The detailing of the column *capitals* gives the large flat roof the appearance of hovering over the building.

Commercial & Industrial buildings

The **AEG Turbine Shop, Huttenstrasse, West Berlin** (1909), by Peter Behrens, was one of the major works of the New Architecture. Although Behrens exploited steel framing techniques he still needed to create a feeling of mass rather than lightness, hence the huge concrete corners and polygonal *gable*. The **Fagus Factory, Alfeld an der Leine** (1911-14), by Walter Gropius and Adolph Meyer, is the antithesis of Behrens's massively powerful shed; it is a light, delicate steel skeleton with glass and slender brick columns. It rejected symbolism, banned ornamentation and was the first truly *Functionalist* building.

Architecture in the early 1920s searched for a strong image or expression. Frequently symbolic motifs were applied to building frames, as in the ship-like **Chilehaus, Hamburg** (1923), by Fritz Hoeger. The search for functionally expressive forms is seen at its best, however, in the **Cowshed, Gut Garkau Farm, Lübeck** (1923), designed by Hugo Häring, where the form is entirely functional. The major element — 41 stalls for cows — is planned in a pear shape around the mangers and is surrounded by an aisle. In the middle is the feeding table, where hay can be delivered directly from the loft above. The diagonally-sloped tower houses the hay shredder. Another *Expressionist* building is the **Anzeiger-Hochaus, Hannover** (1927-28), a publishing house with a domed cinema on top, designed by Fritz Hoeber.

Interesting recent buildings include the **DLRG Station Pichelsdorf, West Berlin** (1969-72), and the **Wasserversuchsanstalt, Technische Universität, West Berlin** (1976), both by Ludwig Leo, and the **Turmrestaurant** and **Station, Berlin Steglitz** (1972), designed by Ralph Schüler and Ursula Schüller-Witte.

National Gallery, West Berlin *Designed by Ludwig Mies van der Rohe, the gallery stands to the west of the Philharmonic. It is raised on a* podium *and has the mathematical purity of proportion of the Parthenon in Greece.*

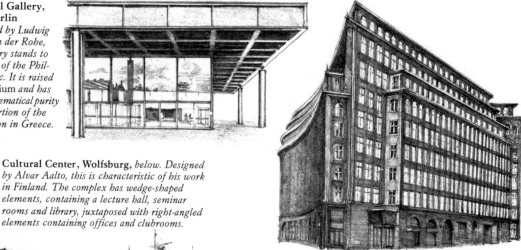

Cultural Center, Wolfsburg, *below. Designed by Alvar Aalto, this is characteristic of his work in Finland. The complex has wedge-shaped elements, containing a lecture hall, seminar rooms and library, juxtaposed with right-angled elements containing offices and clubrooms.*

Chilehaus, Hamburg *This magnificent building, designed by Fritz Hoeger as shipping offices and headquarters, is a fine example of the* Expressionist *style. The pointed front, the highest point of the building, symbolizes the prow of a ship, seemingly ploughing its way through the city.*

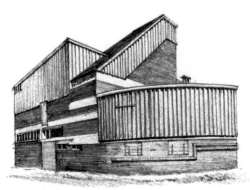

AEG Turbine Shop, Huttenstrasse, West Berlin *This work by Peter Behrens is one of the most celebrated of the Functionalist buildings. The workshop has a steel-frame with* curtain walls *and heavy concrete corners.*

Cowshed, Gut Garkau Farm, Lübeck
Designed by Hugo Häring, this is a marvelously sculptured design in which modern technology and Expressionist ideas are happily combined. The building is constructed of brick and of concrete and wood.

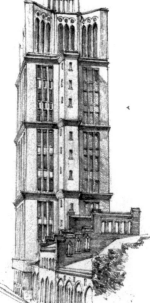

German Maritime Museum, Bremerhaven
(1969-75). View from the sea wall promenade on the south side. This is one of Hans Scharoun's most brilliantly designed buildings. It expresses its function exactly, even to the crowning ship's bridge which contains the Maritime Museum's radar room.

Fagus Factory, Alfeld an der Leine *By Walter Gropius and Adolf Meyer, this is one of the seminal works in modern architecture. With its glass curtain walling and stark cubic blocks, it was one of the first buildings to use features that became fundamental to the International Style.*

Kleines Atelier, West Berlin *(1972-74). The plan, right, shows the rectangular studio block next to the long garden terrace with its round end, within which stands the tree, below.*

Hochhaus, West Berlin, *(1927), in Tegel. This is a powerfully* articulated *Expressionist building with bold* cornices *and a concave top story with* Gothic-style *lancet windows. The building was designed by Eugen G. Schmohl.*

Central Germany

Religious buildings

The damage of two world wars led to the building of many churches in Germany. For architects the problem was to find an original and yet suitable form. In **St. Rochus-Kirche, Düsseldorf** (1953-54), designed by P. Schneider-Esleben, the principal problem of building a new *nave* onto the 19th-century *Romanesque* revival tower was overcome by the use of a bold dome. Both the **Church of Peter and Paul, Dettingen** (1923), by Dominikus Böhm, and the **Frauenfrienden-skirche, Frankfurt** (1928-29), have spreading west towers evocative of the medieval tradition. **St. Engelbert, Cologne** (1930-31), also designed by Böhm, is more *Expressionist* in its appearance and has a centralized plan.

Domestic buildings

There are a number of fine modern domestic buildings in central Germany. The **Mathilden-höhe Estate, Darmstadt** (1900-7), is an artists' colony planned by Joseph Maria Olbrich and one of the rare examples of *Art Nouveau* town planning. The **Hermann Lange House, Krefeld** (1928), is a fine brick-built house by Ludwig Mies van der Rohe, while the old people's home, **178, Friedrich-Ebert-Strasse, Kassel** (1930-32), designed by O. Haesler and Karl Völker, is a sensitive *International Style* building. It consists of two parallel, four-story blocks with the south facing façades completely glazed. A continuous balcony runs along each level and a two-story communal wing links the blocks.

60, Belvederestrasse, Cologne-Müngersdorf (1959), was designed by Mathias Ungers for himself. It is a remarkably well-planned house and a good example of *Brutalism*. **Housing, Marl** (1964-67), designed by Peter Faller and Herman Schröder, is an interesting project consisting of a large tent-like structure, five stories high. The terraces on both sides are stepped back to give an abundance of light.

St. Rochus-Kirche, Düsseldorf *Designed by P. Schneider-Esleben, this is a curious building with no obvious architectural precedent. With its tall dome, the building seems to have been inspired by the 17th-C Puritan's hat.*

Hermann Lange House, Krefeld *View of the garden front. This fine brick villa with its plain façades pierced by crisp windows was designed by Ludwig Mies van der Rohe. It is now used as a museum of modern art.*

Progymnasium, Lorch *(1972-73). By Gunter Behnisch and his partners, the building consists of three main elements of wedge and crescent shape grouped around a central courtyard. The construction is deliberately unostentatious in appearance and is without ornamentation.*

Behren's House, Mathildenhöhe *(1901), Darmstadt. This house was built by Peter Behrens for himself. Its ordered and compact plan is in complete contrast to the overall picturesqueness of the estate, planned by Joseph Maria Olbrich.*

Ernest Ludwig House, Mathildenhöhe *(1900-1), Darmstadt. This striking house is a long, low, shed-like building and was the exhibition building of the Mathildenhöhe estate. The ornamentation is concentrated around the entrance portal and has statues by Ludwig Habich.*

Civic & Public buildings

The **Primary School, Marl** (1960-68), designed by Hans Scharoun, is interesting for its fragmentary form. Each part is allowed to develop its own particular quality and character while the spaces are used to provide coherence. Scharoun also designed the **Geschwister School, Lunen** (1958-62).

The **Rathaus, Bensberg** (1962-64), by Gottfried Böhm, is a memorable building. It takes the Brutalist style of Unger's house much further in a powerful and Expressionist manner to produce an almost medieval fantasy.

Commercial & Industrial buildings

The influence of the North American skyscraper came fairly late in this field. An example of its influence is the **Phoenix-Rheinrohn A. G. Building, Düsseldorf** (1960), a 22-story metal-sheathed office building.

Many German architects of the inter-war period turned their talents to commercial buildings, such as warehouses and office blocks. A notable example is Peter Behrens, who worked in a number of European countries but chiefly in Germany where a good example of his work is the warehouse at **66, Essener Strasse, Oberhausan** (1921-25). Olbrich was yet another architect who designed other than purely domestic buildings, notable examples of his work being the **Kauthof, Düsseldorf** (1907-8), and his last major work before his death in 1909, the **Tietz Department Store, Düsseldorf.** Further examples of buildings in this category include the **I. G. Farben Administrative Building, Hochst** (1921-25), and the **Trades Union Building, Frankfurt** (1931).

I. G. Farben Administrative Building, Hochst *Interior of the Administrative Building, designed by Peter Behrens. With its flowing lines, this is a fine* Expressionist *building into which Behrens introduced a number of bold* Gothic *elements.*

60, Belvederestrasse, Cologne-Müngersdorf *The style of the house, with its use of bare-faced brick and raw concrete, is a good example of the* Brutalist *movement. It was designed by Matthias Ungers.*

Primary School, Marl, *left. This school is one of a number by Hans Scharoun. Here Scharoun's use of spaces between each unit is particularly interesting, as they give cohesion to the building.*

Wedding Tower, Mathildenhöhe *(1907), Darmstadt. The tower is a dominant feature of the town. It was designed by Olbrich and anticipates* Art Deco. *It was built to celebrate the wedding of the Grand Duke Ernst-Ludwig.*

Rathaus, Bensberg *The new town hall, designed by Gottfried Böhm. The building is notable for its rawness of materials but lively molded forms. With its rather medieval Expressionist style, it fits in with its historic surroundings without discord.*

Southern Germany

Domestic buildings

Housing and the search for new styles and designs to meet new needs have been the concern of many leading architects since the 1920s. The **Weissenhof Estate, Stuttgart** (1927), was a pioneering housing scheme. It was planned by Ludwig Mies van der Rohe and the architects who collaborated on it included Walter Gropius, Hans Scharoun, Le Corbusier and Jacob Oud. The theme was housing for all, and the radical architectural ideas propagated in Berlin and elsewhere were developed on a remarkably poetic level. The scheme was seen as an expression of a new way of life; stylistic elements of traditional architecture disappeared and were replaced by pure, gleaming white villas, designed both for economy and mass production.

The **Schmitz Housing, Biberach** (1950), is a notable group of houses by Hugo Häring. Häring advocated a theory of organic architecture, not of curved shapes but one based on right-angled plans. The decisive criterion was that form was determined by function.

During the 1960s and 1970s much interesting housing was produced by the partnership of Peter Faller and Hermann Schroder. They developed the idea of a "housing hill" — a tent-like structure with terraces on the outside and servicing inside the void. Their **Housing, Täpachstrasse, Stuttgart** (1965-68), makes use of this idea although only one side of the "hill" is used, with a group of courtyard houses at its base. They developed their idea further in the **Schmitz Housing, Stuttgart** (1972-74), in Neugereut, where a basic support

Schmitz Housing, Biberach *The plan and form of these houses designed by Hugo Häring continue his thesis that function should determine the form of a building.*

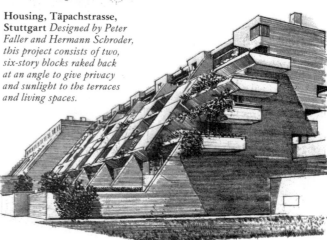

Housing, Täpachstrasse, Stuttgart *Designed by Peter Faller and Hermann Schroder, this project consists of two, six-story blocks raked back at an angle to give privacy and sunlight to the terraces and living spaces.*

Weissenhof Estate, Stuttgart

These are magnificent examples of the modern architecture of the 1920s. The split-level floors, large areas of glass and free planning were particularly radical features. Originally planned as an exhibition of housing for all in 1927, it was built along the contours of the southeast slope of the Kellesburg.

Housing by Le Corbusier

Apartment housing by Ludwig Mies van der Rohe

Housing by Hans Scharoun

structure was designed in which each occupant then planned his own apartment layout. However, the most recent tendency has been the return of recognizable stylistic elements to the architectural form. This can be seen in the **House, Malchin** (1976-77), by Ante Josip von Kostelac. The volumes owe much to 1920's modernism, but they are split in an unorthodox manner. The key window has an elaborate semicircular molded *pediment* and one side of the house has an almost *Neoclassical colonnade*. By contrast, the **Weidman House, Stuttgart** (1975), designed by Robert Krier, with its small pierced openings and double height terrace, is notable for its simple but nonetheless extremely powerful design.

There is another interesting housing project in **Osterwaldstrasse, Munich** (1976), designed by Otto Steidle and others. This consists of a basic support structure but each unit has its own particular arrangement.

The **Housing for the Elderly, Stuttgart,** (1973-76). in Reutlingen, designed by Günter Behnisch and others, is a sensitive housing scheme, consisting of a large four- and five-story block attached by a main entrance pavilion to existing accommodation for the elderly. The whole is grouped with some new housing around a gently undulating garden. The garden has two façades, that on the housing side having balconies and walls faced with wood shingles, that on the public road side having asbestos tiling. The principal passageway inside the main block is lighted by skylights and has views to the outside.

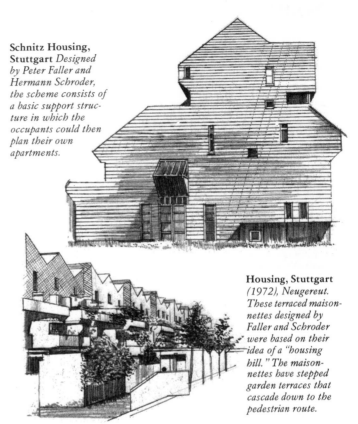

Schnitz Housing, Stuttgart *Designed by Peter Faller and Hermann Schroder, the scheme consists of a basic support structure in which the occupants could then plan their own apartments.*

Housing, Stuttgart *(1972), Neugereut. These terraced maisonnettes designed by Faller and Schroder were based on their idea of a "housing hill." The maisonnettes have stepped garden terraces that cascade down to the pedestrian route.*

House, Malchen, *left. The house, designed by Ante Josip von Kostelac, consists of two rectangular boxes split around the main entry hall.*

Housing for the Elderly, Stuttgart *In this fine housing scheme, the main façades on the garden side are multifaceted, creating privacy and a sense of enclosure for the occupants.*

Housing, Genterstrasse, Munich *(1971). One of a series of projects by Otto Steidle, it consists of a basic support structure into which a series of individual units are plugged. Much of the character is in the play of solids and voids, as frame sections are left exposed.*

Southern Germany

Civic & Public buildings

There are a number of fine modern college and school buildings in southern Germany. One example is the **School of Design, Ulm** (1953-55), which was designed by Max Bill, who was also its founding principal. The various buildings were made up of industrialized units and yet the overall effect has been to create a particularly pleasant and sympathetic environment on a hilly site. The **Freie Waldorfschule, Stuttgart** (1965-67), designed by Rolf Gutbrod, is another notable building, characterized by its use of concrete technology.

Gunter Behnisch also designed some notable works. An early example of his work is the **Engineering School, Ulm** (1961-63), which is still very much part of the *International Style*. By comparison, in the **Hymnus-Chor-Schule, Stuttgart** (1969-70), Behnisch used asbestos tiles and also an exposed steel frame with which to create a remarkably delicate building.

Behnisch and his partners also designed the **Olympic Park, Munich** (1967-77). Here the various elements are partially covered by magnificent tensile roof structures forming a canopy. Even more interesting is their **Sports Hall, Sindelfingen** (1976-77), in which giant *portal* frames of tubular steel carry the roof covering the stadium. The frames, triangular in section, are glazed with external blinds to cut out any glare and prevent excessive gain in heat.

The **Kurhaus, Badenweiler** (1962-67), by Klaus Humpert, is a quite exceptional building. A multiplicity of recreational activities are served by a free-form plan that has been shaped both by the specific uses required and by the topography. Winding paths move in, out and around the buildings. Although influenced by the work of other architects. Humpert's innovations have produced an entirely original work.

Commercial & Industrial buildings

The **Railway Station, Stuttgart** (1914-22), is an interesting building, very much a creation of its time. The station's starkly simple solids and voids, with the *colonnaded* side elevation, greatly influenced the younger theorists of the 1970s. More recently, there have been some interesting commercial buildings by Kammerer, Bolz & Partners in **Stuttgart**. Of particular interest is the **Calwer Strasse and Passage** (1974), with buildings grouped around a glazed *arcade*. The style is reminiscent of the *Brutalist* movement.

The **Architects' Office, University of Ulm**, (1970), by Walter Heinrich, is a fine *timber-frame* building raised on stilts and consisting of a series of right-angle planned studios and offices of receding and projecting planes. These are grouped around a central courtyard and also stepped down the side of a hill. The effect is reminiscent of Japanese architecture, particularly the way in which the building seems to float above ground.

The **Schneider Store, Freiburg** (1975), by Heinz Mohl, is a good example of how sensitive many German architects are to environment and context. Despite the building's obviously modern style, it looks at home in its medieval surroundings.

Hymnus-Chor-Schule, Stuttgart. *Here the component parts seem to come gently together under the lean-to roofs, giving the building an almost temporary feel. It was designed by Gunter Behnisch and his partners.*

Freie Waldorfschule, Stuttgart, *above. Designed by Rolf Gutbrod, the building is characterized by its non-right-angled geometry and use of concrete technology. The building symbolizes the free-form philosophy or "soul architecture" developed by Rudolf Steiner.*

Romeo and Juliet Flats, Stuttgart-Zuffenhausen *(1954-59). By Hans Scharoun, the flats comprise a 19-story point block and a lower terrace in a horseshoe-shaped plan. The façade is multifaceted and has numerous decorative projecting balconies.*

Kurhaus, Badenweiler.
Designed by Klaus Humpert, it stands on the
lower slopes of a castle hill, around which are a
network of footpaths. The design, consisting of a
café, gallery space, small concert hall, reading
rooms and external terracing, is molded between
and around the paths so that the hillside seems to
become part of the roof.

View from the base of the castle ruin

Main foyer and gallery space

**Schneider Store,
Frieburg,** *below.*
*This obviously modern
building stands on a
corner of the Munster-
platz blending
perfectly into its
historic surroundings,
a remarkable example
of how this may
be achieved.*

**Architects' Office,
Ulm,** *right.*
*This is the archi-
tectural office for the
planning and construc-
tion of the University
of Ulm. It is a modest
timber-frame building
raised on stilts
and is the work of
Walter Heinrich.*

**Sports Hall,
Sindelfingen**
*This very fine
project was designed
by Behnisch and
his partners. The
building's chief
attraction lies in
the careful juxta-
position of fabric
and structure.*

367

Switzerland

Domestic buildings

The first house designed by Adolf Loos was the **Villa Karma, Clarens-Montreux** (1904-6). It represents the beginning of his search for a pure, undecorated architecture. In complete contrast is the sculptural organic use of reinforced concrete in the **Duldeck House, Dornach** (1914-16), by Rudolf Steiner. The sculptural qualities of this latter building owe much to preparatory models which were made in clay. Le Corbusier designed several villas in and around **La Chaux-de-Fonds**, including the **Villa Fallet** (1905-7), the **Villa Stotzer** (1908), the **Villa Jaquemet** (1908), and the **Villa Jeanneret** (1912). Characteristic of all these buildings is Le Corbusier's reinterpretation of the vernacular tradition and the subsequent inclusion of *hipped roofs,* deep *eaves,* and *gable* ends, and the use of natural materials. The **Apartments, Doldertal, Zürich** (1935-36), by A. and E. Roth and M. Breuer, continued the stark architecture developed by Loos. Awnings and wooden roller blinds to give protection from the sun are the only trimmings on an otherwise unadorned building.

A remarkable series of terraced houses have been built in Switzerland since the 1950s. Good examples include **Terraced Housing, Zug** (1958-61), by Stucky & Meuli. The **Siedlung Halen, Berne** (1960-61), by Atelier 5, is planned in a grid system around a communal square. A major feature is the incorporation of large planting boxes

Duldeck House, Dornach *This powerfully sculpted house is articulated by a string course, pilasters, and a boldly curved entablature which reinforces the concave and convex forms.*

Villa Karma, Clarens-Montreux *The house, designed by Adolf Loos, is a simple rectangular block. The form has been enlivened by the articulation of a piano nobile and by surrounding terraces and numerous projecting corner towers.*

Apartments, Doldertal, Zürich *The scheme is divided into two blocks, with a garden space in between. The blocks are set at such an angle to the road that the terraces and the sitting-rooms face toward the south.*

Goetheanum, Dornach *The building is constructed entirely of concrete. The manner in which it has been molded, in an almost sculptural fashion, would only have been possible with such a material as this.*

Housing, Brugg *These houses are built on the side of a hill and consist of two rows of three-story terraces. The complex culminates at the top of the slope with a seven-story apartment block. The apartments are joined by a path which winds its way through the development.*

along the terraces which provide privacy. Other interesting housing schemes include **Terrace Housing, Flamatt** (1957-60); **Housing, Brugg** (1970-71); **Uberhauung Lorraine, 12, Burgdorf** (1976), and **62-68, Brunnadernstrasse; Bern** (1970-72), all by Atelier 5. Alvar Aalto designed the **Schonbuhl Apartment Building, Lucerne** (1963-66), which is a development of his earlier work at Bremen in Germany. It consists of wedge-shaped apartments planned in a fan arrangement around a main service core. There are some interesting houses in **Ticino** designed by Mario Botta which make their impact through the use of simple, monumental forms. An excellent example is the **Tower House** (1971-73).

Civic & Public buildings

The architecture of Rudolf Steiner, the founder of the Anthroposophical Society, incorporates his philosophical ideas, which were concerned with freedom from traditional architectural and educational constraints. These ideas were manifested in a break with the right-angle plan. The **Goetheanum, Dornach** (1925-28), consists of one large and one smaller hall, with adjacent lecture, reading and exhibition rooms. The **Center Le Corbusier, Zürich** (1963-67), is a pavilion and the last building which Le Corbusier designed before his death in 1965. The Center consists of an umbrella roof with the main volumes planned in a flexible manner underneath.

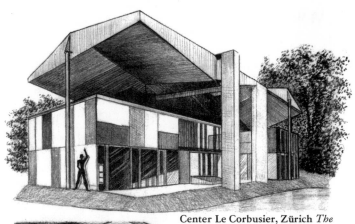

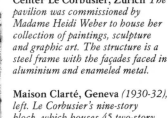

Center Le Corbusier, Zürich *The pavilion was commissioned by Madame Heidi Weber to house her collection of paintings, sculpture and graphic art. The structure is a steel frame with the façades faced in aluminium and enameled metal.*

Maison Clarté, Geneva *(1930-32), left. Le Corbusier's nine-story block, which houses 45 two-story apartments. Each flat has a large, glazed façade which can be protected from the sun by external roller blinds. Their haphazard use gives added interest to the architectural frame.*

Tower House, Ticino *Standing on sloping ground, the house resembles a medieval tower house. The entrance to the building is reached from the crest of a hill via a metal gangway.*

Siedlung Halen, Berne *A privately owned estate of 74 terraced houses built on the wooded slopes above the Halen bridge. The manner in which the paths wind through the scheme is reminiscent of many Mediterannean hill towns.*

Terraced Housing, Zug *The scheme consists of 25 single-story apartments stepped on the side of a hill. They are so arranged that the terrace of each flat forms the roof of the flat beneath it.*

Austria

Domestic buildings

The **Majolika House, Vienna** (1898-99), is a six-story apartment block designed by Otto Wagner. The name is derived from the majolica slabs which were used for the facing. The building consists of a structural frame covered with a skin of *polychrome* work and some fine examples of *Art Nouveau* decoration. Josef Hoffman was one of the most gifted architects to emerge from the Viennese Sezession. In his **Primavesi House, Vienna** (1913-15), classical elements, including *pediments* and *pilasters,* are combined with *Art Deco*-style molded *cornices.* The building itself is treated as a series of cubes massed on and around each other. One of the most radical of Austrian architects of the early 20th century was Adolf Loos. He worked in the United States of America for three years from 1893 and then returned to Austria to become a pioneer of the modern movement. His work is a synthesis of Louis Sullivan's purist ideals and Wagner's *Functionalist* theories. Of particular interest is his design for the **Steiner House, Vienna** (1910), in which these ideas can be seen at their best. The house was one of the first to be built of reinforced concrete. In the **House, Nothartgasse, Vienna** (1913), also by Loos, the half *vault* which was employed at the rear of the Steiner House is here used to cover the whole house. The *eaves* on one side extend out and line up with the terrace which serves the rooms in the roof space. His **Strasser House, Vienna** (1919), manifests a similar play of curved and straight lines. Between 1923 and 1928 he lived in Paris, and in the **Moller House, Vienna** (1928), the controlled and simple volumes demonstrate his assimilation of French purism. In the **Khuner House, Payerbach** (1930), Loos began to return to the vernacular interests of his youth, using natural materials such as timber and incorporating alpine roofs.

As elsewhere in Europe, the modern movement was concerned primarily with housing schemes rather than single, private houses. One of the major projects was the **Karl-Marx-Hof, Vienna** (1930), by Karl Ehn, then the city architect. It stands as a monolithic wall, punctuated by giant archways and decorated with *keystones,* crowned by sculptures. Also of interest are the designs of the **Werkbund Exhibition, Vienna** (1930), which included work by Loos, Hoffman and Richard Neutra, who had then left Austria to work in the United States of America.

Civic & Public buildings

The young avant-garde of late 19th-century Vienna revolted against the existing art establishment and formed the Sezession Movement in 1897. The group had its own exhibition building, the **Sezession Building, Vienna** (1898-99), designed by Josef Maria Olbrich. The key elements are the play of cubic forms and the juxtaposition of decorated and undecorated elements. The simplicity of the basic geometry foreshadows Frank Lloyd Wright's Unity Temple, Illinois. The building was nevertheless criticized by the young modernist Loos, on his return from the United States of America, who considered it to be overdecorated.

Commercial & Industrial buildings

The **Exchange, Vienna** (1869-77), by Theophil von Hansen, is an Italianate-style building similar to the Royal Exchange, London. The **Post Office Savings Building, Vienna** (1904-6), by Otto Wagner, is in stark contrast and reveals how revolutionary the modern architects of the early 20th century were. Unlike the older buildings, which rely on mass, this is a light and strictly functional work, with a glass-covered hall. It is stripped of all superfluous detail, even the structural columns being left bare. The **Goldman Commercial Building, Vienna** (1910-11), by Loos, was originally a clean, undecorated design. The shop windows and the window boxes are a later addition. The absence of decoration was greatly disliked by the establishment of the day.

Church of the Steinhof, Vienna *(1903-7). Designed by Otto Wagner, it comprises a series of simple, coherent masses with* Art Nouveau *decoration. This is one of the few great churches built in the 20thC.*

Steiner House, Vienna *Unlike most contemporary Austrian architects, Adolf Loos rejected ornament. This is a remarkable house in that it predates much of the work of the modernists in Europe and the USA. The rounded elevation on the roadside belies the large scale of the house behind.*

Primavesi House, Vienna *View of the garden front. Of particular interest is the use of balconies and the cutting away of form. The decorative language is typical of the work which developed out of the Viennese Sezession.*

Moller House, Vienna *Here Loos employed simpler forms than in the Steiner House. The stark symmetrical quality of the building is reminiscent of* Neoclassicism.

House, Nothartgasse, Vienna, *right. This house has the geometry of straight and curved lines first employed in the Steiner House. The great curled* barrel-vaulted *roof appears to tie the building to the ground.*

Post Office Savings Building, Vienna, *above. In this refined, sleek interior Wagner dispensed with the decorative details of Art Nouveau then prevalent in Viennese architecture. The reductive quality of the modern movement is clearly evident here.*

Sezession Building, Vienna *The dominant feature is the circular dome, which is* articulated *by the four tapering corner towers. Although this building represented a radical departure from contemporary designs, it is far removed from the work of Loos which followed.*

Purkersdorf Sanatorium, Vienna *(1903-06). A detail of the main entrance by J. Hoffman, with its remarkably simple and utilitarian elements. The modest design, which is comparatively modern, was due to economic constraints as well as to the purpose of the building.*

Goldman Commercial Building, Vienna *This structure was the only major public commission given to Loos. Both a store and an apartment block, the two functions are clearly articulated externally by a* cornice *controlling the juxtaposition of diverse images.*

371

Belgium

Domestic buildings

A leading figure of the Belgian *Art Nouveau* movement was Victor Horta. The first notable building which he designed was the **Tassel House, Rue Paul-Emile Janson, Brussels** (1892-93). It was revolutionary both in its form and structure. The novelty exists in its plan which dispensed with the through passage — a prerequisite of most terraced houses — so that the rooms are arranged around an octagonal hall. Horta's use of iron is also of interest. Like Louis Sullivan in the United States, he used it as an architectural means of expression and not merely as a structural material. His **Solvay House, 224, Avenue Louise, Brussels** (1895-1900), which was built for an industrialist, combines both classical and *Baroque* elements, having as it does a symmetrical front and an asymmetrical garden elevation. It is a five-story house and has a stone façade. The second and third stories have a concave center with large curved windows and these are *articulated* by a decorative iron balcony.

Horta built numerous other houses in Brussels. A characteristic feature includes the extensive use of iron, which reduced the necessity of load-bearing walls and thus allowed the inclusion of large glazed surfaces. Buildings designed by him include the **Hôtel van Eetvelde, Avenue Palmerston, Brussels** (1896); the **Hôtel Dubois, Avenue Brugmann** (1901), and **Maison Horta, Rue Américaine** (1898), both in **Saint Gilles**. Other buildings of interest include the **Hôtel Otlet, Rue de Florence, Brussels** (1894) a building of distinctly Baroque origin, designed by Octave van Rysselberge. He also designed the **Hôtel d'Alcantara, Brussels** (1882), a classical building in the style of the Italian *Renaissance.* At the house of Saint-Cyre, the painter, in **Place Ambiorix, Brussels** (1903), designed by Gustave Straven, the classical restraint of Horta has disappeared and has been replaced by a more flamboyant interpretation of Art Nouveau.

Another important figure in 20th-century Europe, particularly in Belgium, was Henry Van der Velde. He was a theorist, painter and typographer, who eventually became an architect. Critical of the environment in which most people lived, he advocated reforms which reflected those of William Morris and the English *Arts and Crafts* movement. His own House, the **Bloemenwerf House, Uccle** (1895), reflected his theories, for he designed everything, from the curtains to the carpets and the dinner service, as an integral part of the complete design.

The theories of the Arts and Crafts movement were further developed when the Austrian architect, Josef Hoffman, was commissioned to design the **Palais Stoclet, Avenue de Tervuren, Brussels** (1905), it is one of the architectural masterpieces of the early 20th century and consists of a series of two- and three-story blocks, planned over a grid of squares. It is rich and refined almost to the point of decadence. The simple rectangular masses and the angular bay windows are faced with white marble slabs, while the edges of the volumes are lined with ornamental metal *friezes.*

Bloemenwerf House, Uccle *The house is an amalgam of the English* Arts and Crafts *movement as well as* Art Nouveau. *Not only was the architect responsible for the design of the house but also for the entire contents, from the joinery and furniture to the hardware and furnishing fabrics.*

Maison du Peuple, Antwerp *(1898). Of particular interest in this house by Emile van Averbeke and Van Asperen is the careful symmetry of the front façade and of the central oval window. The curvature of the latter is typical of the stylistic motifs of Art Nouveau.*

Tassel House, Rue Paul-Emile Janson, Brussels *The house is one of the classic buildings of the Art Nouveau movement. The main rooms are in the center of the building and are* articulated *by an intricately designed iron and glass bay, above.*

Hôtel van Eetvelde, Avenue Palmerston, Brussels *One of a series of houses which Victor Horta built in Brussels before World War I.* Baroque, *classical, romantic and utilitarian elements appear harmoniously together.*

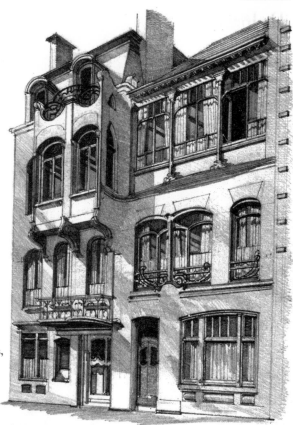

Hôtel Max Hallet, Brussels *(1903). This façade by Victor Horta is particularly notable for its amalgam of bays and quasi-classical motifs. Though at first glance the bays appear as no more than unnecessary appendages they acquire vitality when seen against the bland façade behind.*

Maison Horta, Rue Américaine, Saint-Gilles, *right. These two houses were amalgamated into one, the Horta Museum. At one time it was Horta's own residence. The cramped exterior belies a profusion of airy, mirrored rooms inside.*

Housing, Rue Marconi, Forest *(1903), left. This section of the building shows how elements of Art Nouveau design have been added to a somewhat drab façade in order to create a more coherent and colorful whole.*

Palais Stoclet, Avenue de Tervuren, Brussels *This building was constructed in the tradition of the town palazzo, built from the Renaissance onward and displaying the owner's wealth and importance. Inside there are friezes painted in the Art Nouveau style by Gustave Klimt.*

Hotel, Schilderstraat and Plaatsnijderstraat, Antwerp *(1905). This building is an amalgam of elements including Art Nouveau features like the horseshoe-shaped window frames. Most unusual however is the boat balcony which protrudes above the first floor.*

Belgium

The influence of Dutch architects in their *articulation* of volumes and the overlapping geometry of horizontal and vertical elements, was considerable in Belgium. Good examples are the **Hôtel Wolfers, Ixelles** (1926), by Jean-J. Eggericx; Robert Putteman's own **House, Rue Camille Lemmonier, Brussels** (1930), and the **House, Avenue della Faille, Antwerp** (1928), by Paul Smekens.

The major *International Style* buildings are those designed by Louis de Koninck, such as the **House, Avenue Brassine, Auderghem** (1928-29). It was the first house in Belgium to have been built of reinforced concrete. Also of interest in **Uccle** are his own house, **105, Avenue Fond'Roy** (1926-70); the **Dr. Ley House** (1934); the **House, Avenue du Fort Jaco** (1937), and **Housing, Place Coghen** (1934-36). Victor Bourgeois designed the house of the sculptor Oscar Jespers, **149, Avenue du Prince Heritier, Woluwé Saint Lambert** (1928), and the **Cité Moderne, Berchem Sainte-Agathe** (1922-25). Le Corbusier designed the house for the painter René Guiette in the **Avenue Peupliers, Antwerp** (1927).

One of the more interesting Belgian architects is Antoine Pompe. He produced a series of projects all of which were executed with craftsmanlike care, such as the **Institute of Dr van Neck, Saint Gilles** (1910); the **Villa Grunewald, Uccle** (1925), and the **House, Avenue Jean Sermon, Ganshoren** (1922). In these buildings Pompe resorted to the ideas propogated by the *Arts and Crafts* movement.

An amalgam of traditional vernacular forms, *Art Nouveau* and *Functionalist* elements can be seen in a number of suburban housing schemes, such as **Kapelleveld Garden City, Woluwé Saint Lambert** (1922-26), by Pompe. It includes 124 houses and commercial premises. The second floor is contained in huge pitched roofs, punctuated by *gabled dormers* and staircase towers. He also designed the **Garden City, Hautrage-Nord** (1921). On similar lines, but with a stronger vernacular content, is the **Garden City, Boitsfort** (1920-29), by Eggericx and Louis van der Swallman. The scale of the latter is considerably larger and consists of 1,600 houses. The earlier schemes were far smaller. All three were influenced by the British garden city ideas of Sir Ebenezer Howard, which were first developed at Letchworth in 1903. The projects were intended to remedy the squalor and social alienation of the big cities.

A reaction against the orthodoxy of International Style architecture is most clearly seen in the **Medical Faculty Building, Woluwé Saint Lambert** (1969-74), by Lucien Kroll. The interest is centered on the picturesque quality of the building. Attention is drawn, not to the structural framework, but the separate elements which seem to grow in an almost organic fashion. Such romantic associations were taken further in the development of the university town of **Louvain la Neuve** (1971-73), laid out under the direction of Professor R. M. Lemaire. The scheme, with its crooked streets, resembles the old Béguinage, Louvain, the extensive restoration of which was another of Lemaire's projects.

Villa Grunewald, Uccle *Though the building is strongly traditional in its use of motifs from the English Arts and Crafts movement, it is a highly intuitive and romantic building. The powerful blocks which make up the lower two stories owe something to modern Functionalism.*

129, Rue des Atrébates, Brussels *(1922). On one level this building by Antione Pompe is simple and utilitarian. On close inspection, however, the articulation of the façade is quite complex. Asymmetrical in its design, each section is carefully balanced by the others.*

House, Avenue Brassine, Auderghem *A house designed in the manner of the International Style, the main rooms are on the first floor and are defined by the long, horizontal band of windows. All the internal spaces are expressed on the façade.*

Institute of Dr van Neck, Saint Gilles *The building combines both a clinic and an apartment. The whole building is air-conditioned, the system being secreted in the six pilasters on the façade.*

Garden City, Boitsfort, *left. The scheme consists of 1600 terraced and semi-detached houses, like the one shown, arranged in an irregular manner. The houses are characterized by tiled roofs,* stuccoed *walls, gabled* dormers *and roofs drawn from the vernacular tradition.*

Medical Faculty Building, Woluwé Saint Lambert *The building serves as accommodation for the medical faculty of the university of Louvain la Neuve. The building appears as a collage of disparate parts, carefully combined into a mammoth complex.*

House, Avenue della Faille, Antwerp *The clearly* articulated *volumes and the play of geometric shapes, as well as the cubist form of the house, are motifs derived from traditional Dutch and early 20th-C German architecture.*

Palais de Justice, Brussels *(1968-73). The entry staircase, which is contained within a deep recess behind the giant front* colonnade. *By Joseph Proelaert, the building is a* monumental Baroque *edifice, designed with a vigor which is reminiscent of Sir John Vanbrugh.*

Galeries Saint Hubert, Brussels *(1839-46), right. By J. P. Cluysenaer, it is one of the finest glass structures built in Belgium in the 19thC and consists of a series of galleries, each linked to another. All the galleries are articulated by Tuscan and* Ionic *pilasters.*

Housing, Place Coghen, Uccle, *left. These finely proportioned houses were designed in the International Style. They are characterized by corner windows and stucco walls.*

Holland

Domestic buildings

In the years which followed World War I Dutch architecture was dominated first by the *Expressionist* movement and later by *de Stijl.* The earlier style amounted to a revival of vernacular architecture, the leading members of which were Michael de Klerk, P. L. Kramer and M. van der Maes. Schemes such as the **Eigen Haard Housing, Zaarnstraat, Amsterdam** (1913-21), by de Klerk, are characterized by the use of natural materials and the incorporation of decorative detail. The bold angular designs of Frank Lloyd Wright represented an alternative style to the vernacular. Robert van t'Hoff, a Dutch architect who once worked in Wright's office, adopted Wright's solutions in the **Heide House, Utrecht** (1917). Its forms, however, are simpler, and Wright's textured surfaces have been replaced by a smooth, elegant finish. It was a seminal building in a new style of architecture which was to come to fruition in the de Stijl movement. This movement, founded in 1917, was concerned primarily with space, color and functionalism and is represented best by the geometric styles of the Dutch painters Piet Mondrian and Theo van Doesburg. The architectural style developed largely as a reaction against the picturesque style of de Klerk and is epitomized by the **Schröder House, Utrecht** (1924), by Gerrit Rietveld. The walls, roof and balconies are all composed of interlocking planes of concrete. J. J. P. Oud sought to impose this method of building in prefabricated concrete in large-scale housing schemes, notably in **Spangen Housing, Rotterdam** (1919-20). Part of it, the **Spaanischebocht** (1919-20), by M. Brinkman, incorporates long, communal courtyards, and became a prototype for public housing throughout northern Europe. Contemporary design, often eclectic and sometimes bizarre, can be seen in the **Gabled Housing, Zwolle** (1975-77), by Aldo van Eyck and Theo Bosch, where the picturesque terraces and *gables* introduce a feeling of seclusion.

Civic and Public buildings

Functionalism, particularly suited to public buildings, is seen in the **Zonnestraal Sanatorium, Hilversum** (1926-28), by Johannes Duiker. All the buildings in the complex are characterized by reinforced concrete frames, white walls and large, glazed façades. Another building by Duiker, and equally radical in its turn, is the **Open Air School, Amsterdam** (1930-32).

Heide House, Utrecht, *above. With its advancing and receding planes this house represents a brilliant European interpretation of the prairie houses of Frank Lloyd Wright, though the forms belie an overworked interior.*

Open Air School, Amsterdam *The school represents a radical departure from traditional school buildings of the period. Within the concrete frame is a stair-well flanked by classrooms.*

Workers' housing, Hook of Holland *(1924-27). This scheme is probably one of the best examples of the* Functionalist *architecture of J. J. P. Oud. Typical features are the uncluttered wall surfaces and the crisp fenestration.*

Van Slobbe House, Heerlen *(1970). A view toward the main garden terraces on the southwest side of the house. On this side the interior has been opened up through the extensive use of glass, while on the opposite side, which faces north, the interior is closed in.*

Spangen Housing, Rotterdam
Several blocks in this scheme were designed by M. Brinkman and in them he incorporated the first access balconies to have been developed since the classical world.

Town Hall, Hilversum *(1928-30). Designed by Willem Dudok, who was the city architect from 1915. He developed a personal style which deployed powerful horizontal and vertical brick masses and bold, simple cornices. His style has been imitated both at home and abroad.*

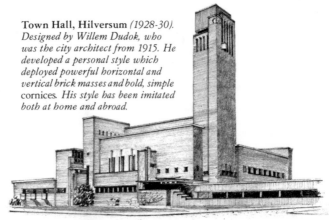

Eigen Haard Housing, Amsterdam

Michael de Klerk's solution for Amsterdam's housing problems, the scheme was constructed with an amalgam of traditional materials such as slate, tile and brick and incorporated eccentricities of form and detail. The *picturesque* qualities were deliberately incorporated to humanize the urban environment.

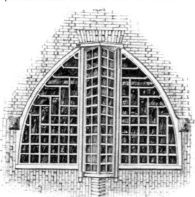

Window to hall

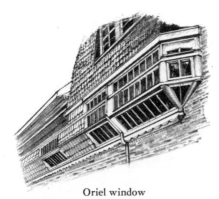

Oriel window

Schröder House, Utrecht *The pure forms which are employed in this building are reminiscent of the work of Walter Gropius and the* Bauhaus, *while the manner in which the shapes are superimposed on each other owes something to* Cubist *painting of the previous decade.*

House, Venlo *(1970). Designed by Aldo van Eyck, the ground floor of the house consists of a square enclosure, the corners of which are softened by two entrance* loggias. *The first floor is contained in an elongated, hexagonal roof, punctuated by* dormer windows.

Holland

The **Municipal Museum, The Hague** (1919-34), by H. P. Berlage, consists of large, box-like volumes which are interlocked around a central garden courtyard. The *articulation* of the forms owes much to the **Town Hall, Hilversum,** by W. M. Dudok. The **De Drie Hoven, Amsterdam** (1975), by Herman Hertzberger, is a residential complex for the physically and mentally handicapped. At first glance the façades seem harsh and unappealing, but on closer inspection the simple and rational layout gives the interior a more hospitable feeling.

Commercial & Industrial buildings

The architecture of late 19th-century Holland was immersed in *Romantic Nationalism* which is perhaps best represented by the monumental **Rijksmuseum, Amsterdam** (1885), and the **Railway Station, Amsterdam** (1889), both of which were designed by P. J. H. Cuijpers. By the turn of the century such an eclectic and decorative style had been replaced by a more functional one.

The major commercial building to be erected at the beginning of the century was the **Exchange, Amsterdam** (1897-1903), by Hendrick Petrus Berlage. It is a strictly utilitarian building but with an imposing, glazed roof. The brick walls are undecorated save for the use of a light-colored stone and brick *balustrade, capitals* and window surrounds. Its tall tower is a dominant feature of the town. The influence of the building was considerable, particularly in the works of the Amsterdam School.

The **Van Nelle Factory, Rotterdam** (1928-30), by Johannes Andreas Brinkman and L. C. van der Vlugt, exemplifies the utilitarian tradition. The administrative offices, a lower structure with a concave façade, and the factory itself were designed as two separate entities and then linked by bridges. The factory was divided into three sections for the processing of tobacco, tea and coffee. The transfer of products to the shipment area was via long sloping bridges. The **Handelsblad Cineac Cinema, Amsterdam** (1934), occupies a corner site. It is of a straightforward box-shape housing an auditorium, but the façade on the street front is incised at one of its angles to provide an entrance. The roofscape is embellished with a system of bright, electrical signs, reminiscent of Russian constructivist designs. The **Centraal Beheer Offices, Apeldoorn** (1975), by Herman Hertzberger, is open plan and was designed for an insurance company. It is built on a grid system and based on a standard *module.* The central section is taken up by seating areas, coffee shops and conference rooms. Wells, lighted from above, penetrate the floors at critical points. The creation of a sympathetic environment was of paramount importance in the architect's design. The **Lijnbaan Shopping Center, Rotterdam** (1953), was one of the city's first redevelopments after World War II. The complex consists of an "L"-shaped shopping mall which is traffic free, and was conceived of at a time when the idea of pedestrian precincts was far from common. The center was designed by J. H. van den Broek and J. B. Bakema.

Van Nelle Factory, Rotterdam
The Functionalist *style which emerged after World War I was particularly suited to the design of factories. The curved block on the left houses the administrative offices of the factory.*

Arts Center, Helmond *(1907). By Piet Blom, this highly individualistic building was designed as a reaction against the sterility of much postwar Dutch architecture. It consists of timber-framed cubes, impaled on brick piers and organized into a circular plan.*

Children's Home, Ysbaarnpad, Amsterdam *(1955-60), above. By Aldo van Eyck, the home is constructed from prefabricated concrete units arranged around this major square and seven secondary squares.*

Exchange, Amsterdam
This building marks the birth of modern Dutch architecture for, despite the sobriety of the design, it lay the foundations for the more Expressionistic *buildings designed by Michel de Klerk.*

Spain

Religious buildings

The architectural styles which proliferated in 19th-century Spain were diverse. Some buildings were conceived in the *Classical* style while others, like the **Cathedral, San Sebastian** (1888), were *Gothic Revival*. In the 1870s Antoni Gaudi emerged as an architect of exceptional originality and he produced some of the most individualistic and audacious buildings in Europe at that time. Influenced by the philosophy of Milà y Fontanels, in his veneration of the Middle Ages, Gaudi sought to emulate the honesty and the craftsmanship of medieval building.

His school and convent, **Santa Teresa, Barcelona** (1889-94), is a simple, formal building. Rectangular in shape, its walls are of rubble, framed by brick panels. The main focal points are the projecting entrance bay and the top story with its saw-toothed *arcading,* and the windows, which are crowned with motifs suggesting castellation and reflecting the battlements above.

For the last 30 years of his life Gaudi was increasingly preoccupied with the **Church of the Sagrada Familia, Barcelona** (1883-1926). It is raised on a 12 ft high terrace and surrounded by a dry moat so that it must be approached by steps. Though *Gothic* in spirit, the plan is radical in that it dispenses with the traditional *choir screen* and makes provision for a *cloister* to encircle the church. Like the medieval cathedrals, work was intended to continue in the years which followed the architect's death. Construction was halted by the Civil War and though it was resumed in 1952 the church remains incomplete. The three main *portals*, however, are finished and are known as the Portal of Glory, The Portal of the Nativity and the Portal of the Passion. Each is a narrative, carved in stone, depicting scenes from the New Testament. The **Church of Santa Coloma de Cervello, Barcelona** (1898-1914), also by Gaudi, was likewise never completed. Only the *crypt*, a dark semieliptical space carried on four inclined pillars, was finished. Built in brick and surmounted with a red, terracotta tile roof, it seems to grow out of the low hill on which it stands.

Castles & Palaces

The **Güell Palace, Barcelona** (1885-90), by Gaudi, is a stronghold which was built as an extension of the client's town house. It is infused with the spirit of the Middle Ages. Consisting of six stories, the principal feature is the entrance, designed in the manner of *Art Nouveau*. The interior is dominated by a square living room which carries through three stories and is crowned with a tiled dome. This is disguised on the exterior by a tall spire. Gaudi was also responsible for the **Archbishop's Palace, Astorga** (1887-93), a white granite palace with cylindrical corner towers and splayed hoods over the entrance *portico*.

Santa Teresa, Barcelona *The simple, rectangular form of the whole structure is enlivened by decorative turrets at the four corners. The use of contrasting elements, the spiral against the angularity of the surrounding parts, is typical of Antoni Gaudi's work.*

Church of Santa Coloma de Cervello, Barcelona *The decorative hoods of the windows are covered with ceramic mosaics while the grills of the windows are constructed from the discarded parts of obsolete cotton spinning machines.*

Church of the Sagrada Familia, Barcelona *The* Portal *of the Nativity which punctuates the east transept. In his desire to emulate the medieval cathedrals, Gaudi intended the church to be taller than all the surrounding buildings. The spires rise to more than 348 ft.*

Güell Palace, Barcelona *The entrance portal. Gaudi's use of detail is often extravagant and fantastic, incorporating motifs from diverse cultures. The medley of styles here includes a hint of the architecture of Morocco as well as the Spanish Baroque.*

Spain

Domestic buildings

Antoni Gaudi designed a wide range of domestic
buildings. Among them is the **Güell Pavilion,
Barcelona** (1884-88). It consists of an octagonal
caretaker's house and a rectangular stable block
flanking the entrance gate to the Güell estate at
Pedralbes, on the outskirts of the city. The
influence of Moorish architecture is much in
evidence. The **Casa Calvet, Barcelona** (1898-
1904), also by Gaudi, is remarkably restrained,
consisting of a *gabled* façade with *Baroque* style
fenestration. His **Casa Battló, Barcelona** (1905-
07), with its twisting stone window frames and
the texture of its roof which resembles dragon's
scales, is considerably more flamboyant. The **Casa
Milà, Barcelona** (1905-10), is the most sculptural
of all of Gaudi's projects. It is a six-story apartment block and in it there is hardly a straight line
to be found. The **Park Güell, Barcelona** (1900-
14), was conceived by Gaudi as a garden suburb.
Though it was to have had 60 houses, only two
were built. It is now a municipal park and consists
of a maze of meandering paths. The walls and the
fountains in the park have tile mosaics.

Civic & Public buildings

The **Thau School, Barcelona** (1972-75), by
Martorell, Bohigas & Mackay, is built on a
narrow sloping site. It consists of three elements:
a large block steps up the slope and contains the
nursery, primary schools and the library; a single
story porter's lodge at 45° to this steps up to the
third element, the secondary school. The **School**
and **Social Center, Irun** (1975-76), by Miguel
Garay and José Ignacio Linazasoro, is the complete
antithesis to this, being smooth and streamlined,
even austere. This rationalist approach to design
is typical of recent Spanish architecture.

*Casa Vicens,
Barcelona (1878-80).
A rubble, stone and
brick building by
Antoni Gaudi, which
bristles with corbeled
turrets, chimneys and
brick fins. The garden
fence illustrated has
cast-iron leaves.*

*El Capricho, Comillas
(1883-85). The walls
of Gaudi's building are
enlivened with decora-
tive floral bands. The
main entrance is given
extra prominence by a
decorative tower
which is carried on a
four-columned porch,
which is in turn raised
above the ground.*

Galleried Houses, La Coruña

A characteristic of the houses on the Atlantic coast
of Spain is their galleries with glazed façades. The
best examples are to be found in La Coruña. Usually
projecting about 3½ ft, they provide additional living
space as well as protection from the sea spray.

Avenida de la Marina

Riego de San Nicolas

Thau School, Barcelona *The school buildings serve 1500 pupils of all ages. The flight of steps joins the diverse elements which make up the school complex.*

Almirall House, Lá Garriga *(1975-77), Barcelona. A house by Martorell, Bohigas & Mackay based on the square. The fireplace and chimney are at the center.*

Casa Milà, Barcelona *An apartment building which was laid out around two courtyards. The fluidity of the forms makes it seem as if the building is an organic growth rather than a man-made structure. Its roof, which resembles a rolling landscape, is adorned with giant chimneys.*

Casa Battló, Barcelona *Detail of the façade which was added by Gaudi to a comparatively ordinary house, owned by a textile manufacturer. It was transformed into a flamboyant, jewel-like design, its curves derived from Art Nouveau.*

Walden 7, Sant Just *(1973-75), d'Esvern. A group of apartments by Ricardo Bofill and others, it is arranged in a medieval style around courtyards. The façades, which are 18 stories high, are enriched by numerous semicircular turrets and balconies.*

School and Social Center, Irun *The first stage of the development. It is an uncompromisingly rationalist design, with a large three-sided colonnaded courtyard terminated by two austere, porticoed pavilions, which are square and angular.*

Denmark

Religious buildings

Architecture in Europe at the turn of the 20th century was dominated first by *National Romanticism* and then by austere classicism. The new generation of architects developed a purer feeling for space and form. In Denmark, one of the more interesting examples resulting from this is the **Grundtvig Church, Copenhagen** (1920-40). It has the monumentality of the *Romanesque* style, combined with a feeling for space, which clearly belongs to the 20th century. As the century progressed references to past architecture were dropped and unequivocally modern forms and materials drawn from industrial technology were used. The **Bagsvåerd Church, Copenhagen** (1974-76), by Jorn Utzon, provides a fine example of this development.

Domestic buildings

The major factors in modern Danish domestic architecture are a simplicity of form, the architects' preference for natural materials and the successful blending of the new work with the surroundings. The **Bellavista Housing Estate, Klampenborg** (1934), by Arne Jacobson, with its projecting balconies and flat roof line is typical.

In the years following World War II, the complementary influences of Ludwig Mies van der Rohe's machined precision and Frank Lloyd Wright's humanism produced an architectural style characterized by formal simplicity and conscientious craftsmanship. The **Søholm Housing Estate, Klampenborg** (1950-55), became a prototype for housing schemes throughout Europe. Other examples of modern domestic building projects include the **Court Houses, Elsinore** (1957-60), by Utzon, and the **Center Point Housing, Farum** (1970-74).

Civic & Public buildings

In reaction to the stiff classicism of the early 19th century, Danish civic architecture in the later part of the century became increasingly eclectic, as illustrated by the **Thorwaldsen Museum, Copenhagen** (1839-48), and the **Town Hall, Odense** (1880-83). The end of the century saw a return to traditional styles and to classicism before the appearance of the first modern movement public buildings, such as the **Town Hall, Aarhus** (1938-42), by Arne Jacobson and Erik Moller. Its openwork tower is a reinterpretation of a medieval style, in horizontal and vertical concrete slabs. Also of interest is the **Louisiana Museum, Humlebaek** (1958), by Bo & Wohlert, comprising a series of pavilions linked by corridors.

Bagsvåerd Church, Copenhagen
The church stands on a long narrow site, surrounded by streets on three sides. Most of the building is one story high, but at the east end it rises to a stepped gable over the church hall. Inside, the walls of the hall are decorated with cascades of sprayed concrete shells.

Grundtvig Church, Copenhagen *By P. V. J. Klint, this fine church has its stepped gables boldly articulated by long vertical recessed panels. Inside, the clearly defined volumes are distinctly 20th-C in feeling.*

Søholm Housing Estate, Klampenborg *The 14 houses are planned in a sharply staggered terrace. The simple yellow brick gable ends and clerestory sections create a simple, picturesque overall outline.*

House, Sorgenfri *(c. 1959). By Eva and Nils Koppel, the house is a rectangular block with pitched and lean-to sections to the roof and a central glazed courtyard. There are few windows in the external walls, except on the side facing the garden and Lake Lyngby.*

Court Houses, Elsinore *The estate comprises 63 houses. Each unit is based on a square plan, with the living quarters on two sides in an "L" shape about a court- yard in the angle. The walls of the court face out onto the common parkland beyond.*

Summer House, Rørvig *(c. 1972). By Bertel and Vibe Udson, its principal feature is the inter- secting lean-to roofs, built on the outside of the right angle formed by the two main walls. The bedrooms are separated from the main house by a raised sun deck.*

Center Point Housing, Farum *A "low-rise" housing scheme, designed by Sorensen, Moller-Jensen & Arnfred, it was intended as an alternative to high-rise blocks. The stepped terrace units run in six parallel rows, connected by a network of walkways.*

Homes built by hand

One reaction to the restraints of planning regulations and building codes is the hand-made house ingeniously built with materials found in junk yards and on rubbish heaps. The hand-made structures built in **Christiana, Copenhagen,** in the 1970s are good examples.

House made from scrap

Dome house

Odense University *(1971-80). Courtyards within the campus provide light to the laboratories and study rooms on either side. The facing material is steel sheeting fixed to a steel framework. The architects were Krohn and Hartvig Rasmussen and Knud Holscher.*

Sweden

Domestic buildings

International modernism dominated Swedish architecture in the first part of the 20th century. However, by 1940 a reaction against such formalism had started and a style developed dependent on the simple use of natural materials, such as decorative brickwork, timber, stone and sheet materials. Houses were no longer designed to standard plans, but tailor-made to the client's needs. The work of Sven Backström and Leif Reinius who designed the **Winter House, Västberga, Stockholm** (1939), illustrates this trend. Also of interest is the work of Ralph Erskine, in particular the **Villa, Sorunda** (1955-56), Lisön; the **Villa, Storvik** (1947-48), Hammarby, and the forestry workers' **Houses, Jädraas** (1951). His six prefabricated **Apartments, Växsjö** (1954), are interesting for the way in which his design grew out of the process of production and construction as well as being determined by climatic restraints. The balconies are suspended by steel rods from concrete beams in the roof, both to reduce structural complications and also to eliminate heat loss from the interior to the exterior. Erskine's housing schemes at **Bruket, Sandviken** (1970-80); **Barberaren, Sandviken** (1962-70), and at **Svappavard** (1963-64), all demonstrate the strong influence of social concerns on domestic Swedish buildings and architecture.

Civic & Public buildings

Eclecticism and *Neobaroque* styles characterized civic architecture in Sweden at the end of the 19th century, and classical influences continued to be important until well into the 20th century.

Forest Crematorium, Emskede, Stockholm *(1934-40). Designed by Gunnar Asplund, it stands at the top of a gently sloping hill and comprises a simple but dramatic group of buildings linked by a portico of plain shafts.*

Winter House, Västberga, Stockholm *The architects Sven Backström and Leif Reinius wanted to create an indoor all-year-round garden for an owner who had moved to a drab, treeless site. The accommodation is "L"-shaped on two floors. The double-story living-room is in the angle of the "L" and opens out onto a greenhouse.*

Houses, Jädraas *The tiny hamlet of 16 timber dwellings was built for forestry workers. The houses are grouped in an irregular plan around a clearing in the forest. Their design recreates the simplicity and utility of traditional styles.*

Villa, Storvik, *below. Projecting terraces, overhanging eaves around most sides of the house and the exaggeratedly tall chimney stack are the major features of this compact timber built domestic building.*

Villa, Sorunda, *below. The house, a welded steel dome, stands on a raised terrace beside the water. The design was originally intended as a prototype for mass production.*

Another element in determining the development of a modern style was the influence of the English *Arts and Crafts* movement.

The first major figure of the modern movement was Carl Bergsten, who designed the **Liljeralch Gallery, Stockholm** (1916). In the 1920s and 1930s a style marked by simple forms and materials evolved. Buildings of interest of the period include the **City Hall, Stockholm** (1923), with its austere wall face relieved only by the very simple *fenestration*, and the **Maritime Museum, Stockholm** (1934), both by Ragnar Östberg; the **City Library, Stockholm** (1927), and the **Court House, Gothenburg** (1937), by Gunnar Asplund, and the **Concert Hall, Halsingborg** (1932), by Sven Markelius, who also designed the **Folkets-hus, Linköping** (1954), and was responsible for setting up the **Satellite Town, Vällingby** (1953).

Commercial & Industrial buildings

The most successful architecture is often shaped by functional requirements. A good example is the **Cardboard Factory, Fors** (1953), by Erskine, designed around the linear plan of the machinery and providing for maximum ventilation. The result is a building with a long horizontal façade, dramatically marked by projecting cylinders and the convex and concave bays which house the ventilation system. Other interesting projects by the same architect include the **Shopping Center, Lulea** (1955), and the **Sports Hotel, Borgafjäll**, (1955), Lapland, where in the winter months the sloping roof combines with the hillside to provide a beginners' ski slope, while the snow of the roof acts as an insulator.

Housing, Bruket
This group of houses is part of an estate of 750 dwellings. The façades, with their balconies and varied skyline, create an interesting and picturesque environment.

Apartments, Växsjö, *left. Detail of the balconies of one of this group of six prefabricated apartments. The balconies are suspended by steel rods from concrete beams in the roof, partly for ease of construction.*

Court House, Gothenburg *By Gunnar Asplund, this is a remarkably refined addition to an existing classical building. The* articulation of *pilasters in the original building is matched by the expression of the frame structure of the new. The horizontal* cornice *lines and* entablature *are picked up in the new structure.*

Cardboard Factory, Fors, *above. The long horizontal line of the building is dictated by the requirements of the manufacturing process. The casing for the ventilating machinery adds bold relief to the façade.*

Sports Hotel, Borgafjäll, *right. The overriding concern of the design is to harmonize with the surroundings. The building is made of local materials and its form reflects and blends in with the mountainous landscape behind.*

Finland

Religious buildings

There are two exceptionally fine churches in the *Gothic* style, adapted to the skills of local carpenters. One of them, the **Church, Kerimäki** (1848), E. B. Lohrmann and A. E. Granstedt, is a wooden church, and thought to be the largest in the world. Built by the parishioners themselves, it is cruciform in plan with a crowning polygonal dome on a square *drum*. The most notable feature of the interior decoration is the marbling on the timber columns. The other church is at **Kajaarni** (1898), by J. Ahrenberg, and has a particularly impressive interior.

Around the turn of the century the Gothic period gave way to the *National Romantic* movement, which was characterized by a more free-form, fluid style of architecture. The **Cathedral, Tampere** (1902-7), by Lars Sonck, is a typical example of this new style, with its irregular plan and picturesque skyline. The boldness of its form, and of the materials used to build it, are reminiscent of H. H. Richardson's work in New England. The first stirrings of the monumental classicism which succeeded the National Romantic movement in Finland are seen in Lars Sonck's church at **Helsinki**, the **Kallio Church** (1902-12). While bearing the hallmarks of the National Romantic movement in its bold masonry and ornamentation, the controlled form of the building is akin to the new classicism.

A rapid series of changes in architectural style took place during the years following World War I: monumental classicism gave way to *Functionalism* in the 1920s, which was in turn usurped by a more free-ranging style in which the use of natural materials predominated. This latter movement, started in the 1940s, has continued up to the present day. A typical example of this school of architecture can be seen in the **Chapel, Technical University, Otaniemi** (1957). It was destroyed by fire in 1975 but was rebuilt in 1977. One of the most interesting features of Kaija and Heikki Siren's design is the way that the intimate scale of the building blends into its wooded setting. Two other churches of interest built at almost the same period are, however, remarkably different in concept. The Sirens' design for the church at **Orivesi** (1961) is much bolder; the most outstanding feature is the curving brick-walled *chancel,* which projects from the rest of the structure and is lit at the sides. The other striking example is the **Kaleva Church, Tampere** (1966), which dominates the surrounding area. It seats more than 1000 and has a choir of 80.

Domestic buildings

Some of the best examples of the work of the National Romantic movement are to be seen in domestic buildings. There are also some fine examples of Gothic vernacular architecture to be found, particularly along the coast and islands of the Gulf of Bothnia. Turku is especially rich in *Art Nouveau* buildings, while outstanding among the houses of the modern romantic period is the **Villa Mairea, Noormarkku** (1938-39), designed by Alva Aalto on the Ahlström estate.

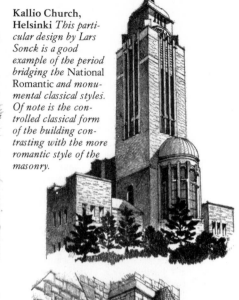

Kallio Church, Helsinki *This particular design by Lars Sonck is a good example of the period bridging the* National Romantic *and monumental classical styles. Of note is the controlled classical form of the building contrasting with the more romantic style of the masonry.*

Church, Kajaarni *View of the interior of this particularly fine carpenter's* Gothic *church, showing the pews and the raised gallery and pulpit. The church has a* hammer beam *roof and a boarded ceiling. The style reflects the frontier spirit of the small town in which it is situated.*

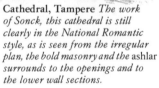

Cathedral, Tampere *The work of Sonck, this cathedral is still clearly in the National Romantic style, as is seen from the irregular plan, the bold masonry and the* ashlar *surrounds to the openings and to the lower wall sections.*

Church, Vuoksenniska *(1959). The most striking feature of this white-*stuccoed *church with a copper roof is its tower, which has been given a sculptured form to distinguish it from the factory chimneys of the surrounding industrial area. The interior can be partitioned off to allow a number of simultaneous functions.*

Chapel, Technical University, Otaniemi *Kaija and Heikki Siren's church has exposed timber trusses. They are shown here near the large, high-level west window, behind the congregation. The church has a completely glazed* chancel *which looks out over the woodland in which the church is situated.*

Kaleva Church, Tampere, *above. By Reima Pietilä, this church stands on high ground dominating the area around it. The* nave of the church *is formed by a series of jagged concave curves which are joined by long, narrow glazed panels. Like the church at Vuoksenniska, the interior can be split into several areas.*

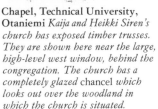

House, Mariehamm *(19thC), Aland Islands. The balcony of this house in Mariehamm is typical of many along this part of the coast and in the islands of the Gulf of Bothnia. It has* barge boards, corbeling *and classical* pediments *in the best carpentry traditions. Most of the houses are either of one or two stories in height.*

Church, Orivesi *(1961), above. The major source of lighting is the* clerestory *light and the windows which flank this projecting chancel wall. The church is oval in plan and is formed by five curved, brick walls.*

Villa Mairea, Noormarkku, *below. The house, standing in a clearing in a pine forest, is a marvelous collage of parts. "L"-shaped in plan, it has a number of distinctive features, in particular the raised first-floor studio with its curving walls.*

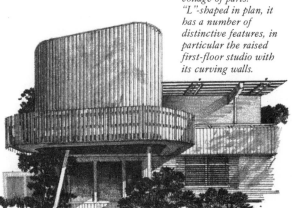

House, Turku *(1902). A typical example of the many fine* Art Nouveau *buildings to be found in Turku, this is a timber house designed by F. Strandell. Of particular interest is the corner* oriel *window with its crowning turret.*

387

Finland

Some of the earliest examples of the *National Romantic* movement are to be seen in the pioneer work done by Gesellius, Lindgren & Saarinen in their series of houses and studios built at **Hvitträsk** from 1901. The irregularity of the plan, the use of huge boulder bases, and the *stuccoed* walls and *shingled* upper stories successfully retain the spirit of local vernacular styles while translating it into a more modern form.

The eventual reaction to this particular style can be seen, for example, in the **Doctors' Housing, Sanatorium, Paimio** (1929-33), by Alvar Aalto. That Aalto had by this time become influenced by the international modern movement is demonstrated most clearly in his design for the nearby staff housing, which consists of interlocked "L"-shaped blocks enclosing small courtyards. He carried on with much the same ideas in his design for the **Industrial Village** and **Pulp Mill, Sunila** (1937-38). Although the village has no real center or focal point, some of the individual blocks are interesting, notably the three-story, stepped, terrace housing and the fan-shaped row of housing for managerial and technical staff. His **Apartments, Ahlström Company, Kauttua** (1938), are a similar series of stepped terraces. Aalto's reaction to the *Functionalist* tradition was a more overtly humanist style, as is demonstrated by his own house at **Munksnäs, Helsinki** (1935-36). This has white-washed brick walls, upper level terraces and hollow steel columns filled with concrete. This particular style, developed in the Villa Mairea, was taken a stage further in the 1950s in Aalto's **Summer House, Muuratsalo** (1953, built on the edge of a forest. Designed about a courtyard with

rooms on two sides, the house is built on the edge of a lake, with the courtyard opening onto it. The grouping of outbuildings taper off in an irregular line as the plan of the house receded into the dense woods beyond.

This informality is also to be seen in his later **Studio, Munnkkiniemi** (1953-55). It consists of a central block with a drawing office raised above ancillary accommodation, and irregular shaped wings projecting from each side of it. On a more heroic scale is the **Students' Hostel, Institute of Technology, Otaniemi** (1962-66), which consists of two five-story blocks radiating from a main entrance around which the communal facilities of the institute are grouped.

Other buildings of interest are contained in the **Housing, Suvikumpu, Tapiola** (1952-c. 1970). The architects include Auluis Blomstedt, Kaija and Heikki Siren and Reima Pietilä.

Civic & Public buildings

The National Romantic style is best seen in buildings such as the **Telephone Building, Helsinki** (1905), and the **Eira Hospital, Helsinki** (1905), both by Lars Sonck; the **National Theatre, Helsinki** (1902), by Onni Tarjanne, and the **National Museum, Helsinki**, (1905-12), by Gesellius, Lindgren & Saarinen. Another quite remarkable building is the **Working Men's Club, Jyväskylä** (1925), by Aalto, an austere *Neoclassical* building with a *colonnaded* ground story. In **Tampere**, the **Fire Station** (1907) by Vivi Lönn is notable for its *Art Nouveau* detailing. The textural quality of the building is, however, typical of the National Romantic movement.

Apartments, Ahlström Company, Kauttua *This group of houses, stepped down a hillside, allows the roof of the lower dwelling to form the terrace of the one above. Interesting features are the rails on the balconies.*

Apartments, Sunila *(1937-38). This stepped, three-story terrace housing was designed by Alvar Aalto for the employees of the Sunila Cellulose Factory. One of the earliest* Functionalist *buildings, it is part of the industrial village and is linked to the Pulp Mill by a bridge.*

Studio, Munnkkiniemi, Helsinki *(1953-55). By Aalto for himself. A feature picked up by many European architects in the 1960s is the* mullioned, clerestory *window on the end wall of the studio.*

Summer House, Muuratsalo *The private retreat that Aalto designed for himself on the edge of a lake. The house is centered on a courtyard.*

Students' Hostel, Institute of Technology, Otaniemi *The faceted, five-story block illustrated joins the two rectilinear blocks which splay out around the courtyard beyond. Communal facilities are grouped around the entrance. This project by Aalto was originally begun as early as 1949.*

Housing, Suvikumpu, Tapiola *This fairly orthodox arrangement of units, designed by Reima Pietilä, is made more interesting by the way it is staggered along a ridge of land. The walls are of concrete and wood boarding.*

Summer House, South Coast *(1965). One of the chief delights of this group of small houses by Lindq Vist, Lögström & Vosu Kainen is the way in which it blends into its surroundings in a forest clearing by the sea.*

Vacation House, Lingonsö Island *(1966-69). This house by K. and H. Siren is built of logs in the standard Finnish tradition and consists of an irregular group of detached pavilions on the water's edge, which are connected by a verandah.*

Working Men's Club, Jyväskylä, *below. In this building the particular features worth noting are the ground-story* Doric colonnade *and the plain* stuccoed *wall above, pierced by a* Palladian-*style window. The auditorium is encased in the stuccoed box.*

Telephone Building, Helsinki *This romantic granite-faced building by Lars Sonck is notable for its gable entrance and its boldly corbeled projecting bays. A special feature is the massive columns which serve to emphasize the horizontal band of windows of the principal floor.*

Finland

Civic & Public buildings

Early in the 20th century the *Neoclassical* tradition was again much in evidence in Finland. The **Civil Guard Building, Seinäjoki** (1925), by Alvar Aalto, is an example of the style. It consists of a rectangular block with an almost circular assembly hall at the front. The main stairs and entrance are arranged at the rear of the building. Two huge columns support the offices above the entrance hall. Another impressive Neoclassical building is the **Parliament Building, Helsinki** (1927-31), by J. S. Sirén. It is a huge, rectangular, red granite block, with a high circular chamber in the center. A giant *colonnade* runs the length of one of the façades, which is approached by an imposing flight of steps in the ancient Roman style.

The first major modern building in Finland was the **Tuberculosis Sanatorium, Paimio** (1929-33). By Aalto, it shows a break with the Neoclassical tradition. Influenced by the works of the Dutch architect Johannes Duiker, it is a fine collage of buildings, with the hospital areas —the quiet zones of the design—and the service points separated from one another by gardens. The buildings radiate out from a long main corridor, which accommodates the right-angled shapes of the individual volumes.

Aalto's later designs show his sympathetic concern for the users of his buildings. In the **Town Hall, Säynätsalo** (1950-52), he grouped together commercial, public, and civic needs in two-story brick buildings with lean-to roofs, and centered them around a pleasant first floor grassed square. A glazed corridor runs along two sides of the enclosure. At **Jyväskylä University** (1950-64) his planning is freer and more open. He added to existing 19th-century buildings, grouping his new structures in an irregular "V" formation around a sports field. Classrooms and leisure rooms open onto the enclosed field, while the entrances are on the other side of the buildings. Aalto's later buildings are for the most part constructed of red brick.

During the 1950s and 1960s, Aalto experimented with the juxtaposition of disparate forms created by the use of fan and wedge shapes. Good examples are the **Town Hall, Seinäjoki** (1953-67), and the **Town Hall, Alajärvi** (1966-69). **The Civic and Cultural Center, Rovaniemi** (1963-68), consists of a long rectangular block, with shallow projections which contain work rooms, studies, conference and small reading rooms, and a gallery. The main reading room radiates out from this block in a fan shape. The **Library, Seinäjoki** (1963-65), is similar in plan but smaller in scale.

Aalto's influence was enormous: his handling of materials, his ability to juxtapose disparate shapes, the boldness of his forms, were all emulated by younger architects. The undulating shape of the **Meilahti Primary School, Helsinki** (1952), by Viljo Rewell and Osmo Sipari, obviously owes a great deal to him, even if the direct model by Aalto, the Baker House Dormitory, Massachusetts Institute of Technology, was in fact in New England in the United States.

Civil Guard Building, Seinäjoki, *left. By Alvar Aalto, the low semicircular terrace is the roof of the assembly hall, which is a semi-basement and juts out into the parade ground itself.*

Parliament Building, Helsinki, *right. This monumental* Neoclassical *building by J. S. Sirén has a long, deep entrance which is emphasized by the bold projecting* colonnade *and the surrounding* entablature.

Tuberculosis Sanatorium, Paimio, *left. View of the ward block of Aalto's sanitorium, which has a reinforced concrete framework* rendered *and then painted white.*

Town Hall, Seinäjoki, *below. This interesting civic building is a good example of Aalto's later work, with its wide range of disparate forms including fan and wedge shapes. The high roof of the hall crowns the council chamber.*

Town Hall, Säynätsalo (1950-52)
The complex, designed by Alvar Aalto, includes civic offices, a council chamber, and a public library built around a raised square. Under the library, on the opposite side to the square, are the shops. The enclosure is reached by steps.

Council chamber

Steps to council chamber

Civic and Cultural Center, Rovaniemi, *right. Aalto designed these* clerestory *windows for the main reading room of the Civic and Cultural Center. The library was the first part of the center to be built.*

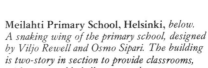

Meilahti Primary School, Helsinki, *below. A snaking wing of the primary school, designed by Viljo Rewell and Osmo Sipari. The building is two-story in section to provide classrooms, with an assembly hall at one end.*

Jyväskylä University, *above. A characteristic feature of Aalto's work in the 1950s and 1960s was the way he used the space between disparate blocks. In the university complex he found room for this handsome foyer, in between the auditorium and the classroom block.*

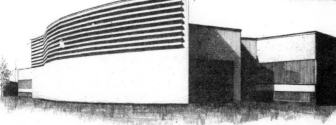

Library, Seinäjoki, *left. This library by Aalto forms part of the administrative and cultural center. With its strong concave and convex external walls it fans out, like the library at Rovaniemi, from the main rectangular block.*

Finland

Civic & Public buildings

Alvar Aalto's treatment of façades, with their continuous bands of windows, has had a considerable influence on European architects, though their works do not often match his refinement of proportion and detail. The **National Pensions Institute, Helsinki** (1952-56), a fine complex of offices set around an open forecourt, has a good example of Aalto's façades. Aalto also designed many auditoria and civic complexes throughout Finland. The **House of Culture, Helsinki** (1958), has a high, curved auditorium with seating for 1500. The **Institute of Technology, Otaniemi** (1955-66), is a vast complex designed by Aalto but also including work by Reima Pietilä. The Institute was designed as a staggered grid of parallel blocks, linked together at right angles by lower blocks. The blocks are located at the rear of a huge auditorium. Parkland runs up to the fragmented line of buildings.

Aalto's **Finlandia Hall, Helsinki** (1971), was intended as part of the new city center. The fan-shaped forms of his earlier works are reversed, so that the wide end of the fan faces in toward the building itself. In addition to the main auditorium there is a conference hall, a chamber music hall and a restaurant. The **Lappia Theatre and Radio Building, Rovaniemi** (1969-75), Aalto's second work in Rovaniemi, is a juxtaposition of disparate shapes. Another fine building is Timo Penttilä's **City Theatre, Helsinki** (1967).

Lappia Theatre and Radio Building, Rovaniemi *A complex by Alvar Aalto, it is divided into two main sections: a large block built around three sides of a square, and a wedge-shaped block. The complex includes a museum, a theatre with seating for 400, a music school and a conference hall.*

Institute of Technology, Otaniemi *Dominating the institute's red-brick buildings is this auditorium. Aalto planned the whole complex, grouping the other buildings in parallel blocks at the rear of the auditorium.*

Students' Union, Institute of Technology, Otaniemi, *left. Contrasted to the naturalism of Aalto's work, this part of the complex, by Reima Pietilä, seems in spirit to belong more to the* National Romantic *movement.*

Finlandia Hall, Helsinki *Aalto's last major work. The main auditorium, above, seats 1750. In 1975 the complex was extended to include a conference hall, left, whose north façade forms a series of convex and concave curves, contrasting with the more solid main block.*

Commercial & Industrial buildings

The *National Romantic* style gradually gave way in the 20th century to more austere, symmetrical compositions. In the **Railway Station, Helsinki** (1907-14), Eliel Saarinen displayed the assured manner found in Lars Sonck's Kallio Church. Romantic influences are no longer in evidence. The plan, with the exception of the tower, is symmetrical. The massive *vaults* of the central hallway are constructed from reinforced concrete, the first time that this material had been used in a major building in Finland.

Two of Sonck's Helsinki buildings typify the change of style from the romantic to the more austere classical designs: the **Mortgage Bank Building** (1908), with its recessed middle two stories *articulated* by giant columns, and the **Stock Exchange** (1911), which has handsome *piers* and slightly projecting end bays. Both are more formal than his earlier work.

One of the most interesting aspects of industrial buildings is the way their functions usually dictate the eventual shape. Examples among a number of buildings by Aalto are the **Pulp Mill, Sunila** (1936-39); the **Sawmill, Varkaus** (1945-46), and the **Boiler House, The Institute of Technology, Otaniemi** (1962-63). Another example of functions dictating shape is the **Marimekko Clothing Factory, Herttoniemi** (1973), by Erkki Kairamo and other architects.

Railway Station, Helsinki *This station by Eliel Saarinen has a cruciform-shaped plan. The central hall is flanked at right angles by two secondary halls. The main entrance is through a giant archway leading into the* vaulted *hall.*

Sawmill, Varkaus
Designed by Aalto, the sawmill has a light, steel framework and is covered, appropriately enough, with timber. This is an example of a building where its shape is entirely dictated by its commercial function.

Outdoor Museum, Seurasaari *(1909). View of the store sheds. These agricultural buildings came originally from Uusimaa and Häme. Architects of the 1940s and 1950s emulated this simplicity of design.*

Hamburger Bors Hotel, Turku *(1903-8), left. A handsome* Art Nouveau *hotel designed by F. Strandell. It stands at the corner of the market square. The unusual central window is reminiscent of the work of contemporary architects in Brussels and Paris.*

Valtion Hotel, Imatra *(1903). Although this is an Art Nouveau building, designed by Usko Nyström, its strange corbeled* turrets, *strong granite arches and round towers evoke the style of the National Romantic movement.*

Eastern Europe

Domestic buildings

An outstanding example of the *International Style* is the **Tugendhat House, Brno** (1930), Czechoslovakia, built by Ludwig Mies van der Rohe. It pioneers the concept of the open plan in which space is seen as something continuous, with walls and partitions merely *articulating* its flow. Its influence was enormous, particularly in North America. Of the few private houses built in the Soviet Union, one of the most unusual is **Melnikov's House, Moscow** (1927), with a plan based on two interconnecting cylinders.

Housing, not houses, was the main concern in eastern Europe in the late 1920s and the 1930s. One of the most elegant examples was the **Apartment Block, Breslau** (1928), Poland, by Hans Scharoun, which has a central communal hall, with the apartment wings turned in at each end. In the Soviet Union, new housing design was intended to improve the way of life, as the architect Moishe Ginsburg advocated. Experimenting in mass production with new materials and standardized plans, his major International Style work was the **Apartment Block, Novinsky Boulevard, Moscow** (1928-29), an austere design reminiscent of the work of Le Corbusier.

By the 1930s, the modern movement had given way to socialist realism. The most modern techniques were used to achieve monumentality, as in the **Skyscraper, Kotelnicheskaya Naberezhnaya, Moscow** (1949-53), by D. N. Chechulin and A. K. Rostovsky, which seems to emulate the *Gothic* fantasies of some Chicago and New York skyscrapers built in the 1920s.

Civic & Public buildings

The Russian Revolution precipitated a radical revision in architectural ideas. Freed from restricting traditions of the past, architects began to define the style of a workers' Utopia. Using industrial materials, the emphasis was on dynamism with both structure and form expressed. Of particular interest are the many workers' clubs, which were designed as centers to develop the creative talents of the working class and as places where party propaganda could be disseminated. The Vesnin brothers built the club for the **Society of Political Prisoners, Ulitza Vorovskovo** (1931-34), and the much larger and more lavish **Zili Palace of Culture, Likhachev Automobile Works** (1930-37), both in Moscow. Other good examples in Moscow include the **Frunze Club** (1927) and the **Burevestnik Club** (1929) by Konstantin Melnikov. Characteristic of such works is the bold articulation of volumes and the dramatic contrasts of opaque and transparent materials.

The **Planetarium, Moscow** (1927-29), by Michael Barshch and Michael Sinyavsky, was designed to serve as an educational and entertainment center for workers, besides fulfilling its scientific function. Le Corbusier designed the **Centrosoysus Building, Kirova Ulitsa, Moscow** (1928-36), now the Ministry of Light Industries, a huge reinforced concrete complex of which only part was finished. But as with domestic building the Stalinist era brought the modern movement to an end and ushered in an eclectic, monumental style with works like the **Moskva Hotel** (1932-33), by A. V. Shchusev and others.

Villa, Prague-Vysehrad *(1913), Czechoslovakia. Built by Josef Chocol, the basically simple set of volumes are brought alive by their faceted, geometrical treatment.*

Melnikov's House, Moscow, *left. Designed by Konstantin Melnikov for himself, it consists of two cylinders linked by a spiral staircase. The study has a huge plate-glass window, while the studio has a wall of small diamond-shaped windows.*

Parliament Building, Budapest *(1882-1902), Hungary. This strange, fairy-tale* Gothic Revival *building by Imre Steindl has a 950 ft frontage along the Danube. It is crowned by turreted towers,* gables *and a giant central dome.*

Workers' clubs in the USSR

A prerequisite of the social revolution, many were started in converted stately homes. But purpose-built clubs soon became necessary, comprising theatres, meeting rooms, libraries and ancillary accommodation.

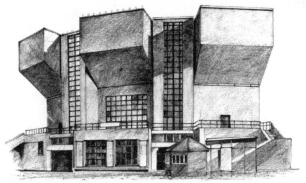

Rusakov Club, Moscow (1927)

Zuyev Club, Moscow (1928)

Postal Savings Bank, Budapest *(1882-1902), Hungary. Detail of the fine* Art Nouveau *building by Odon Lechner. The bank has flamboyant panels, such as the one illustrated, which are reminiscent of Antoni Gaudí's.*

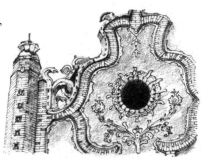

GUM, Red Square, Moscow *(1889-93), above. One of three* barrel-vaulted *iron and glass galleries that run for some 985 ft through this huge state-owned department store designed by A. N. Pomerantsev. The multilevel walkways are linked by numerous iron bridges.*

Commercial Building, Breslau *(1911), Poland. Designed by Hans Poelzig, it was one of the first office blocks in Europe to make use of a skeleton structure of reinforced concrete —a technique developed in North America.*

Red Army Theatre, Moscow *(1934-40). The theatre was designed by K. Alabyan and N. Simbutzev with its plan in the shape of the Army's five-pointed star. It has the monumentality of Filippo Juvarra's work.*

New England

Religious buildings

Trinity Church, Boston (1872-77), Massachusetts, by Henry Hobson Richardson, with its boldness and slightly medieval appearance, is the most outstanding late 19th century church in New England. The **Chapel, Massachusetts Institute of Technology, Cambridge** (1955), by Eero Saarinen, is an interesting modern work.

Domestic buildings

During the 19th and 20th century domestic styles moved from bold terraces and arched bays, through the *shingle* style to modern buildings. The shingle style dominated domestic architecture during the 1870s and 1880s. Essentially it was a mixture of the Queen Anne style of the English architect Norman Shaw, and the American *Colonial Style*.

Richardson dominated the architecture of the period, and his buildings were the pioneer examples of the shingle style. These include the **W. Watts Sherman Residence, Newport** (1874-76), Rhode Island, and the **Stoughton Residence, Cambridge** (1882-83), Massachusetts.

William Ralph Emerson also helped to perfect the shingle style in buildings such as **Loring House, Prides Crossing** (1881), Massachusetts; **Alexander Cochrane Residence, Prides Crossing** (1881), Massachusetts, and his own personal house in **Milton**, Massachusetts (1880).

Some of the very best examples of the shingle style are in **Newport**, Rhode Island. These include **31 Old Beach Road** (1873), by Champlin Mason, which incorporates the basic chalet style with the English half-timber look; **Southside** (1883), and the **Isaac Bell, Jr., Residence** (1881-83) by Charles Follen McKim, W. R. Mead and Stanford White.

There are also some interesting examples in Newport of the early work of Richard Morris Hunt. One is **72 Bellevue Avenue**, a handsome house where the *frame* is expressed externally, the stick style. But clients looking for summer cottages wanted something more ostentatious and European in style. In catering to these requirements, architects such as Hunt precipitated academicism that held back the advance of modern architecture in the United States for some years. Examples of the sort of work that Hunt produced include **Ochre Court** (1889-91); the **Breakers** (1892-95), perhaps the most magnificent of all Newport's summer residences, and **Marble House, Bellevue Avenue** (1893-95).

Other notable residences in Newport include **Rosecliff, Bellevue Avenue** (1902), designed by McKim, Mead & White in a French *Renaissance* style, and the **Elms** (1901) by H. Trumbauer, which was modeled on the 18th-century Château d'Asnières in France. Trumbauer also designed **Clarendon Court** (1904), which was modeled on an 18th-century English mansion, and the **Mirimar** (1961), the last of the great Renaissance-style mansions to be built in Newport.

Many of the Newport residences were modeled on Elizabethan manor houses. Most notable are **Bonniecrest, Harrison Avenue** (1912-18), by John Russell Pope, and **Wakehurst, Ochre Point Avenue** (1888), by Dudley Newton.

Trinity Church, Boston *This is one of the most memorable late 19th-C buildings in the USA. It was designed by Henry Hobson Richardson and established him as the leading architect of the time. The porch was added in the 1890s.*

Loring House, Prides Crossing *This is an outstanding shingle-style house. Points of interest include its turreted corner tower,* gabled *roofs and* dormers. *It was designed by William Ralph Emerson.*

Isaac Bell, Jr., Residence, Newport *One of the most famous of the shingle-style houses, the architects were Charles McKim, W. R. Mead and Stanford White. Its outstanding features include the gabled roofs, round tower and arched verandah. Above the verandah is a gallery.*

Rosecliff, Bellevue Avenue, Newport *View of the interior, showing the arched hallway. This striking residence was designed by McKim, Mead & White in the French* Renaissance *style. It was modeled on the Grand Trianon, Versailles.*

Marble House, Bellevue Avenue, Newport *This imposing mansion was designed by Richard Morris Hunt for William K. Vanderbilt. The design comprises a simple rectangular block* articulated *by a giant* Corinthian portico *and crowning* balustrade.

Hodgson House, New Canaan *(1951), Connecticut. Designed by Philip Johnson, this house is outstanding for its apparent simplicity. The design is* Palladian *in its axiality and symmetrical proportions.*

Cottage, Wayland *(1941), Massachusetts. This is a utilitarian* timber-frame *house faced with Douglas fir and raised above a stone basement. It was designed by Walter Gropius and Marcel Breuer, whose work greatly influenced American architecture of that time.*

H. C. Bradley Residence, Woods Hole *(·1912), Massachusetts. This arresting building was designed by Purcell & Elmslie. The various elements are articulated, with the one-story curved bay at the front set off against the main rectilinear section of the building.*

Methodist Camp, Oak Bluffs (*c.* 1860)
These decorative *gingerbread* cottages were built to replace the tents that originally made up this religious settlement on Martha's Vineyard, Massachusetts. Of the original 1000 cottages only 300 now remain but they are fine examples of American folk architecture.

Gabled façades

Verandahs and galleries

New England

Frank Lloyd Wright is regarded as the greatest American architect of the 20th century, and there are a number of his houses in New England. Two of the most outstanding are the **Darwin D. Martin Residence** (1904), and the **Heath Residence** (1905), both in **Buffalo**, New York, and both of which are in the prairie style of rectangular forms and oversailing roofs that he created. An example of his later work is the **Baird Residence, Amherst** (1940), Massachusetts.

The major influence of the early 1940s and 1950s, however, was the work of European refugee architects, such as Walter Gropius. Outstanding houses by the Europeans include the **Chamerlain House, Wayland** (1940), Massachusetts, by Gropius and Marcel Breuer, and **Caesar Cottage, Lakeville** (1952), Connecticut by Breuer. Both are characterized by their simplicity.

Philip Johnson was a leading member of the modern European movement. The **Johnson Residence, New Canaan** (1949), Connecticut, which he built for himself, is a sophisticated glass walled container in the style of Ludwig Mies van der Rohe's work. Subsequently, in his **Wiley House, New Canaan** (1953), he raised the glass box onto a stone basement story and added a roof terrace. By contrast, the **Smith House, Darien** (1965-67), Connecticut, by Richard Meier, is an interesting white painted timber villa that combines the style of Le Corbusier with the aura created by a *Palladian* building.

During the 1970s much east coast architecture continued to be influenced by Europe. Two exceptions are the **Trubek** and **Wislocki Houses, Nantucket** (1971-72), Massachusetts, by Robert Venturi and John Rauch, both an architectural interpretation of everyday America.

Civic & Public buildings

The work of Henry Hobson Richardson has a boldness and vigor that in some ways is uniquely American. Key buildings by him are the **Oak Ames Memorial Library** (1877-79), and **Town Hall** (1879), both in **North Easton**, Massachusetts, the **Crane Memorial Library, Quincy** (1880-83), Massachusetts, and the **Billings Memorial Library, University of Vermont** (1883-85), Burlington. Other works by him are at **Harvard University, Cambridge**, notably **Austin** (1881-83) and **Sever Halls** (1878-90).

One of the most important civic buildings of this period is the **Boston Public Library, Boston** (1887-95), by Charles Follen McKim, W. R. Mead and Stanford White. It was the first notable Italian *Renaissance* style building in the United States.

New England has some memorable 20th-century work, among it a number of buildings by Louis Kahn. These include the **Library, Phillips Exeter Academy** (1967-72), Exeter, New Hampshire, which consists of a cube with *splayed* corners. The four main façades are treated as if they are free-standing and are propped up by the splayed corners, which have open balconies. Other buildings by Kahn in **New Haven**, Connecticut, are the **Yale Art Gallery** (1951-54), and the **Center for British Art and Studies** (1969-74).

Johnson Residence, New Canaan *Designed by Philip Johnson for himself, it is a plain glass-walled container in the style of Ludwig Mies van der Rohe. The house established Johnson's architectural repute.*

Smith House, Darien *Standing on a waterfront, the main façade is broken up by a pattern of huge glass windows, giving panoramic views. The house was designed by Richard Meier.*

Trubek House, Nantucket *One of two adjacent houses designed by Robert Venturi and John Rauch. In contrast to many of the European influenced styles of the time, the houses are mainly influenced by New England traditions. The shingle style can also be seen.*

Boston Public Library, Boston *Designed by Charles Follen McKim, W. R. Mead and Stanford White, this is their best-known work. The façade is modeled on Henri Labrouste's Bibliothèque Sainte-Geneviève, in Paris.*

Crane Memorial Library, Quincy
This is a bold and massive building, notable for its turreted staircase tower and portal *in the Syrian style. The library was designed by Henry Hobson Richardson, whose powerful and original style spread and influenced a number of later architects in the United States.*

Baker Dormitory, Massachusetts Institute of Technology, Cambridge *(1947-49). The building's rear is right-angled in plan with the stairs boldly* articulated. *The front façade is undulated in order to give as many rooms as possible a river view. The architect was Alvar Aalto.*

Lang House, Washington *(1972-74), Connecticut, right. By Robert Stern, the free application of molding to articulate the façade is characteristic of much work in the 1970s. The pediment is reminiscent of 16th-C Italy.*

Carpenter Center, Harvard University, Cambridge *(1961). Le Corbusier's last major work and his only American building, it was erected by Sert, Jackson & Gourley. The center consists of a crisply articulated set of curved and right-angled volumes. A ramp winds its way at first floor level through the building.*

Phillips Exeter Academy, New Hampshire *The Library, an outstanding building by Louis Kahn with a memorable brick façade. The building is notable for the proportions of the façades with their* parapet.

City Hall, Boston *(1962-69). A powerful building by Kallman, McKinnell & Knowles. Like many other buildings of the time, it was heavily influenced by Le Corbusier's Monastery, Eveux.*

399

New England

In **Boston** notable modern civic buildings include the **Schools of Law and Education, Boston University** (1964), by Sert, Jackson & Gourley; the **New England Aquarium, Central Wharf** (1969), by Cambridge Seven, and the strangely medieval **Health, Education and Welfare Center, Government Center** (1970), with Paul Rudolph as co-ordinating architect. **South End Branch Library, Tremont Street** (1971), by Mitchell & Giurgola, is basically a brick box but with occasional sharply pointed geometry.

Commercial & Industrial buildings

Henry Hobson Richardson applied his highly original style to a number of commercial buildings. One is the **Cheney Building, Hartford** (1875), Connecticut, with its tiers of *arcading* and bold *cornices*. It is outstanding for the way in which Richardson was able to *articulate* an *astylar* pallazzo-type façade. Utilitarian work appealed to Richardson and he also designed a number of small railroad stations in the area.

Stanford White and Charles McKim were both pupils of Richardson until, in 1879, they set up their own office with W. R. Mead. One of their first major commercial projects was the **Newport Casino, Newport** (1881-88), Rhode Island. This has a *gabled* front façade with the central gable over the entrance articulated by a *Palladian* window motif. The front incorporates shops and the main entrance leads to a courtyard.

Also of interest from this period are the **Ames Building, Boston** (1892), by Shepley, Rutan & Coolidge, which is influenced by Richardson's style, and the **Custom-house, State Street** (1837-47), Boston, notable for its striking tower.

Round Barn, *near* **Passumpsic, Vermont** *(19thC). This characteristic round barn with central silo is an arresting piece of agricultural architecture. Of particular interest is the way in which the narrow clapboard is laid horizontally.*

Newport Casino, Newport, Rhode Island *By Charles McKim, W. R. Mead and Stanford White, it was their first major project. Of particular interest are the* Palladian *motif in the gable, and the courtyard in which the far side is enclosed by a covered crescent-shaped verandah.*

Diner, Boston *(1950s). An archetypal diner, characterized by its railway restaurant-car appearance. Built as packages in the 1930s, 1940s and 1950s, they were shipped to vacant sites along the main highways, where many remain to this day.*

Covered bridges of Vermont
During the early 1800s many bridges were built, covered in with a *shingle* roof, such as those shown here. This protected the costly framework and a greater strength against gales was ensured by the addition of *braces* connecting the side frames of the bridge with roof trusses.

Upper Bridge, East Charlotte

Barnet Village Bridge, Stephen's River

Mid-Atlantic States

Religious buildings

St. Patrick's Cathedral, New York City (1853-77), by James Renwick, with its cruciform plan and monumental twin-towered west front is the classic American *Gothic Revival* building. It was completed in the years after the Civil War and relied heavily on European Gothic Revival ideas.

Among 20th-century buildings the **Beth Sholom Synagogue, Elkins Park** (1954-59), Pennsylvania, by Frank Lloyd Wright, and the **First Unitarian Church, Rochester** (1962), New York, by Louis Kahn, are the most outstanding.

Domestic buildings

Late 19th-century buildings were clearly influenced by the styles of the European past. Good examples are the **Vanderbilt Mansion, Hyde Park** (1895-99), New York, by Charles McKim, W. R. Mead and Stanford White; the **Andrew Mellon House, Woodland Road** (1897-1917), Pittsburgh, a picturesque Tudor-style mansion; **Olana, Hudson** (1874), New York, an eclectic fantasy with brightly ornamented towers, porches and gazebos, and the **Frick Mansion, 5th Avenue, New York City** (1913-14), a French-style town house with an English interior designed by Carrère & Hastings.

In complete contrast, the **William Lescaze Residence, 211 East 48th Street** (1934), New York City, is a magnificent *International Style* town house. It has a white frame front, curving walls, bands of windows and large areas of glass block. **Fallingwater, Mill Run** (1935), Pennsylvania, by Wright, was equally daring with its hovering horizontal planes of reinforced concrete *cantilevered* out over a waterfall.

Beth Sholom Synagogue, Elkins Park
View of the interior. This is a giant translucent tent with seating for 1,214. Completely dominating its hilltop site, it was designed by Frank Lloyd Wright and is one of his most notable later works.

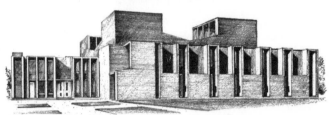

First Unitarian Church, Rochester
Designed by Louis Kahn, this is a beautifully articulated building. The church consists of a central area for worship with four corner towers that are designed to admit light. Flanking the central area are two stories of classrooms.

Lowell, 63rd Street, New York City *(1926). View of the covered entrance. This marvelous apartment building was designed by H. Churchill and H. Lippman. It is a steel-framed building with a glazed terracotta ground story that is articulated in an attractive* Art Deco *manner.*

Fallingwater, Mill Run *Designed by Wright and dramatically* cantilevered *over a waterfall, it was built as a weekend retreat for Edgar J. Kaufmann, whose family called it Bear Run.*

Esherick House, Chestnut Hill *(1959-61), Pennsylvania. A house designed by Louis Kahn. Its dark stucco walls, stained wood reveals and refined articulation greatly influenced American architects.*

401

Mid-Atlantic States

The **Wright Residence, Bethesda** (1953), Maryland, by Frank Lloyd Wright, is a two-story hemicycle of blockwork faced in horizontal boards. It is one of his later works and is a good example of how much his style had changed from the early style of his prairie houses.

The **Jesse Oser House, Melrose Park** (1940), Pennsylvania, is one of the earliest houses designed by Louis Kahn. It is a simple, utilitarian structure of timber and stone. Slightly more formal is his **Norman Fisher House, Philadelphia** (1960), which consists of two great cubes, one rotated at 45° to the other.

The influence of Kahn can be seen in the work of Robert Venturi, notably in the **Vanna Venturi House, Chestnut Hill** (1962-64), Philadelphia. The split façade over the entry point, however, is also reminiscent of the work of the modern Italian architect, Luigi Moretti. A characteristic of Venturi's work is the introduction into a building of quite unconventional elements. Examples include the exaggerated roof line and windows in the **Leib House, Loveladies** (1967), New Jersey; the *Baroque* curves of the **Brandt House, Greenwich** (1973), Connecticut, or the extraordinary *dormer* of the **Tucker House, Westchester County** (1975), New York.

The white box architecture of Richard Meier, however, provides a complete contrast. Examples of his work include the **Hoffman House, East Hampton** (1966-67), Long Island; private residence, **Old Westbury, Long Island** (1969-71), and the particularly perceptive design of **Twin Parks Northeast Housing, The Bronx** (1969-74), New York, in which he created a most effective complex for mass housing.

Civic & Public buildings

The dramatic molding of interior spaces is one of the major American contributions to modern architecture. **The Peabody Institute Library, Baltimore** (1875-78), Maryland, by E. G. Lind, with its cathedral-like six-story high central space, is an outstanding example. Equally impressive is the great hall in the **Old Pensions Building, Washington, D.C.** (1881-87), by General Montgomery Meigs, which was modeled on the Farnese Palace, Rome.

Other late 19th-century buildings of interest are the **Pennsylvania Academy of Fine Arts, Philadelphia** (1872-76), by Frank Furness; the **Jefferson Market Library, New York City** (1876), by Calvert Vaux and Fred Withers, and the **Allegheny County Courthouse and Jail, Pittsburgh** (1883), by Henry Hobson Richardson.

Buildings of interest by Robert Venturi and John Rauch are the **Guild House, Spring Gardens Street** (1960-65), and the **Faculty Club, Pennsylvania State University** (1974-76), both in **Philadelphia**. Another of their works is the **Humanities Building, State University of New York, Purchase** (1968-73), New York.

Leib House, Loveladies Despite its unconventional appearance, this house, by Robert Venturi, has the structure of an ordinary shed. The building's interest lies in the exaggerated roof lines and unconventional window shapes.

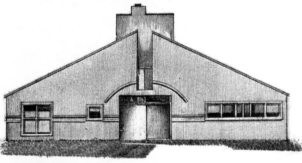

Vanna Venturi House, Chestnut Hill, *above. This is a classic example of post-modern movement architecture with its applied molding, split* pediment *and front façade. It was designed by Robert Venturi and John Rauch and was influenced greatly by the work of Louis Kahn.*

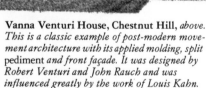

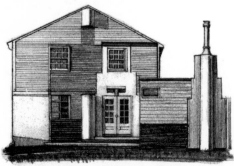

Schulman House, Princeton
(1976), New Jersey, left. By Michael Graves, this is an extension to an existing two-story suburban house. The new section, on the right hand side, overlays the old section. The stucco of the chimney is repeated over the portal.

Hoffman House, East Hampton
View toward the two-story living room. The design of this dwelling by Richard Meier consists of interlocking right-angled elements. The design depends on the way one set of elements in the complex is rotated 45° along the entry path.

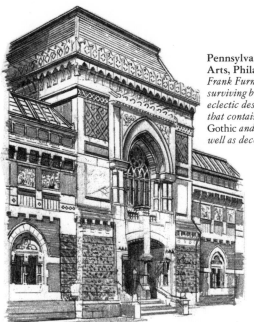

Pennsylvania Academy of Fine Arts, Philadelphia *Designed by Frank Furness, this is his finest surviving building. It is a bold, highly eclectic design with a striking façade that contains a mixture of Islamic,* Gothic *and* Renaissance *motifs as well as decorative* polychrome *work.*

Statue of Liberty, New York City *(1871-86). This world-famous, colossal bronze statue, nearly 165 ft high, was designed by the French sculptor Frédéric Auguste Bartholdi as a memorial to Franco-American friendship. The structural skeleton was the work of the French engineer, Alexandre Gustave Eiffel.*

Guggenheim Museum, 5th Avenue, New York City *(1956-59). View of the interior showing the magnificent spiraling ramp that circles the entire height of the museum. Designed by Frank Lloyd Wright, it is one of his more controversial works.*

Richards Medical Center, Philadelphia *(1957-61), below. A highly dramatic building, it is notable for its lift and ventilation towers that rise above the central core. It was designed by Louis Kahn and established his reputation.*

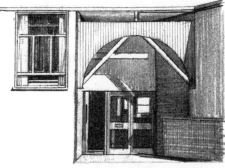

North Pennsylvania Visiting Nurses Association HQ, Ambler *(1960), Pennsylvania, above. View of the entrance* portal. *By Venturi & Rauch, the entrance portal and applied molding are characteristic of their work, while* flush *windows are more typical of Louis Kahn.*

Haughwot Building, New York City *(1857). View of front façade. This is a marvelous cast iron building designed by J. P. Gaynor. Its façades and arched windows were modeled on the Library in Venice, designed by Jacopo Sansovino in 1536.*

403

Mid-Atlantic States

The **Cloisters, Ford Tryon Park, New York City** (1934-38), by Charles Collens, is an unusual example of civic architecture. It consists essentially of a collage of imported medieval French and Spanish monastic *cloisters* and was created to house the medieval art collection of the Metropolitan Museum of Art.

A more recent civic building of interest is the *Neoclassical* **Lincoln Center for the Performing Arts, Columbus Avenue, New York City** (1962-68), the co-ordinating architect of the project being Wallace K. Harrison.

Commercial & Industrial buildings

There are a number of monuments to the industrial achievements of the late 19th and early 20th century. Perhaps the most spectacular is **Brooklyn Bridge, New York City** (1869-73). Designed by John A. Washington Roebling, it is a magnificent steel and cable structure.

The major railway stations, too, are highly spectacular. Two of the finest are **Grand Central, New York City** (1913), by Whitney Warren and Charles Wetmore, and **Union Station, Washington, D.C.** (1907), by Daniel H. Burnham. Both have memorable interiors and façades based on the triumphal arches of ancient Rome.

But it is in the field of office building that the most notable examples of commercial architecture exist. The **Executive Office Building, Washington, D.C.** (1871-88), by A. B. Mullett, was the largest office building in the world when built. The interior is enriched by paired libraries which wrap around multistory light-wells. The 12-story **Prudential**, or **Guarantee Building, Buffalo** (1895), New York, by Louis Sullivan

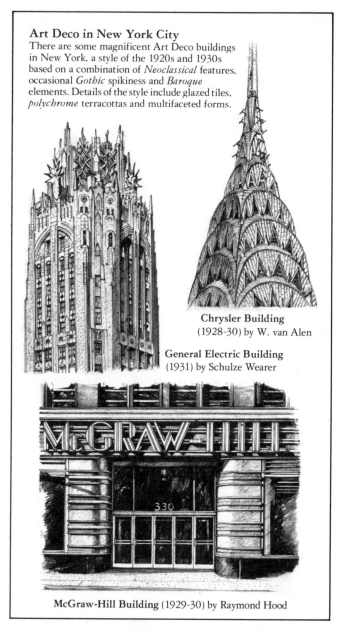

Art Deco in New York City

There are some magnificent Art Deco buildings in New York, a style of the 1920s and 1930s based on a combination of *Neoclassical* features, occasional *Gothic* spikiness and *Baroque* elements. Details of the style include glazed tiles, *polychrome* terracottas and multifaceted forms.

Chrysler Building (1928-30) by W. van Alen

General Electric Building (1931) by Schulze Wearer

McGraw-Hill Building (1929-30) by Raymond Hood

Grand Central Station, New York City
Designed by Whitney Warren and Charles Wetmore, this monumental façade is a magnificent interpretation of the grand structures of ancient classical Rome. The interior of the station is a vast, cavernous hall.

Prudential, *or* **Guarantee Building, Buffalo** *Details of façade decoration. The building is particularly notable for the lush, flower-like patterns that decorate the façade. The buiding has classical features, including a bold, capping cornice, but on a new giant scale made possible by the steel skeleton structure.*

and Dankmar Adler, was the first great office building. It is steel framed with marvelous decorative work on the façade and is one of the finest examples of early modern American architecture. Other relatively early skyscrapers of note in **New York City** include the fine **Flatiron Building** (1902) by Daniel H. Burnham and the **Woolworth Building** (1913) by Cass Gilbert.

The **Empire State Building**, 5th Avenue (1930-32), is possibly the most potent symbol of the Manhattan skyscraper. The last of the pre-Depression skyscrapers, the Empire State is 1470 ft high with an observatory on the 86th floor.

The **Rockefeller Center** (1931-40) by Reinhard & Hofmeister, Corbett, Harrison & MacMurray and Hood & Fouilhoux, is possibly the most successful grouping of buildings. They are planned around a handsome urban plaza.

The **Lever House** (1952) was designed by Skidmore, Owings & Merrill, one of the leading firms of architects in the United States, and was a pioneer office building with an all-glass façade.

The **Seagram Building** (1958) by Ludwig Mies van der Rohe is the most refined of all the tall New York City buildings but perhaps the most typically American is the **Ford Foundation Building** (1967) by Roche & Dinkerloo, with offices wrapped around a giant conservatory.

Interesting offices in **Washington, D.C.** include the **H.Q. for the AIA**, Pennsylvania Avenue (1973), by Mitchell & Guirgola, which is notable for accommodating an already existing house designed in 1800 by William Thornton. The **Watergate** (1964-72), a complex of hotel offices and apartments, is notable for being the last project of the great Italian architect, Luigi Moretti.

Tribune Review Building, Greensburgh *(1958-61), Pennsylvania, above. Handsome newspaper offices, designed by Louis Kahn. The building is rectangular in plan and is notable for the way in which the central core is* articulated *by escape stairs. The windows are cleanly cut into blockwork walls.*

Lever House, New York City *A pioneer building by Skidmore, Owings & Merrill that established an international trend for metal and glass* curtain-walled *skyscrapers. The building rises from a* podium, *in the middle of which is a garden court.*

Empire State Building, New York City *(1930-32). By Shreve, Lamb & Harmon, this was, at the time, the tallest building in the world. Built of standardized components, it was opened during the Depression and remained largely unlet.*

Seagram Building, New York City, *right. This has perhaps the most sophisticated design of all New York City skyscrapers. It is a bronze and bronze-glass tower of refined proportions, designed by Ludwig Mies van der Rohe. The interiors were designed by Philip Johnson.*

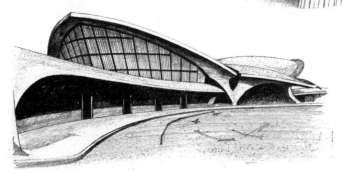

TWA Terminal, Kennedy Airport, New York City *(1962). Looking much like a bird about to take flight, this dramatic building was designed by Eero Saarinen. The intention was to create a design with forms analogous with flight.*

Great Lakes States

Religious buildings

Much religious architecture in late 19th- and 20th-century America is of a bizarre nature, somewhat akin to John Nash's extravaganza, Brighton Pavilion, in England. One of the most outlandish is the **Isaac Wise Temple, Cincinnati** (1866), Ohio, an amalgam of oriental and *Gothic* imagery by James Wilson, the front façade of which is flanked by twin minarets. The **Bahai House of Worship, 112 Linden Avenue, Wilmette** (1920-21), Illinois, is another eclectic building, chiefly oriental in spirit. Other bizarre churches include the saucer-shaped **Greek Orthodox Church, Wauwatosa** (1959), Wisconsin, by Frank Lloyd Wright, and the bulbous **Roofless Church, New Harmony** (1960), Indiana, by Philip Johnson.

There are two buildings, however, that stand out above all these. One is the **Getty Tomb, Graceland Cemetery, Chicago** (1890), Illinois, a simple volume, beautifully designed by Louis Sullivan. The other is the **Unity Temple, Oak Park** (1906), Illinois, by Wright. The form of the church consists of a crisply *articulated* set of cubes and was determined by the material, concrete, which was used because it was the cheapest.

Domestic buildings

One of the great houses of the late 19th century is the **Glessner House, South Prairie Avenue, Chicago** (1885-86), Illinois, by H. H. Richardson. It has a granite façade with *gables,* a turret, and the bold arched entrance typical of his work. The

deliberate asymmetry of the design is a feature which anticipates the style of *Art Nouveau.*

The early work of Wright in the Chicago area was characterized by picturesque plans, high-pitched roofs with a turreted corner tower and *dormer windows,* as in the **Walter Gale House, Oak Park** (1893), Illinois. Wright's early work was completed while still employed by Sullivan; including a large number of commissions in **Oak Park, Highland Park,** and **River Forest.** His first commission after leaving Sullivan was the **Winslow Residence, River Forest** (1893), Illinois. Its deep overhanging *eaves* foreshadow the first prairie-style house, the **Willits Residence, Highland Park** (1901), Illinois. The **Robie House, Chicago** (1909), Illinois, epitomizes the prairie style. This, and the **Emil Bach Residence, Chicago** (1915), Illinois, became a major influence in the *de Stijl* movement in Europe.

Wright later gave more emphasis to simplicity and utility. The strict orthogonal geometry of the prototype **Jacobs House, Madison** (1936), Wisconsin, gave way to the more free-form planning of the **Second Jacobs Residence, Middleton** (1942), Wisconsin, and the **Curtis Meyer Residence, Galesburg** (1948), Michigan. The **Ford House, Aurora** (1948), Illinois, by Bruce Goff, shows the influence of Wright but seems more primitive. At this time Ludwig Mies van der Rohe was designing refined high-rise apartment towers, such as the two **Apartment Towers, Lake Shore Drive, Chicago** (1948-51), Illinois.

First Unitarian Church, Madison *(1947-51), Wisconsin. An excellent example of Wright's creation of spectacular interior space. The pitched roof rises up over the pulpit. The primary materials used in the church are limestone and oak.*

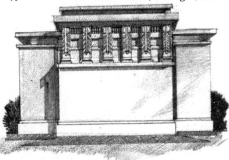

Unity Temple, Oak Park *The main street façade of this church, designed by Frank Lloyd Wright, displays a geometry of enclosing squares and cubes. The main entrance, at the rear, also serves the parish house.*

Jacobs House, Madison, *above. The first of what Wright called his "Usonian" (a term implying thoroughly American) houses. The main characteristic features of this type are the "L"-shaped plan, the oversailing roof, and the horizontal boarding with recessed battens.*

Curtis Meyer Residence, Galesburg, *right. Constructed from concrete, with boarding for the balconies, this is one of a series of Galesburg dwellings by Wright. The predominant geometry is the circle, or segments of a circle. The hemicycle section faces east.*

Commonwealth Promenade Apart-ments, Chicago *(1953-56), Illinois, below. A detail of this high-rise block shows aluminium and glass curtain walls which Ludwig Mies van der Rohe deployed in front of the reinforced concrete structure.*

Ford House, Aurora, *right. Bruce Goff designed this striking house. Made from intersecting domes, it was constructed with surplus steel frames from army huts. Goff conceived the plan from the circular for-mation often adopted by people in groups.*

Farnsworth House, Fox River *(1946-50), Illinois, above. This sophisticated pavilion embodies Mies van der Rohe's style at its most refined. Constructed from white-painted steel and glass, it appears to float above the ground.*

Frank Lloyd Wright's Chicago Houses

From his own **House and Studio, Oak Park** (1889-95), Illinois, Wright designed many houses in the early 1900s, including the charac-teristic prairie houses. With façades of long, low horizontals, their main rooms are raised above a basement story with generous central fireplaces and continuous bands of windows.

Winslow Residence, River Forest

Robie House, Chicago (1909)

Emil Bach Residence, Chicago (1915)

Great Lakes States

In the late 1960s the differences between the designers of free-form buildings, who seem concerned primarily with the folk vernacular styles, and those who see architecture as an aesthetic exercise, became more marked. The first approach is represented by buildings such as the **Glen Harder House** (1970) and the **Jacob Harder House** (1971), both near **Mountain Lake**, Minnesota, and both by Bruce Goff. The second style is typified by the **Hanselman House** (1967) and the **Snyderman House** (1972), both in **Fort Wayne**, Indiana, and both by Michael Graves, and the **Dayton Residence, Wayzata** (1970), Minnesota, by Mitchell & Giurgola. Characteristics of these buildings are the interplay of solids and voids, white walls which are occasionally eroded to expose the frame, and the rotation of one right-angled element of the plan against another.

Civic & Public buildings

The great Chicago fire of 1871 gave architects an unprecedented opportunity for reconstruction. Skyscrapers developed with the works of Burnham & Root at the turn of the century and culminated in the refinements of Ludwig Mies van der Rohe's buildings in the mid-20th century. Once only considered for commercial design, skyscrapers were eventually put to civic use, as seen in the **Federal Center and Plaza, Chicago** (1959-73), by Mies van der Rohe or the **Richard J. Daley Center, Chicago** (1964), by C. F. Murphy. Mies van der Rohe's configuration of the high ground floor with a black *colonnade* has become as potent a symbol in buildings of corporate bodies, civic or commerical, as the temple *portico* was in the early 19th century in the United States.

Also of interest are the steel-framed campus buildings, an example of which is the **Illinois Institute of Technology, Chicago** (1940-58), by Mies van der Rohe. Buildings there, such as the **Crown Hall** (1952), are refined examples of the skeletal type of construction with a skin-like, non-loadbearing covering.

Commercial & Industrial buildings

During the early years of the Chicago School, William le Baron Jenney's buildings, in particular his **Home Insurance Building** (1883-85), greatly influenced contemporary architects in **Chicago**. An example of a transitional building is the **Rookery, South La Salle Street** (1885-87), by Burnham & Root, with its part masonry, part skeletal frame construction. It was one of the earliest examples of a public foyer with shops around a glass-roofed square. One of the most celebrated achievements of this period is the **Auditorium Building and Theatre, Michigan Avenue** (1886-89), by Dankmar Adler and Louis Sullivan. A combination hotel, office and auditorium, the masonry-built structure is *articulated* in the manner of H. H. Richardson. Sullivan's **Carson Pirie Scott Store, South State Street** (1899-1904), with its light frame and broad horizontal bands of windows, anticipates the *International Style* of architecture which was to dominate building for some years after 1920.

Douglas House, Harbor Springs *(1971-73), Michigan. A white villa by Richard Meier, suggesting closed and open spaces. It stands above the conifers and overlooks Lake Michigan.*

Walter Rudin Residence, Madison *(1957), Wisconsin. One of four prefabricated houses built for the Marshall Erdman Co. It is constructed in concrete, with board and batten placed horizontally.*

Snyderman House, Fort Wayne, *above. The architecture of the building is determined by its exposed structural frame. The interaction of flat and curved solids, the external staircase and spaces behind and in front of the frame accentuate the building's* open-work *quality.*

Water Tower, Michigan Avenue, Chicago *(1867-69). A castellated* Gothic-*style water-tower by William W. Boyington. The tower was constructed from rough-faced yellow limestone and encloses a 150 ft-high wrought iron standpipe which is 3 ft in diameter.*

Arcade, Cleveland
(1890), Ohio. Probably the finest 19th-C arcade in North America. Designed by George H. Smith, the first floor section of the arcade is recessed in order to allow maximum light to penetrate from the glazed roof.

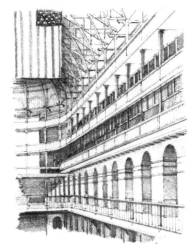

River Forest Women's Club, River Forest *(1913), Illinois. Designed by L. Guenzal and W. Drummond, who had both worked for Frank Lloyd Wright. Finished in board and batten, it resembles Wright's Unity Temple, Oak Park, Illinois, with its design of interconnecting rectangles.*

Crown Hall, Chicago *An architectural school designed in neo-Palladian style by Ludwig Mies van der Rohe. It has an uninterrupted floor space, 120 ft by 220 ft, and a roof suspended from four girders carried on steel columns.*

Sears Tower, Chicago, Illinois *(1974). By Skidmore, Owings & Merrill, it is 110 stories high and consists of nine separate sections of different height, tied together. The steel frame is sheathed in black aluminium.*

Monadnock Building, West Jackson Boulevard, Chicago *(1889-91) left. This 16-story office building by Burnham & Root was the last of the skyscrapers to be built using load-bearing masonry. The lower two stories lean inward, and the projecting polygonal bays create a vertical harmony.*

Reliance Building, Chicago *(1890-95), right. The basic elements of the 20th-C skyscrapers are incorporated in this building by Burnham & Root: a skeletal steel frame, internal bracing against the potential force of the wind in the city, and glass curtain walls.*

Great Lakes States

Commercial & Industrial buildings

Chicago was not alone in sponsoring early modern architecture. The **National Register Company Building, Dayton** (1888-1906), Ohio, by Frank M. Andrews, is a particularly fine glass-walled building. But the most handsome office complex in the area is the **Johnson Wax Company Buildings, Racine,** Wisconsin, with offices (1936-39) and tower (1950) designed by Frank Lloyd Wright. Both projects are known for their pleasant working environments. Also of interest are the **General Motors Technical Center, Warren** (1952-55), Michigan, and the **Deere & Company Building, Moline** (1962-64), Illinois. both by Eero Saarinen & Associates.

Architecture by the late 1960s was seen either in terms of dramatic structural techniques, as in the **John Hancock Center, Michigan Avenue,** Chicago (1966-68), Illinois, by Skidmore, Owings & Merrill, then the second tallest building in the world, or in multistory spaces, as in the **Hyatt Regency, Chicago** (1971), Illinois, by John Portman, or in bland geometrical statements such as the **College Life Insurance Company of America,** near **Indianapolis** (1972), Indiana, by Roche & Dinkerloo.

The ability to *articulate* façades of the quality of Louis Sullivan's **Security Bank and Trust Company, Owatonna** (1908), Minnesota, with its boldly projecting *cornice,* its crisp interplay of semicircles on rectangles, and its enriching decorative banding, seems lost to all but a few architects. Robert Venturi, however, displays that ability with his **Fire Station 4, Columbus** (1965), Indiana, which has an appropriate scale for its role in the public realm.

Merchants' National Bank, Winona *(1911), Minnesota. The architects, Purcell, Feick & Elmslie, had all worked for Louis Sullivan in Chicago. The brick façade is crisply* articulated.

Security Bank and Trust Company, Owatonna, *below. The most brilliant of a series of banks designed by Louis Sullivan for small midwestern towns. It has an austere, rectangular façade.*

John Hancock Center, Chicago, Illinois *(1970). A 100-story structure by Skidmore, Owings & Merrill, it has prominent diagonal wind bracing externally and inclined façades. The multiplicity of uses include shops, cafés, recreational facilities, offices and apartments.*

Tribune Tower, Chicago *(1922-25), Illinois, right. The imagery of medieval European cathedrals had a strong influence on architects Mead Howells and Raymond Hood, as can be seen in their spikey crowning lantern on this building.*

Offices, Johnson Wax Company, Racine *By Frank Lloyd Wright, the roof of the three-story central office area is carried on mushroom columns. Natural light filters in through tubular glass skylights.*

Plains States

Domestic buildings

There are several interesting houses by Frank Lloyd Wright in Iowa, and all are characterized by flat roofs and right-angled geometry. They include the **Stockman Residence, Mason City** (1908); the **Walter Residence, Quasqueton** (1946); the **Grant Residence, Cedar Rapids** (1945), and the **Millar Residence, Charles City** (1946-50). His **Bott Residence, Kansas City** (1956), Missouri, is more post-modern with its cut corner, rubble-stone wall and metal roof. The angular design was taken to extremes by Bruce Goff in his **Nicol House, Kansas City** (1965-67), Missouri.

Civic & Public buildings

The sheer magnitude of certain modern civic works in the plains states is impressive. The **State Capitol, Lincoln** (1922-32), Nebraska, by B. G. Goodhue, has a huge tower, while the **Climatron, St. Louis** (1961), Missouri, by Murphy & Mackey, has a giant dome sheltering the botanic garden. Eero Saarinen's **Gateway Arch, St. Louis** (1965), Missouri, is an extraordinary stainless steel arch 630 ft high.

Commercial & Industrial buildings

The classic monuments of the plains states are the giant grain elevators. However, there are also some magnificent commercial buildings, such as the **Wainwright Building, St. Louis** (1890-91), Missouri, by Louis Sullivan and Dankmar Adler, and the **Katz Building, Kansas City** (1908), Missouri, an early, non-load bearing curtain wall building by L. Curtiss.

Dodge City, Kansas *Part of a modern reconstruction of the city as it was in 1872, when the linkup with the Santa Fé railroad turned the city into the major shipping center for cattle in the area.*

Woodbury County Courthouse, Sioux City *(1918), Iowa. A magnificent* Art Deco *building by Steel, Purcell & Elmslie. It has exuberant terracotta decorative work, and* Neoclassical *sculptures crown the pillars which flank the courthouse entrance.*

Wainwright Tomb, St. Louis *(1882), Missouri, left. Louis Sullivan and Dankmar Adler designed this limestone mausoleum crowned with a dome. It seems a forerunner to Joseph Olbrich's Sezession Gallery, Vienna (1898-99).*

Merchants' National Bank, Grinnell *(1914), Iowa. The façade, an example of how in Sullivan's later work his aim was to give life to box shapes by the use of ornament, especially contrasting geometric shapes, here seen above the* portal *and dominating the façade.*

Wainwright Building, St. Louis, *above. An unusual amalgam by Louis Sullivan and Dankmar Adler of the* Functionalist *skyscraper, with its seven stories of red-brick piers and the* Renaissance *formalism of the palazzo, with its differentiated ground floor, its projecting roof cornice and terracotta frieze.*

411

The South

Domestic buildings

The colonial inheritance of European styles of architecture permeated North American building into the late 19th and early 20th century. A notable example is **Biltmore, Asheville** (1890-95), North Carolina, recreated in the style of 16th-century Blois, France, and incorporating an external spiral staircase and high-pitched roofs. Similarly, **Ca'd'zan, Sarasota** (1916-26), Florida, by Thomas R. Martin, included *arcaded* windows modeled on the Doge's Palace, Venice, and **Vizcaya, South Miami Ave.** (1916), Miami, a Venetian-style palazzo, was planned to accommodate a series of modern classical rooms.

However, by the 1880s attempts were being made to reflect in architecture those qualities unique to the American experience. Though some projects proved bizarre, such as the **Doullut Houses, New Orleans** (1905), Louisiana, built in a style reminiscent of the Mississippi river boats, it is later, in the works of Frank Lloyd Wright and Bruce Goff, that the cultural constraints of Europe were abandoned and truly indigenous architecture emerged.

This transfiguration is reflected in Wright's "Usonian" (a word he coined to describe wholly American architecture) houses developed from his theoretical projects designed for suburbia, and built to a compact "L"-shaped plan with gardens on the inside angle. Both the **Pope-Leighey House, Mount Vernon** (1939, 1964), Virginia, and the **Rosenbaum Residence, Florence** (1939), Alabama, show how his work is highly structured yet conveys an air of informality and freedom. Similarly, Goff's projects, including **Wilson House, Pensacola** (1951-53), Florida, and **Gutman, House, Gulfport** (1958-60), Mississippi, though formally planned, seem to be hand-built rather than architect designed.

Civic & Public buildings

A notable example of this building type is **Florida Southern College, Lakeland** (1938-54), Florida. In Wright's master plan, the dynamism of the project derives not from the overall structure of the complex but from the individual buildings, such as the **Pfeiffer Chapel** (1939), the **Roux Library** (1941) and the **Industrial Arts Building** (1942). They are all geometrically sharp and angular, and characterized by a diamond motif. Linked by esplanades throughout the campus, the buildings combine to form an impressive infrastructure. Also of interest is the **Old City Hall, Richmond** (1894), Virginia, and **Flagler College, St. Augustine** (1888), Florida.

Commercial & Industrial buildings

The strongly utilitarian nature of many American buildings is evident in this sphere of architecture, the most radical example being the **Vehicle Assembly Building, Cape Canaveral** (1962-66), Florida, built for the space program. A more aesthetic illustration is **Dulles International Airport**, near **Washington, D.C.** (1958-62), by Eero Saarinen, which is designed to provide travelers with the maximum comfort.

Florida Southern College, Lakeland *The striking geometric form of Pfeiffer Chapel, designed by Frank Lloyd Wright, is based on a diamond or double triangle. This design is repeated in other combinations elsewhere on the campus.*

Ca'd'zan, Sarasota *A late example of European-influenced North American architecture, it is dominated by an elaborate polychrome tower with Venetian-style windows. The luxurious mansion was built for John Ringling, a circus impresario.*

Pope-Leighey House, Mount Vernon *One of Wright's "Usonian" houses incorporating such characteristic details as horizontal boards with sunken battens built around a brick core. The house was relocated on its present site, having been originally built at Falls Church.*

Zimmerman House, Fairfax County *(1974-75), Virginia. A conventional wood frame house, designed by William Turnbull, that is encased in a redwood trellis and encircled by a verandah. The porches and skylight are designed to provide an abundance of light.*

Dulles International Airport, near Washington, D.C., *right. An impressive terminal building, designed by Eero Saarinen, with a high front façade, canted columns, and a hung roof. Passengers go from the terminal to their flights in mobile lounges.*

Biltmore, Asheville, *left. Richard M. Hunt, one of several architects in the late 19th and early 20thC influenced by European styles, created this impressive mansion for George Vanderbilt in the style of a French Renaissance palace.*

Dormitories, Woodberry Forest School (1978)
These buildings in Virginia by Robert Vickery & Partners are typical of the style of architecture with distinct fronts and backs to buildings which was evolved in the 1970s. The brick front is in the grand manner, but the rear elevation is domestic in scale and is embellished with *stuccoed* and painted walls.

Burroughs Wellcome Company Building, Research Triangle Park *(1972), North Carolina. Offices by Paul Rudolph for the Burroughs Wellcome Company. The elaborate tent-like structure of the building forms a lobby that is reminiscent of a church interior.*

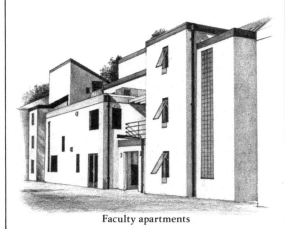

Faculty apartments

Lawn façade

Doullut House, New Orleans *One of two houses built by Paul Doullut on the edge of the Mississippi. The decorative railings, posts and galleries imitate the style of the great Mississippi river boats of the mid-19thC.*

413

Mountain States

Religious buildings

The tabernacles and temples of the Mormon Church are plentiful in Utah. The strongly eclectic **Mormon Temple, Manti** (1877-88), by William Folsom, incorporates such *Gothic Revival* features as the tall *buttresses* and crowning battlements, while the flanking towers, *Neoclassical* in style, are crowned with French château-style roofs. The most monumental of religious buildings is the walled complex, more than 12 acres in extent, in **Salt Lake City**, which includes the **Tabernacle** (1868) by Folsom and the **Temple** (1893) by T. Angell, with its towers strangely stepped and crowned with sharp pyramids. Another impressive religious building is the *multifaceted,* aluminium-clad **Air Force Academy Chapel, Colorado Springs** (1952-62), Colorado, by Skidmore, Owings & Merrill.

Civic & Public buildings

A peculiarity of the buildings of the frontier lands is the manner in which architectural motifs are often combined to bizarre effect. This can be seen in the **Civic Center, Helena** (1920), Montana, by Link & Haire, which is a converted temple complete with Islamic style minaret, domes and horseshoe arch. Also of interest are the numerous "ghost" towns of Nevada and Montana, where empty saloons and false-fronted stores reminiscent of gold rush days line the deserted streets.

Commercial & Industrial buildings

A spectacular building is the **Brown Palace Hotel, Denver** (1892), Colorado, by Frank Edbrooke & Partners. Nine stories of balconies open out onto a central, glass-roofed lobby, a space which became the prototype for the giant lobbies of the late 1960s and 1970s. In contrast to the usual city skyline is that of **Las Vegas, Nevada,** where attention is focused mainly on the electric signs. Despite the vitality of these buildings, they are not so much architecture as commerical art.

The Ames Monument, Sherman *(1879), Wyoming. The monument is more than 60 ft tall and constructed of rough stone. It was designed by H. H. Richardson as a memorial to the Ames brothers, who financed the building of the Union Pacific Railroad.*

Sheldon Jackson Memorial Chapel, Fairplay *(1874), Colorado. A small-scale, wooden church built of board and batten walling in the* Gothic *style by local carpenters.*

Brant-Johnson House, Vail *(1976), Colorado. By Venturi & Rauch, it is a tower house built among the trees. The boarded walls are inward sloping, while the roof has dormer windows.*

Las Vegas

The town, with its gas stations, motels and gambling places, represents the extreme development of the American Main Street. Though the neon lights and glittering façades may seem unattractive to many, the town is rooted in the tradition of urban America.

Caesar's Palace

The Flamingo

414

The West Coast

Religious buildings

The **Christian Science Church, Berkeley** (1910), designed by Bernard Maybeck, is one of many churches built in California during the early part of the 20th century. It is an amalgam of *Gothic,* Oriental and *Romanesque* motifs, molded together under pitched roofs and deep *eaves.* Also of interest is **St John's Presbyterian Church, Berkeley** (1910), by Julia Morgan; the **Bethlehem Baptist Church, Los Angeles** (1944), by R. M. Schindler, and the **Wayfarer's Chapel, Palos Verdes** (1951).

Domestic buildings

Numerous styles were employed by architects in California during the 19th century. Among the most interesting buildings are the magnificent terraced houses in San Francisco, with their narrow façades and combination of exotic styles. Other interesting buildings include the **Governor's Mansion, Sacramento** (1878), by N. Goodell, and the **William Carsen Residence, Eureka** (*c.* 1885), by S. and J. Newsan. The *gabled dormers,* asymmetrical plan and high central tower, are typical of grand mansion architecture during the 19th century. Of the early 20th-century architects, the buildings of Charles and Henry Greene are perhaps, with their boldly projecting roofs and *shingled* walls, the most distinctive. Good examples are the **R. R. Blacker House, 1177 Hillcrest** (1907), and the **Gamble House, 4 Westmoreland Place** (1908), both in Pasadena.

Gamble House, Westmoreland Place, *Pasadena. The masterpiece of Charles and Henry Greene. The overhanging eaves, shaded porches, shingle board and batten exterior, as well as the exposed junctions of the posts and lintels, are typical ingredients of their work.*

1347 McAlister, San Francisco *(1880). This is an extraordinary town house for its date, built in the style of the French Baroque Revival. The house was designed for a tobacco merchant, who had a ballroom built on the top floor.*

Hearst Castle, San Simeon *(1919-47). The outdoor swimming pool is surrounded by stepped terraces and classical colonnading. This vast mansion was designed by Julia Morgan for William Randolf Hearst.*

Lovell Beach House, Newport Beach *(1926), Los Angeles. This is R. M. Schindler's most famous building and one of the great modern houses in North America. It is raised on concrete stilts above the sand.*

1597 Fulton, San Francisco *(1892). The houses built in San Francisco during the second half of the 19th C were usually flamboyant and incorporate a variety of styles. This house was built in the Queen Anne style.*

The West Coast

Much of the 20th-century domestic architecture in California has relied on diverse motifs and styles from other cultures. The houses of Irving Gill, such as the **Bailey House, La Jolla** (1907), the **Miltmore House, Pasadena** (1911), and the **Morgan House, North Arden** (1917), are a mixture of the Spanish mission stations of California and the volumetric geometry of the work of Frank Lloyd Wright. Bernard Maybeck, in houses like the **Roos House, San Francisco** (1909), or the **Kennedy House, Berkeley** (1923), was even more eclectic and was prepared to combine oriental motifs with *Neoclassical* elements. Frank Lloyd Wright's work was equally romantic, as is seen in his **Madison Millard House, Pasadena** (1921), and the **Storer House, Hollywood** (1922), both monumental blockwork houses with Mayan and Islamic overtones. A romantic element is seen in **Thornsberg Village, Berkeley** (1928), and the **Goss House, Piedmont** (1925), both by W. R. Yelland.

One of the main architects to emerge in California after World War I was Richard Neutra, an immigrant from Vienna who brought with him the ideas of Adolf Loos and Otto Wagner. With Rudolph Schindler, he introduced the sophisticated, new European architecture to the United States. Examples by Schindler are his own **House, Kings Road** (1929), Hollywood; the **Sachs Apartment House, Los Angeles** (1928), and the **Wolfe Residence, Catalina Island** (1928). Buildings of interest by Neutra include the **Kahn House, San Francisco** (1939), and the **Tremaine House, Santa Barbara** (1948). A key building was the **Eames House, Santa Monica** (1947-49), by Charles Eames. It was built of standard components and has been one of the major influences in the high technology buildings of the younger European architects of the 1970s.

In the late 1940s two important houses were designed in Los Angeles by Schindler, the **Janson House, Hollywood**, and the **Tischler House, 175 Greenfield**, both of 1949. The frames, which are clearly expressed, and the angular geometry seem to belong to roadside American architecture, the small town architecture of garages, cafés and wooden domestic houses. Indeed, they represent the beginnings of "pop" architecture. The incorporation of roadside architecture is seen in later buildings, such as the **Talbert House, Oakland** (1962), by Charles Moore, and the **Falk House, Berkeley** (1974), by Richard Peters. Both are characterized by their white walls with bays and balconies which project from a central core. This synthesis of low and high art rapidly deteriorated in the jumble of roofs and modish vernacularisms, seen in North California at **Sea Ranch**, developed by Moore, Turnbull & Esherick from 1965 onward.

Civic & Public buildings

Mann's or **Grauman's Chinese Theatre, Los Angeles** (1927), by Heyer & Hollen, is an exotic cinema which dates from the heyday of Hollywood and is indicative of the fantasy which surrounds the world of film production.

Thornsberg Village, Berkeley *The scheme is now commonly referred to as Normandy Village but is more an apartment block than a village. Its plan is "H"-shaped, while the eccentric motifs give the complex a somewhat humorous quality. The scheme looks back to the medieval architecture of the Auvergne, France.*

The Lovell House, 4616 Dundee *(1929), Los Angeles. By Richard Neutra, it is a three-story house built around a light, prefabricated steel frame. Despite its angular qualities, it blends into the surrounding landscape.*

Tischler House, Los Angeles *A geometrical pattern of shapes is set in front of a gable-roofed central core. The roof was made originally of corrugated fiberglass and was shaded by rows of eucalyptus trees.*

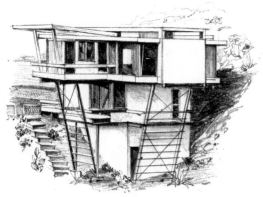

Janson House, Hollywood
The house shocked the architectural establishment of the period due to its wooden stilts and roadside character. However, it was a low budget house and this is reflected by the spindly, stilt construction.

Cary House, Mill Valley *(1960). By Joseph Esherick, the walls are of shingle and the terraces are shaded by trellis work. The house is a simpler and more utilitarian interpretation of the buildings which were designed by the Greene brothers.*

Talbert House, Oakland
The style of the house was described by the architect as "saddle bag" architecture for the bays and balconies are hung outside the central core. This style is characteristic of much of the recent architecture in the area.

Palace of Fine Arts, San Francisco
(1915). Built for the Panama Pacific Exhibition, it consists of a giant domed rotunda which is articulated by Corinthian columns. At the rear there is a semicircular colonnade.

Sleeping Beauty's Castle, Disneyland *(1955). This park was the first in the USA to be devoted to a theme. The castle combines motifs taken from the vernacular revival and the Gothic Revival. These parts are incorporated with a number of more bizarre features.*

Watts Towers, 1765 E. 107th Street
(1921-54). Los Angeles. By Sam Rodia, they consist of metal frames covered with bits of tile, bottles and china, which were collected over a period of some 30 years.

The Maritime Museum, Beach Street
(1939), San Francisco. By William Mooser and his son, the building is reminiscent of Mendelsohn's De la Warr Pavilion, Bexhill, England, although the conscious styling of the curved walls lacks the tension of the English example.

417

The West Coast

A classic example of fantastic architecture is to be found in the film lots of **Universal Studios, Hollywood** (1930s), where false fronts and sham buildings were used to create palatial cities or highly exotic environments.

One of the few civic buildings which was designed by Frank Lloyd Wright is the **Marin County Civic Center, San Rafael** (1957-62). Two long blocks, *articulated* by tiers of arches — wide at the bottom and smaller at the top — shoot out from a domed library at the center. The **Salk Institute, La Jolla** (1959-65), by Louis Kahn, is one of the architectural masterpieces of the West Coast. The laboratory buildings are organized as two parallel blocks with a central court lined with study rooms. The plan has classical simplicity. **Kresge College, University of Southern California, Santa Cruz,** (1974), by Moore, Turnbull & Associates, is articulated by elaborate stageset *porticos,* while parts of the façade are lined with wafer-thin *colonnades* that look as if they were cut from card. Between the formalism of the former and the picturesqueness of the latter lies a whole range of buildings, such as Alvar Aalto's **Library, Mount Angel Abbey, St. Benedict** (1967-79), Oregon; the **University Art Museum, Berkeley** (1967-70), by M. J. Ciampi; the **Oakland Museum, Oakland** (1968), by Roche & Dinkerloo, where a balance between the orthodoxy of the Salk Institute and the picturesqueness of Kresge College is achieved, and the *Neoclassical* **Getty Museum, Malibu** (1970-75).

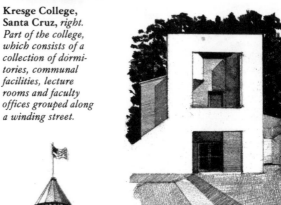

Faculty Club, Santa Barbara *The building is an amalgam of the Spanish colonial style and streamlined modern forms wrapped around a* Renaissance-*style courtyard. The combination of diverse styles has resulted in a design somewhat lacking in vitality.*

Salk Institute, La Jolla *The study rooms are organized as a series of pavilions with* multifaceted *façades. The boldness of forms and* articulation *is reminiscent of the Marchiondi Spagliardi Institute, Milan.*

Kresge College, Santa Cruz, *right. Part of the college, which consists of a collection of dormitories, communal facilities, lecture rooms and faculty offices grouped along a winding street.*

Marin County Civic Center, San Rafael *One of the largest projects designed by Frank Lloyd Wright. The building, which extends across the rolling landscape, is arranged underneath a long, sky-lit spine.*

Hotel de Coronado, Coronado *(1888), California. By James and Merrit Reid, it is the last great Californian resort hotel to be built in the 19thC. When it was opened it comprised nearly 800 rooms and spread over nearly 5 acres. The scheme was designed as a quadrangle enclosing an interior courtyard.*

The eclectic buildings of the late 1960s and the 1970s lost much of the vitality of the earlier works. A comparison between the **Faculty Club, Santa Barbara** (1967-68), by Moore, Turnbull & Associates, and Irving Gill's **La Jolla Women's Club, La Jolla** (1913), for example, shows that the more recent examples have become so stylized that they have lost a sense of visual identity.

Commercial & Industrial buildings

Of the early office buildings in **San Francisco** the **Hallidie Building** (1918) by Willis Polk is one of the most interesting, with its all-glass façade and superimposed decorative cast iron fire-escapes. There are also a number of fine streamlined modern buildings, such as the **Coca Cola Bottling Plant, Los Angeles** (1936), by R. Derrah.

One of the most deceptively simple but ingenious designs is Frank Lloyd Wright's **V. C. Morris Store, Maiden Lane, San Francisco,** (1947), which consists of a large cube with a brick façade articulated by a bold, arched *portal* set on a raised brick panel which itself mirrors the main façade. The inside of the shop is lighted by a skylight in the roof, while added drama is created by a large spiral ramp which winds itself up the interior.

There are two fine examples in San Francisco of the rehabilitation of late 19th-century and early 20th-century industrial buildings, that in **Ghiradelli Square** (1970), by Wurster, Bernardi & Emmons, and the **Cannery** (1968) by Joseph Esherick, both consisting of shops and cafés.

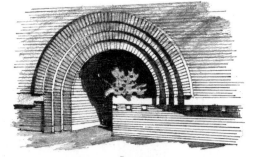

Hyatt Regency Hotel, San Francisco *(1973). This central lobby of John Portman's building is the most spectacular part of the Hyatt hotel. The space is vast and is surrounded by oversailing balconies from which the rooms lead off.*

L. C. Smith Building, Seattle *(1914), Washington. The building makes an inspired use of a tight, awkward site. Unlike most West Coast architecture there are few reminders of the past, the only historic elements being the arched roof and the corbeled cornices.*

V. C. Morris Store, San Francisco *The only relief in the plain brick-walled façade is the bold, arched entrance, and the pattern of the brickwork itself.*

Los Angeles Pop architecture

Though these works are unadulterated Kitsch, their very scarceness helps them to gain a certain charm and individuality. The designers of the **Tail-o-Pup Hot-dog Stand** and the **Brown Derby Café** have simply created symbols which attract customers.

Brown Derby Café, Wilshire (1926)

Tail-o-Pup, La Cienga (c. 1936)

The Southwest

Religious buildings

There are several interesting churches in the
southwest, outstanding examples being Frank Lloyd
Wright's **First Christian Church, Phoenix**
(1950-77), Arizona; Bruce Goff's **Hopewell
Baptist Church, Edmond** (1952), Oklahoma,
and Anshen & Allen's **Chapel of the Holy Cross,
Sedona** (1950-57), Arizona.

Domestic buildings

Adobe houses, such as the **Zimmerman House,
Albuquerque** (1929), New Mexico, by Miles
Brittelle, dominated the region. The first major
modern house was Wright's winter home, **Taliesin
West, Scottsdale** (1938-59), Arizona. His later
work includes some remarkable free-form build-
ings, such as the **Norman Lykes Residence,
Phoenix** (1950-52), Arizona. Even more informal
are houses by Goff, such as the **Dale House,
Beaver** (1964), Oklahoma.

Civic & Public buildings

Fine civic works include the **Kalita Humphreys
Theatre, Dallas** (1955-56), Texas, by Wright,
and the **Outdoor Theatre, Institute of American Indian Art, Santa Fé** (1970), New Mexico,
by Paolo Soleri.

Commercial & Industrial buildings

It is the architecture of the boldly *articulated*
commercial buildings of the southwest that will
probably most influence building in the area over
the next decades. A particularly fine example of
this structurally disparate style is the **Reunion
Hotel, Dallas** (1977), Texas, by Welton
Becket Associates.

David Wright Residence, Phoenix
*(1950-52), Arizona, above. A free-
form building designed by Frank
Lloyd Wright for his son. The curved
forms of concrete block are characteristic of his architecture at this
period. The living spaces are raised
above the ground and are reached by
a spiral staircase.*

Price Tower, Bartlesville *(1952-
56), Oklahoma. This was the only
skyscraper designed by Wright. Built
of reinforced concrete, it has an "X"
shaped structural spine from which
the floors are* cantilevered. *The
exterior consists of copper* louvers
and gold-tinted glass.

Galleria, Houston *(1978), Texas,
above. View of an escalator in this
50 acre shopping, office and
hotel complex, designed by Hell-
muth & Obata. There is a huge
covered mall with upper level streets,
linking bridges and an ice rink.*

**Richard Lloyd-Jones
House, Tulsa** *(1929),
Oklahoma, right. A
handsome glass and
block house designed
by Wright. It contains
a raised inner court-
yard which has a pool
set into it. The glazed
bays were originally
used as aviaries.*

**Bavinger House,
Norman** *(1950-55),
Oklahoma, left. Bruce
Goff designed a volute
plan for this house.
The free stone wall is
higher at the center.
The roof is suspended
by cables from a giant
central mast.*

Canada

Domestic buildings

Canadian domestic building followed closely the east and west coast schools of the United States, from the late 19th century until the 1970s. Academic design until the early 20th century favored the monumental proportions of medieval architecture. A good example is the **Casa Loma, Toronto** (1911-13), Ontario, by Edward J. Lennox. In contrast, **Habitat, Montreal** (1966-67), Quebec, by Moshe Safdie and others, is a complex of prefabricated boxes, with terrace gardens on the stepped rooftops.

Civic & Public buildings

The best civic building of the mid-19th century is the *Gothic*-style **Library, Parliament Buildings,** Ottawa (1859-67), Ontario, by Fuller & Stent. The library is the only part to have escaped destruction by fire in 1916. The other parliament buildings were rebuilt by Pearson & Marchand. The early 20th century was characterized by such *Classic* works as the **Legislative Buildings** for the city of **Winnipeg** (1913-20), Manitoba, by F. W. Simon, and for **Edmonton** (1907-12), Alberta, by A. M. Jeffers. The bold zig-zag plan of **Scarborough College, Toronto** (1964-66), by John Andrews and other architects, resembles commercial works of the United States west coast and southwest states.

Commercial & Industrial buildings

The French château style of the **Château Frontenac, Quebec** (1890), by Bruce Price, was a prototype for numerous railway hotels. Recent works, such as the **Place Bonaventure, Montreal** (1967), Quebec, have discarded European influences and are more akin to the 1970s' commercial buildings of Texas.

Casa Loma, Toronto
A mansion in the Scottish baronial style, designed by Edward J. Lennox. Today many see its monumental size and vulgar flamboyance, previously out of favor, as having a certain beauty.

Civic Center, Scarborough *(1973), Ontario, left. The plan of this civic center, designed by Raymond Moriyama & Partners, is based on arc shapes. There is a multi-story central foyer.*

Library, Parliament Buildings, Ottawa, *right. A delightful* Gothic-*style building designed by Fuller & Stent. The medieval English chapter-house seems to have been its model. The library was the only part of the complex to survive a fire in 1916.*

Château Frontenac, Quebec, *above. The French château of the 16thC was the primary influence on this hotel, designed by the Boston architect Bruce Price. It stands on a spectacular hill-top site. The tower was added in 1923.*

Barn, *near West Brome (19thC), Quebec, right. This barn of the late 19thC has the typical characteristics of circular and polygonal barns of North America: a flat site and a broad ramp, sometimes covered over, leading up to the wagon doors. The turret here crowns a central silo.*

Maps

The maps on the following pages show the geographical areas into which Europe and North America have been divided for the purposes of this book. Although the architectural coverage goes back to early classical times, the maps reflect current political boundaries.

———————	County boundary
▪–▪–▪–▪–▪	National boundary
▬▬▬▬▬	Regional boundary

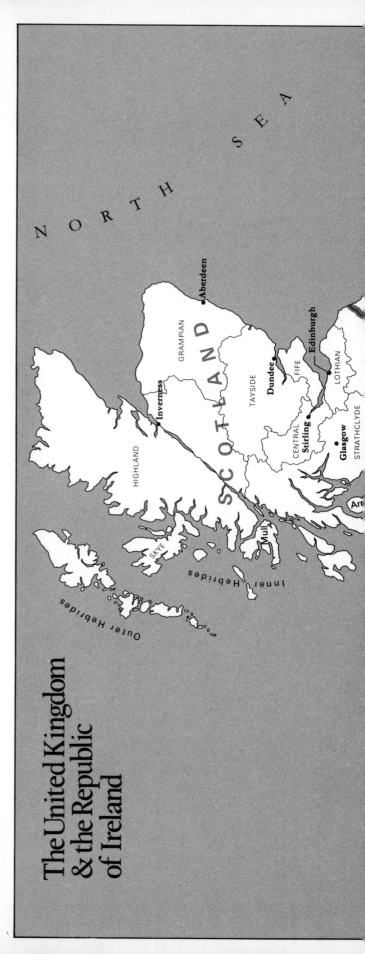

The United Kingdom
& the Republic
of Ireland

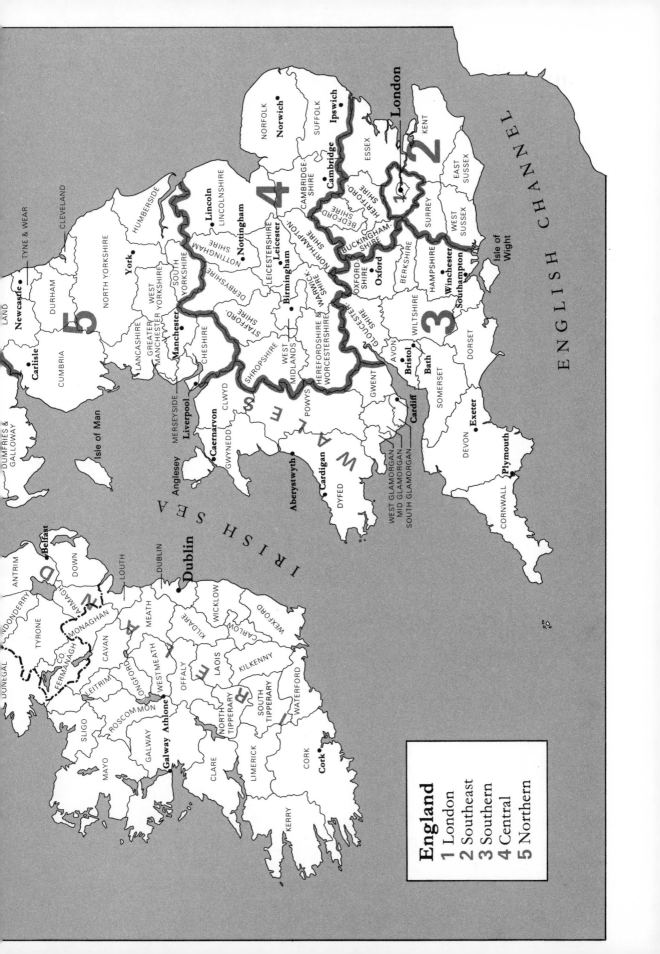

ENGLISH CHANNEL

IRISH SEA

England
1 London
2 Southeast
3 Southern
4 Central
5 Northern

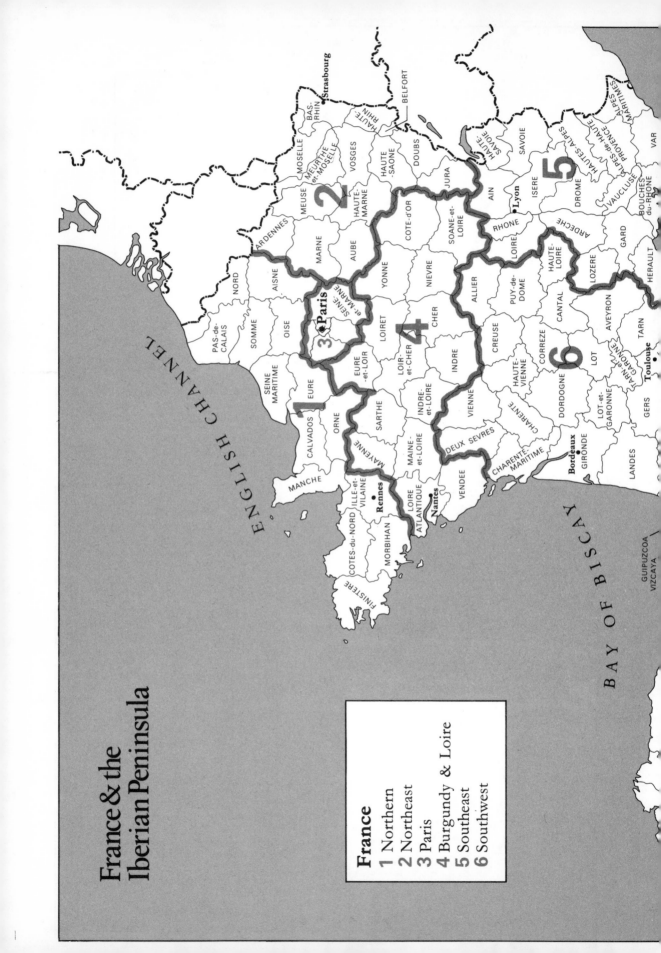

France & the Iberian Peninsula

France

1 Northern
2 Northeast
3 Paris
4 Burgundy & Loire
5 Southeast
6 Southwest

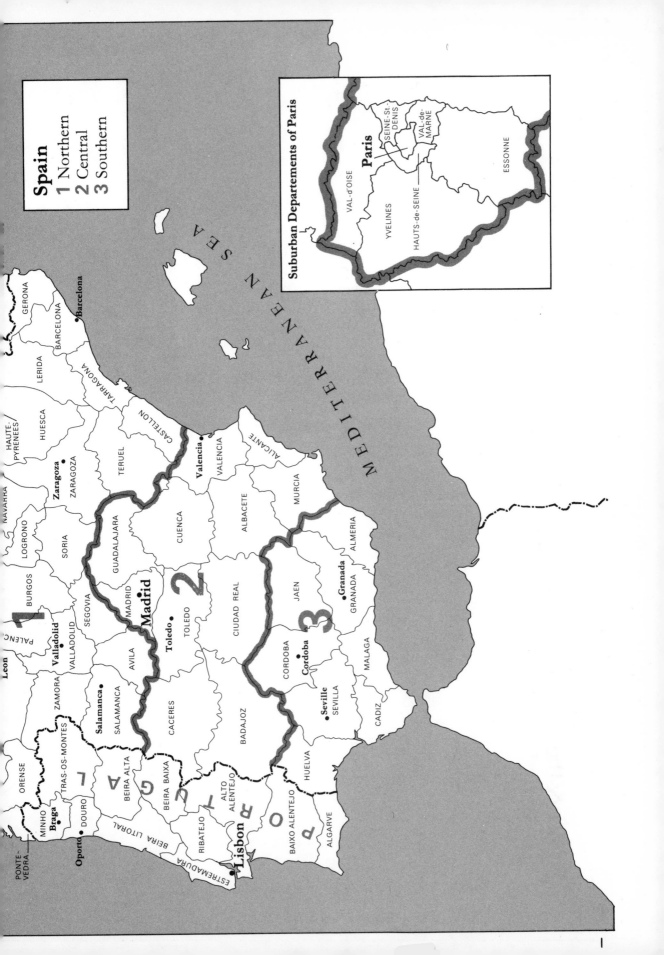

Spain
1 Northern
2 Central
3 Southern

Suburban Departements of Paris

Paris

VAL-d'OISE

SEINE-St.-DENIS

VAL-de-MARNE

ESSONNE

YVELINES

HAUTS-de-SEINE

MEDITERRANEAN SEA

GERONA

BARCELONA

Barcelona

LERIDA

HAUTE-PYRENEES

HUESCA

TARRAGONA

CASTELLON

NAVARRA

ZARAGOZA

Zaragoza

TERUEL

VALENCIA

Valencia

VALENCIA

ALICANTE

LOGRONO

SORIA

GUADALAJARA

CUENCA

ALBACETE

MURCIA

BURGOS

SEGOVIA

MADRID

Madrid

ALMERIA

Leon

PALENC.

VALLADOLID

Valladolid

AVILA

TOLEDO

Toledo

CIUDAD REAL

JAEN

GRANADA

Granada

1

2

3

ZAMORA

SALAMANCA

Salamanca

CACERES

BADAJOZ

CORDOBA

Cordoba

MALAGA

ORENSE

TRAS-OS-MONTES

BEIRA ALTA

BEIRA BAIXA

ALTO ALENTEJO

HUELVA

SEVILLA

Seville

CADIZ

PONTE-VEDRA

MINHO

Braga

DOURO

Oporto

BEIRA LITORAL

RIBATEJO

BAIXO ALENTEJO

ALGARVE

ESTREMADURA

Lisbon

PORTUGAL

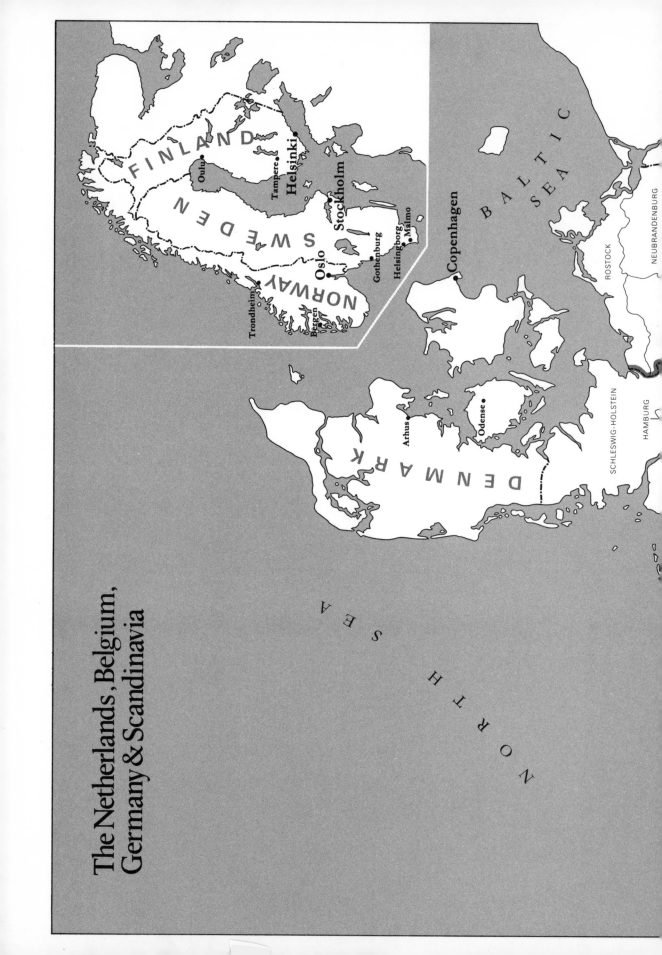

The Netherlands, Belgium,
Germany & Scandinavia

FINLAND

SWEDEN

NORWAY

Oulu

Tampere

Helsinki

Stockholm

Gothenburg

Malmö

Helsingborg

Oslo

Trondheim

Bergen

Copenhagen

BALTIC SEA

ROSTOCK

NEUBRANDENBURG

DENMARK

Århus

Odense

SCHLESWIG-HOLSTEIN

HAMBURG

NORTH SEA

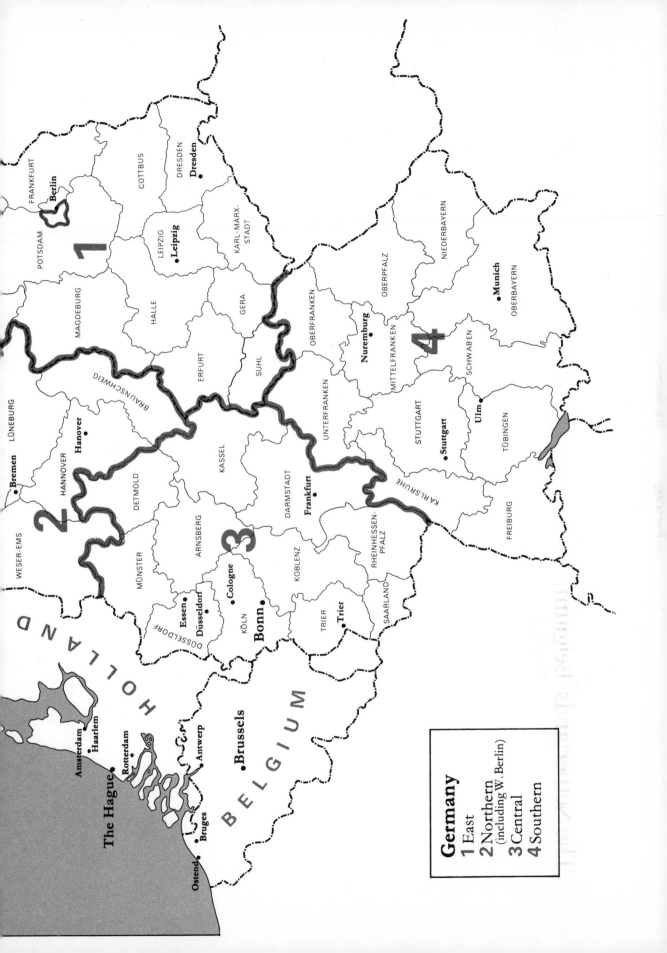

FRANKFURT

Berlin

COTTBUS

DRESDEN

Dresden

POTSDAM

1

LEIPZIG

Leipzig

KARL-MARX-
STADT

NIEDERBAYERN

MAGDEBURG

HALLE

GERA

OBERFRANKEN

OBERPFALZ

Munich

OBERBAYERN

LÜNEBURG

ERFURT

SUHL

Nuremburg

MITTELFRANKEN

SCHWABEN

BRAUNSCHWEIG

4

Bremen

Hanover

HANNOVER

DETMOLD

KASSEL

UNTERFRANKEN

STUTTGART

Stuttgart

Ulm

TÜBINGEN

WESER-EMS

DARMSTADT

Frankfurt

3

ARNSBERG

KOBLENZ

RHEINHESSEN-
PFALZ

KARLSRUHE

FREIBURG

MÜNSTER

2

Essen

Cologne

KÖLN

Bonn

TRIER

Trier

SAARLAND

Düsseldorf

DÜSSELDORF

H O L L A N D

Amsterdam

Haarlem

Rotterdam

The Hague

Bruges

Ostend

Antwerp

Brussels

B E L G I U M

Germany
1 East
2 Northern
(including W. Berlin)
3 Central
4 Southern

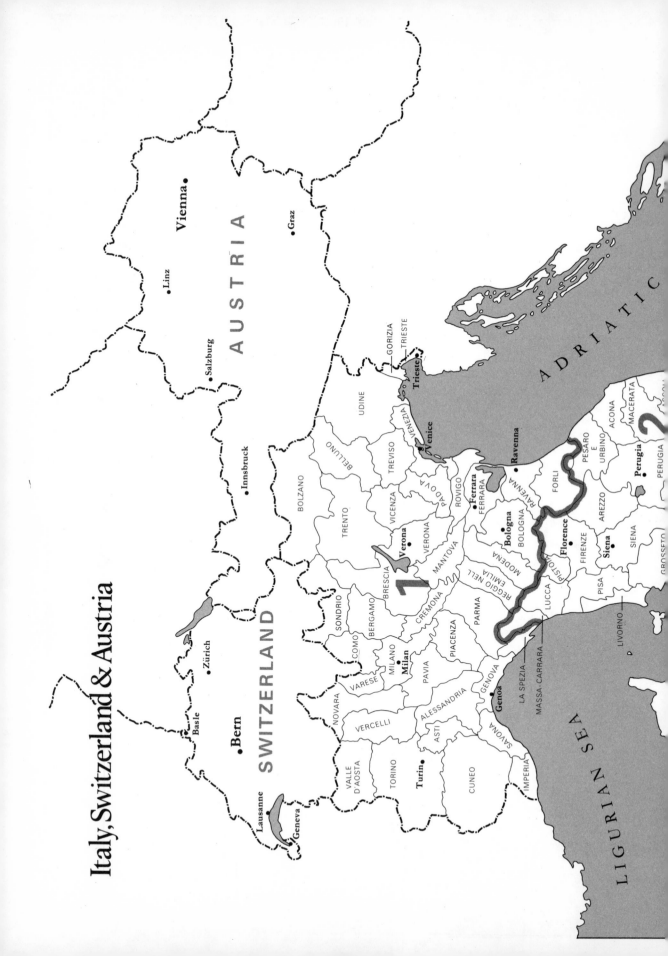

Italy, Switzerland & Austria

AUSTRIA

Vienna

Linz

Graz

Salzburg

Innsbruck

SWITZERLAND

Zürich

Basle

Bern

Lausanne

Geneva

ADRIATIC

GORIZIA

TRIESTE

Trieste

UDINE

BELLUNO

BOLZANO

TRENTO

VENEZIA

TREVISO

VICENZA

Venice

PADOVA

ROVIGO

Verona
VERONA

Ferrara
FERRARA

Ravenna

RAVENNA

ACONA

MACERATA

PESARO
E
URBINO

PERUGIA

Perugia

FORLI

Bologna
BOLOGNA

MODENA

REGGIO NELL'
EMILIA

AREZZO

Florence
FIRENZE

Siena
SIENA

GROSSETO

PISTOIA

LUCCA

BRESCIA

SONDRIO

BERGAMO

MANTOVA

CREMONA

PARMA

PIACENZA

PISA

COMO

Milan
MILANO

PAVIA

MASSA-CARRARA

LA SPEZIA

LIVORNO

VARESE

NOVARA

ALESSANDRIA

GENOVA

Genoa

SAVONA

IMPERIA

VERCELLI

ASTI

VALLE
D'AOSTA

TORINO

Turin

CUNEO

LIGURIAN SEA

SEA

MEDITERRANEAN SEA

Brindisi
LECCE
BRINDISI
Taranto
TARANTO
Bari
BARI
MATERA
CATANZARO
COSENZA
4
REGGIO DI CALABRIA
FOGGIA
Foggia
POTENZA
AVELLINO
SALERNO
BENEVENTO
CHIETI
CAMPOBASSO
CASERTA
NAPOLI
Naples
Messina
PESCARA
FROSINONE
L'AQUILA
LATINA
Sicily
RIETI
3 Rome
ROMA
Palermo
VITERBO

TYRRHENIAN SEA

Sardinia

Italy
1 Northern
2 Central
3 Rome
4 Southern

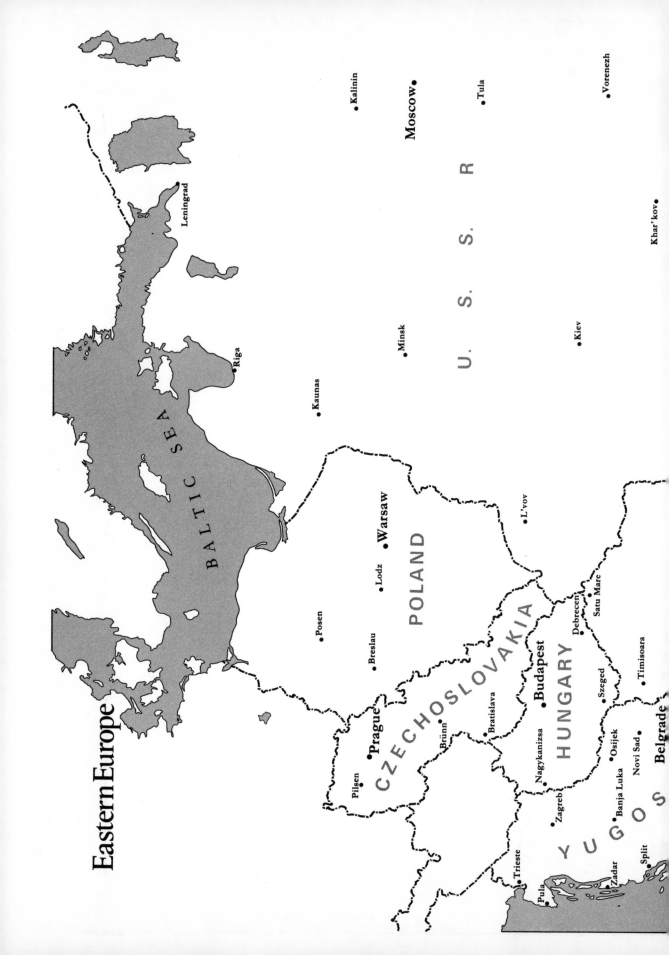

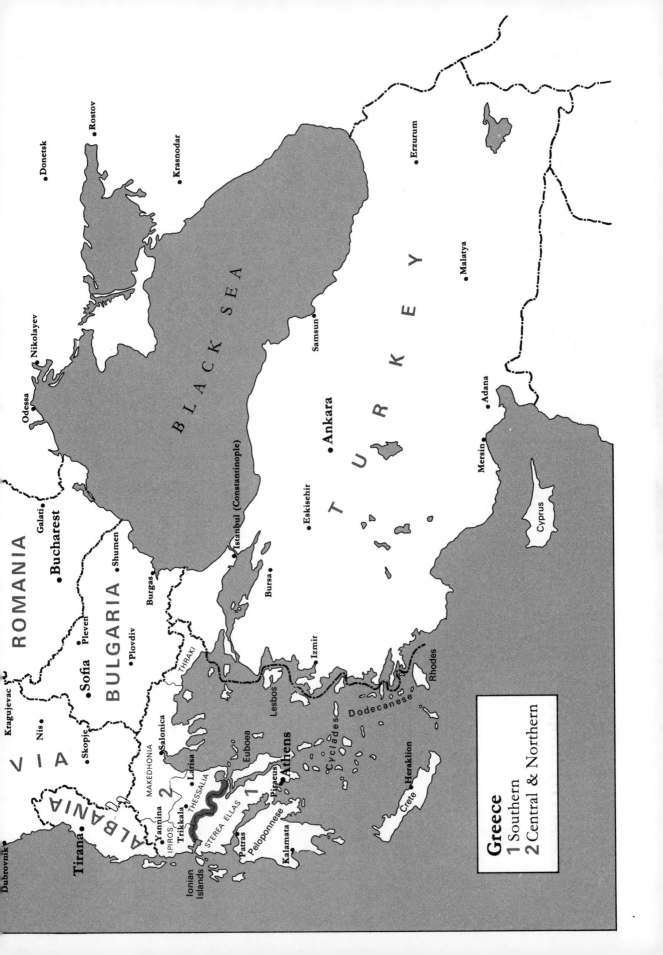

ROMANIA

Rostov

Donetsk

Krasnodar

Nikolayev

Odessa

Galati

Bucharest

Shumen

Sofia

Pleven

BULGARIA

Plovdiv

Burgas

B L A C K   S E A

Istanbul (Constantinople)

Samsun

Erzurum

Malatya

Ankara

T U R K E Y

Eskisehir

Mersin

Adana

Bursa

Cyprus

Izmir

Rhodes

Dodecanese

Lesbos

THRAKI

Cyclades

Salonica

MAKEDHONIA

Larisa

Euboea

Crete

Heraklion

Athens

Piraeus

STEREA ELLAS

THESSALIA

Trikkala

Yannina

IPIROS

Patras

Peloponnese

Kalamata

Ionian
Islands

1

2

Kragujevac

Nis

Skopje

Dubrovnik

Tirana

ALBANIA

V I A

Greece
1 Southern
2 Central & Northern

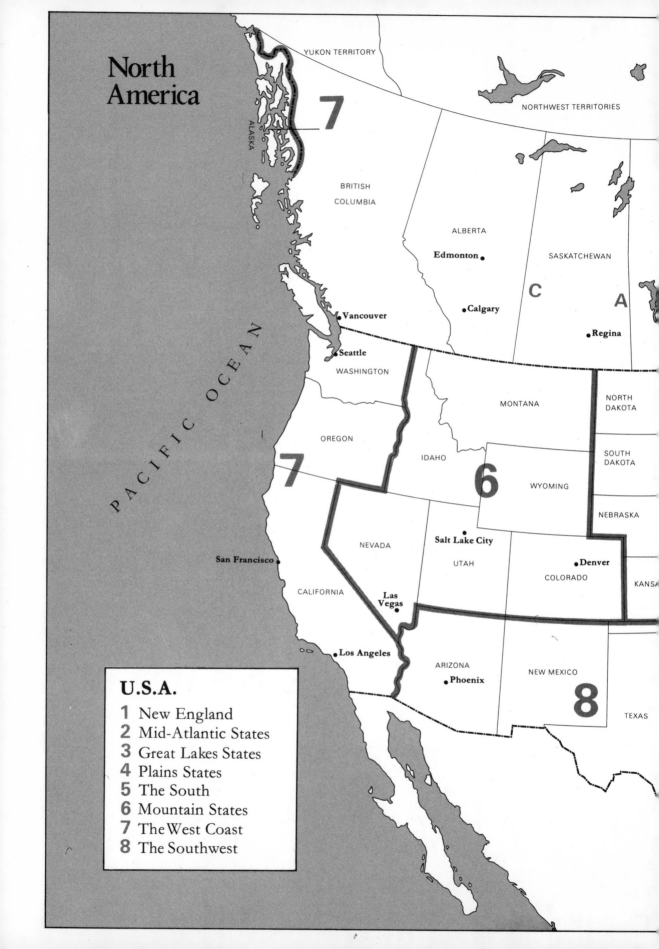

Glossary

Words in *italic* type cross-refer to other Glossary terms.

A

Acropolis In Greek architecture, the citadel, or elevated central part of the city, containing the major religious and public buildings.

Adam style Style associated with Robert Adam (1728-92). His architectural approach was an interpretation of English *Palladianism* but his classical studies led to a preference for picturesque classical forms, such as the *rotunda* and Imperial Roman Baths. However, much of his style is associated with his work as a designer of interiors and furniture, also much influenced by classical forms.

Adobe Form of clay brick, traditionally used in Spain and Spanish America, which is not baked but left to dry in the sun.

Aisle Division of a church, usually flanking the nave on each side, and divided from it by columns or *piers*.

Ajimez Spanish term for paired, round-headed windows, a recurring late *Gothic* and *Renaissance* element.

Altis Classical Greek sanctuary enclosure.

Ambulatory Continuation of the side *aisles* around a *chancel* or *apse,* providing space for processions around the *sanctuary* or presbytery.

Apse Vaulted end portion of a *nave, transept* or *aisle,* usually circular or polygonal. It often forms a chapel or part of the *chancel.*

Arcade Row of arches supported by free-standing or engaged *piers* or columns.

Architrave 1. In Classical architecture, the lowest division of the *entablature,* resting directly upon the *capitals* of the supporting columns. 2. Collective term for the elements comprising the molding around a door or window.

Archivolt 1. Continuation of *architrave* moldings around the curving face of an arch. 2. Lower face of an arch.

Art Deco Eclectic style of the 1920s and 1930s based on a decorative combination of *Neoclassical, Gothic* and *Baroque* features. Buildings were often covered in glazed tiles and polychrome work.

Artesonado Style of inlaid or marquetry ceiling in which raised ridges or fillets define star-shaped patterns, widely used in Spanish ecclesiastical architecture during the 15th and 16th centuries.

Articulation The means of giving clarity or distinction to the architectural elements of a building.

Art Nouveau Decorative style developed in Europe during the 1890s and widespread until the advent of World War I. It was basically the stylized adaptation of plant and floral forms into graceful linear patterns and broad areas of bright color.

Arts and Crafts Movement based on a veneration of medieval craftsmanship, first developed by William Morris and the Pre-Raphaelites in 19th-century England.

Ashlar Squared masonry blocks laid regularly in parallel courses.

Atrium Open central courtyard or hall, surrounded on all sides by roofed areas, often *colonnaded* in larger houses. Found in Roman domestic architecture, this original form was adapted in Early Christian and medieval architecture as an open quadrangle or colonnade on the front of a church.

Attic 1. Style or elements of architecture pertaining to Attica, a region of Ancient Greece, the capital of which was Athens. 2. In Classical architecture, the upper story, above the main *entablature.* 3. Small rooms directly beneath the roof.

Axial Said of a building when its parts are organized symmetrically around a central axis.

Azulejos Type of glazed tile painted with colors, often on a blue ground.

B

Bailey Initially, the walls surrounding a *keep,* but later used to mean a courtyard enclosed by fortified walls.

Baluster Short, decorative column, often bulging at the base and tapering at the top.

Balustrade Strictly, a structure composed of *balusters* supporting a coping. However, the term is often applied to any range of uprights supporting a rail.

Banding Decorative linear incisions, often laid in parallel horizontal, vertical or diagonal courses.

Baptistery Part of a church, sometimes apart from the main building, containing the baptismal font.

Barbican Projection on a fortification defending an approach or gateway.

Bargeboards Decoratively carved boards often attached to the *gable* ends of a roof.

Bargeboard

Baroque General term for the style of art and architecture in the 17th century, originally from Rome, in which strict adherence to *Classical* canons was replaced by a more subjective approach. It combined classical and imaginative motifs in unusual juxtaposition to achieve an effect of monumentality, theatricality and awe. Lighting, paintings and sculpture were all devices used to involve the viewer.

Barrel vault Continuous *vault,* semicylindrical in section and uninterrupted by any cross vaults. Also known as a tunnel vault.

Base Molded section of a Classical *Order,* resting on the *plinth,* and supporting the *shaft.*

Basilica 1. Ancient rectangular hall with apses, supported by double *colonnades.* 2. In Christian architecture, a basic church ground-plan. 3. Term applied to the seven main Roman churches founded by Constantine.

Bastide Fortified town built in medieval France or Wales.

Bastion Projection, usually on the corner of a fortified building, enabling the defenders to see the ground below the ramparts on two sides.

Bauhaus Name of a radical arts and crafts design school established in Weimar, Germany, by Walter Gropius in 1919. The aim of the school was to achieve modern design but determined by the main functions of a building.

Beakheads Decorative additions to *Norman* moldings of beaked animal or human heads.

Bee-hive huts Primitive dome-shaped buildings, circular in plan, where stone courses of diminishing size were constructed on top of each other.

Black and white work Contrasting patterning on a *timber-frame* structure when the timbers have been stained black and the wall in-fill painted white.

Blind 1. *Tracery* or *arcading* laid directly onto a wall surface. 2. An opening which has been filled in.

Box-frame Cellular method of concrete construction, where stories of regular rectangular spaces are built up, the load being carried on cross-walls. Also known as cross-wall construction.

Brace Lower element of a *timber-framed* roof, composed of a small diagonal support, straight or arched, springing from the wall or wall post, and supporting the *hammerbeam* or *tie-beam.*

Broach spire Octagonal spire rising directly from a tower, common in *Early English* architecture.

Brutalism Term developed in England during the mid-1950s to describe the contemporary style of Le Corbusier and his followers. It is characterized by the extensive use of unfinished concrete, the use of materials in their natural form, undisguised application of the service elements to a building, and a juxtaposing of large, heavy forms.

Bulwark Any large, raised fortification.

Buttress Supporting structure to give greater strength to a wall, usually built of stone or brick.

Byzantine First flourish of Christian architecture which sprang from the establishment of Constantine's Empire at Byzantium (later Constantinople) in 330 AD, and which was characterized by the gradual rejection of pagan classical forms while still matching its splendor. By the 5th century two basic forms had evolved: the *basilican* plan, and the centralized Greek Cross surmounted by a *cupola.* The style embodied a complex symbolism evident in the interplay of light and dark and richly embellished surfaces to induce a sense of mystery, and in the careful mathematical and geometric structure of the plans and elevations. Although limited to eastern Europe, the influence on early medieval Italian architecture was considerable.

C

Caldarium Hot-bath room, originally Roman.

Campanile Italian term for a belltower, often freestanding.

Cantilever Horizontal projection counterbalanced by the pull of gravity about a fulcrum, thus giving the impression of being self-supporting.

Capital Decorated section of an *Order* on top of the *shaft,* and directly below and supporting the *architrave.*

Carolingian Relating to the Christian classical revival inspired by Charlemagne, which took place between the late 8th century and the early 10th century and affected most art forms. The style included the imitation of *Classical* features, such as columns with decorated *capitals* and semicircular arches, with emphasis on the west façade of churches and ground plans based on the multiplication of square units.

Cartouche Ornamental painted and carved or molded panel in the form of a scroll, containing an inscription or emblem.

Caryatid Sculpted female figure functioning as a column or *pier.*

Cella Central body of a *Classical* temple.

Centralized Term usually applied to ecclesiastical architecture, where the elements of a building are symmetrically organized around a regular central space.

Chancel Screened area at the eastern end of a church around the high altar and reserved for the officiating clergy.

Chantry chapel Chapel established and reserved by endowment for the celebration of masses for the benefactor and his family.

Chapter-house Main secular meeting hall of a monastic community, often adjoining a *cloister.*

Chevron Medieval decorative molding forming a zigzag pattern.

Choir Area of a church reserved for the singers.

Choir screen Screen separating the *choir* from the congregational area of a church, usually decoratively carved or ornamented.

Clapboard American term for *weatherboarding.*

Classical Relating to the architecture of the ancient Greek and Roman Empires. Classical architecture is characterized by *pillar* and *lintel* or pillar and arch structures, and by strict adherence to a system based on the use of proportion and ornament.

Clerestory Upper story of a church wall, pierced by windows and below the main *eaves* yet above any projecting subsidiary roofs.

Cloisonné Intricate inlaid enamel surface in which enamels are used in separate cells.

Cloister Roofed or vaulted passage-way surrounding an open quadrangle which connects domestic areas within a monastic building.

Cob Wall-filling material composed of straw bonded by gravel, clay and sand.

Coffering Recessed square or polygonal moldings or panels decorating a ceiling or lower face of an arch.

Colonette Small, slender column used for the *articulation* of such elements as window surrounds.

Colonial style Architectural style which developed during the 18th century throughout the British Empire and America, which derived its basic form from the English country house of the Queen Anne period or, for public buildings, English *Palladianism*.

Colonnade Range of columns supporting arches or an *entablature*.

Composite Latin Roman *Order*, loosely combining features of the *Ionic* and *Corinthian* Orders.

Compound pier *Pier* comprising a number of shafts, common in *Gothic* architecture. Also known as a clustered pier.

Console Type of *corbel* or ornamental bracket.

Corbel Projection of wood or stone, supporting a horizontal or springing member.

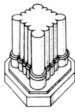

Compound pier

Corbel-table Continuous row of *corbels* supporting the *eaves*, usually found in *Norman* architecture.

Corinthian *Classical Order* comprising a plain *plinth*, cushioned base, *fluted shaft*, intricately molded *capital*, slightly projecting *architrave frieze* and more heavily projecting *cornice*.

Cornice 1. Uppermost projecting part of an *entablature* surmounting the *frieze* and often decorated with molding and dentils on its lower face. 2. Any continuous projecting decorative moldings surmounting an architectural feature.

Corps de logis French term for the main body of a building or complex as distinct from the outlying or service buildings.

Cortile Italian term for an internal, *arcaded* open courtyard.

Course Any continuous horizontal layer of building material. When emphasized by a molding, it is called a string course.

Crafting Concern of an architect, designer or craftsman for the degree of detail and quality of finish on a building.

Crenellation Alternating pattern of raised blocks and gaps along the upper edge of a fortified wall, giving protection to the defenders.

Crocket *Gothic* decorative feature of carved leaf shapes placed on the angles of *gables*, canopies and spires.

Crocketed capital Early *Gothic capital*, often polygonal, with projecting carved leaf forms or *crockets*.

Crossing In a church, the area of intersection between the *nave*, *transepts* and *chancel*, usually topped by a dome or tower.

Cruck-frame Method of construction where pairs of large curved timbers, set in the foundation and rising to meet in a pointed arch, provide the framework for a building.

Crypt Space below the main body of a church, often containing a chapel, relics or tombs.

Cubism Abstract art form developed by Picasso and Braque during the first decade of the 20th century, which emphasized the surfaces of solid objects by developing a more conceptual approach to the use of line and color. It stimulated interest in abstract forms, geometrical logic and restrained use of color, later seen in the *International Style*.

Cufic Style of Arabic calligraphy often used in oriental decoration.

Cupola Dome, usually springing from a circular or octagonal base.

Cupola

Curtain wall 1. Outer wall of a castle.
2. Non-structural cladding (such as metal or glass) applied to a framed structure and employed widely in the construction of 20th-century high-rise blocks.

Cushion capital Simple *Romanesque capital*, cubic in form, but with the lower corners chamfered to fit the round column.

Cusping Carved points or spurs intruding on a glazed space in decorative *tracery*.

Cushion capital

D

Decorated Term applied to the late *Gothic* style, characterized by a proliferation of ornate, detailed carving and open-work.

De Stijl Group of Dutch artists and architects formed in 1917 to discuss and develop theories of geometric abstraction, as seen in the paintings of Mondrian. The importance of careful balance and proportion, based on an understanding of the laws governing reality, made great impact on design in all fields.

Diapers Surface decoration made up of repeated small squares, rectangles or lozenges.

Domical vault *Vault* sprung from a square or polygonal base, approximately hemispherical, but composed of ascending flat segments divided by *groins*.

Donjon French term for a *keep*.

Doric 1. Pertaining to the ancient Greek region of Doria. 2. Greek *Order*, characterized by the absence of a *plinth* or base, but with a *fluted shaft*, simple *cushion capital*, plain abacus and *architrave*, *frieze* of alternating metopes and triglyphs, and a projecting, unadorned *cornice*.

Dormer window Roofed window projecting vertically from a sloping roof.

Dorter Dormitory of a monastery.

Double splay *Splaying* of a recess by cutting back the edge of the corner in two angled faces, rather than a single diagonal splay.

Dormer window

Dressing Smooth finish given to the surface of masonry blocks or moldings, usually used to emphasize features such as doors and windows.

Drip moldings Moldings usually projecting from a *cornice*, allowing rain water to run off the roof without touching the wall below.

Drum 1. Vertical walls supporting a *cupola* or dome, either square, circular or polygonal in plan. 2. Cylindrical segments comprising a column.

E

Early English Term for the early English *Gothic* style, which developed from the last quarter of the 12th century. It is unique for its emphasis on horizontality, lack of *apses*, and development of intricate *vaulting* systems such as the star vault.

Eaves Lower edge of the roof, projecting over and beyond the supporting walls.

Egg and dart patterning Style of molding decoration often applied to interior *cornices* and characterized by alternate oval and arrow-head shapes.

Engaged column Column adjoining, or sunk into, a wall and sometimes known as an attached or applied column.

Entablature Horizontal elements of an *Order* supported by the column, comprising the *architrave*, the *frieze* and the *cornice*.

Entasis Technique invented by the ancient Greeks where such upright structures as columns or *piers* are made to bulge slightly to compensate for the optical illusion of concavity which occurs if they are straight.

Ephebeum In classical Roman architecture, the gymnasium of public baths.

Estipite Type of late Spanish *Renaissance* *pilaster* which tapers toward the base

Etruscan Pertaining to the ancient Italian country of Etruria, now known as Tuscany, whose civilization (750-100 BC) immediately preceded, and greatly influenced, that of classical Rome. The Etruscans were notable for the massive scale of their fortifications, built from large blocks of hewn rock set without mortar, many of which remain today.

Expressionism Style based on expression by exaggeration of forms and distortion of line and architectural space, prevalent in Germany from the beginning of the 20th century until the 1930s. It is characterized by a broad range of imaginative, often sculptural, structures, frequently inspired by biological forms.

F

Faceting Type of finish given to a material such as dressed stone, made up of regular shapes with smooth, flat surfaces.

Facing Finished surface of building material.

Fan vaulting Technique of *vaulting* developed in the *Perpendicular Gothic* style. It is essentially *rib vaulting* in which the diagonal ribs are replaced by a semiconical spread of small ribs forming, in each corner of the vault, a smooth, inverted, partial cone.

Federal style Style of American architecture dating from the early 19th century, widely used for public buildings. It combined aspects of English *Palladianism* with the more grandiose, idealized interpretation of *Neoclassical* architecture popularized by Thomas Jefferson.

Fenestration Manner in which windows are distributed on a building.

Finial Molded or carved ornament, often floral, surmounting a pinnacle or *gable*.

Flamboyant Highly decorated late French *Gothic* style characterized by a proliferation of curvilinear forms in structures, *tracery* and openwork.

Fleche Slim wooden spire, usually rising from the ridge of a roof.

Flint and ashlar Decorative squared and *faced* masonry (or sometimes brick) for dressing the surrounds to windows, doors and other major elements, and flint for the main wall surface.

Flushwork Decorative surface patterning or inlay using *ashlar* or brick in conjunction with *knapped flint*.

Fluting Regular, parallel, vertical grooves used to decorate the shaft of a column, *pier* or *pilaster*.

Flying arch Arch, usually placed between two buildings such as towers, which springs directly from the outer walls of the buildings.

Font 1. In Christian architecture, an open topped stone receptacle for holy water, used in baptismal rites. 2. A fountain.

Forechoir Structure with *aisles*, often added to the west end of a church.

Forum In Roman town planning, an open space, piazza or square, surrounded by *colonnaded* public buildings.

Framed building Method of building in which the load and thrust is carried on a framework rather than by load bearing walls. Once wooden, now they are mostly steel.

Fresco General term for the technique of decorative wall and ceiling painting where water-based pigments are applied to plaster.

Fretwork Decorative band of regular, repetitive rectilinear surface ornamentation or molding.

Frieze 1. Middle section of the *entablature* of a classical *Order*, above the *architrave* and below the *cornice*. 2. Band of relief, molded or painted decoration usually high on a wall.

Functionalism Commitment to the basic requirements of a building, devoid of any stylistic, aesthetic or emotional expression by the architect.

G

Gable Upper part of a wall, supporting the end of a pitched roof.

Gallery arcade Range of columns or *colonettes*

along the open side of a gallery.

Gambrel roof Roof which rises initially as a four-sided pyramid, surmounted by a *gabled* and pitched section, often at a different angle.

Dutch gable

Georgian General term encompassing the popular architectural styles prevalent in Britain and its colonies during the reigns of the first four Hanoverian Kings, from George I to George IV (1714-1830). It represents the first major attempts to establish a classical style in England. See also *Palladian*.

Gingerbread Intricate *fretwork* patterning of *bargeboards*, especially common in 19th century American domestic timber buildings.

Gothic Style of architecture, mainly ecclesiastical, prevalent in Western Europe from the late 12th century until the advent of the *Renaissance*. The style was characterized by the pointed arch and the *rib vault*, longitudinal or cruciform plans, and tall, spacious and light side *aisles*, supporting a triforium gallery, and surmounted by a glazed *clerestory*. See also *Early English*.

Gothic Revival Late 18th and 19th century style, mostly in England and America, which promoted the revival of the Gothic style in answer to the post-*Renaissance* adulation for classical architecture.

Greek Revival Late 18th and 19th century style, prevalent in Protestant countries, which promoted the revival of the classical Greek style of architecture.

Grisaille Illusionistic decorative painting, usually in shades of grey, giving the impression of details in relief.

Groin vault *Vault* formed by the right-angled intersection of two equally proportioned tunnel or *barrel vaults*.

H

Hall church Church, longitudinal in plan, in which the *nave* and *aisles* are of equal height.

Hammerbeam Short, lower, horizontal member of a hammerbeam roof, partially projecting from the top of the supporting wall, replacing the *tie beam* and providing a base for the rafters, struts and *braces*.

Harmonic proportions System of architectural proportion relating to the structure of musical harmonies and developed in *Classical* architecture. It was based on the mathematical break-down of the relation in pitch of two chords into halves (1:2), two-thirds (2:3) and three-quarters (3:4) in order to achieve an octave, a fifth of an octave and a fourth of an octave respectively. This was seen as the basis for the most successful classical architecture by Alberti, and was to be developed as a standard proportional method by Palladio.

Hellenic Pertaining to *Classical* Greece from c. 800-323 BC. The monumental architectural style was mainly used for temples and included features such as a rectangular main body (*naos*) surrounded by a *colonnade* (*peristyle*), supporting a *pedimented* roof. The whole structure was raised on a stepped platform (*stylobate*), and was elevated by the *fluted* Greek *Doric Order*, without a base and tapering toward the *capital*.

Hellenistic Style of *Classical* Greek architecture prevalent after the death of Alexander the Great in 323 BC and lasting until c. 146 BC, by which time it had greatly influenced Imperial Roman architecture. There was great emphasis on grandiose public, domestic and palatial buildings, and although traditional Greek Classical forms persisted there was more elaboration and development of new motifs, such as the *Ionic* and the *Corinthian Orders*.

Helm roof Sharply inclined roof often used on towers or spires, where four *gables* support

Helm roof

lozenge-shaped sections which rise to meet at a point.

Herm Decorative rectangular pillar rising to terminate in the male torso and head of Hermes.

Hip Outer angle formed by the meeting of two sloping surfaces of a roof.

Impost Upper element of a *pier* or wall from which an arch springs. It can be projecting or concealed.

International Style Style developed in Europe and America prior to World War I and popularized in the 1920s and 1930s. It developed from the *Arts and Crafts* movement combined with the aesthetics of contemporary abstract art, and was characterized by cubic forms, asymmetric planning, horizontal bands of windows, concrete rendered walls painted white and by the absence of applied decoration.

Ionic 1. Pertaining to the ancient Greek division of Ionia. 2. Classical *Order* developed in Asia Minor in c. 6th century BC, characterized by a circular *plinth*, simple molded base, a regular, *fluted shaft*, surmounted by a horizontal *volute*, *capital* and abacus. The *entablature* comprises a sparsely decorated *architrave* and a broad, plain *frieze* surmounted by a deeply projecting *cornice* with large regular dentils.

Isabeline Late *Gothic* style of decoration developed in Spain under Isabel the Catholic (r. 1474-1504), in which Moorish and other exotic motifs were used to elaborate essentially traditional Spanish Gothic elements.

Italic 1. Pertaining to ancient and early Roman Italy, including the Greek colonies in S. Italy. 2. Alternative term for *Composite Order*.

J

Jacobean architecture British architectural style dating from the early 17th century. The style is found mainly in domestic buildings and is characterized by dense decorative brickwork and complex *strapwork*, but modified by the inclusion of classical details.

Jamb Upright framing a doorway, upon which the *lintel* rests.

Jetty Externally projecting floor joists of a *timber-frame* building which support the upper storey *overhang*.

K

Keep The fortified tower of a castle, usually set in a courtyard which is itself encircled by fortified walls.

Keystone Stone segment, often pronounced, at the apex of an arch or *rib*.

Knapped flint Flint split to leave smooth surfaces, used for providing a partially dressed facing to a flint wall.

L

Lancet window Tall, sharply pointed window, characteristic of high and late *Gothic* architecture.

Lantern Open polygonal or circular turret, usually glazed and surmounting a dome or roof to admit overhead light.

Lesene Plain *pilaster* without base or *capital*, commonly occurring in *Romanesque* and Anglo-Saxon architecture, often used to strengthen broad expanses of flat wall. Also known as a pilaster strip.

Lintel Upper, horizontal element spanning a doorway or window, supported at each end by the upright *jambs*.

Loggia Gallery enclosed by a *colonnade* or *arcade*.

Lombardic Pertaining to the north-west Italian region of Lombardy, and especially the early medieval and *Romanesque* architecture which developed after the Germanic invasion in the

6th century and which flourished until the 13th century. The characteristic ecclesiastical style was based on a rectangular groundplan, divided into three *aisles* of equal length, each terminating in an *apse* of equal height. The side aisles tended to be of two stories, the central *nave* of three.

Long and short work Saxon technique of bonding the external corners of buildings. The *quoins* comprise broad, horizontal stones, often extending through the wall, set *alternately* with long, upright stones.

Louver 1. Opening in a roof often surmounted by a cowel used to allow smoke to escape. 2. One of a series of hinged panels set in a wall which, when opened, admit air but exclude rain.

Louver

Lozenge Diamond shape, having four equal sides set as parallels but not at right angles.

Lunette Any flat, semicircular element over a doorway or rectangular window.

M

Machicolation Parapet of a defense work with a pierced floor, through which molten pitch or lead was poured upon the assailants below.

Mannerism Style which developed from the high *Renaissance* and preceded the *Baroque*, principally in Italy. The term was initially used to describe

Machicolation

a degeneration of the Renaissance style, and certainly its characteristic over-adornment, stylization and conspicuous beautification support this. However, the artists and architects were consciously attempting to create a new style which acknowledged and yet exceeded classicism, while avoiding imitation.

Mansard roof Roof with a double slope, the upper angle being less steep than the lower.

Manueline Style of late *Gothic* architecture in Portugal which developed under King Manuel the Fortunate (r. 1495-1521). Highly decorated and ornate, its many ingredients arose from the development of overseas trade.

Martyrium Shrine or church erected on the site of a martyrdom, a martyr's tomb or a site directly connected with the life of Christ.

Model village Idealized rural village, planned and built as a single entity, either as the result of the re-siting of an existing village, or as a social experiment.

Modillion 1. Form of bracket or *console*. 2. One of a series, often paired, of projecting members, applied to *Corinthian* or *Composite Orders* supporting the upper parts of the *cornice*.

Module Standard unit of measurement from which proportions of a building are developed.

Motte and bailey Primitive early medieval and Norman defense works, comprising a raised earthwork mound, the motte, surmounted by a ring wall enclosing a courtyard, the bailey.

Mozarabic Style of Christian architecture which developed in Spain under the Moors from the late 9th century until the

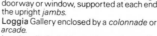

Motte and bailey

middle 11th century. Buildings were usually solitary and employed many elements and motifs of Islamic origin.

Mudejar Style of Spanish Christian architecture which developed in a Muslim style, often including Cufic inscriptions.

It formed the transition between the Mozarabic and Spanish *Gothic* style.

Mullion Fixed vertical members dividing a window.

N

Naos Sanctuary of a Greek temple containing the statue of the deity but adapted in *Byzantine* architecture as the sanctuary of a centrally planned church.

Narthex 1. *Arcaded* transverse porch or vestibule forming the entrance space of a *basilican* church, usually Byzantine. 2. Covered antechamber at the main entrance of a church.

National Romanticism Late 19th-century – early 20th-century movement, concerned with the establishment of a national style based on a romantic view of the vernacular.

Nave Generally, the longitudinal western arm of a Christian church, but more specifically the middle section of the western arm, with *aisles* either side.

Necropolis Ancient Greek burial ground.

Neoclassicism Popular European style during the last quarter of the 18th century and first quarter of the 19th century. It was based on careful study of Roman classical architecture, not as a source for mimicry but rather as inspiration for the creation of a new style.

New Architecture Style that arose from *de Stijl*, where architects proposed a new architecture based on horizontal and vertical slabs and columns, and the use of all the primary colors with black, white and grey.

Newel Post set at the foot of a staircase forming an abutment to the lowest step and supporting the lower end of the *balustrade*.

Nogging Areas of brick in-fill between the external structural wooden members in a *timber-frame* building.

Norman English branch of the *Romanesque* style, originating slightly before, but made more general by, the Norman invasion in 1066. Ecclesiastical architecture is characterized by two-towered façades and square towers over the *crossing*. See also *Romanesque*.

Nymphaeum In classical architecture, a retreat or grotto, often sunken and open, usually containing plants, statues and running water.

O

Ogee "S"-shaped molding, comprising a convex curve flowing into a concave curve.

Oratory Small private chapel.

Order 1. In *Classical* architecture, the column, usually comprising a base, *shaft* and *capital*, and the *architrave* supported by it. 2. One of a series of concentric, semicircular steps approaching a window or door, or layers of *voussoirs* in an arch.

Oriel window Window projecting from the flat face of a wall, on an upper story, and usually curved.

Orientation Siting of a building in relation to the points of the compass.

Outwork Preliminary defense work beyond the main walls of a fortification.

Oriel window

Overhang System of *timber-frame* building where the joists are allowed to protrude over the supporting wall below, while supporting the wall above.

P

Palaestra Classical public building or enclosure for athletic training.

Palladian Derived from the buildings and publications of the Venetian architect Andrea Palladio (1508-80), one of the most important *Renaissance* interpreters of Roman classical architecture. His work was influential throughout Europe and was based, primarily, on his reworking of classical motifs, such as *porticos*, arches and columns.

Panhellenic General term for the architectural styles of *Classical* Greek colonies or settlements.

Pantile Tile with an "S"-shaped section.

Parapet Low wall providing protection from a sudden vertical drop.

Pargetting Exterior plasterwork of a *timber-frame* building, often molded into patterns.

Patio In Spanish architecture, an open inner courtyard.

Pedestal 1. In classical architecture, a large member, square in section, supporting a column or statue, usually comprising a deep *plinth*, a layer of decorative molding, a broad section often decorated with carvings, and surmounted by an *entablature*. Pedestals were often used to preserve the proportions of the *Order* they supported. 2. Any substantial member supporting a superstructure.

Pediment In classical architecture, a triangular or segmented feature surmounting an *entablature*, emphasizing an important feature such as a doorway, window or *portico*, or screening a *hipped* roof.

Pendant Ornamental projection hanging from the intersection of *ribs* of a *vault* or as decoration from a *stucco* ceiling.

Pendentive Triangular curved section by which the transition from the circular base of a dome or *drum* onto the square or polygonally planned supporting *piers* or columns is made.

Pendentive

Peripteral Any building or courtyard surrounded by a continuous range of columns.

Peristyle Continuous range of columns surrounding the main body of a building.

Perpendicular The most prolific and long-lasting variation of the English *Gothic* style, dating from *c.* 1335 – *c.* 1530. It is characterized by straight, slender vertical elements, tall windows divided by *mullions*, and restrained *tracery*, but employing a proliferation of *cusped* arches and foils, both in the windows and in decorative panels. *Rib vaulting*, and later, *fan vaulting* were used.

Piano nobile Main floor of a building, containing the living rooms.

Picturesque Originating in the 18th century, the concept essentially meant that a scene or detail resembled the idealized painting of a classical landscape by such artists as Poussin or Claude. It was characterized by assymetry, informality, bright colors and high texture. The idea was highly influential in the development of the landscaped garden in England by Humphrey Repton, Capability Brown and others.

Pier 1. Main structural support in a building, usually of solid masonry, but larger and less decorative than a column. 2. Any solid mass of masonry between openings. 3. Squat medieval and *Romanesque* forms of column, often changing in section from square to circular or polygonal.

Pilaster Adaptation of any *Classical Order*, rectangular in section and applied to, or emerging from a wall, usually by one sixth of its breadth.

Pilaster strip See Lesene.

Pilotis 20th-century term describing the raising of a building from the ground on widely spaced reinforced concrete columns.

Pinnacle Conical termination of a spire, *parapet* or *buttress*, usually decorated with *crockets*.

Piscina Stone vessel or basin containing water, usually set in a wall to the south of the altar for cleaning Communion utensils.

Plateresque Derived from the ornate working of silverware, the term now refers to the highly embellished style of 16th-century Spanish architecture which combined decorative elements from *Moorish*, *Gothic* and *Renaissance* styles and, like the Portuguese *Manueline* style, included exotic motifs.

Plinth 1. Lowest member of a *Classical Order*, the unadorned raised block upon which the

base stands. 2. Lowest section of a *Classical* pedestal. 3. The base of a wall, giving a broader, stronger support at the foot.

Podium 1. Any uniformly raised block or *pedestal*, often supporting a column. 2. Continuous raised platform encircling the arena of an amphitheatre.

Polychrome Any form of decoration employing several colors.

Porphyry Igneous rock, composed of deep red and white felspar crystals.

Portal 1. Any door or gate, often elaborately decorated. 2. A small door set within a larger door or gate.

Portcullis Reinforced defensive gate found in castles and larger permanent fortifications. It can be raised or lowered vertically in sliding grooves set in the gate *jambs*.

Porte-cochere Porchway large enough to admit the passage of a wheeled vehicle.

Portcullis

Portico *Colonnaded*, covered space projecting from the façade, in front of an entrance.

Postern Small gateway to a fortification, town or church, often concealed at the rear.

Presbytery Generally the area to the east of the *crossing* of a church, reserved for the clergy and containing the main altar and *sanctuary*.

Propylaeum Main gateway or entrance (in classical architecture usually applied to temples or sacred areas).

Proscenium 1. In classical architecture, the main stage of a theatre. 2. In modern architecture, the area between the main curtain and the orchestra.

Prostyle Having a range of free-standing columns, for instance a *portico*.

Pseudo-peripteral Classical Greek temple which lacks a space between the outer walls of the main body of the building and the surrounding *colonnade*.

Q

Quadriga Sculptural group featuring a chariot and four horses, surmounting an architectural element.

Quadripartite vault *Vault* divided, usually diagonally, into four quarters or cells.

Quatrefoil Rosette shape in ornamental *tracery* in which four *cusps* are permitted to intrude upon a circular space.

Quincunx Arrangement of five points in a square or rectangle with one point occupying each of the four corners and the fifth at the center, where the diagonals intersect.

Quoins Emphasized, dressed corner stones, set alternately to present either their long sides or short ends.

Quoin

R

Rampart Outer wall surrounding a fortification.

Redoubt Isolated, self-contained outwork of a fortification.

Regency Style popular during the regency of George, Prince of Wales (1810-20). It was applied mainly to private houses and derives principally from the elegant *rococo* interpretation of the classicism of Robert Adam.

Renaissance Name given to the cultural and social movement which started in Tuscany at the beginning of the 15th century. Architecturally, it manifested itself in a combination of remarkably advanced feats of engineering, such as the building of the dome of the Cathedral in Florence by Brunelleschi, and in a growing fluency in the interpretation of *Classical* principles of architecture, which by the end of the 15th century had spread throughout central and northern Italy and was felt north of the Alps.

Rendering *Stucco* or concrete finish of an exterior wall.

Reredos Screen, usually of carved wood or stone, set behind an altar.

Reveal Surface at right angles to a main wall.

Rib Projecting molded band applied to a ceiling, most commonly used to emphasize and to decorate the structure of *vaults*.

Ribbed vault Development of the *groin vault* in which the groins are replaced by arched *ribs* built across the sides and diagonals of the vaulted bay to form a support for the infilling.

Ridge Line formed by the junction of two sloping angles of a roof.

Rococo Style of ornate decoration applied to architecture, painting and furniture, in which basic motifs were drawn from the free-flowing assymetric forms of plants, shells, corals and garlands, usually realized in delicate gold-painted *stucco* or carving. The style began in the hotels of Paris in the 18th century and quickly spread to most of Europe.

Romanesque Medieval European style preceding *Gothic*. It originated in the 10th century, and flourished until the middle of the 12th century in Europe including England where it was associated with *Norman* architecture. It was fundamentally based on a square bay ground plan *module* and round-headed arch, related barrel and *groin vaults* and longitudinal cruciform plans with radiating *apse* terminations.

Rood-screen Screens across the east end of a church, separating the *chancel* from the *nave*.

Rose window Principally a *Gothic* device, in which curved stone *mullions* reminiscent of petals divide a circular window, permitting elaborate decorative *tracery* and stained glass work. A wheel window is principally a *Romanesque* motif where the mullions radiate from the center of the window like the spokes of a wheel.

Rotunda Circular building, often domed and surrounded by a *colonnade*. Also a round room.

Rustication Method of decorating *ashlar* masonry by recessing the outer edges of the blocks, and often roughening the outer surface. Derived from *Classical* architecture, it was most commonly used in *Renaissance* architecture, applied especially to *quoins* and to basements.

Rustication

S

Sacristy Room in, or attached to, a church, used to store sacred vessels and ceremonial clothing.

Saddle-back roof Term used for a standard pitched roof when it is applied to a tower.

Salomonica Spanish term for a twisted column, popular in late *Renaissance* and *Baroque* architecture.

Sanctuary 1. Any holy or sacred space. 2. From *Byzantine* architecture onward, the area, usually at the east end of a church, containing the main altar.

Scarp Bank found at the foot of the outer walls of a fortification, often formed by the inner face of a ditch or moat.

Scene building The erection of temporary architectural sets on a stage to enhance the illusion of a theatrical event.

Sedilia Seats, often of stone, found on the south wall of the *chancel* and used by officiating clergy.

Sexpartite vaulting Derivation of the simple quadripartite *vault*, where dividing *ribs* have been introduced to two opposite panels, thus dividing the vault bay into six panels or cells.

Shaft 1. Body of a column or *Order* between the base and the *capital*, often *fluted*. 2. In medieval architecture, one of the narrow vertical parts which together form a *pier* or pillar, or window and door surrounds.

Shell keep *Keep* consisting of an enclosure within a *buttressed curtain wall*.

Shingle Wooden tiles, laid or hung in horizontal courses, principally used for the outer skin of roofs or spires. Also popular in late 19th century American architecture as a means of *cladding* for domestic buildings.

Shuttering Temporary mold, usually made of wood, for forming concrete elements, such as columns, beams and walls.

Small framing Method of *timber-frame* building in which the frame is composed of a large number of small *studs* and horizontal members.

Solar Living-room of a medieval domestic house, usually on an upper story.

Solarium An ancient Roman sun-roof or terrace.

Spandrel Triangular space formed by the curve of an arch on one side, the continuation of the vertical line upward from its springing, and the horizontal line drawn through its apex.

Splay Diagonal cutting away of a corner to increase the width of a recess, often containing a door or window.

Springer stone Lowest section at each end of an arch, resting directly upon the *impost*.

Squinch arches Series of arches radiating out diagonally from a corner, to adapt a polygonal or round superstructure to a square ground-plan.

Stave church Style of Scandinavian *timber-frame* church, with upright timber wall *cladding*, and often ornately carved interiors. Common from the mid-11th century.

Strapwork Molded or carved decorative motifs resembling interlaced straps or bands, originating in 16th century Netherlands but soon popular elsewhere, especially in England. Applied to wooden furniture, screens and doors, but most commonly to plaster ceilings.

Strapwork

Stucco Plasterwork, broadly divisible into two types: a fine gypsum and marble-dust based plaster for interior molding, and a coarse limestone-based cement applied externally.

Studs Upright timber members in a *timber frame* building.

Stylobate Raised, stepped structure supporting a *colonnade*; strictly, the top step.

T

Tablinium Room in classical Roman domestic architecture which opened on one side to the central open courtyard.

Tholos Circular dome or a circular domed building.

Tie beam 1. Lowest member of a simple *timber-frame* roof. 2. Single horizontal beam spanning the gap between the walls, and resting directly upon them. Later replaced by the *hammer-beam*.

Timber-framing Method of construction using a timber wall and roof framework, with the wall spaces filled in by plaster, *wattle and daub* or brick (known as *nogging*) or, occasionally, horizontal boarding (*weatherboarding*). Also known as half-timber construction.

Tower house Free-standing fortified house, resembling the *keep* of a medieval castle.

Tracery Decorative working of window *mullions*, common in *Gothic* architecture.

Transept Area of a cruciform church which laterally intersects the main body of the church at the *crossing*.

Transitional Term generally used to describe buildings which display characteristics of the late *Romanesque* style and of the early *Gothic*. Also used for a building in which the change from one style to another is clearly visible.

Trefoil Form of *cusping* used in *tracery*, where three leaves or lobes are allowed to intrude into the open space.

Tribunal Raised platform in an ancient Roman building, reserved for the seating of magistrates.

Tribune 1. *Apse* of a *basilican* plan church. 2. Church gallery.

Triclinium Dining-room in classical Roman domestic architecture.

Truss Any self-supporting structure of jointed timbers, designed to span a gap such as a roof or bridge.

Tufa Grey, porous volcanic building stone, widely used by the ancient Romans.

Turnpike stairs Spiral stairs.

Tympanum 1. Triangular space enclosed by the horizontal base and sloping *cornices* of a *pediment*, often decorated. 2. Space enclosed by the *lintel* and surmounting arch of a doorway.

U

Undercroft *Vaulted* space below the main level of a church or chapel.

V

Vantage court Area between the main entrance to a fortification and the internal entrance, surrounded by galleries from which defenders could fire upon intruders.

Vault Arched ceiling or roof of any space, composed of brick or stone.

Verd-antique Variety of green and white marble widely used for decoration.

Volute Double-spiral scroll of an *Ionic capital*.

Voussoir One of the wedge-shaped blocks comprising an arch or *vault*.

W

Wall pillar Style of church ground plan common in Germany and Austria in pilgrimage churches where the *nave*, *crossing* and *chancel* are surrounded by a continuous range of pillars or *piers*, to set them apart from a continuous processional passage.

Water-leaf Motif of 12th-century *capital* decoration giving the impression of a single, branchless leaf rising to envelop the capital.

Wattle and daub Form of wall-filling composed of thin branches (wattles), interwoven and bonded by clay (daub).

Weatherboarding Cladding of over-lapping horizontal planks.

Westwork Tower-like structure on the west end of *Carolingian* or *Romanesque* churches. It comprises an entrance and vestibule with a chapel above. The central structure is often flanked by stair turrets.

Wheel window See Rose window.

Index

Buildings appear in alphabetical order under their place name. London, Paris and Rome, being regions for the purposes of this book, have page references to periods and building types. Exceptionally important buildings have individual entries.

439

Acknowledgments

Dorling Kindersley would like to thank the following for their special assistance:
Kate Duffield; Judith Escreet; Andrew Heritage; Ann Kramer; Julian Mannering; Hilda Marshall-Johnson; Negs Photographic Services Ltd., Sheilagh Noble; Christopher Pick; Mark Richards; John Smallwood

Artists

Geoffrey Baverstock   96-7; 198; 9; 206-7; 220-1; 224-5; 228-9; 234-5; 250-1; 280-1; 290-1; 324-5; 330-1; 346-7; 356-7; 376-7; 380-1; 394-5; 400-1; 404-5; 410-1

Brian Delf   34-5; 42-3; 54-5; 60-1; 80-1; 84-5; 98-9; 106-7; 126-7; 144-5; 182-3; 196-7; 214-5; 240-1; 252-3; 258-9; 268-9; 282-3; 304-5; 338-9; 396-7

Jeremy Ford   218-9; 298-9; 332-3; 354-5; 384-5; 412-3

Peter Morter   38-9; 50-1; 66-7; 82-3; 86-7; 90-1; 104-5; 110-1; 114-5; 122-3; 128-9; 132-3; 138-9; 148-9; 152-3; 156-7; 162-3; 164-5; 174-5; 180-1; 192-3; 200-1; 204-5; 210-1; 212-3; 216-7; 232-3; 236-7; 238-9; 246-7; 254-5; 262-3; 266-7; 270-1; 272-3; 278-9; 294-5; 296-7; 302-3; 310-1; 326-7; 334-5; 340-1; 342-3; 350-1; 358-9; 366-7; 370-1; 372-3; 382-3; 386-7; 392-3; 398-9; 406-7; 408-9; 418-9

Donald Myall   48-9; 52-3; 56-7; 58-9; 64-5; 78-9; 92-3; 100-1; 112-3; 130-1; 136-7; 150-1; 158-9; 160-1; 168-9; 172-3; 176-7; 194-5; 202-3; 248-9; 276-7; 300-1; 308-9; 314-5; 364-5; 402-3

Peter Nicholls   222-3; 264-5; 284-5; 306-7; 312-3; 328-9; 336-7; 344-5; 390-1; 420-1

Les Smith   322-3; 362-3

Eric Thomas   32-3; 40-1; 44-5; 62-3; 68-9; 102-3; 116-7; 134-5; 142-3; 288-9

John Western   36-7; 46-7; 88-9; 94-5; 108-9; 118-9; 120-1; 124-5; 140-1; 146-7; 154-5; 166-7; 170-1; 178-9; 184-5; 208-9; 226-7; 230-1; 242-3; 256-7; 260-1; 274-5; 286-7; 292-3; 348-9; 352-3; 360-1; 374-5; 378-9; 388-9; 414-5; 416-7

Angus White   244-5; 368-9

Additional illustrations by David Ashby, Nick Hall, Frederick Ford and Michael Pilley of Radius

Photographic sources
Form
1 Michael Holford; 2 Susan Griggs; 3 Zefa; 4 Angelo Hornak; Right : Zefa; Previous page : Zefa
6 Colour Library International; 7 Susan Griggs; Right: Daily Telegraph Colour Library

Facades
1 Angelo Hornak; 2 Ken Randall; 3 Camera Press; 4 David Wild; 5 Michael Holford; Right: Michael Holford
Previous page: Zefa; 6 Canadian Government Office of Tourism; Right: Susan Griggs

Entrances
1 Michael Holford; 2 Scala; 3 Zefa; 4 Angelo Hornak; Right: Michael Holford
5 Angelo Hornak; Right: Angelo Hornak

Structure
1 Ken Randall; 2 Ken Randall; 3 Camera Press; 4 Angelo Hornak; 5 Michael Holford; Right: Michael Holford
6 Sonia Halliday; Right: Susan Griggs

Enclosure
1 Zefa; 2 Zefa; 3 Zefa; 4 Angelo Hornak; Right: Sonia Halliday
5 Susan Griggs; Right: Cooper-Bridgeman Library

Elements
1 Michael Holford; 2 Angelo Hornak; 3 Michael Holford; 4 Susan Griggs; 5 Picture Point; 6 Angelo Hornak; Right: Susan Griggs; Overleaf: Michael Holford

Decoration
1 Michael Holford; 2 Susan Griggs; 3 Picture Point; 4 Zefa; 5 Camera Press; 6 Angelo Hornak; 7 Angelo Hornak; 8 Ken Randall; Right: Susan Griggs
9 Camera Press; 10 Zefa; 11 Susan Griggs; Right: Picture Point; Overleaf: Zefa

Cartography Arka Graphics

Picture researcher Caroline Lucas